WET MOON

FURTHER REALMS of FRIGHT

3

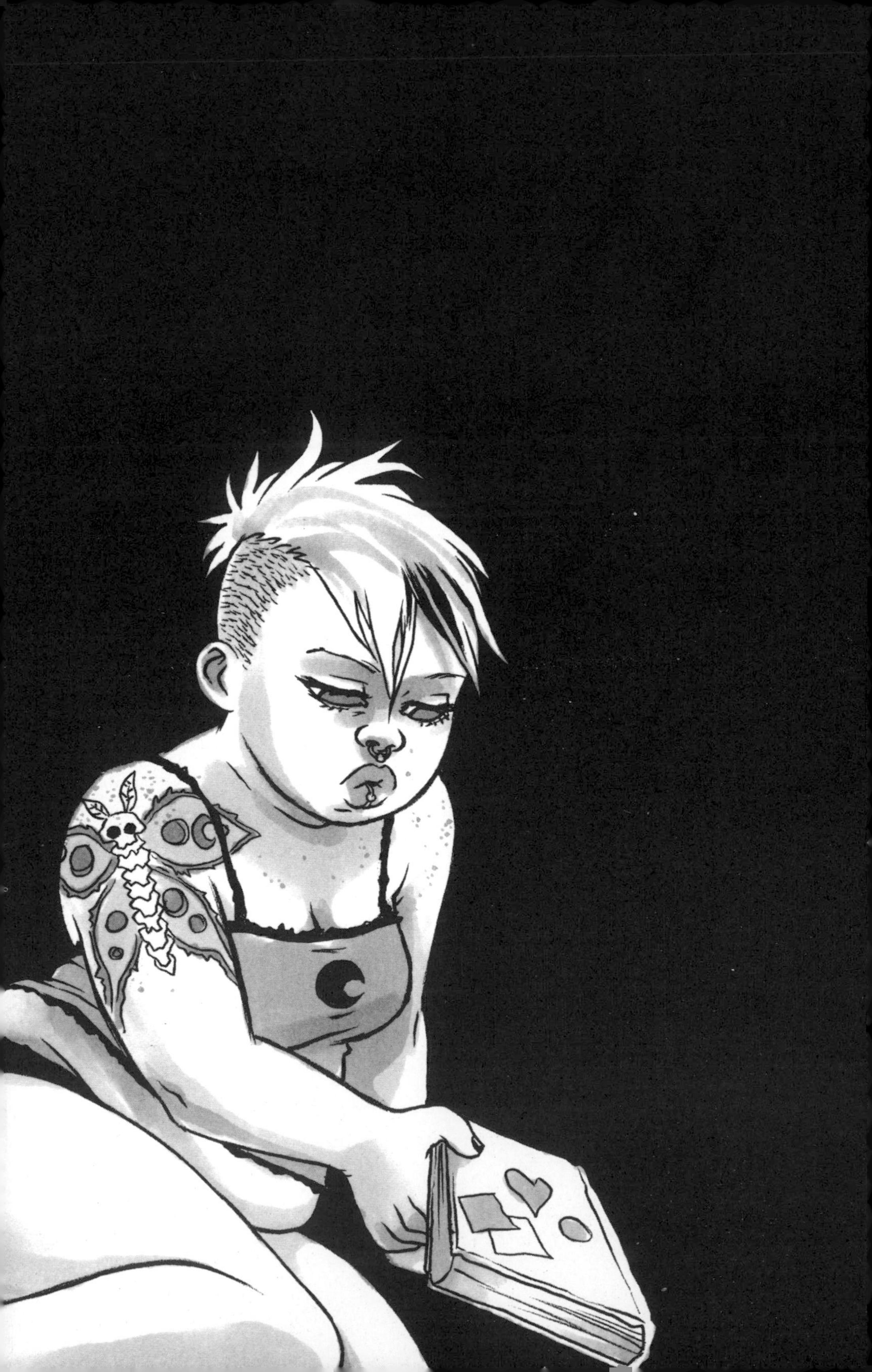

WET MOON

FURTHER REALMS OF FRIGHT

3

written and illustrated by **sophie campbell**
cleo's diary pages by **jessica calderwood**

cover design by **annie mok**
book design by **hilary thompson**
first edition edited by **douglas sherwood & james lucas jones**
new edition edited by **robin herrera**

PUBLISHED BY ONI PRESS, INC.
Joe Nozemack, *publisher*
James Lucas Jones, *editor in chief*
Andrew McIntire, *v.p. of marketing & sales*
David Dissanayake, *director of sales*
Rachel Reed, *publicity coordinator*
Troy Look, *director of design & production*
Hilary Thompson, *graphic designer*
Angie Dobson, *digital prepress technician*
Ari Yarwood, *managing editor*
Charlie Chu, *senior editor*
Robin Herrera, *editor*
Bess Pallares, *editorial assistant*
Brad Rooks, *director of logistics*
Jung Lee, *logistics associate*

ONIPRESS.COM
FACEBOOK.COM/ONIPRESS
TWITTER.COM/ONIPRESS
ONIPRESS.TUMBLR.COM
INSTAGRAM.COM/ONIPRESS

First Edition: April 2017

ISBN 978-1-62010-329-6
eISBN 978-1-62010-365-4

Wet Moon Book Three: Further Realms of Fright, New Edition, April 2017. Published by Oni Press, Inc. 1305 SE Martin Luther King Jr. Blvd., Suite A, Portland, OR 97214.

Printed in China

Library of Congress Control Number: 2016955731

1 2 3 4 5 6 7 8 9 10

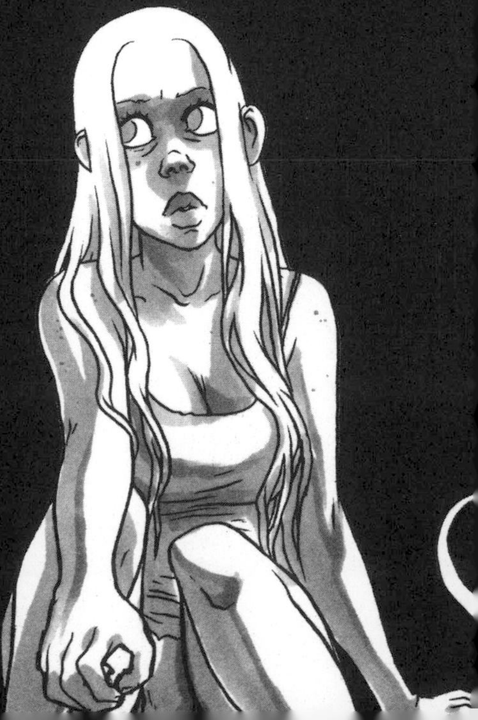

1. Bowden House
2. Vance House
3. Smith House
4. Westmiller House
5. Weitz Hall
6. Polsky Hall
7. Yardley Hall
8. Joseph Hall
9. Simmons Hall
10. Page Hall
11. Meyer Hall
12. Steve Hall
13. Burial Grounds
14. Head-Butt Video
15. House of Usher
16. Denny's
17. Marco's Diner
18. Lo Pan's
19. Swamp Things
20. Flower Power
21. Sundae Best
22. Lorelei Cemetery
23. Zurah Cemetery
24. Trilby's Apartment
25. The Boob Tube
26. Polly Poster
27. Audrey's apartment

wet moon

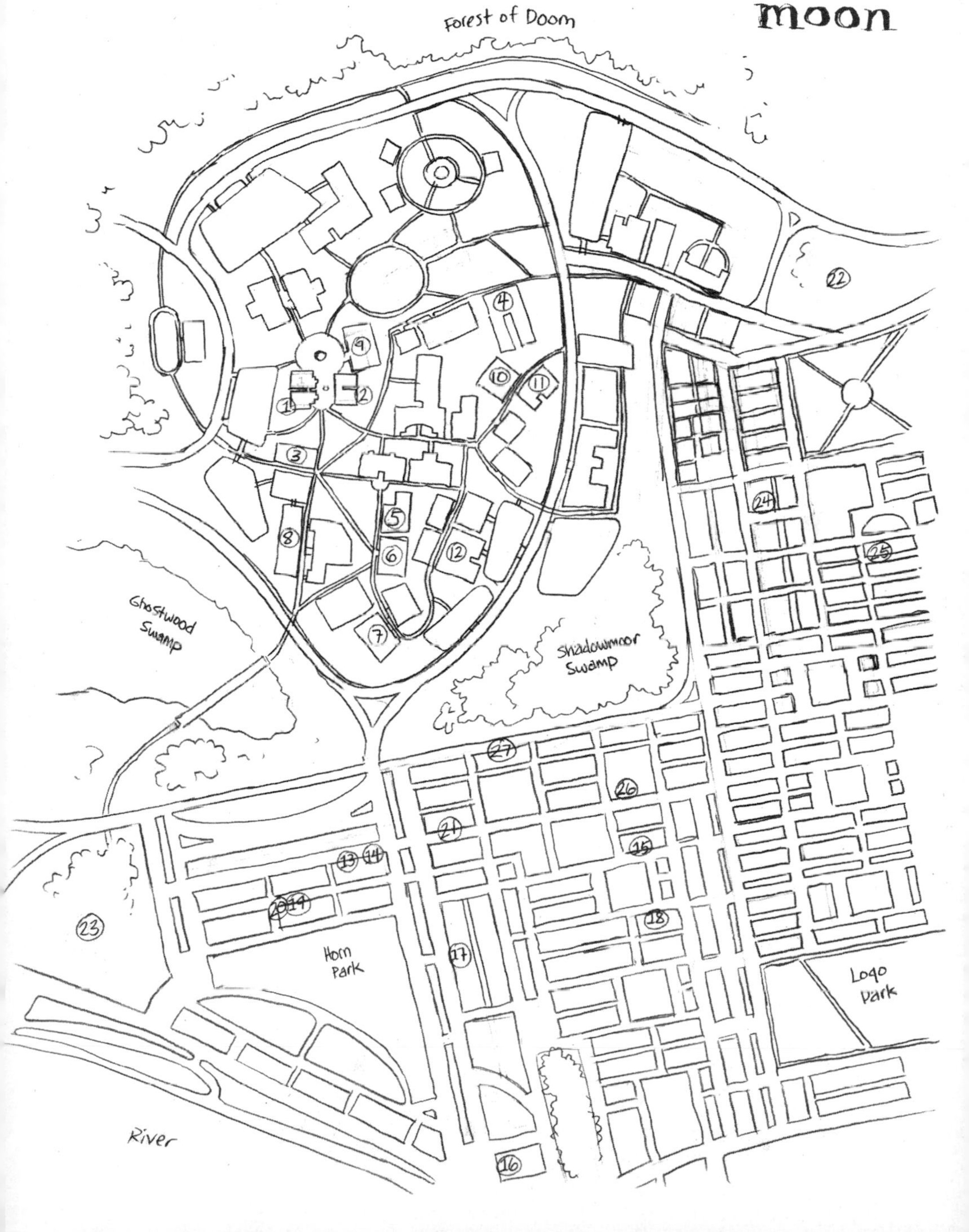
Forest of Doom
Ghostwood Swamp
Shadowmoor Swamp
Horn Park
Logo Park
River

28. The Lovedrop Residence
29. The Swanhilde Residence
30. Wet Moon High School
31. The Shoe Tree
32. The Bernarde Residence
33. The Zuzanny Residence

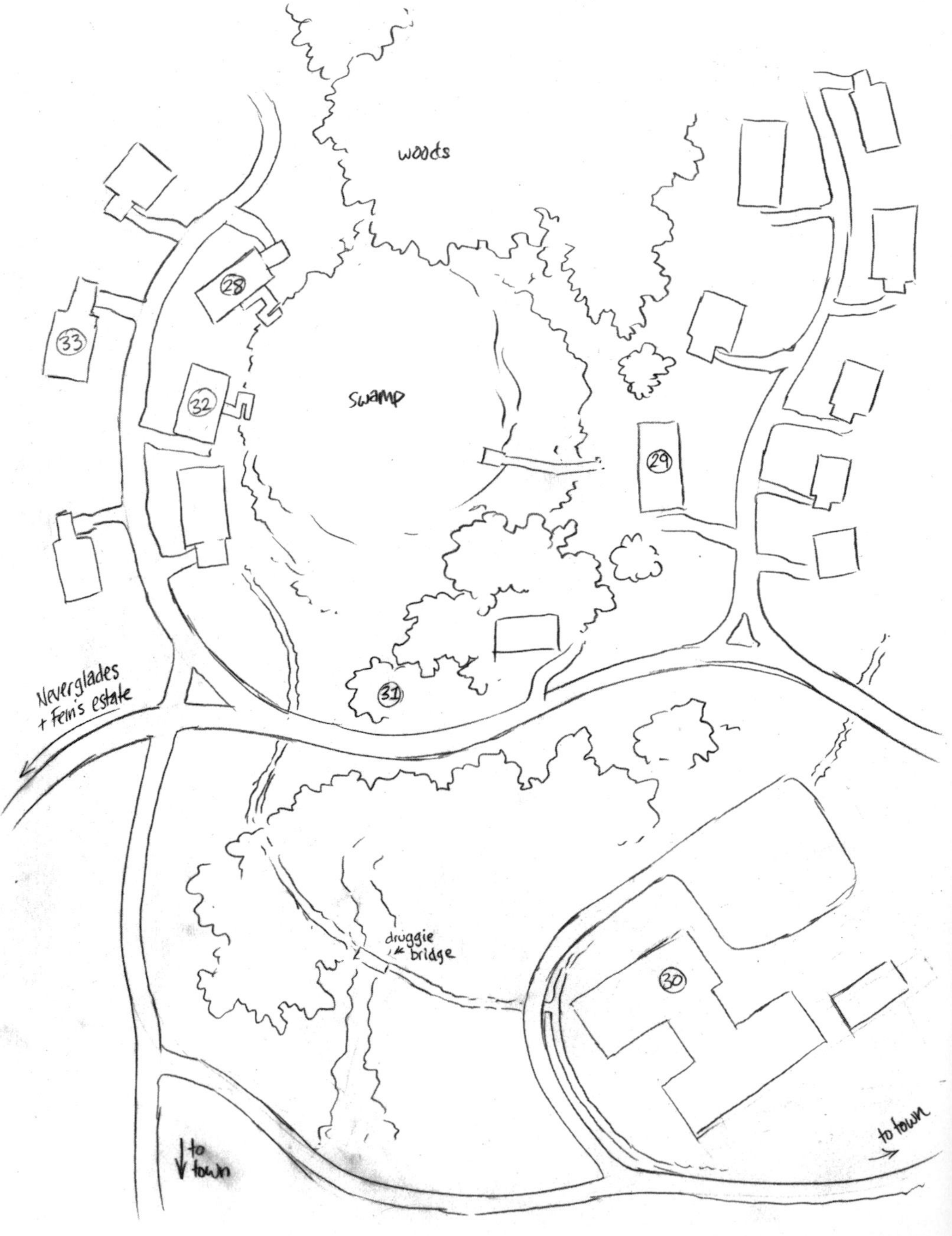

woods
swamp
28
29
30
31
32
33
Neverglades + Fern's estate
druggie bridge
to town
to town

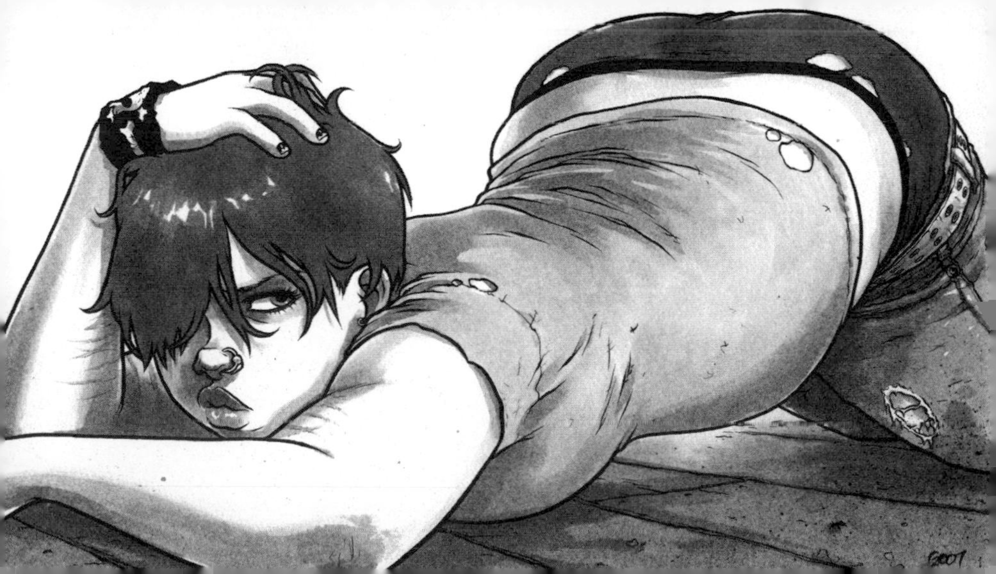

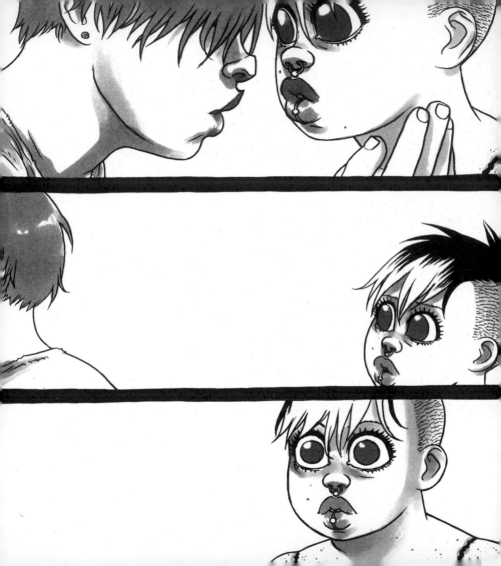

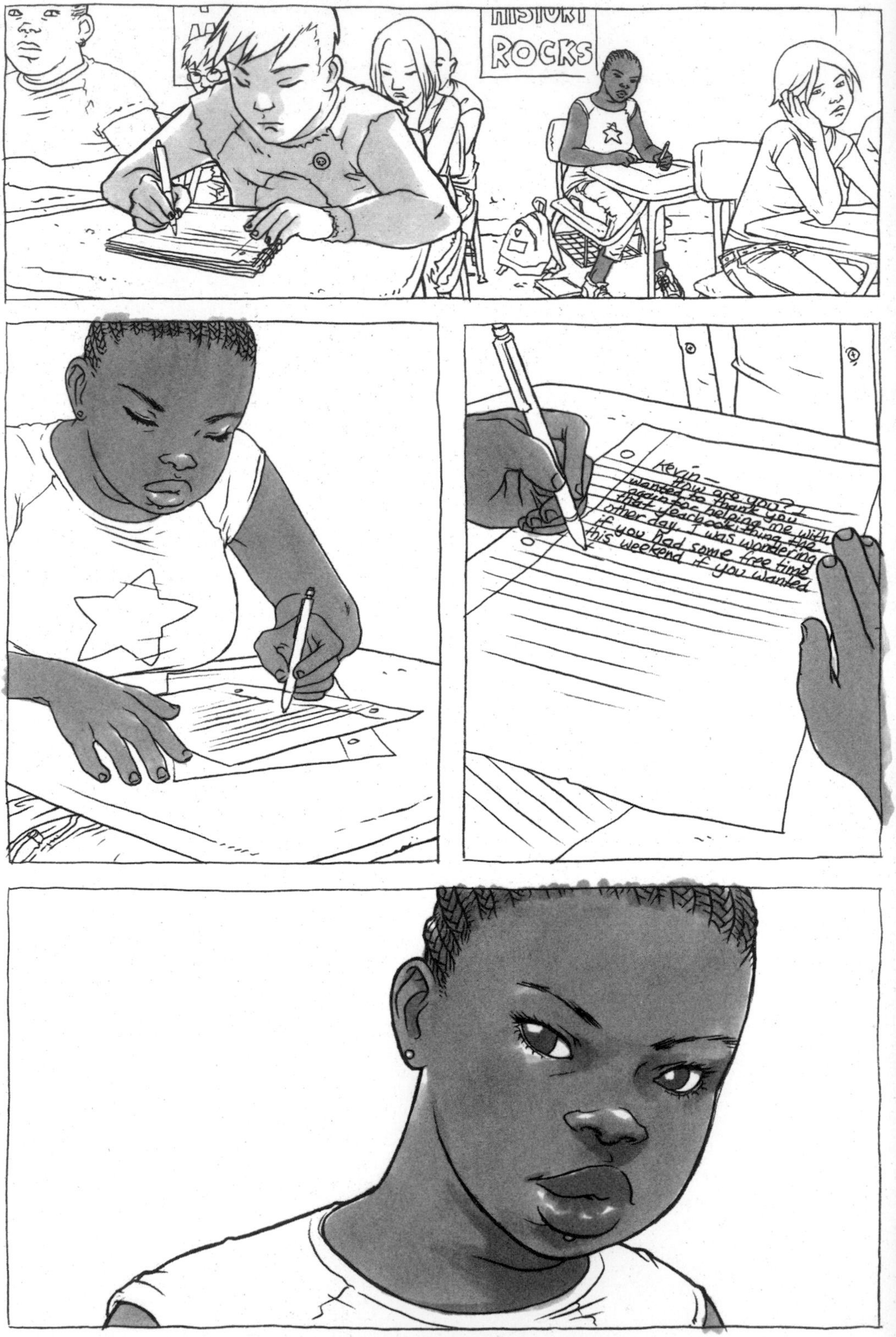
HISTORY
ROCKS
Kevin—
How are you? I
wanted to thank you
again for helping me with
that yearbook thing the
other day. I was wondering
if you had some free time
this weekend if you wanted

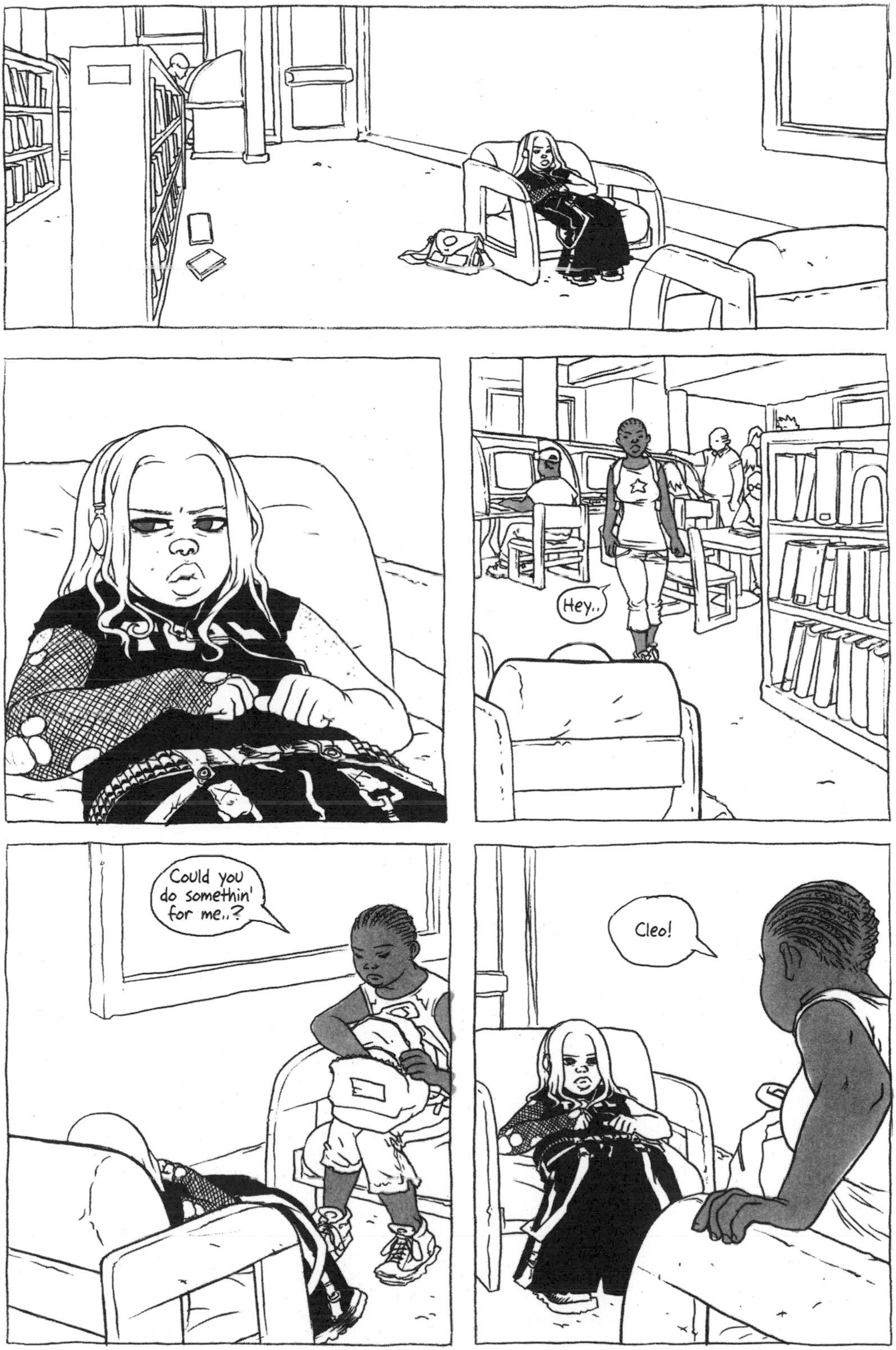
Hey..
Could you do somethin' for me..?
Cleo!

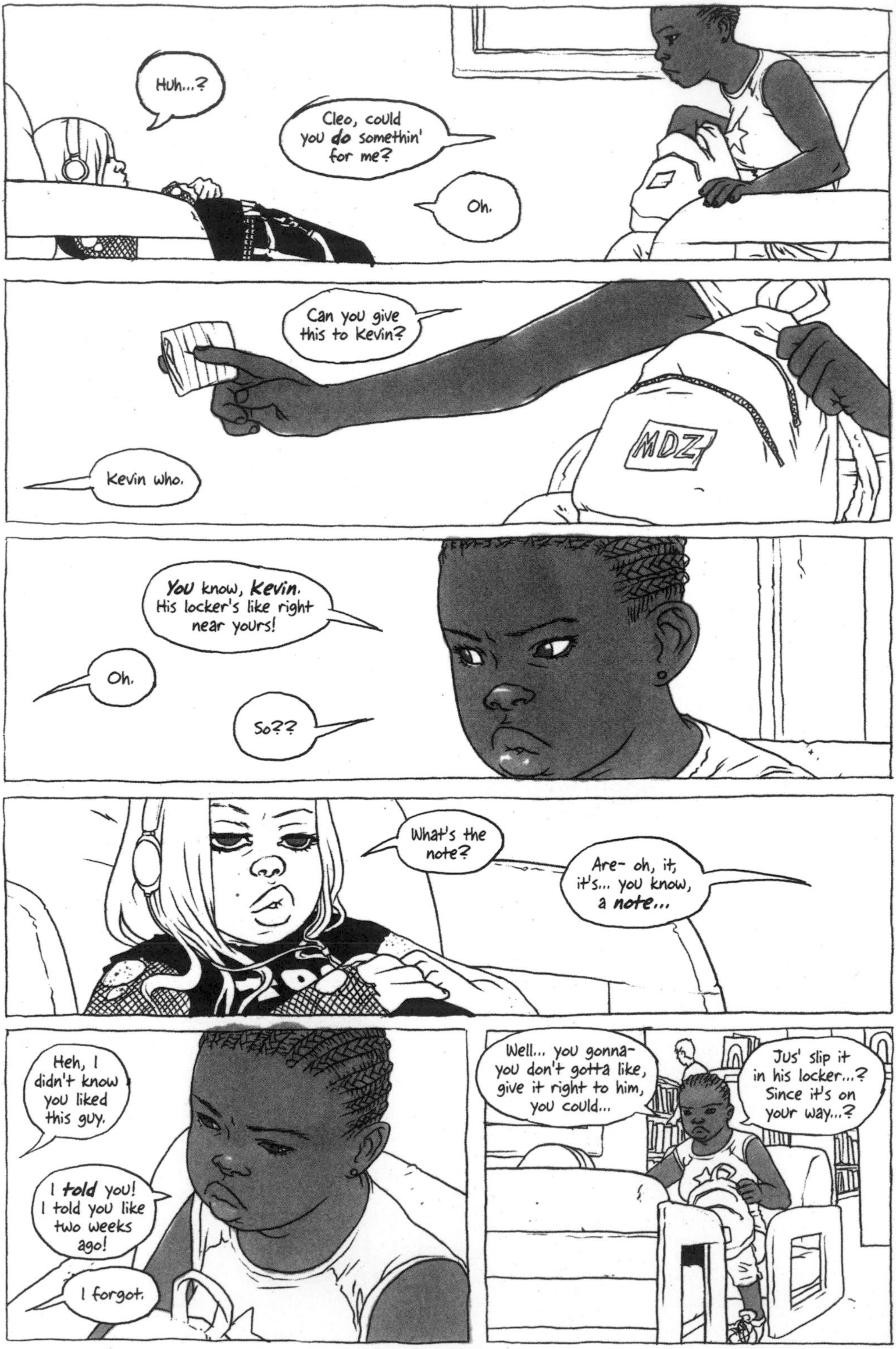
Huh...?
Cleo, could you **do** somethin' for me?
Oh.
Can you give this to Kevin?
Kevin who.
You know, ***Kevin***. His locker's like right near yours!
Oh.
So??
What's the note?
Are- oh, it, it's... you know, a ***note...***
Heh, I didn't know you liked this guy.
I ***told*** you! I told you like two weeks ago!
I forgot.
Well... you gonna- you don't gotta like, give it right to him, you could...
Jus' slip it in his locker...? Since it's on your way...?

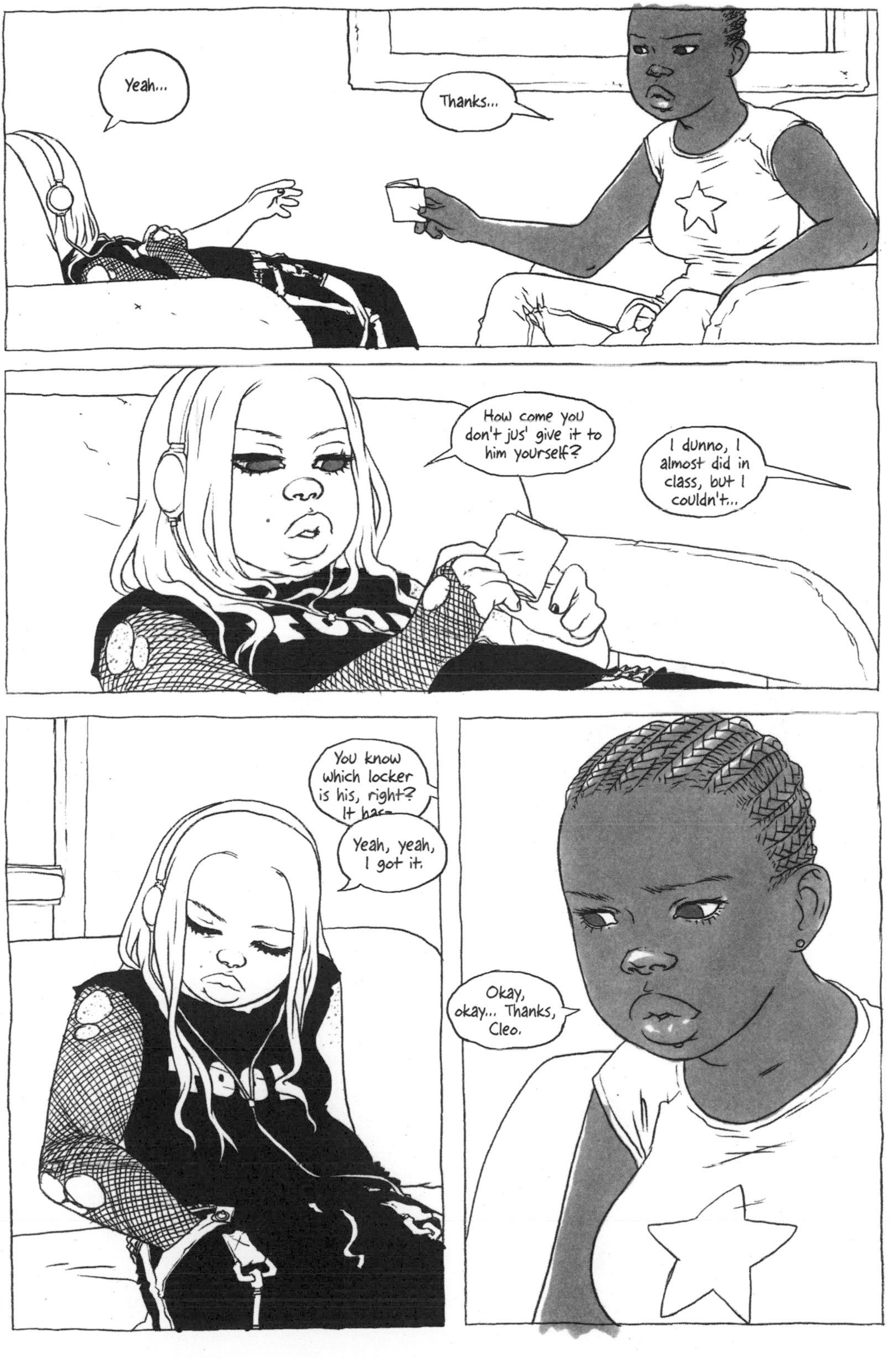
Yeah...
Thanks...
How come you don't jus' give it to him yourself?
I dunno, I almost did in class, but I couldn't...
You know which locker is his, right? It has-
Yeah, yeah, I got it.
Okay, okay... Thanks, Cleo.

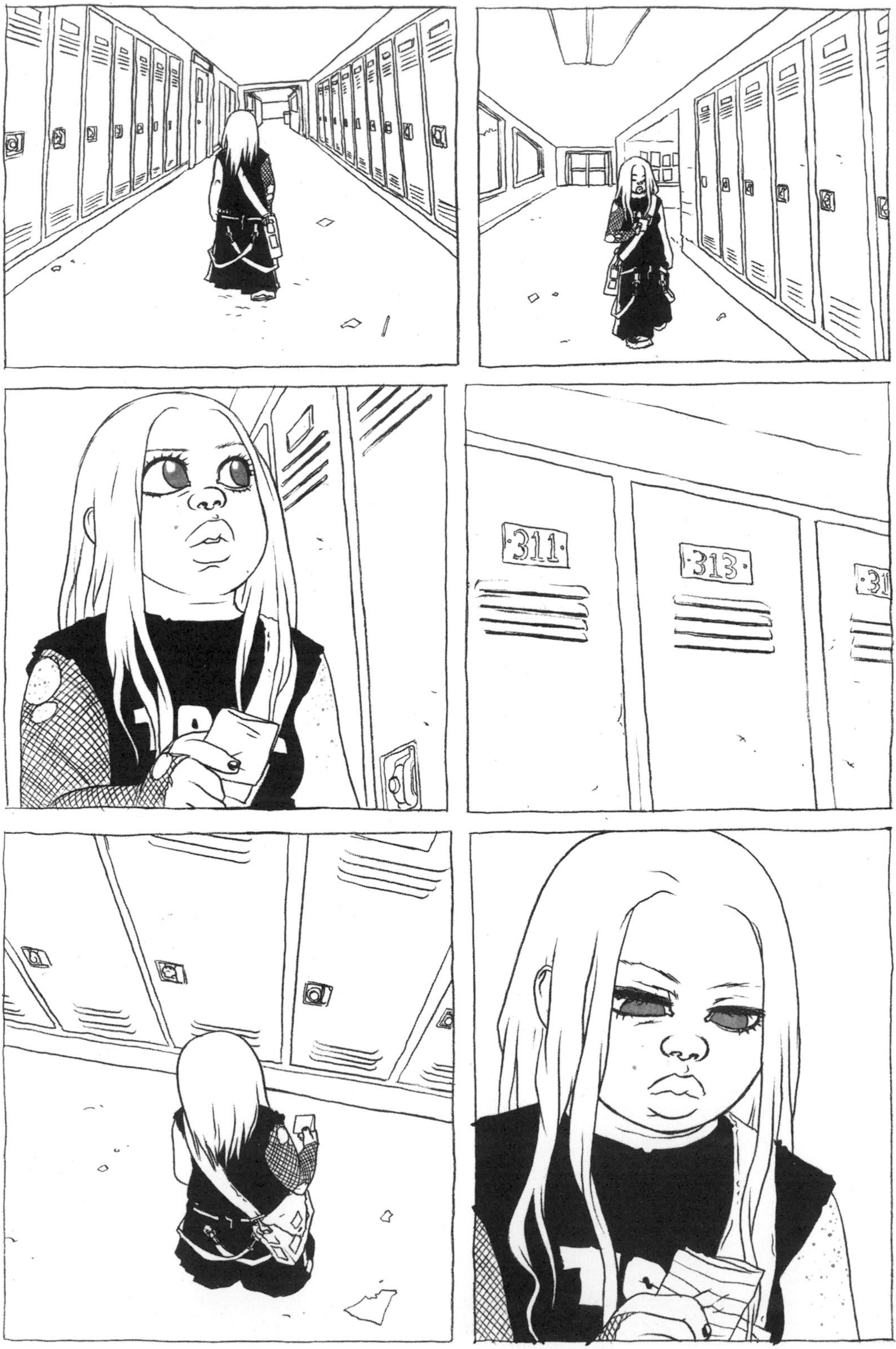
311
313

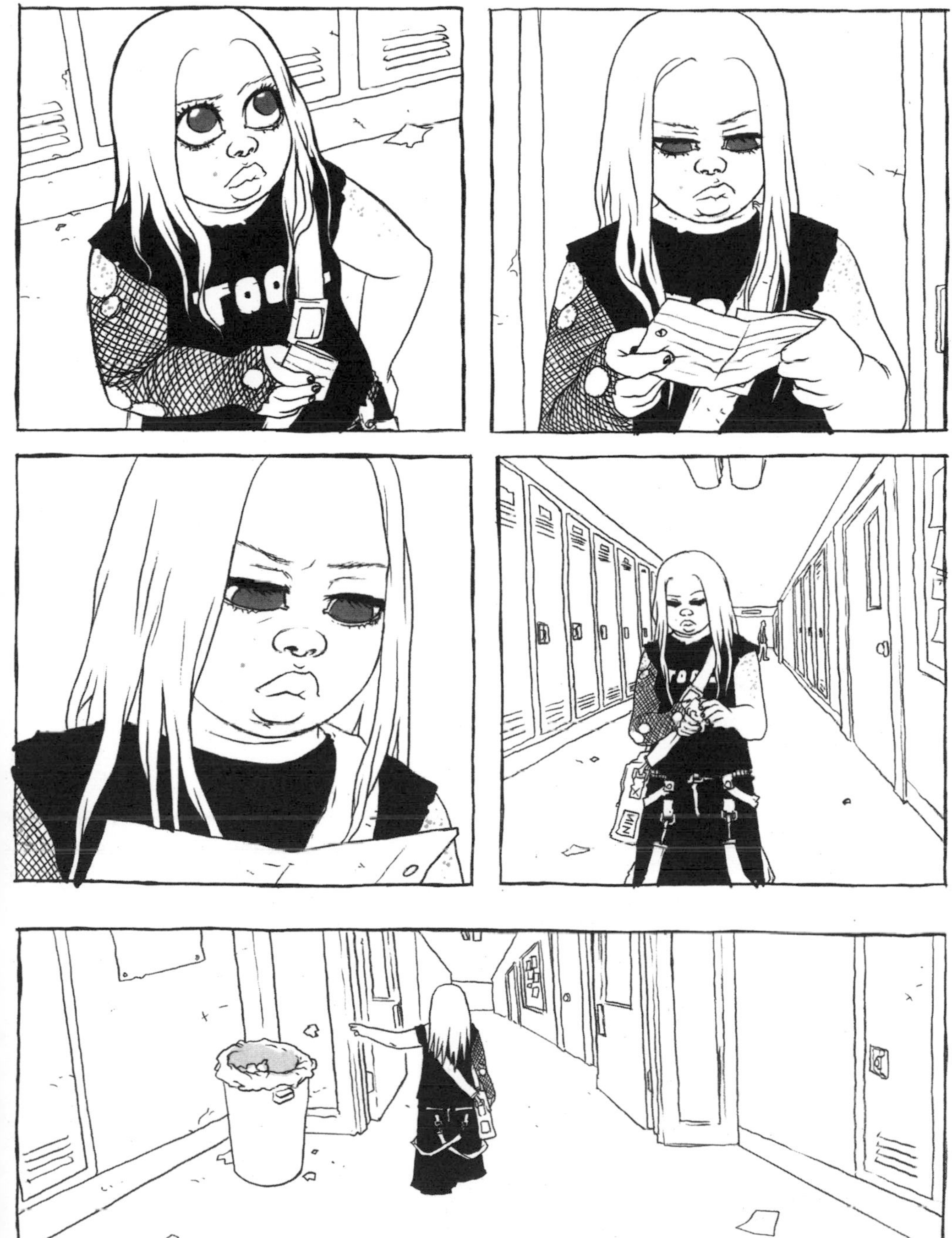

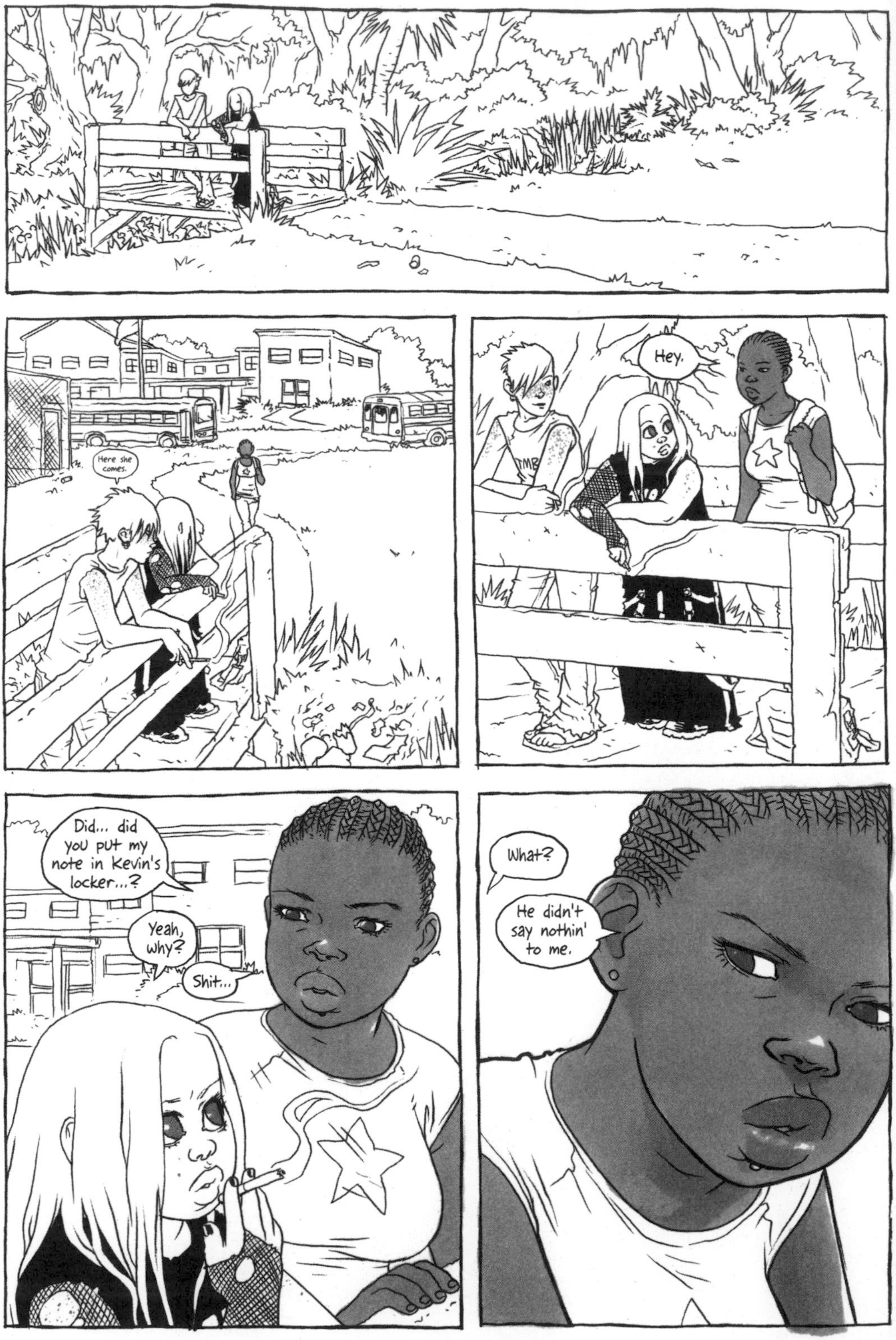
Here she comes.
Hey.
Did... did you put my note in Kevin's locker...?
Yeah, why?
Shit...
What?
He didn't say nothin' to me.

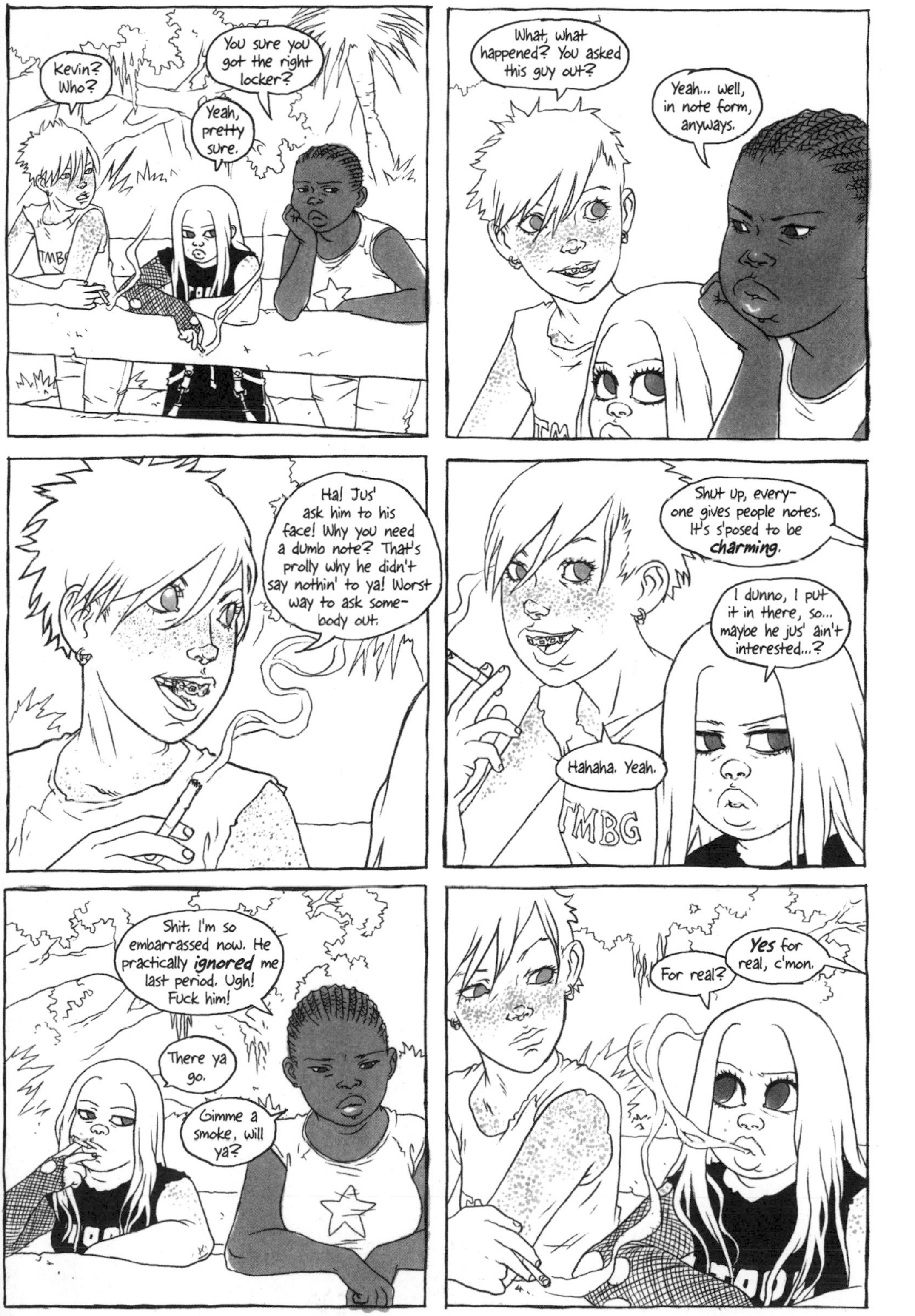
Kevin? Who?
You sure you got the right locker?
Yeah, pretty sure.
TMBG
What, what happened? You asked this guy out?
Yeah... well, in note form, anyways.
Ha! Jus' ask him to his face! Why you need a dumb note? That's prolly why he didn't say nothin' to ya! Worst way to ask somebody out.
Shut up, everyone gives people notes. It's s'posed to be **charming**.
I dunno, I put it in there, so... maybe he jus' ain't interested...?
Hahaha. Yeah.
TMBG
Shit. I'm so embarrassed now. He practically **ignored** me last period. Ugh! Fuck him!
There ya go.
Gimme a smoke, will ya?
For real?
Yes for real, c'mon.

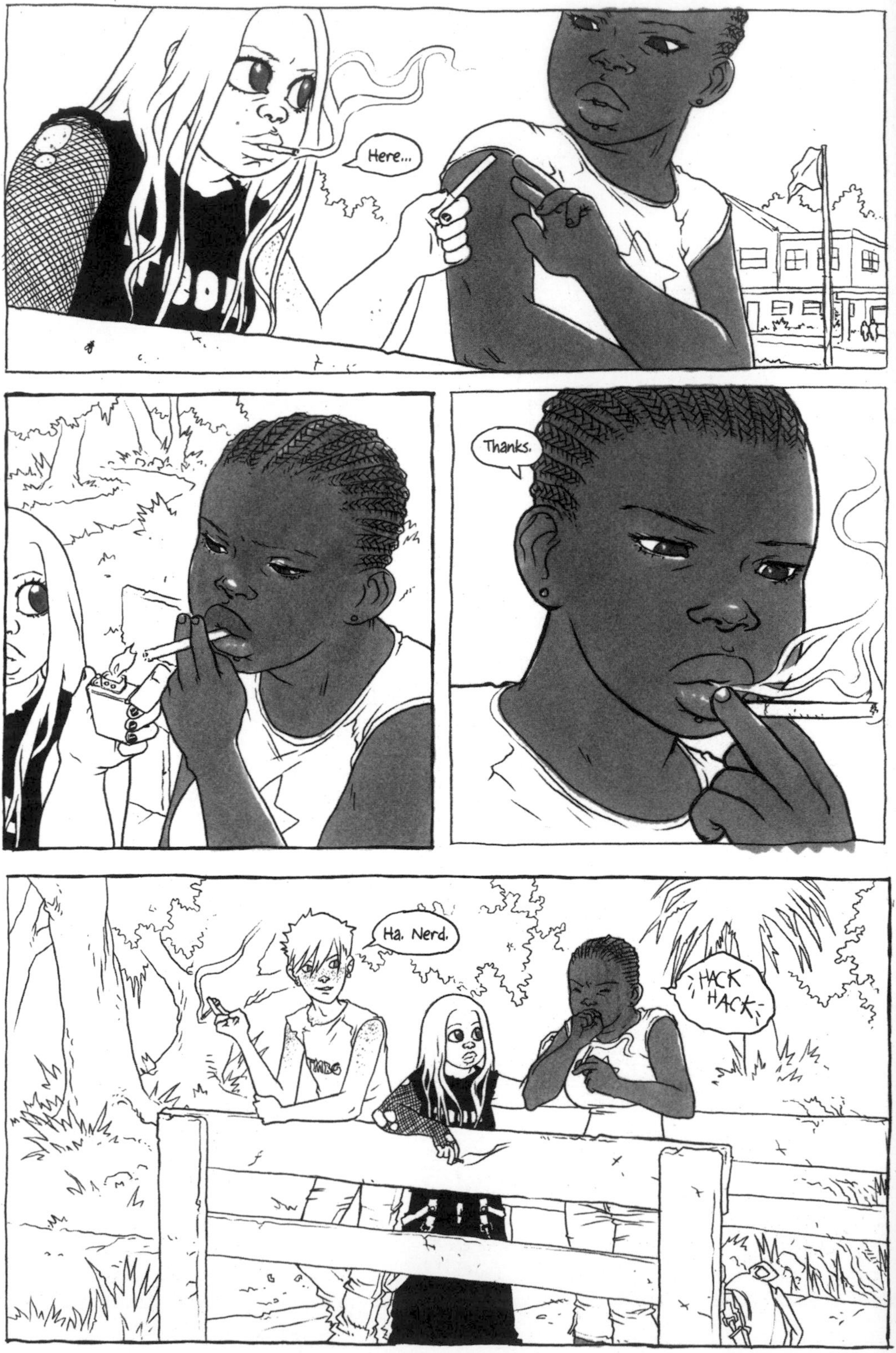
Here...
Thanks.
Ha. Nerd.
HACK HACK

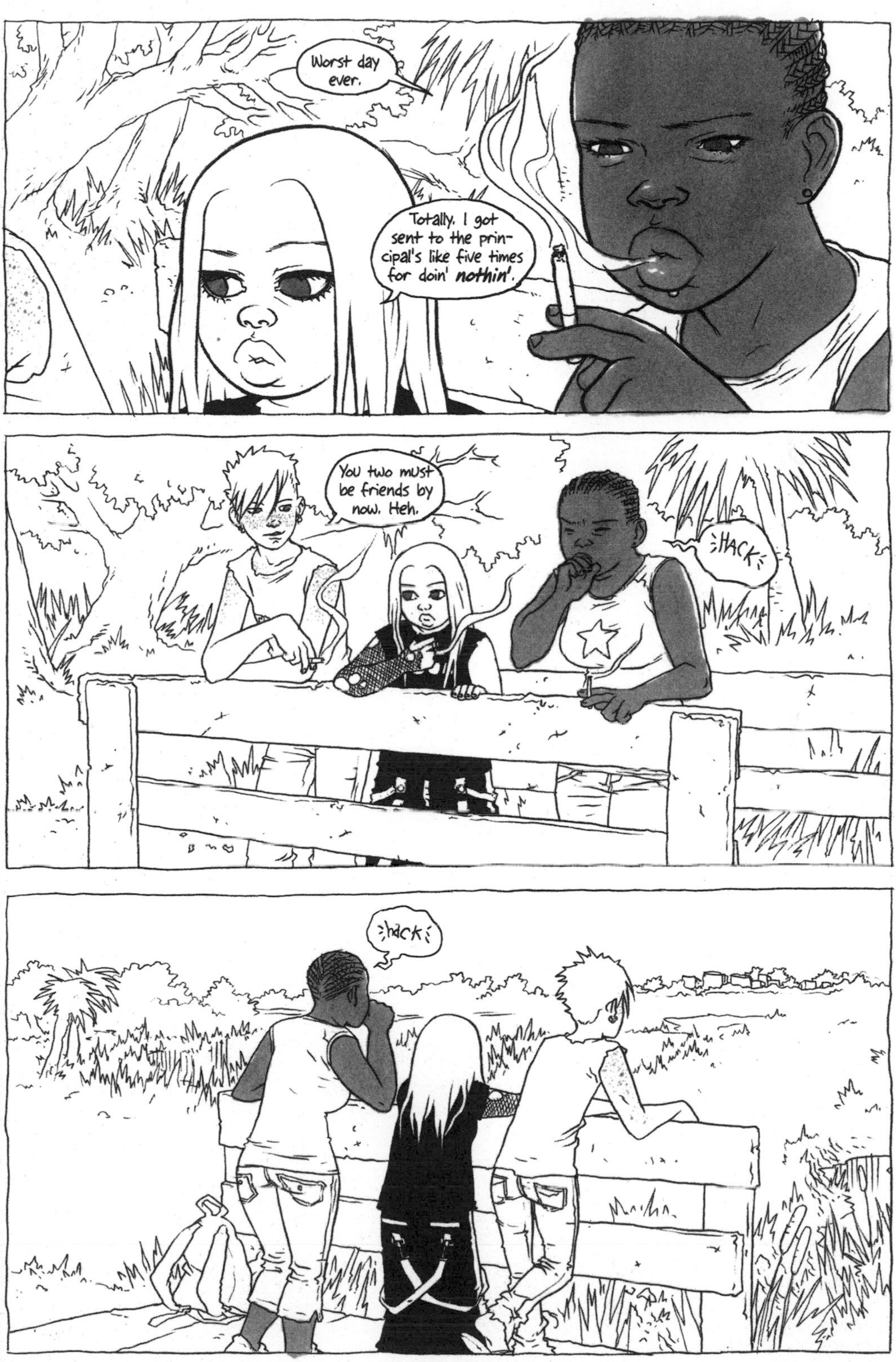
Worst day ever.
Totally. I got sent to the principal's like five times for doin' **nothin'**.
You two must be friends by now. Heh.
HACK
hack

11

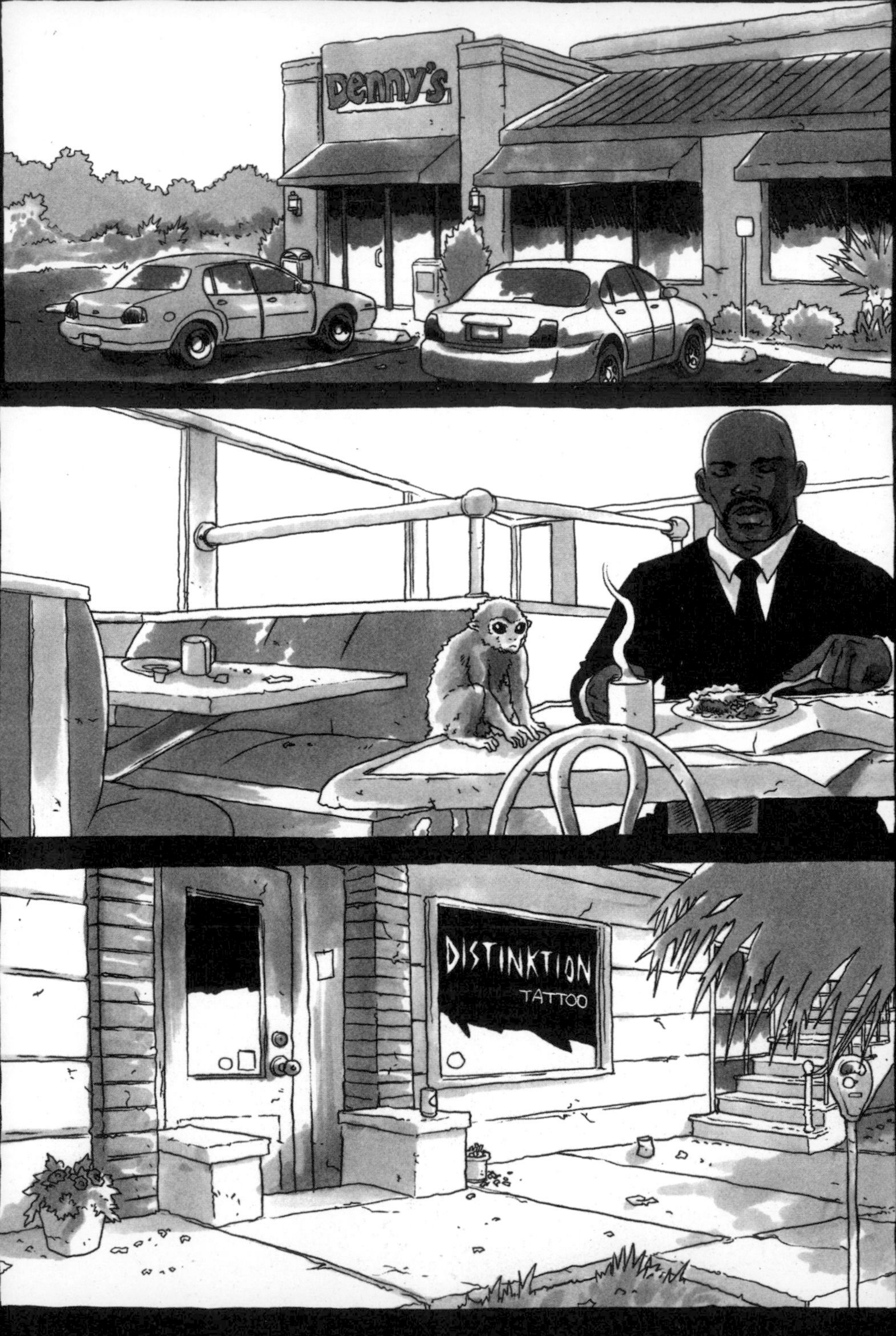
Denny's
DISTINKTION
TATTOO

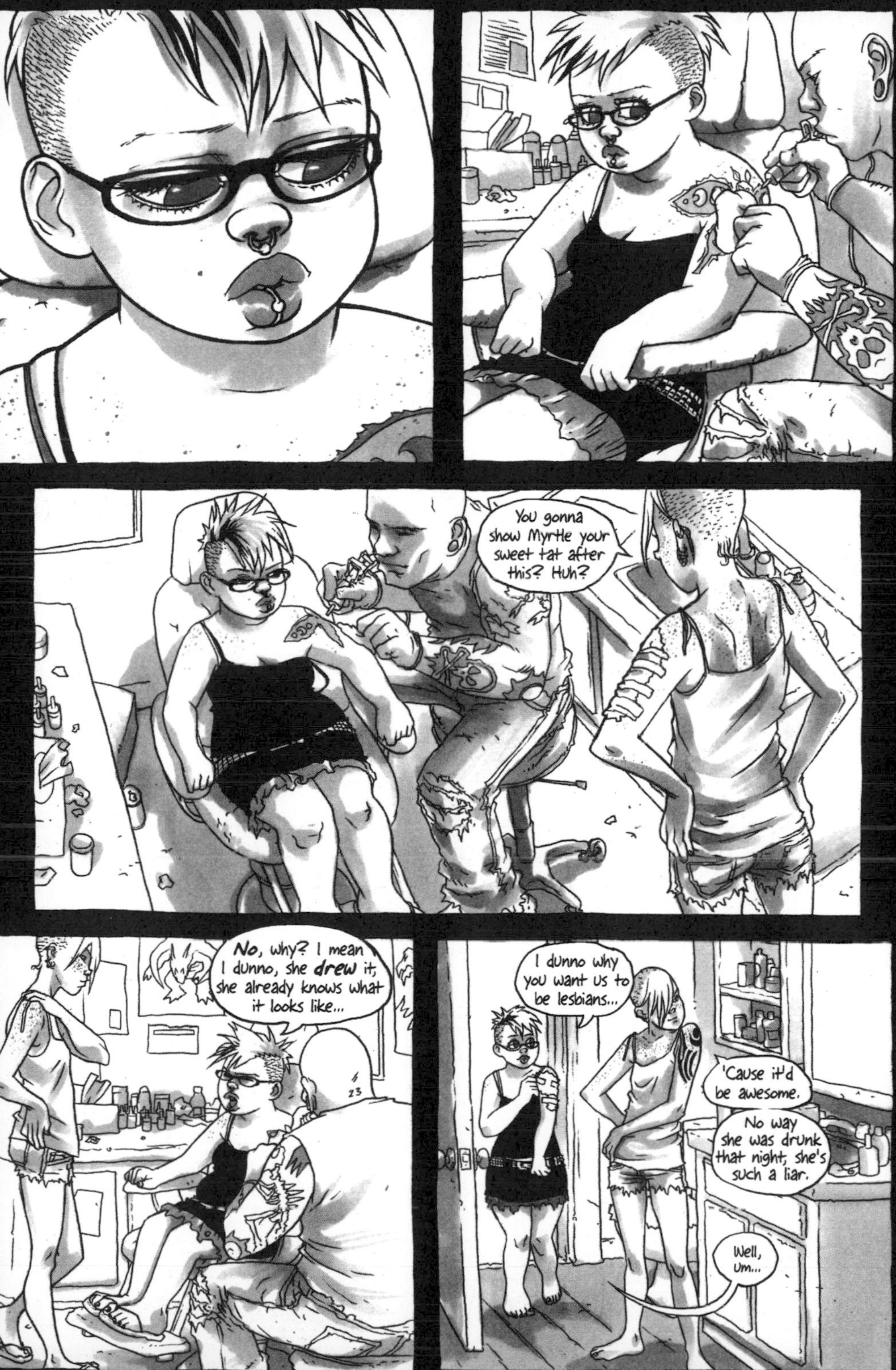
You gonna show Myrtle your sweet tat after this? Huh?
No, why? I mean I dunno, she drew it, she already knows what it looks like...
I dunno why you want us to be lesbians...
'Cause it'd be awesome.
No way she was drunk that night, she's such a liar.
Well, um...

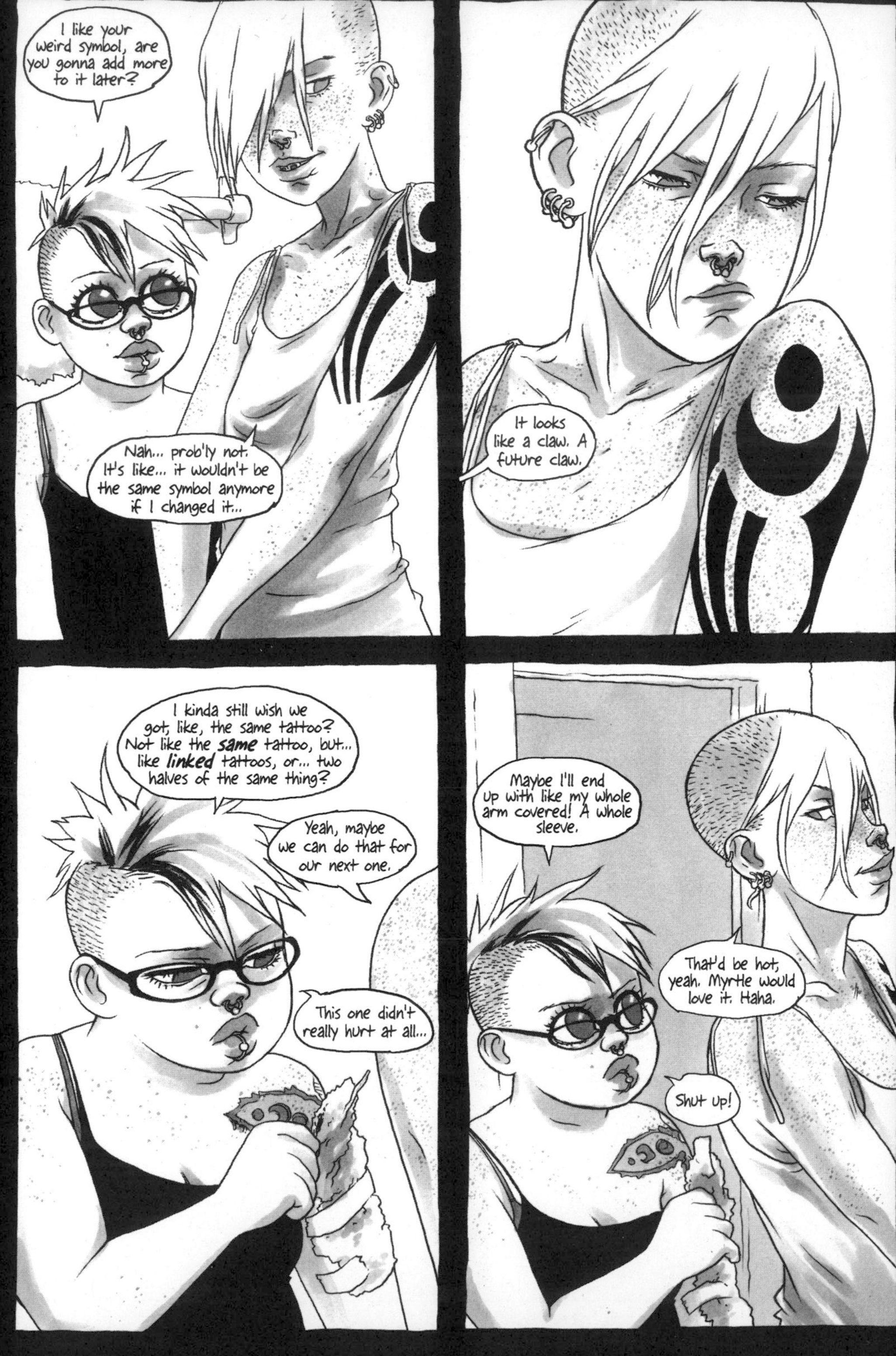
I like your weird symbol, are you gonna add more to it later?
Nah... prob'ly not. It's like... it wouldn't be the same symbol anymore if I changed it...
It looks like a claw. A future claw.
I kinda still wish we got, like, the same tattoo? Not like the **same** tattoo, but... like **linked** tattoos, or... two halves of the same thing?
Yeah, maybe we can do that for our next one.
This one didn't really hurt at all...
Maybe I'll end up with like my whole arm covered! A whole sleeve.
That'd be hot, yeah. Myrtle would love it. Haha.
Shut up!

October 9th

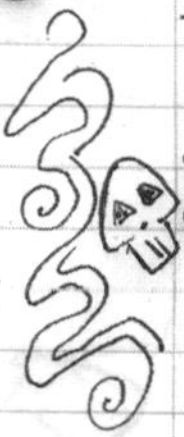

Trilby and I got our tattoos done! We look so good. I decided to get that death's head luna moth design that Myrtle drew for me, and I got it done real big so it even goes onto my chest sort of. I thought it would be a better choice than the bone wings, because Beth just got some bone wing stuff and I didn't want to copy her. The manager guy at the parlor, Erwan, gave us some tattoo care things and a list of what to do. Some of it is kind of a hassle, like putting the lotions on all the time, and right after you get it you have to wipe off the ooze that keeps coming out of your skin,

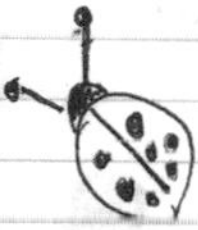

and you're not supposed to stay out in the sun for a long time or even go swimming (or get it wet! no showers! I'm prepared to be stinky). We were supposed to go ~~to~~ the beach sometime this week or next, but now I don't know, maybe if we stay under a big umbrella and go on a cloudy day.

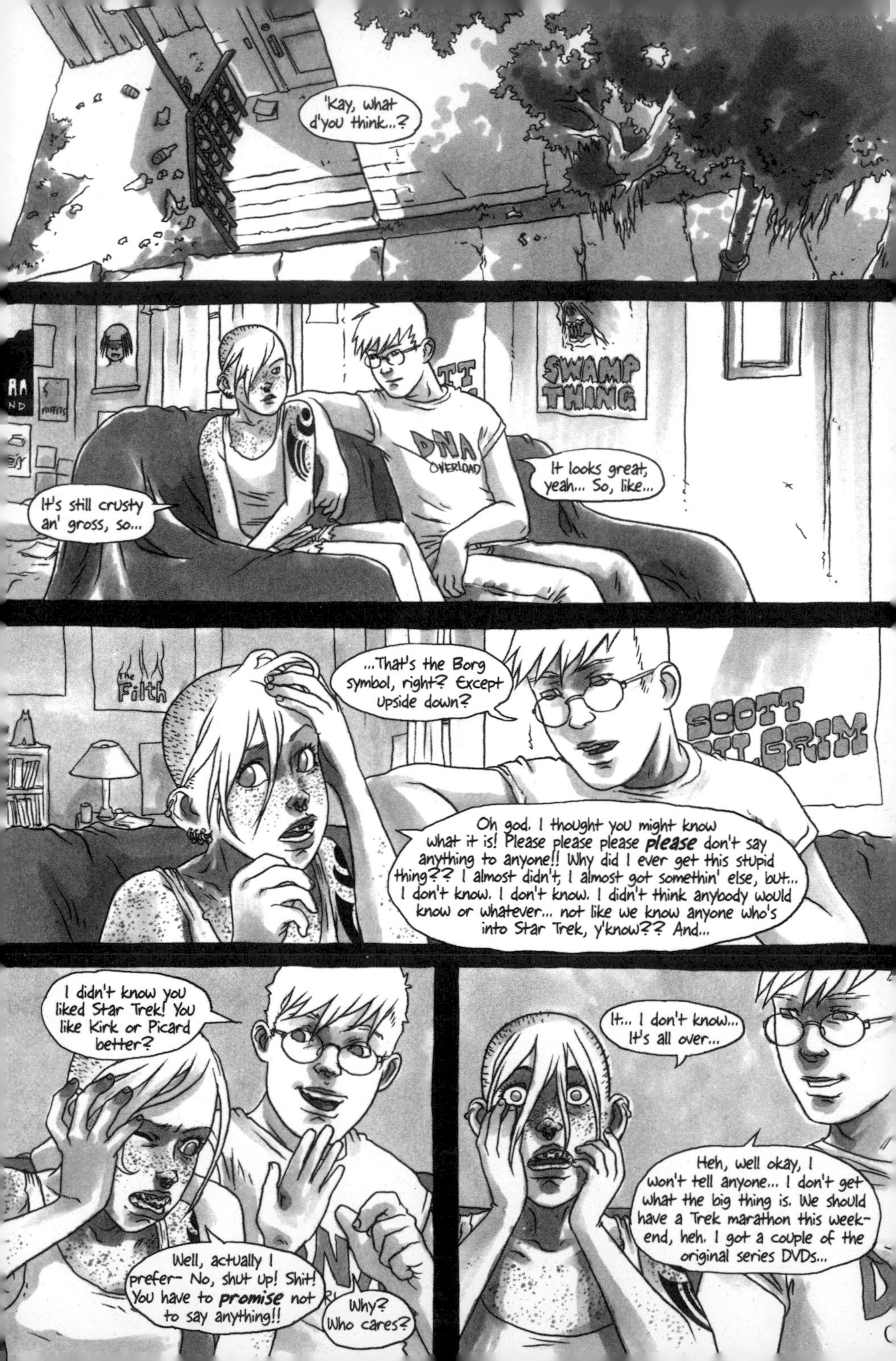

'Kay, what d'you think...?
SWAMP THING
DNA OVERLOAD
It's still crusty an' gross, so...
It looks great, yeah... So, like...
The Filth
...That's the Borg symbol, right? Except upside down?
SCOTT
Oh god. I thought you might know what it is! Please please please *please* don't say anything to anyone!! Why did I ever get this stupid thing?? I almost didn't, I almost got somethin' else, but... I don't know. I don't know. I didn't think anybody would know or whatever... not like we know anyone who's into Star Trek, y'know?? And...
I didn't know you liked Star Trek! You like Kirk or Picard better?
Well, actually I prefer- No, shut up! Shit! You have to *promise* not to say anything!!
Why? Who cares?
It... I don't know... It's all over...
Heh, well okay, I won't tell anyone... I don't get what the big thing is. We should have a Trek marathon this week-end, heh. I got a couple of the original series DVDs...

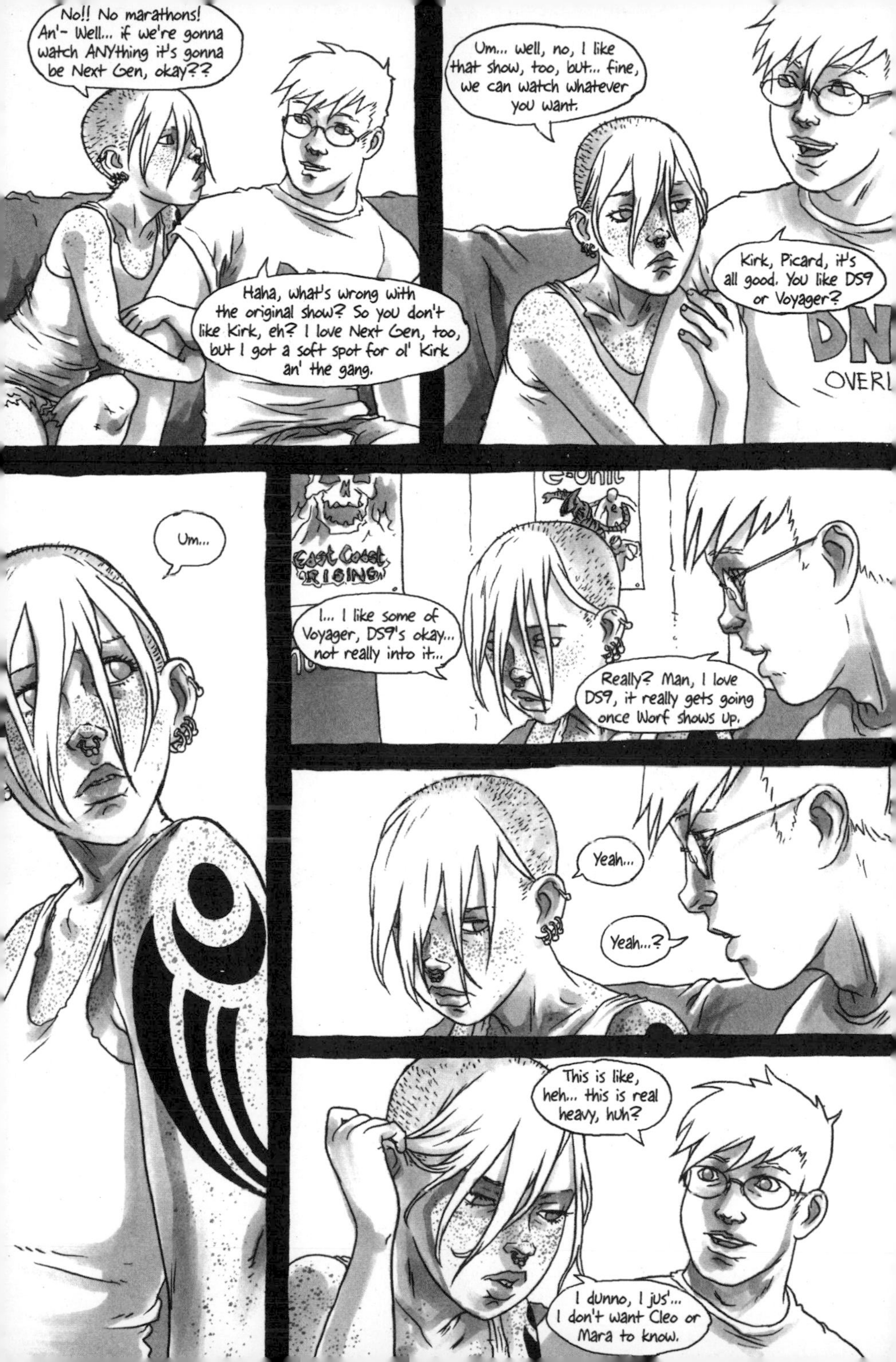
No!! No marathons! An'- Well... if we're gonna watch ANYthing it's gonna be Next Gen, okay??
Haha, what's wrong with the original show? So you don't like Kirk, eh? I love Next Gen, too, but I got a soft spot for ol' Kirk an' the gang.
Um... well, no, I like that show, too, but... fine, we can watch whatever you want.
Kirk, Picard, it's all good. You like DS9 or Voyager?
DN
OVERI
Um...
East Coast RISING
I... I like some of Voyager, DS9's okay... not really into it...
Really? Man, I love DS9, it really gets going once Worf shows up.
Yeah...
Yeah...?
This is like, heh... this is real heavy, huh?
I dunno, I jus'... I don't want Cleo or Mara to know.

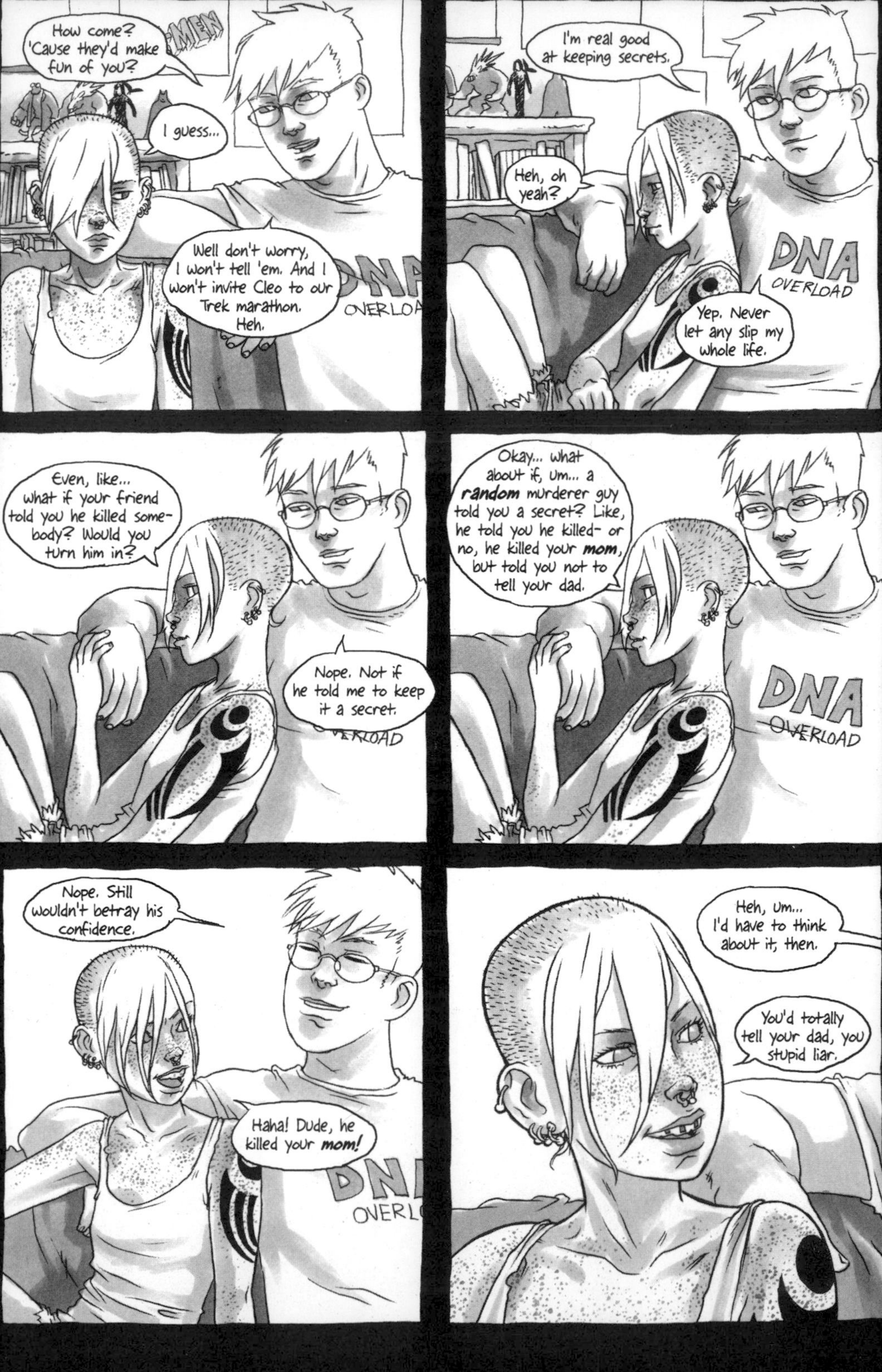

How come? 'Cause they'd make fun of you?
I guess...
Well don't worry, I won't tell 'em. And I won't invite Cleo to our Trek marathon. Heh.
DNA OVERLOAD
I'm real good at keeping secrets.
Heh, oh yeah?
Yep. Never let any slip my whole life.
DNA OVERLOAD
Even, like... what if your friend told you he killed somebody? Would you turn him in?
Nope. Not if he told me to keep it a secret.
Okay... what about if, um... a **random** murderer guy told you a secret? Like, he told you he killed- or no, he killed your **mom**, but told you not to tell your dad.
DNA OVERLOAD
Nope. Still wouldn't betray his confidence.
Haha! Dude, he killed your **mom!**
Heh, um... I'd have to think about it, then.
You'd totally tell your dad, you stupid liar.

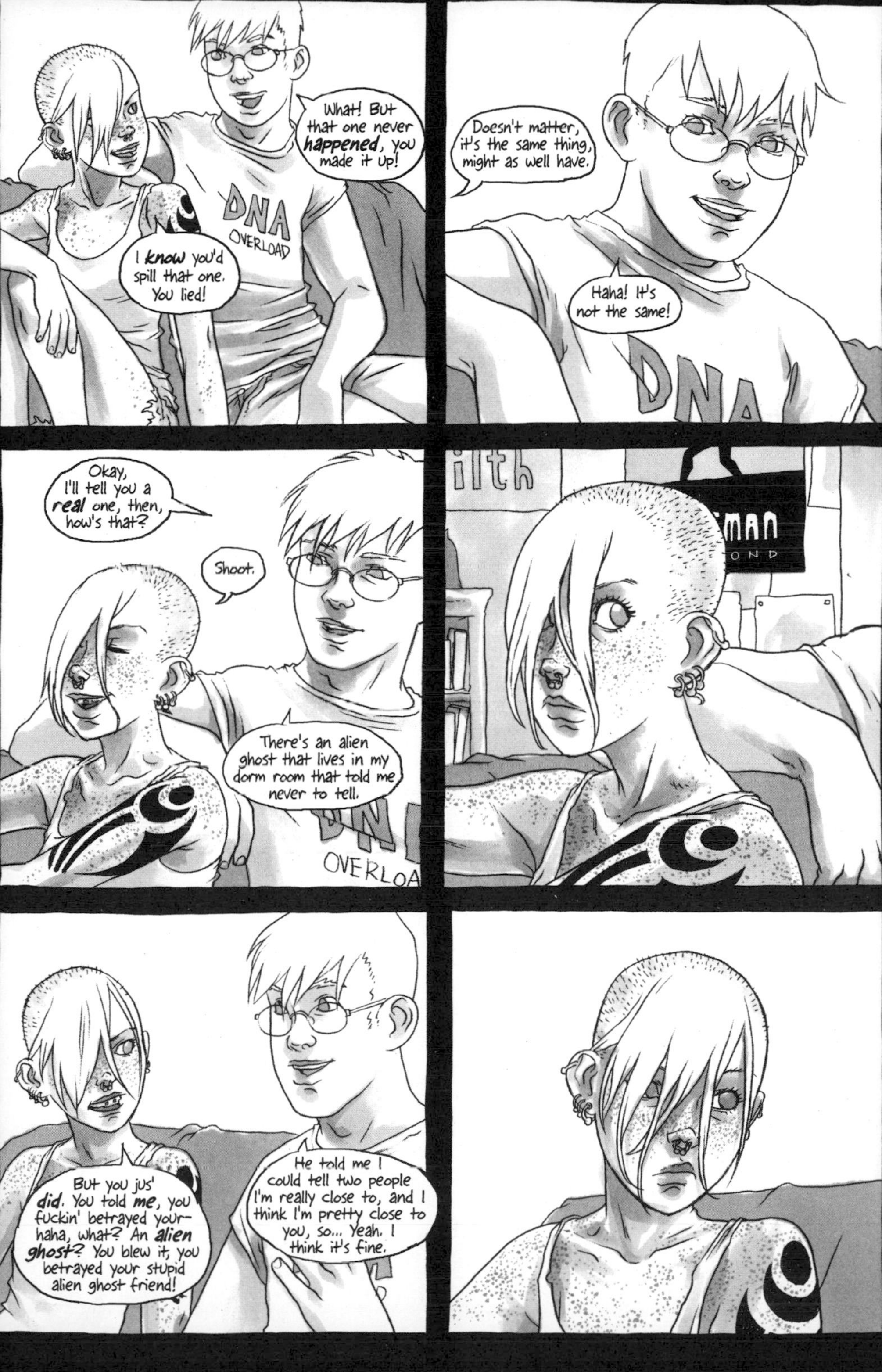
What! But that one never happened, you made it up!
I know you'd spill that one. You lied!
DNA OVERLOAD
Doesn't matter, it's the same thing, might as well have.
Haha! It's not the same!
Okay, I'll tell you a real one, then, how's that?
Shoot.
There's an alien ghost that lives in my dorm room that told me never to tell.
OVERLOA
But you jus' did. You told me, you fuckin' betrayed your- haha, what? An alien ghost? You blew it, you betrayed your stupid alien ghost friend!
He told me I could tell two people I'm really close to, and I think I'm pretty close to you, so... Yeah. I think it's fine.

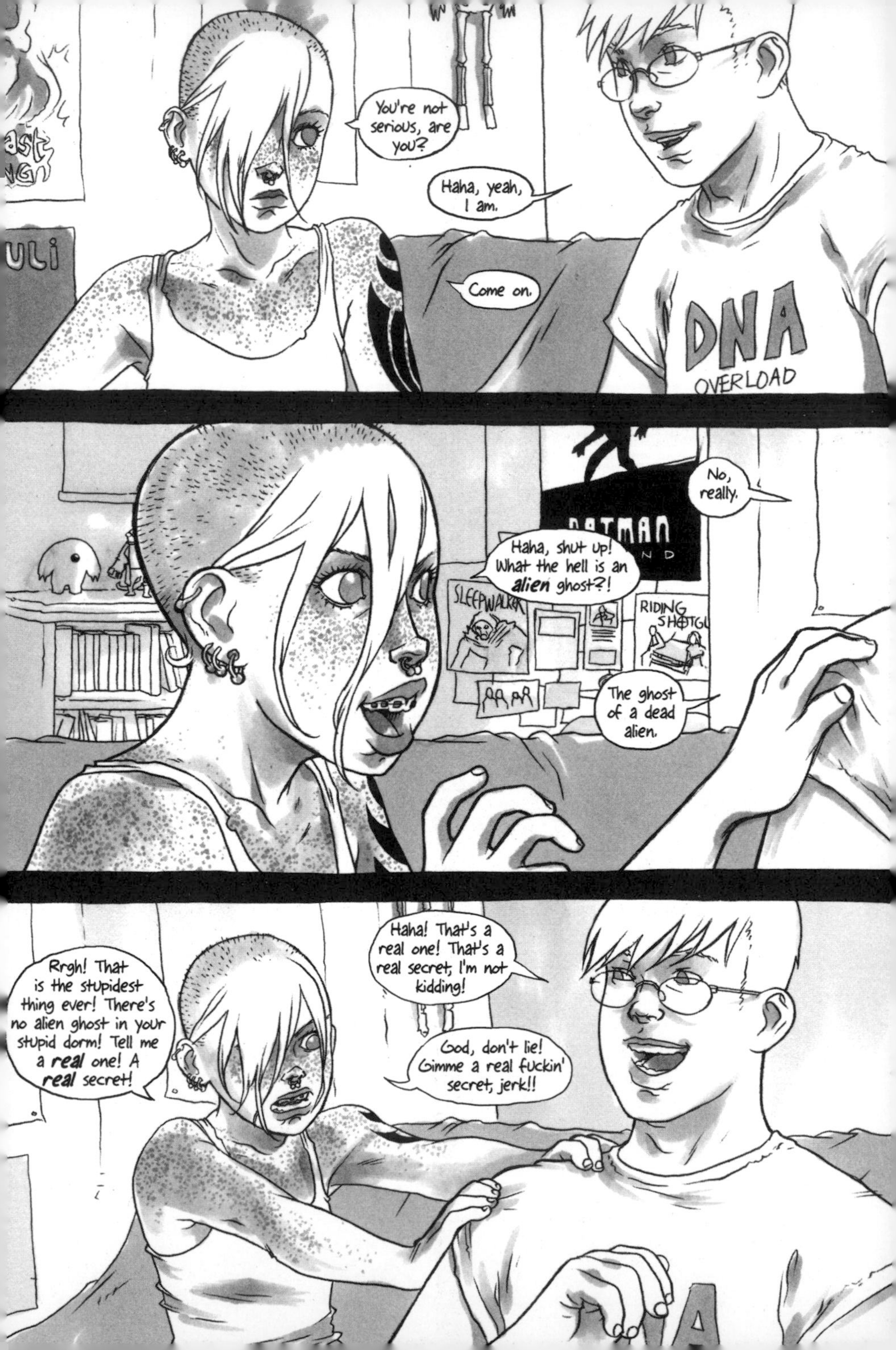

You're not serious, are you?
Haha, yeah, I am.
Come on.
DNA
OVERLOAD
No, really.
Haha, shut up! What the hell is an **alien** ghost?!
SLEEPWALKER
The ghost of a dead alien.
Rrgh! That is the stupidest thing ever! There's no alien ghost in your stupid dorm! Tell me a **real** one! A **real** secret!
Haha! That's a real one! That's a real secret, I'm not kidding!
God, don't lie! Gimme a real fuckin' secret, jerk!!

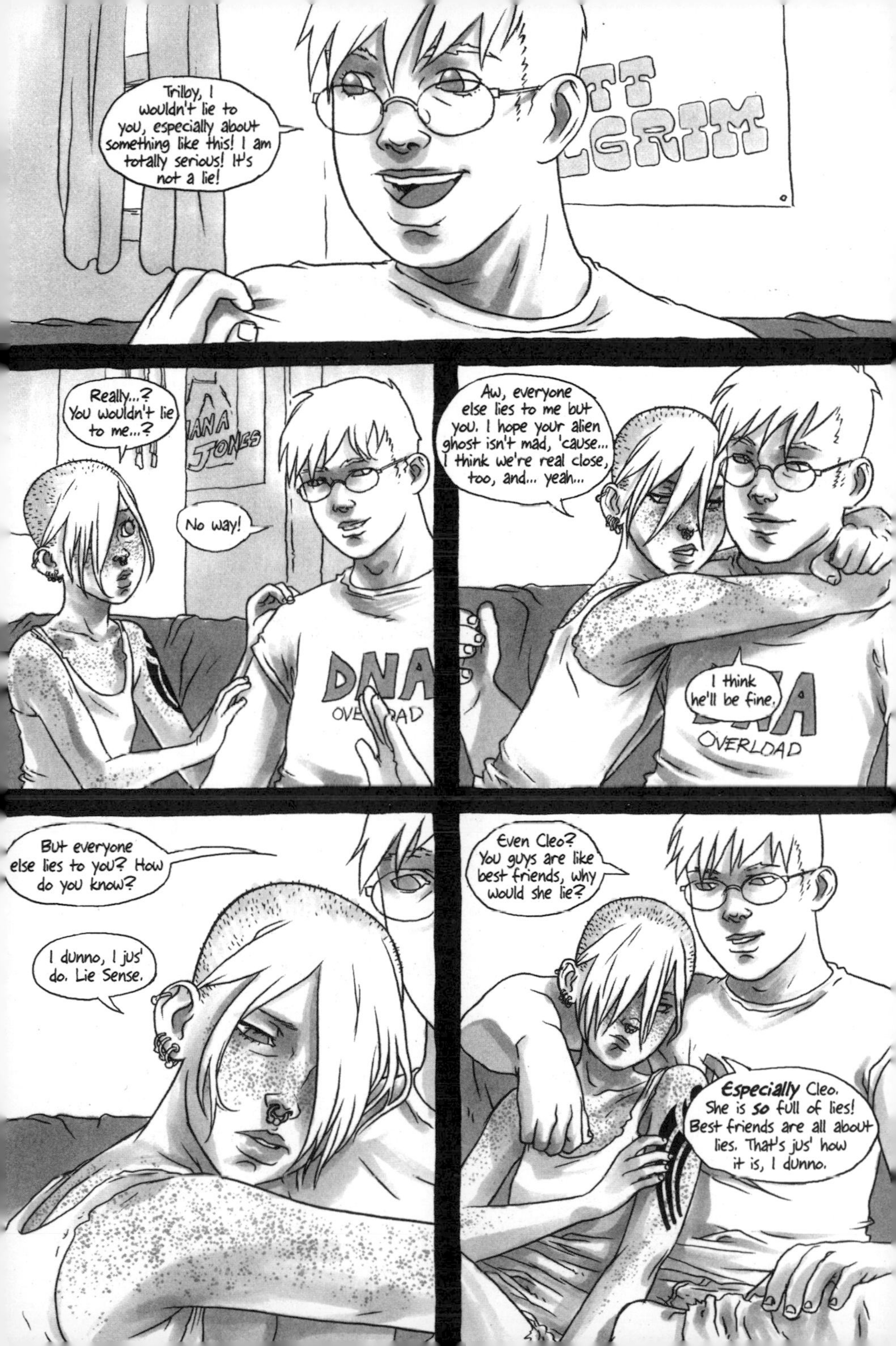
Trilby, I wouldn't lie to you, especially about something like this! I am totally serious! It's not a lie!
Really...? You wouldn't lie to me...?
No way!
Aw, everyone else lies to me but you. I hope your alien ghost isn't mad, 'cause... I think we're real close, too, and... yeah...
I think he'll be fine.
But everyone else lies to you? How do you know?
I dunno, I jus' do. Lie Sense.
Even Cleo? You guys are like best friends, why would she lie?
Especially Cleo. She is so full of lies! Best friends are all about lies. That's jus' how it is, I dunno.

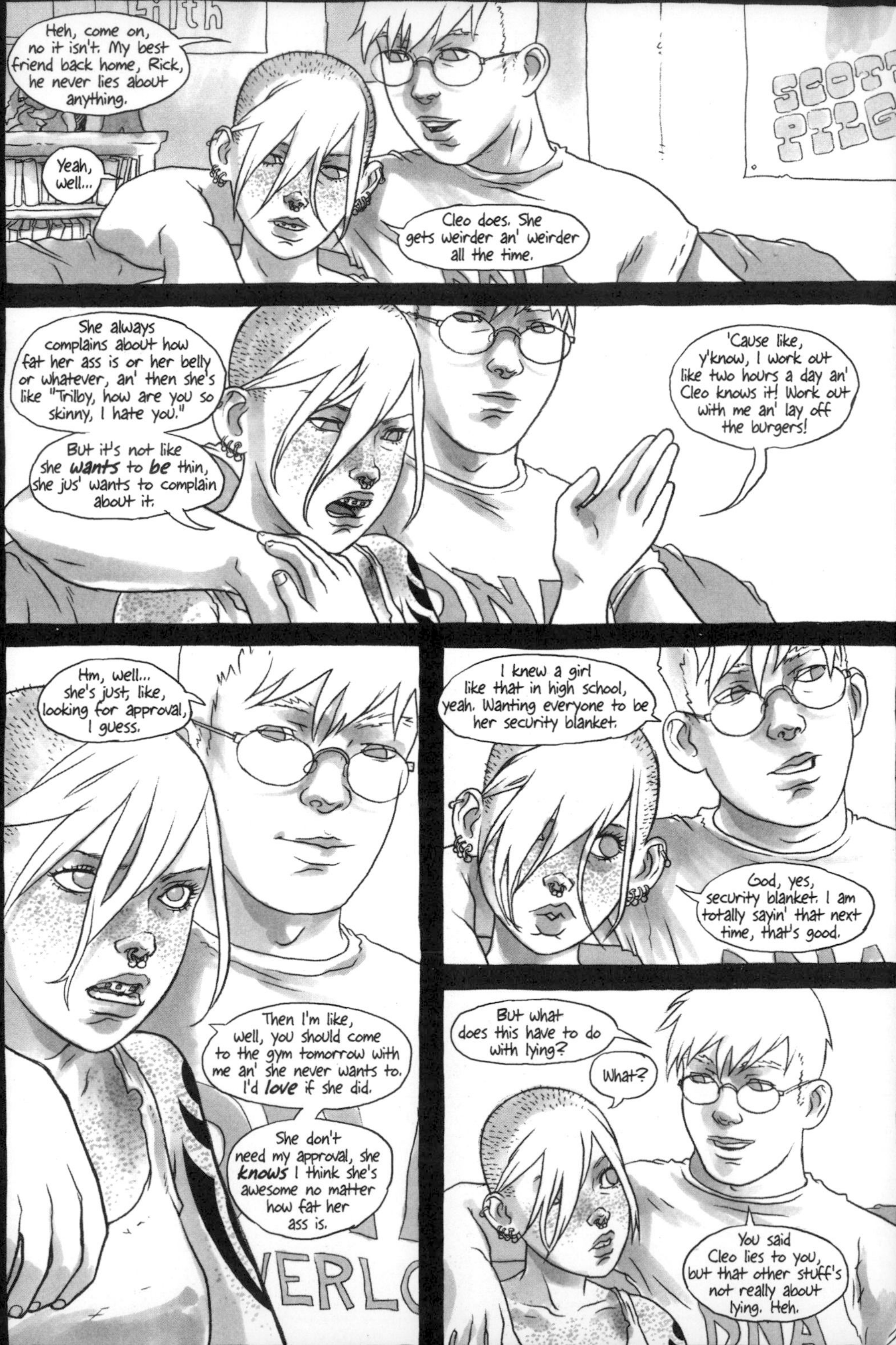

Filth
Heh, come on, no it isn't. My best friend back home, Rick, he never lies about anything.
SCOTT PILG
Yeah, well...
Cleo does. She gets weirder an' weirder all the time.
She always complains about how fat her ass is or her belly or whatever, an' then she's like "Trilby, how are you so skinny, I hate you."
But it's not like she *wants* to *be* thin, she jus' wants to complain about it.
'Cause like, y'know, I work out like two hours a day an' Cleo knows it! Work out with me an' lay off the burgers!
Hm, well... she's just, like, looking for approval, I guess.
Then I'm like, well, you should come to the gym tomorrow with me an' she never wants to. I'd *love* if she did.
She don't need my approval, she *knows* I think she's awesome no matter how fat her ass is.
VERLO
I knew a girl like that in high school, yeah. Wanting everyone to be her security blanket.
God, yes, security blanket. I am totally sayin' that next time, that's good.
But what does this have to do with lying?
What?
You said Cleo lies to you, but that other stuff's not really about lying. Heh.

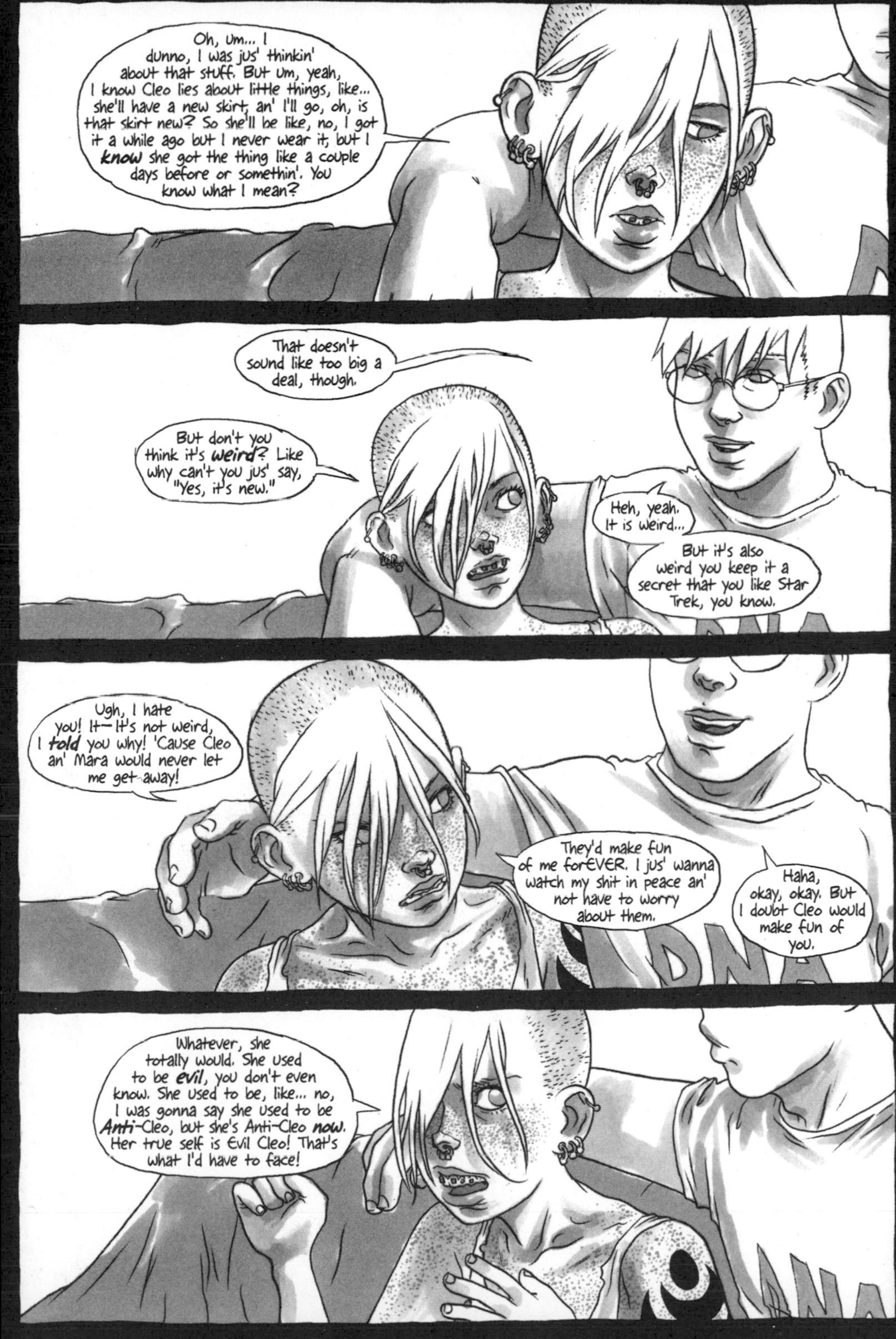
Oh, um... I dunno, I was jus' thinkin' about that stuff. But um, yeah, I know Cleo lies about little things, like... she'll have a new skirt, an' I'll go, oh, is that skirt new? So she'll be like, no, I got it a while ago but I never wear it, but I know she got the thing like a couple days before or somethin'. You know what I mean?
That doesn't sound like too big a deal, though.
But don't you think it's weird? Like why can't you jus' say, "Yes, it's new."
Heh, yeah. It is weird...
But it's also weird you keep it a secret that you like Star Trek, you know.
Ugh, I hate you! It— It's not weird, I told you why! 'Cause Cleo an' Mara would never let me get away!
They'd make fun of me forEVER. I jus' wanna watch my shit in peace an' not have to worry about them.
Haha, okay, okay. But I doubt Cleo would make fun of you.
Whatever, she totally would. She used to be evil, you don't even know. She used to be, like... no, I was gonna say she used to be Anti-Cleo, but she's Anti-Cleo now. Her true self is Evil Cleo! That's what I'd have to face!

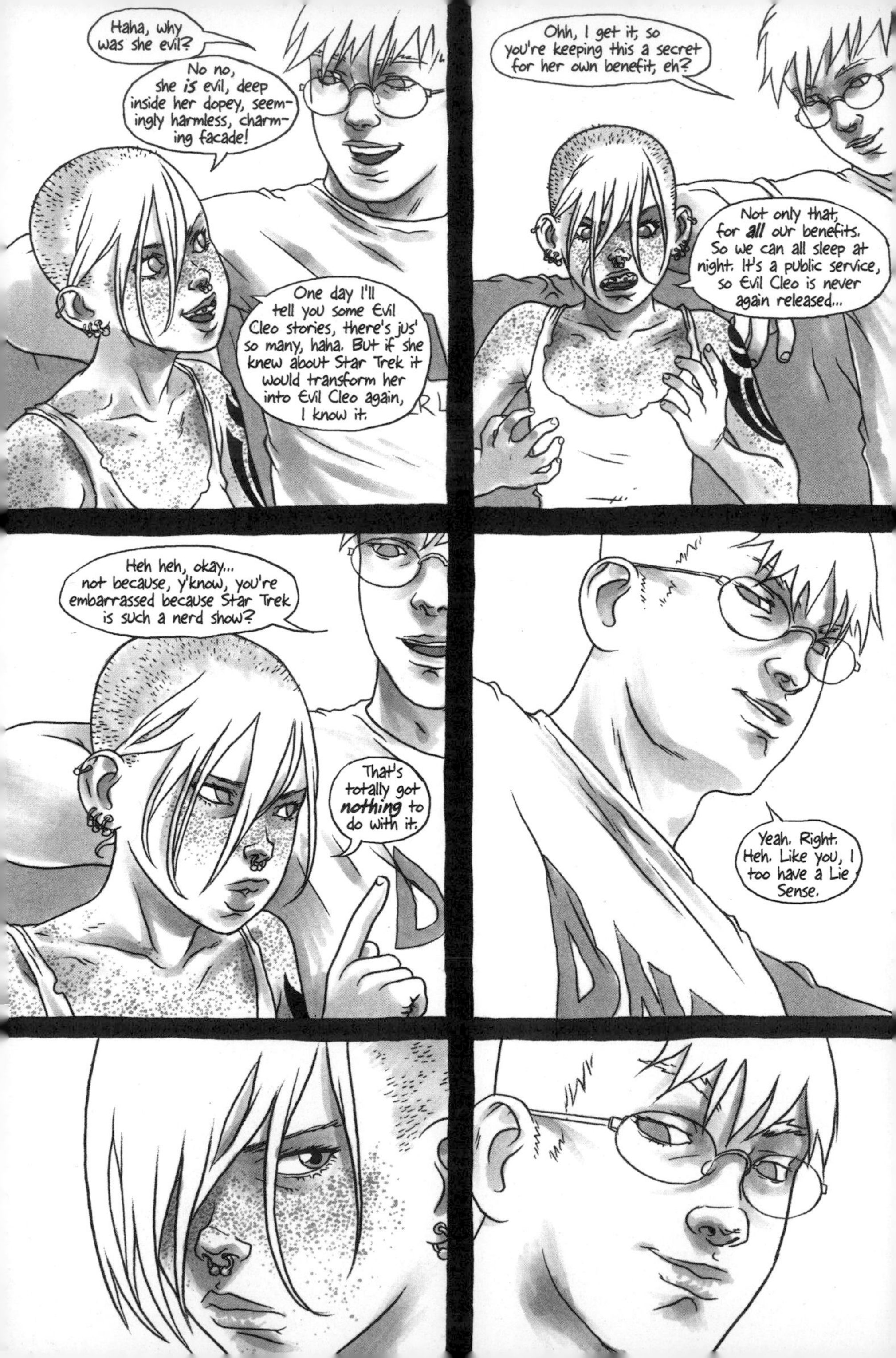
Haha, why was she evil?
No no, she **is** evil, deep inside her dopey, seemingly harmless, charming facade!
One day I'll tell you some Evil Cleo stories, there's jus' so many, haha. But if she knew about Star Trek it would transform her into Evil Cleo again, I know it.
Ohh, I get it, so you're keeping this a secret for her own benefit, eh?
Not only that, for **all** our benefits. So we can all sleep at night. It's a public service, so Evil Cleo is never again released...
Heh heh, okay... not because, y'know, you're embarrassed because Star Trek is such a nerd show?
That's totally got ***nothing*** to do with it.
Yeah. Right. Heh. Like you, I too have a Lie Sense.

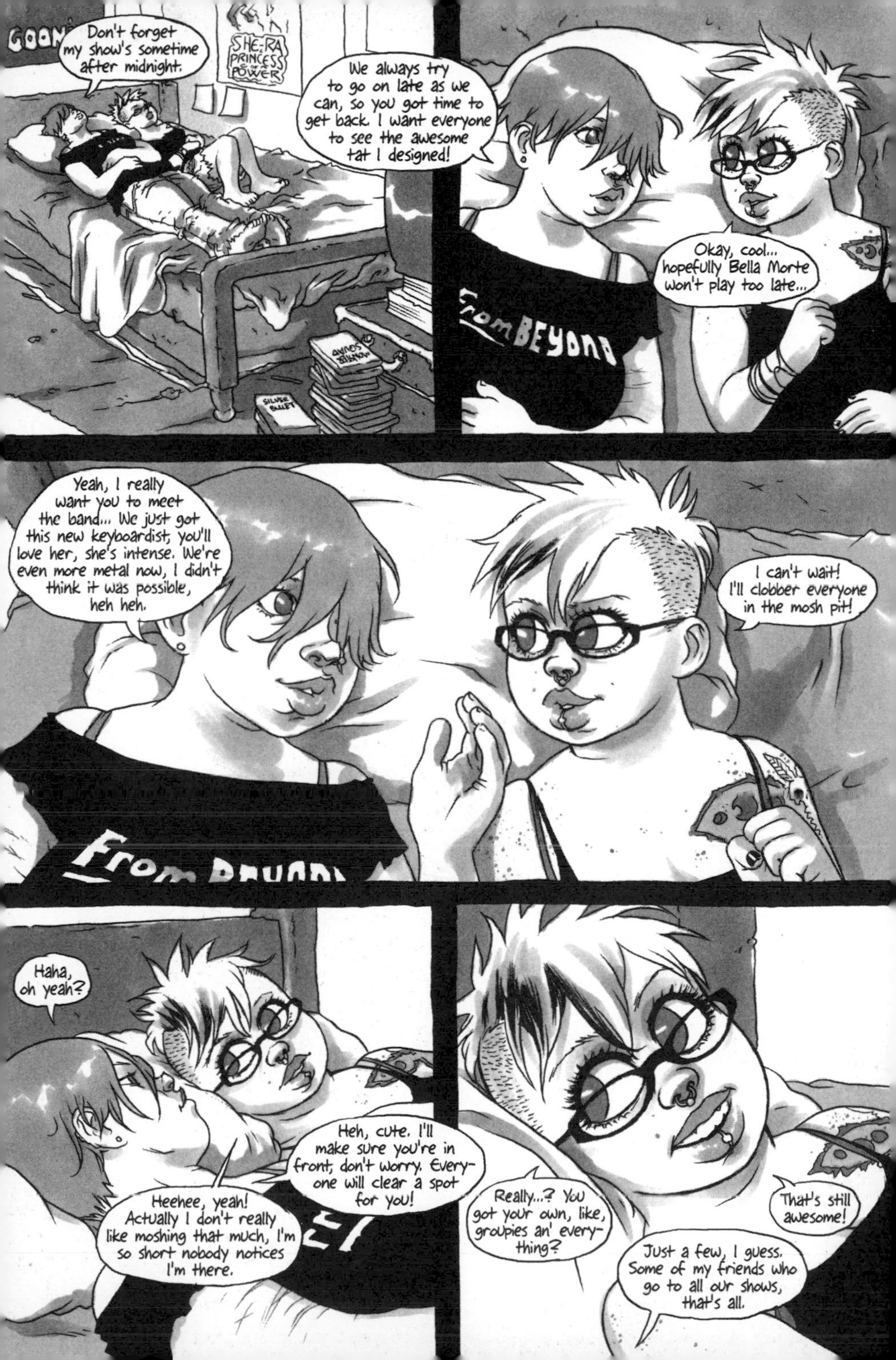
GOON
SHE-RA PRINCESS OF POWER
Don't forget my show's sometime after midnight.
We always try to go on late as we can, so you got time to get back. I want everyone to see the awesome tat I designed!
SILVER BULLET
MONSTER SQUAD
From BEYOND
Okay, cool... hopefully Bella Morte won't play too late...
Yeah, I really want you to meet the band... We just got this new keyboardist, you'll love her, she's intense. We're even more metal now, I didn't think it was possible, heh heh.
I can't wait! I'll clobber everyone in the mosh pit!
Haha, oh yeah?
Heehee, yeah! Actually I don't really like moshing that much, I'm so short nobody notices I'm there.
Heh, cute. I'll make sure you're in front, don't worry. Every-one will clear a spot for you!
Really...? You got your own, like, groupies an' every-thing?
Just a few, I guess. Some of my friends who go to all our shows, that's all.
That's still awesome!

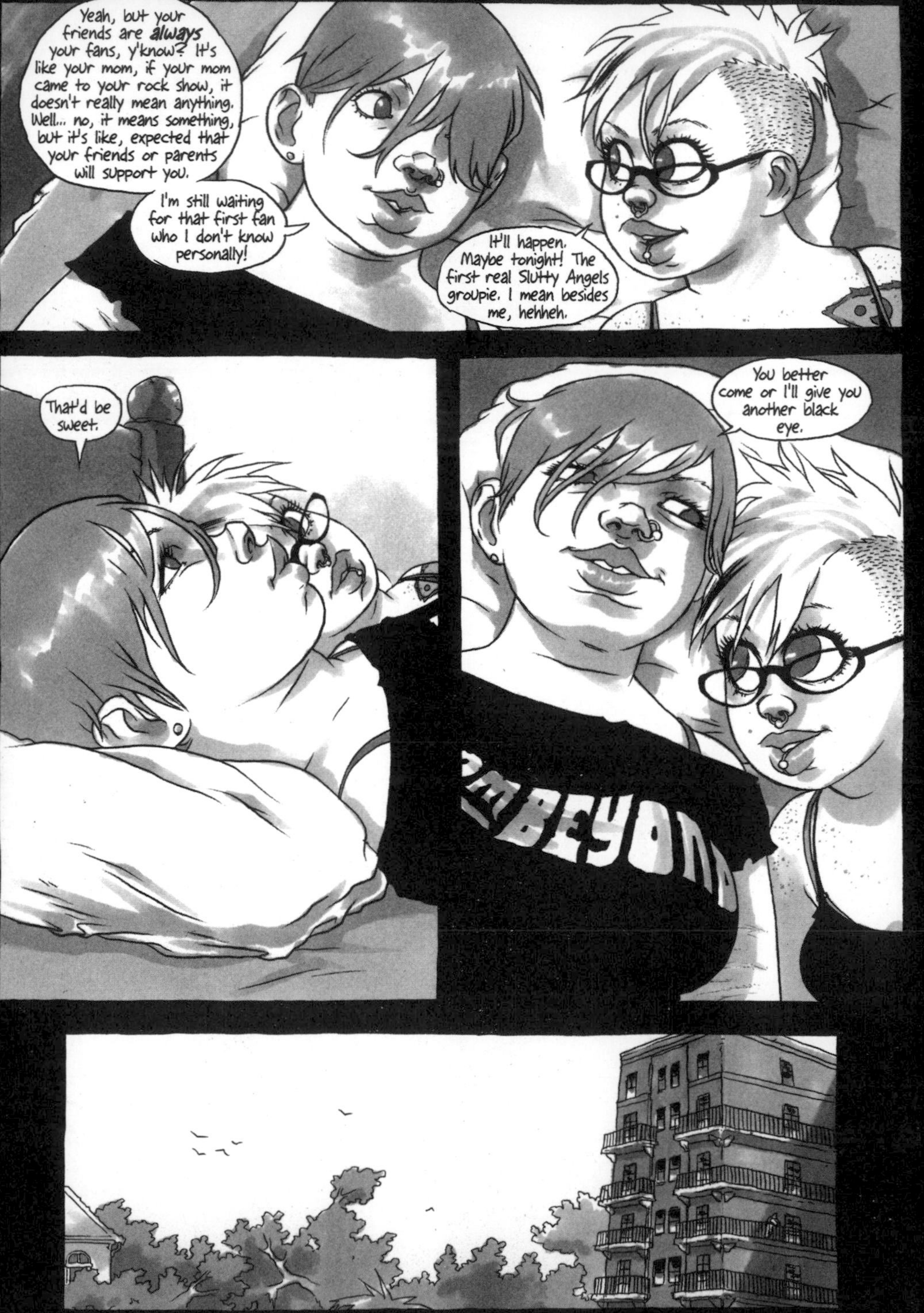
Yeah, but your friends are **always** your fans, y'know? It's like your mom, if your mom came to your rock show, it doesn't really mean anything. Well... no, it means something, but it's like, expected that your friends or parents will support you.
I'm still waiting for that first fan who I don't know personally!
It'll happen. Maybe tonight! The first real Slutty Angels groupie. I mean besides me, hehheh.
That'd be sweet.
You better come or I'll give you another black eye.
BEYOND

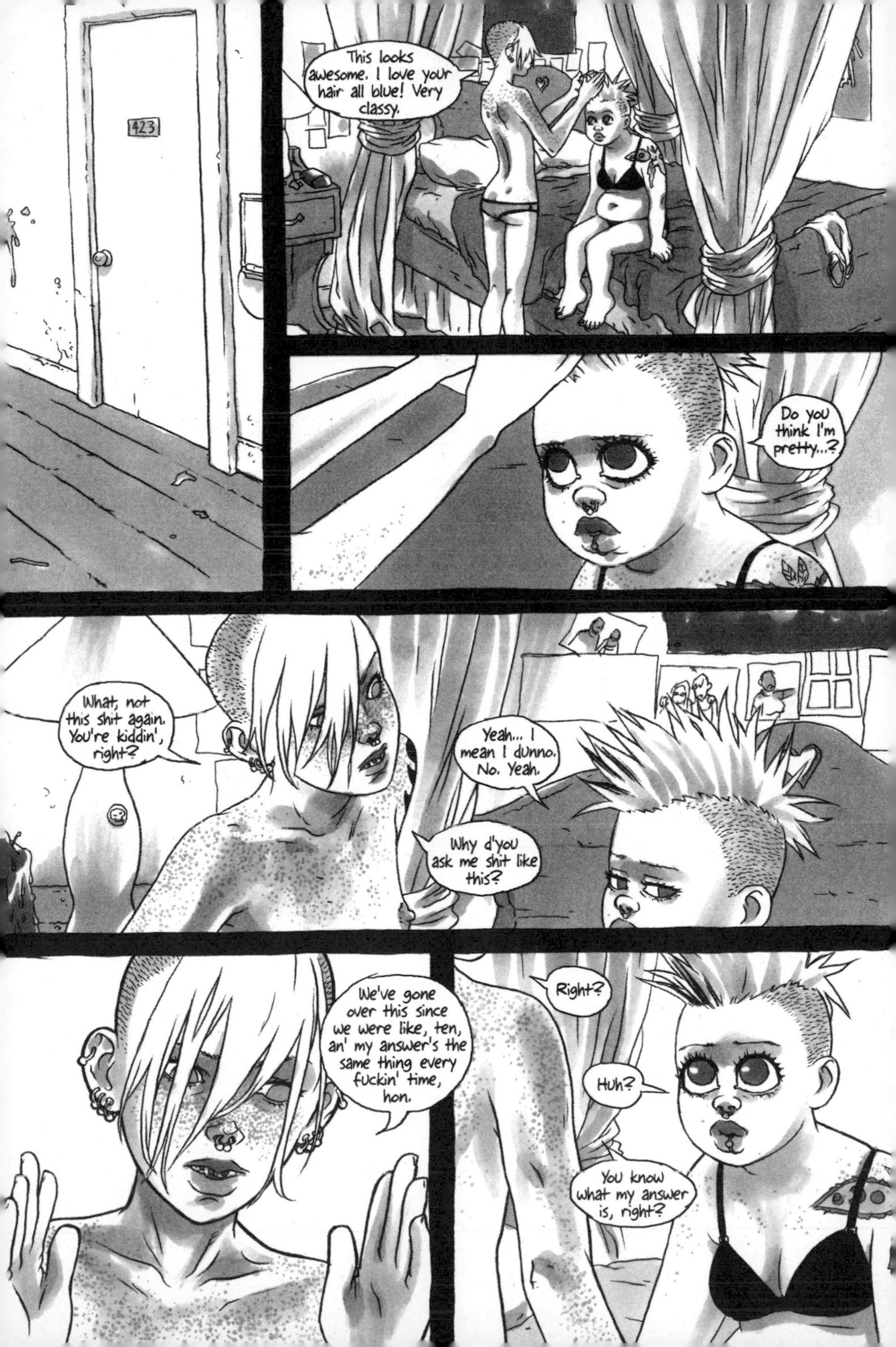
423
This looks awesome. I love your hair all blue! Very classy.
Do you think I'm pretty...?
What, not this shit again. You're kiddin', right?
Yeah... I mean I dunno. No. Yeah.
Why d'you ask me shit like this?
We've gone over this since we were like, ten, an' my answer's the same thing every fuckin' time, hon.
Right?
Huh?
You know what my answer is, right?

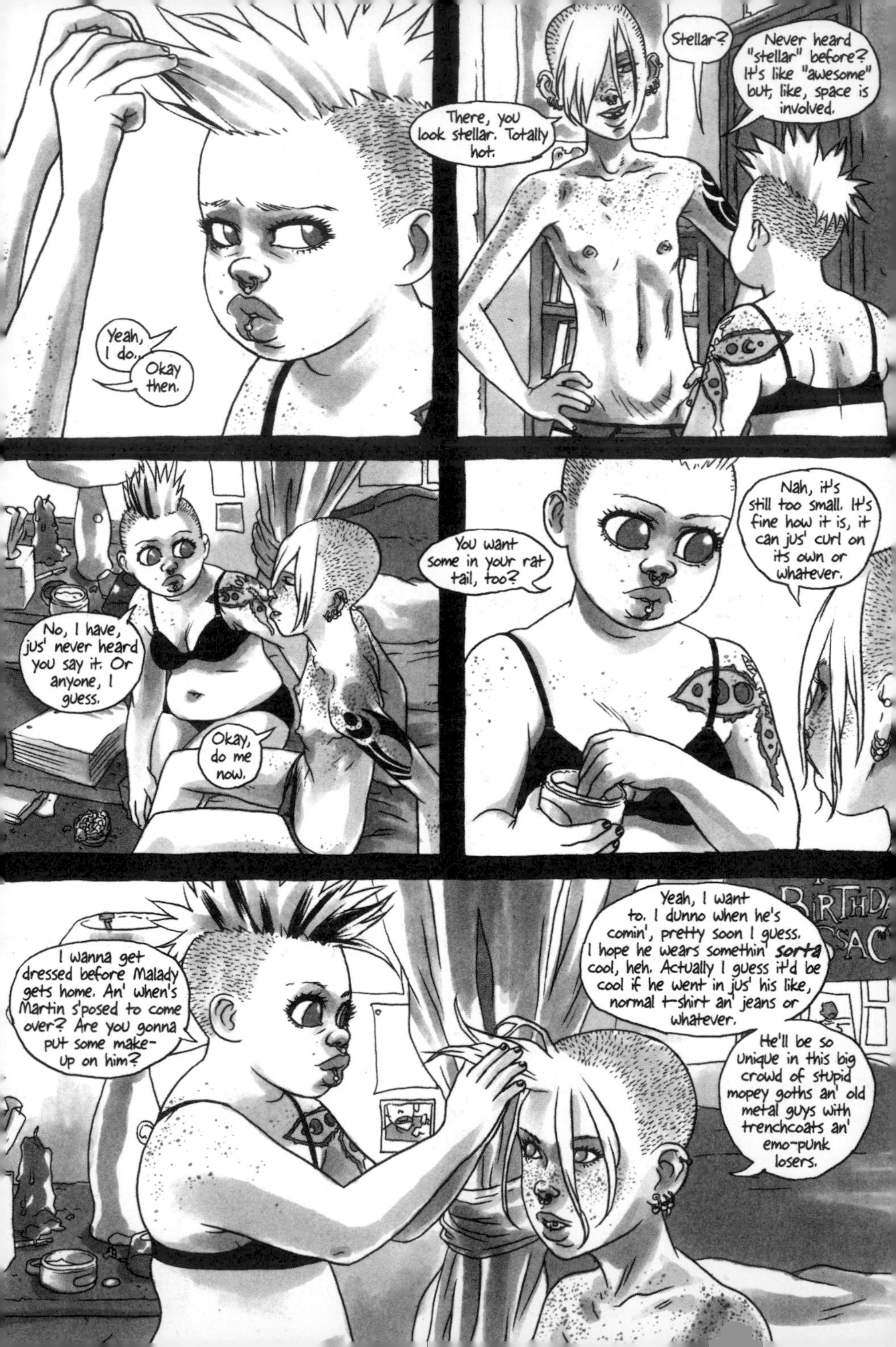
Yeah, I do..
Okay then.
There, you look stellar. Totally hot.
Stellar?
Never heard "stellar" before? It's like "awesome" but, like, space is involved.
No, I have, jus' never heard you say it. Or anyone, I guess.
Okay, do me now.
You want some in your rat tail, too?
Nah, it's still too small. It's fine how it is, it can jus' curl on its own or whatever.
I wanna get dressed before Malady gets home. An' when's Martin s'posed to come over? Are you gonna put some make-up on him?
Yeah, I want to. I dunno when he's comin', pretty soon I guess. I hope he wears somethin' *sorta* cool, heh. Actually I guess it'd be cool if he went in jus' his like, normal t-shirt an' jeans or whatever.
He'll be so unique in this big crowd of stupid mopey goths an' old metal guys with trenchcoats an' emo-punk losers.

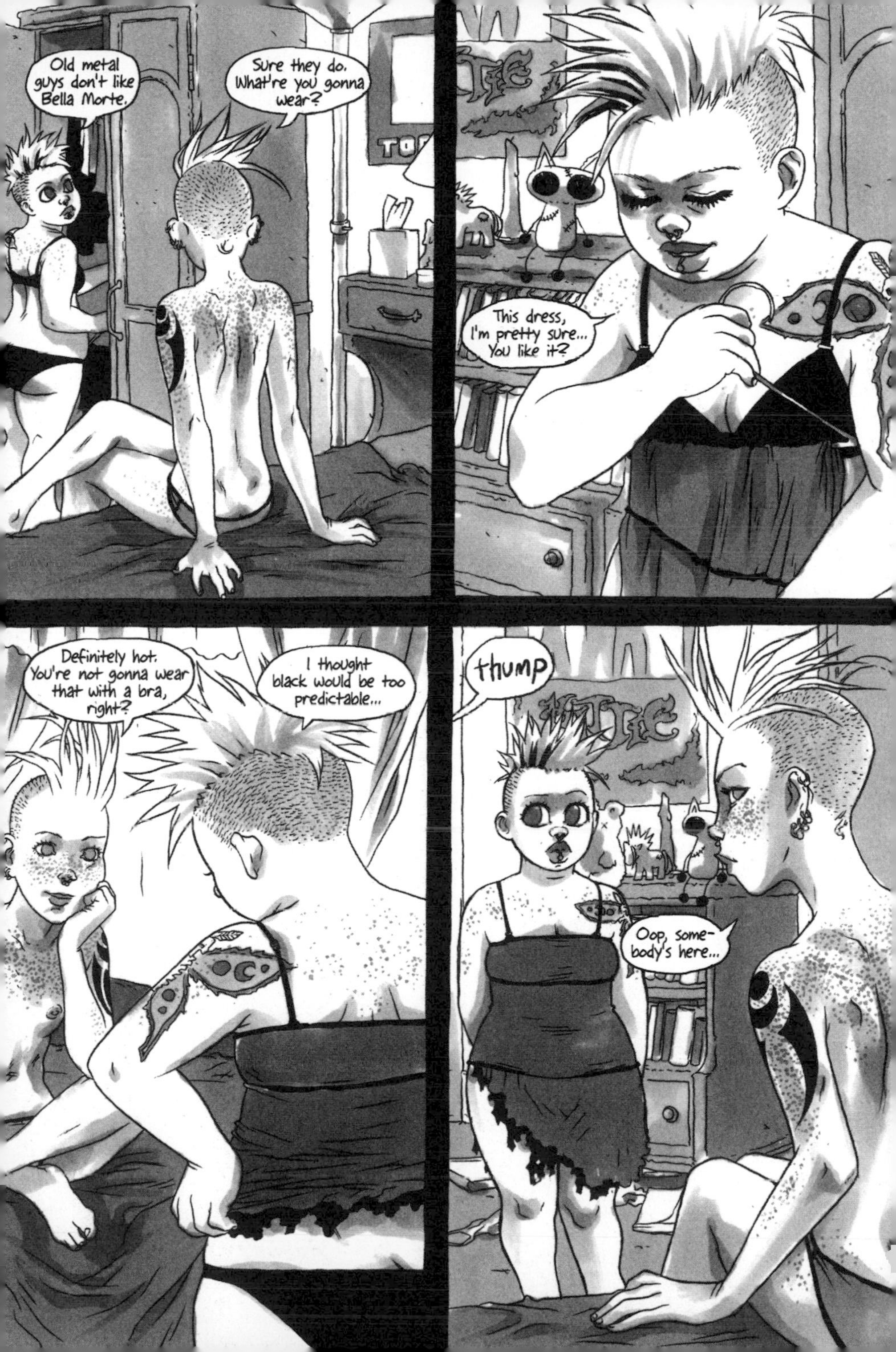
Old metal guys don't like Bella Morte.
Sure they do. What're you gonna wear?
This dress, I'm pretty sure... You like it?
Definitely hot. You're not gonna wear that with a bra, right?
I thought black would be too predictable...
thump
Oop, somebody's here...

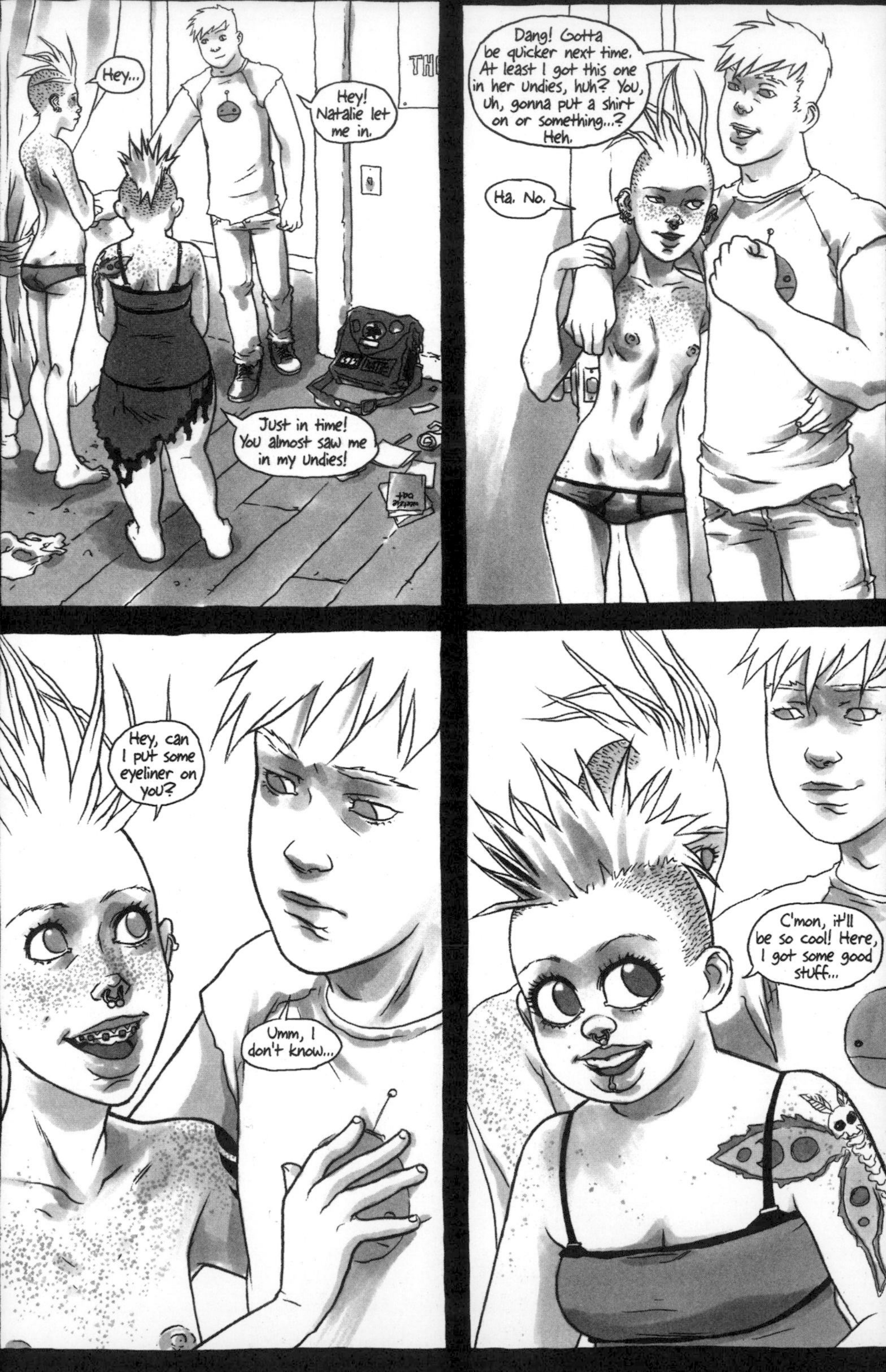
Hey...
Hey! Natalie let me in.
Just in time! You almost saw me in my undies!
Dang! Gotta be quicker next time. At least I got this one in her undies, huh? You, uh, gonna put a shirt on or something...? Heh.
Ha. No.
Hey, can I put some eyeliner on you?
Umm, I don't know...
C'mon, it'll be so cool! Here, I got some good stuff...

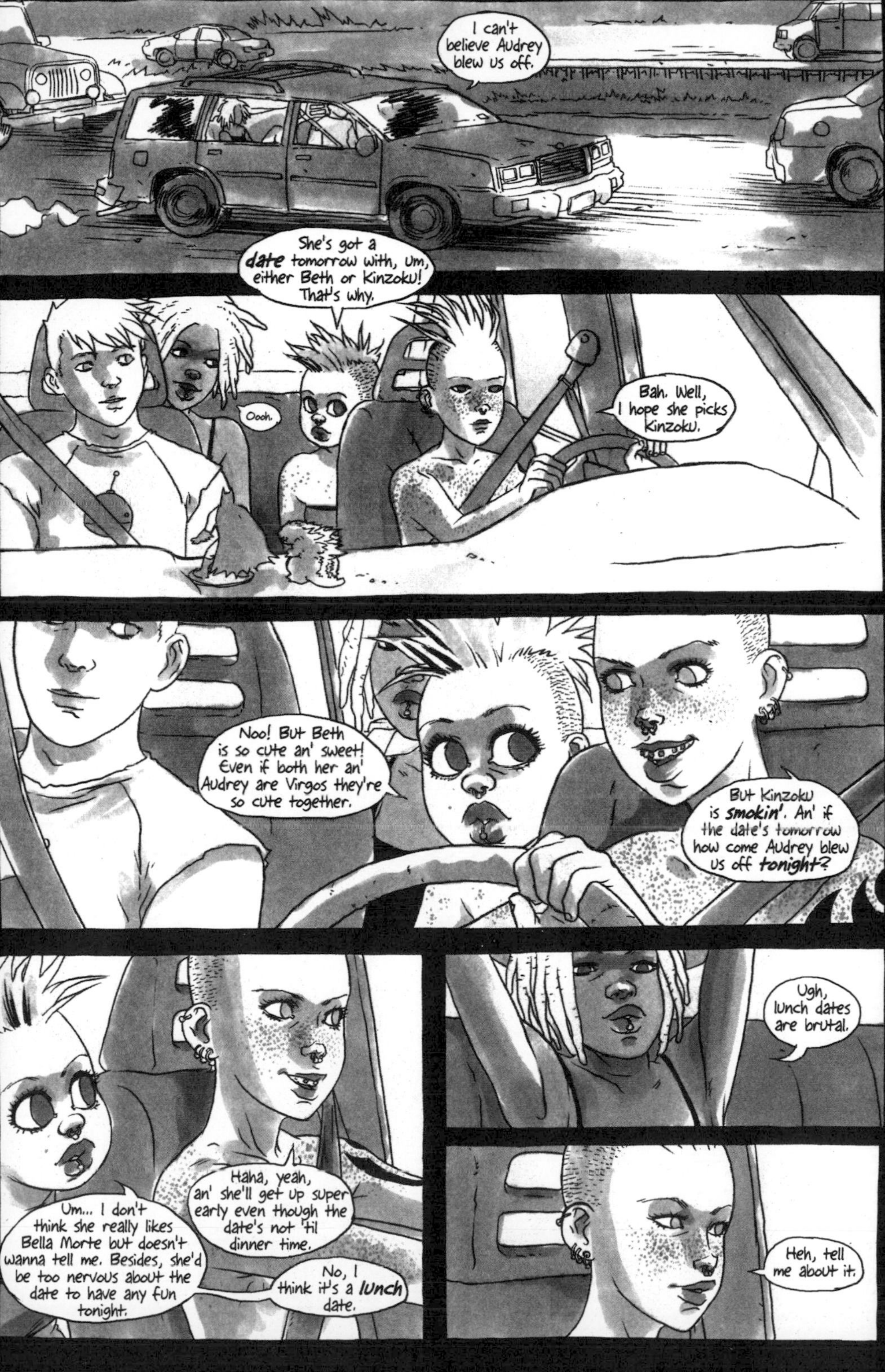

I can't believe Audrey blew us off.
She's got a date tomorrow with, um, either Beth or Kinzoku! That's why.
Oooh.
Bah. Well, I hope she picks Kinzoku.
Noo! But Beth is so cute an' sweet! Even if both her an' Audrey are Virgos they're so cute together.
But Kinzoku is smokin'. An' if the date's tomorrow how come Audrey blew us off tonight?
Um... I don't think she really likes Bella Morte but doesn't wanna tell me. Besides, she'd be too nervous about the date to have any fun tonight.
Haha, yeah, an' she'll get up super early even though the date's not 'til dinner time.
No, I think it's a lunch date.
Ugh, lunch dates are brutal.
Heh, tell me about it.

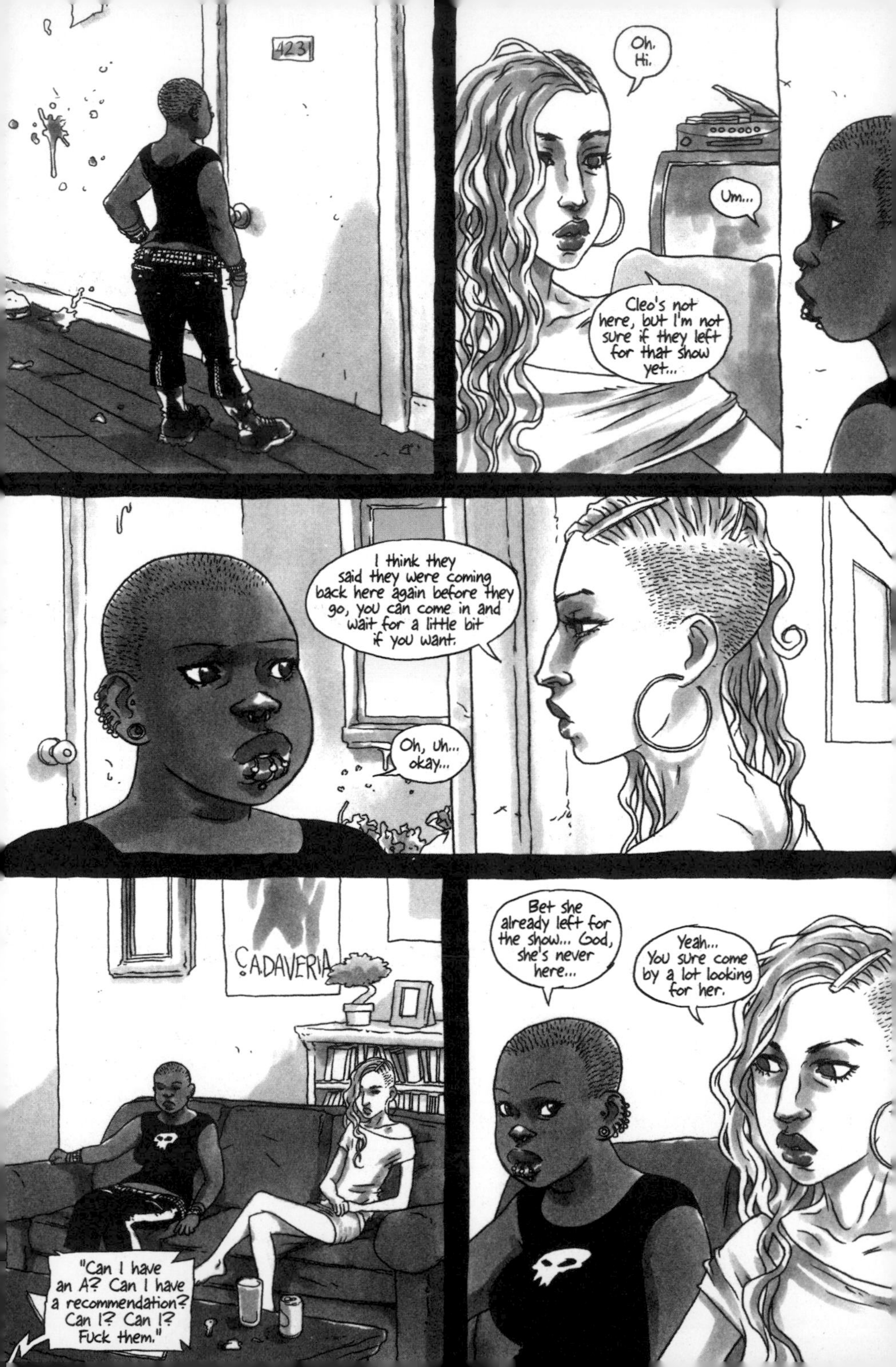
423
Oh. Hi.
Um...
Cleo's not here, but I'm not sure if they left for that show yet...
I think they said they were coming back here again before they go, you can come in and wait for a little bit if you want.
Oh, uh... okay...
CADAVERIA
"Can I have an A? Can I have a recommendation? Can I? Can I? Fuck them."
Bet she already left for the show... God, she's never here...
Yeah... You sure come by a lot looking for her.

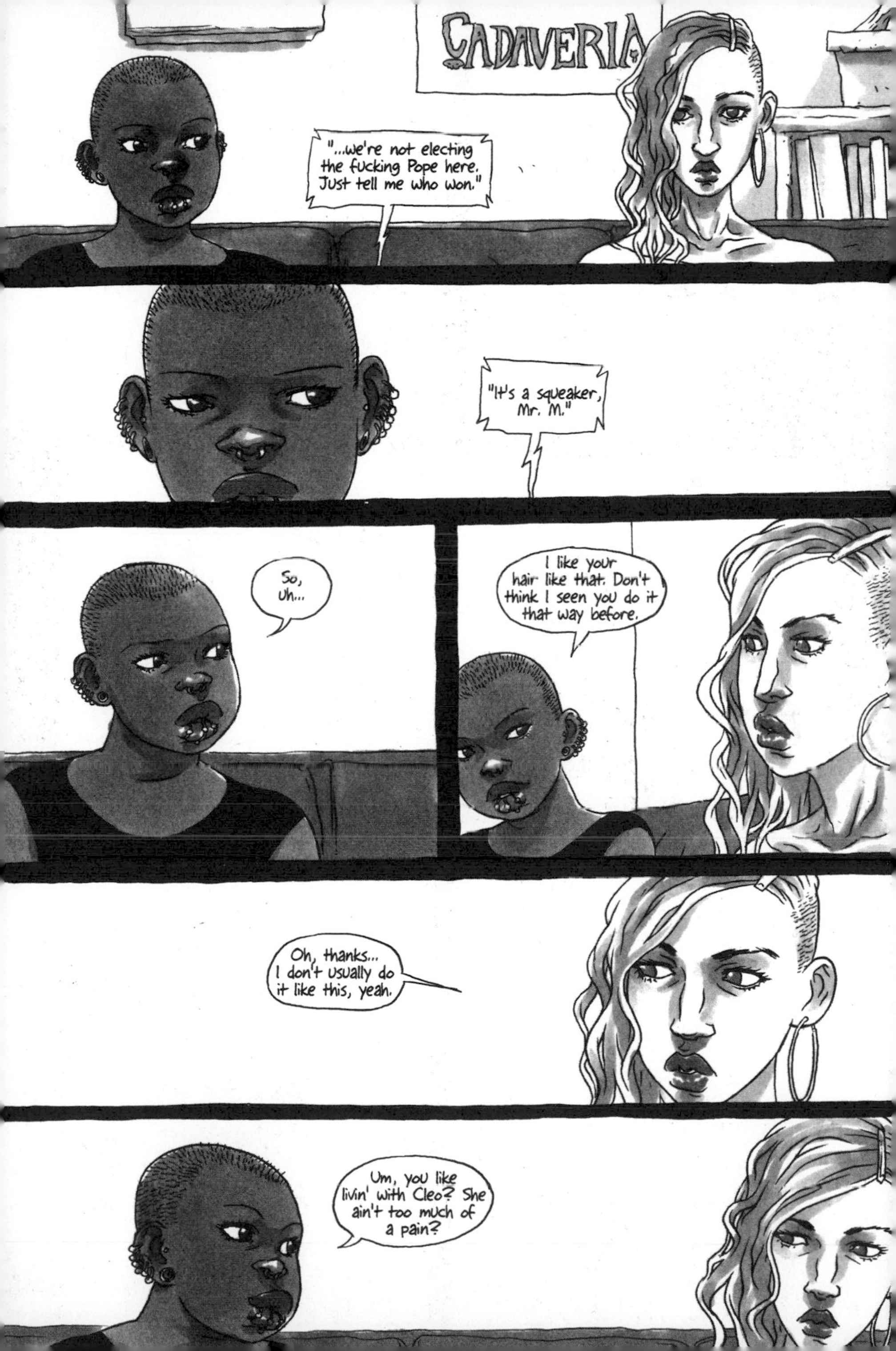

CADAVERIA
"...we're not electing the fucking Pope here. Just tell me who won."
"It's a squeaker, Mr. M."
So, uh...
I like your hair like that. Don't think I seen you do it that way before.
Oh, thanks... I don't usually do it like this, yeah.
Um, you like livin' with Cleo? She ain't too much of a pain?

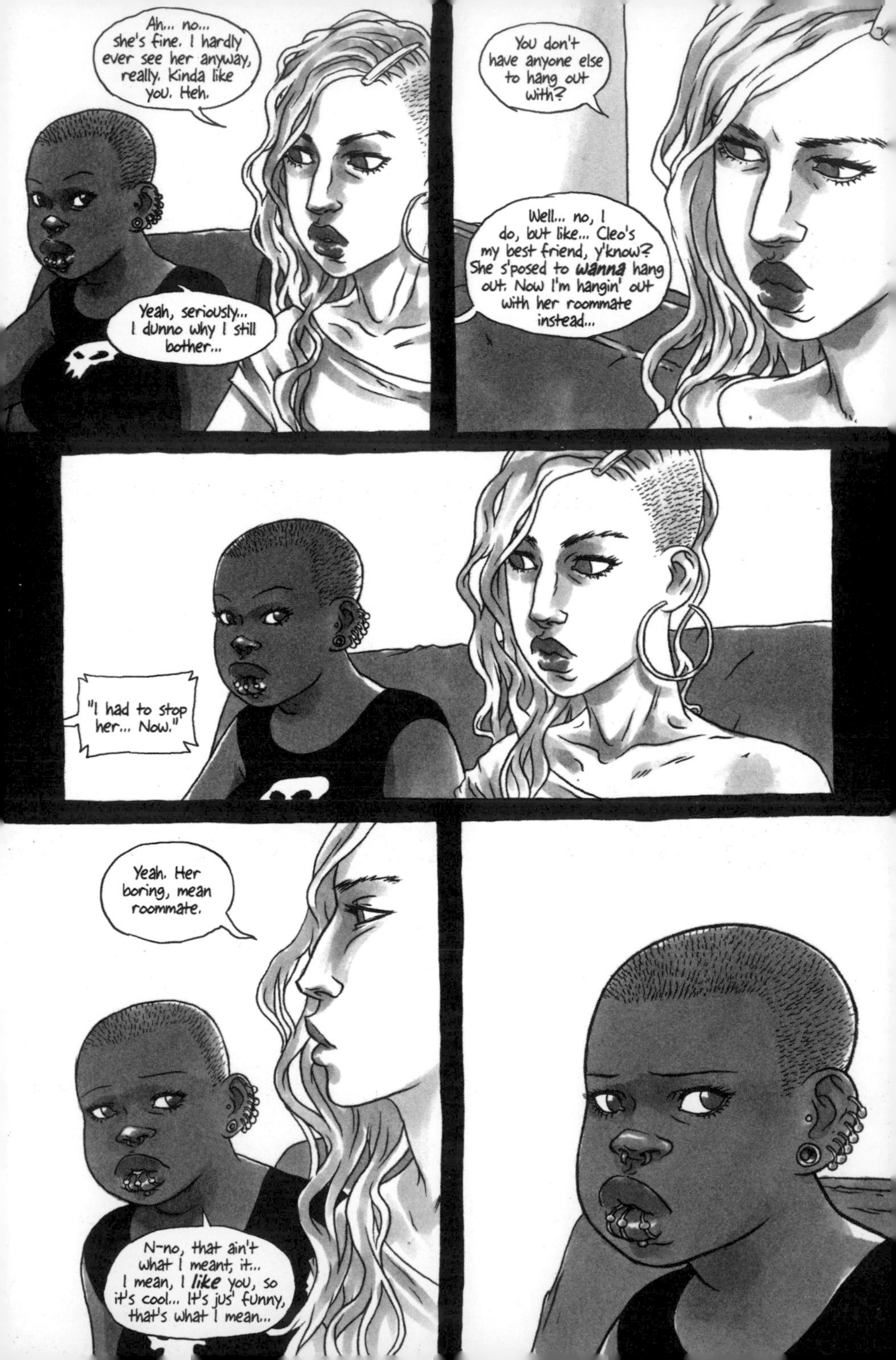
Ah... no... she's fine. I hardly ever see her anyway, really. Kinda like you. Heh.
Yeah, seriously... I dunno why I still bother...
You don't have anyone else to hang out with?
Well... no, I do, but like... Cleo's my best friend, y'know? She s'posed to wanna hang out. Now I'm hangin' out with her roommate instead...
"I had to stop her... Now."
Yeah. Her boring, mean roommate.
N-no, that ain't what I meant, it... I mean, I like you, so it's cool... It's jus' funny, that's what I mean...

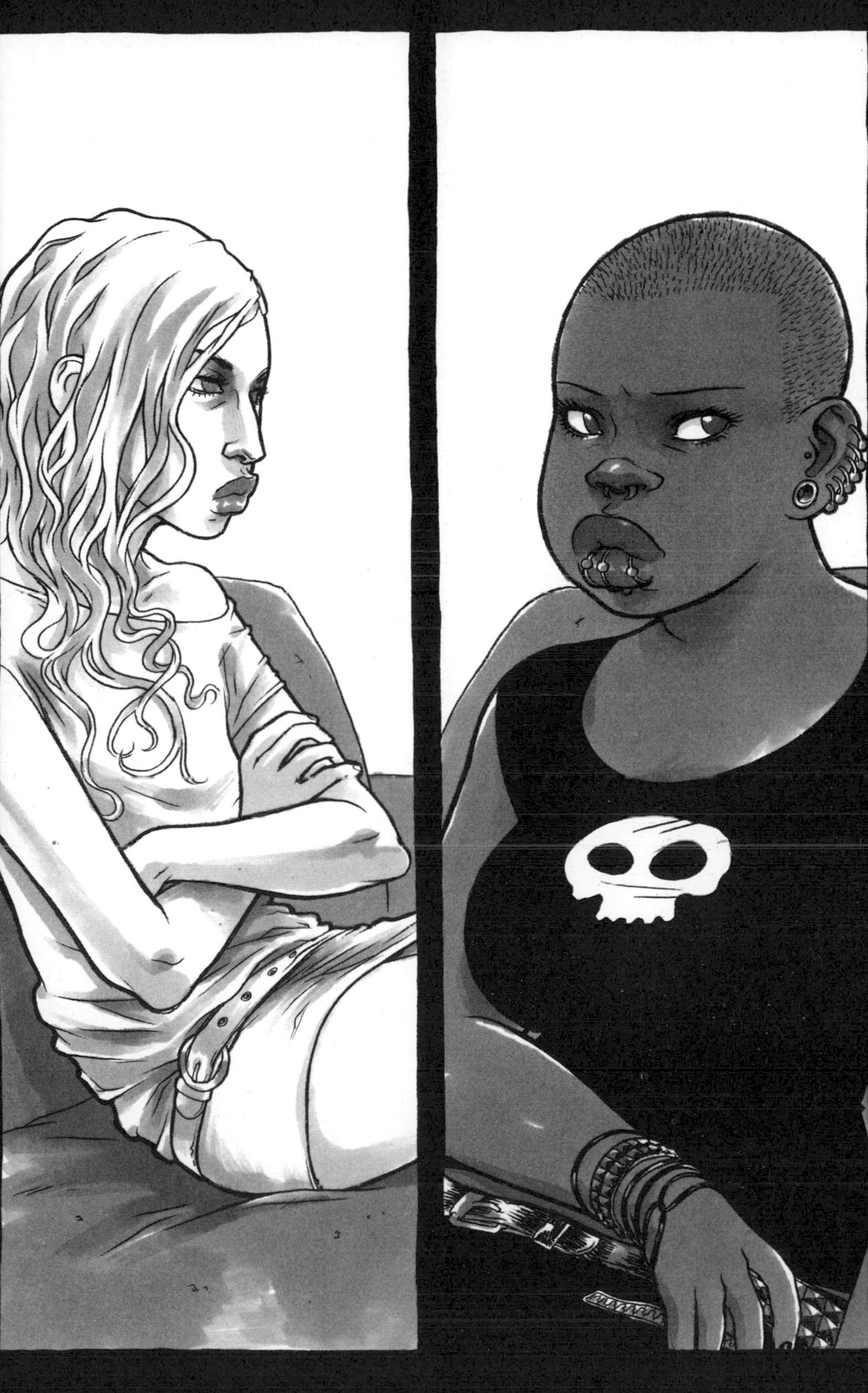

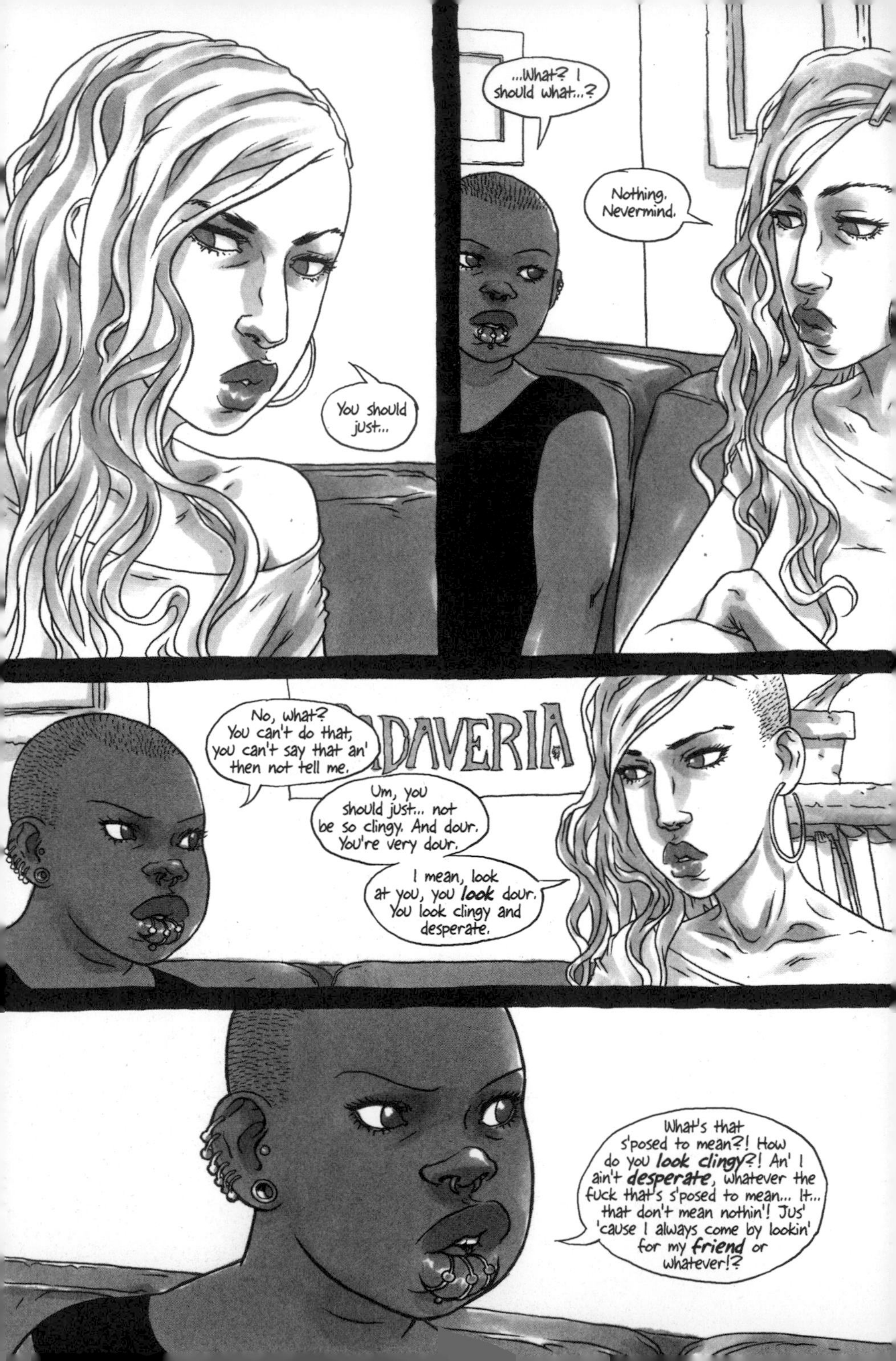
You should just...
...What? I should what...?
Nothing. Nevermind.
DAVERIA
No, what? You can't do that, you can't say that an' then not tell me.
Um, you should just... not be so clingy. And dour. You're very dour.
I mean, look at you, you **look** dour. You look clingy and desperate.
What's that s'posed to mean?! How do you **look clingy**?! An' I ain't **desperate**, whatever the fuck that's s'posed to mean... It... that don't mean nothin'! Jus' 'cause I always come by lookin' for my **friend** or whatever!?

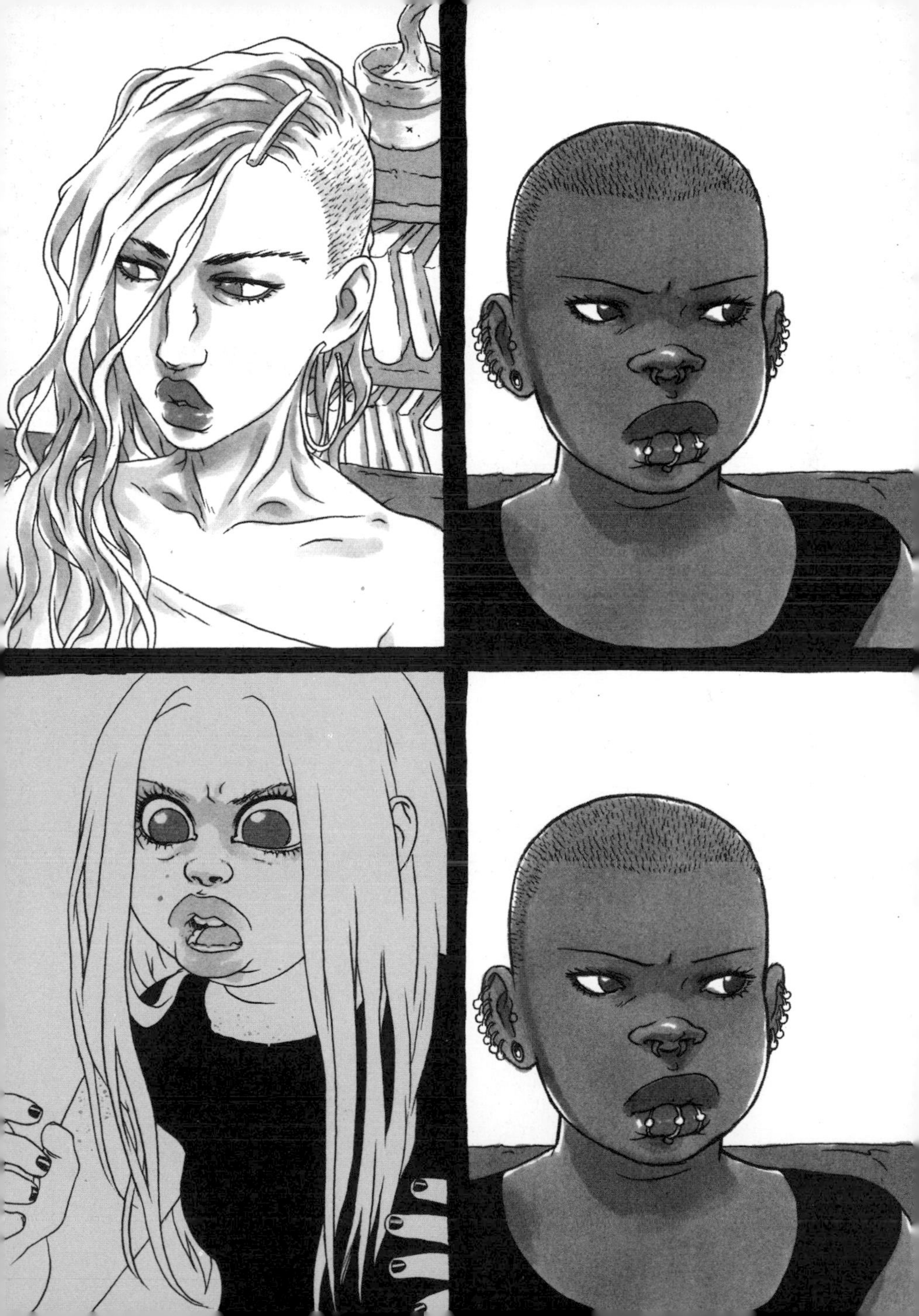

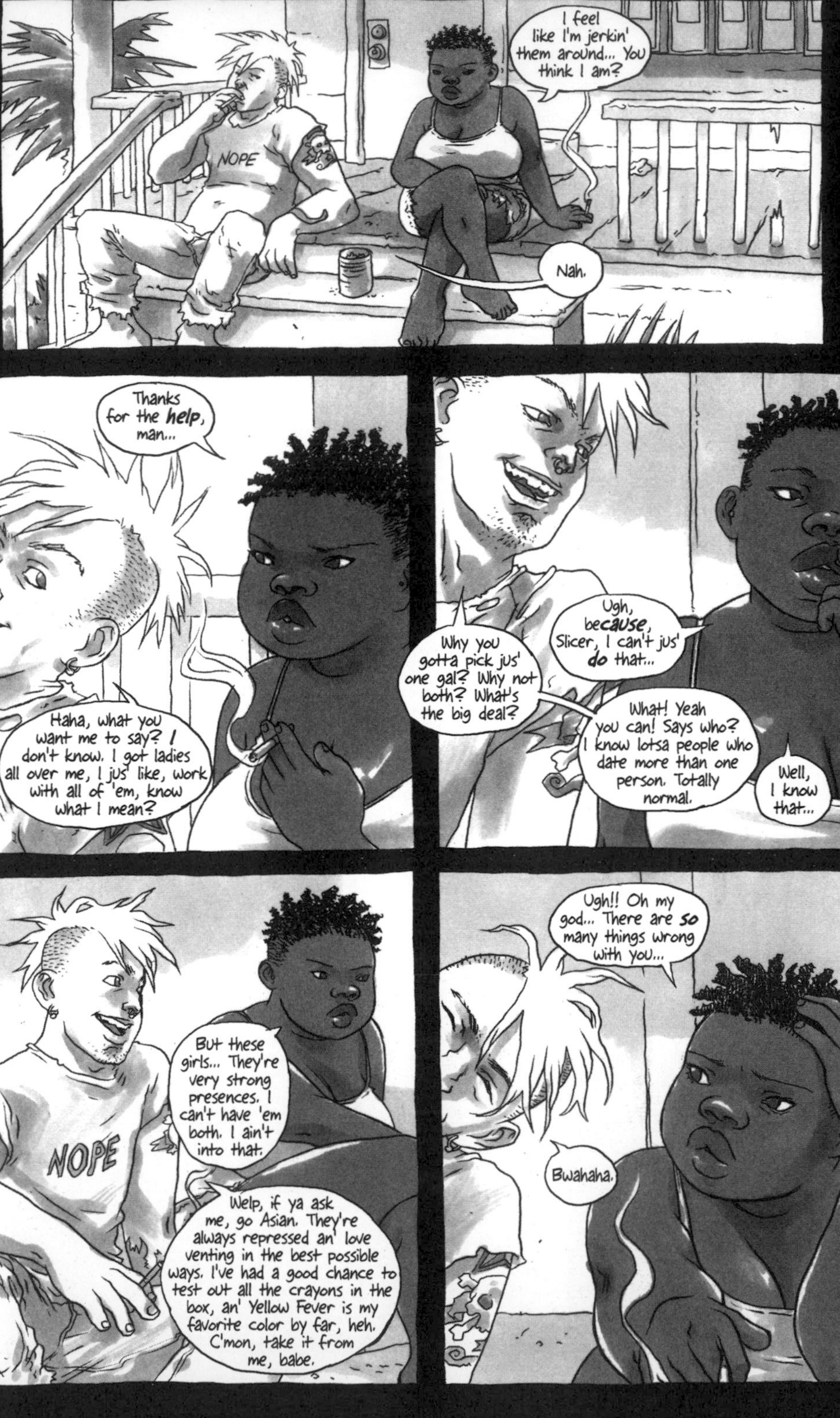

I feel like I'm jerkin' them around... You think I am?
Nah.
Thanks for the **help**, man...
Haha, what you want me to say? *I* don't know. I got ladies all over me, I jus' like, work with all of 'em, know what I mean?
Why you gotta pick jus' one gal? Why not both? What's the big deal?
Ugh, be**cause**, Slicer, I can't jus' **do** that...
What! Yeah you can! Says who? I know lotsa people who date more than one person. Totally normal.
Well, I know that...
But these girls... They're very strong presences. I can't have 'em both. I ain't into that.
Welp, if ya ask me, go Asian. They're always repressed an' love venting in the best possible ways. I've had a good chance to test out all the crayons in the box, an' Yellow Fever is my favorite color by far, heh. C'mon, take it from me, babe.
Ugh!! Oh my god... There are **so** many things wrong with you...
Bwahaha.

The Wonders At Your Feet

[friendtoroaches@gmail.com]

Recent Entries Archive Friends User Info

mara's journal

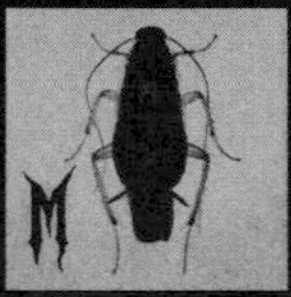

profile

October 11th, 3:23am

I'M MY ENEMY

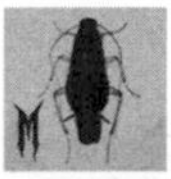

today probably one of the most awkward things that has ever happened to me happened. not only am i completly embarassed now to go over to Cleo's dumb dorm because she's never there but now her stuck-up roomate Natalie thinks i'm the biggest douche on the planet. i always show up there and Cleo is never home so this girl Natalie answers the door and tells me Cleo isn't home every fucking time. then today she told me to wait inside for Cleo so i did, whatever, seemed like a good thing to do. Cleo's gotta come home sometime, right? so i waited with Natalie on the couch, watching some Matthew Broderick movie, the Ferris Bueller guy except now he's old but still looks oddly the same. Reese Witherspoon was in it too. anyway, so we sat there watching this movie, and it's really awkward and totally weird, and then she said like "don't you have anyone else to hang out with?" like i don't have any other friends. of course i do, bitch. who has just ONE friend? well no, i guess some people must have, but she's obviously seen me with other people like Trilby and Audrey, even though Trilby's been seriously pissing me off recently. that's a whole other entry.

anyway, then she goes to say something but stops herself and says "oh, nevermind." i fucking hate it when people do that. especially online. because online, you have all this time to think about what your going to type and you have to hit enter to send what you type, so it doesn't make any sense when people do that shit on MSN, but people still do it. it's all really just to get the other person, in this case me, to go "no, what? tell me!" and beg the person to tell them. the person just does it to have this fucked up kind of control over the other person, like withholding information that the other person obviously is going to want to hear. well normally i'd say fuck that, i don't want to hear your fucking information and play your games, my interest is not piqued, except that's exactly what I did. I go "no, what? tell me!" and she does, of course, and she tells me i look dour and desperate and clingy what the fuck does that mean. i'm glad that i look dour, dour is cool, but i don't look desperate. i don't know, who cares. but so after that i obviously didn't stay, Cleo would never show up anyways, so i just ignored her after that and fucking left. i couldn't stop thinking about her and what she said, it was like eating my brain, so i went for a walk and stopped in at Arcana and found this old copy of *Nightlust* by Edward Lee, so that was cool. i heard it's pretty bad but i'm still interested, and it's tough to find his really old stuff so i had to get it. i'm still in the middle of his book *Portrait of the Psychopath as a Young Woman* and so far it's awesome. i don't know what i'm going to do about Cleo and Natalie. i don't want to be like this.

mood: sad
current music: hocico - spirits of crime

[0 comments | leave a comment]

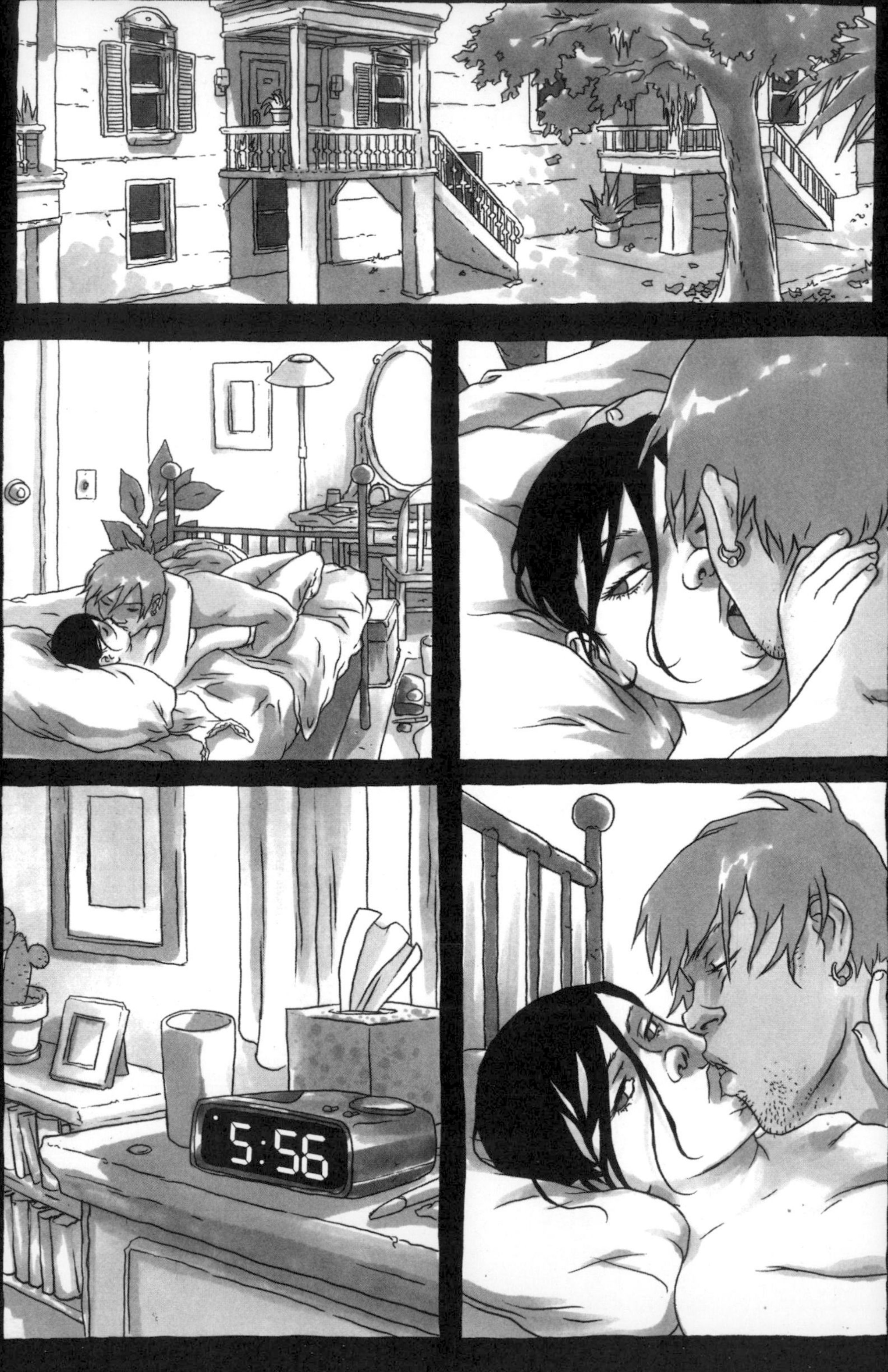
5:56

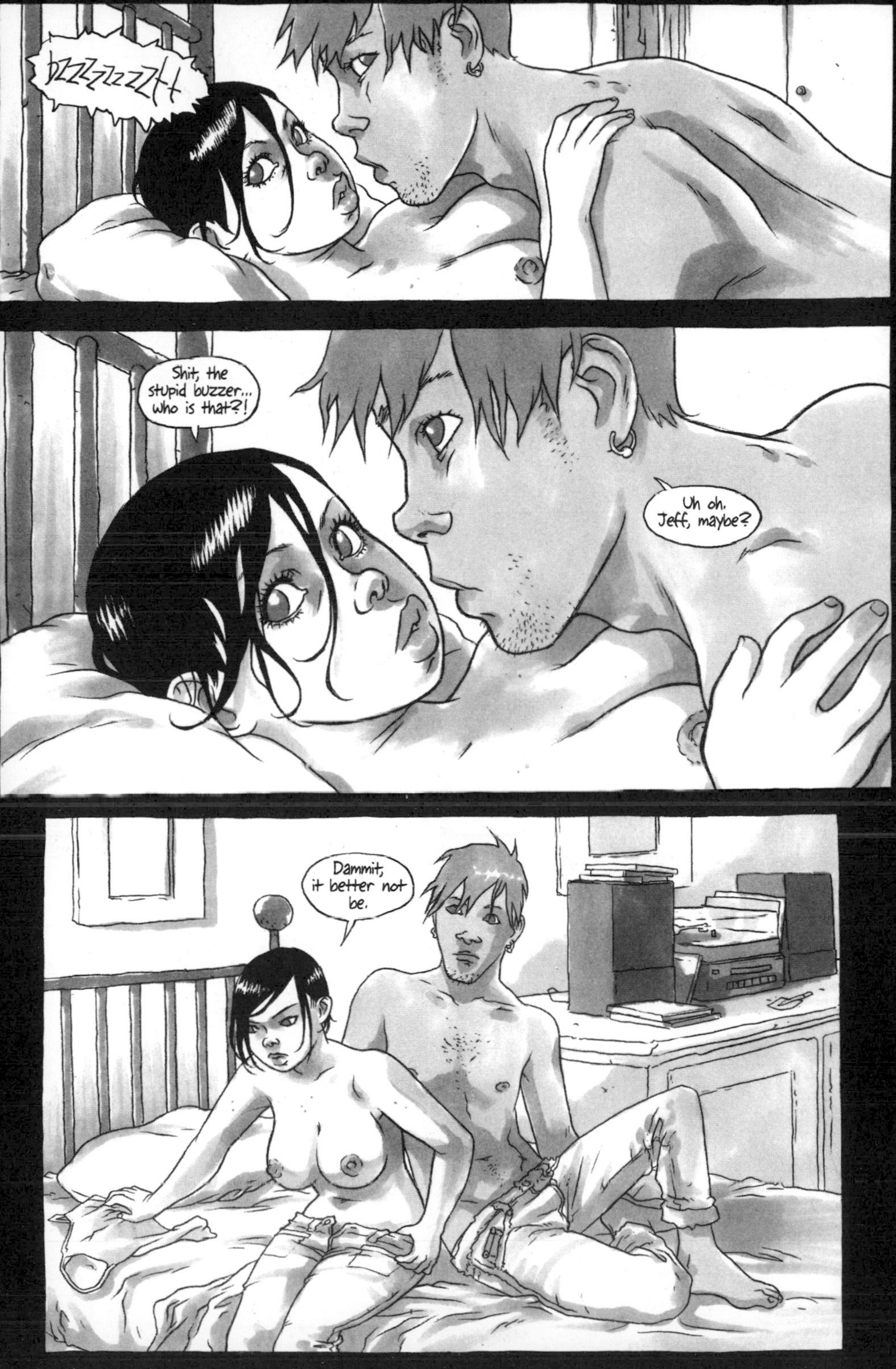
bzzzzzzzzt
Shit, the stupid buzzer... who is that?!
Uh oh. Jeff, maybe?
Dammit, it better not be.

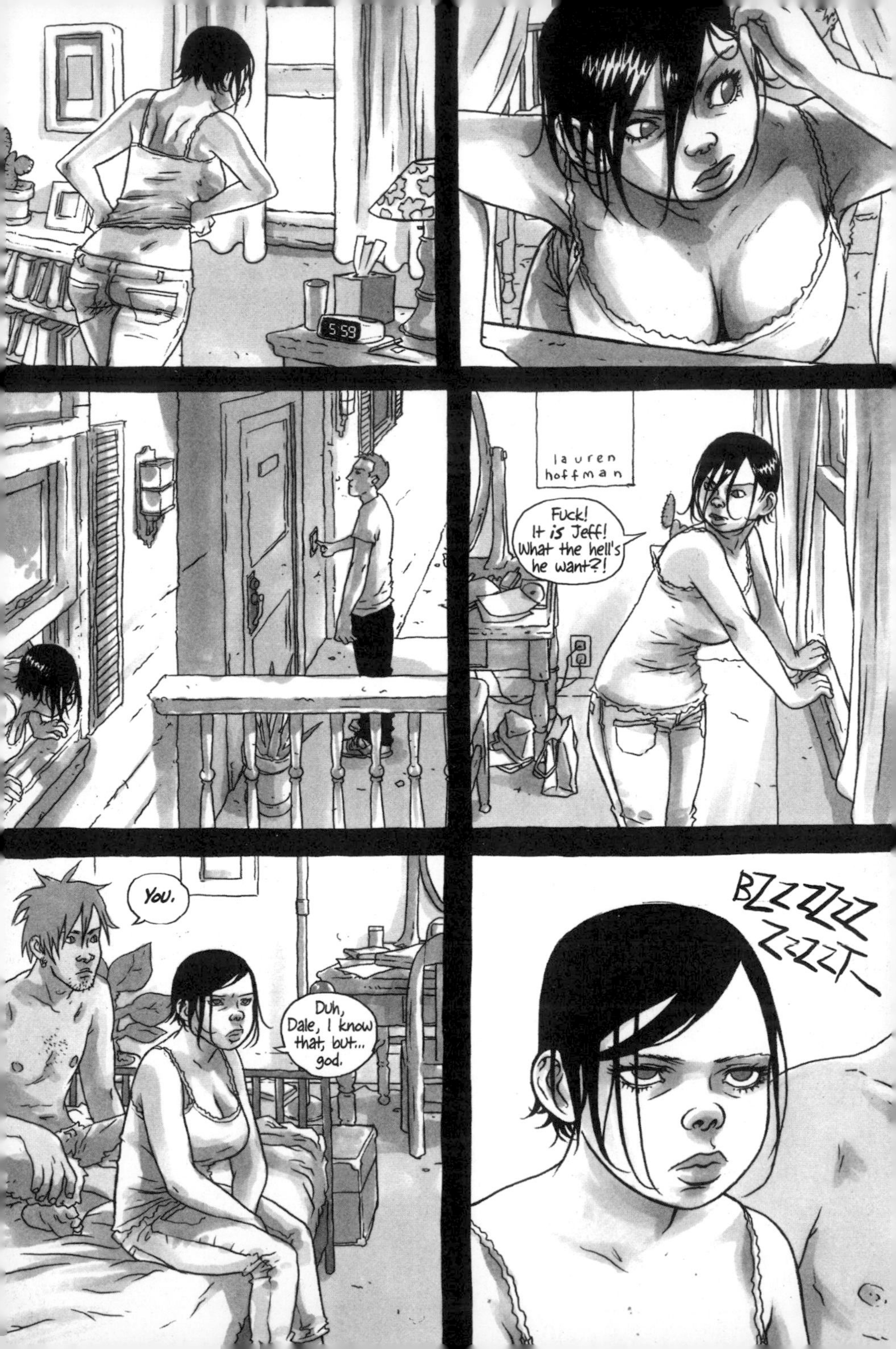
5:59
lauren hoffman
Fuck! It *is* Jeff! What the hell's he want?!
You.
Duh, Dale, I know that, but... god.
BZZZZZZ ZZZZT

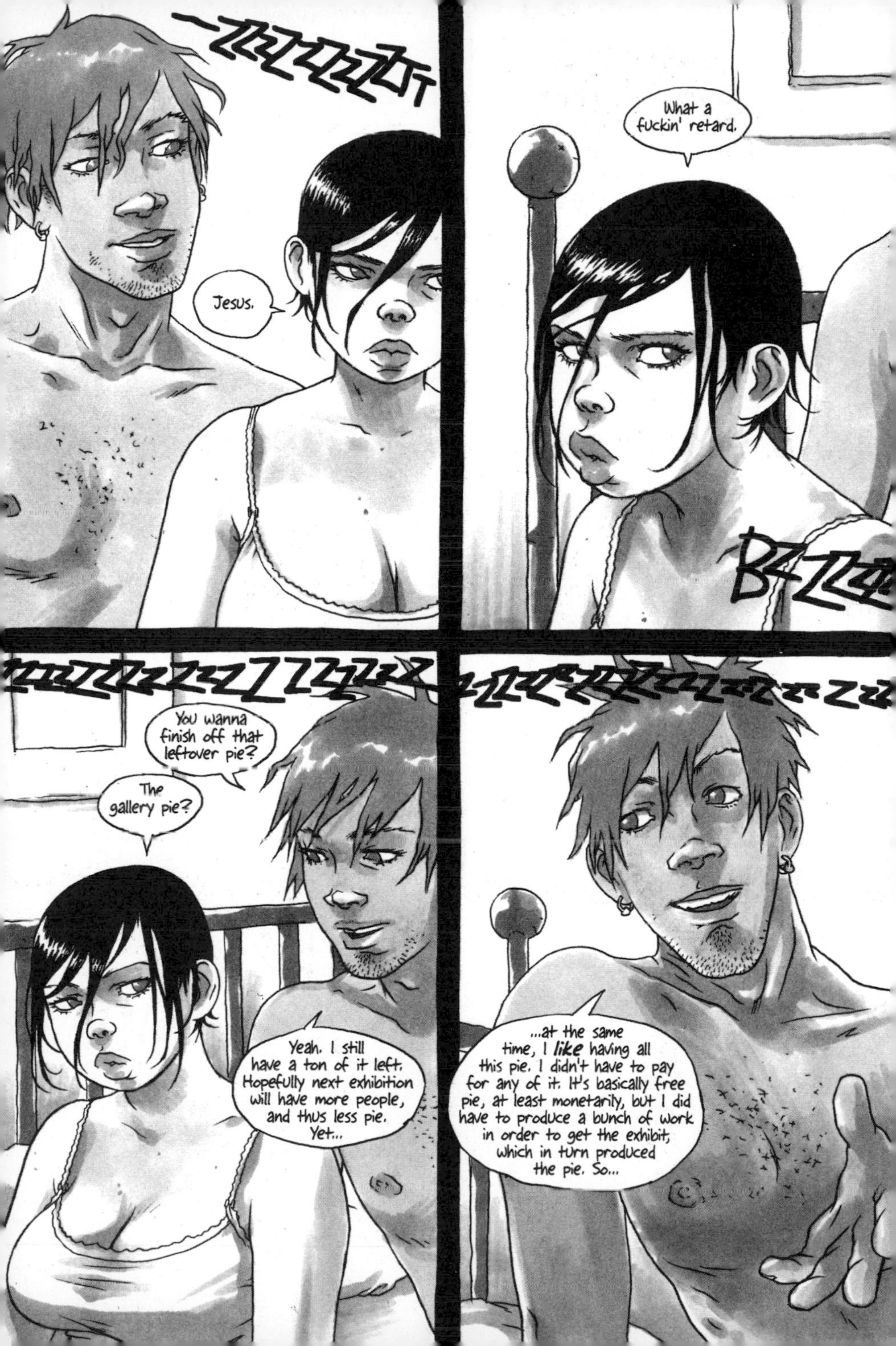
ZZZZZZZZZZT
Jesus.
What a fuckin' retard.
BZZZ
ZZZZZZZZZZZZZZZZZZ
You wanna finish off that leftover pie?
The gallery pie?
Yeah. I still have a ton of it left. Hopefully next exhibition will have more people, and thus less pie. Yet...
ZZZZZZZZZZZZZZZZZZZZZZZ
...at the same time, I *like* having all this pie. I didn't have to pay for any of it. It's basically free pie, at least monetarily, but I did have to produce a bunch of work in order to get the exhibit, which in turn produced the pie. So...

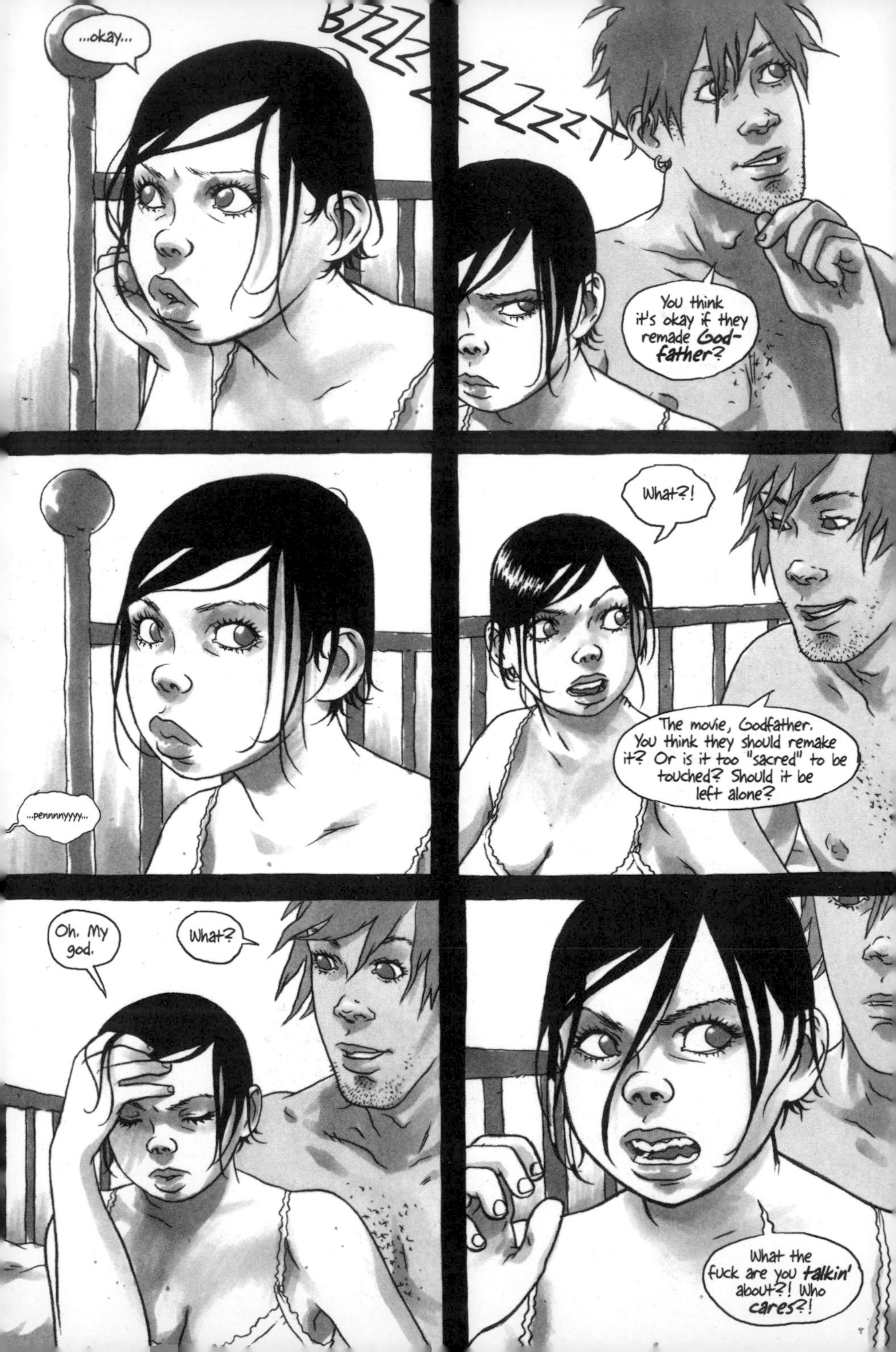
...okay...
BZZZZZZZZZZZT
You think it's okay if they remade Godfather?
...pennnnyyyy...
What?!
The movie, Godfather. You think they should remake it? Or is it too "sacred" to be touched? Should it be left alone?
Oh. My god.
What?
What the fuck are you talkin' about?! Who cares?!

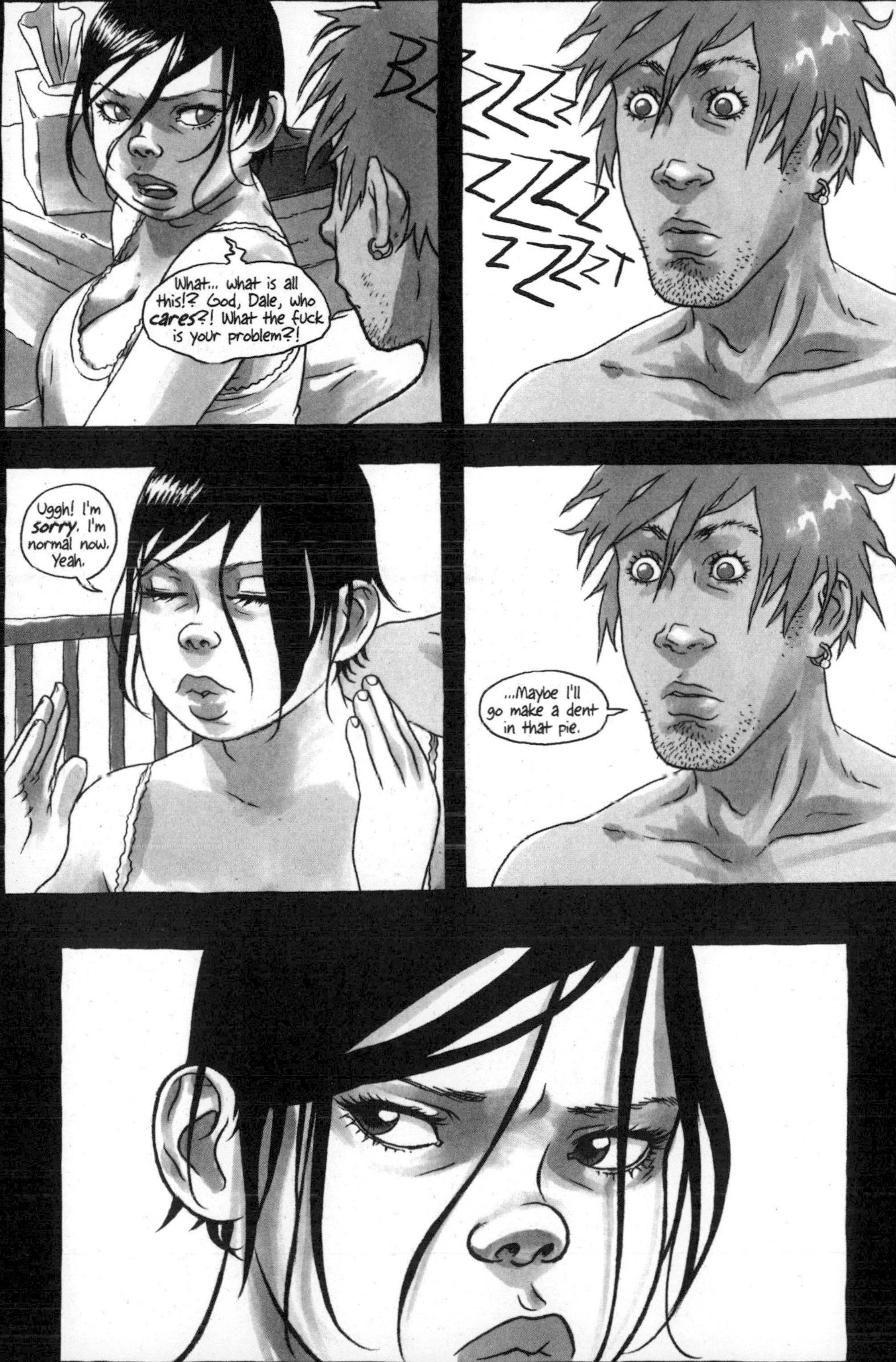

What... what is all this!? God, Dale, who **cares**?! What the fuck is your problem?!
BZZZZZZZZZZZZZZZZT
Uggh! I'm **sorry**. I'm normal now. Yeah.
...Maybe I'll go make a dent in that pie.

12

October 12th

I wish Audrey wasn't Miss Big Mouth. I need some relationship advice and Audrey is always the best person for it. And because I'm sort of dating a girl. Audrey really does have a big mouth like Trilby says, you can't tell her ANYthing. There was this one time, which I wrote about in my previous diary but I'll write again here, when both me and Tril had a crush on this guy Walter, and we both wanted him pretty bad but he asked me out and I didn't know what to do. I really wanted to say yes but I knew Trilby would be upset, so I told Audrey about it thinking maybe she'd give me some advice, but of course like in a matter of hours after that she'd already told Trilby. So the whole thing with Walter got messed up and I never called him back and so neither me or Trilby got with him. I wonder what happened to him.

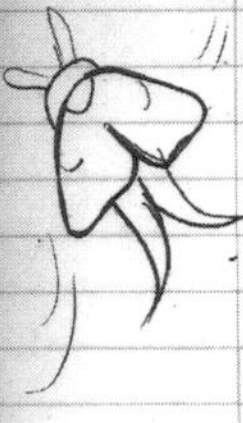

Trilby keeps bugging me to dress up with her for Halloween as a character from a sort of spooky, monstery video game she likes called Darkstalkers. The characters are all real cute but they have tiny, skimpy outfits that I could never wear. Trilby would look adorable, but... I don't think I could do it. Going to the beach in a swimsuit or bikini is one thing, but dressing up all scandalously in a Halloween costume is for some reason totally different. I couldn't pull off that sort of thing. I think I might be lazy this year and just go as a zombie or maybe a mummy. That could be cute, all wrapped up in bandages.

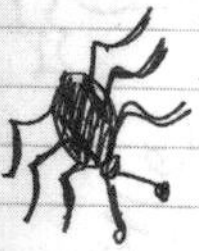

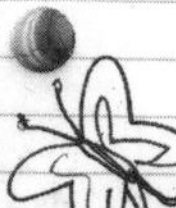

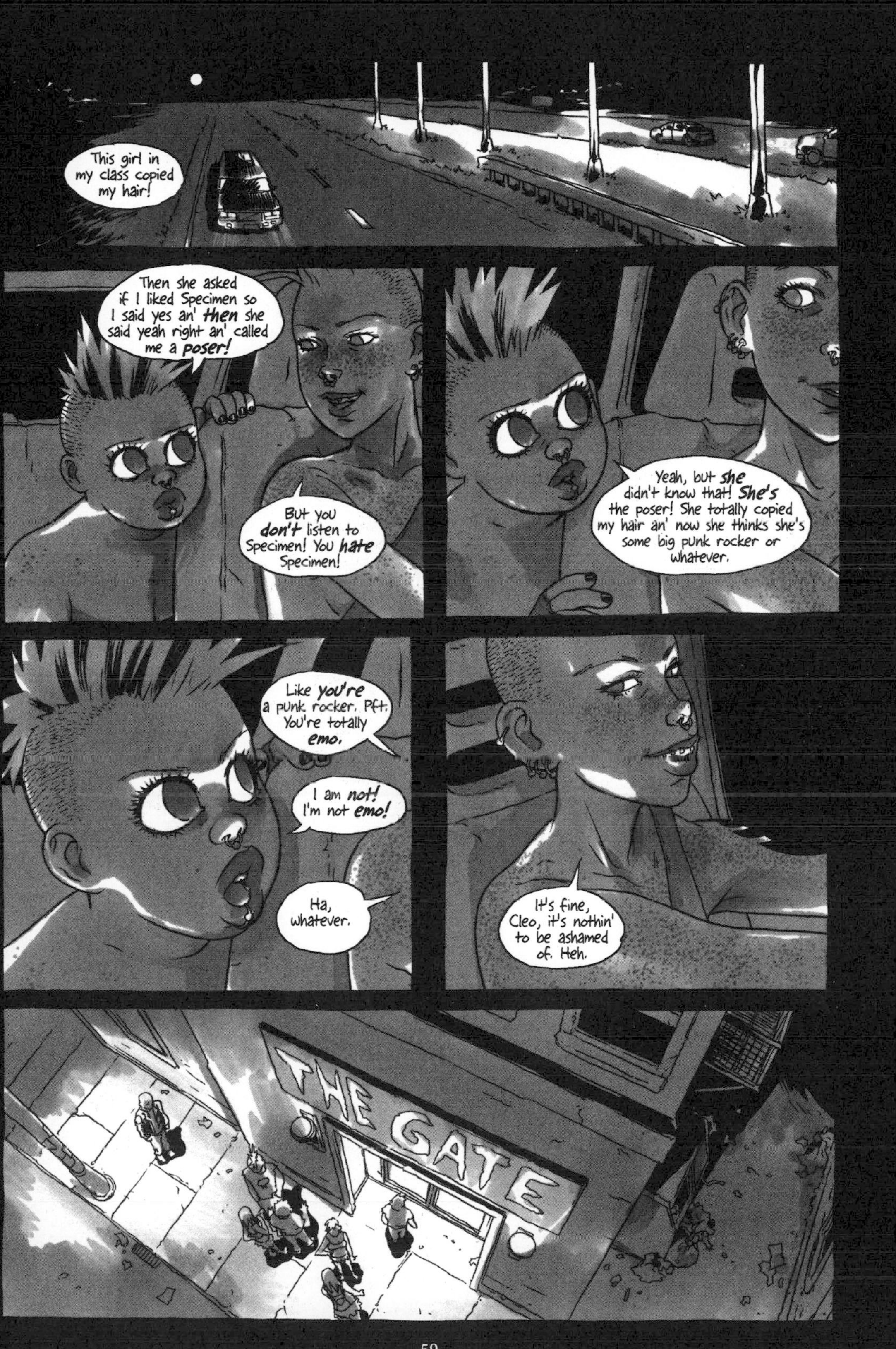
This girl in my class copied my hair!
Then she asked if I liked Specimen so I said yes an' then she said yeah right an' called me a poser!
But you don't listen to Specimen! You hate Specimen!
Yeah, but she didn't know that! She's the poser! She totally copied my hair an' now she thinks she's some big punk rocker or whatever.
Like you're a punk rocker. Pft. You're totally emo.
I am not! I'm not emo!
Ha, whatever.
It's fine, Cleo, it's nothin' to be ashamed of. Heh.
THE GATE

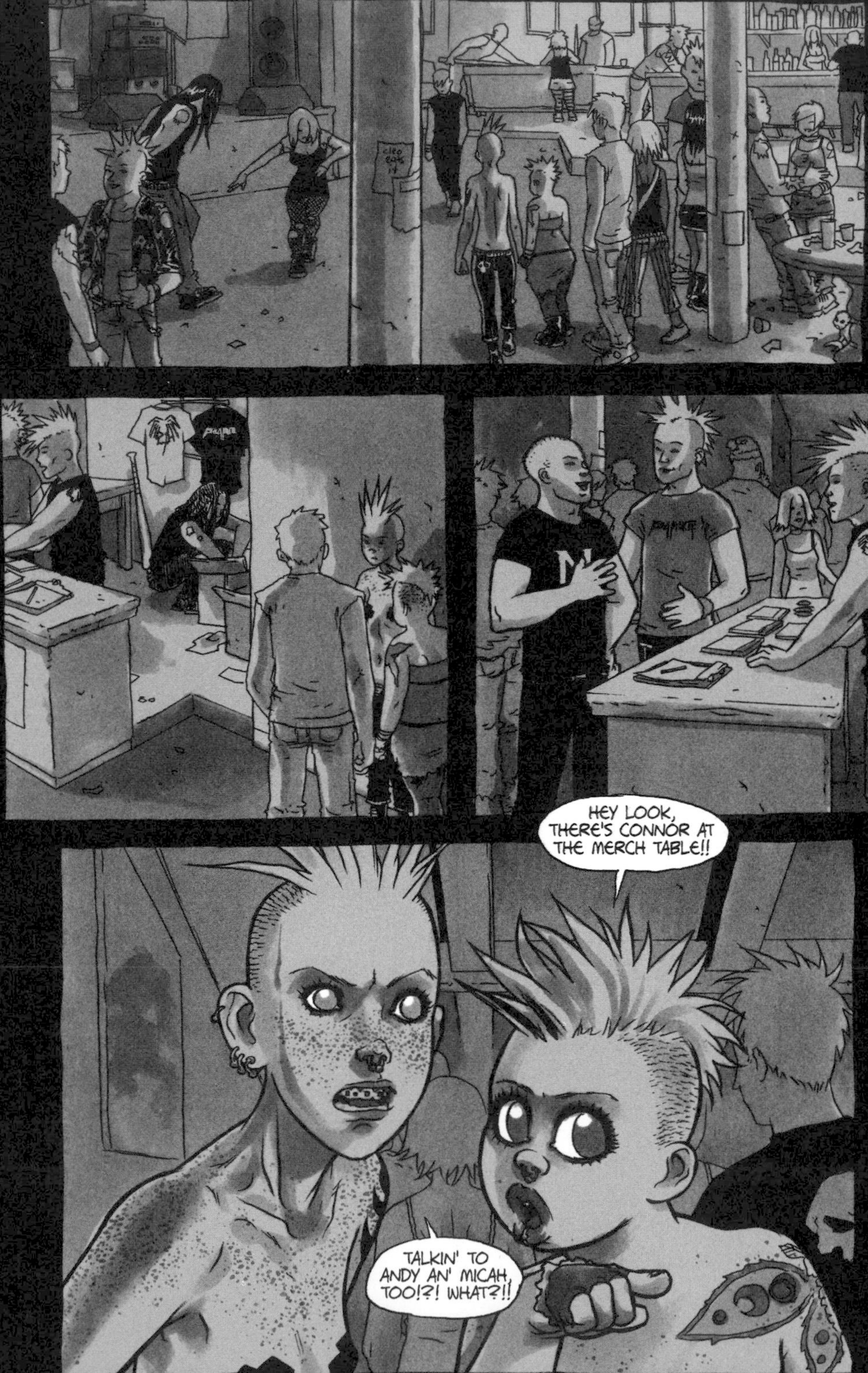
cleo eats it
HEY LOOK, THERE'S CONNOR AT THE MERCH TABLE!!
TALKIN' TO ANDY AN' MICAH, TOO!?! WHAT?!!

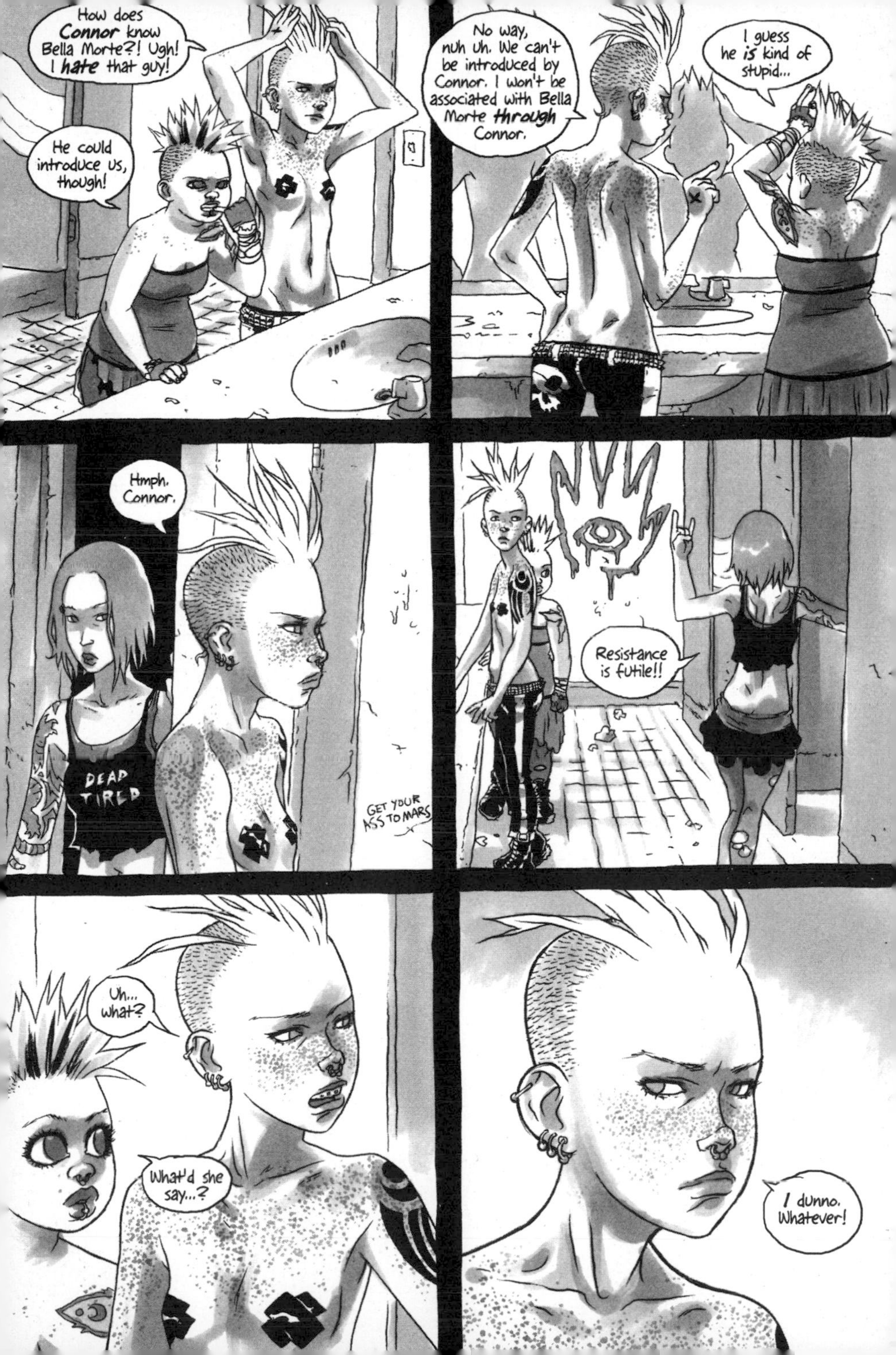
How does Connor know Bella Morte?! Ugh! I hate that guy!
He could introduce us, though!
No way, nuh uh. We can't be introduced by Connor. I won't be associated with Bella Morte through Connor.
I guess he is kind of stupid...
Hmph. Connor.
GET YOUR ASS TO MARS
DEAD TIRED
Resistance is futile!!
Uh... what?
What'd she say...?
I dunno. Whatever!

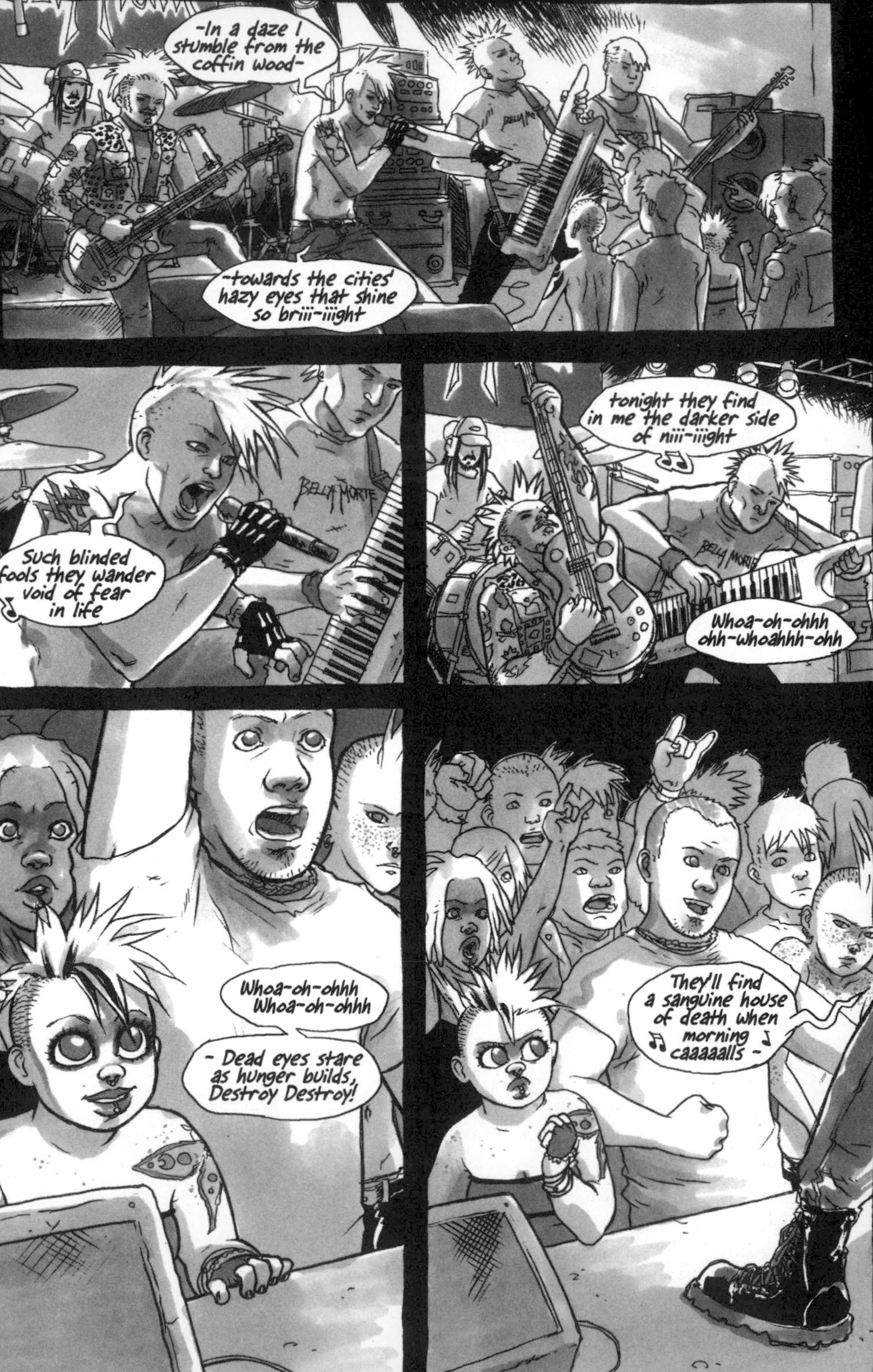
-In a daze I stumble from the coffin wood-
-towards the cities' hazy eyes that shine so briii-iiight
Such blinded fools they wander void of fear in life
tonight they find in me the darker side of niii-iiight
Whoa-oh-ohhh ohh-whoahhh-ohh
Whoa-oh-ohhh Whoa-oh-ohhh
- Dead eyes stare as hunger builds, Destroy Destroy!
They'll find a sanguine house of death when morning caaaaalls -

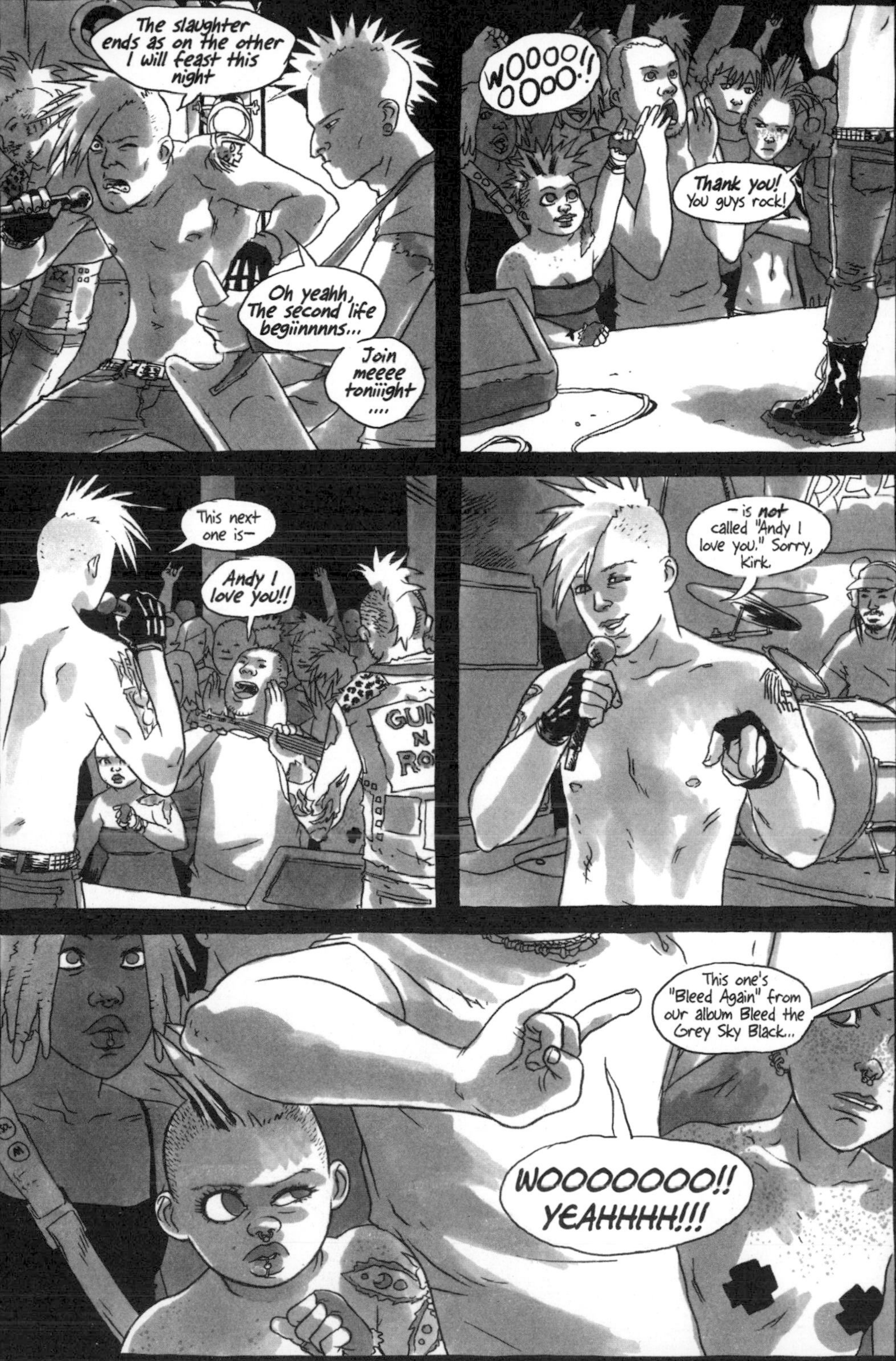
The slaughter ends as on the other I will feast this night
Oh yeahh, The second life begiinnnns...
Join meeee toniiight ....
WOOOO!! OOOO!!
Thank you! You guys rock!
This next one is—
Andy I love you!!
GUN N RO
—is not called "Andy I love you." Sorry, Kirk.
This one's "Bleed Again" from our album Bleed the Grey Sky Black...
WOOOOOOO!! YEAHHHH!!!

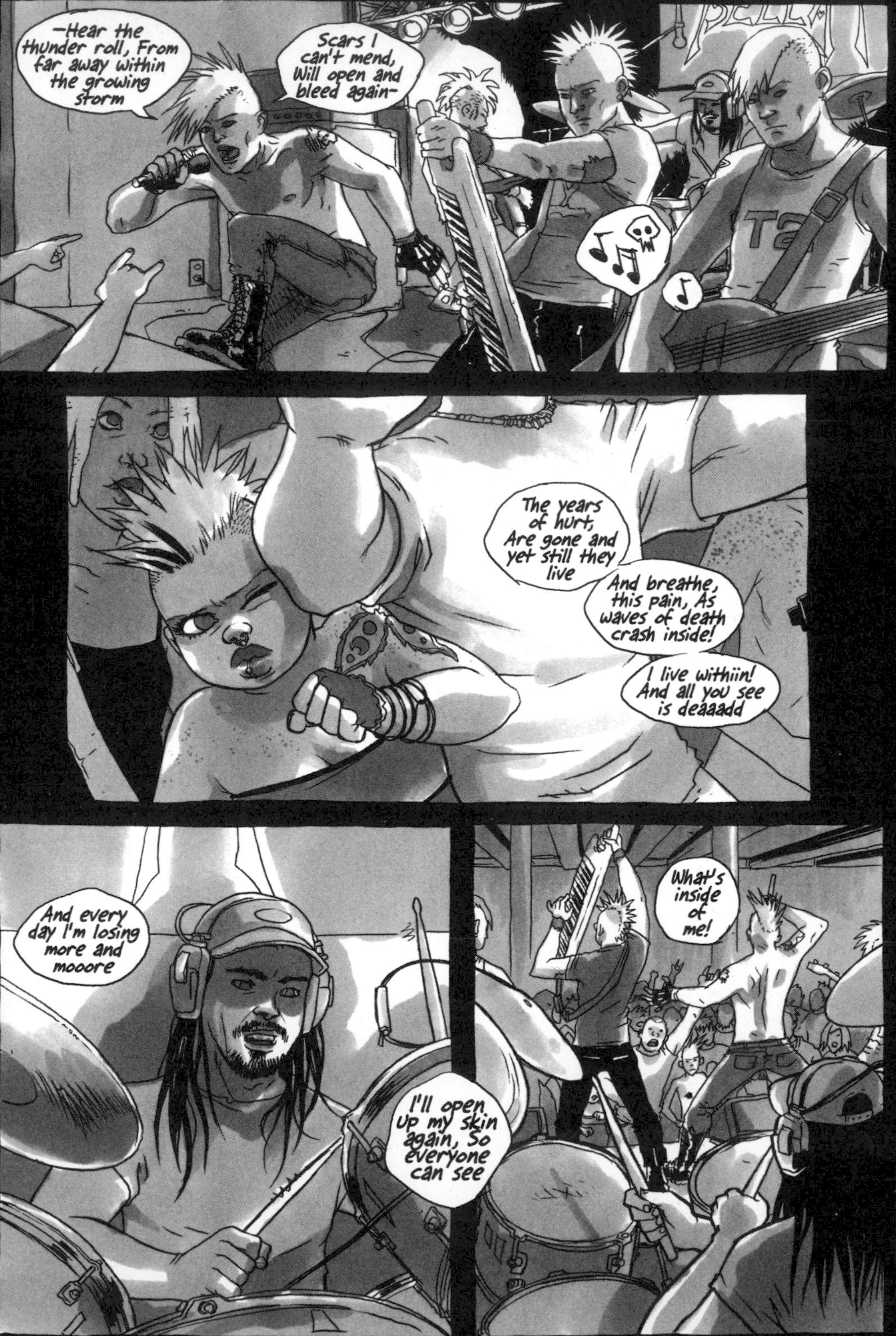
—Hear the thunder roll, From far away within the growing storm
Scars I can't mend, Will open and bleed again-
The years of hurt, Are gone and yet still they live
And breathe, this pain, As waves of death crash inside!
I live withiin! And all you see is deaaadd
And every day I'm losing more and mooore
I'll open up my skin again, So everyone can see
What's inside of me!

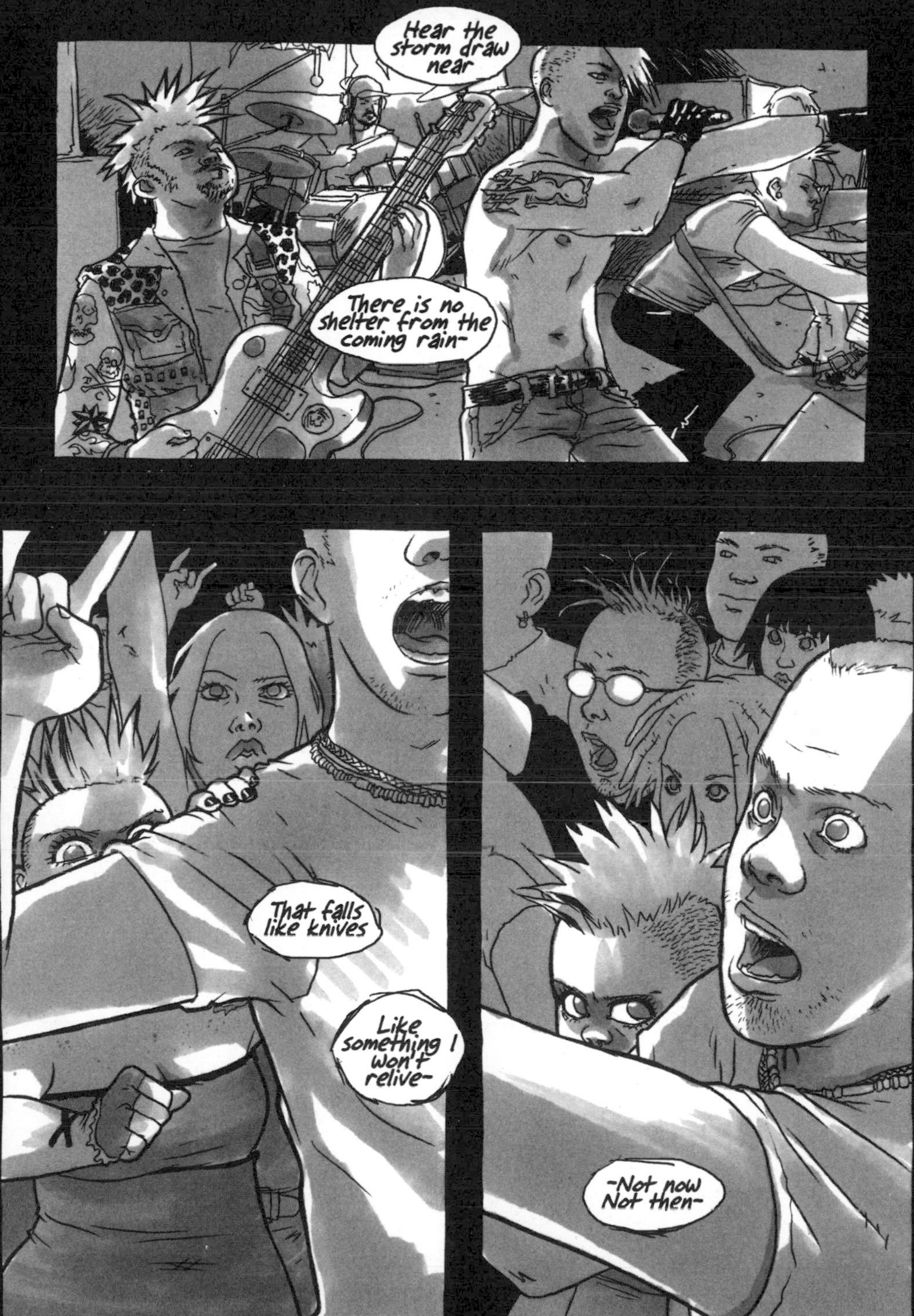
Hear the storm draw near
There is no shelter from the coming rain-
That falls like knives
Like something I won't relive-
-Not now Not then-

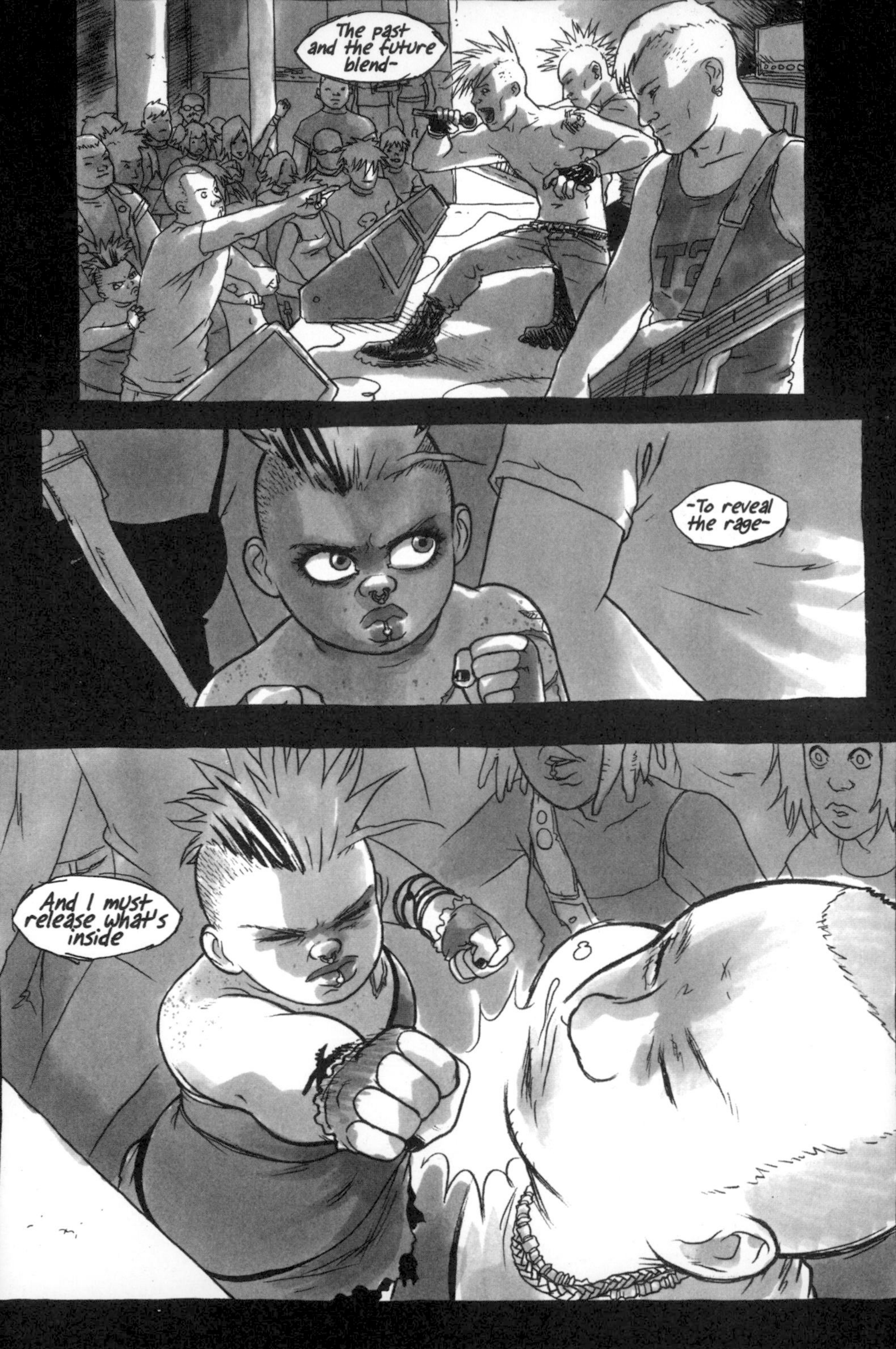
The past and the future blend-
-To reveal the rage-
And I must release what's inside

TSOL

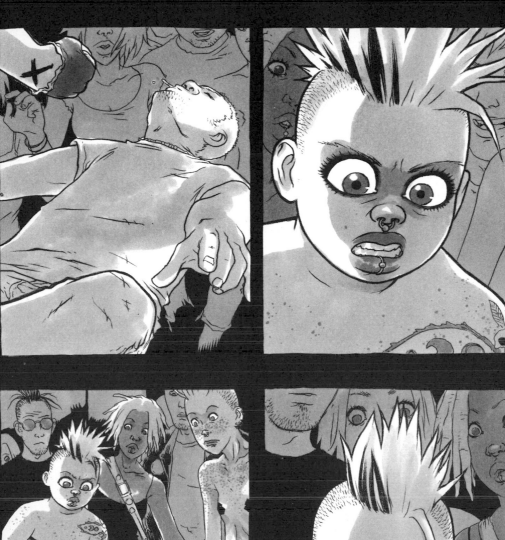

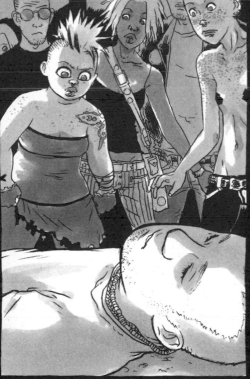

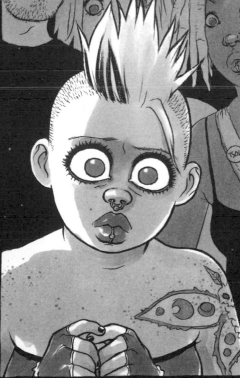

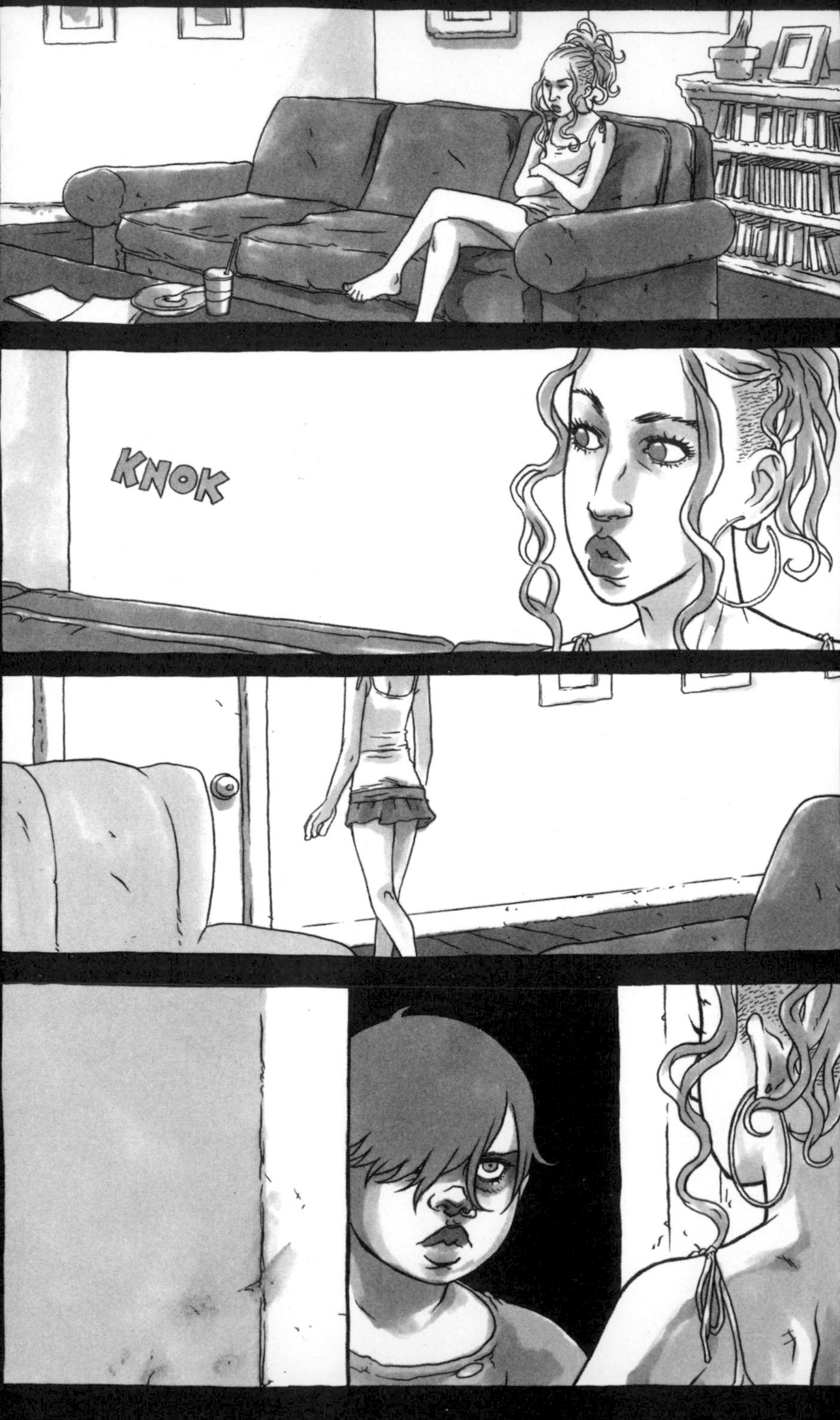
KNOK

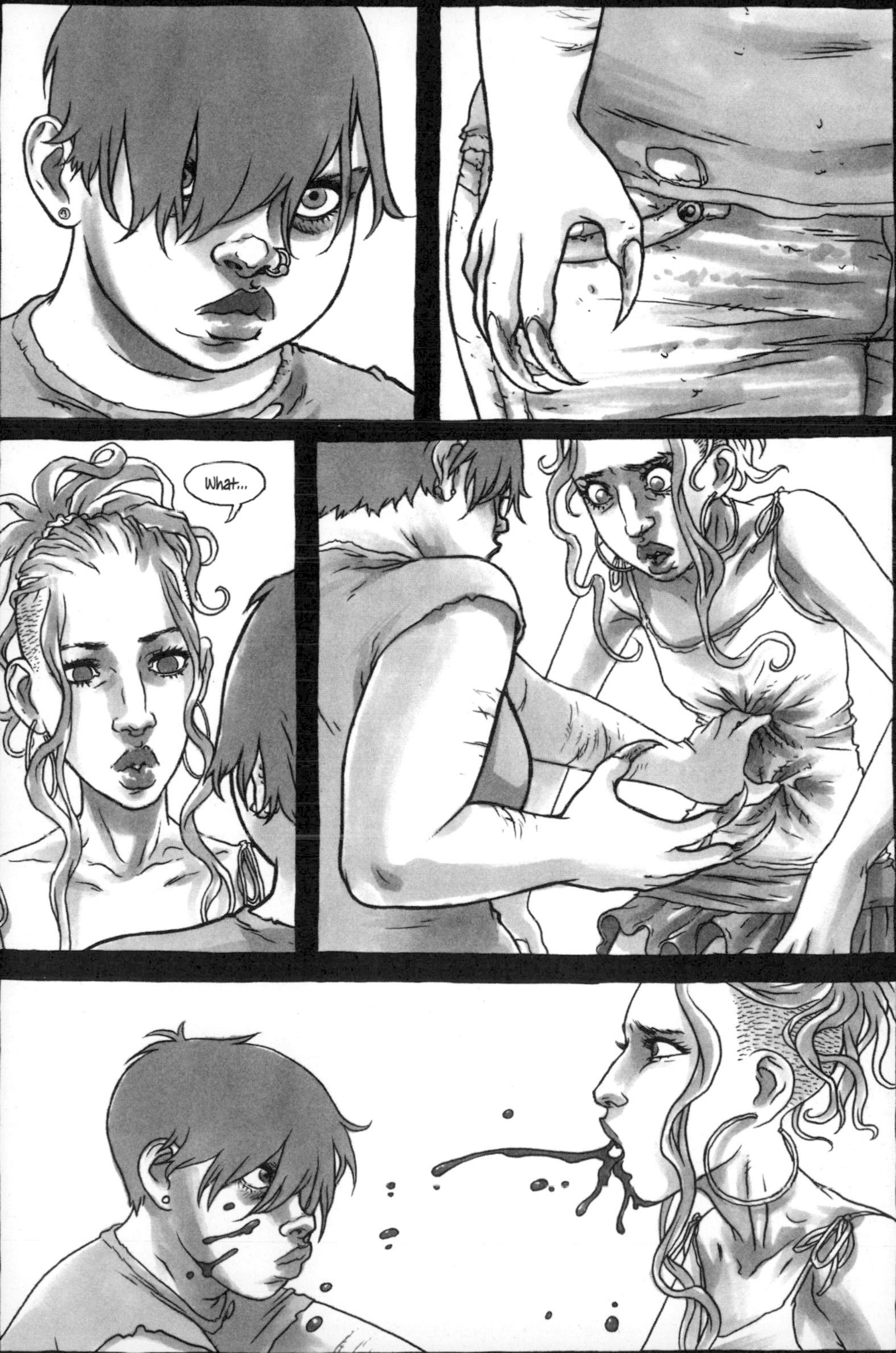
What...

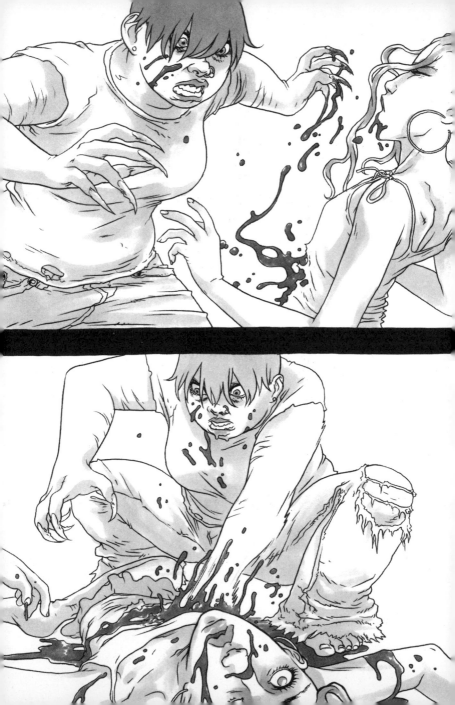

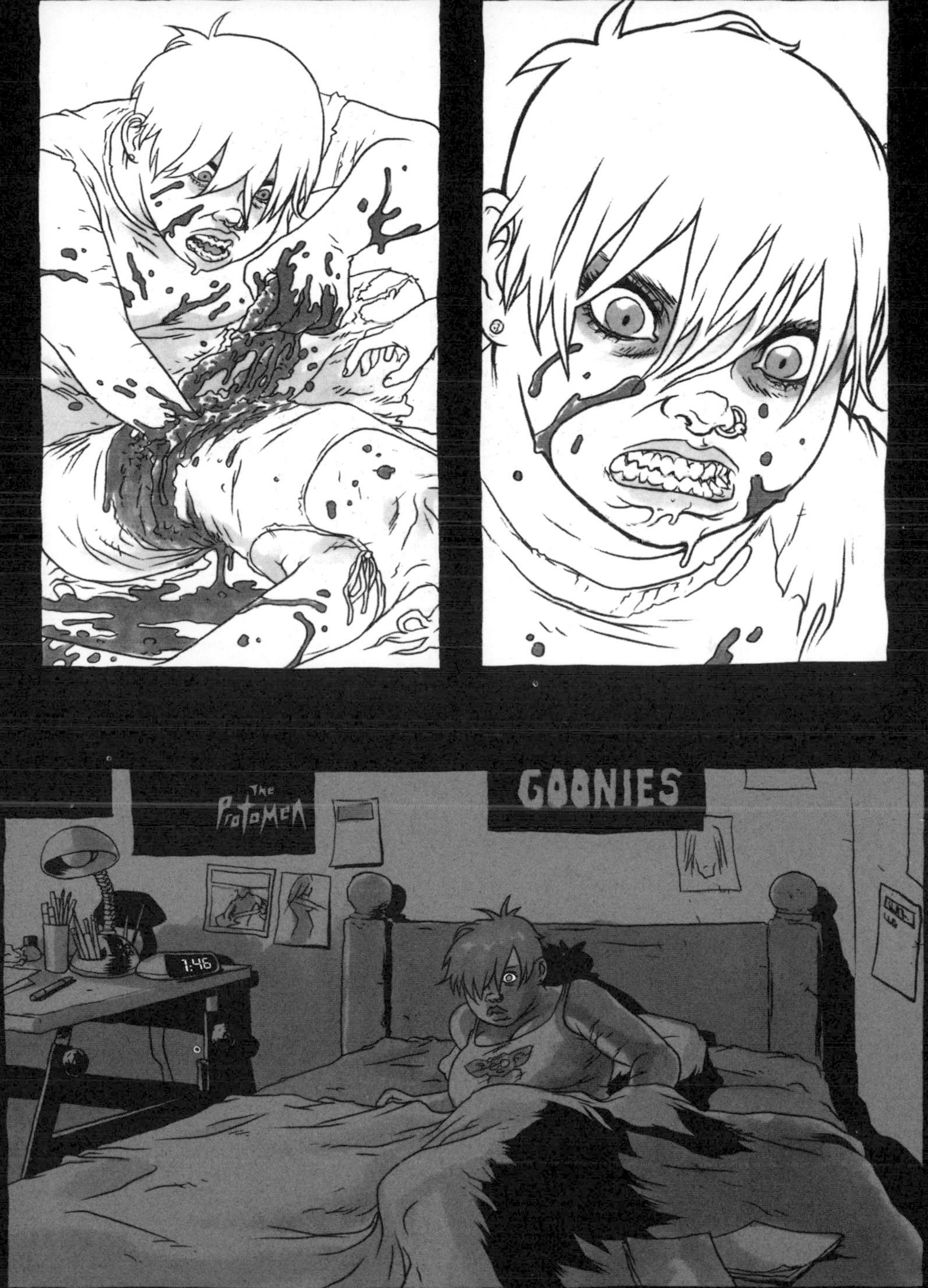
The Protomen
GOONIES
1:46

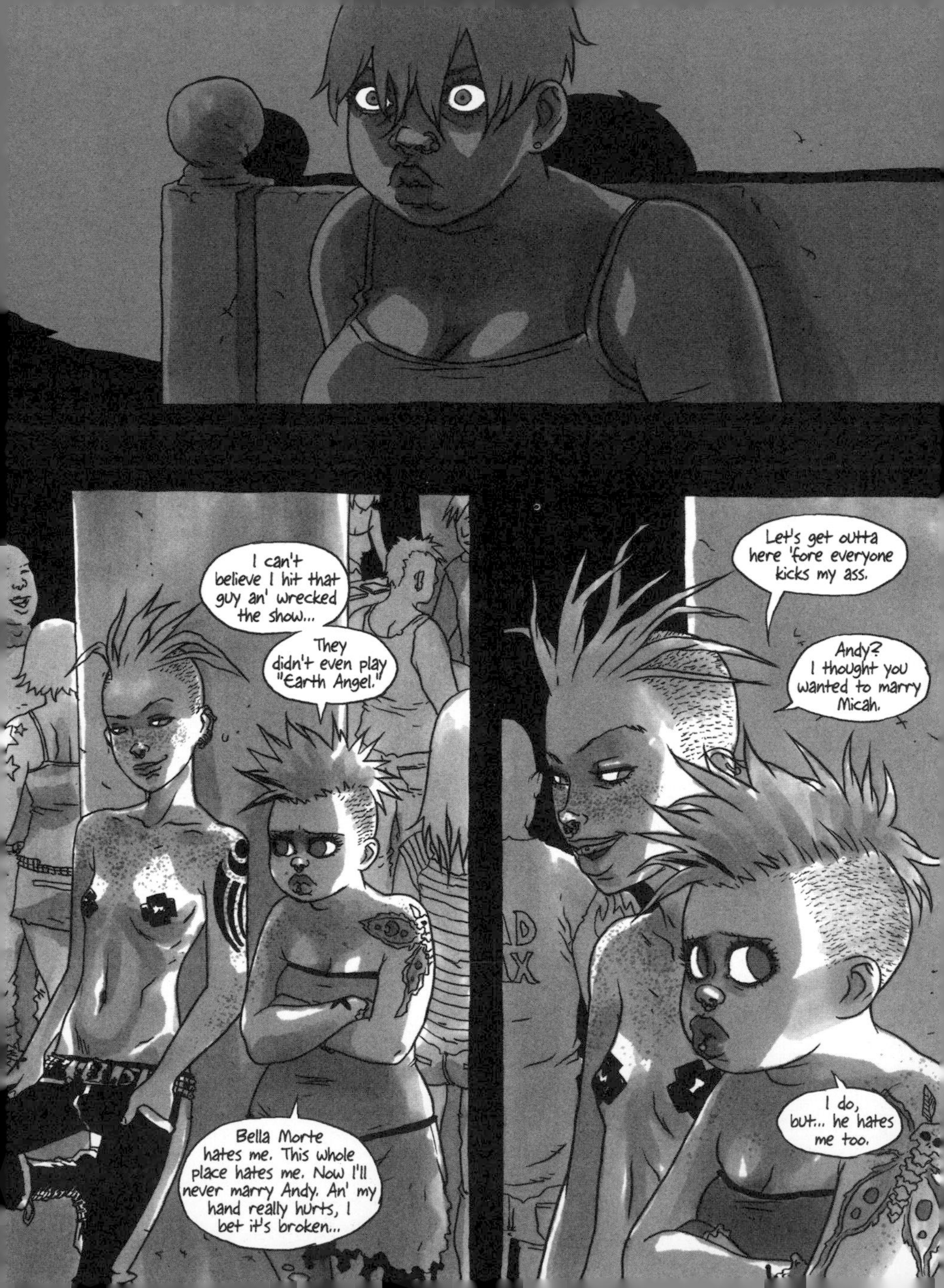
I can't believe I hit that guy an' wrecked the show...
They didn't even play "Earth Angel."
Bella Morte hates me. This whole place hates me. Now I'll never marry Andy. An' my hand really hurts, I bet it's broken...
Let's get outta here 'fore everyone kicks my ass.
Andy? I thought you wanted to marry Micah.
I do, but... he hates me too.

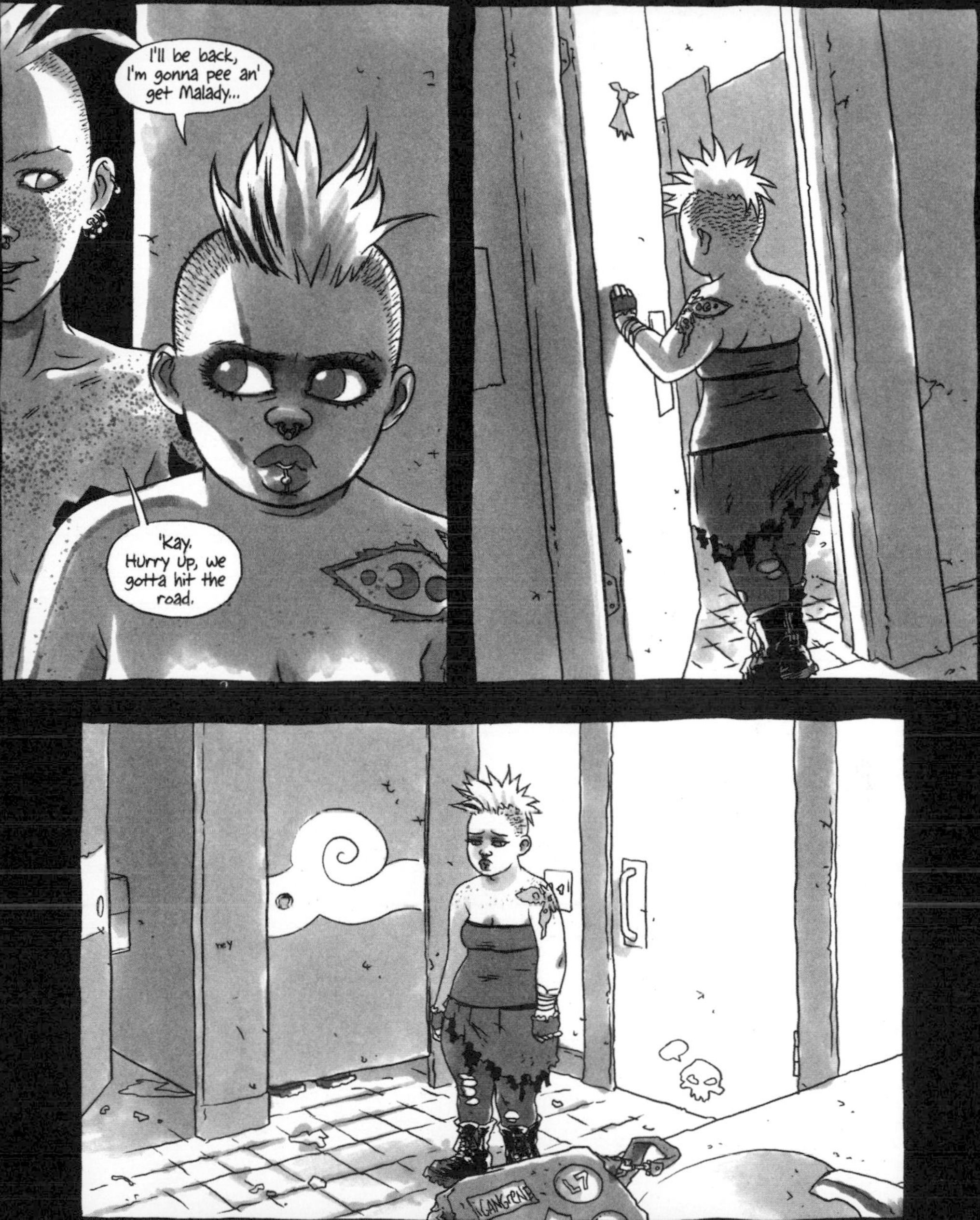
I'll be back, I'm gonna pee an' get Malady...
'Kay. Hurry up, we gotta hit the road.

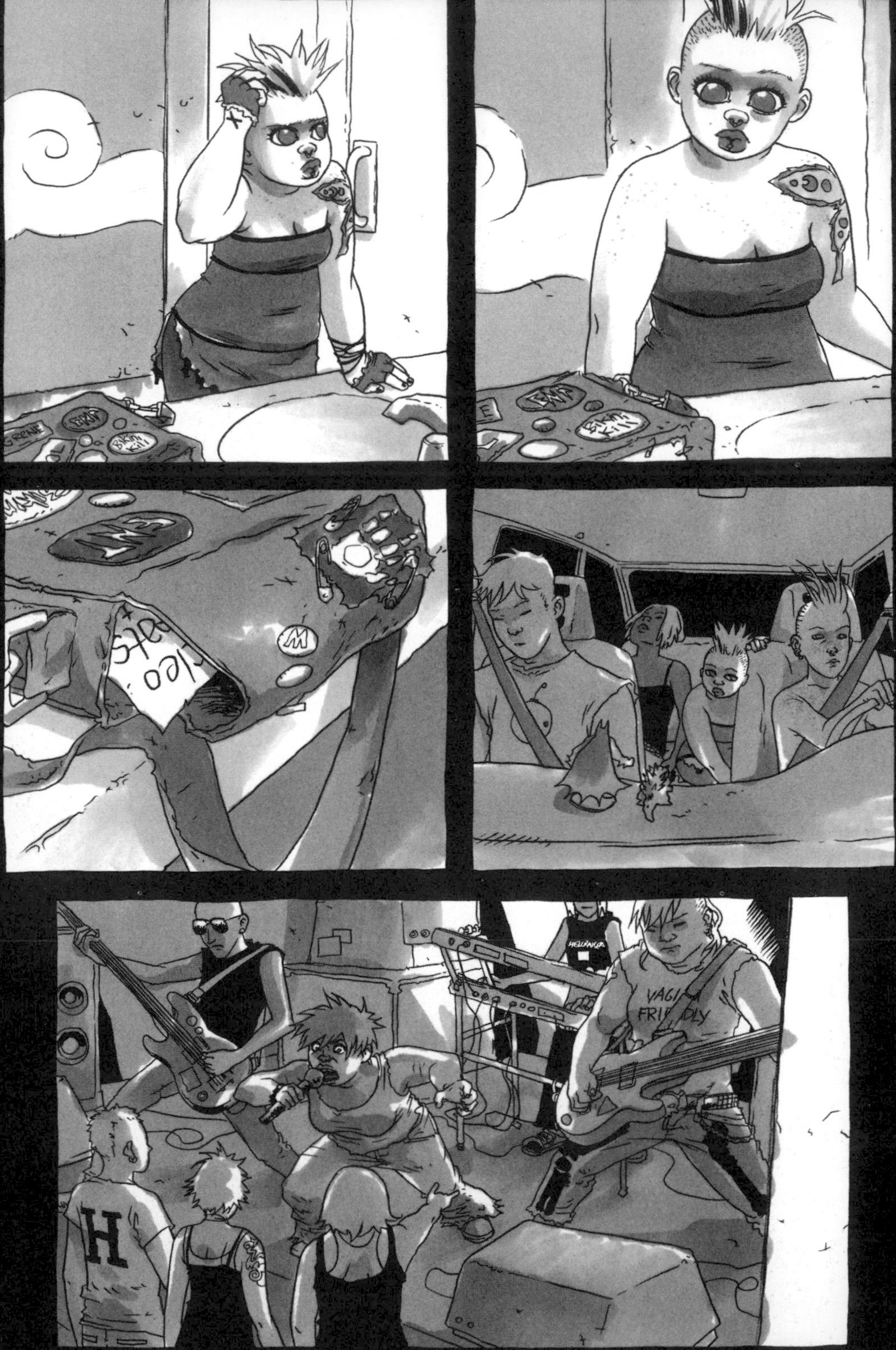
Bikini Kill
H

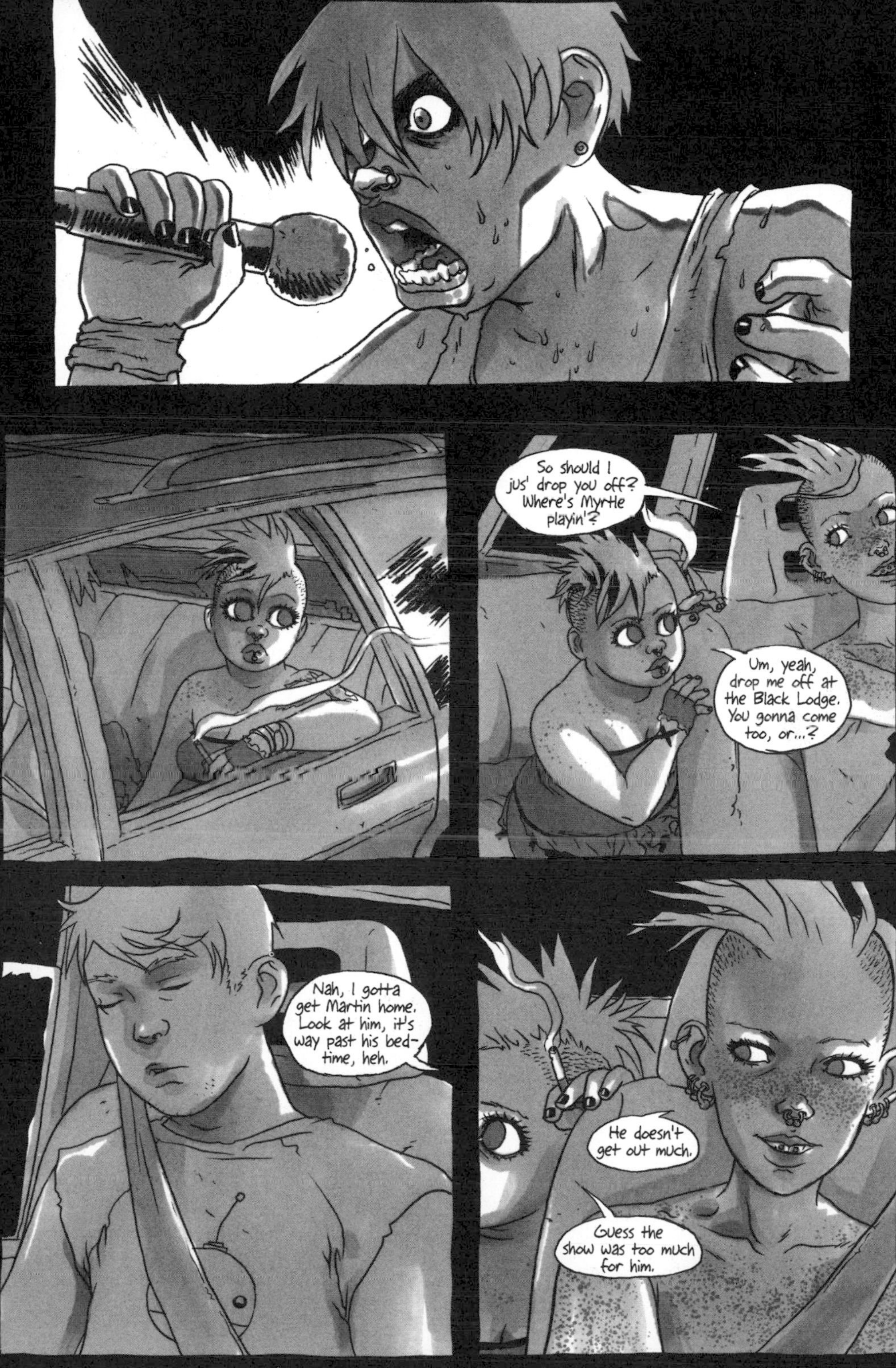
So should I jus' drop you off? Where's Myrtle playin'?
Um, yeah, drop me off at the Black Lodge. You gonna come too, or...?
Nah, I gotta get Martin home. Look at him, it's way past his bed-time, heh.
He doesn't get out much.
Guess the show was too much for him.

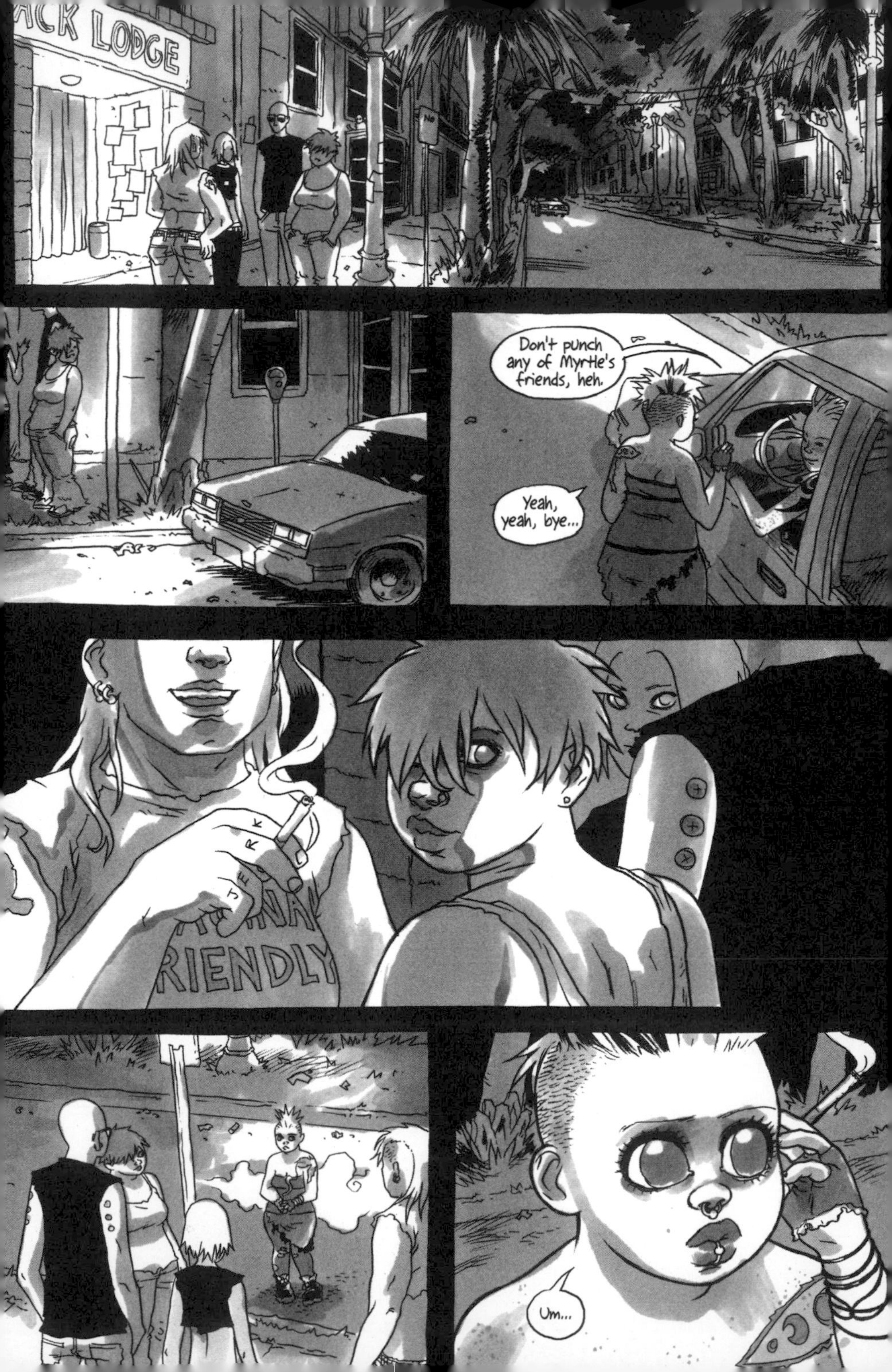
ACK LODGE
Don't punch any of Myrtle's friends, heh.
Yeah, yeah, bye...
JERK
RIENDLY
Um...

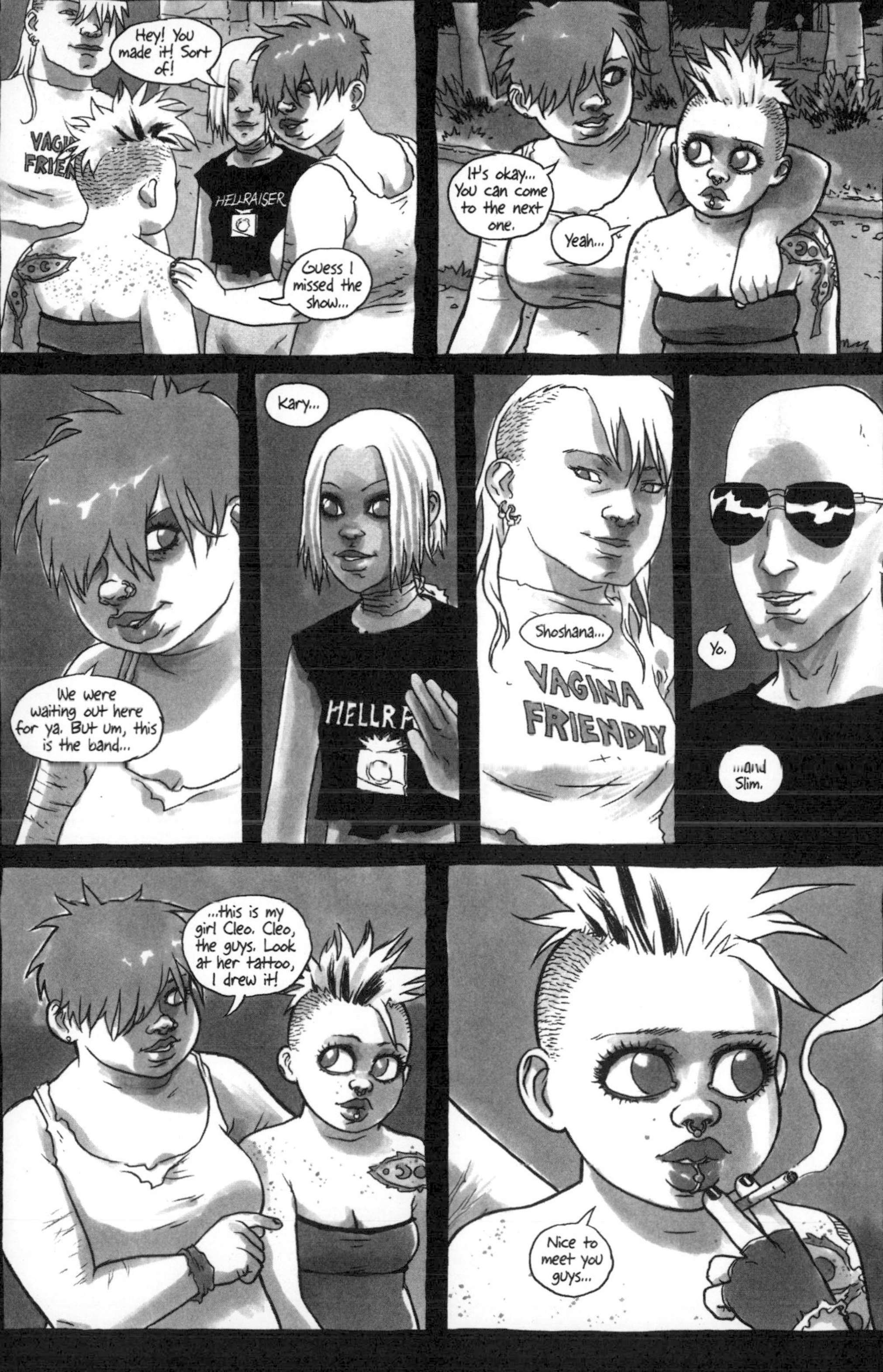

VAGINA FRIEN
Hey! You made it! Sort of!
HELLRAISER
Guess I missed the show...
It's okay... You can come to the next one.
Yeah...
We were waiting out here for ya. But um, this is the band...
Kary...
HELLRA
Shoshana...
VAGINA FRIENDLY
Yo.
...and Slim.
...this is my girl Cleo. Cleo, the guys. Look at her tattoo, I drew it!
Nice to meet you guys...

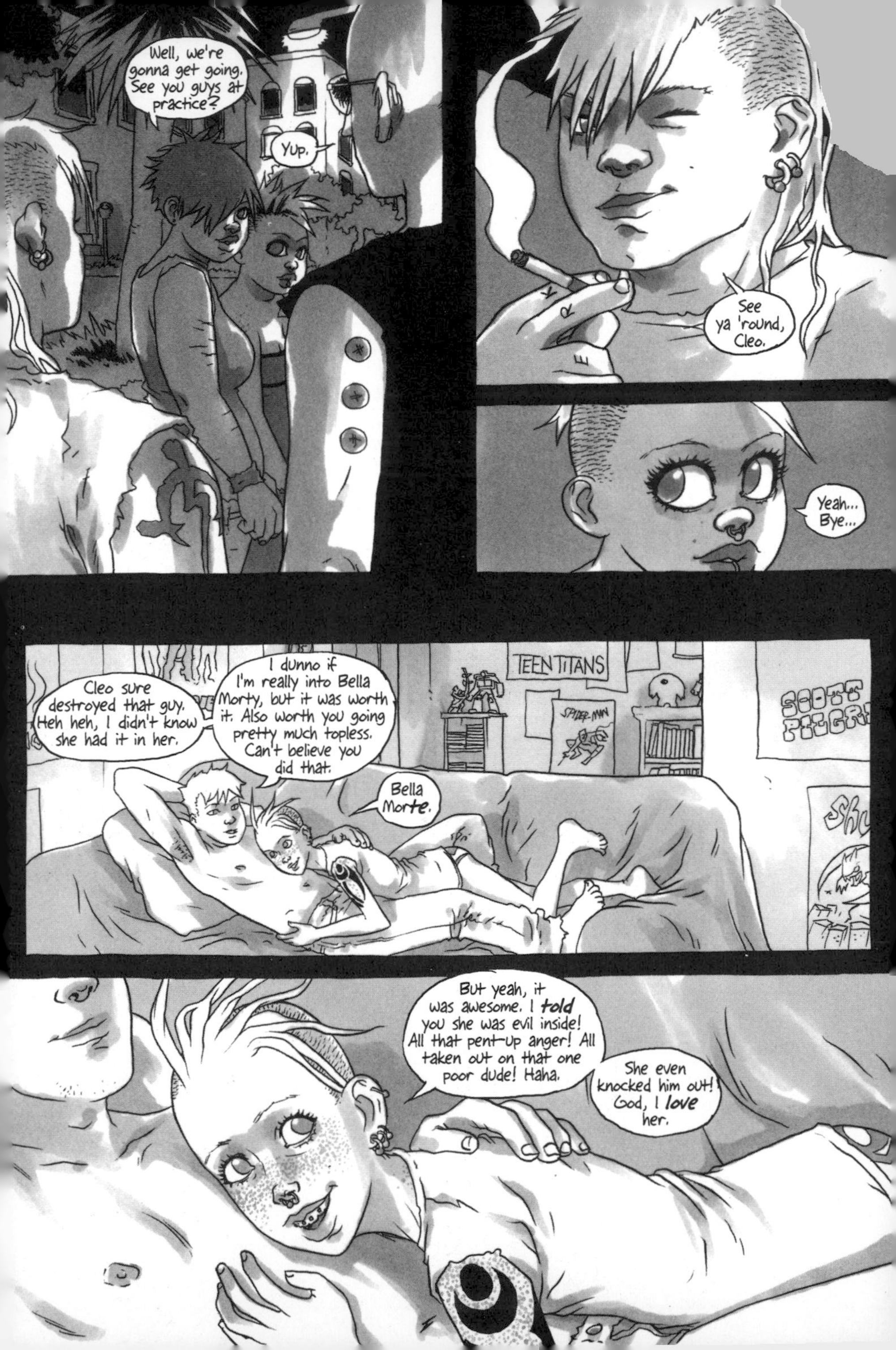
Well, we're gonna get going. See you guys at practice?
Yup.
See ya 'round, Cleo.
Yeah... Bye...
TEEN TITANS
SPIDER-MAN
SCOTT PILGRI
Cleo sure destroyed that guy. Heh heh, I didn't know she had it in her.
I dunno if I'm really into Bella Morty, but it was worth it. Also worth you going pretty much topless. Can't believe you did that.
Bella Morte.
But yeah, it was awesome. I **told** you she was evil inside! All that pent-up anger! All taken out on that one poor dude! Haha.
She even knocked him out! God, I **love** her.

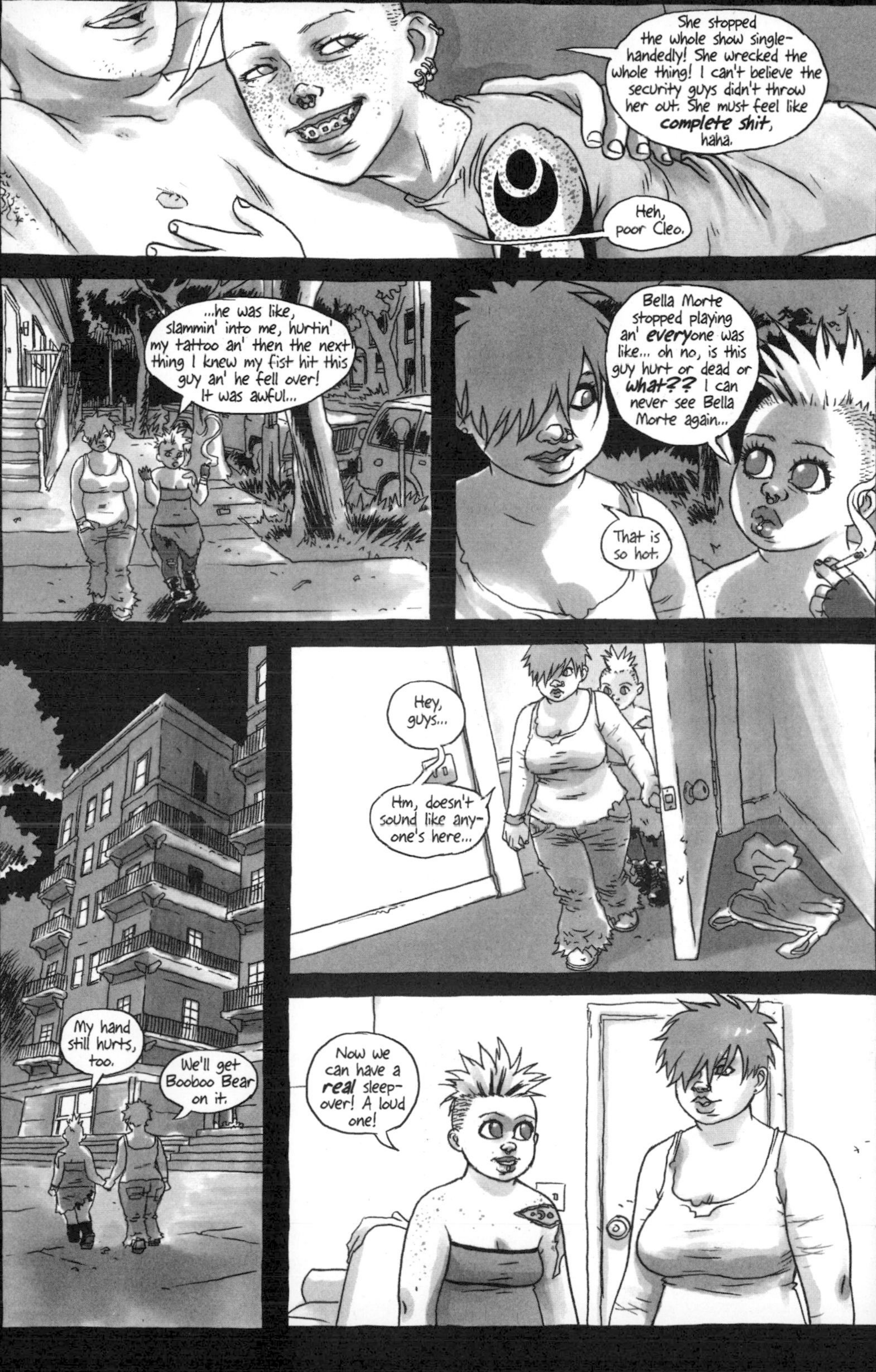
She stopped the whole show single-handedly! She wrecked the whole thing! I can't believe the security guys didn't throw her out. She must feel like **complete shit**, haha.
Heh, poor Cleo.
...he was like, slammin' into me, hurtin' my tattoo an' then the next thing I knew my fist hit this guy an' he fell over! It was awful...
Bella Morte stopped playing an' ***every***one was like... oh no, is this guy hurt or dead or **what??** I can never see Bella Morte again...
That is so hot.
My hand still hurts, too.
We'll get Booboo Bear on it.
Hey, guys...
Hm, doesn't sound like any-one's here...
Now we can have a ***real*** sleep-over! A loud one!

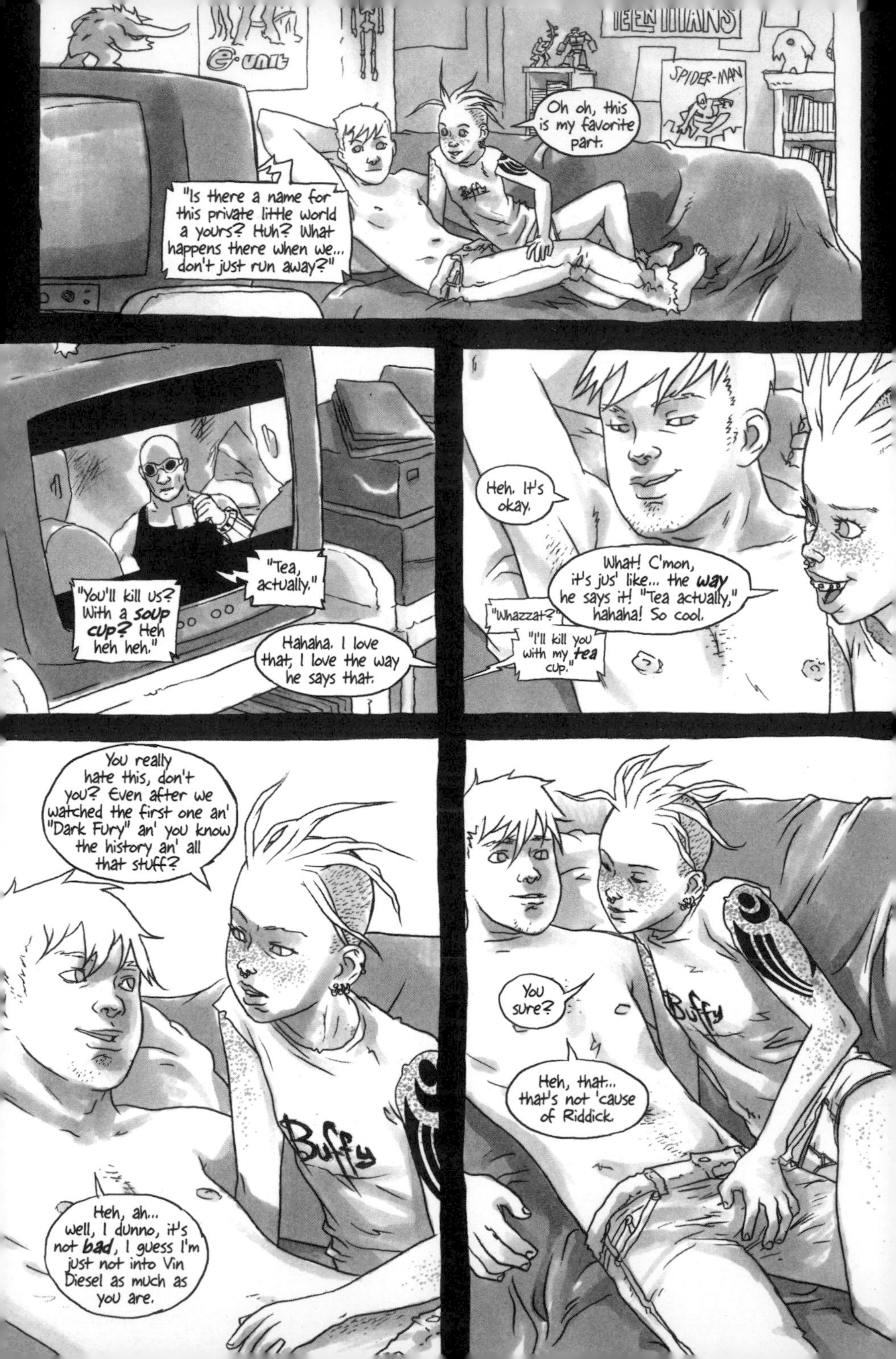
TEEN TITANS
SPIDER-MAN
Oh oh, this is my favorite part.
"Is there a name for this private little world a yours? Huh? What happens there when we... don't just run away?"
Buffy
"You'll kill us? With a soup cup? Heh heh heh."
"Tea, actually."
Hahaha. I love that, I love the way he says that.
Heh. It's okay.
What! C'mon, it's jus' like... the way he says it! "Tea actually," hahaha! So cool.
"Whazzat?"
"I'll kill you with my tea cup."
You really hate this, don't you? Even after we watched the first one an' "Dark Fury" an' you know the history an' all that stuff?
Buffy
Heh, ah... well, I dunno, it's not bad, I guess I'm just not into Vin Diesel as much as you are.
You sure?
Buffy
Heh, that... that's not 'cause of Riddick.

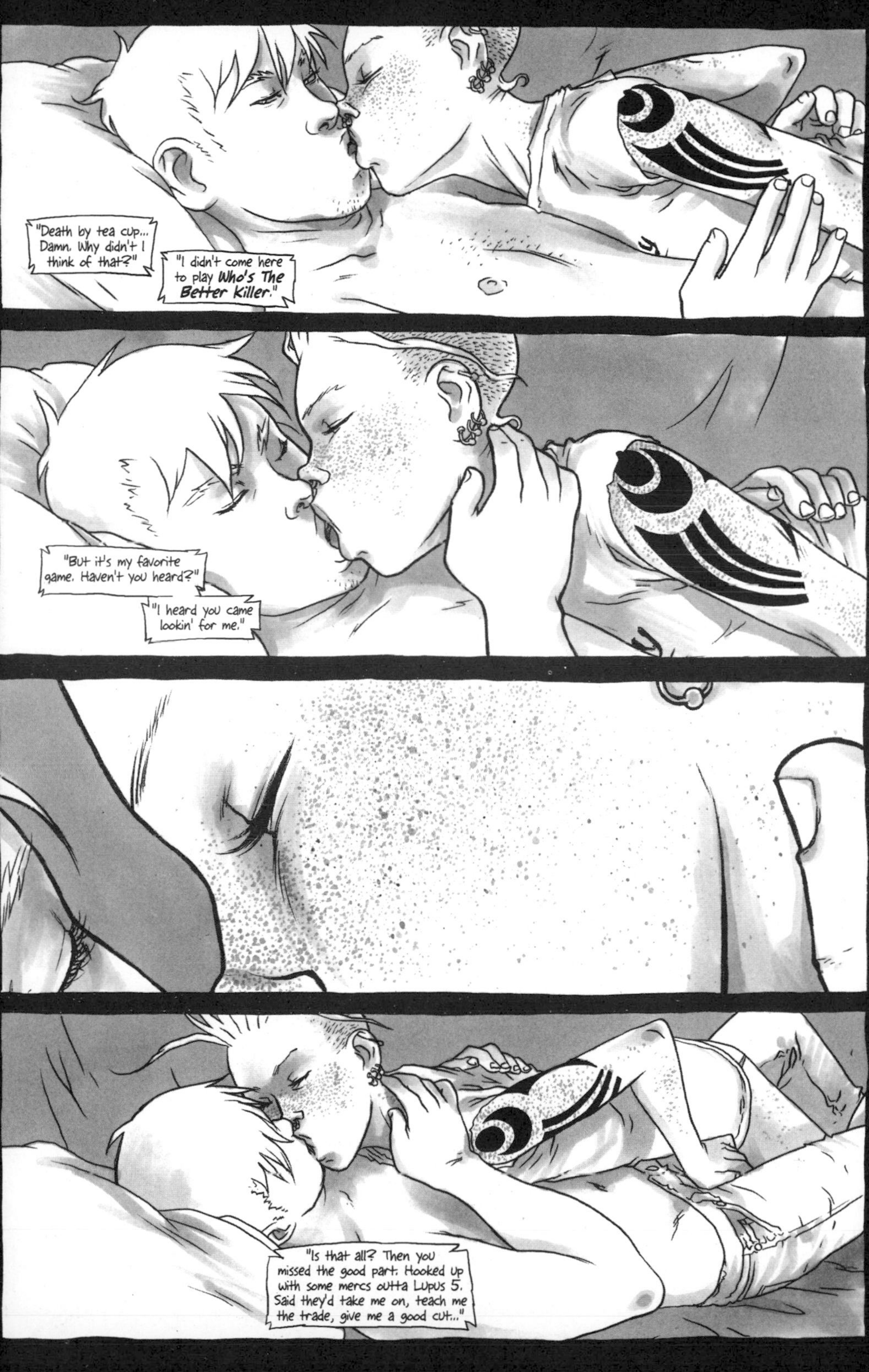

"Death by tea cup... Damn. Why didn't I think of that?"
"I didn't come here to play **Who's The Better Killer**."
"But it's my favorite game. Haven't you heard?"
"I heard you came lookin' for me."
"Is that all? Then you missed the good part. Hooked up with some mercs outta Lupus 5. Said they'd take me on, teach me the trade, give me a good cut..."

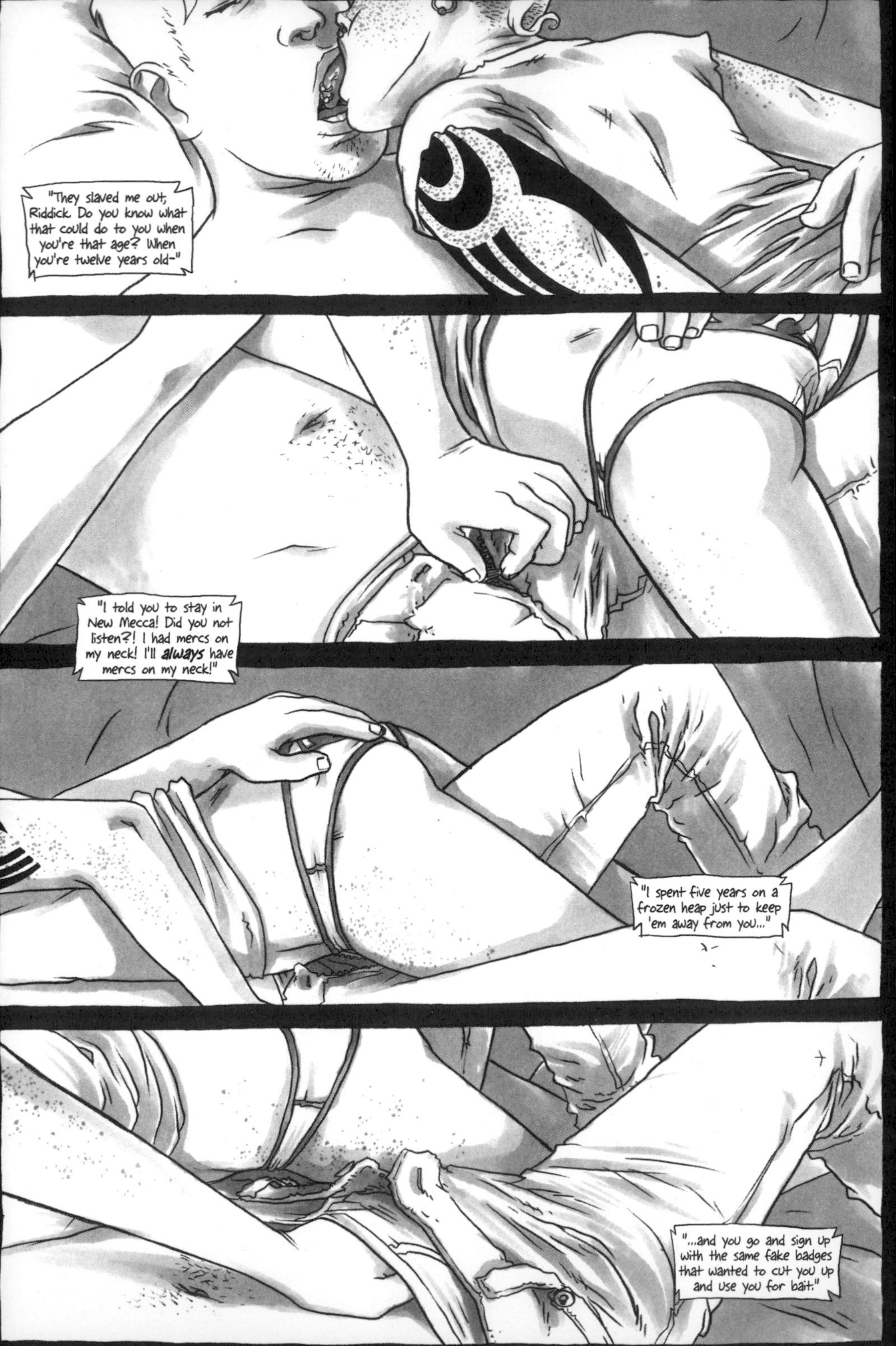
"They slaved me out, Riddick. Do you know what that could do to you when you're that age? When you're twelve years old-"
"I told you to stay in New Mecca! Did you not listen?! I had mercs on my neck! I'll *always* have mercs on my neck!"
"I spent five years on a frozen heap just to keep 'em away from you..."
"...and you go and sign up with the same fake badges that wanted to cut you up and use you for bait."

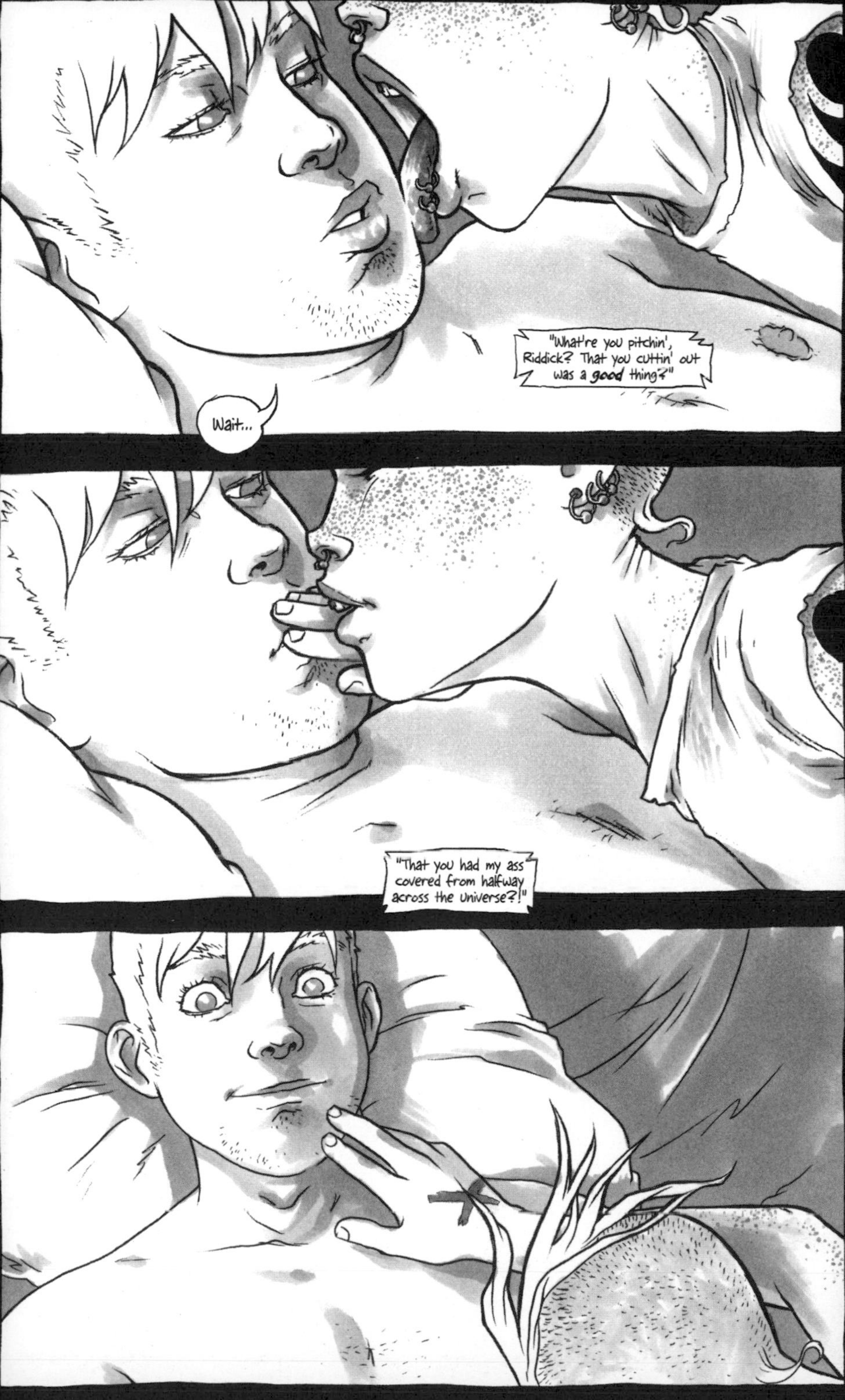
"What're you pitchin', Riddick? That you cuttin' out was a good thing?"
Wait...
"That you had my ass covered from halfway across the Universe?!"

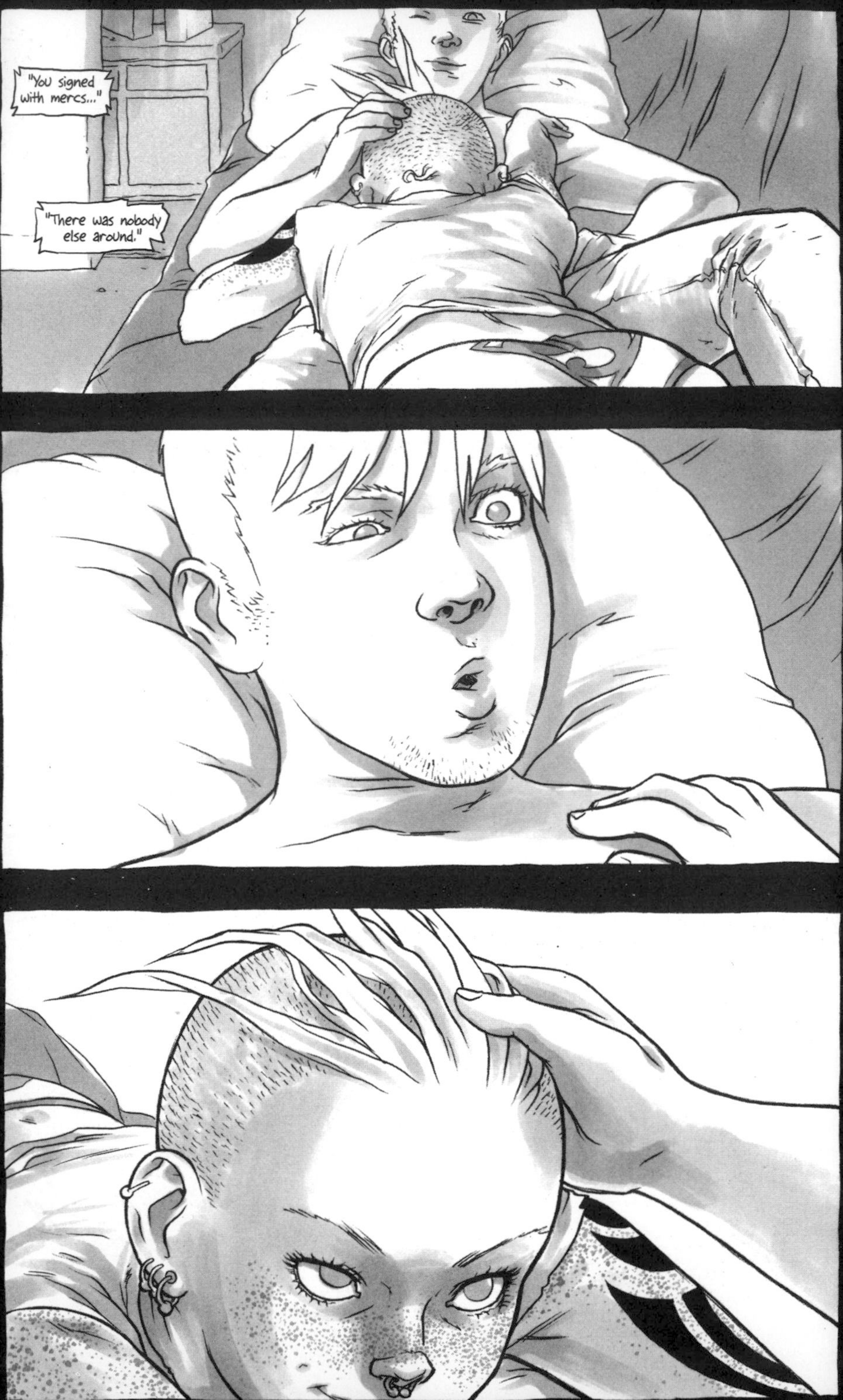
"You signed with mercs..."
"There was nobody else around."

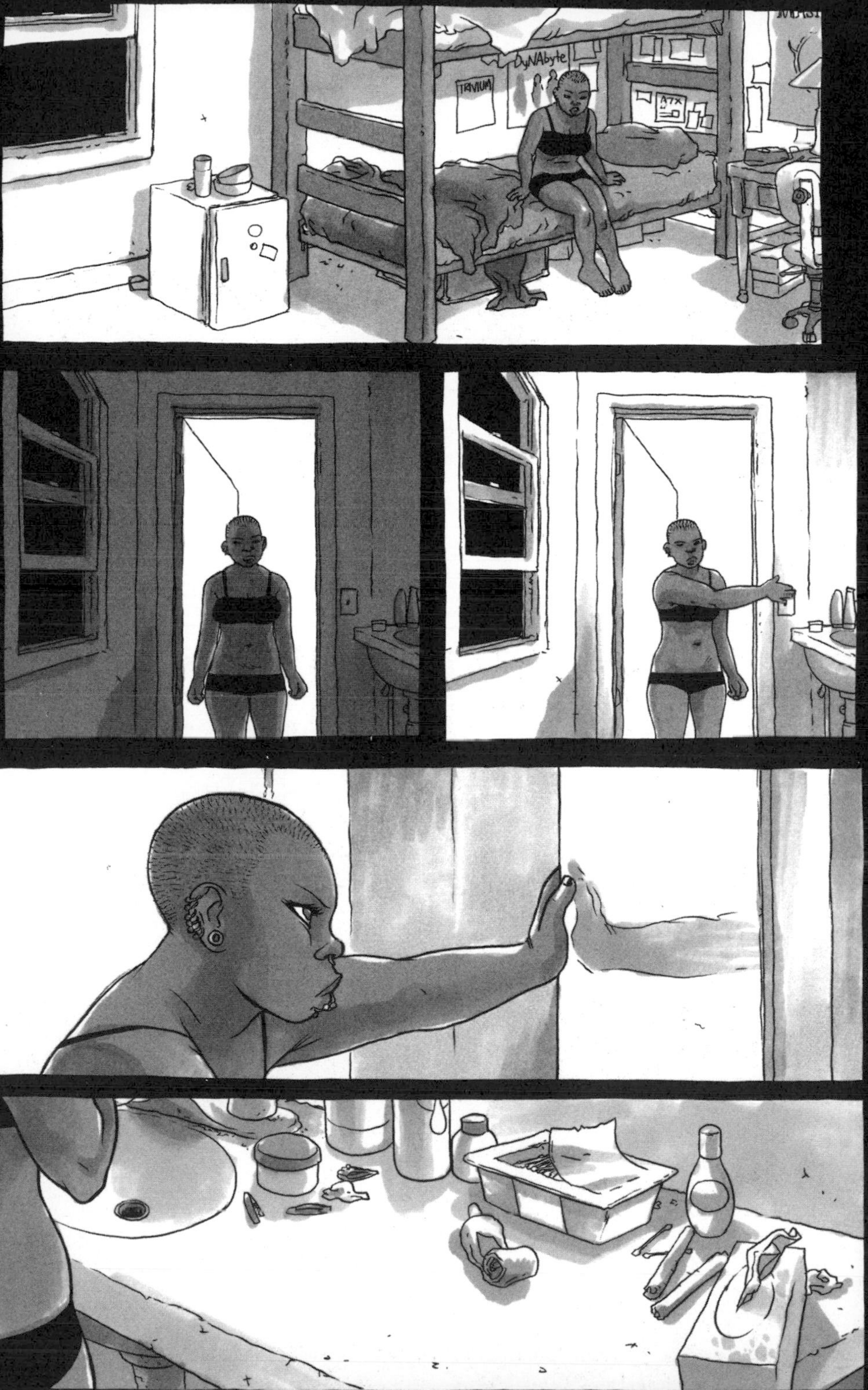
DyNAbyte
TRIVIUM
A7X

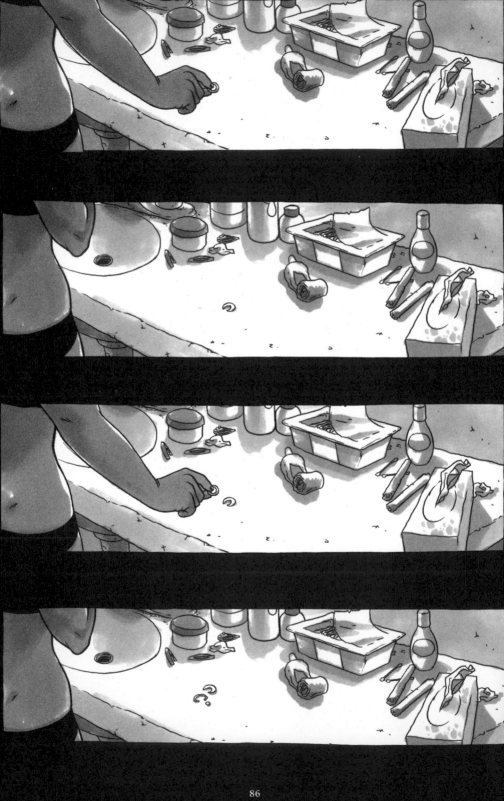

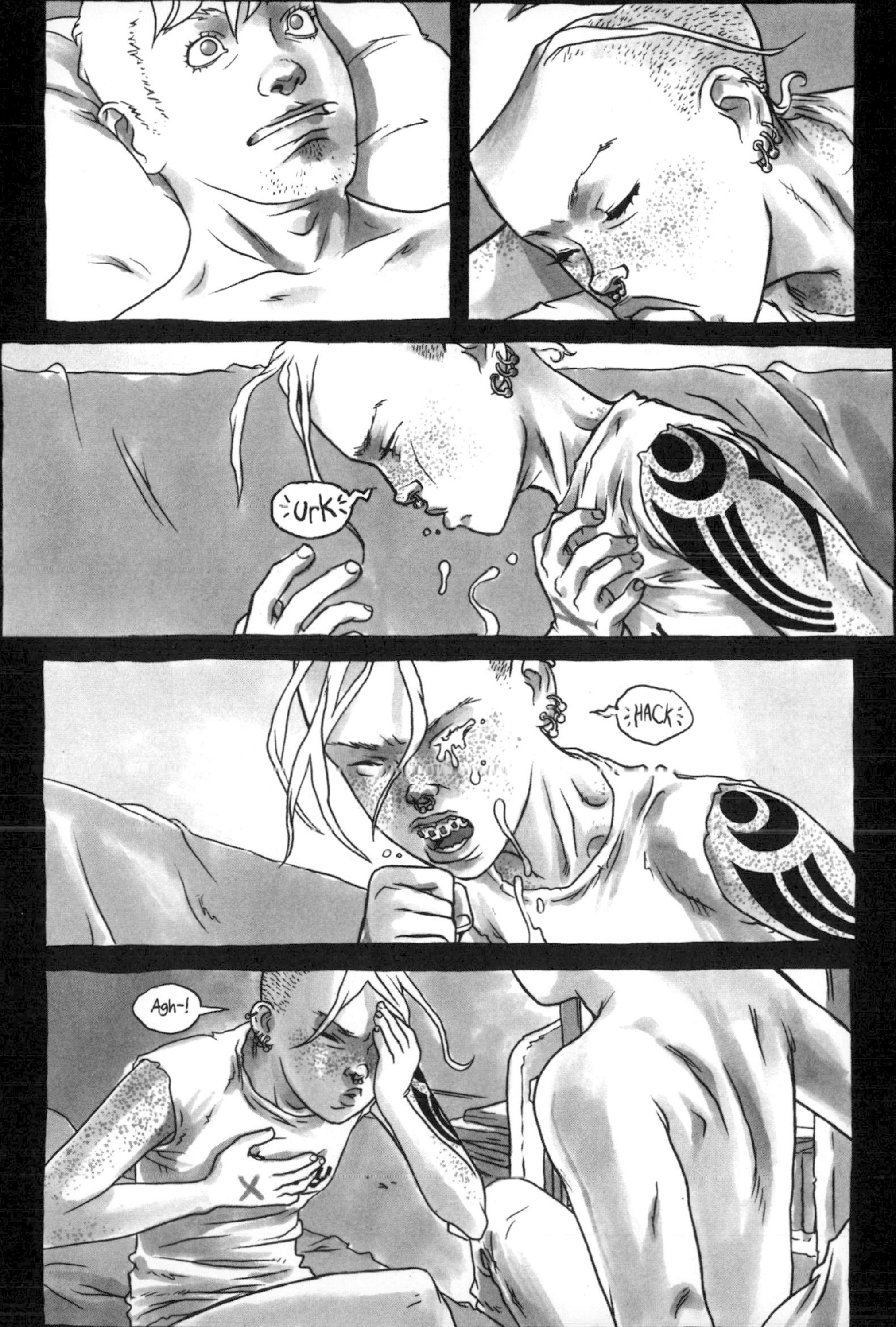
Urk
HACK
Agh-!

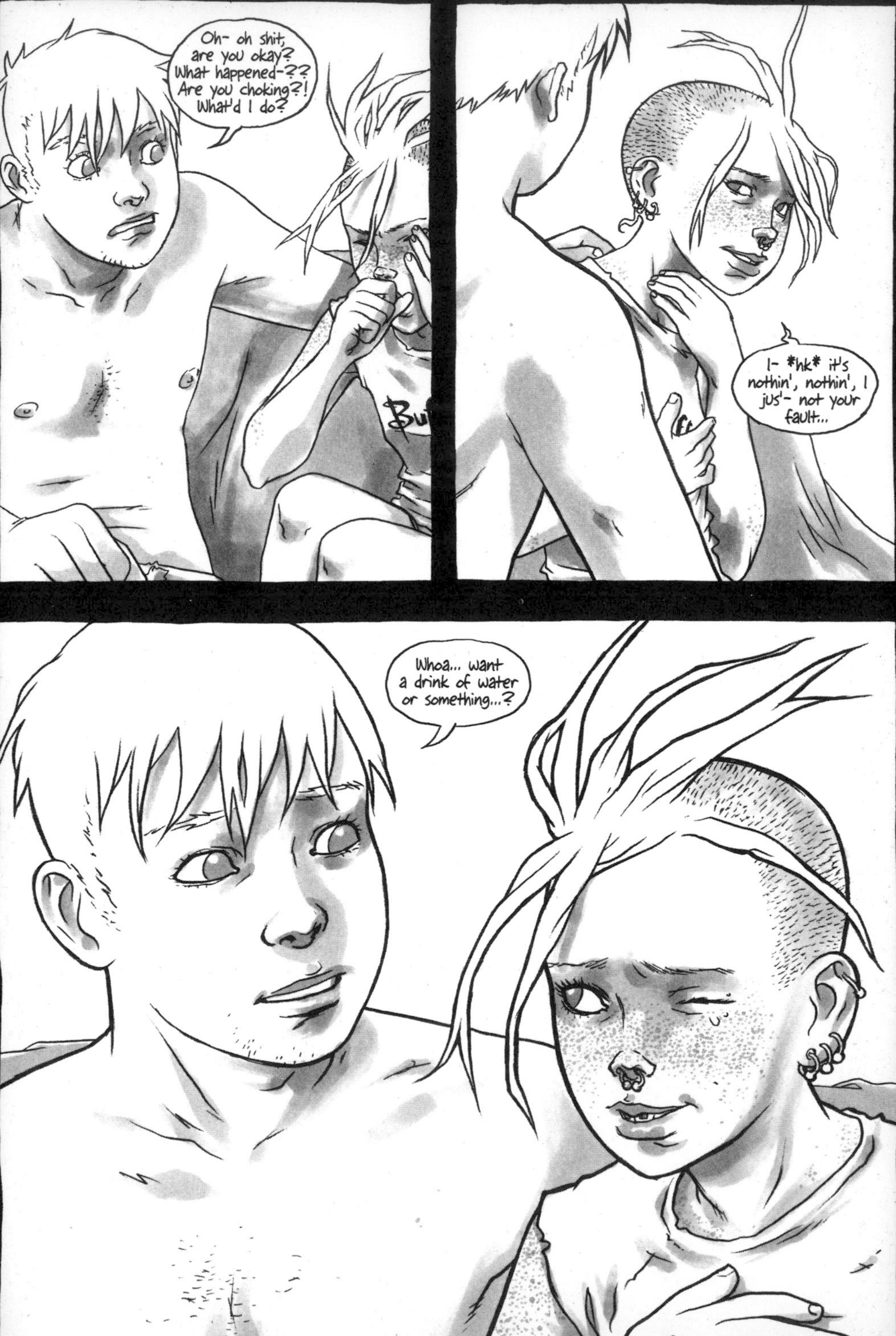
Oh- oh shit, are you okay? What happened-?? Are you choking?! What'd I do?
I- *hk* it's nothin', nothin', I jus'- not your fault...
Whoa... want a drink of water or something...?

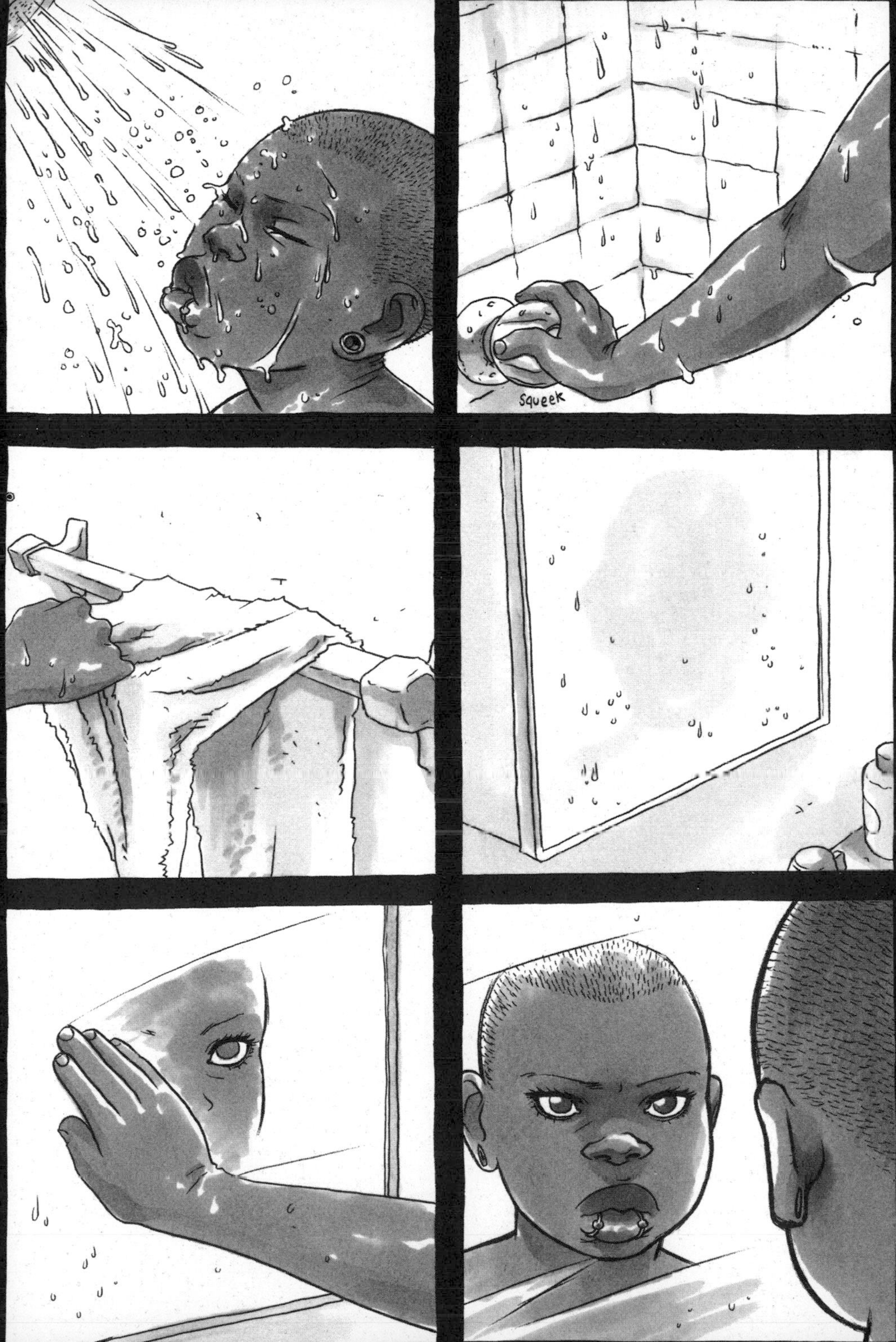
squeek

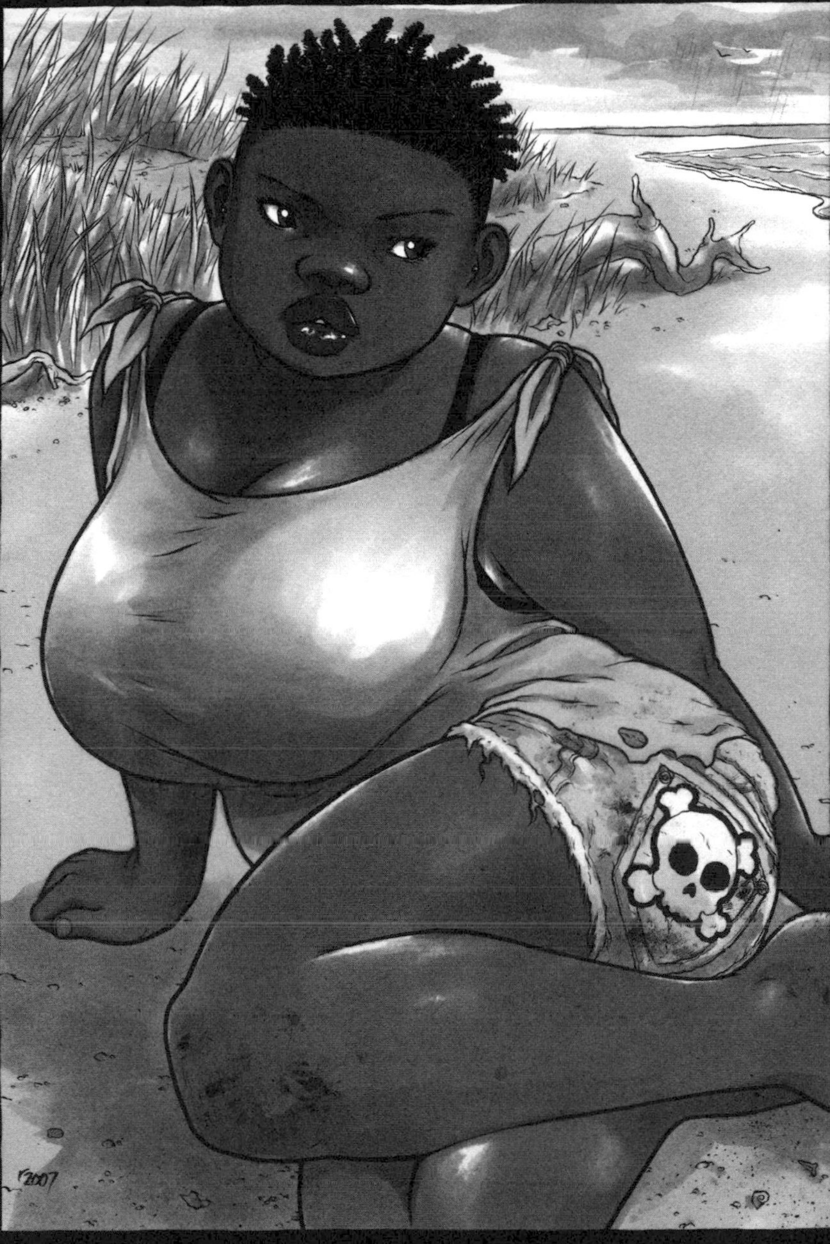

13

The Wonders At Your Feet

[friendtoroaches@gmail.com]

Recent Entries Archive Friends User Info

mara's journal

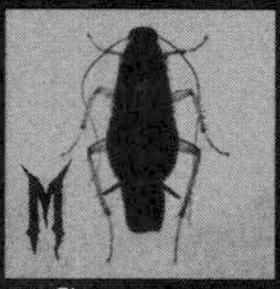

profile

October 13th, 11:32pm

INTRUDER ALERT

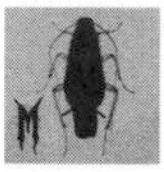

i slept all day. i got up and it was past 10:00pm. i haven't done that in a long time, i used to sleep this late during summer vacation in high school sometimes, but hardly ever anymore. it's a real weird feeling, i can't explain it... it's like you missed something but you don't know what it is and you never will, and you know that you never will, too, so you can't worry about it. and there's something weird but great about after you get up this ridculously late, you take a shower like it's a normal morning. it's both uncomfortable and satisfying at the same time. that's what i just did. i took out a lot of my piercings too, it seemed like the right thing to do, i was getting sick of them... sometimes lately i feel like i don't know who i am anymore. i know that sounds totally lame and emo or whatever, but it's true and i can't lie about it. it seems like once college started, or maybe over the summer after senior year of high school, that everybody started to change real quick except for me. when i think about it, i guess Cleo and Trilby and Audrey are all basically the same, but it doesn't feel like it.

Cleo's been changing a lot in the past few years, so it wasn't a big jump for her, but now i feel like she's all popular or something which is why she's never home. but it's not like she's meeting all these new people, she still hangs out with Trilby, Audrey and Glen and i guess me (sometimes), and i know she doesn't hang out with her roommates, but i guess it's that Myrtle girl who she's always with. it's kind of weird, this whole college thing, because usually you're supposed to go away for school, go away to some other state or at least another city, but all of us stayed in the same town because we had a good school here already that had everything we wanted to do. so instead of being forced to meet entirely new people and make an entirely new group of friends, we don't have to because all our best friends from high school are here with us in college. i wonder if that stunts your growth in some way. is it a natural, necessary thing to go away for college? is it an important learning stage that you should go through? maybe not for all people, but for some people. because a lot of people don't even go to college. and i definately don't think college is necessary, because not everyone knows what they want to do and some people don't have any ambitions that you need a degree for. which is cool. i don't think i need a degree to be a writer either, i think i could do that on my own and become well-known and write for a living without school. i don't know what's going on.

mood: thoughtful
current music: combichrist - lying sack of shit

[0 comments | leave a comment]

October 11th, 3:23am

I'M MY ENEMY

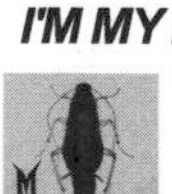

today probably one of the most awkward things that has ever happened to me happened. not only am i completly embarassed now to go over to Cleo's dumb dorm because she's never there but now her stuck-up roomate Natalie thinks i'm the biggest douche on the planet. i always show up there and Cleo is never home so this girl Natalie answers the door and tells me Cleo isn't home every fucking time. then today she told me to wait inside for Cleo so i did, whatever, seemed like a good thing to do. Cleo's gotta come home sometime, right? so i waited with Natalie on the couch, watching some Matthew Broderick movie, the Ferris Bueller guy except now he's old but still looks oddly the same. Reese Witherspoon was in it too. anyway, so we sat there

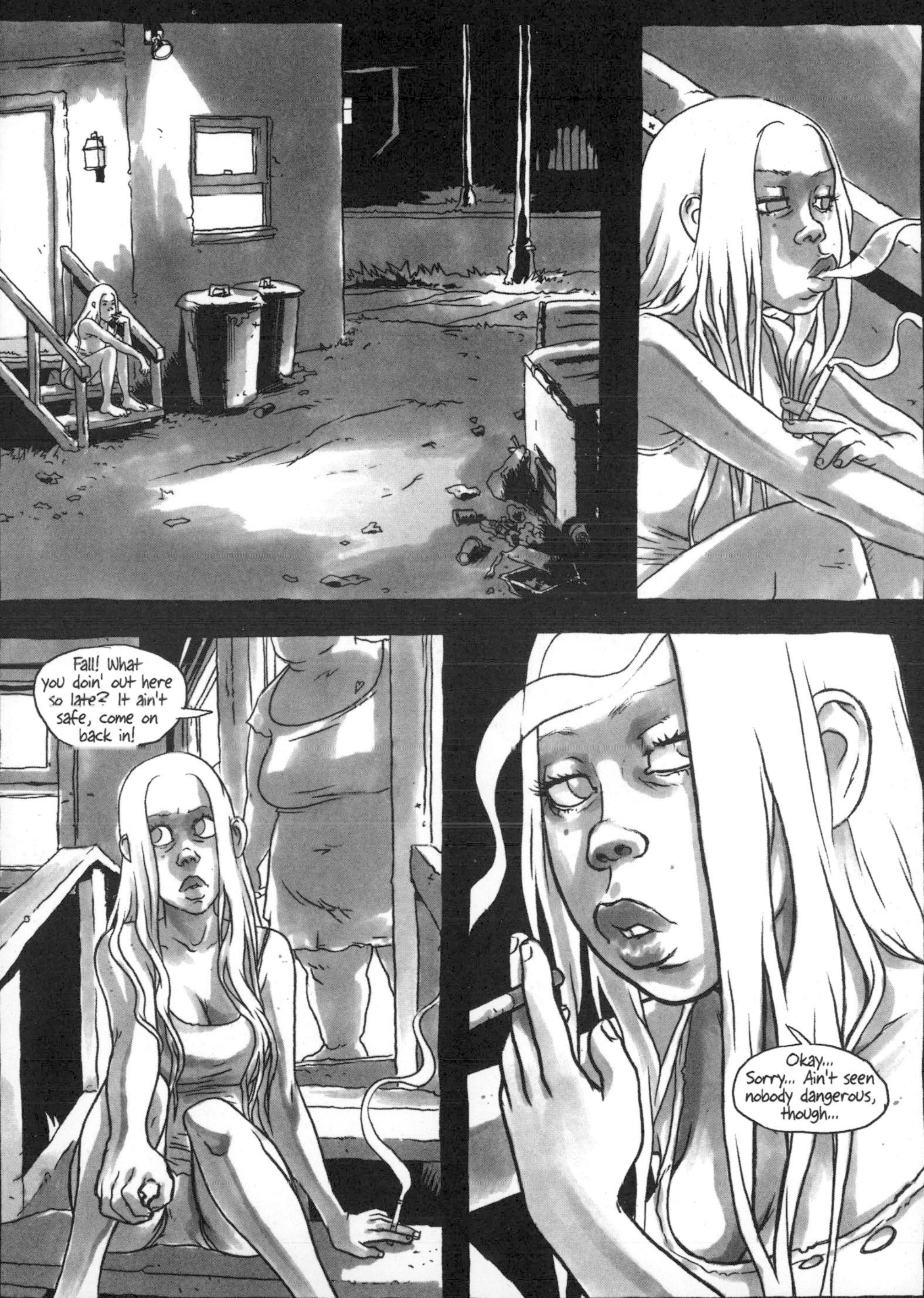
Fall! What you doin' out here so late? It ain't safe, come on back in!
Okay... Sorry... Ain't seen nobody dangerous, though...

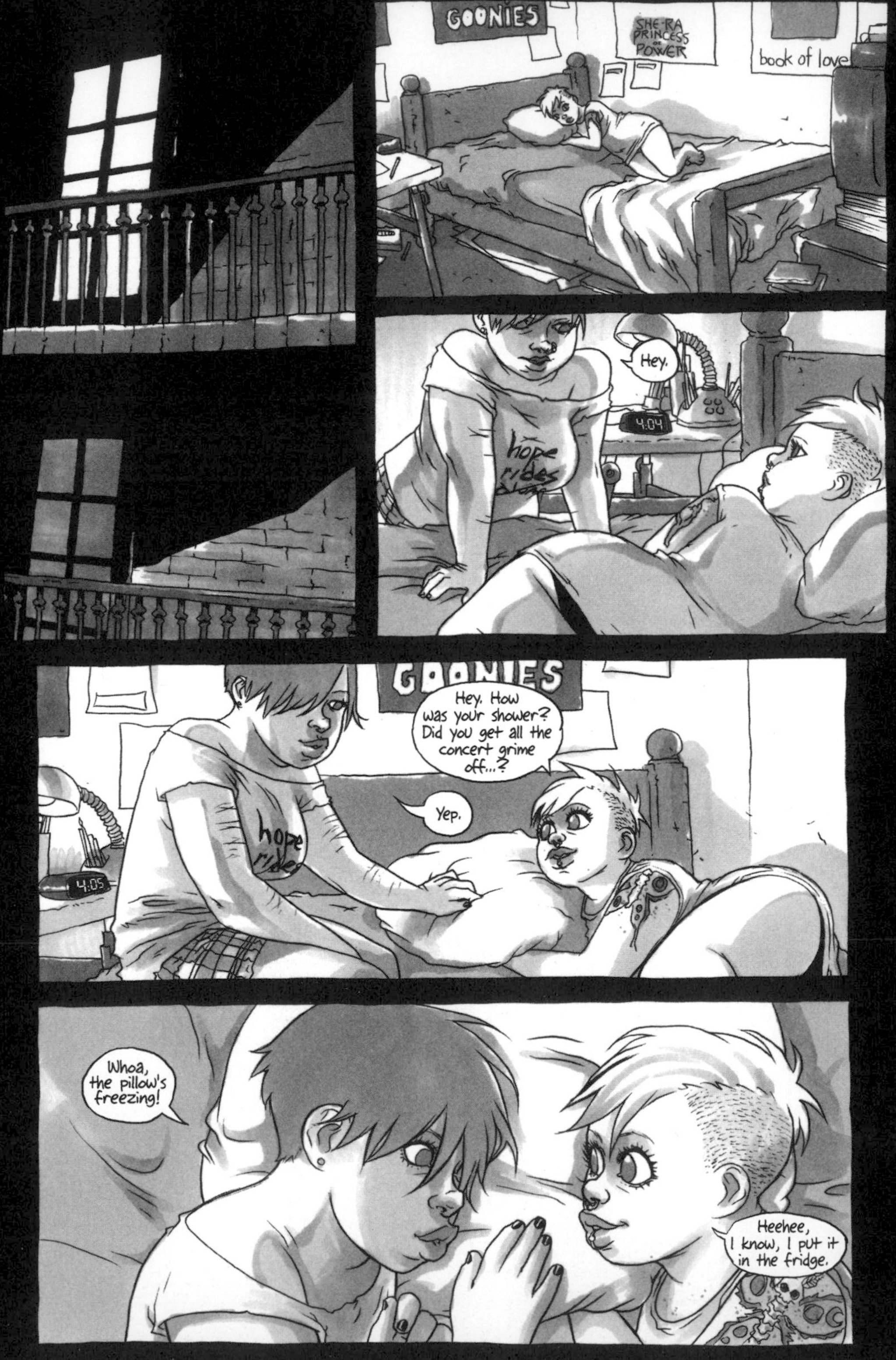
GOONIES
SHE-RA PRINCESS OF POWER
book of love
Hey.
4:04
hope rides
GOONIES
Hey. How was your shower? Did you get all the concert grime off...?
Yep.
hope rides
4:05
Whoa, the pillow's freezing!
Heehee, I know, I put it in the fridge.

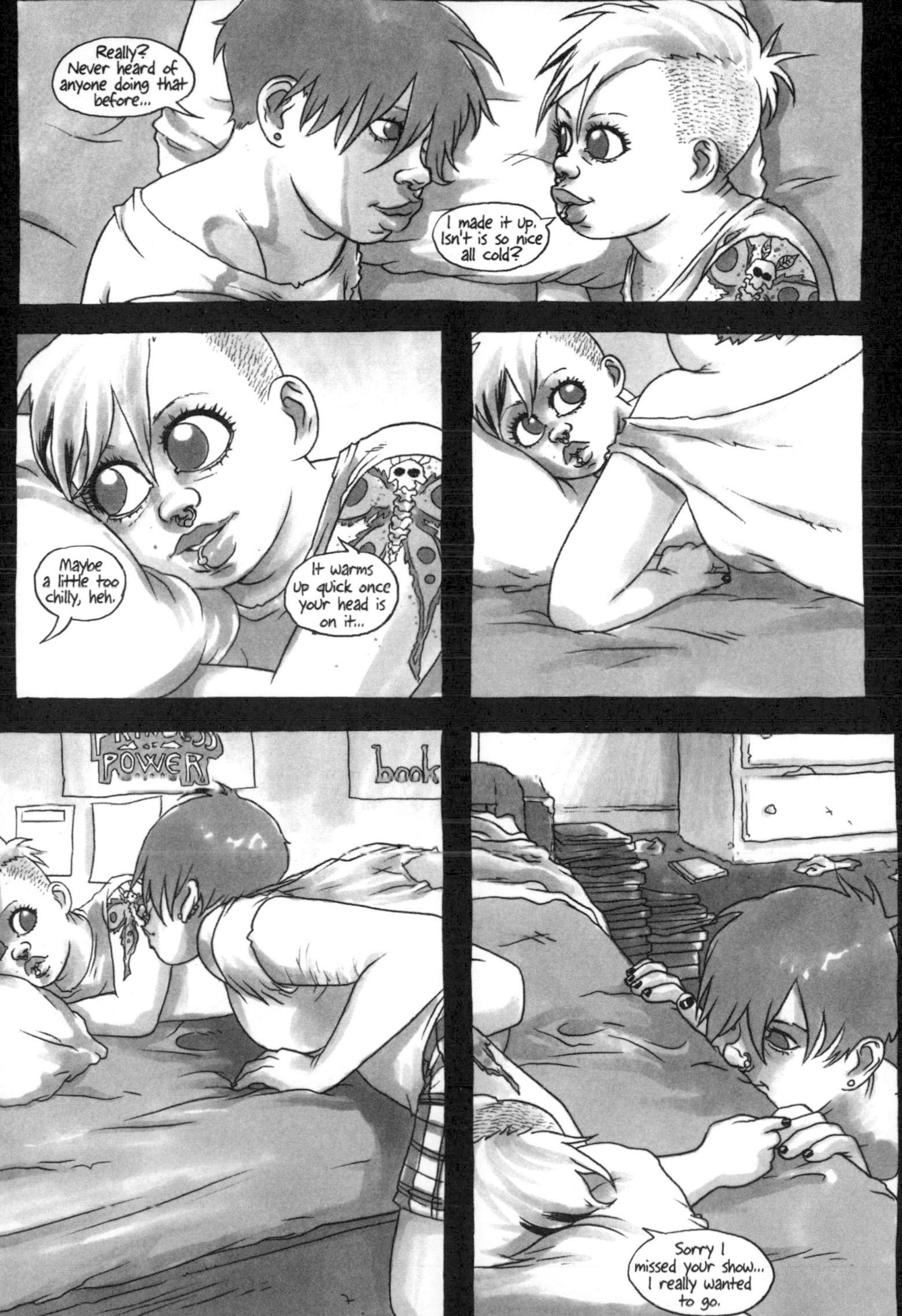
Really? Never heard of anyone doing that before...
I made it up. Isn't is so nice all cold?
Maybe a little too chilly, heh.
It warms up quick once your head is on it...
OF
POWER
book
Sorry I missed your show... I really wanted to go.

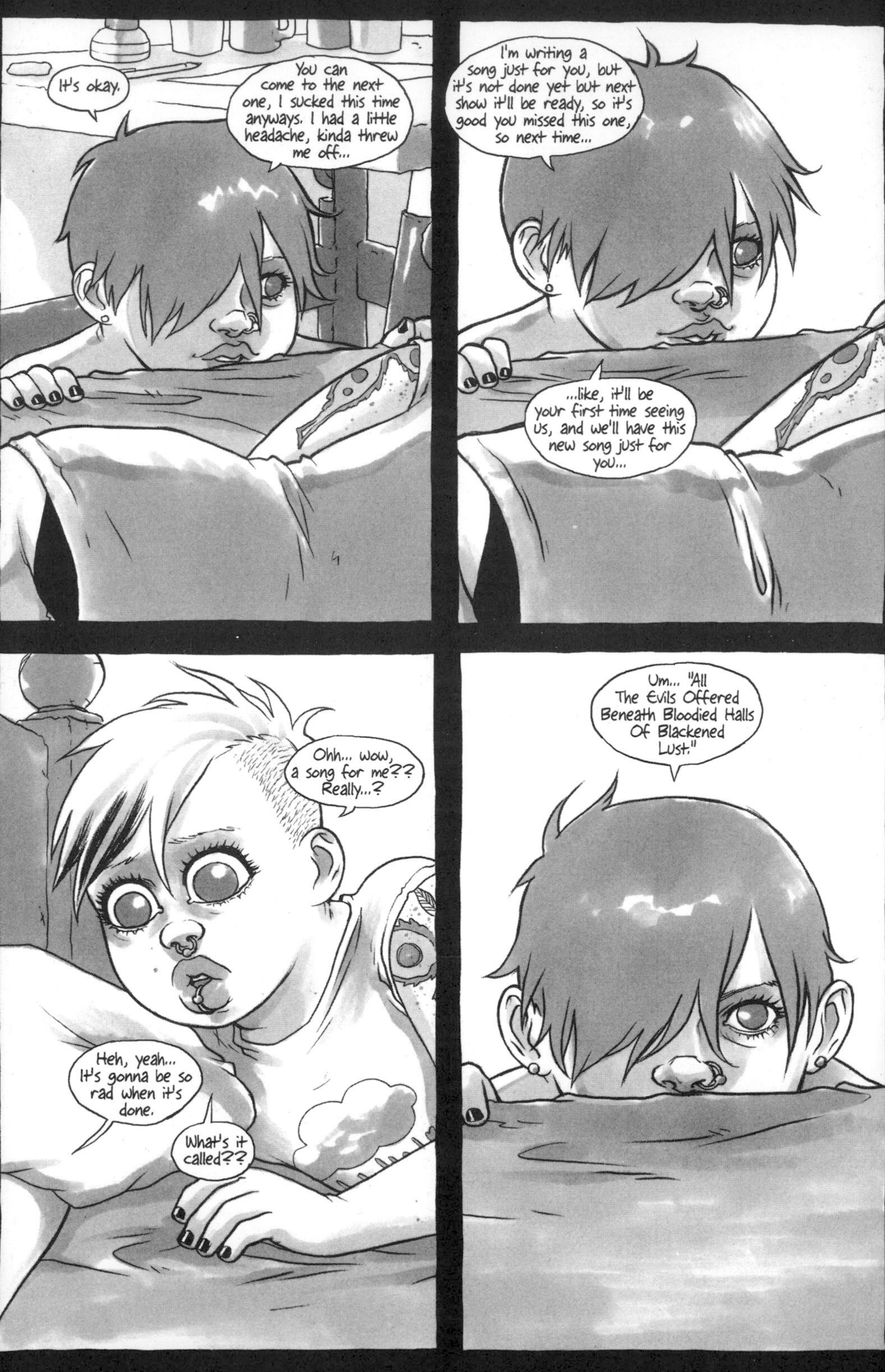
It's okay.
You can come to the next one, I sucked this time anyways. I had a little headache, kinda threw me off...
I'm writing a song just for you, but it's not done yet but next show it'll be ready, so it's good you missed this one, so next time...
...like, it'll be your first time seeing us, and we'll have this new song just for you...
Ohh... wow, a song for me?? Really...?
Heh, yeah... It's gonna be so rad when it's done.
What's it called??
Um... "All The Evils Offered Beneath Bloodied Halls Of Blackened Lust."

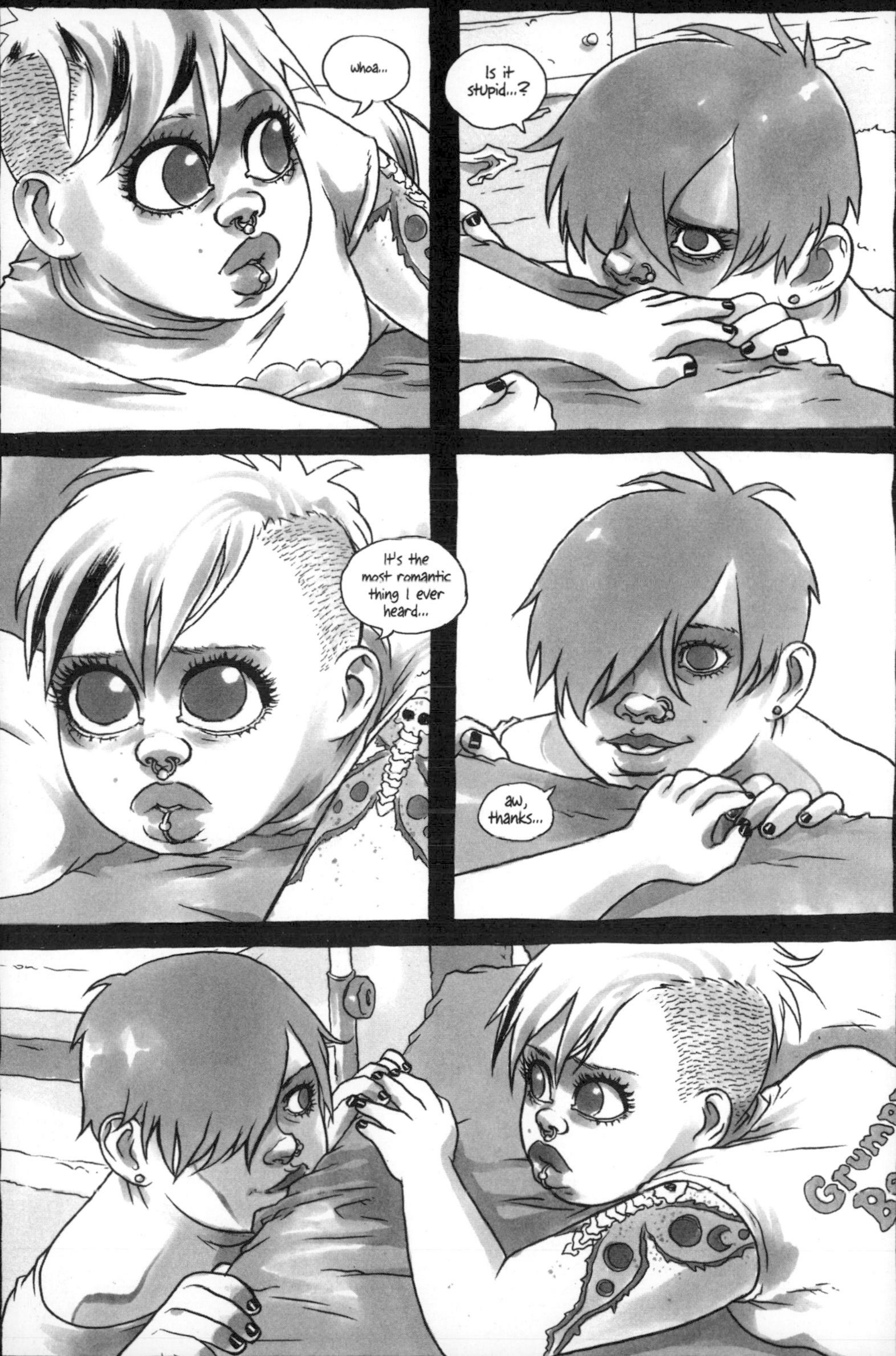
whoa...
Is it stupid...?
It's the most romantic thing I ever heard...
aw, thanks...
Grump
B

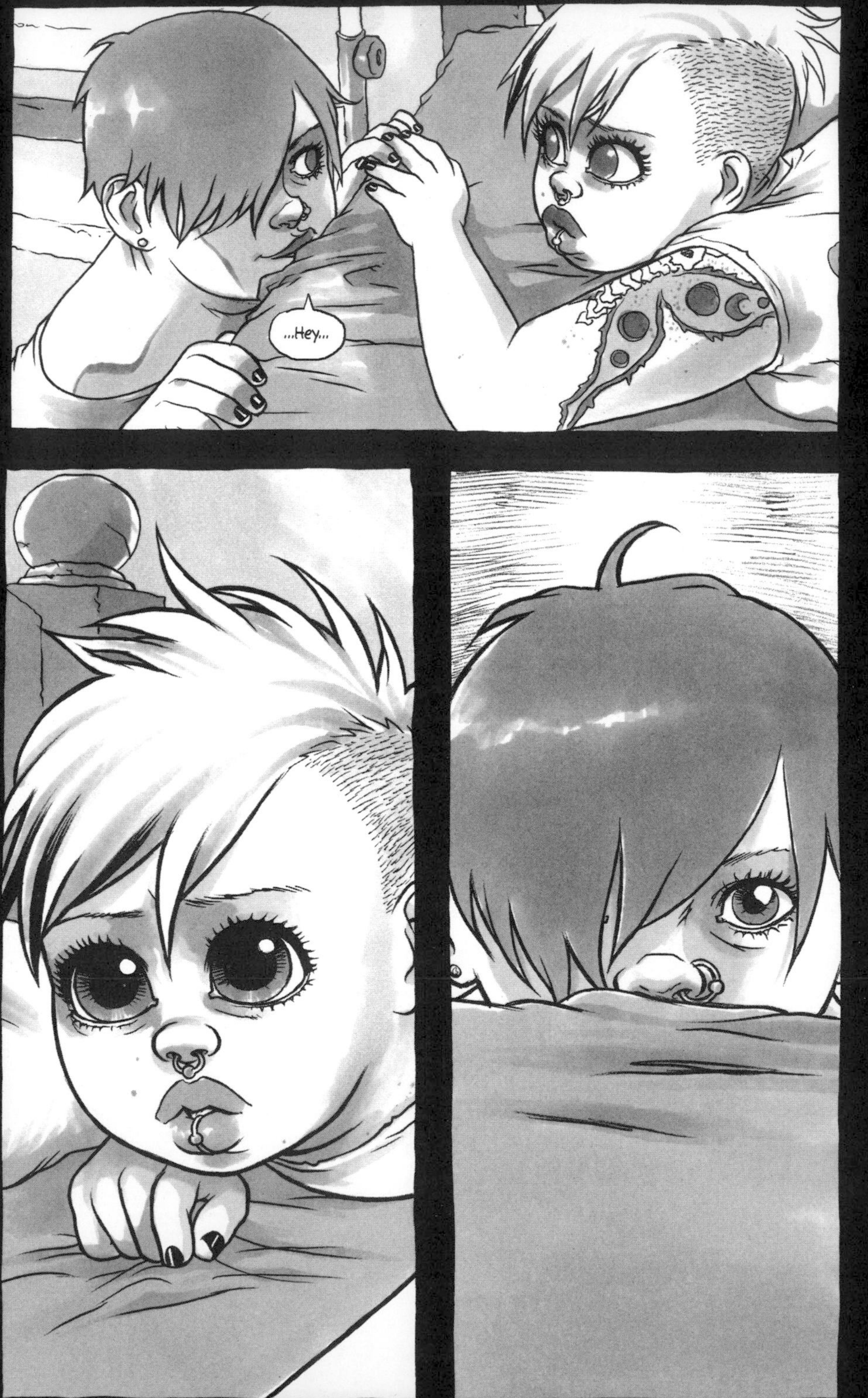
...Hey...

WET MOON
HIGH SCHOOL

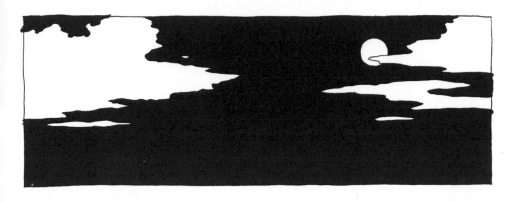

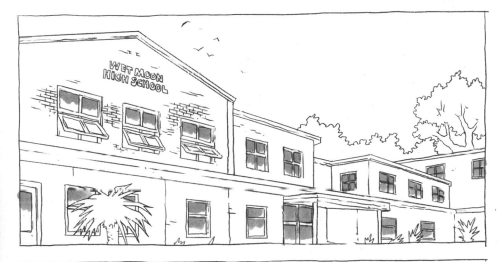

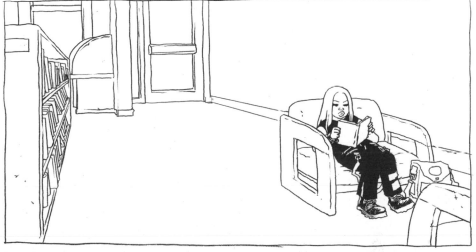

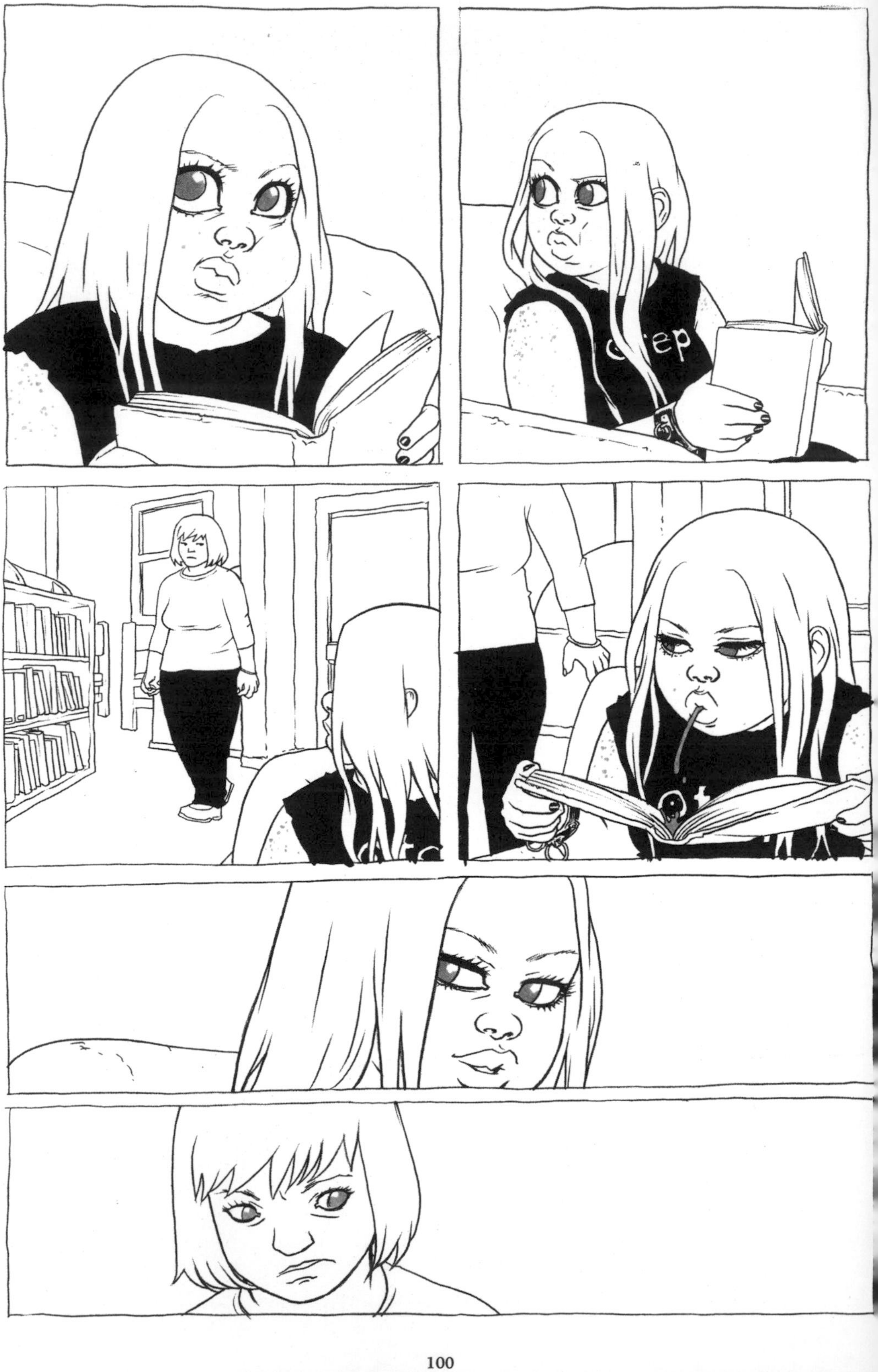

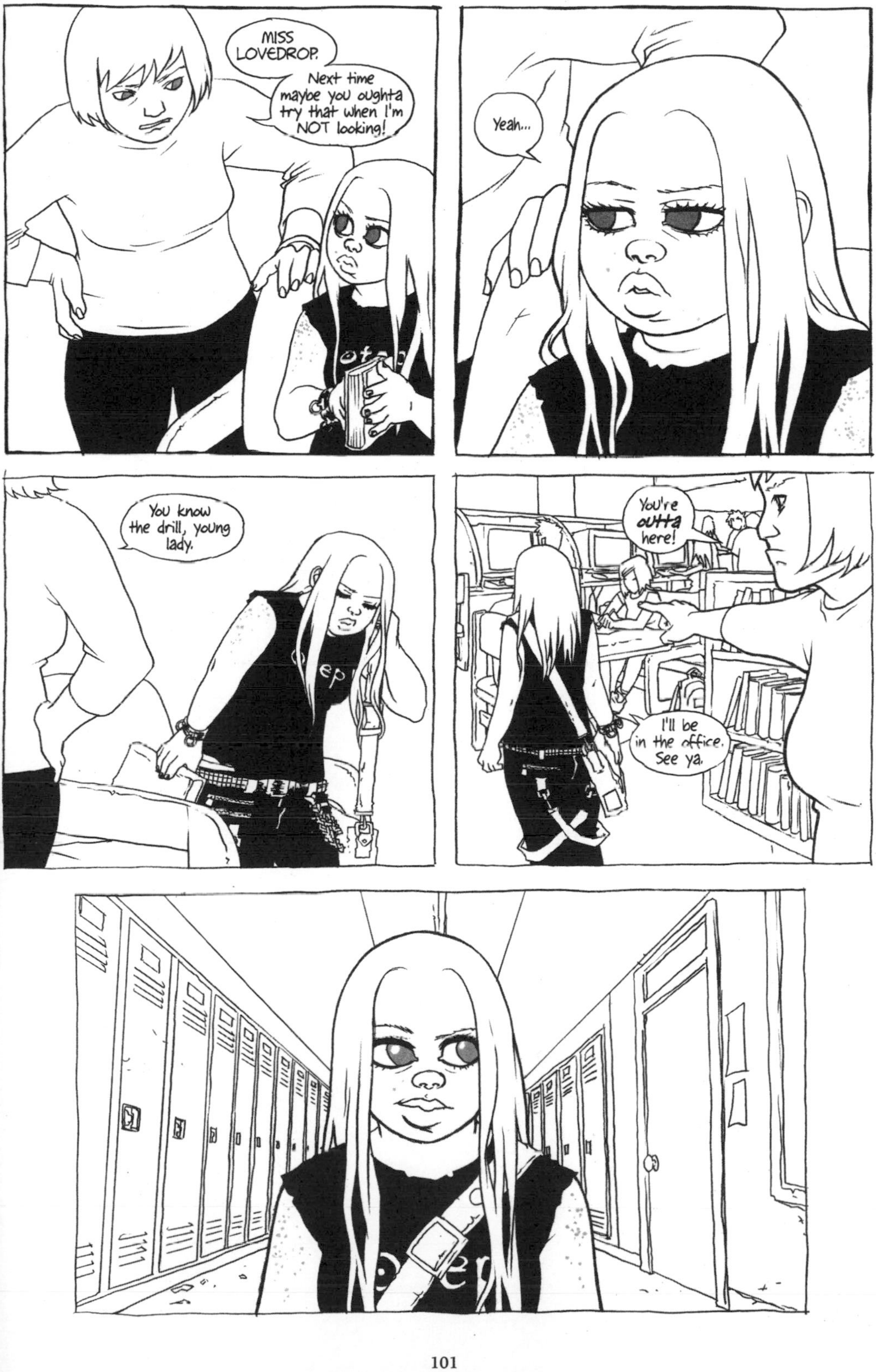
MISS LOVEDROP.
Next time maybe you oughta try that when I'm NOT looking!
Yeah...
You know the drill, young lady.
You're outta here!
I'll be in the office. See ya.

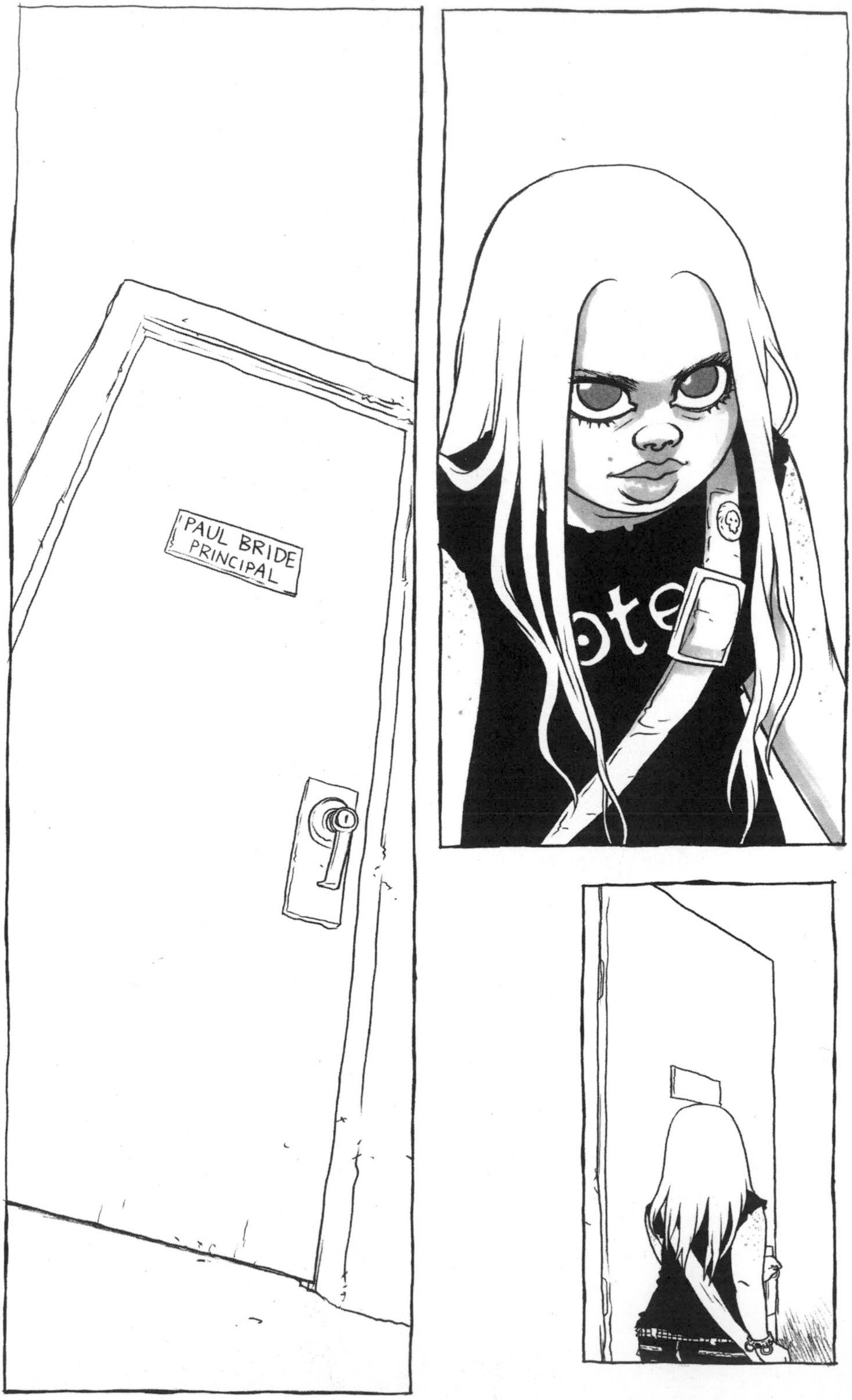
PAUL BRIDE
PRINCIPAL

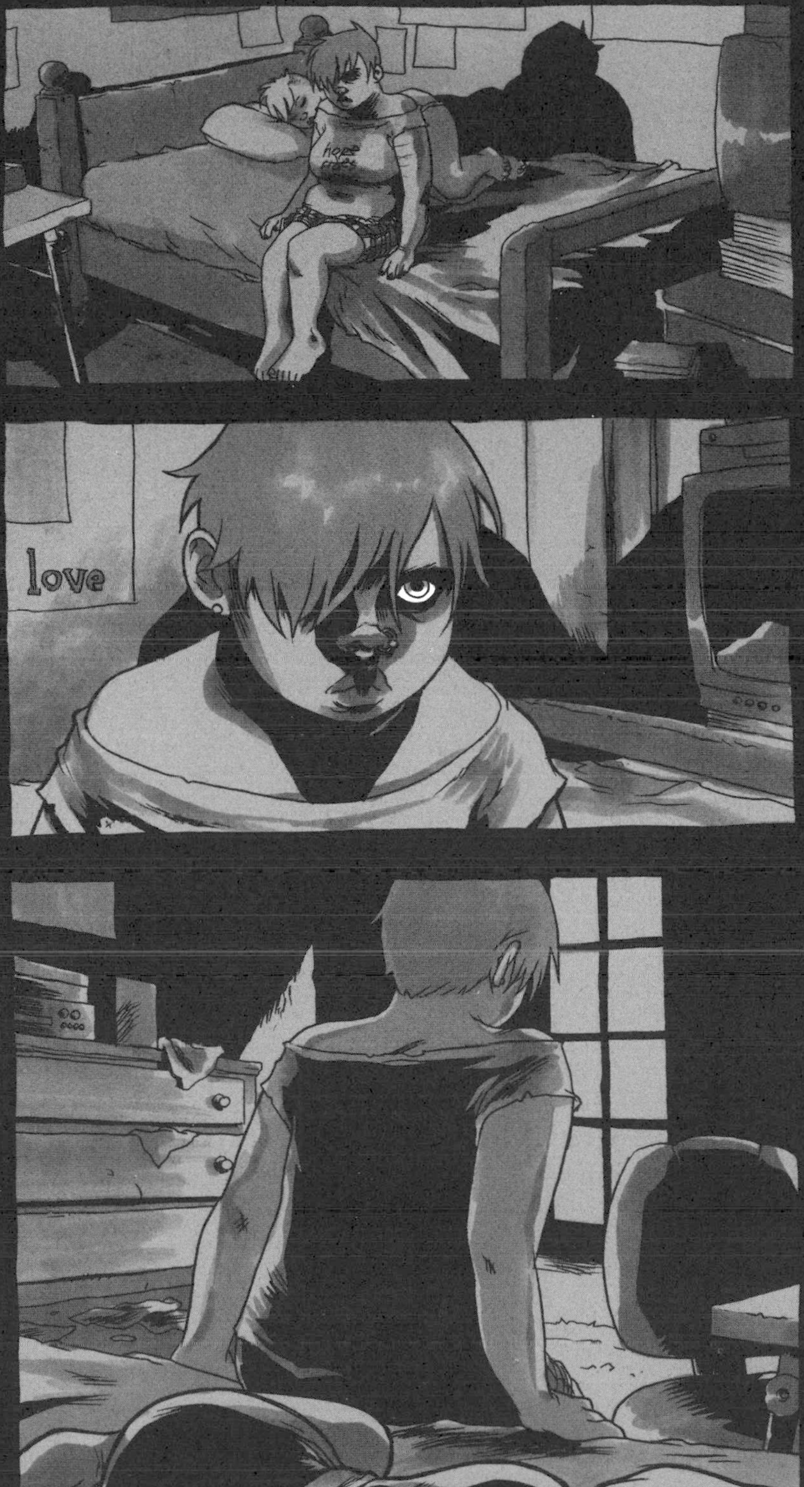
love

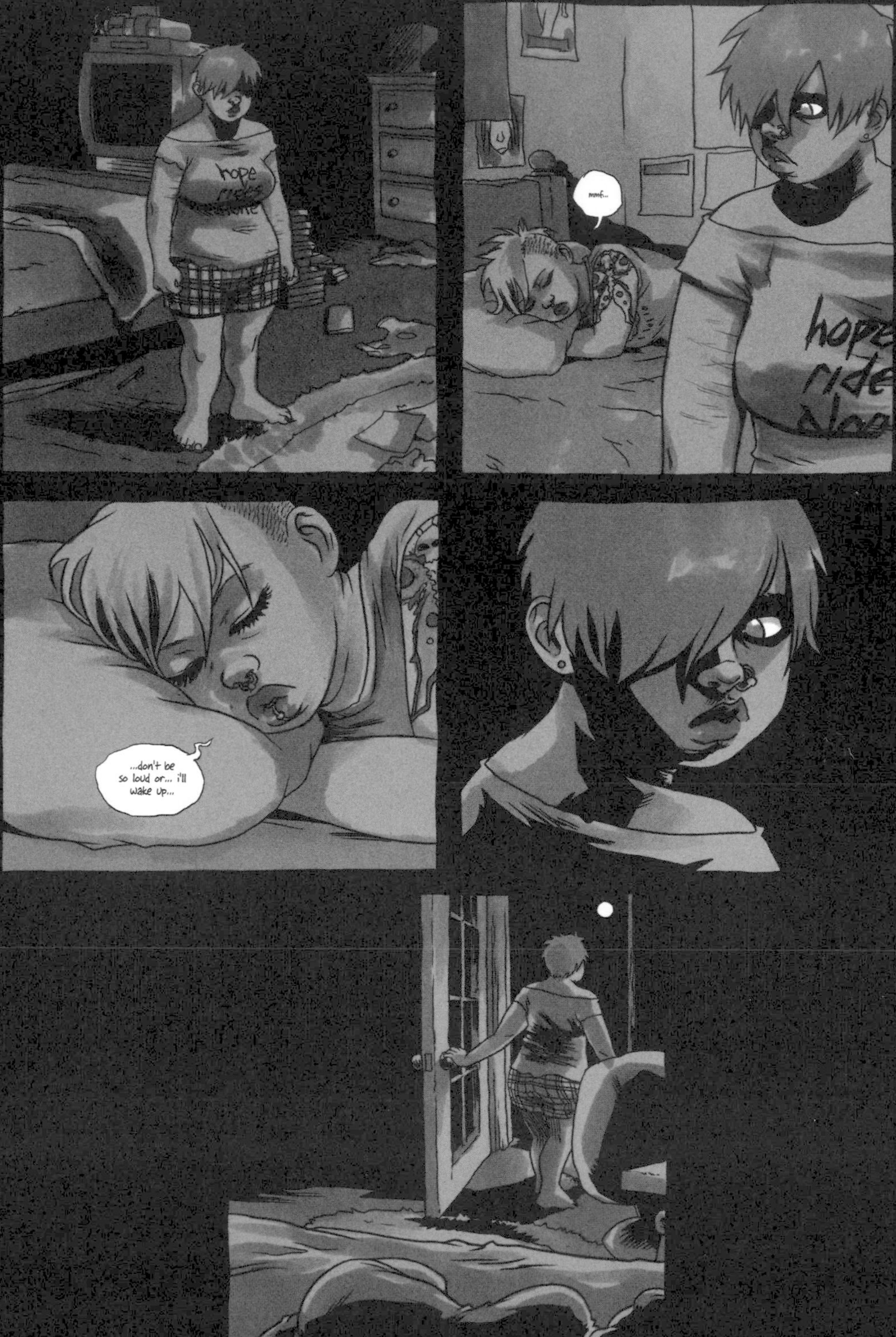
mmf...
...don't be so loud or... i'll wake up...

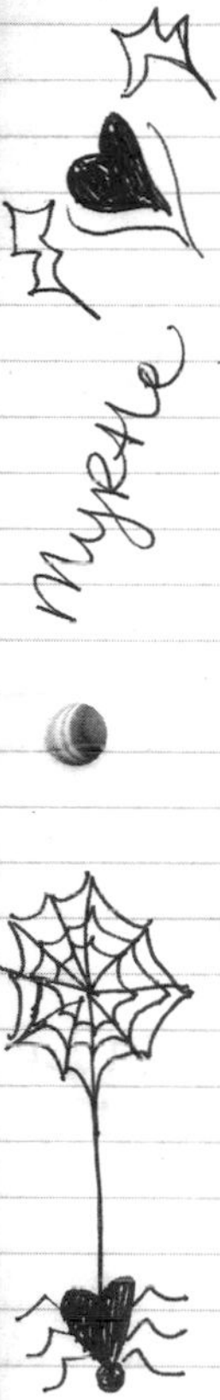
myrtle

October 17th

Myrtle called me her girl!! I guess that means girlfriend. I don't know. That's cool, though, I think I like that. She's doing a song for me!! Wow, so romantic! I can hardly even stand it when I think about it! It takes so much to write a song, it's not like writing a poem or drawing a picture, when you write a song you have to write a poem (the lyrics), and write every layer of music, then get your band to learn the parts, then get everyone together, then play the whole thing and make sure it records the way it's supposed to, or if you're playing a live show make sure not to screw it up because everyone's watching... It seems like such an undertaking! Nobody's ever done anything like this for me before! God what if Myrtle is totally in LOVE with me or something?? I don't know, this could be really serious. Trilby is weird. She says she wants me to get with Myrtle, which I guess I did, but I know that if I told her that she'd make fun of me or tease me or whatever it doesn't make any sense. Trilby's never really made sense, though, ever since I met her. Maybe I don't make sense, either.

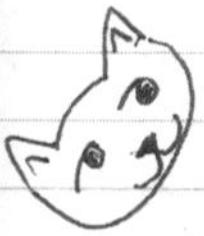

I still can't believe I punched that guy. I feel so bad about it, I wish I could contact him somehow and apologize when he's not unconscious. I really need to get my own computer so I don't have to go to the lab every time. I'm almost <u>positive</u> that Malady must be writing the "Cleo eats it" flyers!! Well, maybe, but at the show I took a peek in her bag in the bathroom and I saw a flyer in there! I know she was collecting them for me, but... it seemed weird that she didn't show me <u>this</u> one... why would she keep this one a secret? Maybe she wrote it and planned to put it up somewhere [redacted] in secret at the show venue before we left. Oh god, how could it be her? I thought we were friends! I don't know, I'll have to do more investigating before I decide... I guess

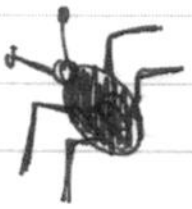

besides the punching thing the show was cool. Bella Morte do such a great show, and they're all so cute... I bet they all have girlfriends, though. Or they could all be gay, maybe with each other. That would be hot. Now I don't think I'll ever get to see them play again, I just know they'll remember me: the girl who punched a guy and ruined the show. And I think they were friends with that guy, too. Andy said something to him during the show but I can't remember what his name was. But that's so even worse, because I punched their friend. Maybe I could do my hair different and wear contacts or dark sunglasses like a mask and wear a big coat, maybe then they wouldn't recognize me. I could be Daray Wilcox, from Kentucky.

Speaking of Daray, I haven't written any on my novel in almost two weeks. School is making me super busy, it feels like I hardly have time for anything else. I have a big

paper to write for my satirical literature class that I haven't even started yet and it's due like next week!

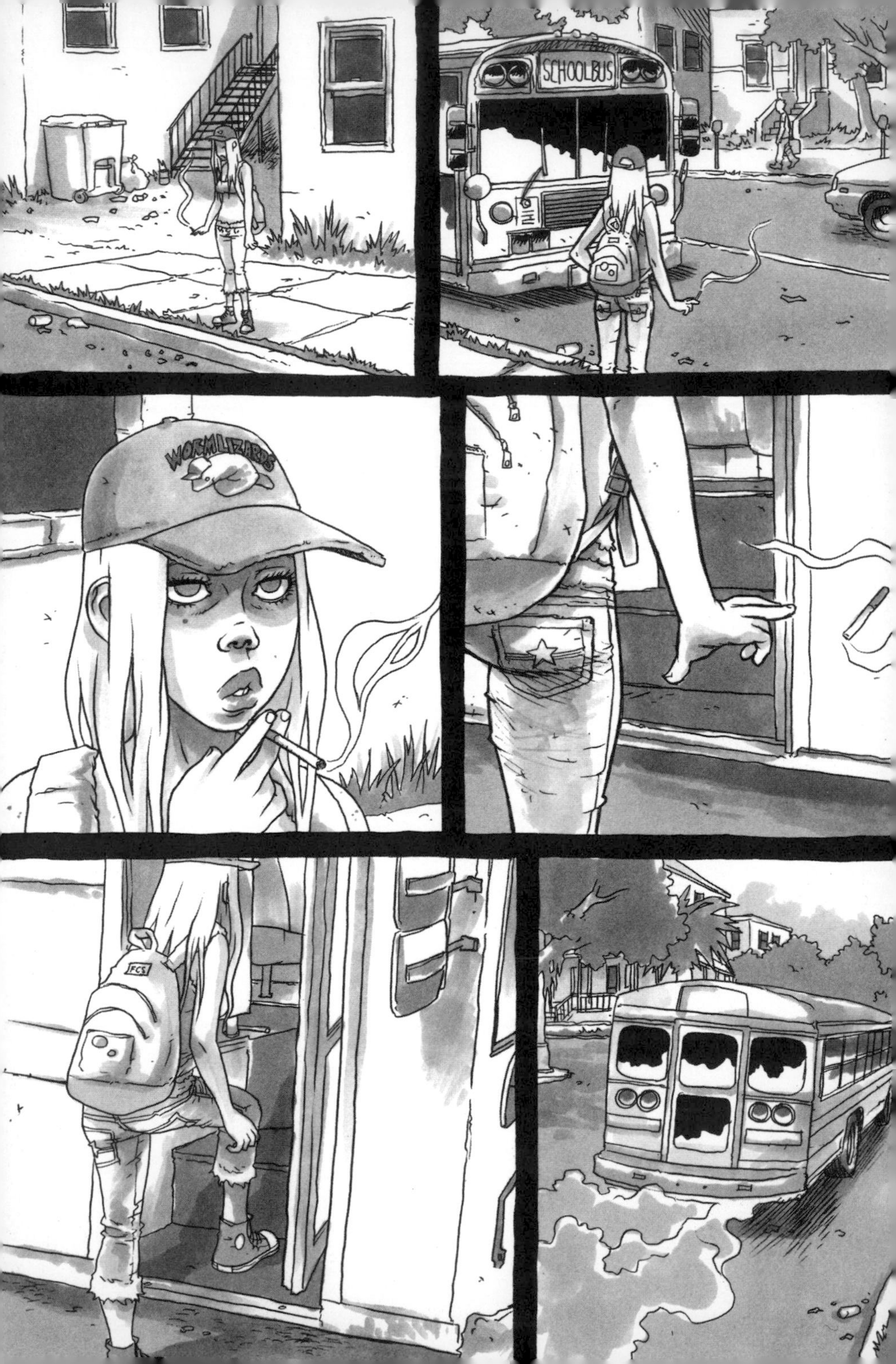
SCHOOLBUS
WORMLIZARDS
FCS

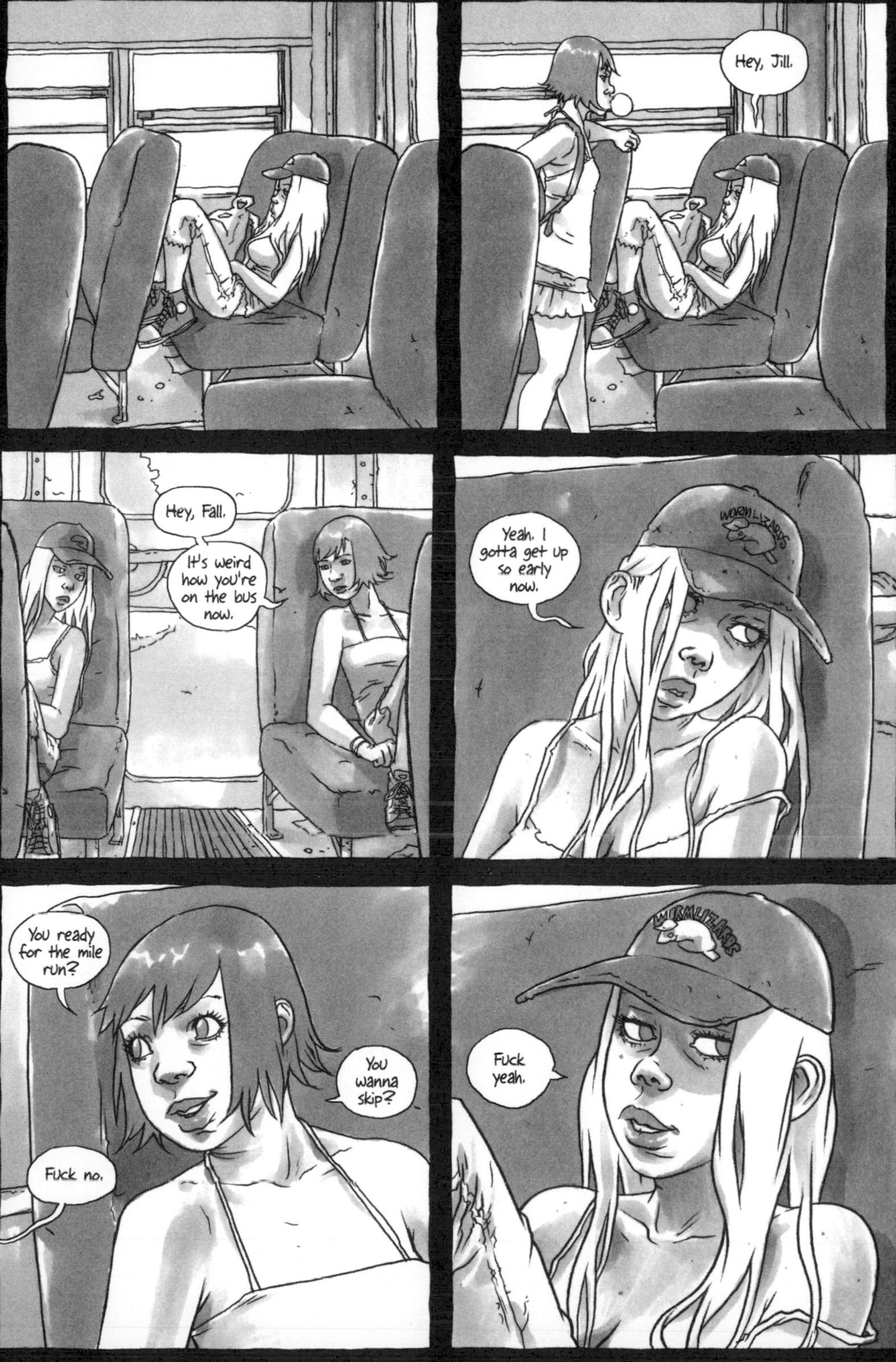
Hey, Jill.
Hey, Fall.
It's weird how you're on the bus now.
Yeah. I gotta get up so early now.
WORMLIZARDS
You ready for the mile run?
You wanna skip?
Fuck no.
WORMLIZARDS
Fuck yeah.

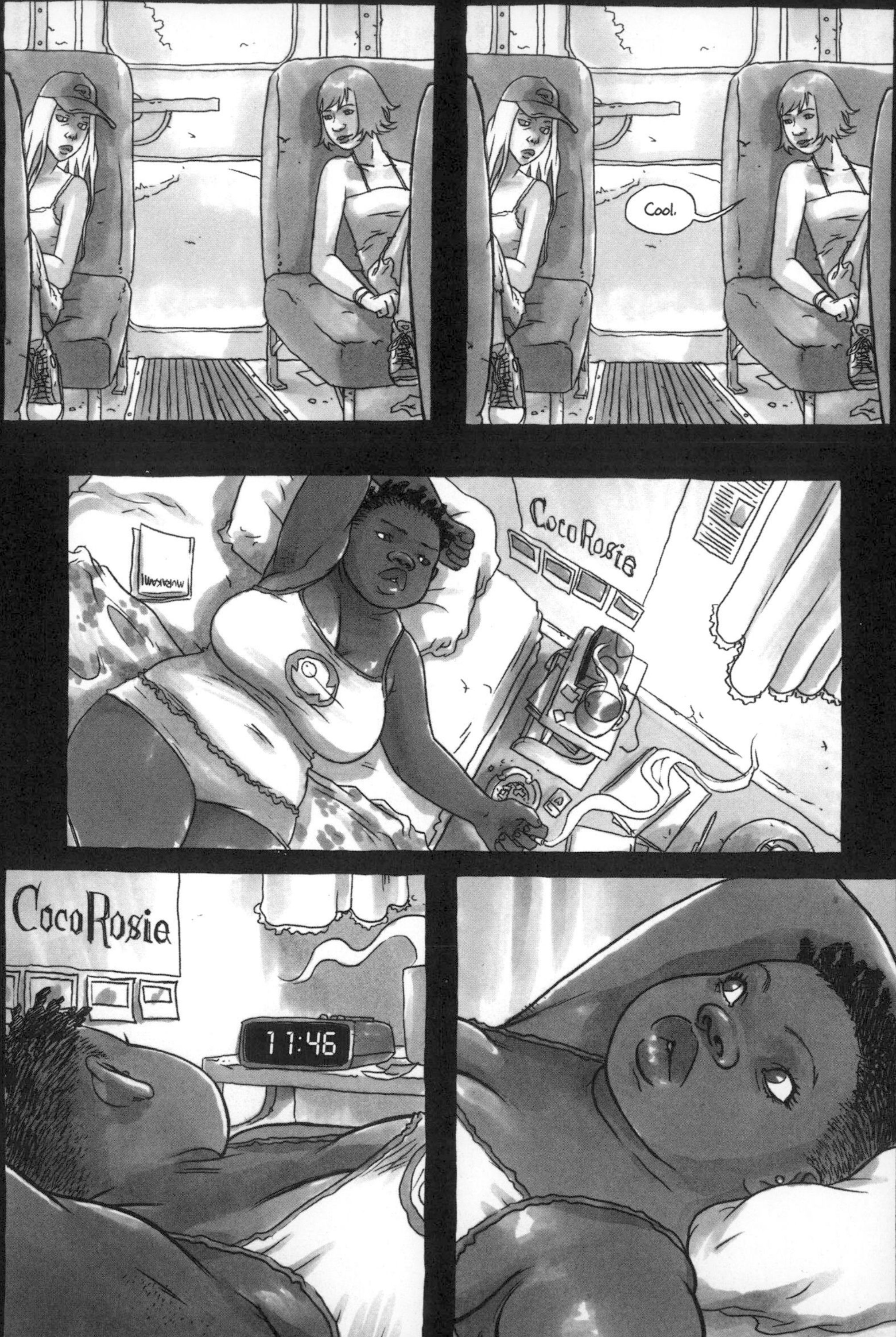
Cool.
CocoRosie
MURAKAMI
CocoRosie
11:46

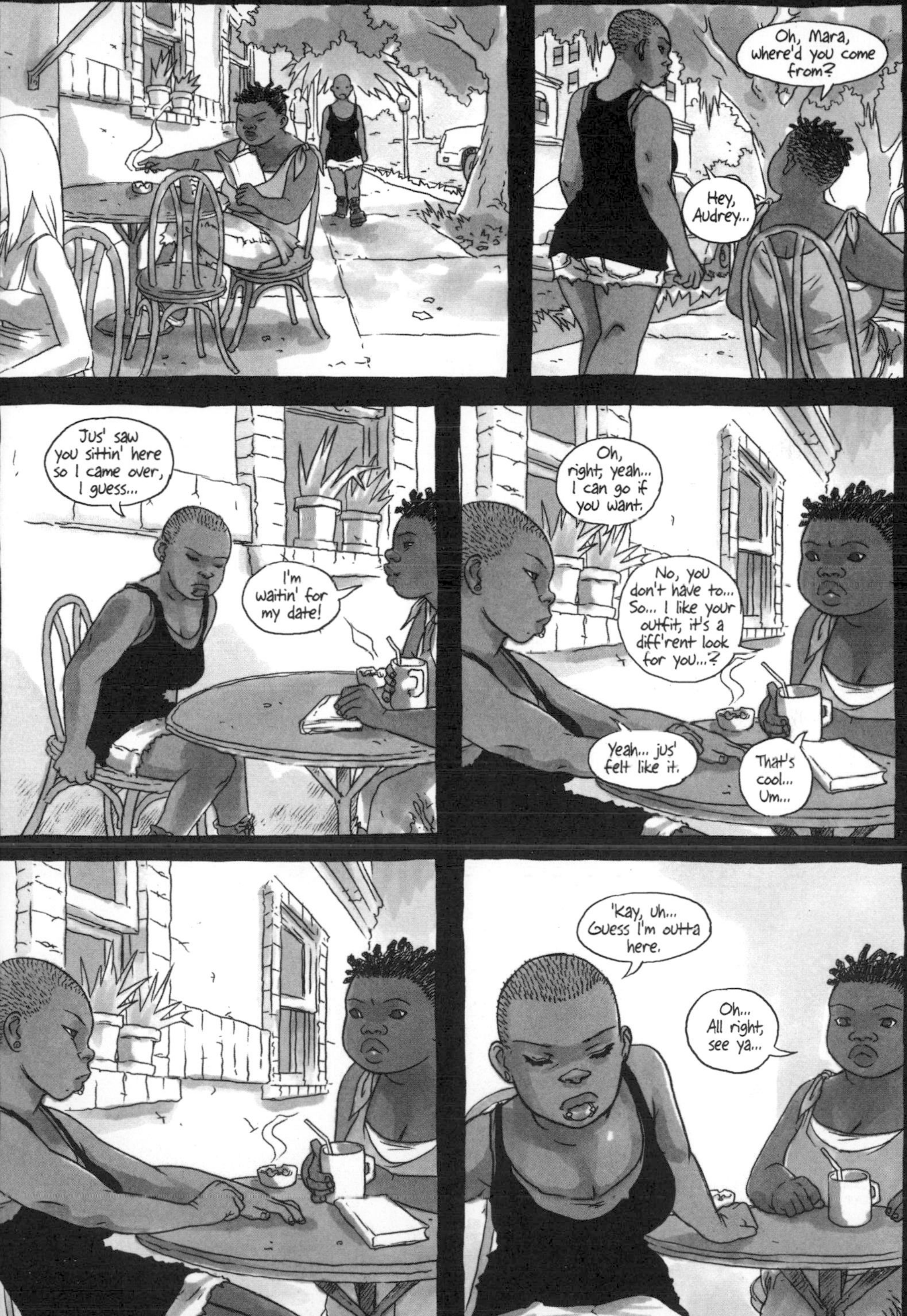
Oh, Mara, where'd you come from?
Hey, Audrey...
Jus' saw you sittin' here so I came over, I guess...
I'm waitin' for my date!
Oh, right, yeah... I can go if you want.
No, you don't have to... So... I like your outfit, it's a diff'rent look for you...?
Yeah... jus' felt like it.
That's cool... Um...
'Kay, uh... Guess I'm outta here.
Oh... All right, see ya...

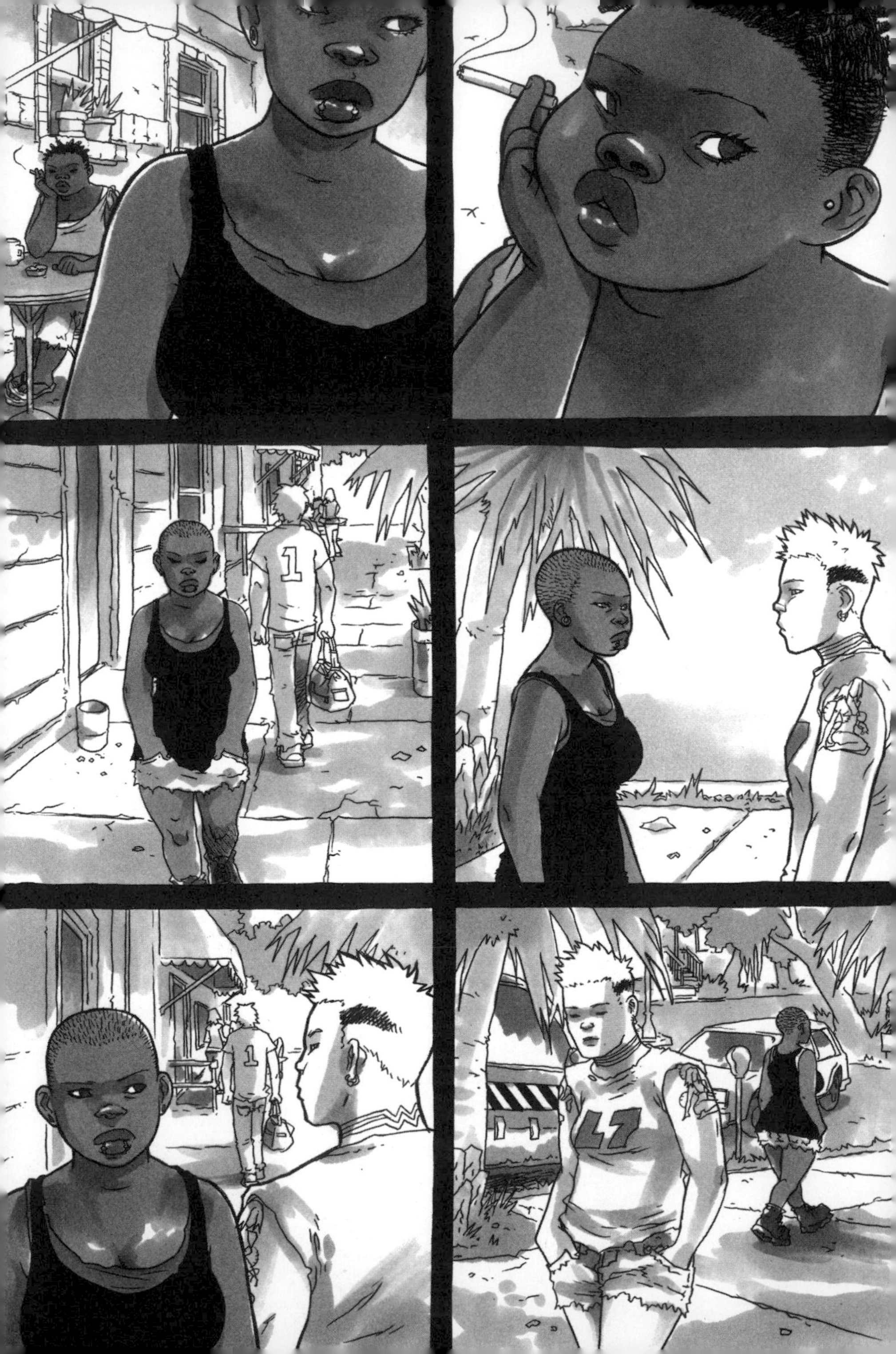

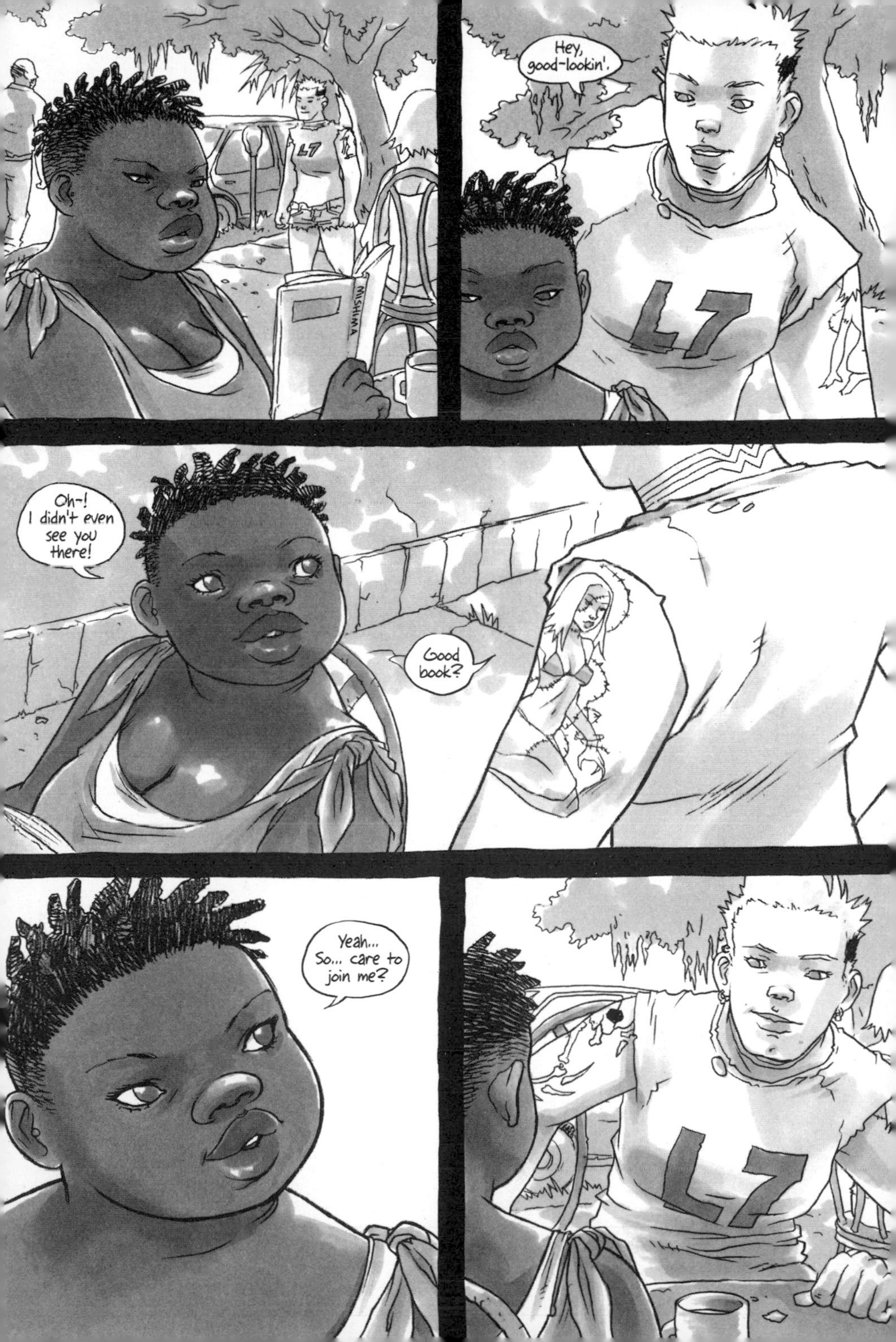
MISHIMA
L7
Hey, good-lookin'.
L7
Oh-! I didn't even see you there!
Good book?
Yeah... So... care to join me?
L7

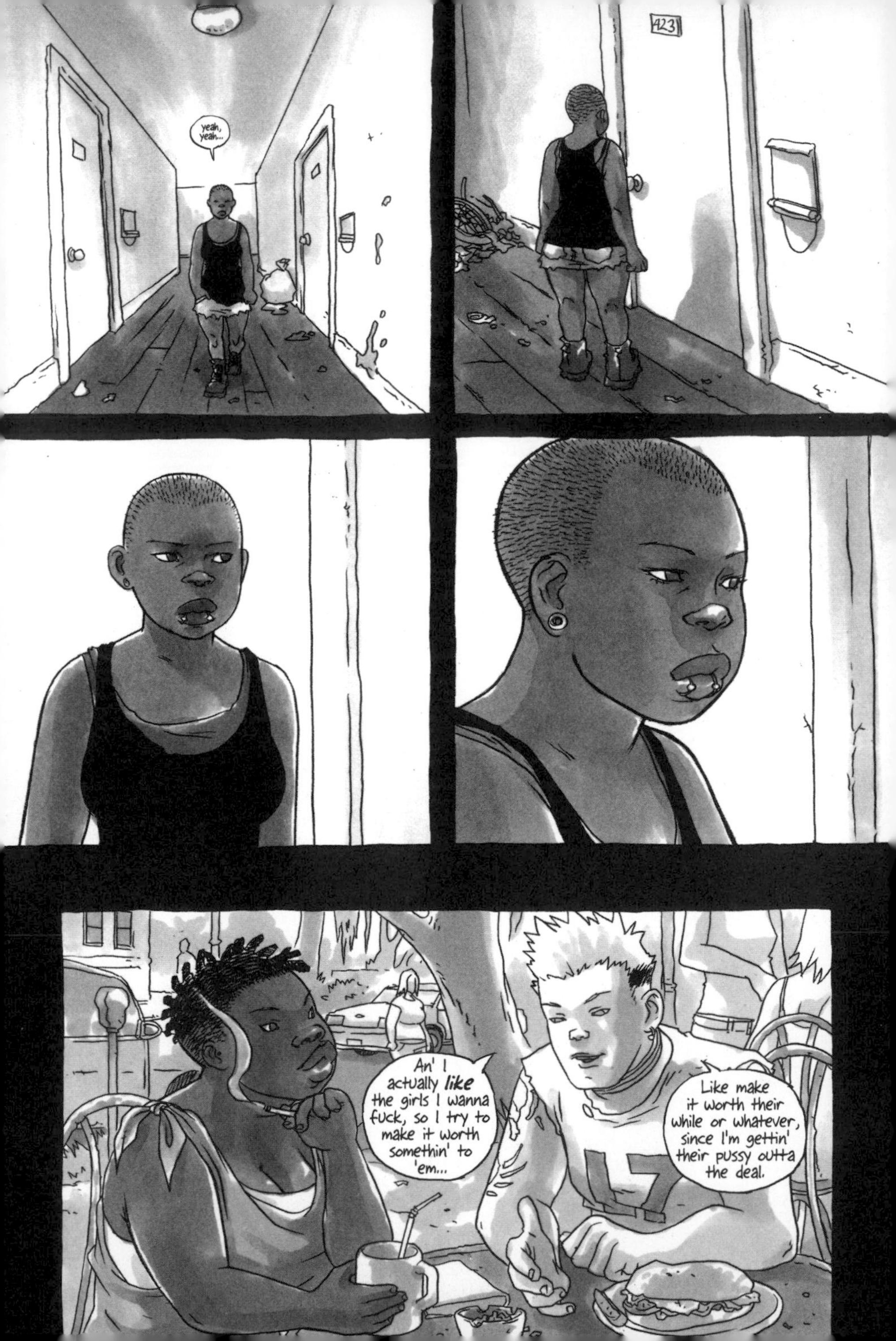
yeah, yeah...
423
An' I actually like the girls I wanna fuck, so I try to make it worth somethin' to 'em...
Like make it worth their while or whatever, since I'm gettin' their pussy outta the deal.

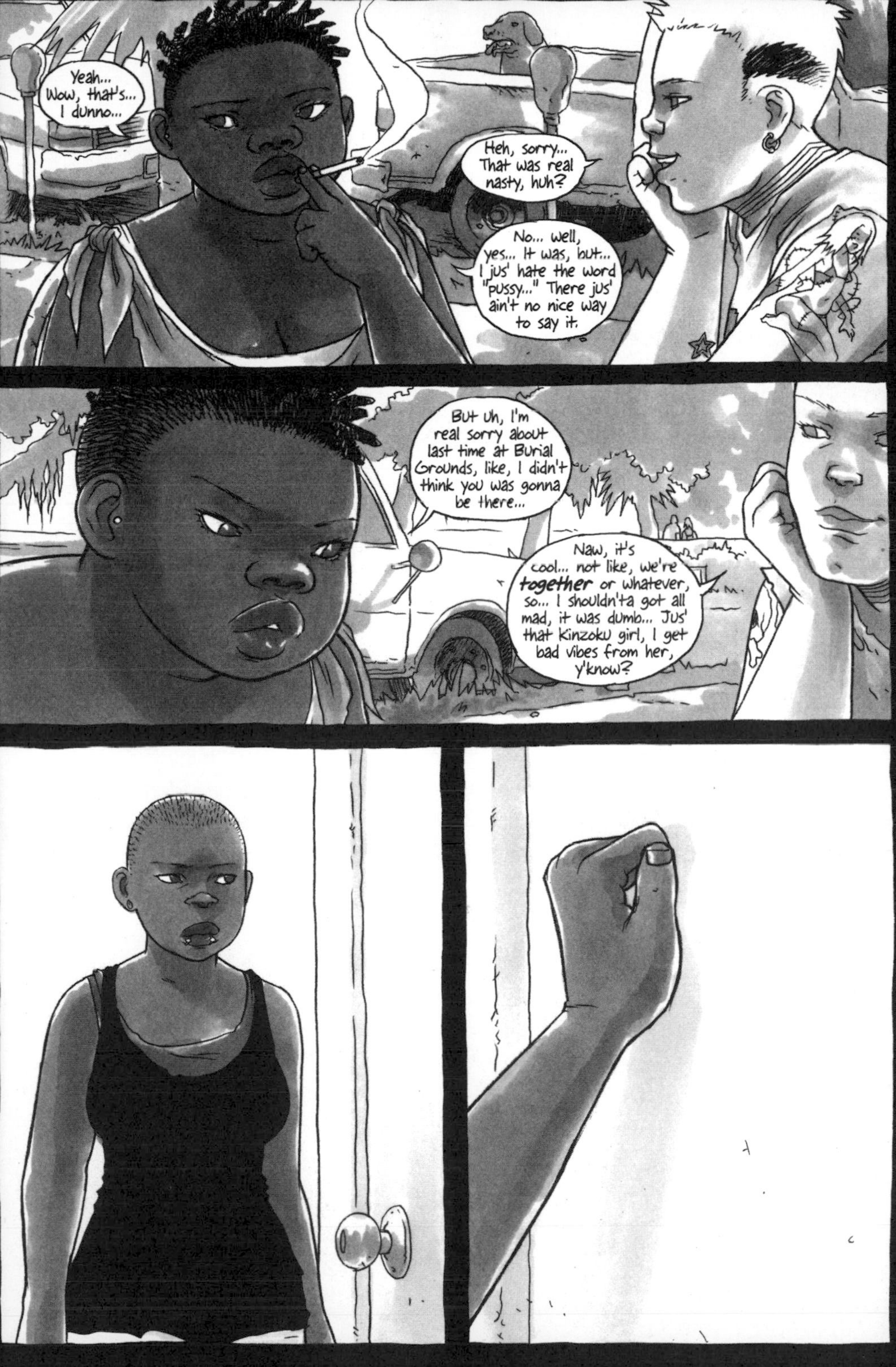
Yeah... Wow, that's... I dunno...
Heh, sorry... That was real nasty, huh?
No... well, yes... It was, but... I jus' hate the word "pussy..." There jus' ain't no nice way to say it.
But uh, I'm real sorry about last time at Burial Grounds, like, I didn't think you was gonna be there...
Naw, it's cool... not like, we're **together** or whatever, so... I shouldn'ta got all mad, it was dumb... Jus' that Kinzoku girl, I get bad vibes from her, y'know?

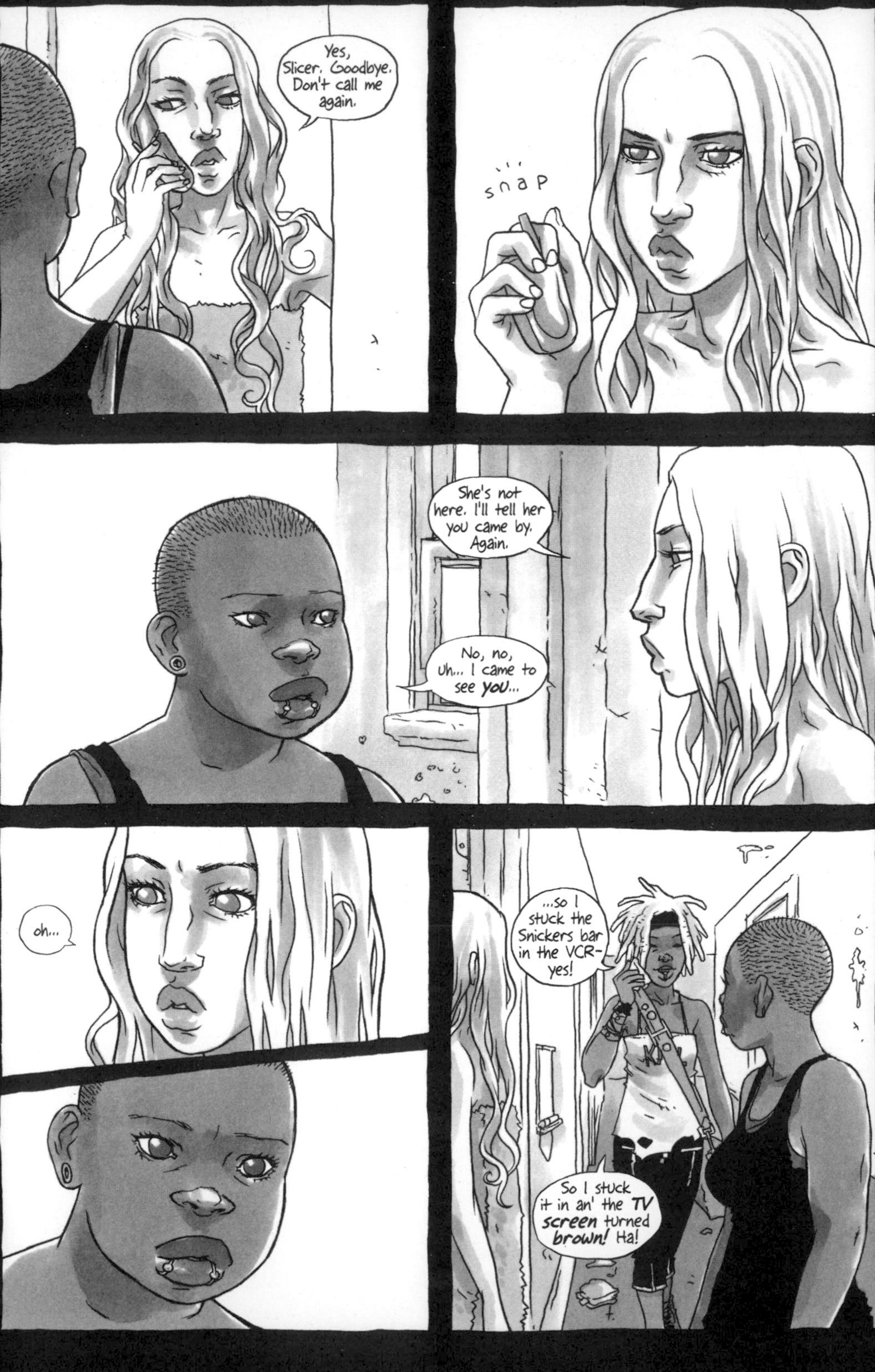
Yes, Slicer. Goodbye. Don't call me again.
snap
She's not here. I'll tell her you came by. Again.
No, no, uh... I came to see ***you***...
oh...
...so I stuck the Snickers bar in the VCR- yes!
So I stuck it in an' the ***TV screen*** turned ***brown!*** Ha!

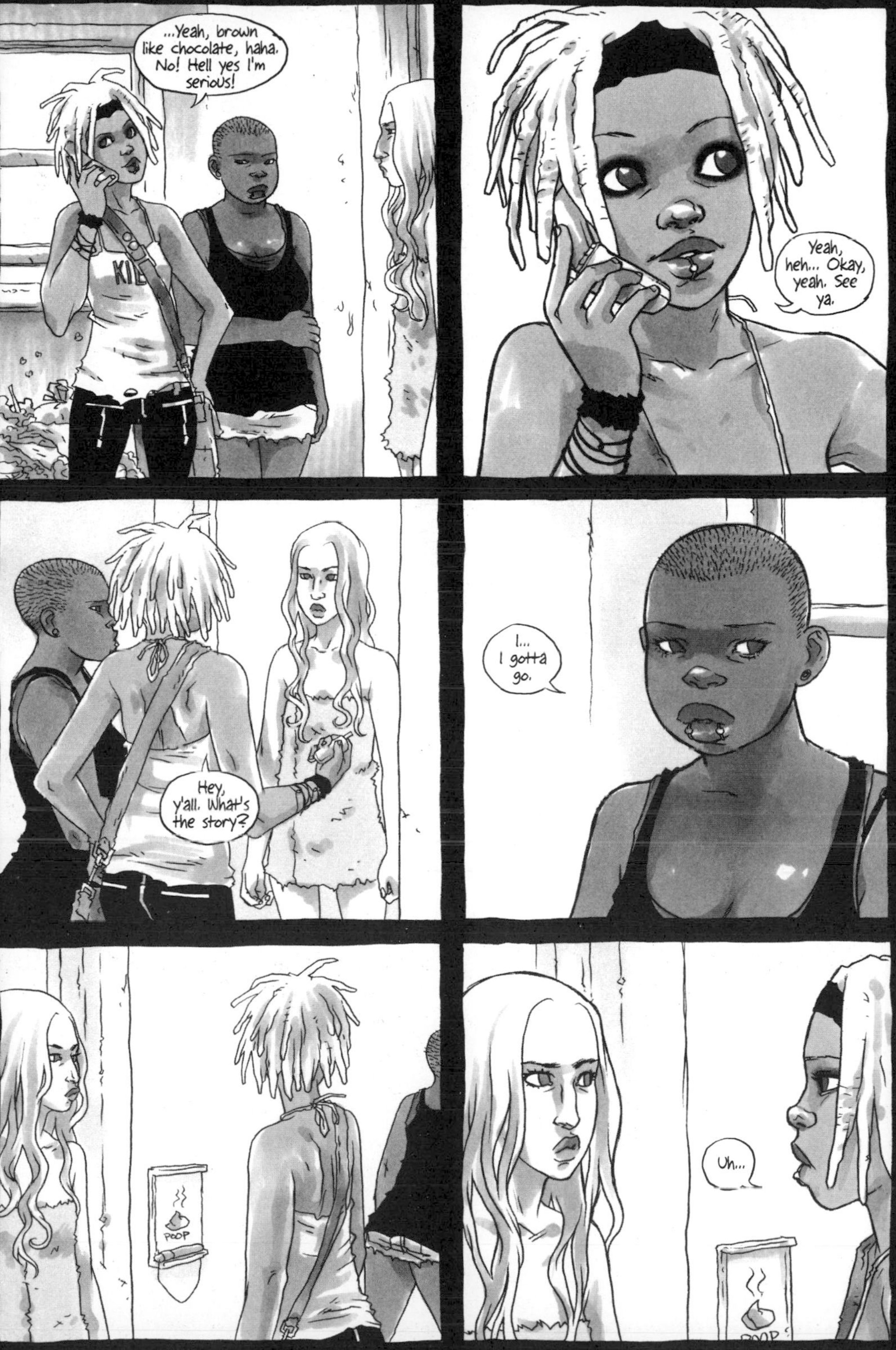
...Yeah, brown like chocolate, haha. No! Hell yes I'm serious!
KIL
Yeah, heh... Okay, yeah. See ya.
Hey, y'all. What's the story?
I... I gotta go.
POOP
Uh...
POOP

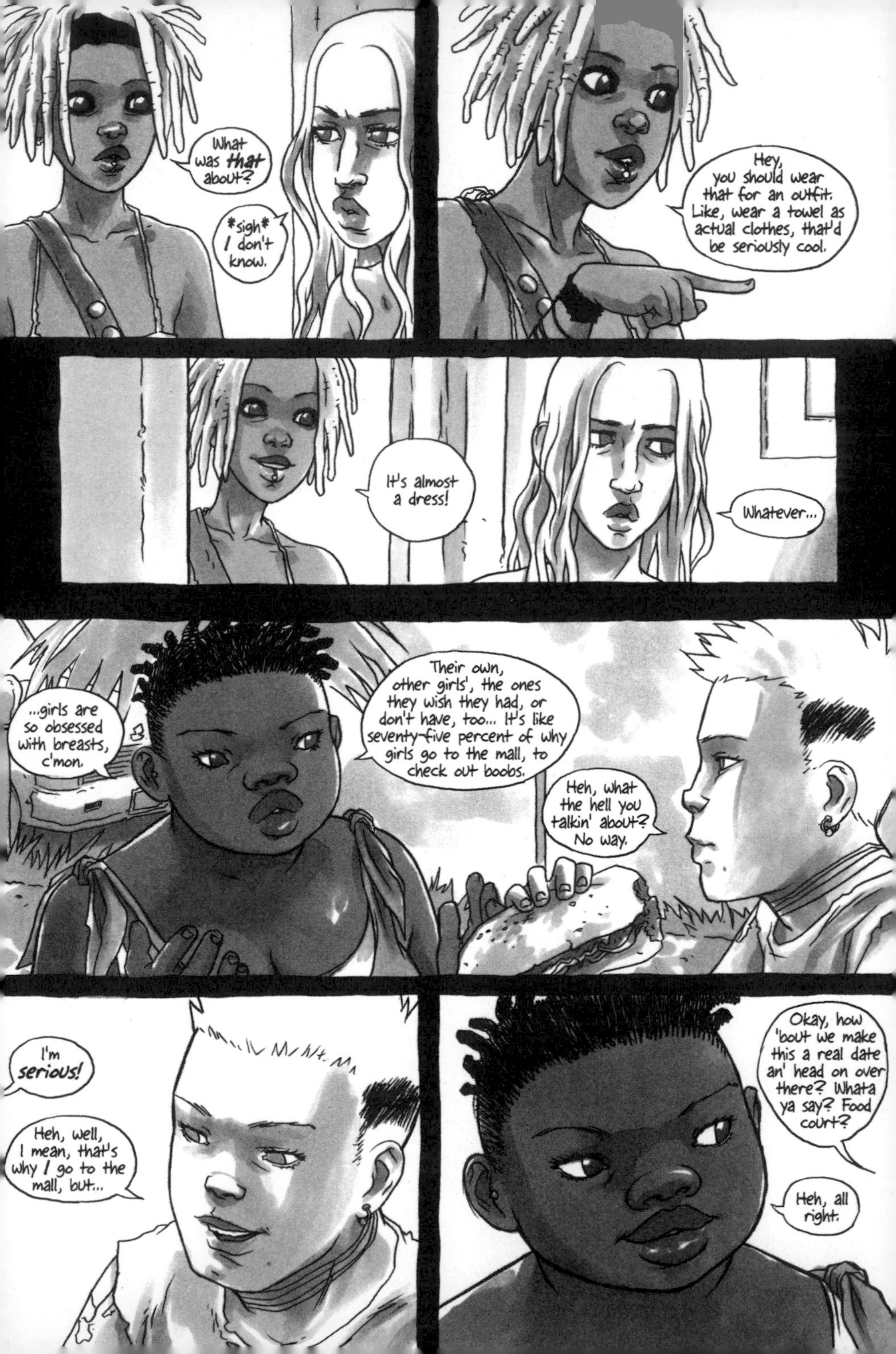
What was that about?
sigh I don't know.
Hey, you should wear that for an outfit. Like, wear a towel as actual clothes, that'd be seriously cool.
It's almost a dress!
Whatever...
...girls are so obsessed with breasts, c'mon.
Their own, other girls', the ones they wish they had, or don't have, too... It's like seventy-five percent of why girls go to the mall, to check out boobs.
Heh, what the hell you talkin' about? No way.
I'm serious!
Heh, well, I mean, that's why I go to the mall, but...
Okay, how 'bout we make this a real date an' head on over there? Whata ya say? Food court?
Heh, all right.

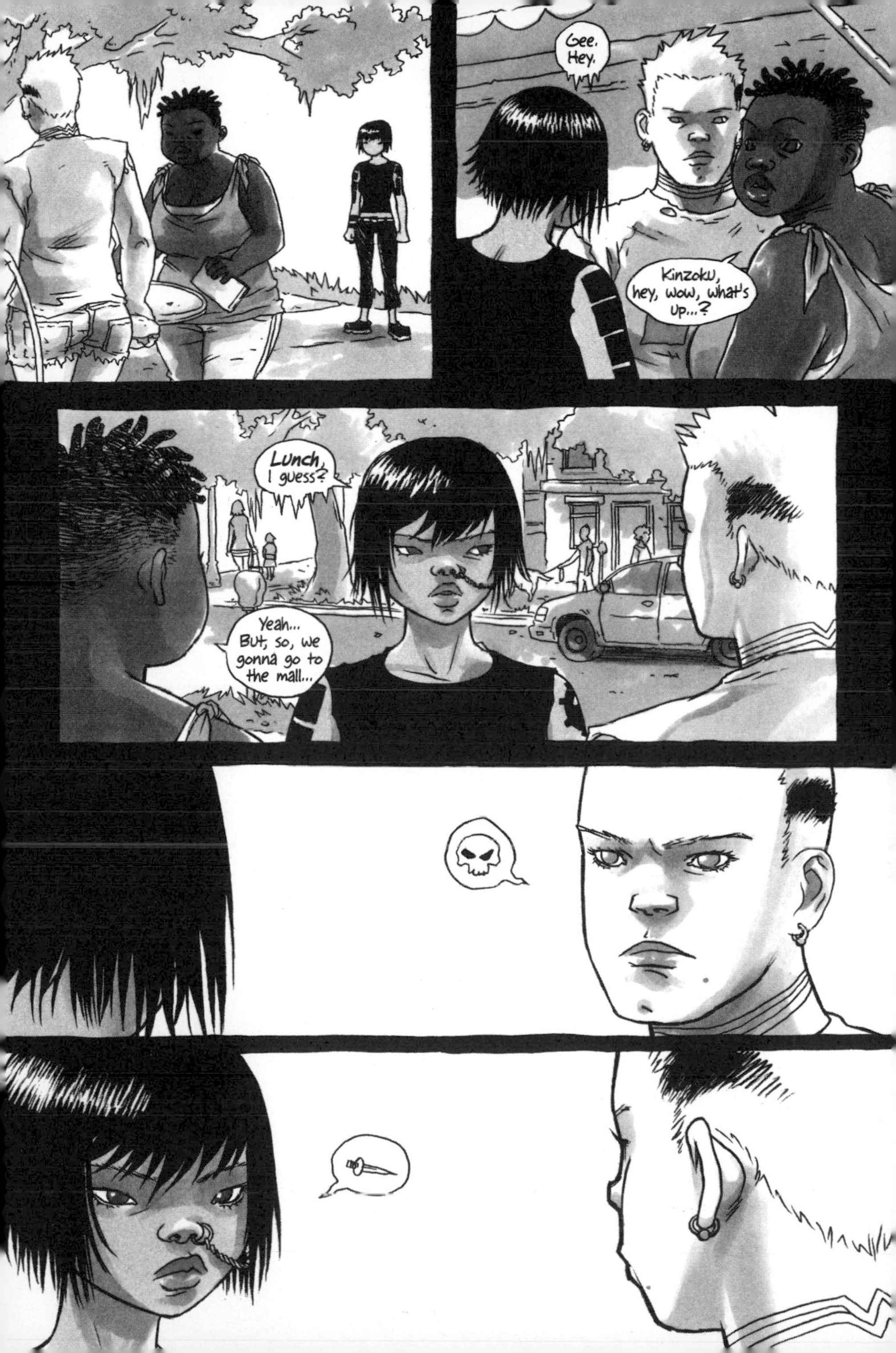
Gee. Hey.
Kinzoku, hey, wow, what's up...?
Lunch, I guess?
Yeah... But, so, we gonna go to the mall...

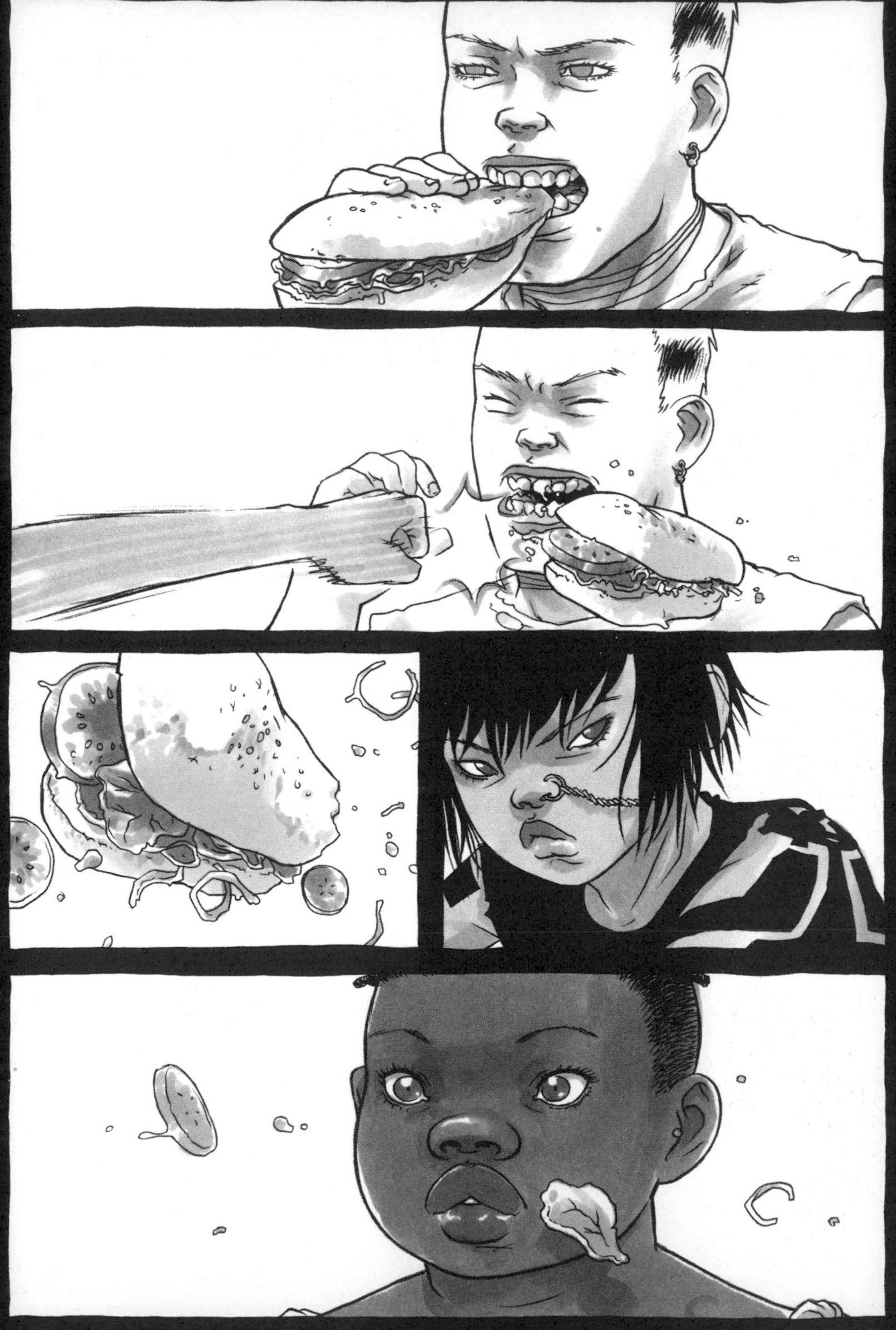

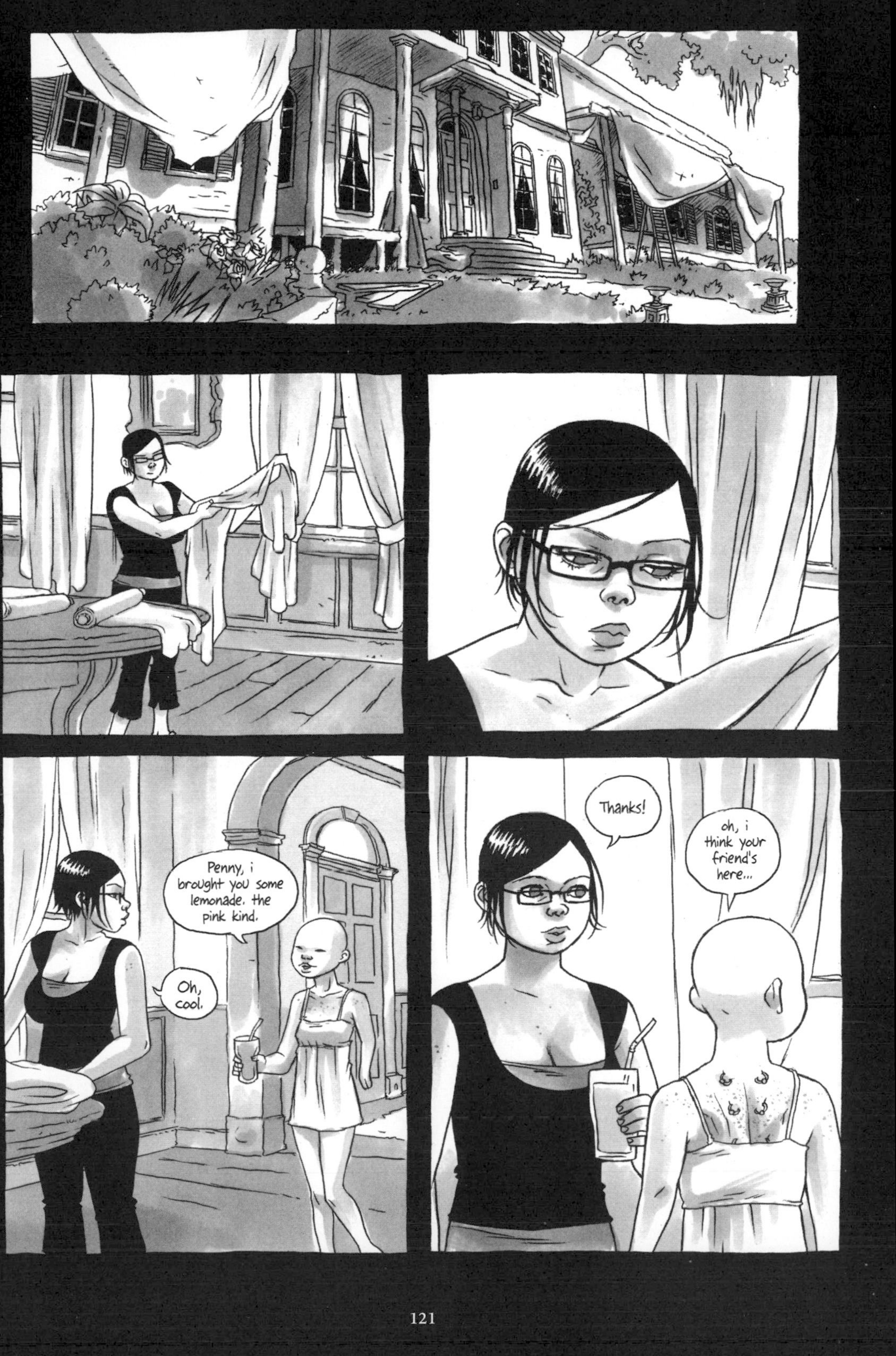
Penny, i brought you some lemonade. the pink kind.
Oh, cool.
Thanks!
oh, i think your friend's here...

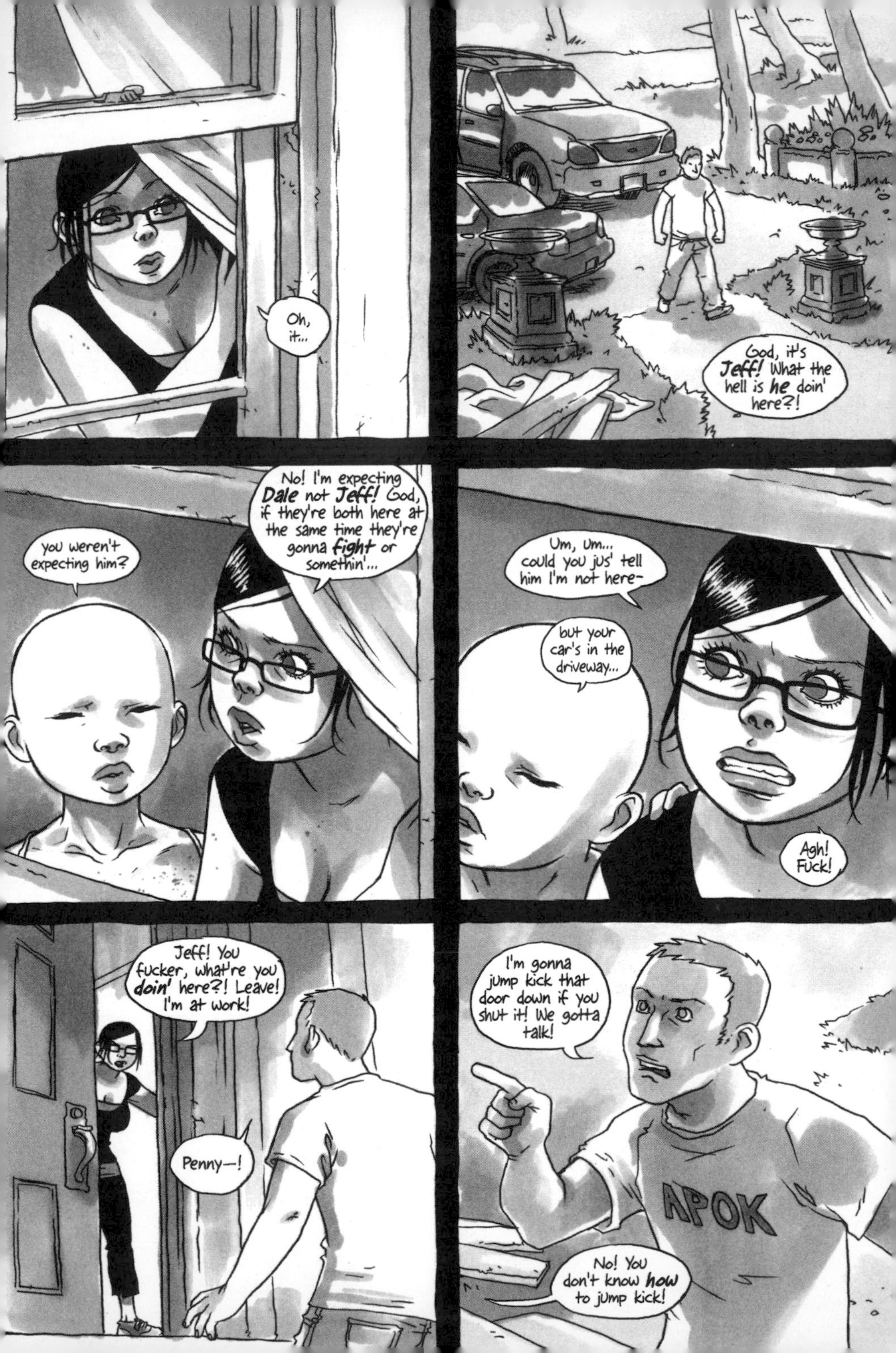
Oh, it...
God, it's Jeff! What the hell is he doin' here?!
you weren't expecting him?
No! I'm expecting Dale not Jeff! God, if they're both here at the same time they're gonna fight or somethin'...
Um, um... could you jus' tell him I'm not here–
but your car's in the driveway...
Agh! Fuck!
Jeff! You fucker, what're you doin' here?! Leave! I'm at work!
Penny–!
I'm gonna jump kick that door down if you shut it! We gotta talk!
APOK
No! You don't know how to jump kick!

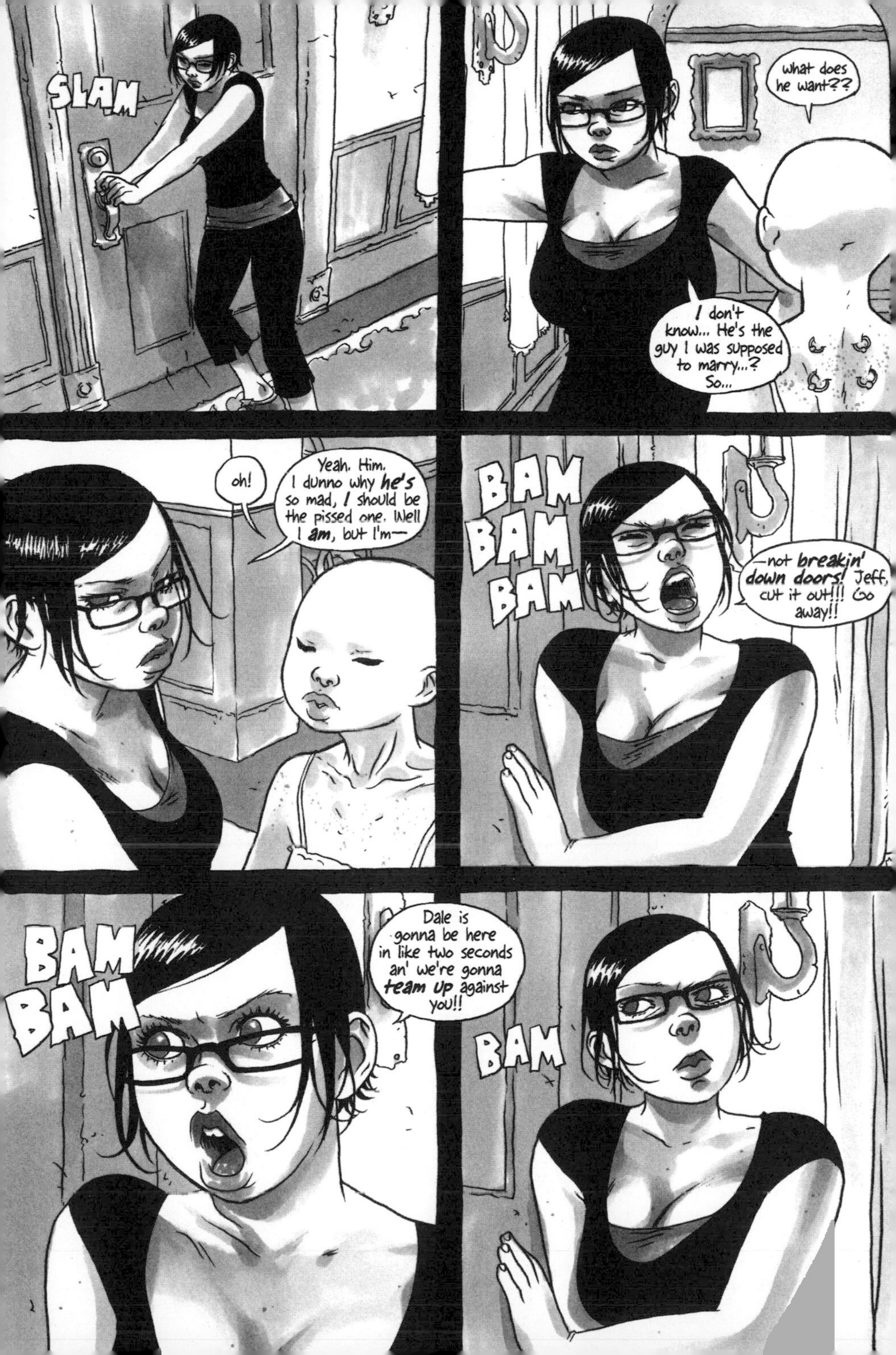
SLAM
what does he want??
I don't know... He's the guy I was supposed to marry...? So...
oh!
Yeah. Him. I dunno why **he's** so mad, **I** should be the pissed one. Well I **am**, but I'm—
BAM BAM BAM BAM
—not **breakin' down doors!** Jeff, cut it out!!! Go away!!
BAM BAM
Dale is gonna be here in like two seconds an' we're gonna **team up** against you!!
BAM

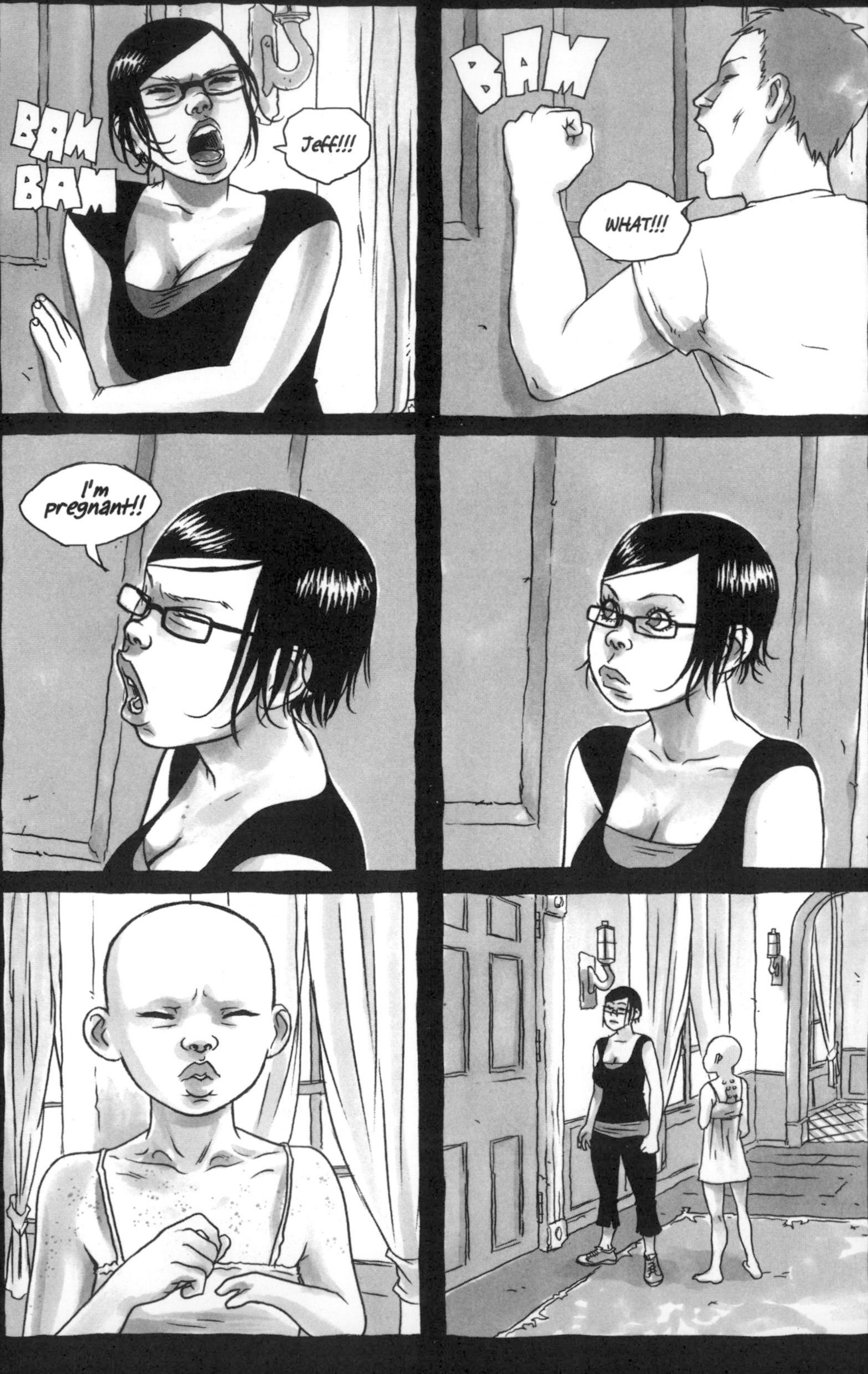
BAM BAM
Jeff!!!
BAM
WHAT!!!
I'm pregnant!!

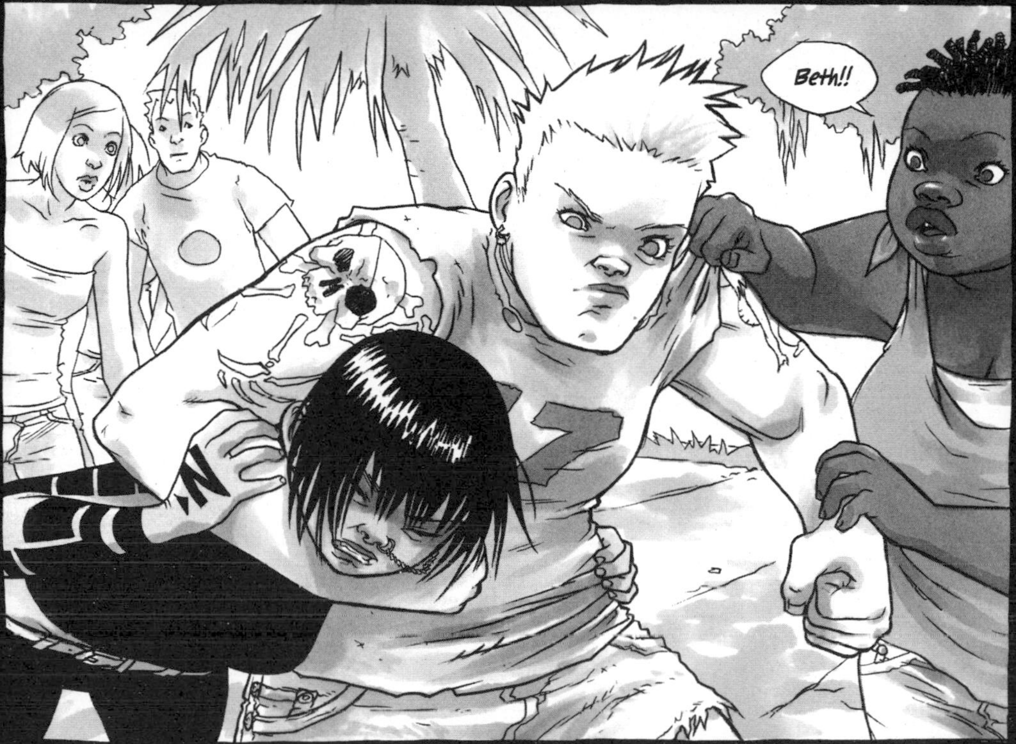
Beth!!

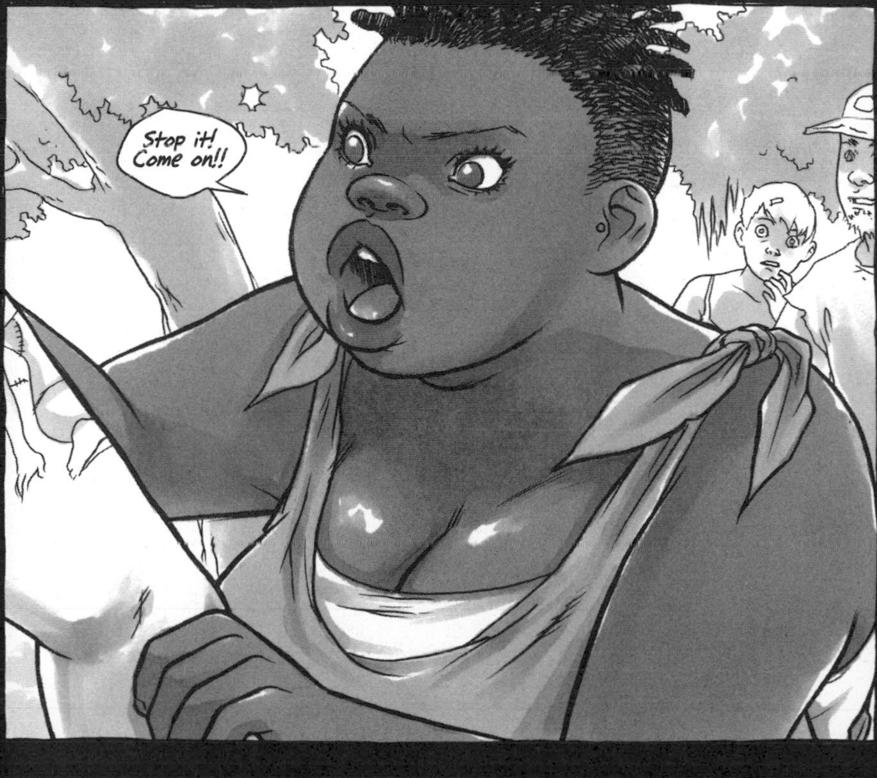
Stop it!
Come on!!

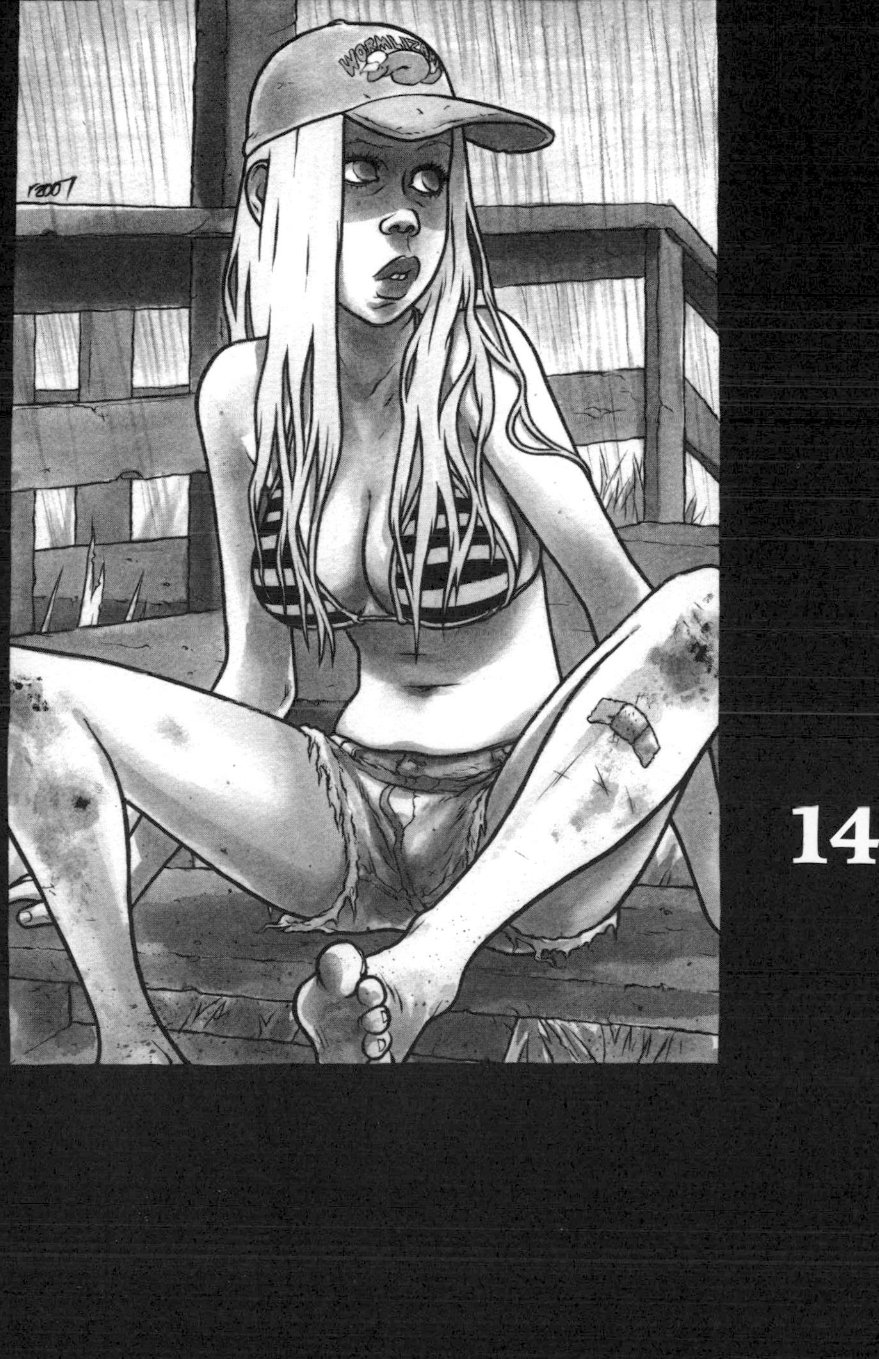
WORMILIZAN
r2007

14

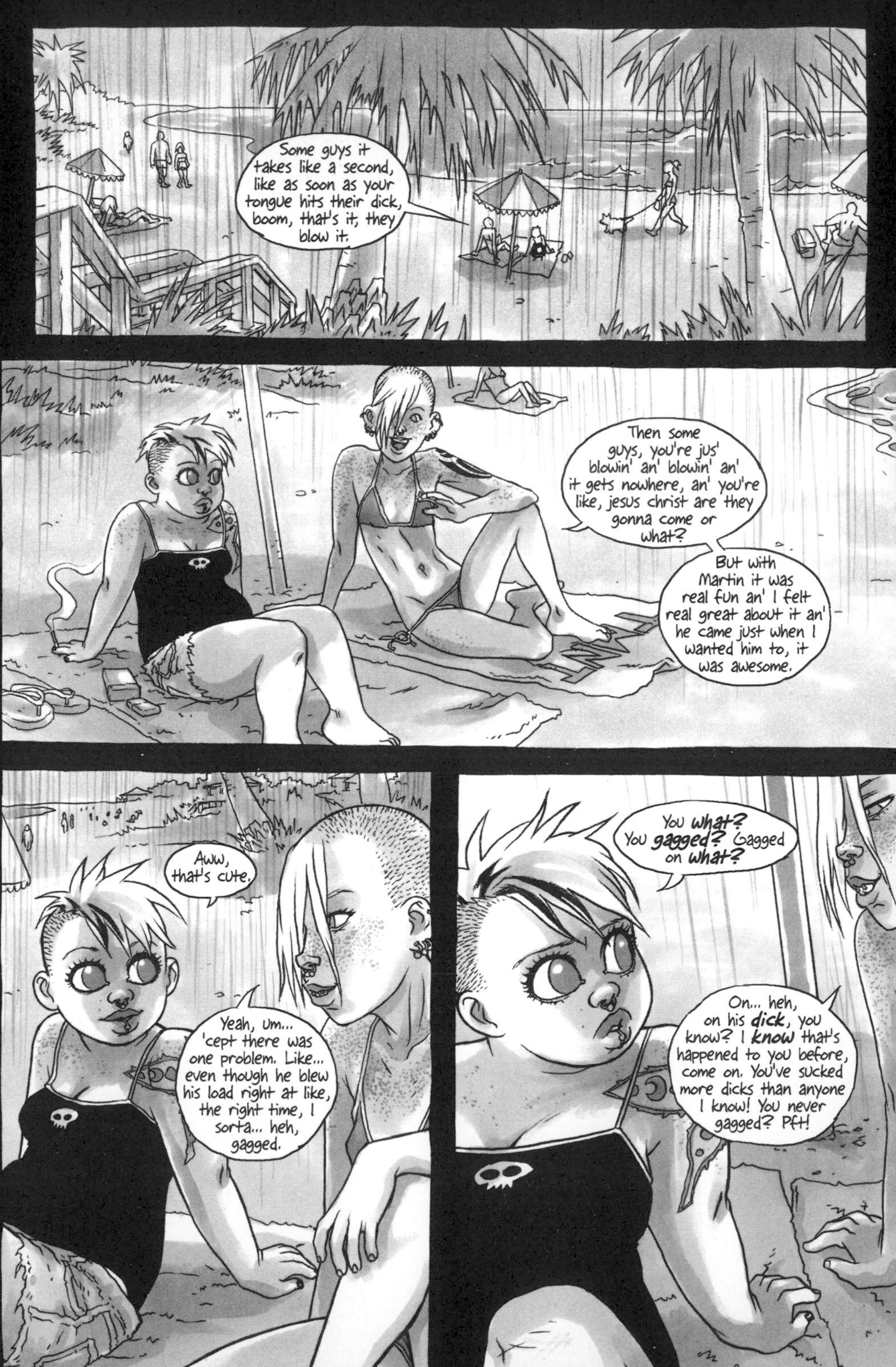
Some guys it takes like a second, like as soon as your tongue hits their dick, boom, that's it, they blow it.
Then some guys, you're jus' blowin' an' blowin' an' it gets nowhere, an' you're like, jesus christ are they gonna come or what?
But with Martin it was real fun an' I felt real great about it an' he came just when I wanted him to, it was awesome.
Aww, that's cute.
Yeah, um... 'cept there was one problem. Like... even though he blew his load right at like, the right time, I sorta... heh, gagged.
You **what?** You **gagged?** Gagged on **what?**
On... heh, on his **dick**, you know? I **know** that's happened to you before, come on. You've sucked more dicks than anyone I know! You never gagged? Pft!

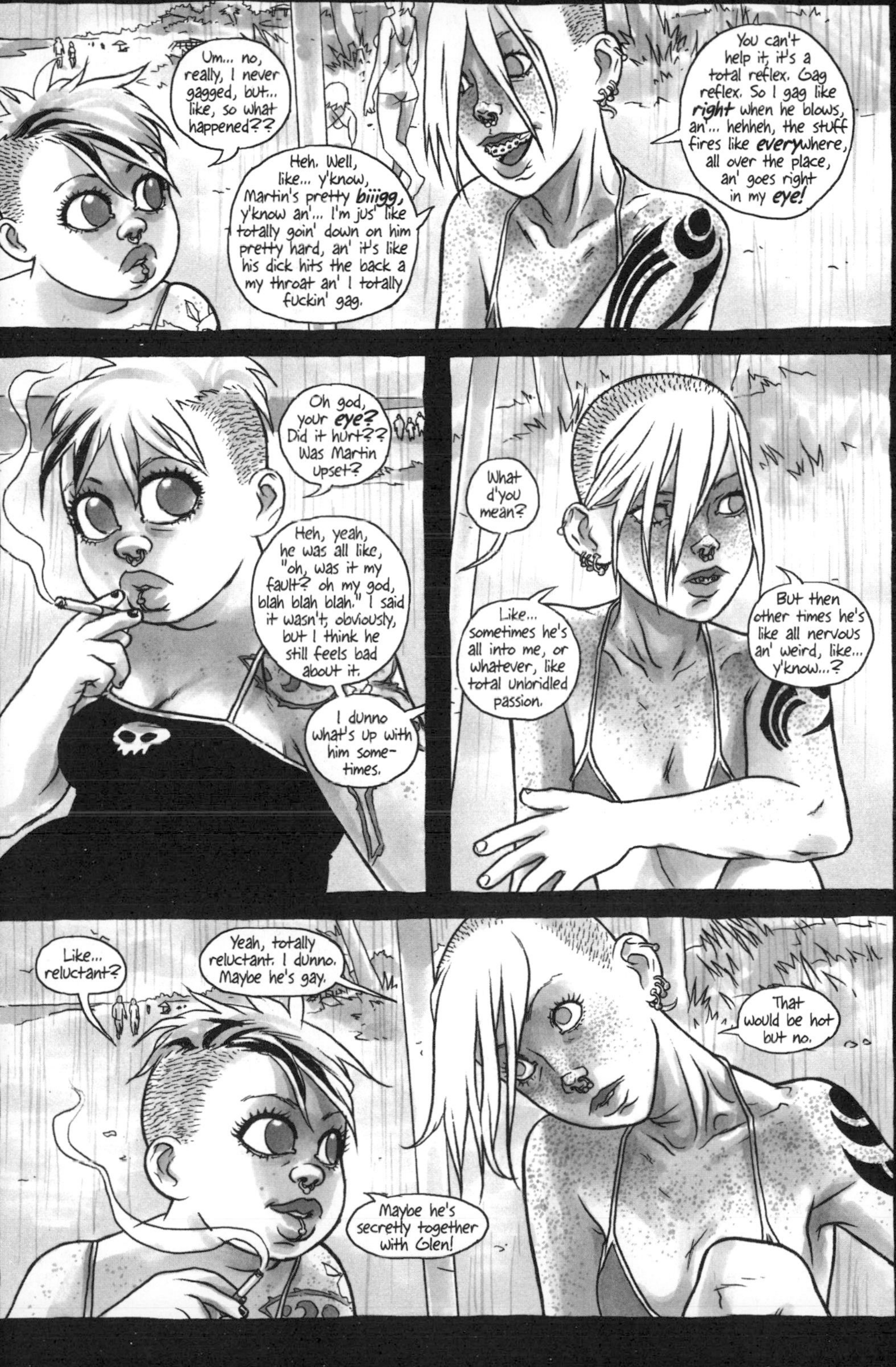

Um... no, really, I never gagged, but... like, so what happened??
Heh. Well, like... y'know, Martin's pretty biiigg, y'know an'... I'm jus' like totally goin' down on him pretty hard, an' it's like his dick hits the back a my throat an' I totally fuckin' gag.
You can't help it, it's a total reflex. Gag reflex. So I gag like right when he blows, an'... hehheh, the stuff fires like everywhere, all over the place, an' goes right in my eye!
Oh god, your eye? Did it hurt?? Was Martin upset?
Heh, yeah, he was all like, "oh, was it my fault? oh my god, blah blah blah." I said it wasn't, obviously, but I think he still feels bad about it.
I dunno what's up with him some-times.
What d'you mean?
Like... sometimes he's all into me, or whatever, like total unbridled passion.
But then other times he's like all nervous an' weird, like... y'know...?
Like... reluctant?
Yeah, totally reluctant. I dunno. Maybe he's gay.
That would be hot but no.
Maybe he's secretly together with Glen!

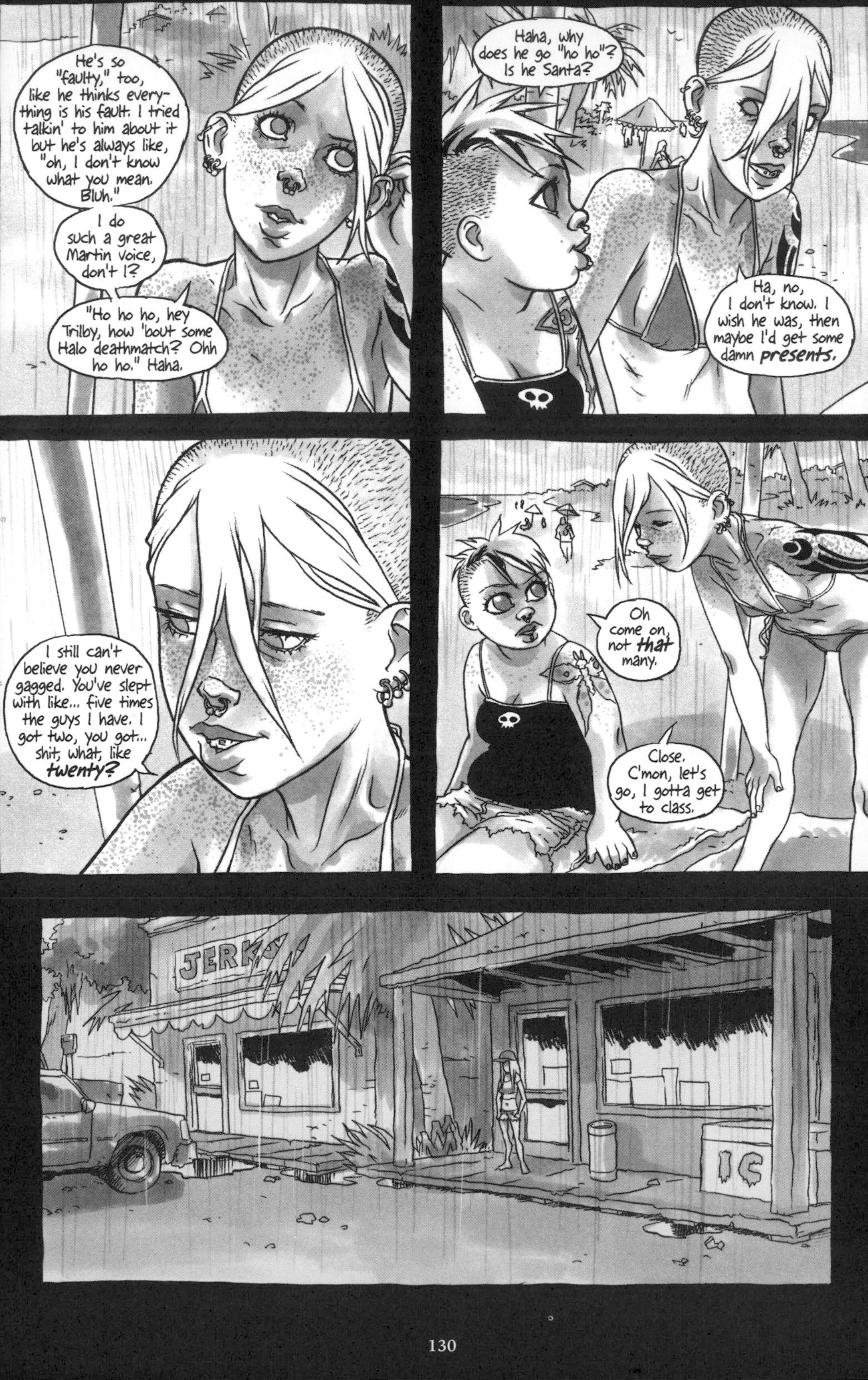

He's so "faulty," too, like he thinks everything is his fault. I tried talkin' to him about it but he's always like, "oh, I don't know what you mean. Bluh."
I do such a great Martin voice, don't I?
"Ho ho ho, hey Trilby, how 'bout some Halo deathmatch? Ohh ho ho." Haha.
Haha, why does he go "ho ho"? Is he Santa?
Ha, no, I don't know. I wish he was, then maybe I'd get some damn presents.
I still can't believe you never gagged. You've slept with like... five times the guys I have. I got two, you got... shit, what, like twenty?
Oh come on, not that many.
Close. C'mon, let's go, I gotta get to class.
JERK
IC

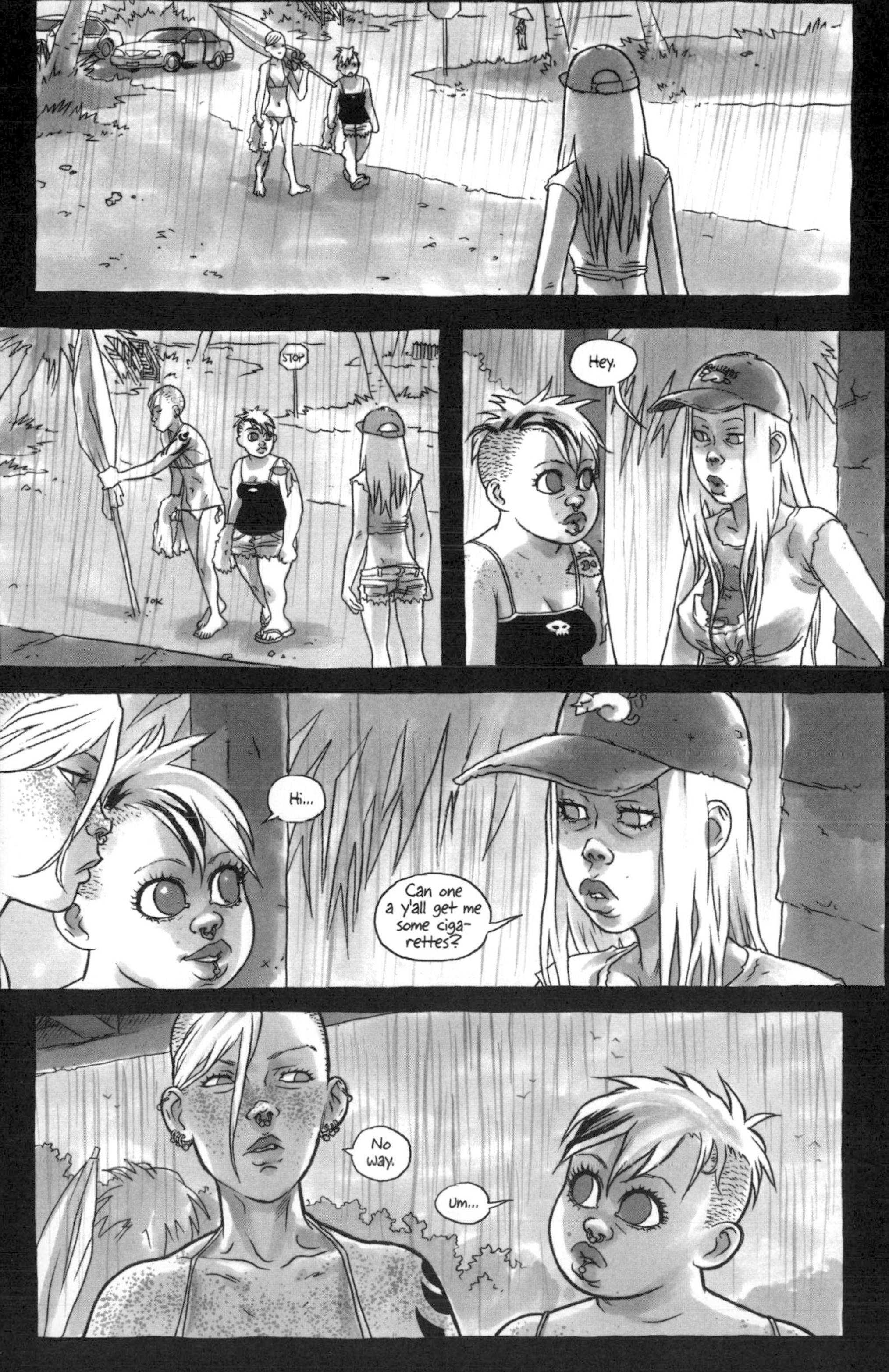
STOP
TOK
Hey.
Hi...
Can one a y'all get me some ciga-rettes?
No way.
Um...

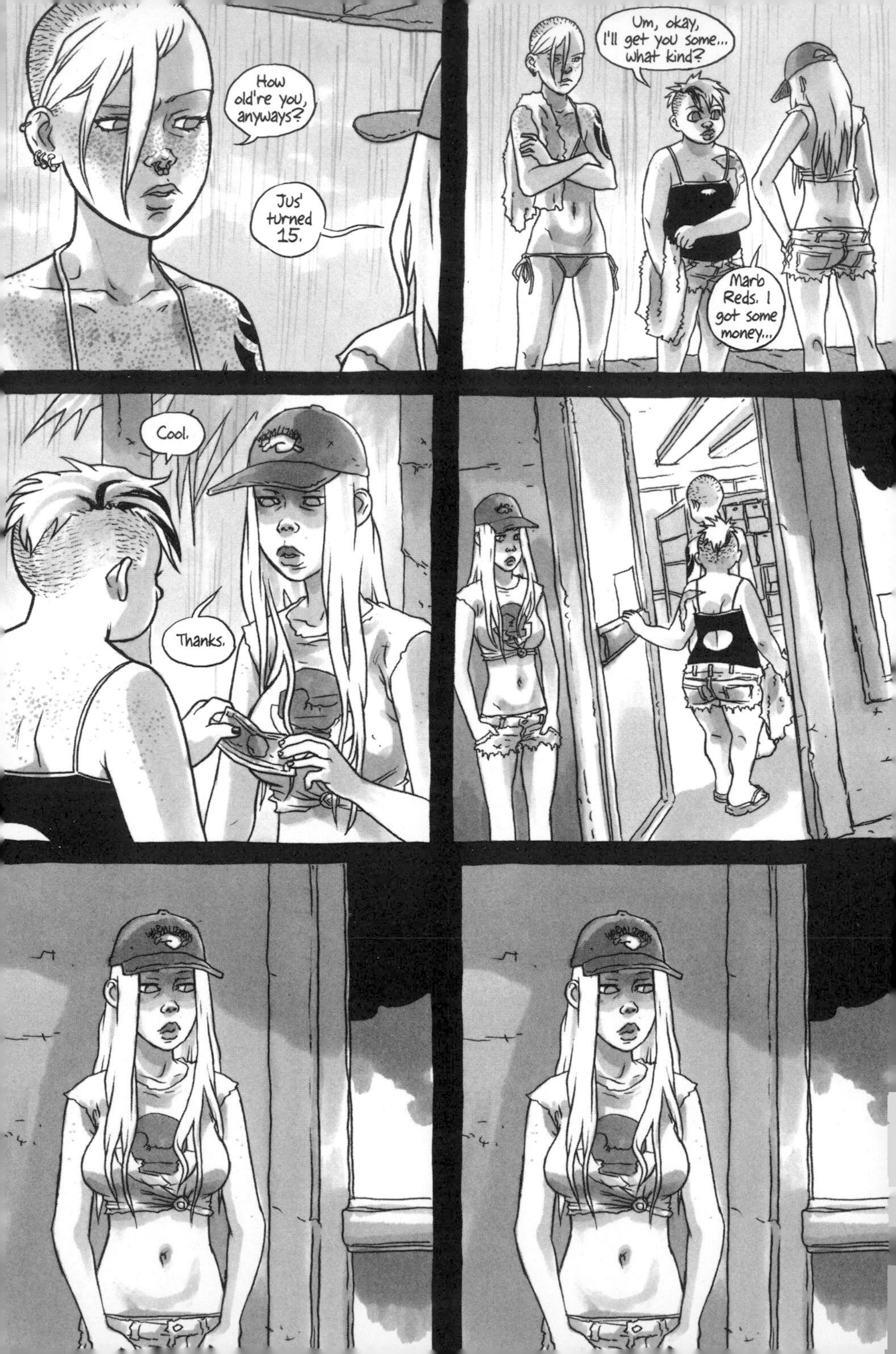
How old're you, anyways?
Jus' turned 15.
Um, okay, I'll get you some... what kind?
Marb Reds. I got some money...
Cool.
Thanks.

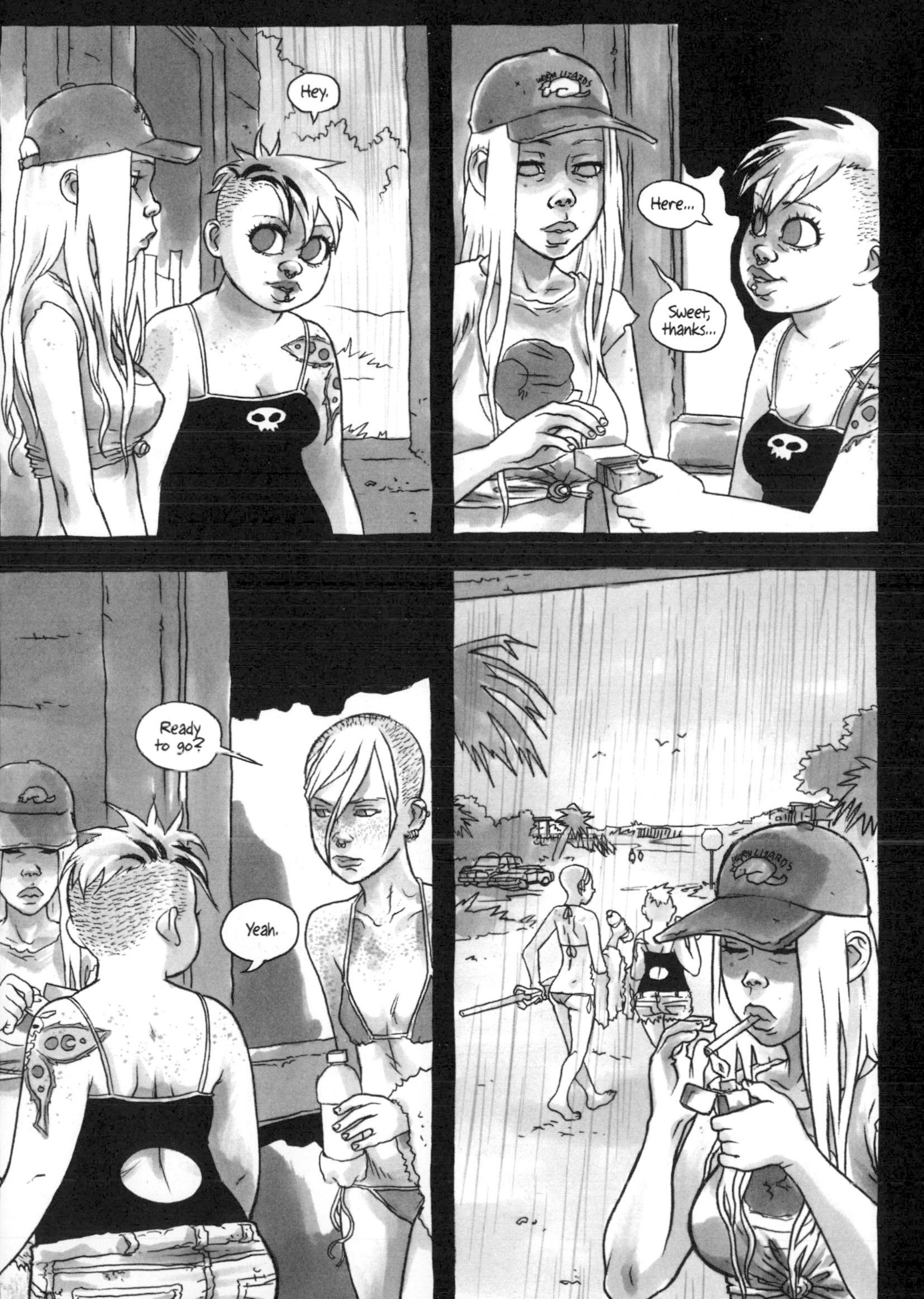
Hey.
Here...
Sweet, thanks...
Ready to go?
Yeah.

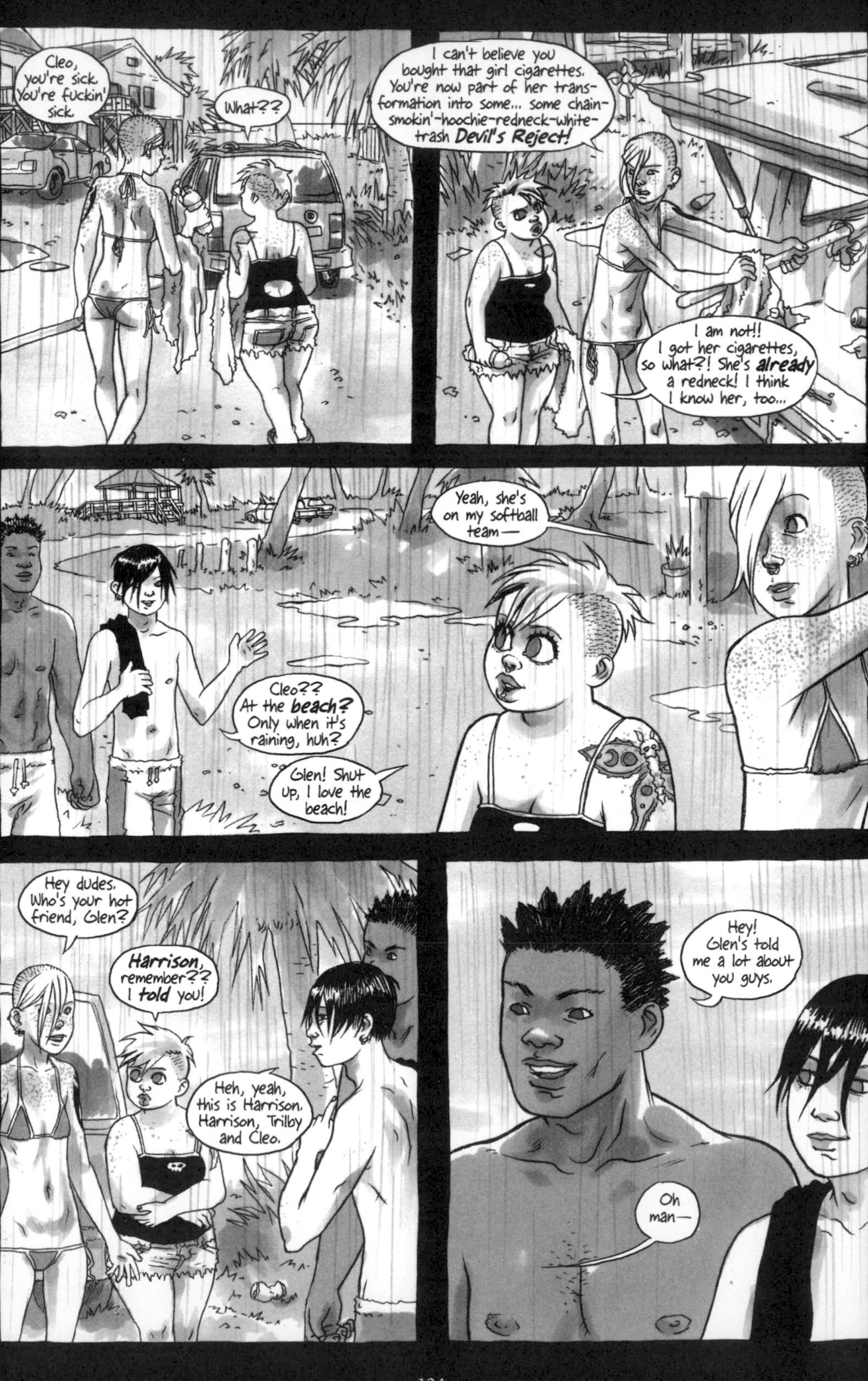

Cleo, you're sick. You're fuckin' sick.
What??
I can't believe you bought that girl cigarettes. You're now part of her transformation into some... some chain-smokin'-hoochie-redneck-white-trash **Devil's Reject!**
I am not!! I got her cigarettes, so what?! She's **already** a redneck! I think I know her, too...
Yeah, she's on my softball team—
Cleo?? At the **beach?** Only when it's raining, huh?
Glen! Shut up, I love the beach!
Hey dudes. Who's your hot friend, Glen?
Harrison, remember?? I **told** you!
Heh, yeah, this is Harrison. Harrison, Trilby and Cleo.
Hey! Glen's told me a lot about you guys.
Oh man—

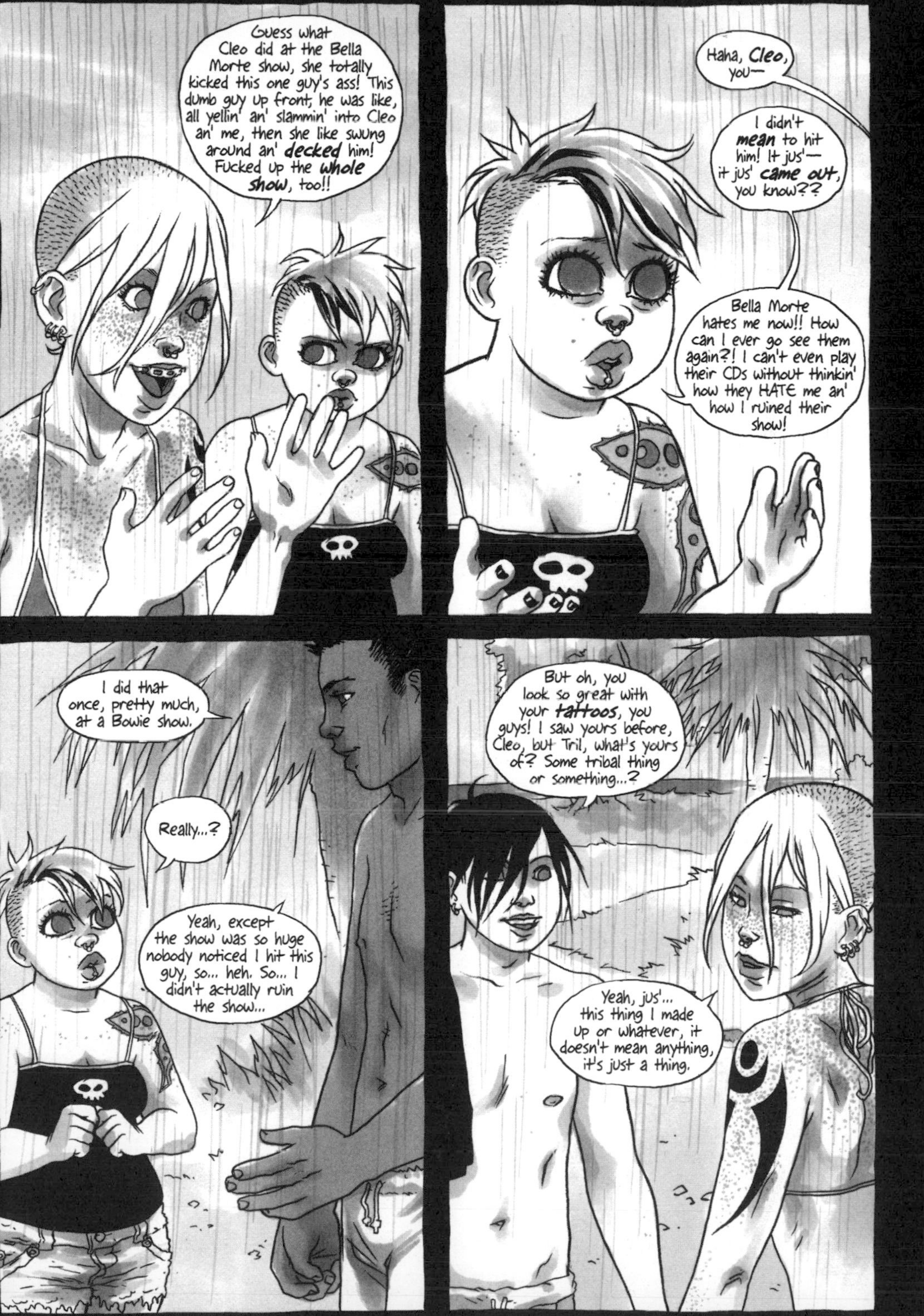
Guess what Cleo did at the Bella Morte show, she totally kicked this one guy's ass! This dumb guy up front, he was like, all yellin' an' slammin' into Cleo an' me, then she like swung around an' **decked** him! Fucked up the **whole show**, too!!
Haha, **Cleo**, you—
I didn't **mean** to hit him! It jus'— it jus' **came out**, you know??
Bella Morte hates me now!! How can I ever go see them again?! I can't even play their CDs without thinkin' how they HATE me an' how I ruined their show!
I did that once, pretty much, at a Bowie show.
Really...?
Yeah, except the show was so huge nobody noticed I hit this guy, so... heh. So... I didn't actually ruin the show...
But oh, you look so great with your **tattoos**, you guys! I saw yours before, Cleo, but Tril, what's yours of? Some tribal thing or something...?
Yeah, jus'... this thing I made up or whatever, it doesn't mean anything, it's just a thing.

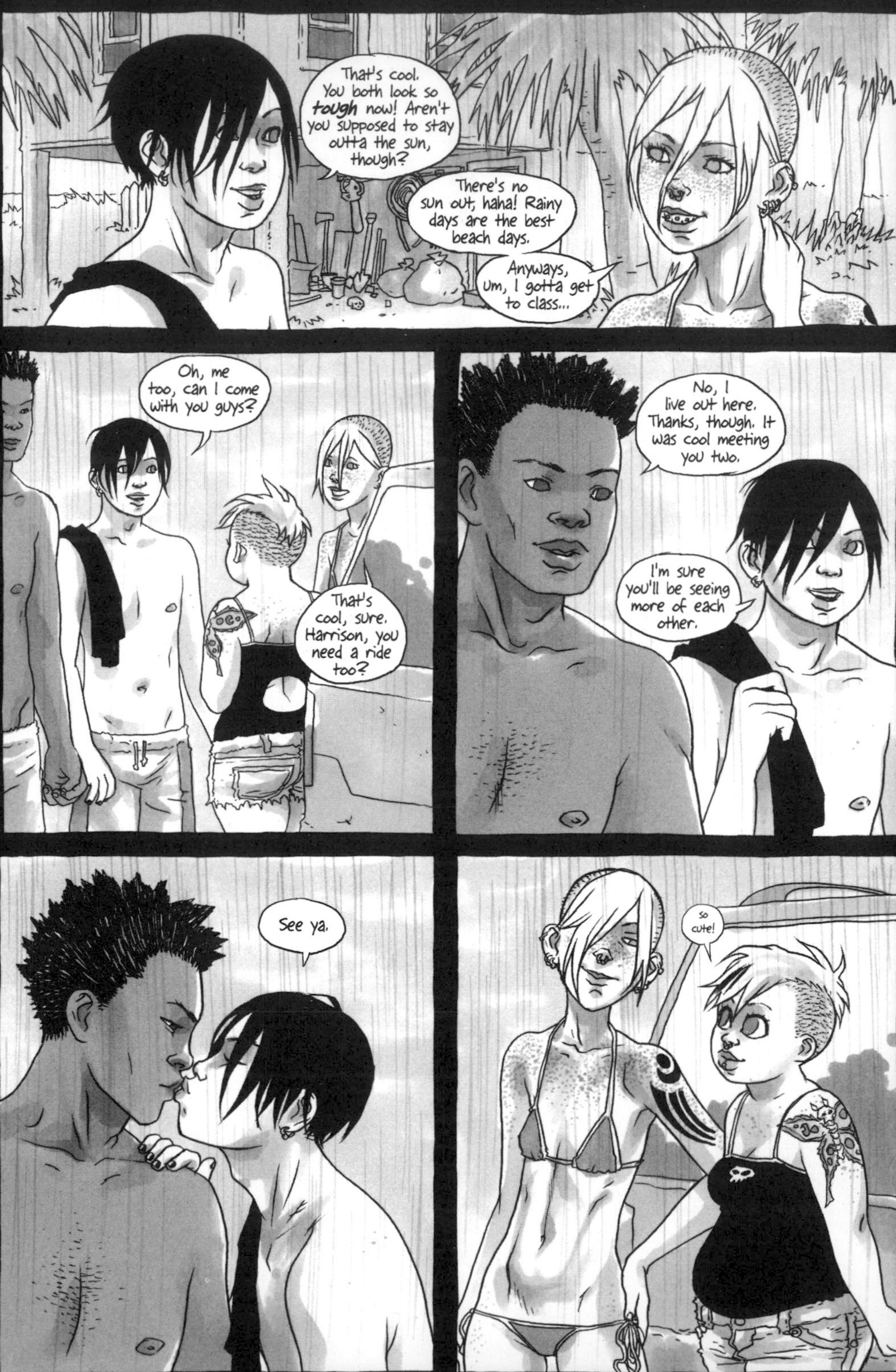
That's cool. You both look so **tough** now! Aren't you supposed to stay outta the sun, though?
There's no sun out, haha! Rainy days are the best beach days.
Anyways, um, I gotta get to class...
Oh, me too, can I come with you guys?
That's cool, sure. Harrison, you need a ride too?
No, I live out here. Thanks, though. It was cool meeting you two.
I'm sure you'll be seeing more of each other.
See ya.
so cute!

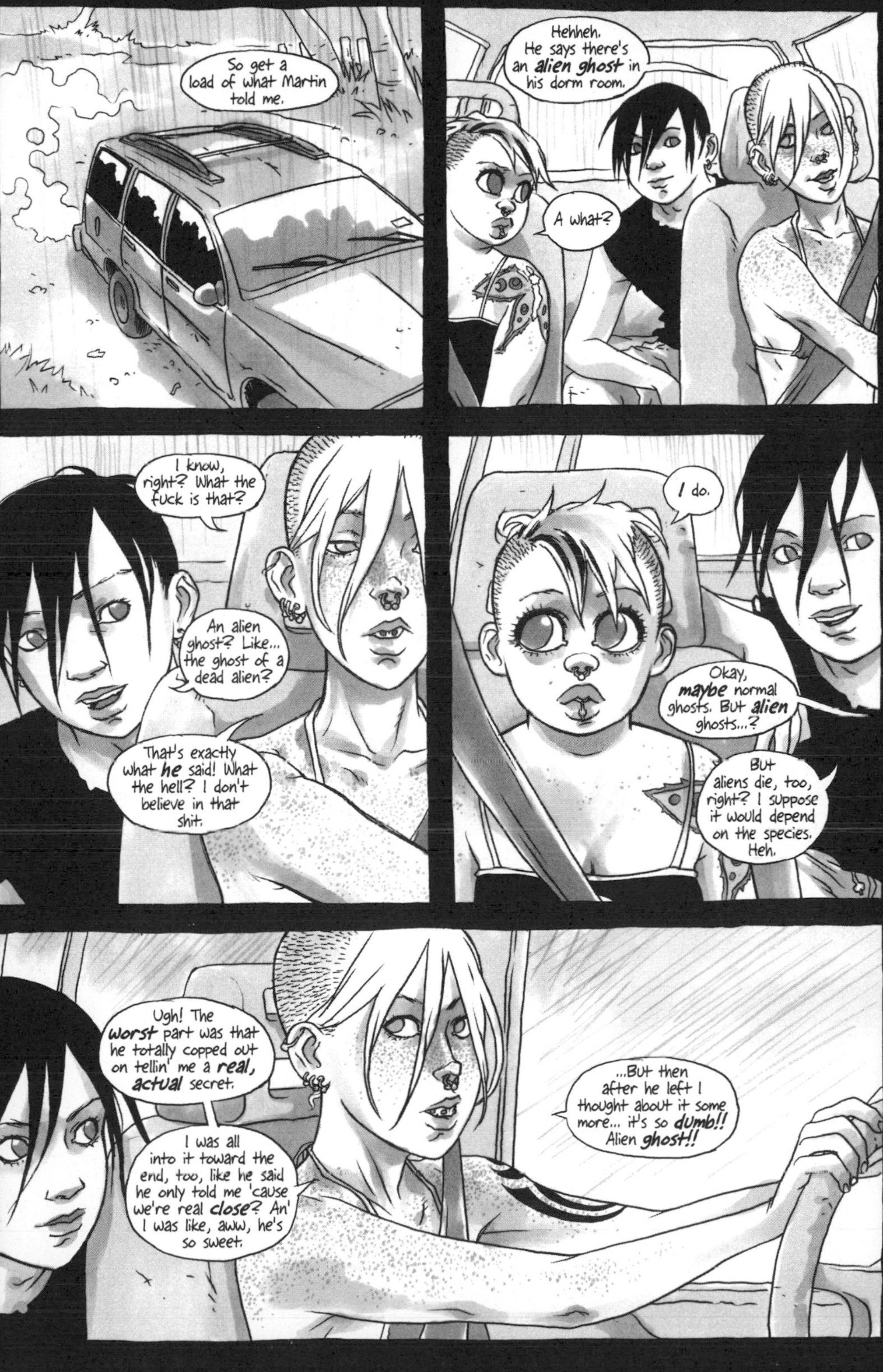
So get a load of what Martin told me.
Hehheh. He says there's an alien ghost in his dorm room.
A what?
I know, right? What the fuck is that?
An alien ghost? Like... the ghost of a dead alien?
That's exactly what he said! What the hell? I don't believe in that shit.
I do.
Okay, maybe normal ghosts. But alien ghosts...?
But aliens die, too, right? I suppose it would depend on the species. Heh.
Ugh! The worst part was that he totally copped out on tellin' me a real, actual secret.
I was all into it toward the end, too, like he said he only told me 'cause we're real close? An' I was like, aww, he's so sweet.
...But then after he left I thought about it some more... it's so dumb!! Alien ghost!!

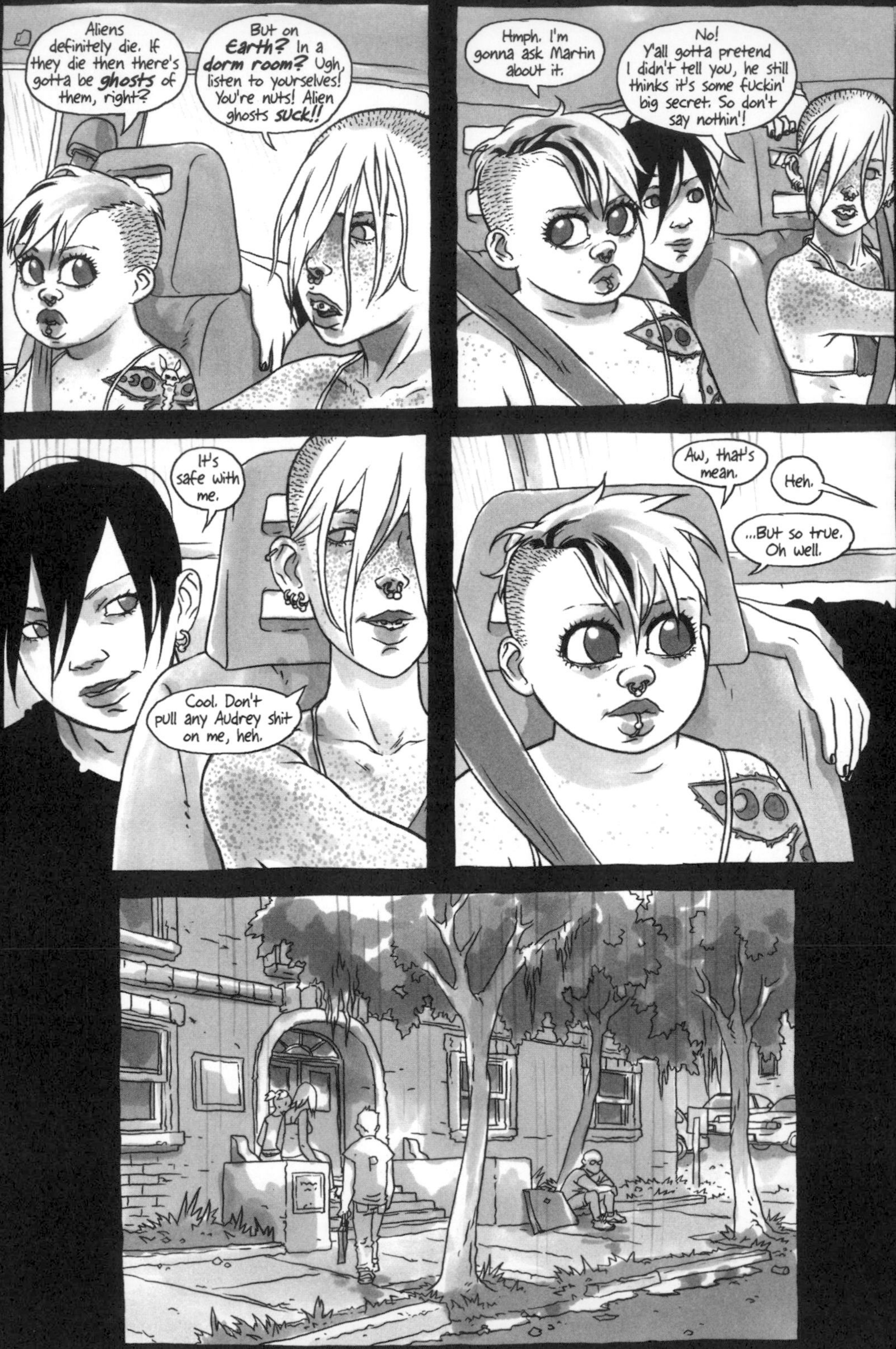
Aliens definitely die. If they die then there's gotta be ghosts of them, right?
But on Earth? In a dorm room? Ugh, listen to yourselves! You're nuts! Alien ghosts SUCK!!
Hmph. I'm gonna ask Martin about it.
No! Y'all gotta pretend I didn't tell you, he still thinks it's some fuckin' big secret. So don't say nothin'!
It's safe with me.
Cool. Don't pull any Audrey shit on me, heh.
Aw, that's mean.
Heh.
...But so true. Oh well.

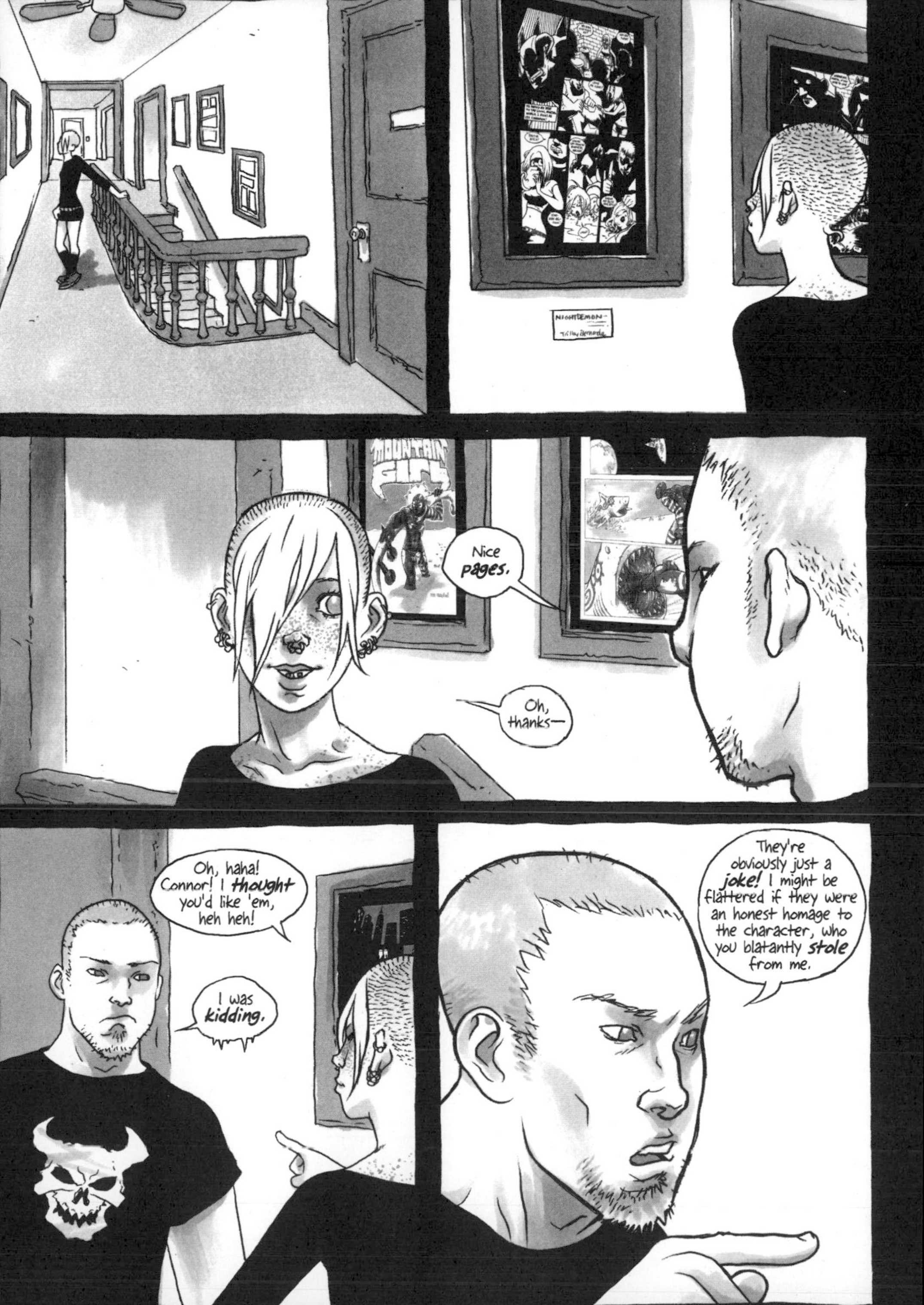
NIGHTDEMON
Nice pages.
Oh, thanks—
Oh, haha! Connor! I thought you'd like 'em, heh heh!
I was kidding.
They're obviously just a joke! I might be flattered if they were an honest homage to the character, who you blatantly stole from me.

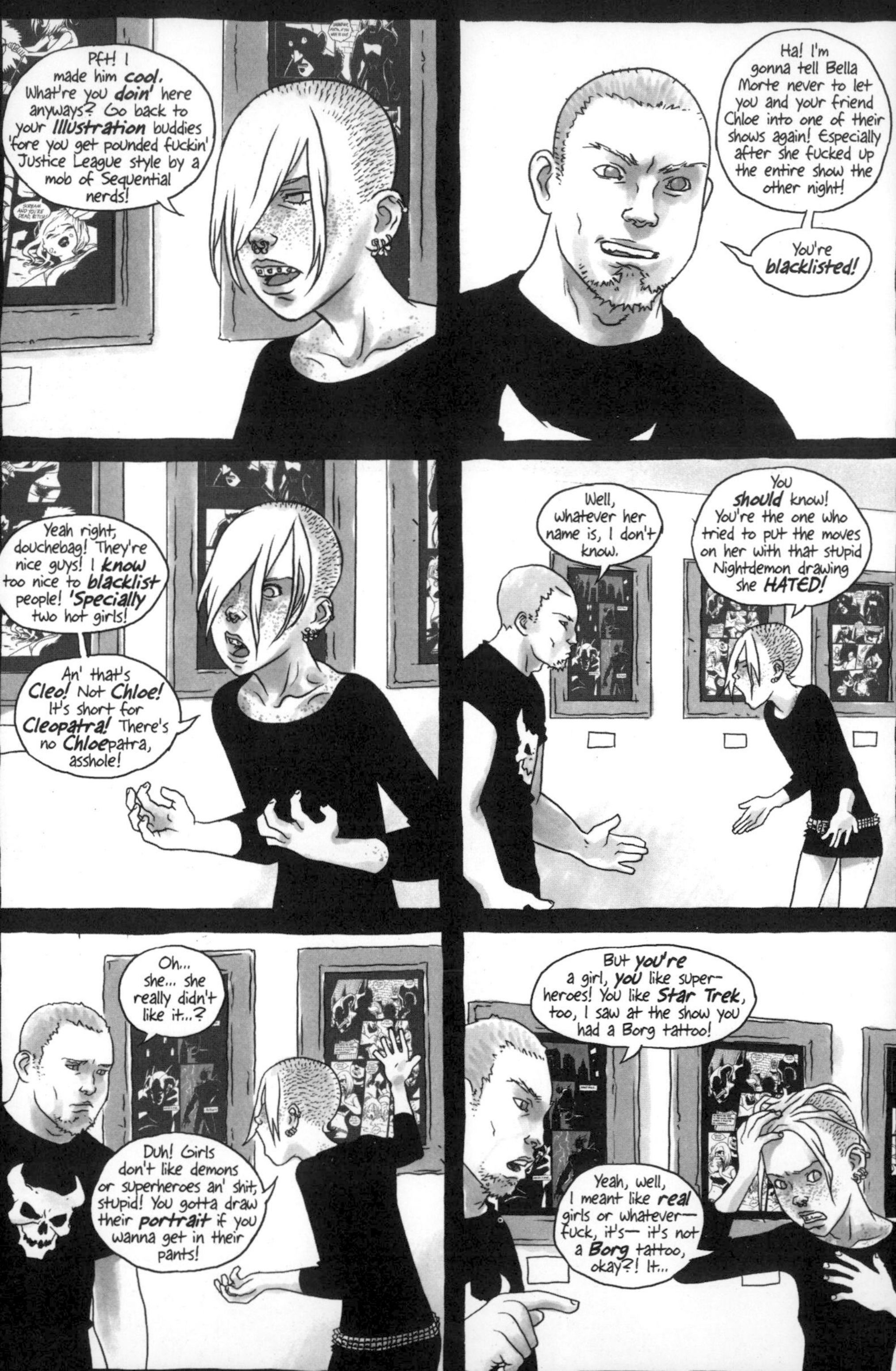

Pft! I made him cool. What're you doin' here anyways? Go back to your Illustration buddies 'fore you get pounded fuckin' Justice League style by a mob of Sequential nerds!
Ha! I'm gonna tell Bella Morte never to let you and your friend Chloe into one of their shows again! Especially after she fucked up the entire show the other night!
You're blacklisted!
Yeah right, douchebag! They're nice guys! I know too nice to blacklist people! 'Specially two hot girls!
An' that's Cleo! Not Chloe! It's short for Cleopatra! There's no Chloepatra, asshole!
Well, whatever her name is, I don't know.
You should know! You're the one who tried to put the moves on her with that stupid Nightdemon drawing she HATED!
Oh... she... she really didn't like it...?
Duh! Girls don't like demons or superheroes an' shit, stupid! You gotta draw their portrait if you wanna get in their pants!
But you're a girl, you like super-heroes! You like Star Trek, too, I saw at the show you had a Borg tattoo!
Yeah, well, I meant like real girls or whatever— fuck, it's— it's not a Borg tattoo, okay?! It...

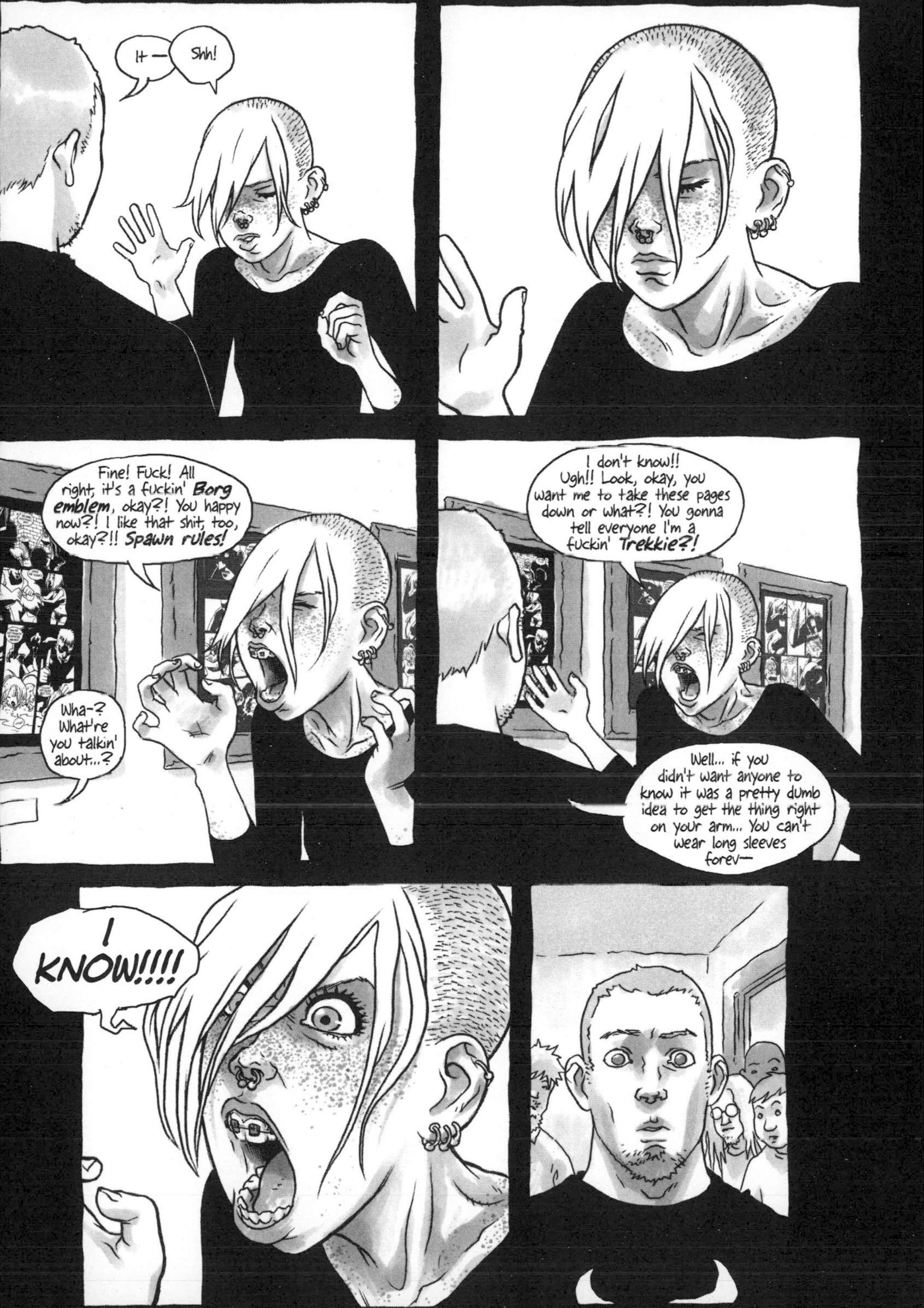
It —
Shh!
Fine! Fuck! All right, it's a fuckin' **Borg emblem**, okay?! You happy now?! I like that shit, too, okay?!! **Spawn rules!**
Wha-? What're you talkin' about...?
I don't know!! Ugh!! Look, okay, you want me to take these pages down or what?! You gonna tell everyone I'm a fuckin' **Trekkie?!**
Well... if you didn't want anyone to know it was a pretty dumb idea to get the thing right on your arm... You can't wear long sleeves forev—
I KNOW!!!!

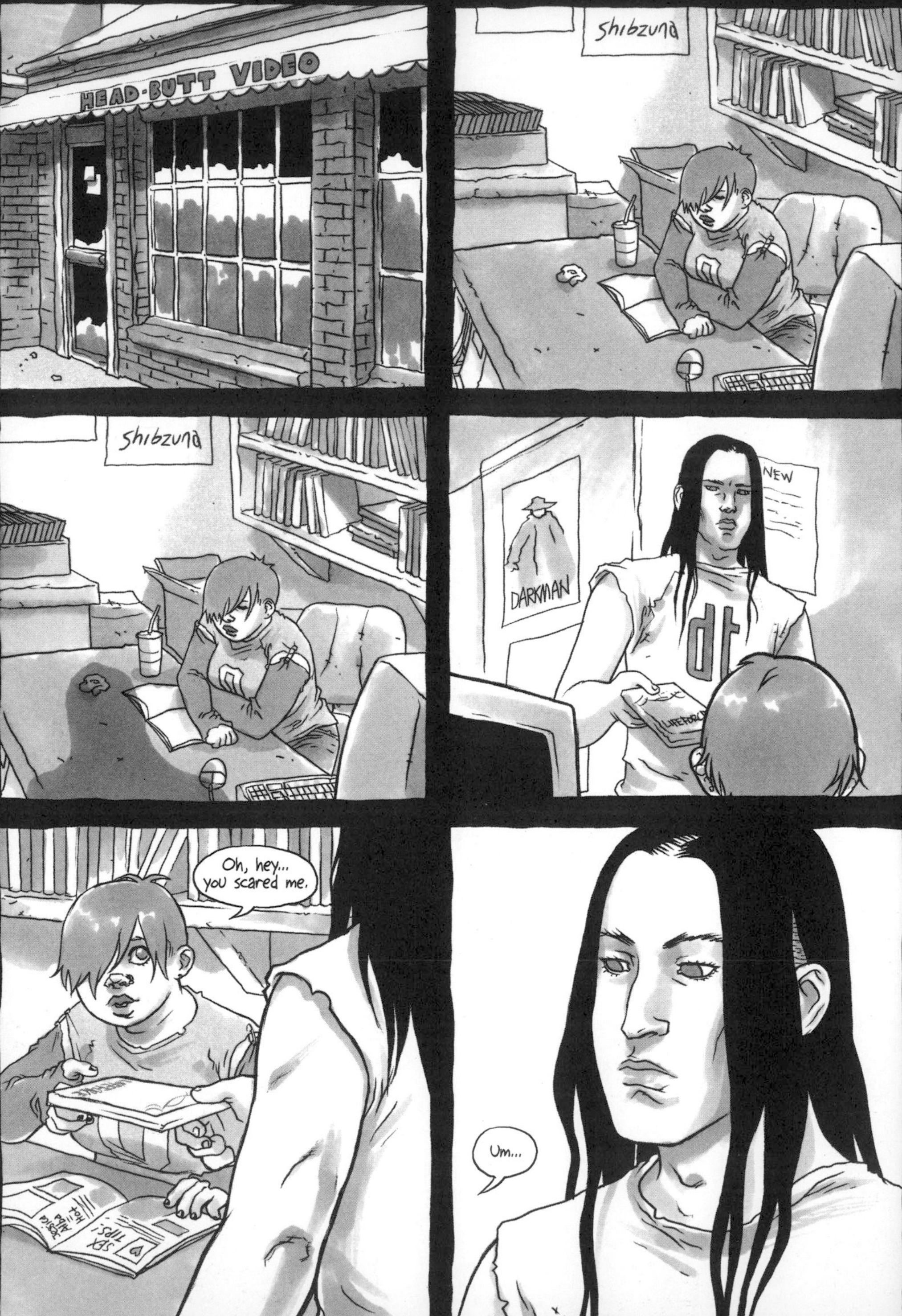
HEAD-BUTT VIDEO
shibzuna
shibzuna
DARKMAN
NEW
Oh, hey... you scared me.
SEX TIPS!
Um...

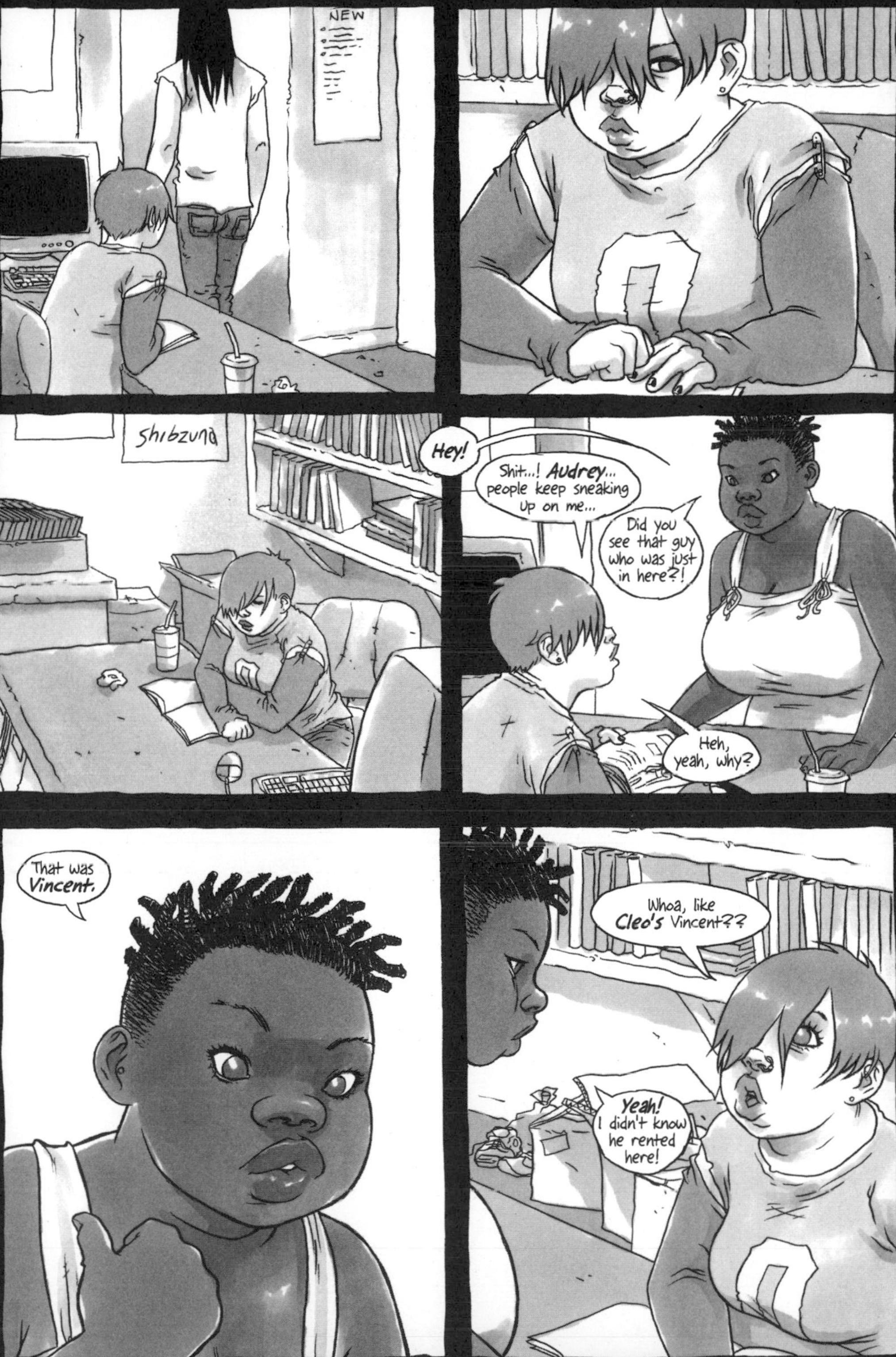
shibzuna
Hey!
Shit...! Audrey... people keep sneaking up on me...
Did you see that guy who was just in here?!
Heh, yeah, why?
That was Vincent.
Whoa, like Cleo's Vincent??
Yeah! I didn't know he rented here!

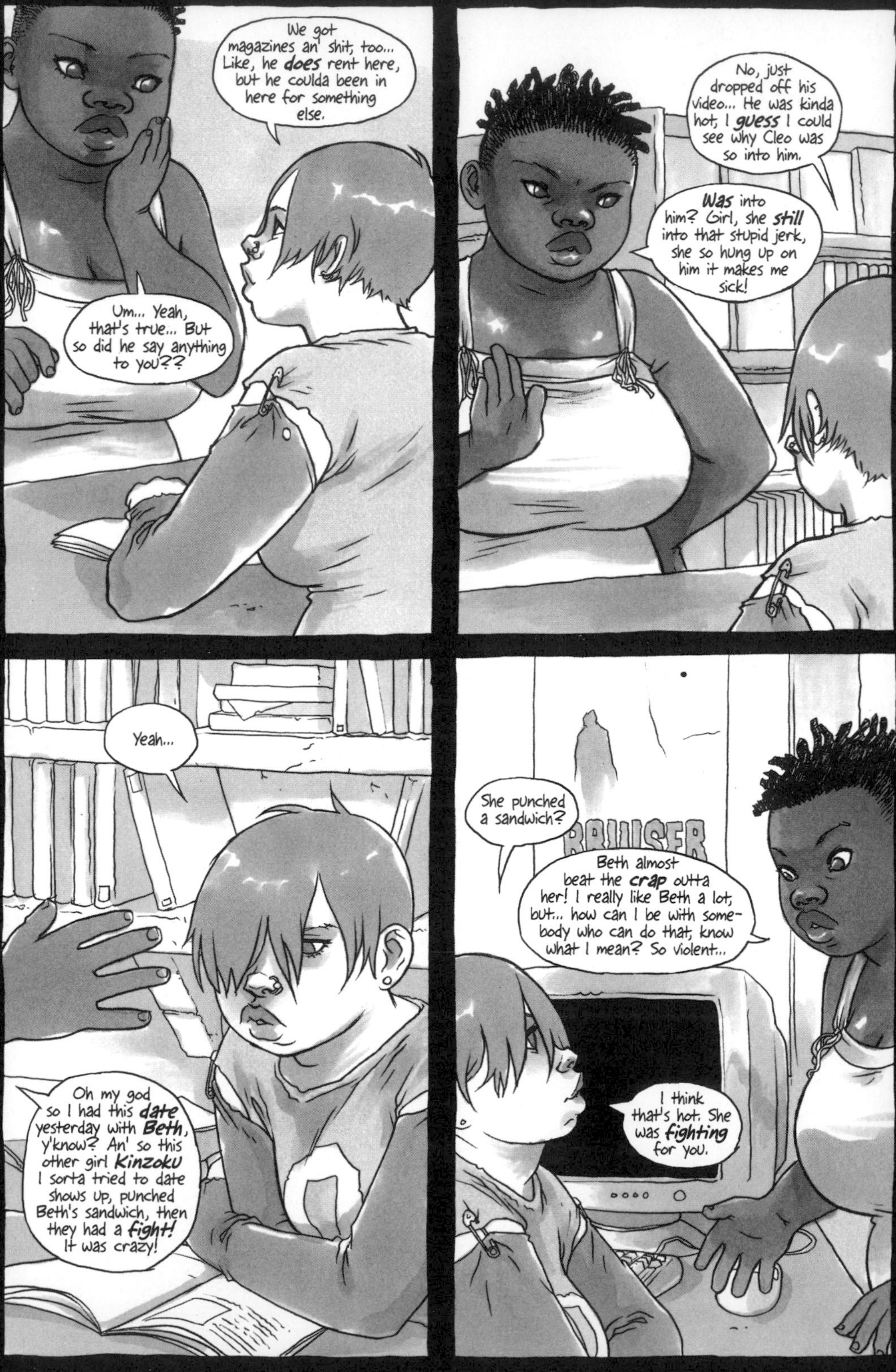
We got magazines an' shit, too... Like, he does rent here, but he coulda been in here for something else.
Um... Yeah, that's true... But so did he say anything to you??
No, just dropped off his video... He was kinda hot, I guess I could see why Cleo was so into him.
Was into him? Girl, she still into that stupid jerk, she so hung up on him it makes me sick!
Yeah...
Oh my god so I had this date yesterday with Beth, y'know? An' so this other girl Kinzoku I sorta tried to date shows up, punched Beth's sandwich, then they had a fight! It was crazy!
She punched a sandwich?
Beth almost beat the crap outta her! I really like Beth a lot, but... how can I be with some-body who can do that, know what I mean? So violent...
I think that's hot. She was fighting for you.

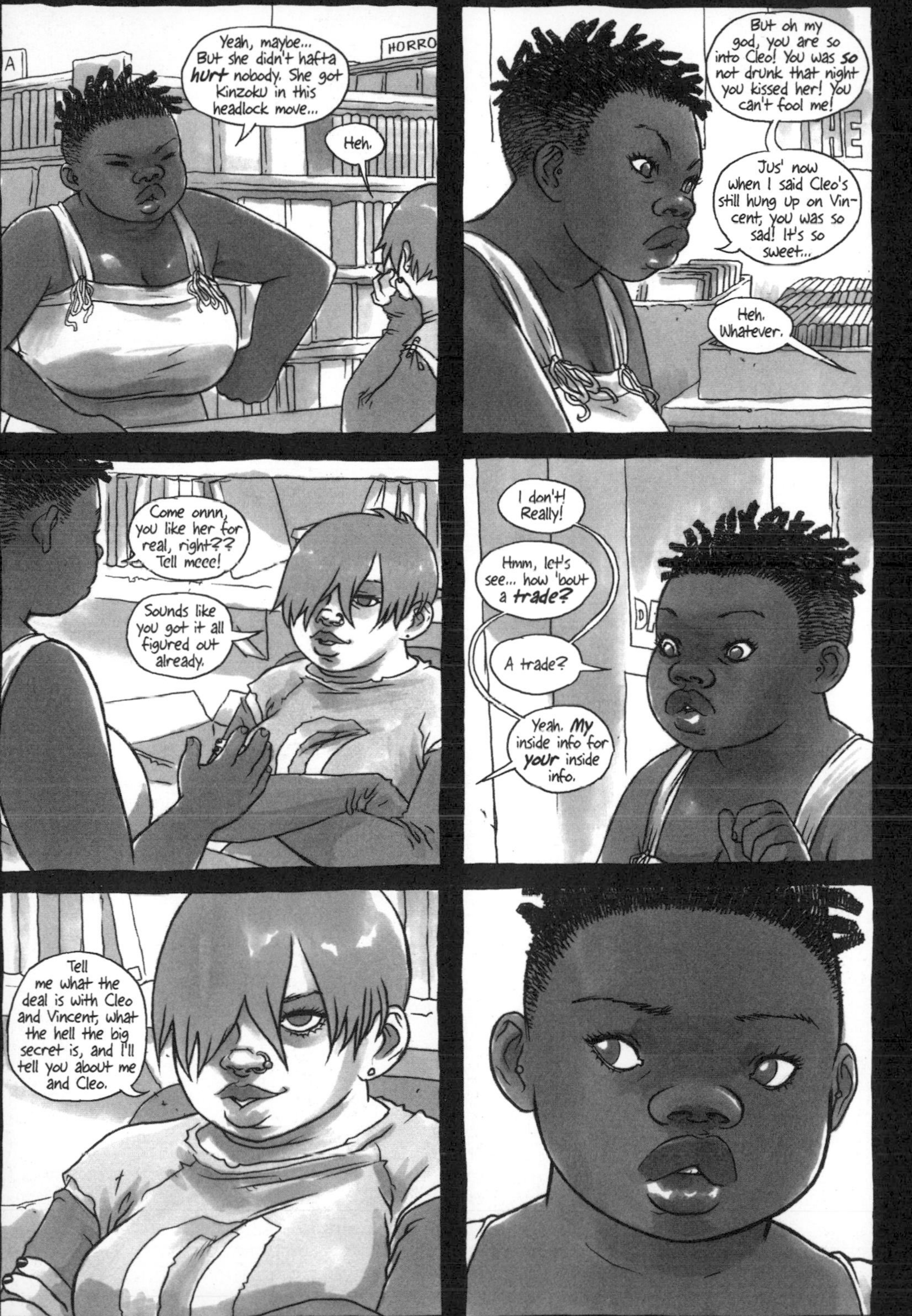
HORRO
A
Yeah, maybe... But she didn't hafta hurt nobody. She got Kinzoku in this headlock move...
Heh.
But oh my god, you are so into Cleo! You was so not drunk that night you kissed her! You can't fool me!
Jus' now when I said Cleo's still hung up on Vincent, you was so sad! It's so sweet...
Heh. Whatever.
THE
Come onnn, you like her for real, right?? Tell meee!
Sounds like you got it all figured out already.
I don't! Really!
Hmm, let's see... how 'bout a trade?
A trade?
Yeah. My inside info for your inside info.
Tell me what the deal is with Cleo and Vincent, what the hell the big secret is, and I'll tell you about me and Cleo.

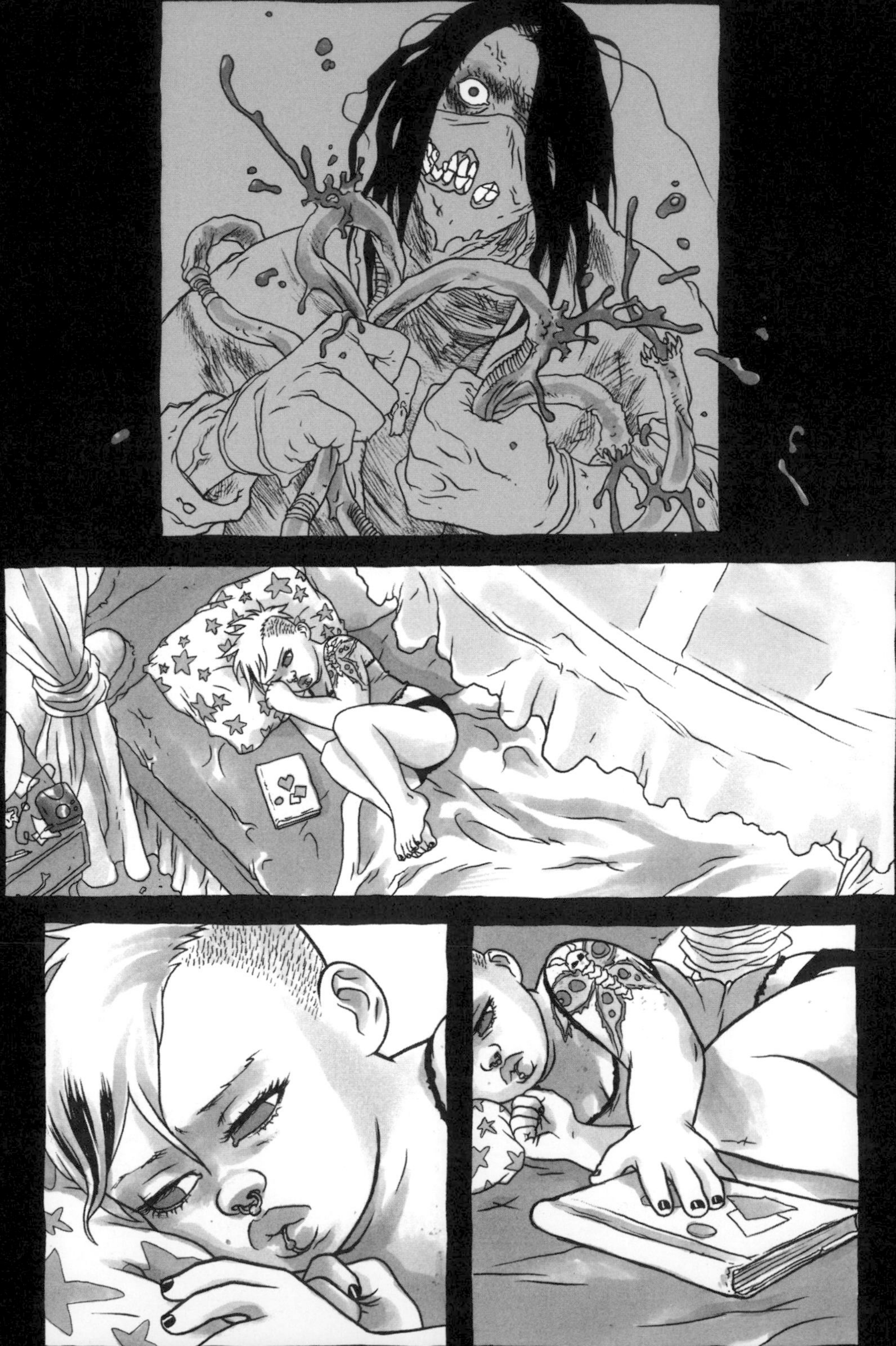

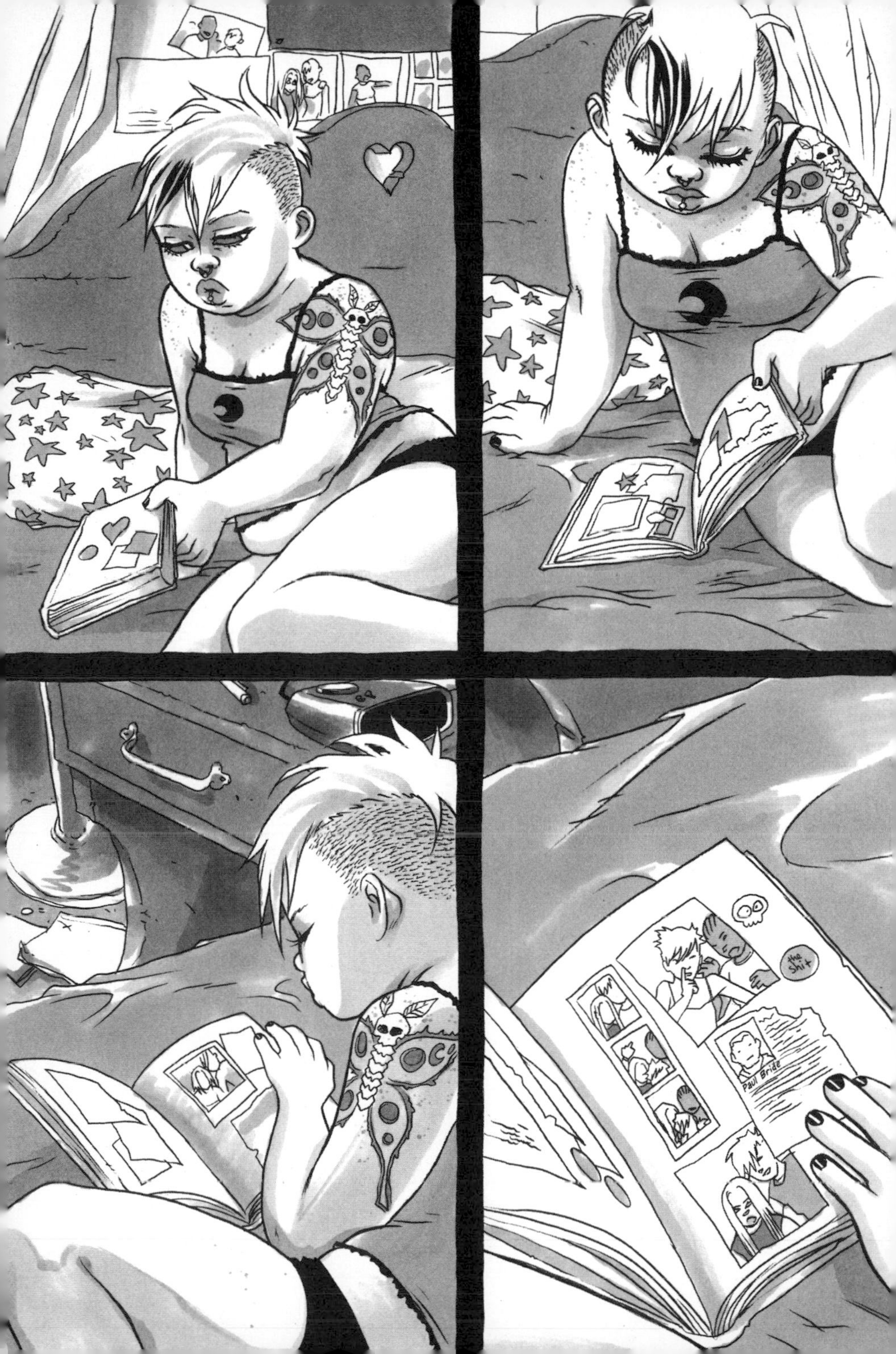
the Shit
Paul Bride

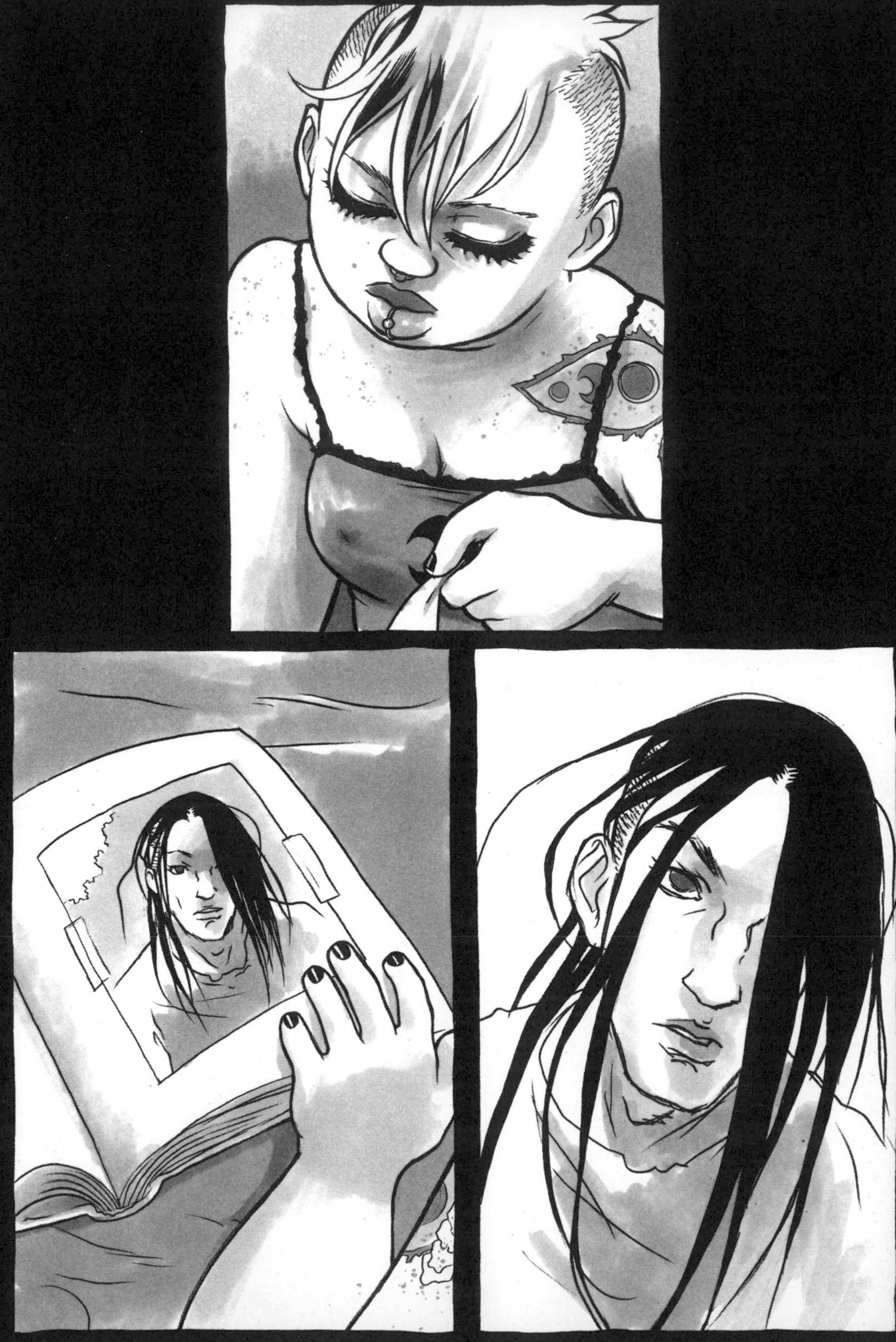

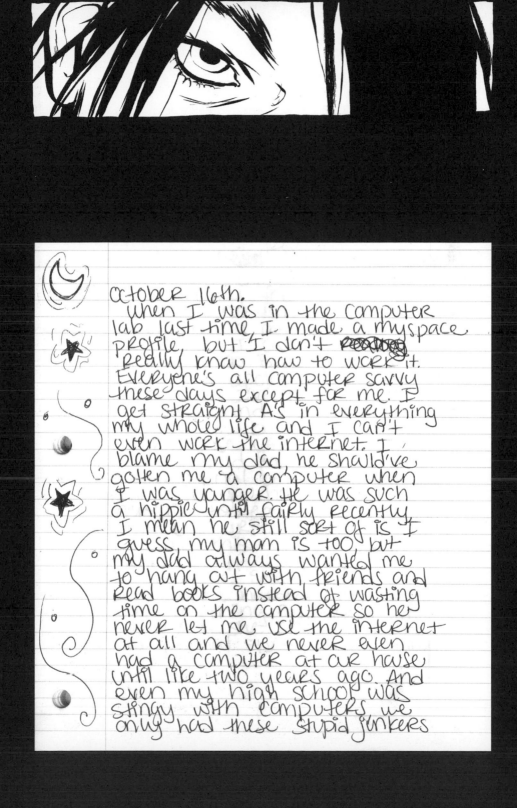

October 16th.

When I was in the computer lab last time, I made a myspace profile, but I don't ~~reeeeeeee~~ really know how to work it. Everyone's all computer savvy these days except for me. I get straight A's in everything my whole life and I can't even work the internet. I blame my dad, he should've gotten me a computer when I was younger. He was such a hippie until fairly recently, I mean he still sort of is I guess, my mom is too but my dad always wanted me to hang out with friends and read books instead of wasting time on the computer so he never let me use the internet at all and we never even had a computer at our house until like two years ago. And even my high school was stingy with computers we only had these stupid junkers

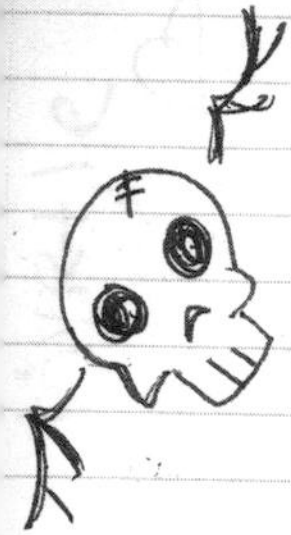

from the 70's or something. I'm so stunted. I'm probably the only person under 25 who doesn't know this shit. But I'm figuring it out really fast, so I'll be savvy in no time, too. I pretty much only made my profile so I could leave comments on Bella Morte's page and apologize for wrecking their show. I've left a couple comments and even sent them a message but there's been no response yet...

Trilby told me Mara has a livejournal but it's "friends only" so you have to be on her list to read it! I wonder what she writes about... Probably all this amazing secret stuff that she doesn't tell anyone. She's such a private person. She hardly even tells me anything anymore. But I think if she knew I read her journal she'd stop writing in it.

I have so much fun with Myrtle. She reminds me of Trilby sometimes since she's sort of bouncy and fun like Trilby is, but in a different way. She makes a lot of jokes but they're not usually at the expense of others and her sense of humor is really different. She also has this darkness to her that I can't put my finger on, but I like it. Even though she seems happy and smiley most of the time, she has a slight sadness to her. I don't want her to be sad, but when I see her show this under-the-surface sadness, it makes me smile. I smile when I think about it, too. I'm not sure if that's bad, since I suppose it's me smiling about somebody being sad, ~~and thinks it~~ and that's mean, but I don't think it's like that... It's not really a happy smile. I guess even though I am happy when she's around and everything, but it's just that I like that aspect of her and I think it's cute. It makes me want to hug her or something, and then me hugging her because of the subtle sadness and I also can't help but smile about that.

I'm taking Myrtle home on Friday to ~~have~~ a late breakfast (brunch?) with dad and Penny. I'm half scared and half excited. I hope Phyllis doesn't act crazy. I hope my dad doesn't tell horrible stories about me but I know he will so I'm prepared for the worst. I don't know if this is one of those times where your significant other meets your family and it's a big deal. things with Myrtle are strange. Actually I think I'm more excited than scared.

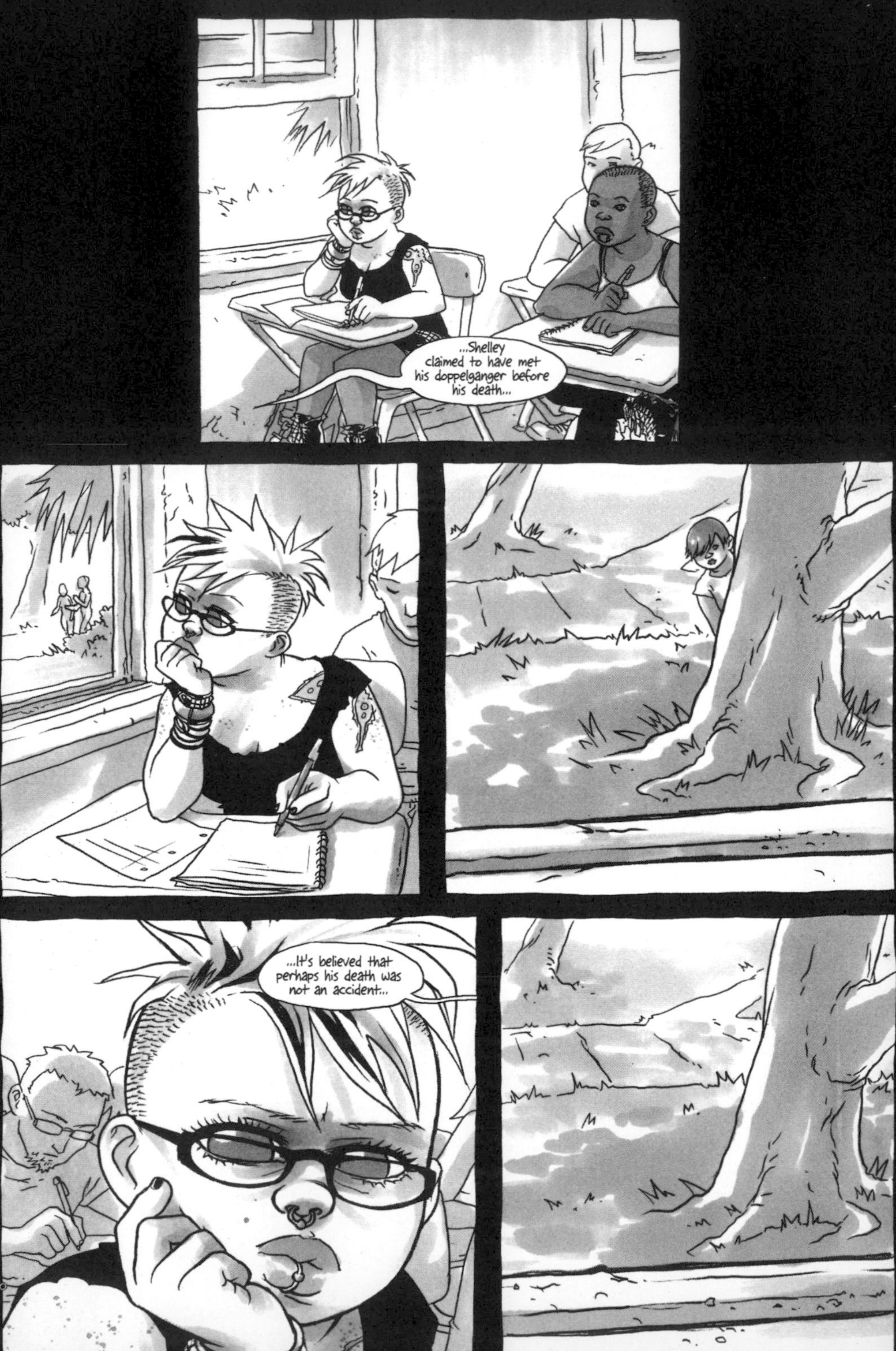
...Shelley claimed to have met his doppelganger before his death...
...It's believed that perhaps his death was not an accident...

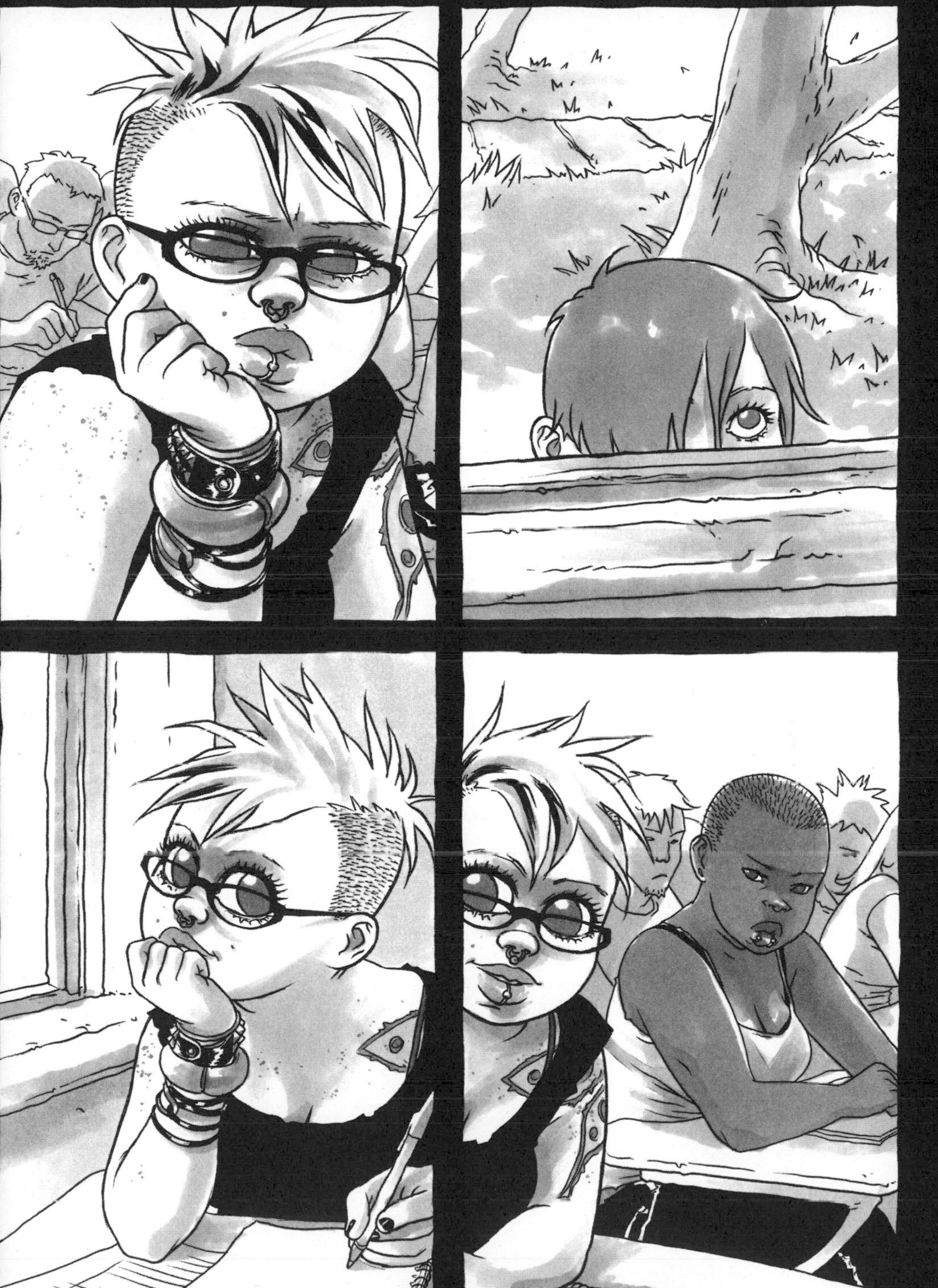

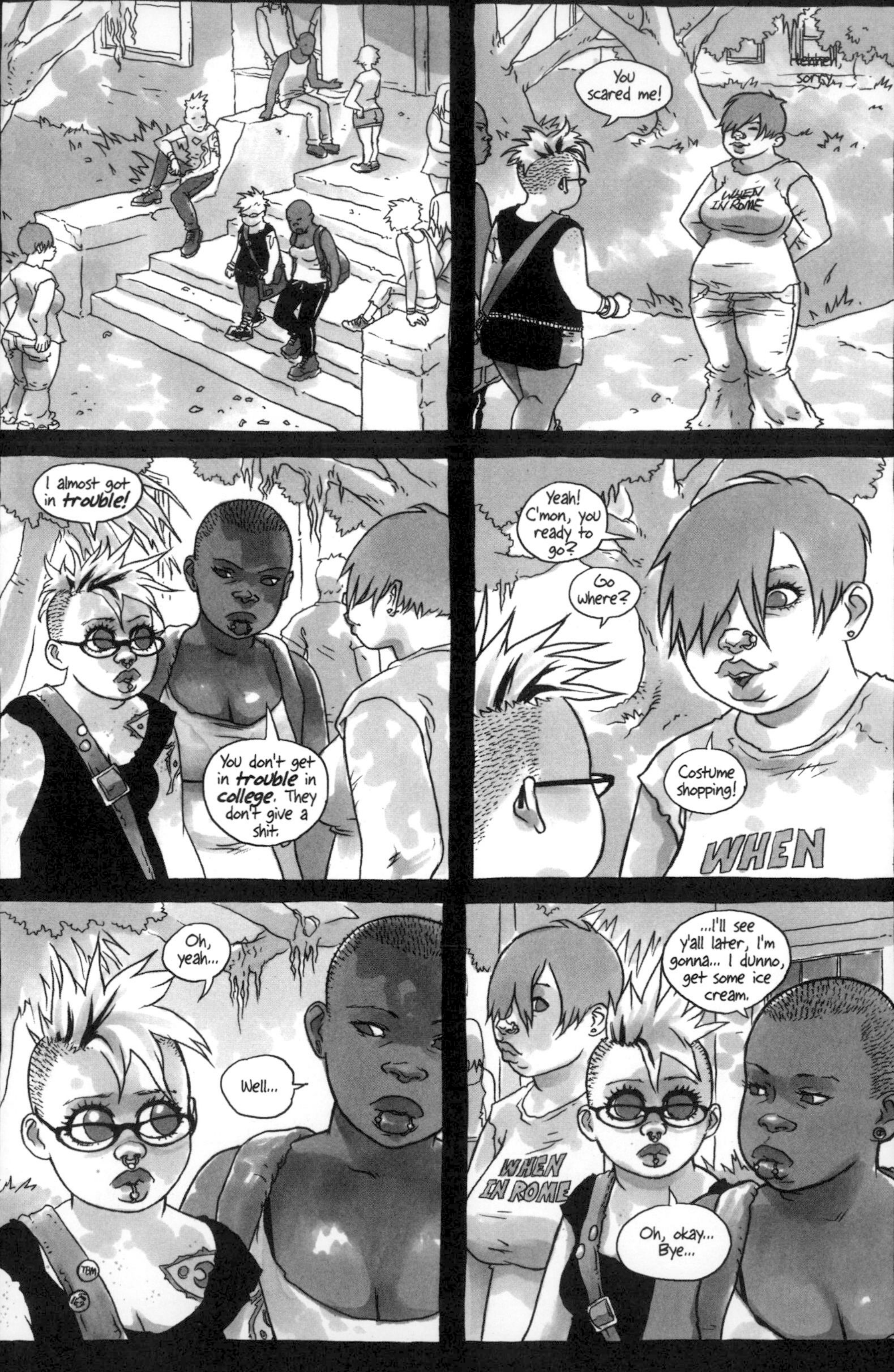
You scared me!
Heheh, sorry.
I almost got in **trouble!**
You don't get in **trouble** in **college**. They don't give a shit.
Yeah! C'mon, you ready to go?
Go where?
Costume shopping!
WHEN
Oh, yeah...
Well...
...I'll see y'all later, I'm gonna... I dunno, get some ice cream.
WHEN IN ROME
Oh, okay... Bye...

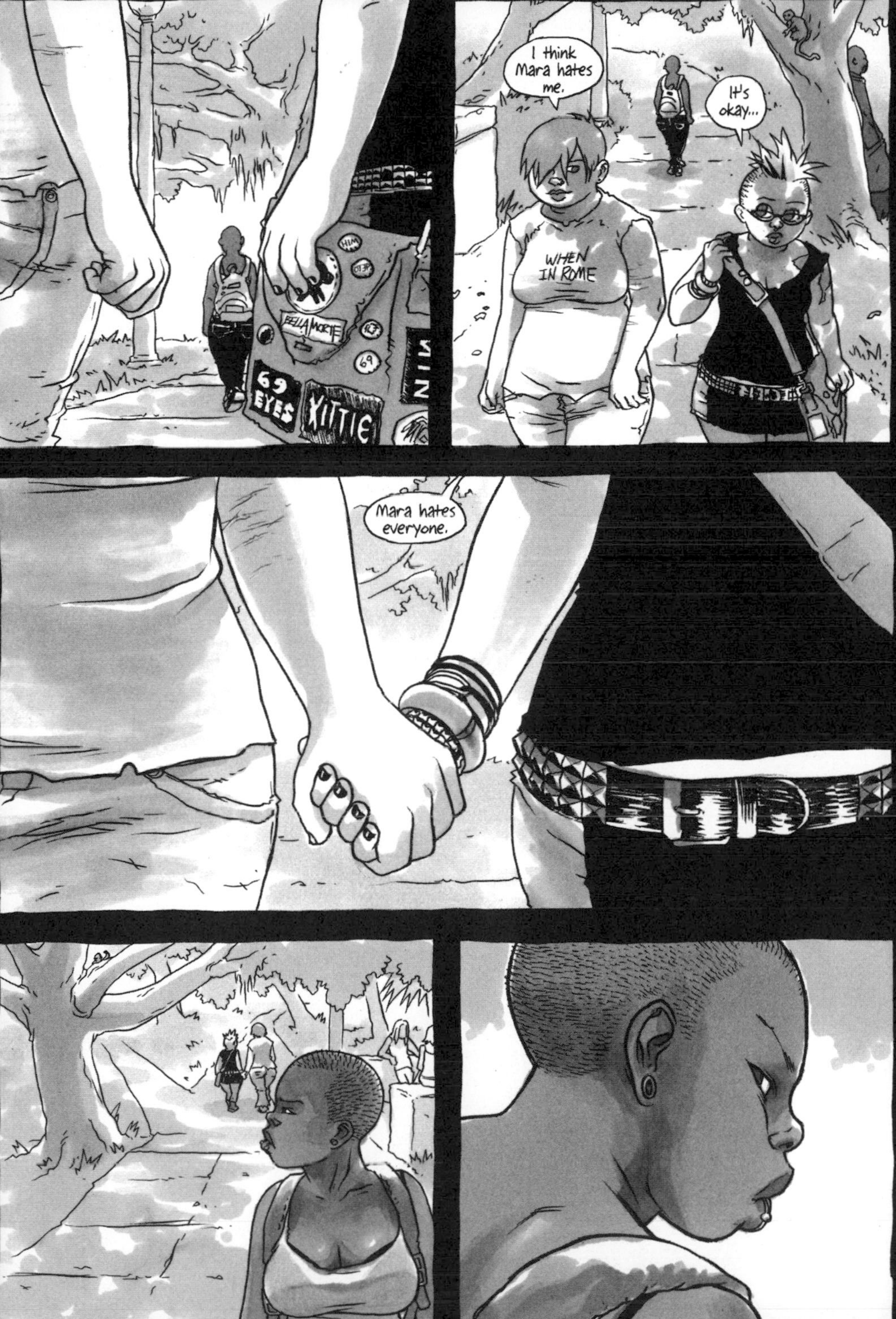
HIM
BELLA MORTE
69
69 EYES
KITTIE
I think Mara hates me.
It's okay...
WHEN IN ROME
Mara hates everyone.

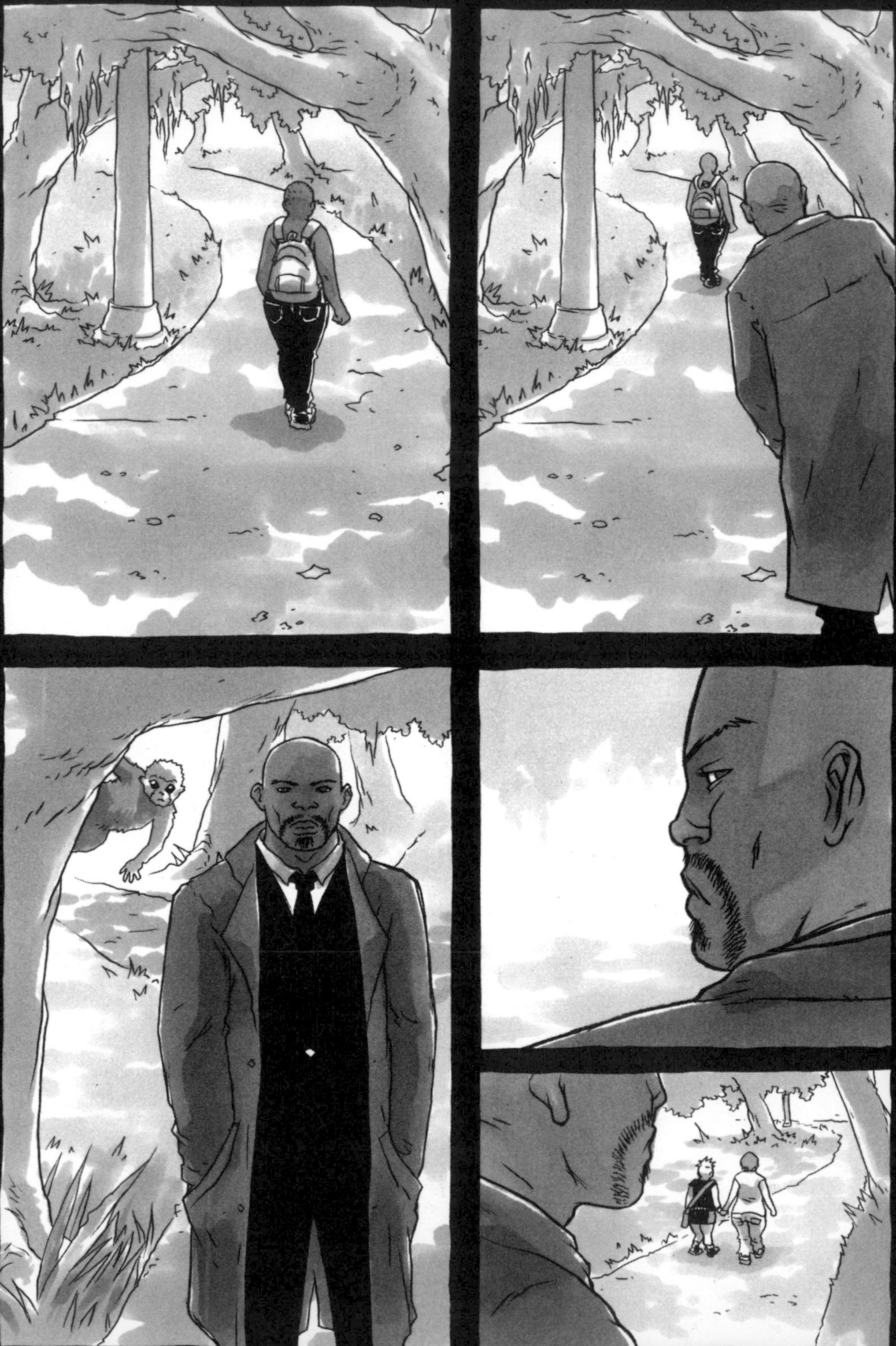

15

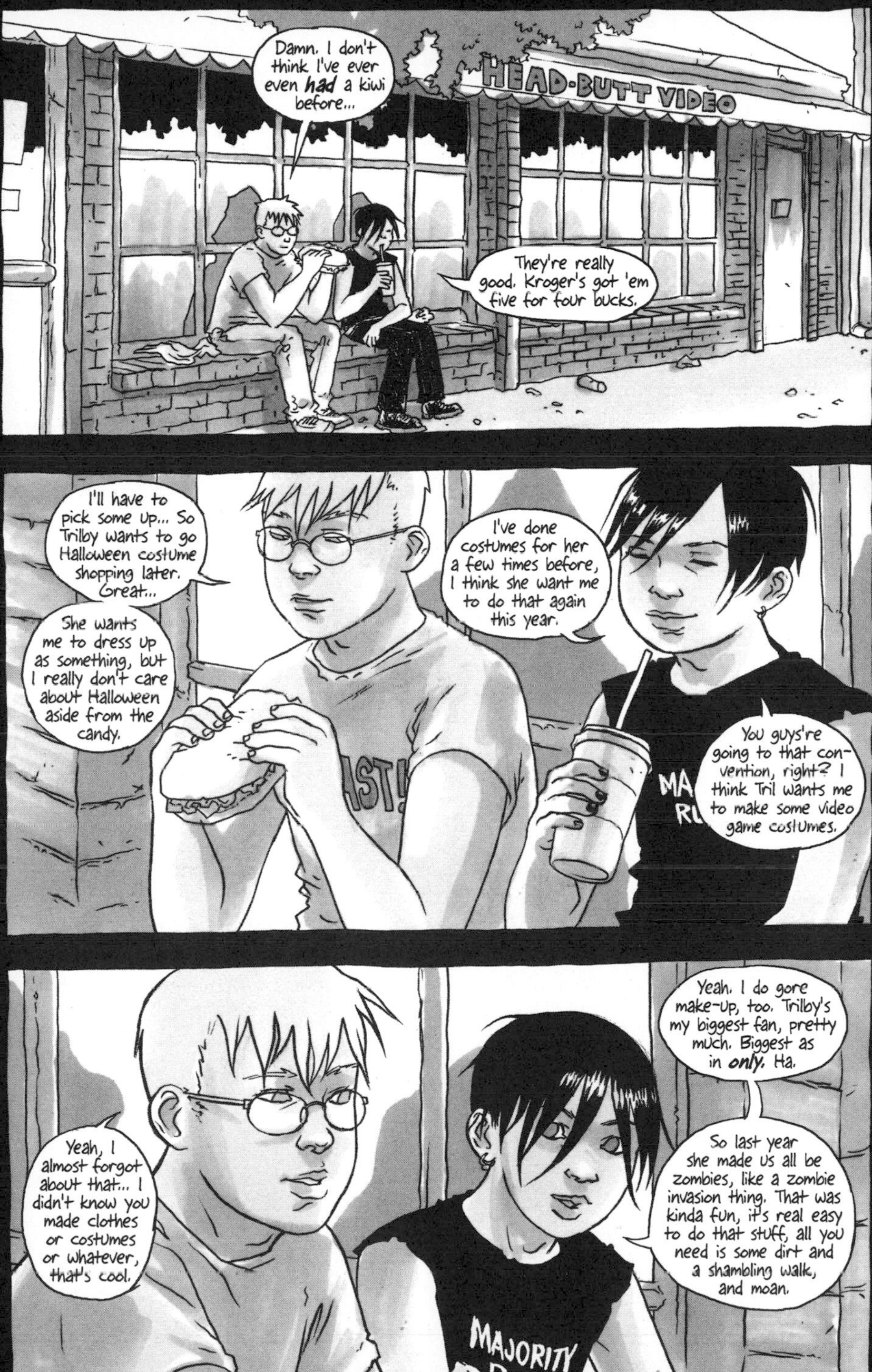
HEAD-BUTT VIDEO
Damn. I don't think I've ever even **had** a kiwi before...
They're really good. Kroger's got 'em five for four bucks.
I'll have to pick some up... So Trilby wants to go Halloween costume shopping later. Great...
She wants me to dress up as something, but I really don't care about Halloween aside from the candy.
I've done costumes for her a few times before, I think she want me to do that again this year.
You guys're going to that convention, right? I think Tril wants me to make some video game costumes.
Yeah, I almost forgot about that... I didn't know you made clothes or costumes or whatever, that's cool.
Yeah. I do gore make-up, too. Trilby's my biggest fan, pretty much. Biggest as in **only**. Ha.
So last year she made us all be zombies, like a zombie invasion thing. That was kinda fun, it's real easy to do that stuff, all you need is some dirt and a shambling walk, and moan.
MAJORITY

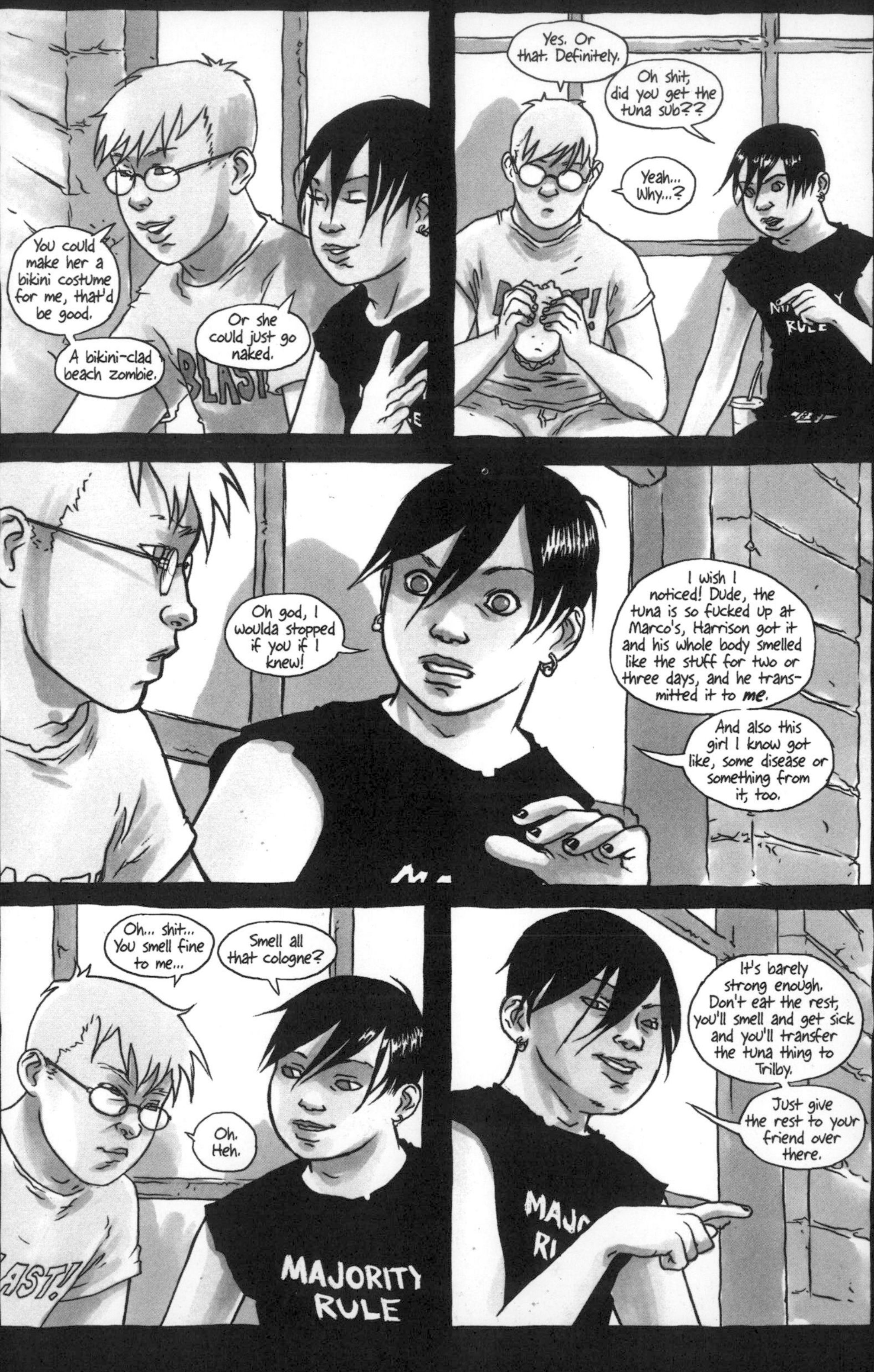
You could make her a bikini costume for me, that'd be good.
A bikini-clad beach zombie.
Or she could just go naked.
BLAST
Yes. Or that. Definitely.
Oh shit, did you get the tuna sub??
Yeah... Why...?
RULE
Oh god, I woulda stopped if you if I knew!
I wish I noticed! Dude, the tuna is so fucked up at Marco's, Harrison got it and his whole body smelled like the stuff for two or three days, and he transmitted it to ***me***.
And also this girl I know got like, some disease or something from it, too.
Oh... shit... You smell fine to me...
Smell all that cologne?
Oh. Heh.
MAJORITY RULE
It's barely strong enough. Don't eat the rest, you'll smell and get sick and you'll transfer the tuna thing to Trilby.
Just give the rest to your friend over there.

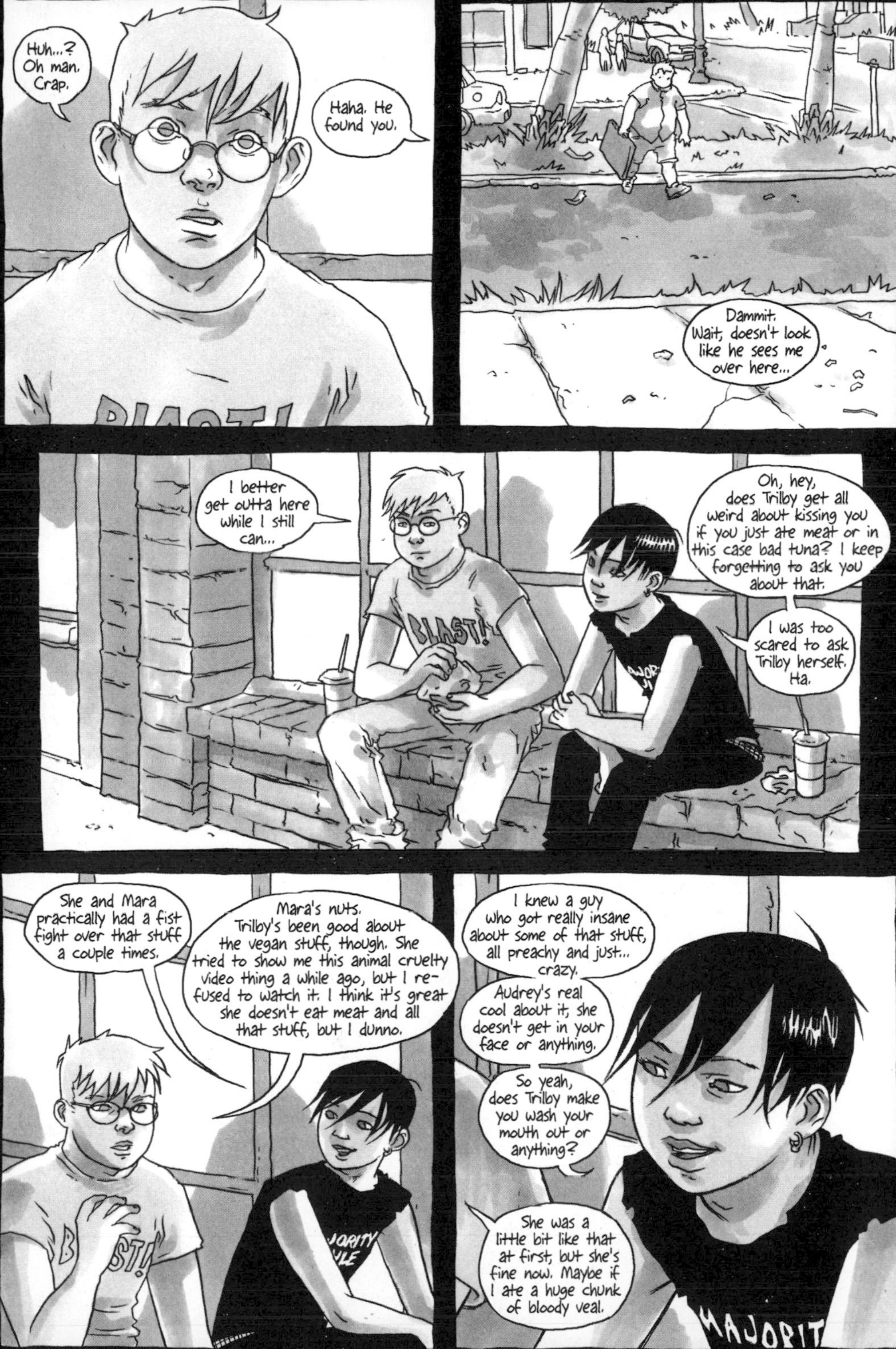
Huh...? Oh man. Crap.
Haha. He found you.
Dammit. Wait, doesn't look like he sees me over here...
I better get outta here while I still can...
Oh, hey, does Trilby get all weird about kissing you if you just ate meat or in this case bad tuna? I keep forgetting to ask you about that.
I was too scared to ask Trilby herself. Ha.
She and Mara practically had a fist fight over that stuff a couple times.
Mara's nuts. Trilby's been good about the vegan stuff, though. She tried to show me this animal cruelty video thing a while ago, but I refused to watch it. I think it's great she doesn't eat meat and all that stuff, but I dunno.
I knew a guy who got really insane about some of that stuff, all preachy and just... crazy.
Audrey's real cool about it, she doesn't get in your face or anything.
So yeah, does Trilby make you wash your mouth out or anything?
She was a little bit like that at first, but she's fine now. Maybe if I ate a huge chunk of bloody veal.

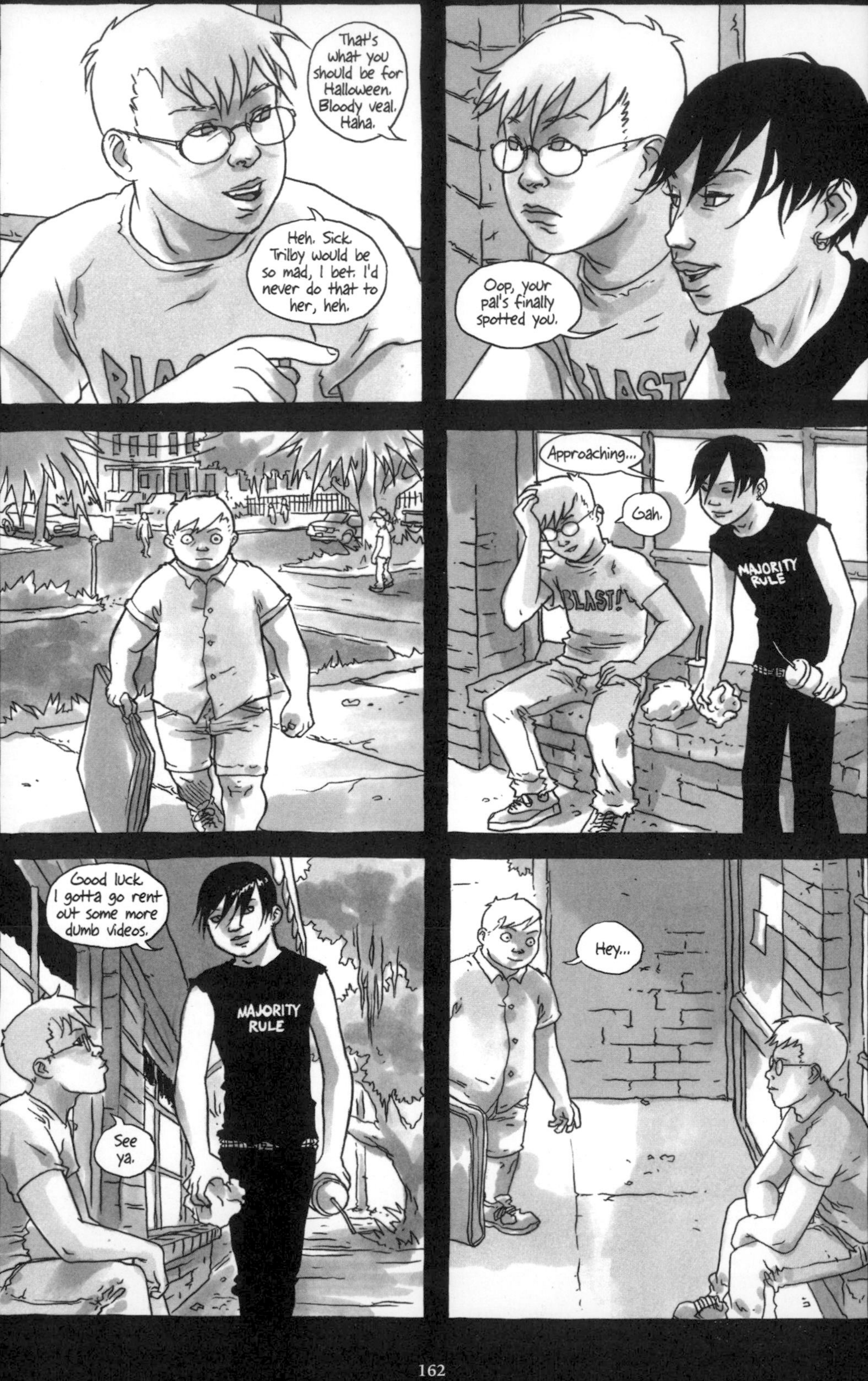
That's what you should be for Halloween. Bloody veal. Haha.
BLAS
Heh. Sick. Trilby would be so mad, I bet. I'd never do that to her, heh.
Oop, your pal's finally spotted you.
BLAST
Approaching...
Gah.
BLAST!
MAJORITY RULE
Good luck. I gotta go rent out some more dumb videos.
MAJORITY RULE
See ya.
Hey...

The Wonders At Your Feet

[friendtoroaches@gmail.com]

Recent Entries   Archive   Friends   User Info

mara's journal

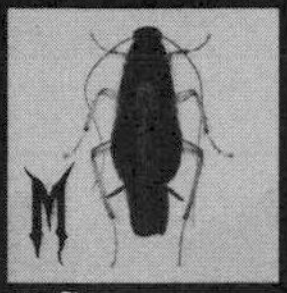

profile

October 16th, 3:47pm

THIS RIVER BANK HOLDS SECRETS

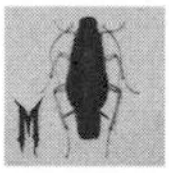

today i got up around 2pm, that's a good start. Cleo is seeing this girl Myrtle, i've mentioned her before. i didn't really think about it at first but i'm pretty much positive now that it's a romantic thing between them. Myrtle actually came up to the window in our European Romanticism class to bug Cleo. who does that? then after that i saw them holding hands. i guess it's cool. i think i'm going to start playing softball again. i walked past the field today and i got all nostalgic and remembering when i used to play. me and Trilby both played and i know Trilby still does so that might be weird with her on the team too. but i know i should really do this, i'm going to tryouts next week. i used to hit some killer home runs. it'll be great to be playing for the Wet Moon Worm Lizards again. maybe this means i'll have to stop smoking.

Trilby being with Martin, Cleo with Myrtle and Audrey with Beth sort of half makes me want to be with someone too, like this subconscious, passive peer pressure. nobody's actively trying to get me to do anything, but it's this presence that's still there. i like being the one single girl though, there's something appealing about it. when all my friends are off with their significant others i'm pretty much left alone, and while i sort of know my roomate Claire i don't really have anyone else to hang out with but i kind of like that, being forced to be by myself and entertain myself. it gives me a lot of time to do things i'd never normally do or read things i wouldn't normally think of to read. there's something also really cool about going out to eat by yourself. either in a restaurant or the dining hall. or even getting takeout alone is cool. i can't imagine myself dating anyone right now anyway, i can't imagine how anyone could really pull me out of this. everyone always rubs me the wrong way or i piss them off and everything goes down the shitter so i might as well keep to myself for now.

mood: nostalgic
current music: thismeansyou - river

[0 comments | leave a comment]

October 13th, 11:32pm

INTRUDER ALERT

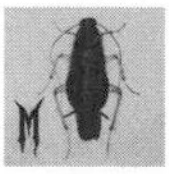

i slept all day. i got up and it was past 10 o'clock. i haven't done that in a long time, i used to sleep this late during summer vacation in high school sometimes, but hardly ever anymore. it's a real weird feeling, i can't explain it... it's like you missed something but you don't know what it is and you never will, and you know that you never will, too, so you can't worry about it. and there's something weird but great about after you get up this ridculously late, you take a shower like it's a normal morning. it's both uncomfortable and satisfying at the same time. that's what i just did. i took out a lot of my piercings too, it seemed like the right thing to do, i was getting sick of them... sometimes lately i feel like i don't know who i am anymore. i know that sounds totally lame and emo or whatever, but it's true and i can't lie about it. it seems like once college started, or maybe over the summer after senior year of high school, that everybody started to change real quick except for me. when i think about it, i guess Cleo and Trilby and Audrey are all basically the same, but it doesn't feel like it.

Cleo's been changing a lot in the past few years, so it wasn't a big jump for her, but now i feel like she's all popular or something which is why she's never home. but it's not like she's meeting all these new people, she still hangs out with Trilby,

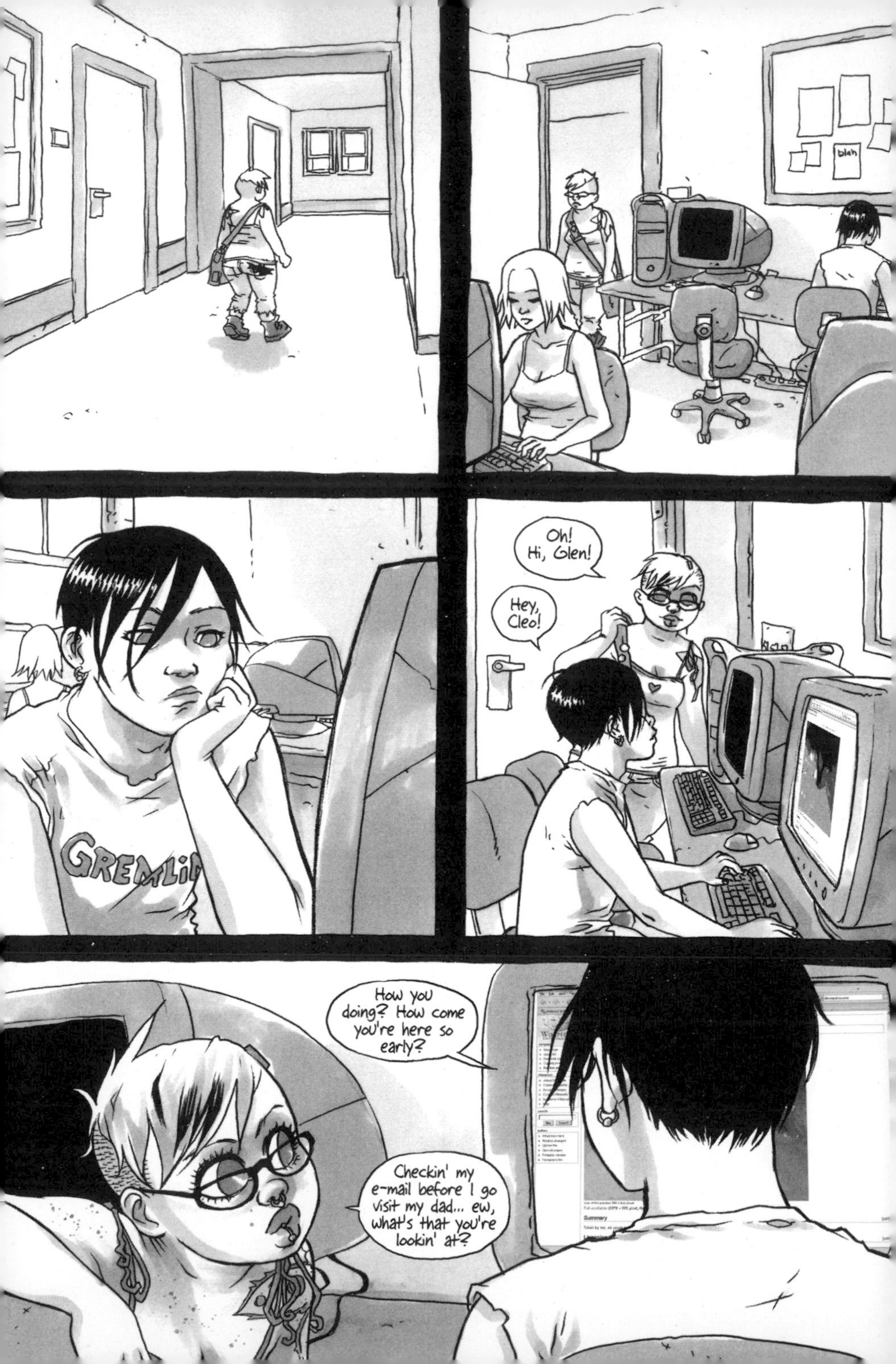
blah
Oh! Hi, Glen!
Hey, Cleo!
GREMLIN
How you doing? How come you're here so early?
Checkin' my e-mail before I go visit my dad... ew, what's that you're lookin' at?

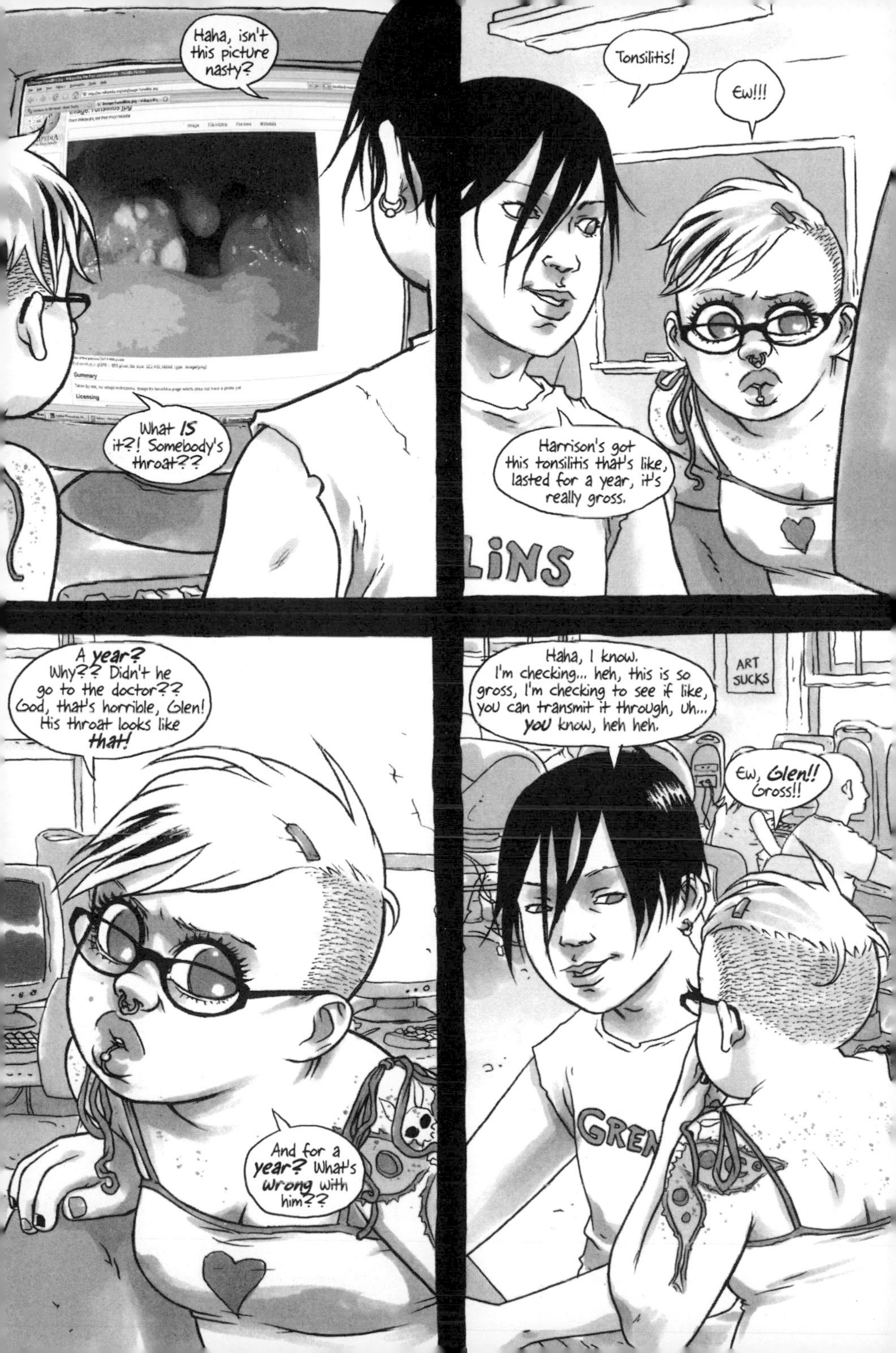
Haha, isn't this picture nasty?
What IS it?! Somebody's throat??
Tonsilitis!
Ew!!!
Harrison's got this tonsilitis that's like, lasted for a year, it's really gross.
LINS
A year? Why?? Didn't he go to the doctor?? God, that's horrible, Glen! His throat looks like that!
And for a year? What's wrong with him??
Haha, I know. I'm checking... heh, this is so gross, I'm checking to see if like, you can transmit it through, uh... you know, heh heh.
ART SUCKS
Ew, Glen!! Gross!!
GREN

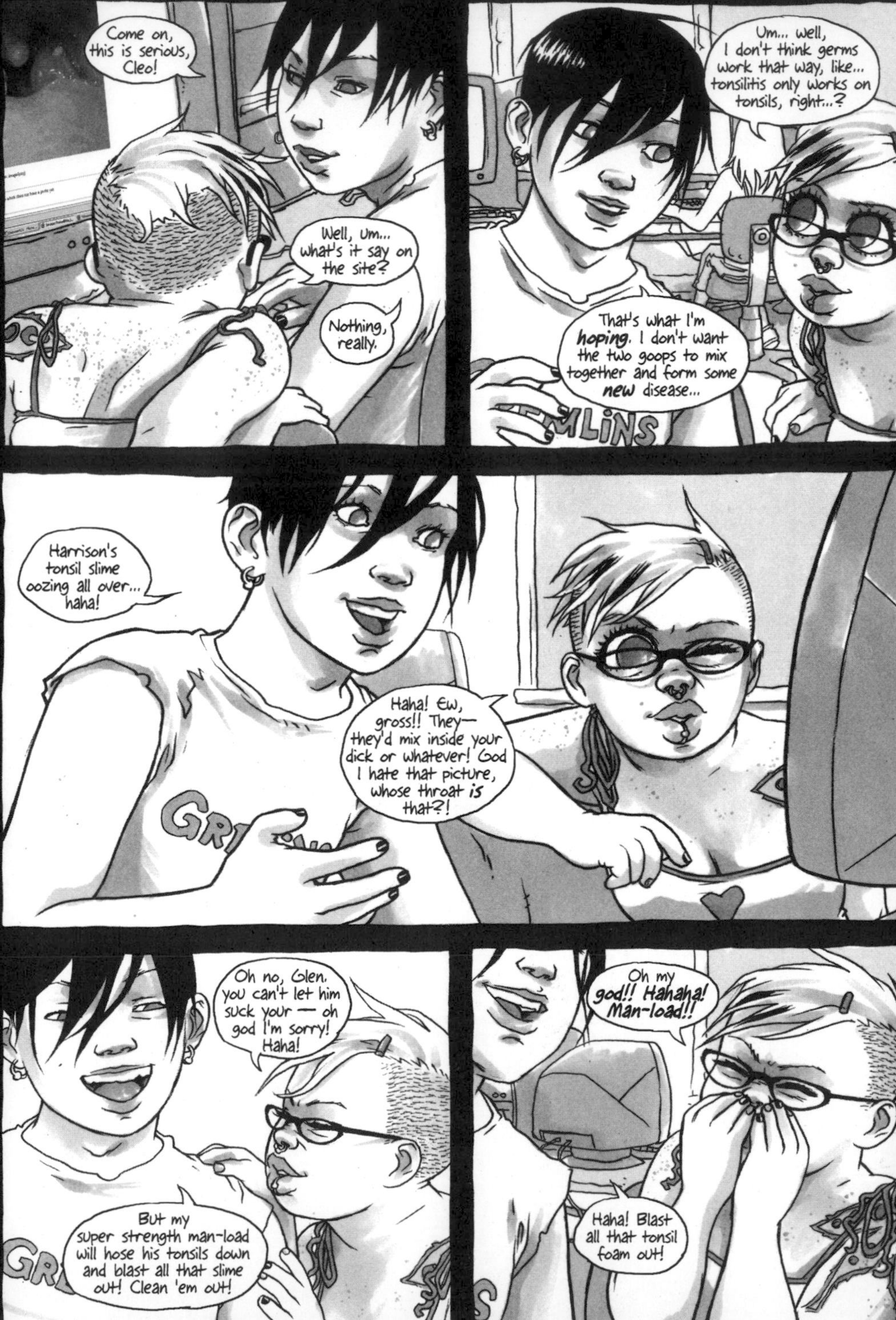
Come on, this is serious, Cleo!
Well, um... what's it say on the site?
Nothing, really.
Um... well, I don't think germs work that way, like... tonsilitis only works on tonsils, right...?
That's what I'm **hoping**. I don't want the two goops to mix together and form some **new** disease...
Harrison's tonsil slime oozing all over... haha!
Haha! Ew, gross!! They— they'd mix inside your dick or whatever! God I hate that picture, whose throat **is** that?!
Oh no, Glen. you can't let him suck your — oh god I'm sorry! Haha!
But my super strength man-load will hose his tonsils down and blast all that slime out! Clean 'em out!
Oh my **god!! Hahaha! Man-load!!**
Haha! Blast all that tonsil foam out!

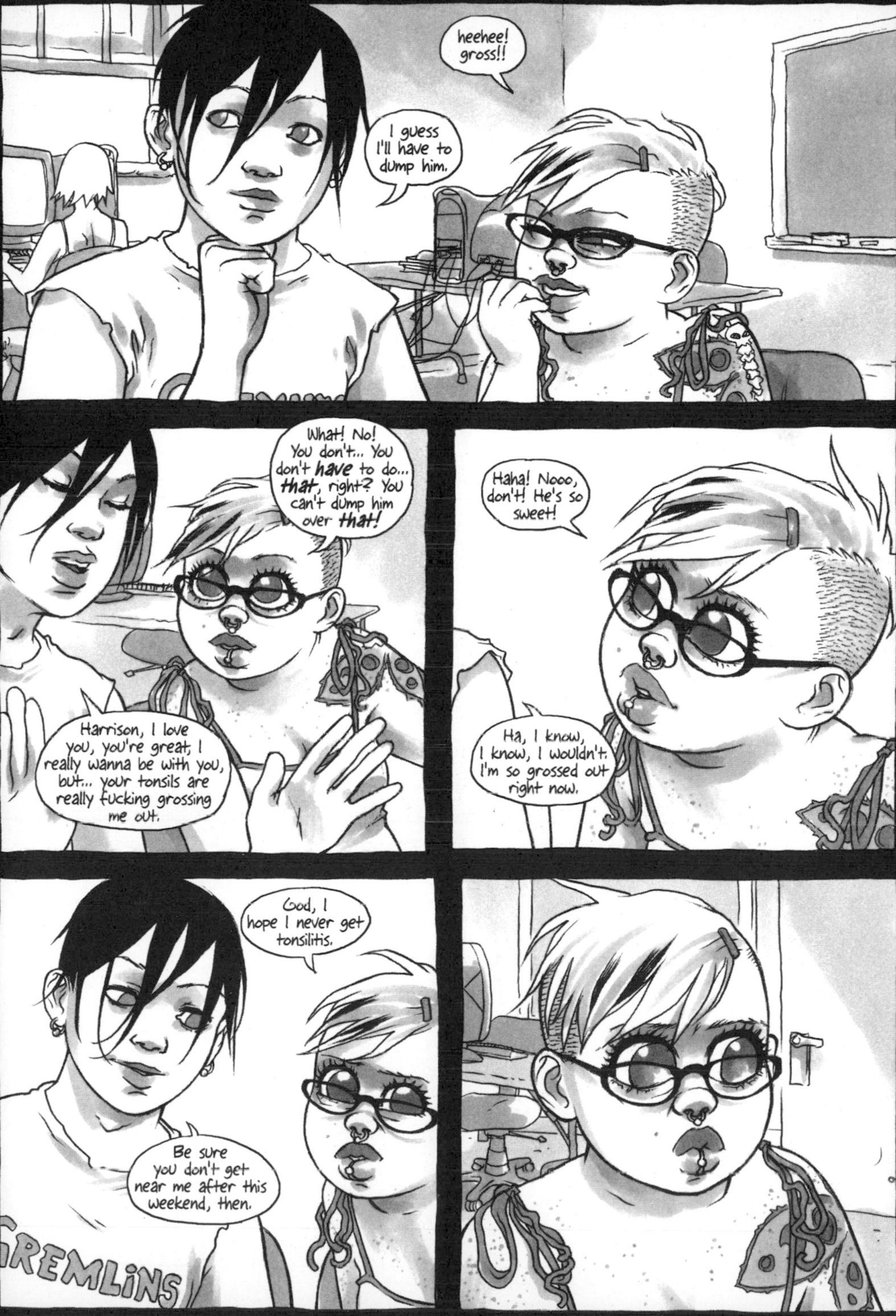

heehee! gross!!
I guess I'll have to dump him.
What! No! You don't... You don't **have** to do... **that**, right? You can't dump him over **that!**
Harrison, I love you, you're great, I really wanna be with you, but... your tonsils are really fucking grossing me out.
Haha! Nooo, don't! He's so sweet!
Ha, I know, I know, I wouldn't. I'm so grossed out right now.
God, I hope I never get tonsilitis.
Be sure you don't get near me after this weekend, then.
GREMLINS

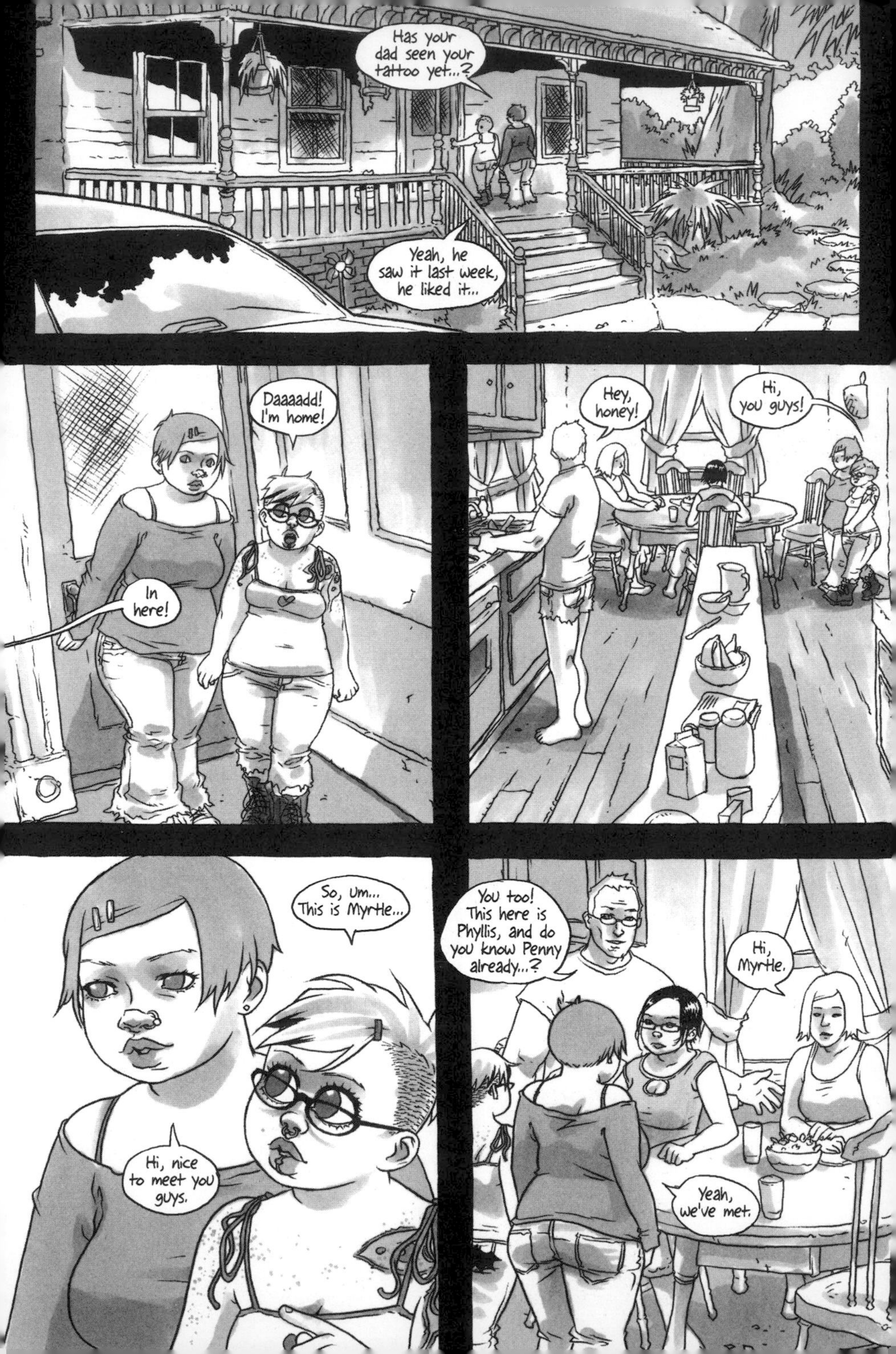
Has your dad seen your tattoo yet...?
Yeah, he saw it last week, he liked it...
Daaaadd! I'm home!
In here!
Hey, honey!
Hi, you guys!
So, Um... This is Myrtle...
Hi, nice to meet you guys.
You too! This here is Phyllis, and do you know Penny already...?
Hi, Myrtle.
Yeah, we've met.

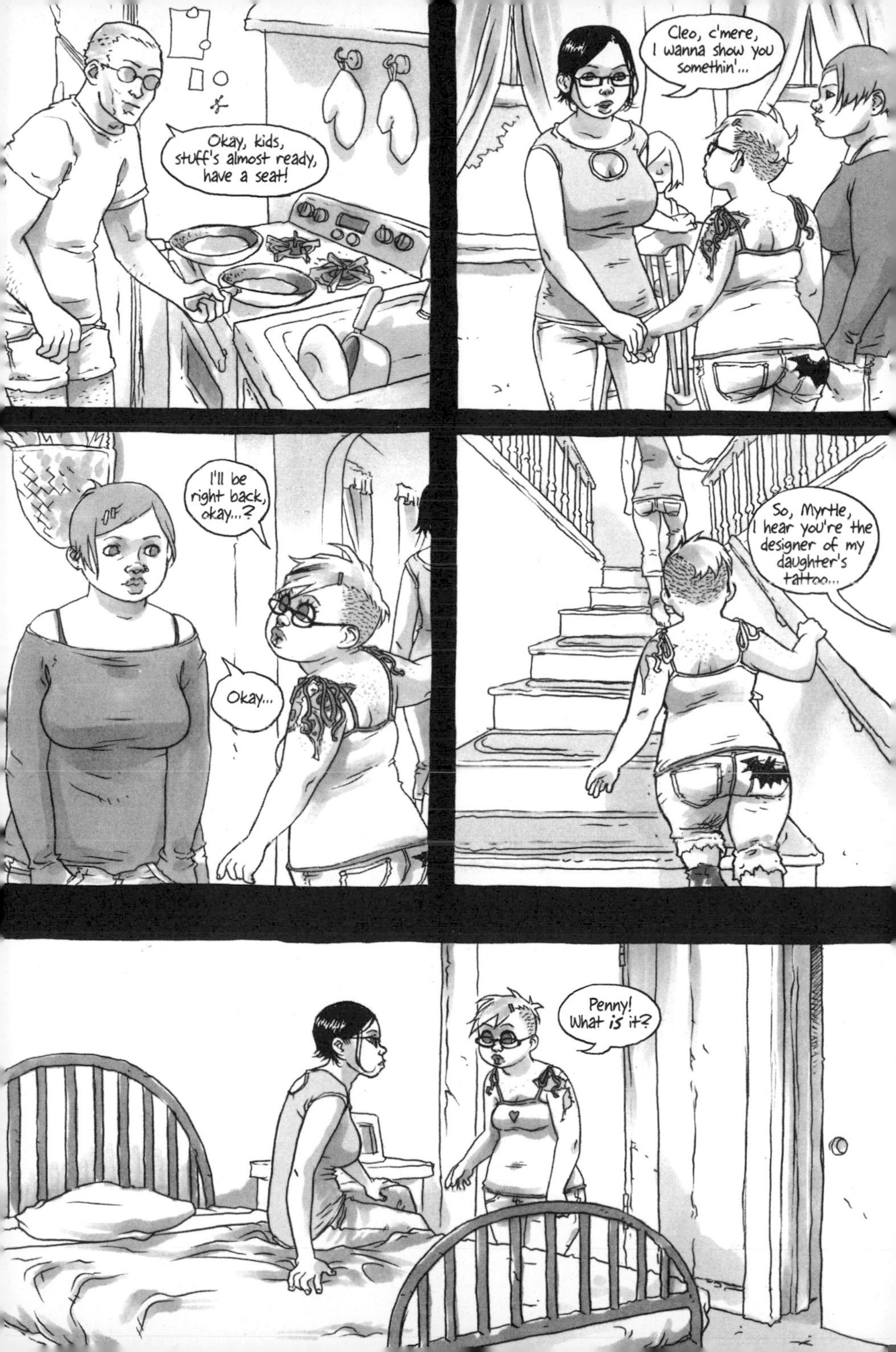
Okay, kids, stuff's almost ready, have a seat!
Cleo, c'mere, I wanna show you somethin'...
I'll be right back, okay...?
Okay...
So, Myrtle, I hear you're the designer of my daughter's tattoo...
Penny! What *is* it?

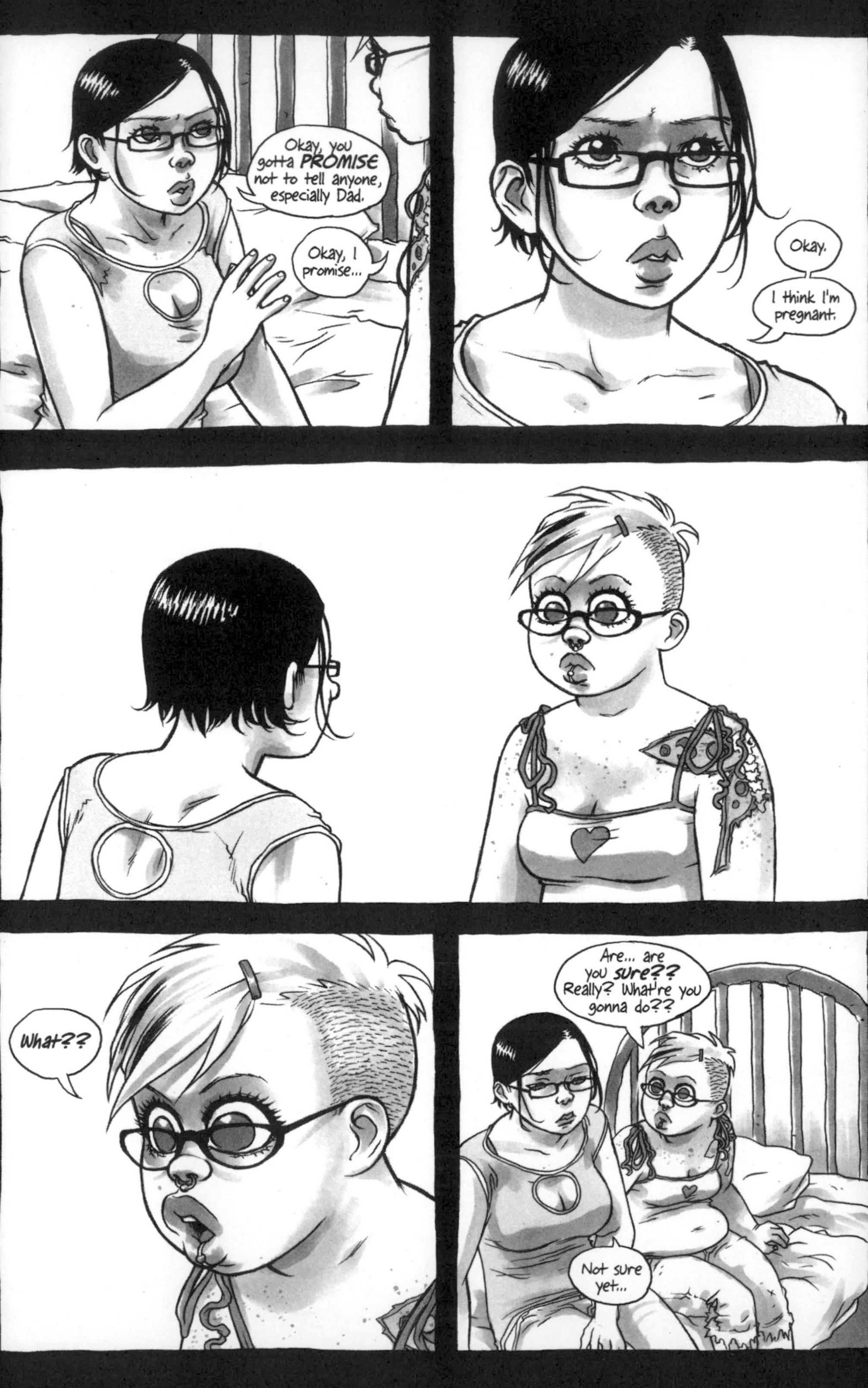
Okay, you gotta PROMISE not to tell anyone, especially Dad.
Okay, I promise...
Okay.
I think I'm pregnant.
What??
Are... are you sure?? Really? What're you gonna do??
Not sure yet...

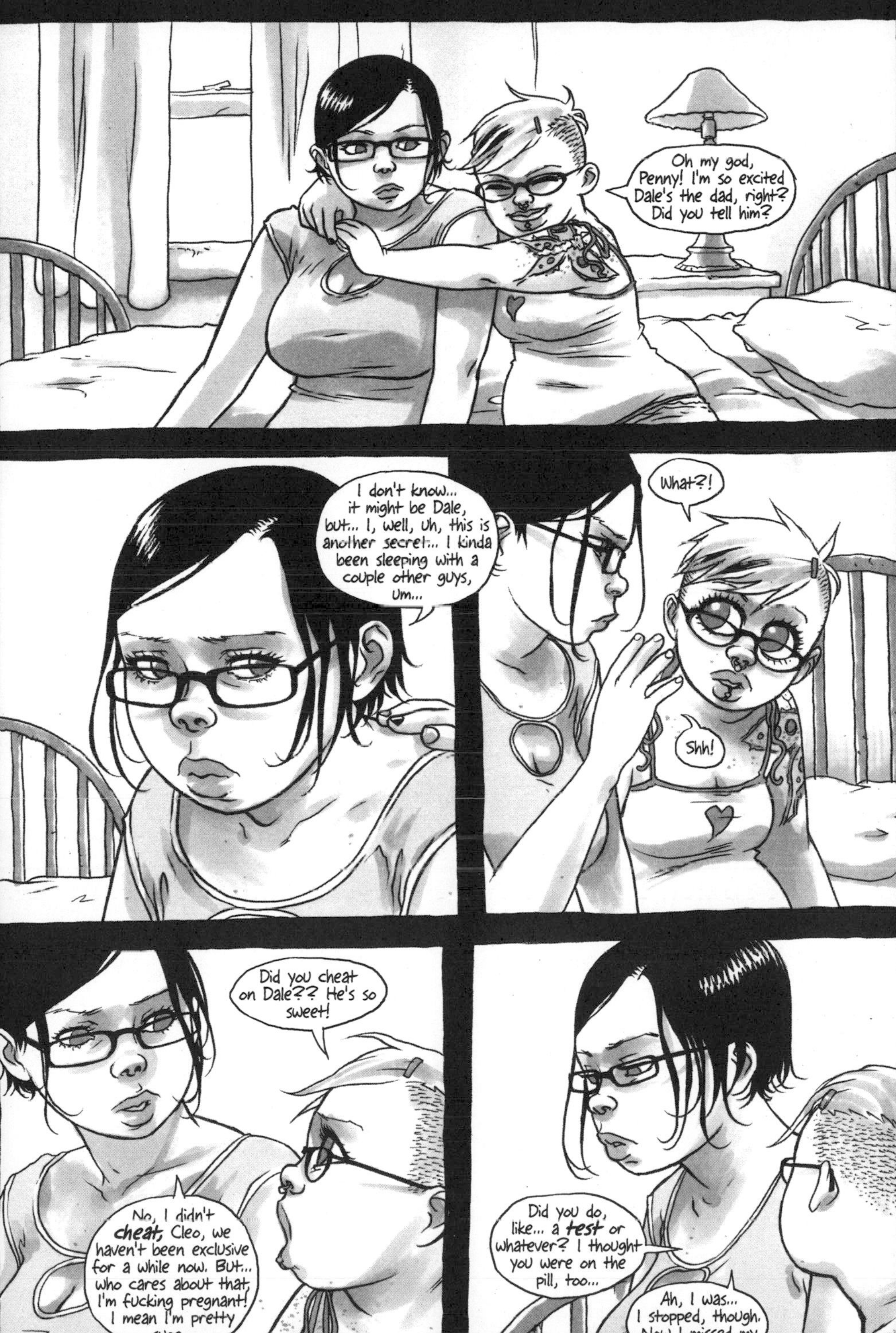
Oh my god, Penny! I'm so excited Dale's the dad, right? Did you tell him?
I don't know... it might be Dale, but... I, well, uh, this is another secret... I kinda been sleeping with a couple other guys, um...
What?!
Shh!
Did you cheat on Dale?? He's so sweet!
No, I didn't **cheat,** Cleo, we haven't been exclusive for a while now. But... who cares about that, I'm fucking pregnant! I mean I'm pretty sure...
Did you do, like... a **test** or whatever? I thought you were on the pill, too...
Ah, I was... I stopped, though. Now I missed my period...

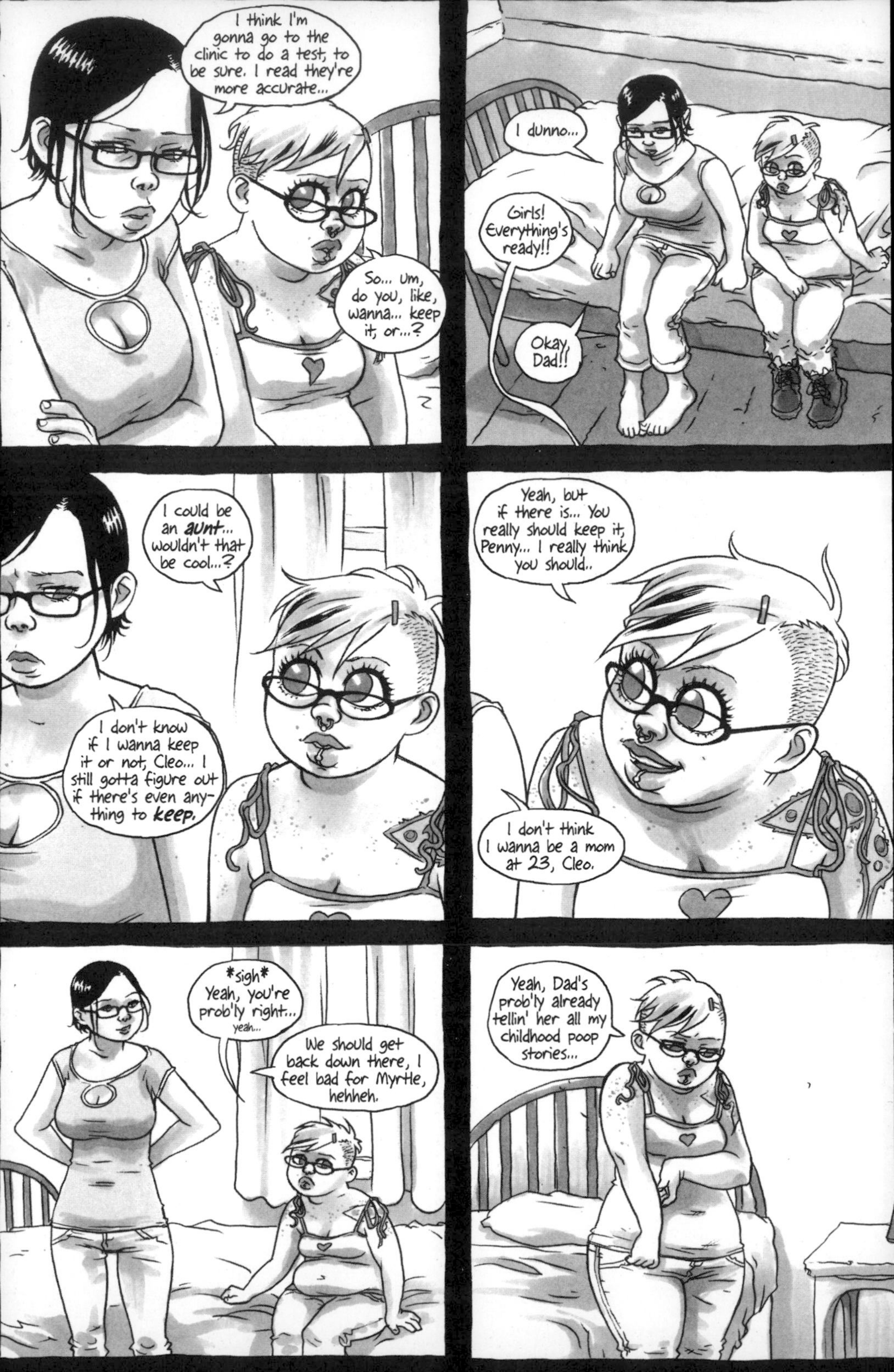
I think I'm gonna go to the clinic to do a test, to be sure. I read they're more accurate...
So... um, do you, like, wanna... keep it, or...?
I dunno...
Girls! Everything's ready!!
Okay, Dad!!
I could be an **aunt**... wouldn't that be cool...?
I don't know if I wanna keep it or not, Cleo... I still gotta figure out if there's even anything to **keep**.
Yeah, but if there is... You really should keep it, Penny... I really think you should..
I don't think I wanna be a mom at 23, Cleo.
sigh Yeah, you're prob'ly right... yeah...
We should get back down there, I feel bad for Myrtle, hehheh.
Yeah, Dad's prob'ly already tellin' her all my childhood poop stories...

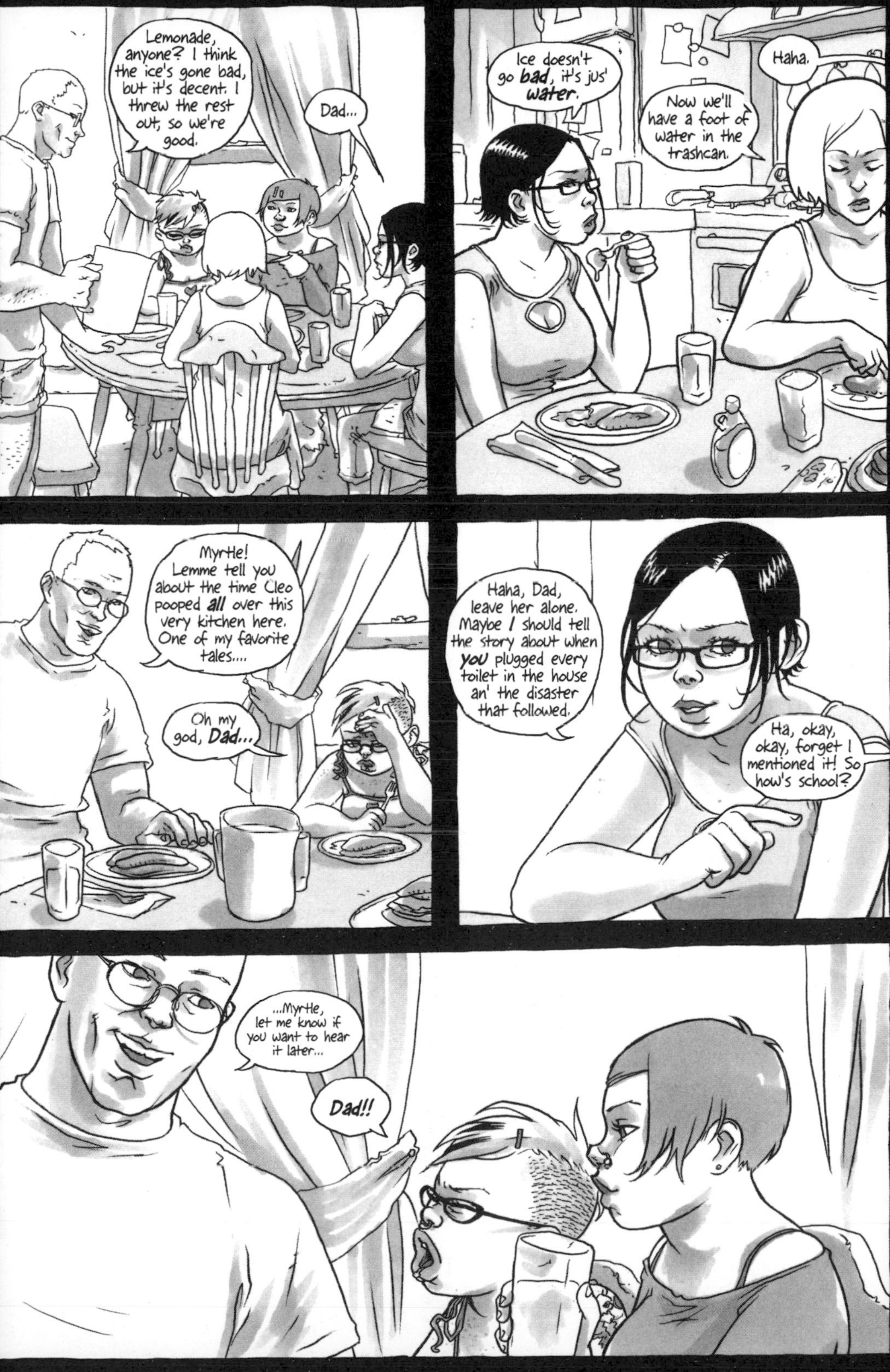
Lemonade, anyone? I think the ice's gone bad, but it's decent. I threw the rest out, so we're good.
Dad...
Ice doesn't go **bad**, it's jus' **water**.
Haha.
Now we'll have a foot of water in the trashcan.
Myrtle! Lemme tell you about the time Cleo pooped **all** over this very kitchen here. One of my favorite tales....
Oh my god, **Dad...**
Haha, Dad, leave her alone. Maybe **I** should tell the story about when **you** plugged every toilet in the house an' the disaster that followed.
Ha, okay, okay, forget I mentioned it! So how's school?
...Myrtle, let me know if you want to hear it later...
Dad!!

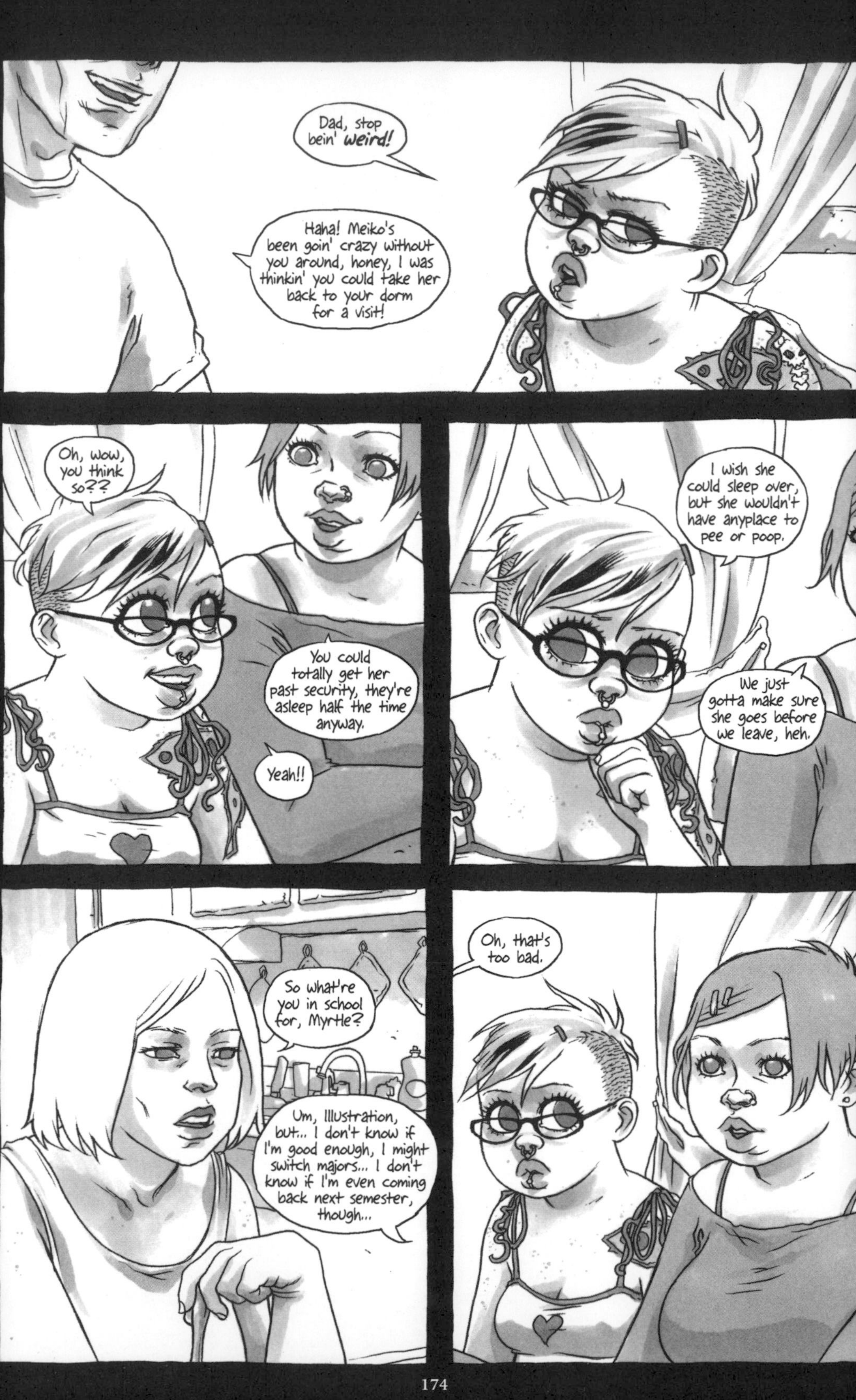
Dad, stop bein' weird!
Haha! Meiko's been goin' crazy without you around, honey, I was thinkin' you could take her back to your dorm for a visit!
Oh, wow, you think so??
You could totally get her past security, they're asleep half the time anyway.
Yeah!!
I wish she could sleep over, but she wouldn't have anyplace to pee or poop.
We just gotta make sure she goes before we leave, heh.
So what're you in school for, Myrtle?
Um, Illustration, but... I don't know if I'm good enough, I might switch majors... I don't know if I'm even coming back next semester, though...
Oh, that's too bad.

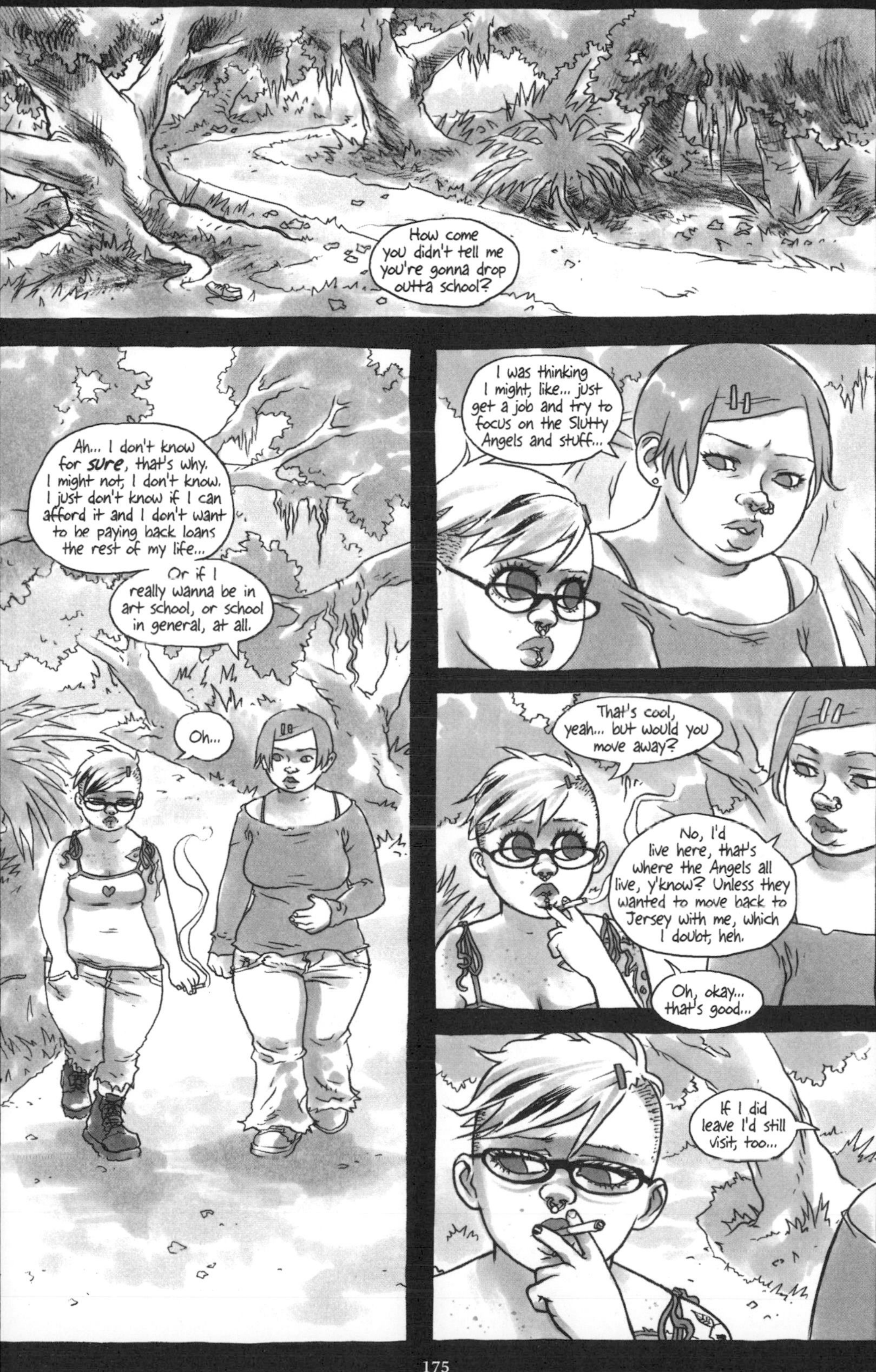
How come you didn't tell me you're gonna drop outta school?
Ah... I don't know for **sure**, that's why. I might not, I don't know. I just don't know if I can afford it and I don't want to be paying back loans the rest of my life...
Or if I really wanna be in art school, or school in general, at all.
Oh...
I was thinking I might, like... just get a job and try to focus on the Slutty Angels and stuff...
That's cool, yeah... but would you move away?
No, I'd live here, that's where the Angels all live, y'know? Unless they wanted to move back to Jersey with me, which I doubt, heh.
Oh, okay... that's good...
If I did leave I'd still visit, too...

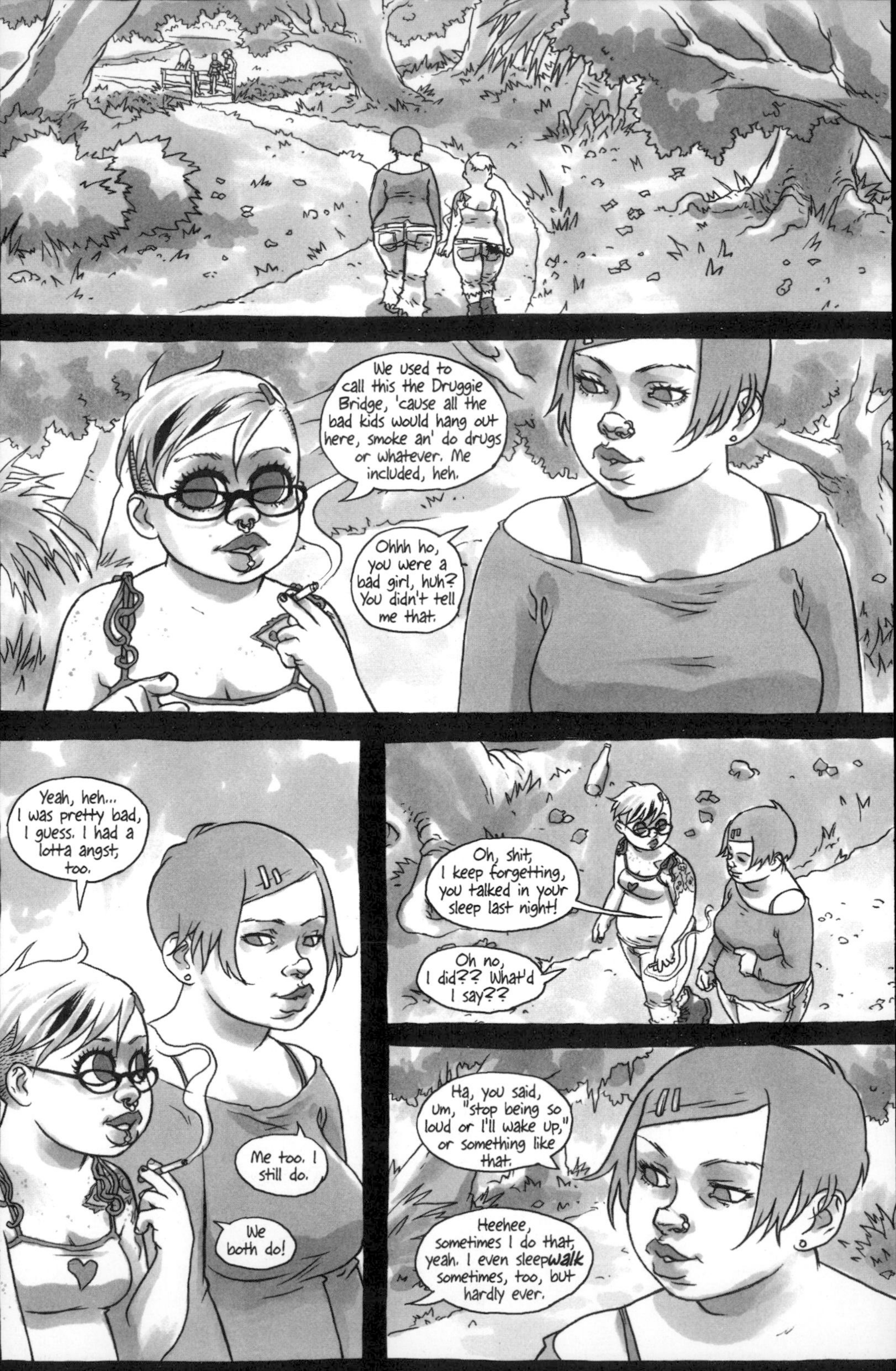
We used to call this the Druggie Bridge, 'cause all the bad kids would hang out here, smoke an' do drugs or whatever. Me included, heh.
Ohhh ho, you were a bad girl, huh? You didn't tell me that.
Yeah, heh... I was pretty bad, I guess. I had a lotta angst, too.
Me too. I still do.
We both do!
Oh, shit, I keep forgetting, you talked in your sleep last night!
Oh no, I did?? What'd I say??
Ha, you said, um, "stop being so loud or I'll wake up," or something like that.
Heehee, sometimes I do that, yeah. I even sleep**walk** sometimes, too, but hardly ever.

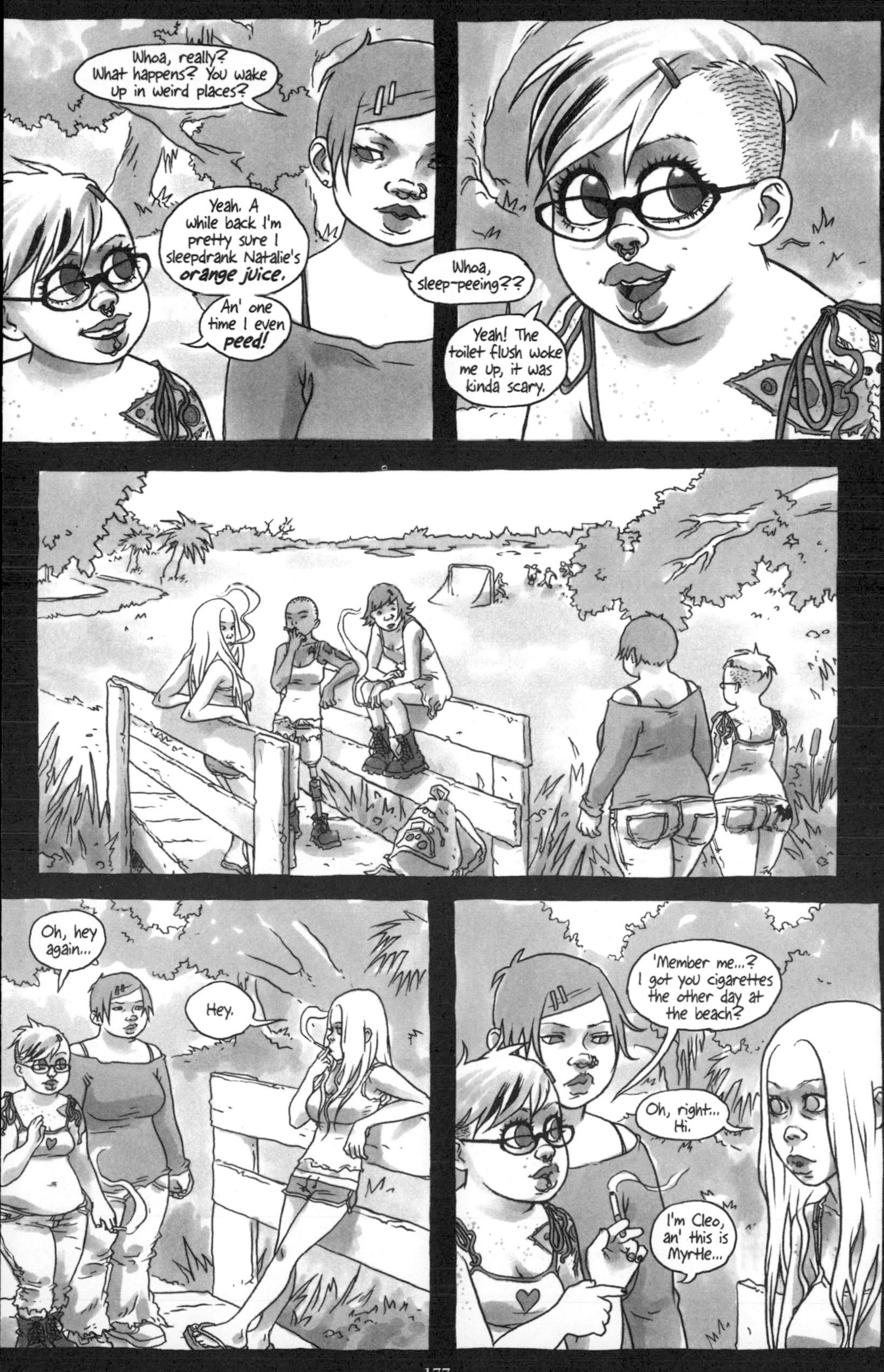

Whoa, really? What happens? You wake up in weird places?
Yeah. A while back I'm pretty sure I sleepdrank Natalie's **orange juice.**
An' one time I even **peed!**
Whoa, sleep-peeing??
Yeah! The toilet flush woke me up, it was kinda scary.
Oh, hey again...
Hey.
'Member me...? I got you cigarettes the other day at the beach?
Oh, right... Hi.
I'm Cleo, an' this is Myrtle...

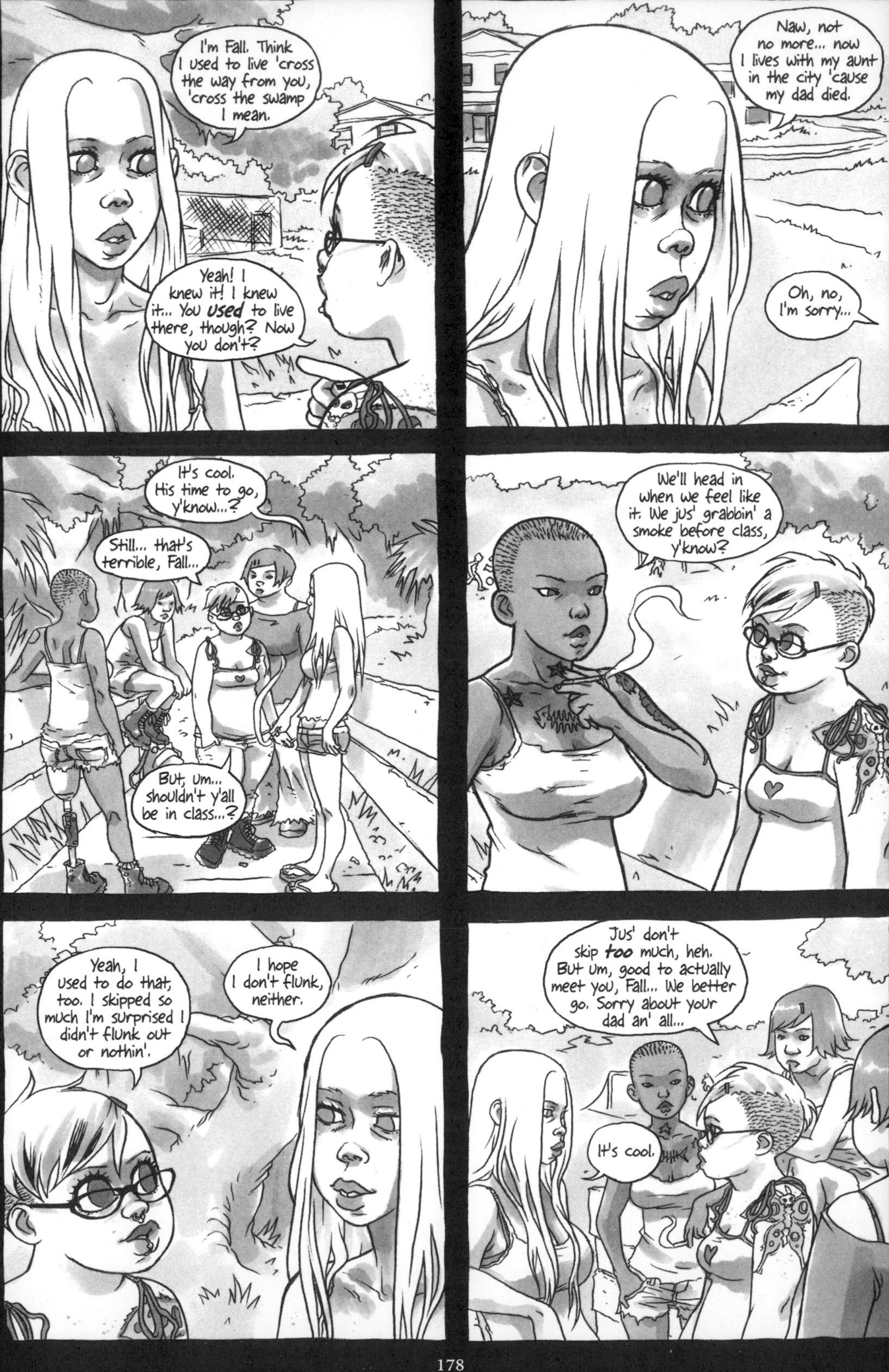
I'm Fall. Think I used to live 'cross the way from you, 'cross the swamp I mean.
Yeah! I knew it! I knew it... You *used* to live there, though? Now you don't?
Naw, not no more... now I lives with my aunt in the city 'cause my dad died.
Oh, no, I'm sorry...
It's cool. His time to go, y'know...?
Still... that's terrible, Fall...
But, um... shouldn't y'all be in class...?
We'll head in when we feel like it. We jus' grabbin' a smoke before class, y'know?
Yeah, I used to do that, too. I skipped so much I'm surprised I didn't flunk out or nothin'.
I hope I don't flunk, neither.
Jus' don't skip *too* much, heh. But um, good to actually meet you, Fall... We better go. Sorry about your dad an' all...
It's cool.

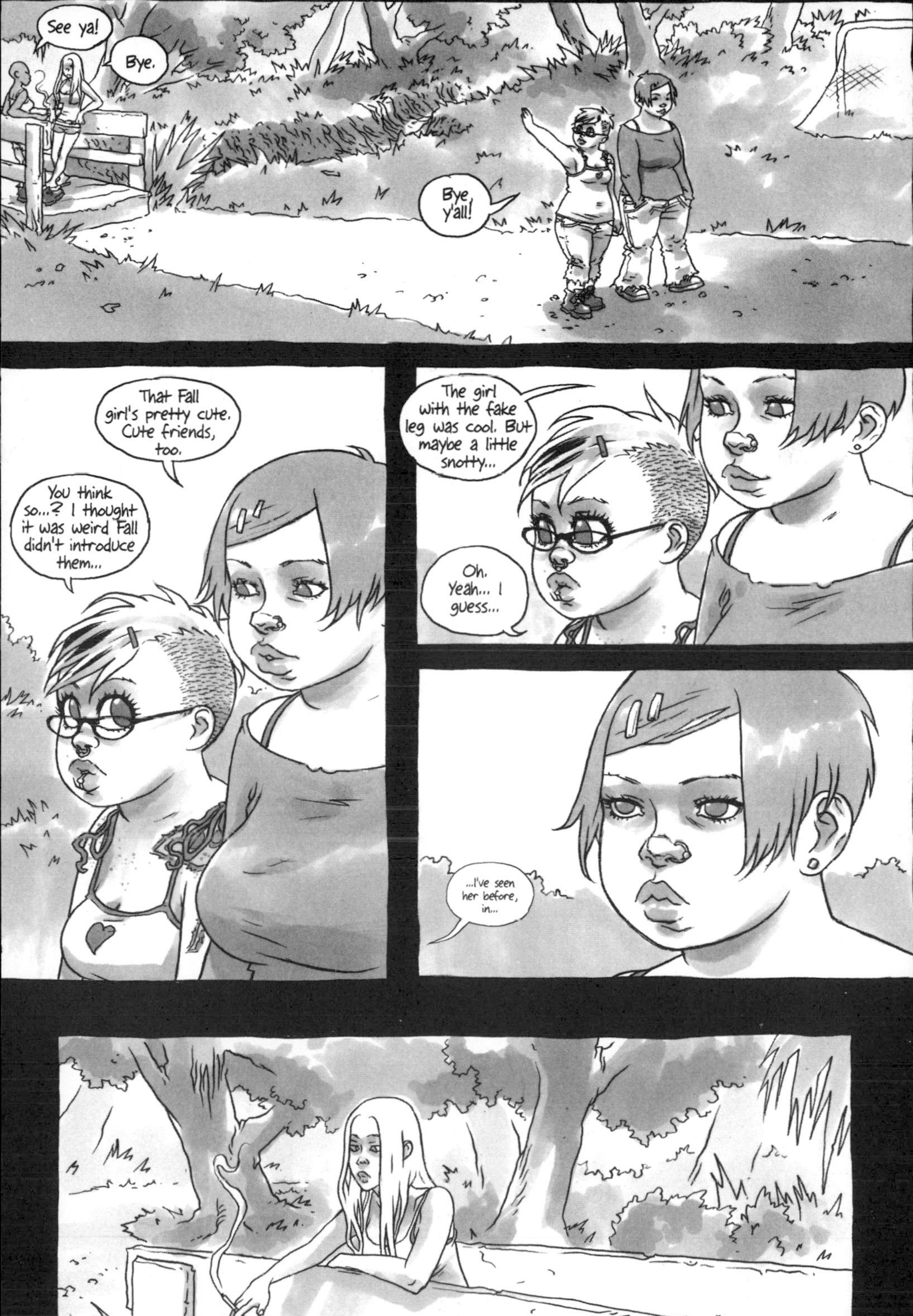
See ya!
Bye.
Bye y'all!
That Fall girl's pretty cute. Cute friends, too.
You think so...? I thought it was weird Fall didn't introduce them...
The girl with the fake leg was cool. But maybe a little snotty...
Oh. Yeah... I guess...
...I've seen her before, in...

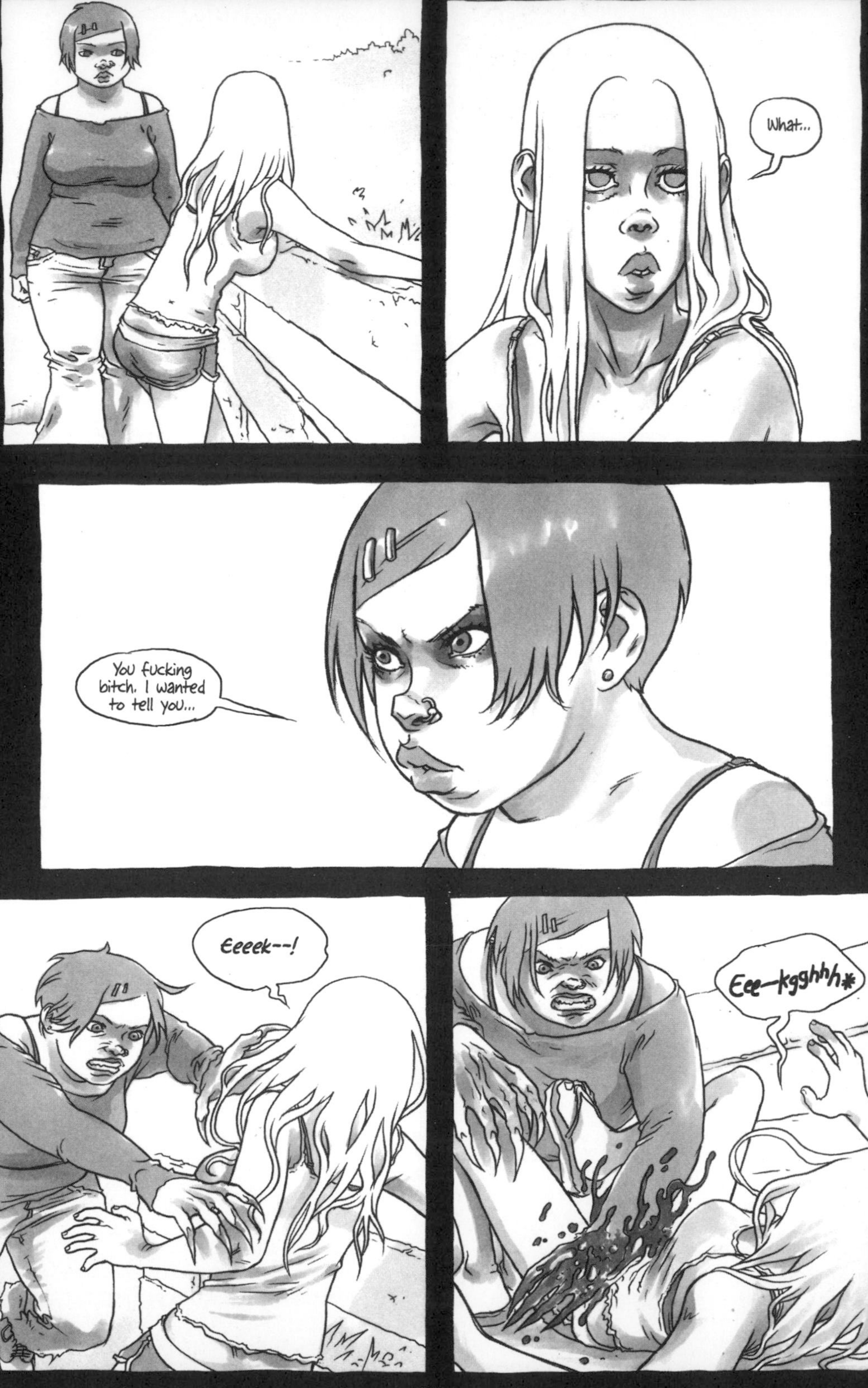
What...
You fucking bitch. I wanted to tell you...
Eeeek--!
Eee-kgghhh*

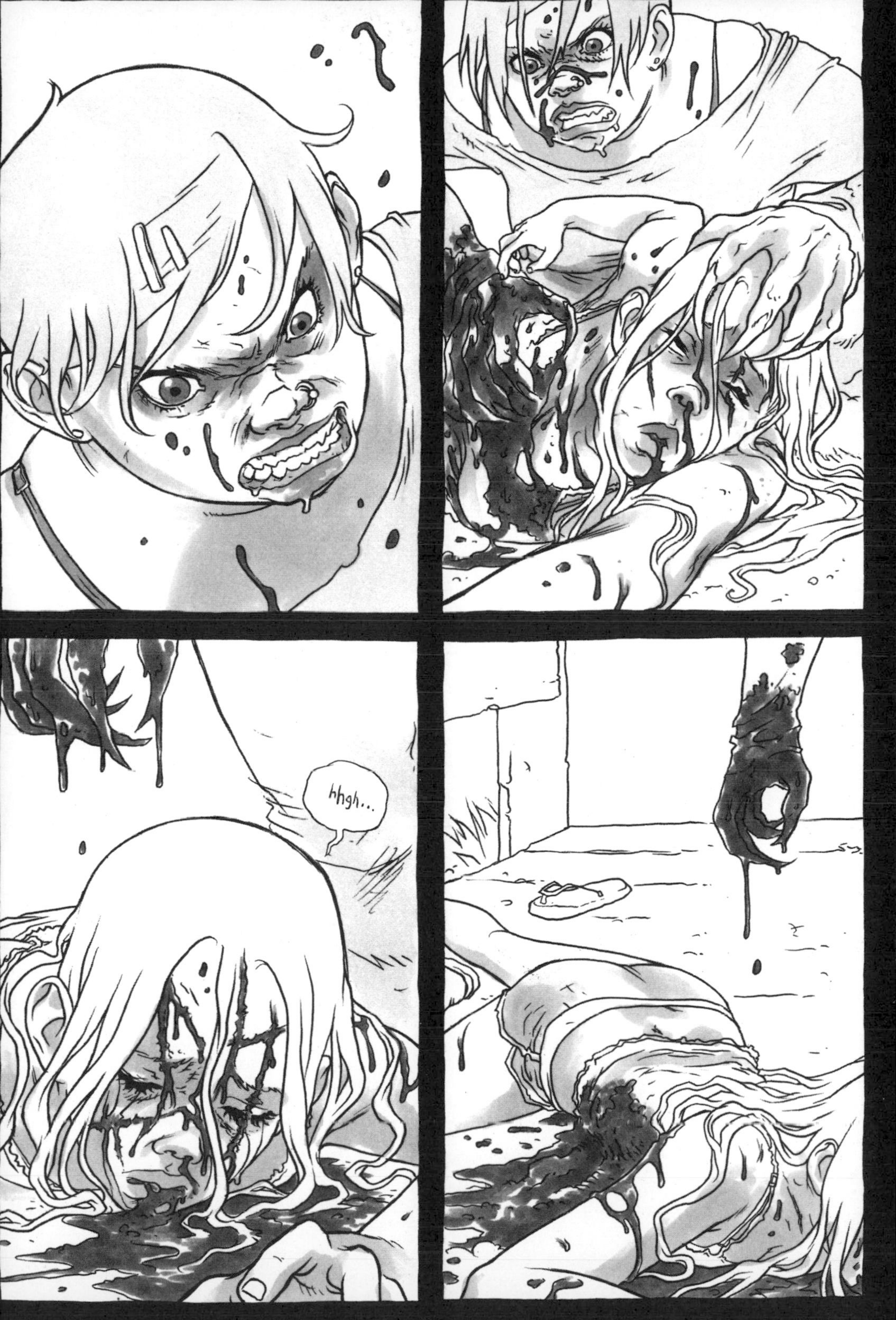
hhgh...

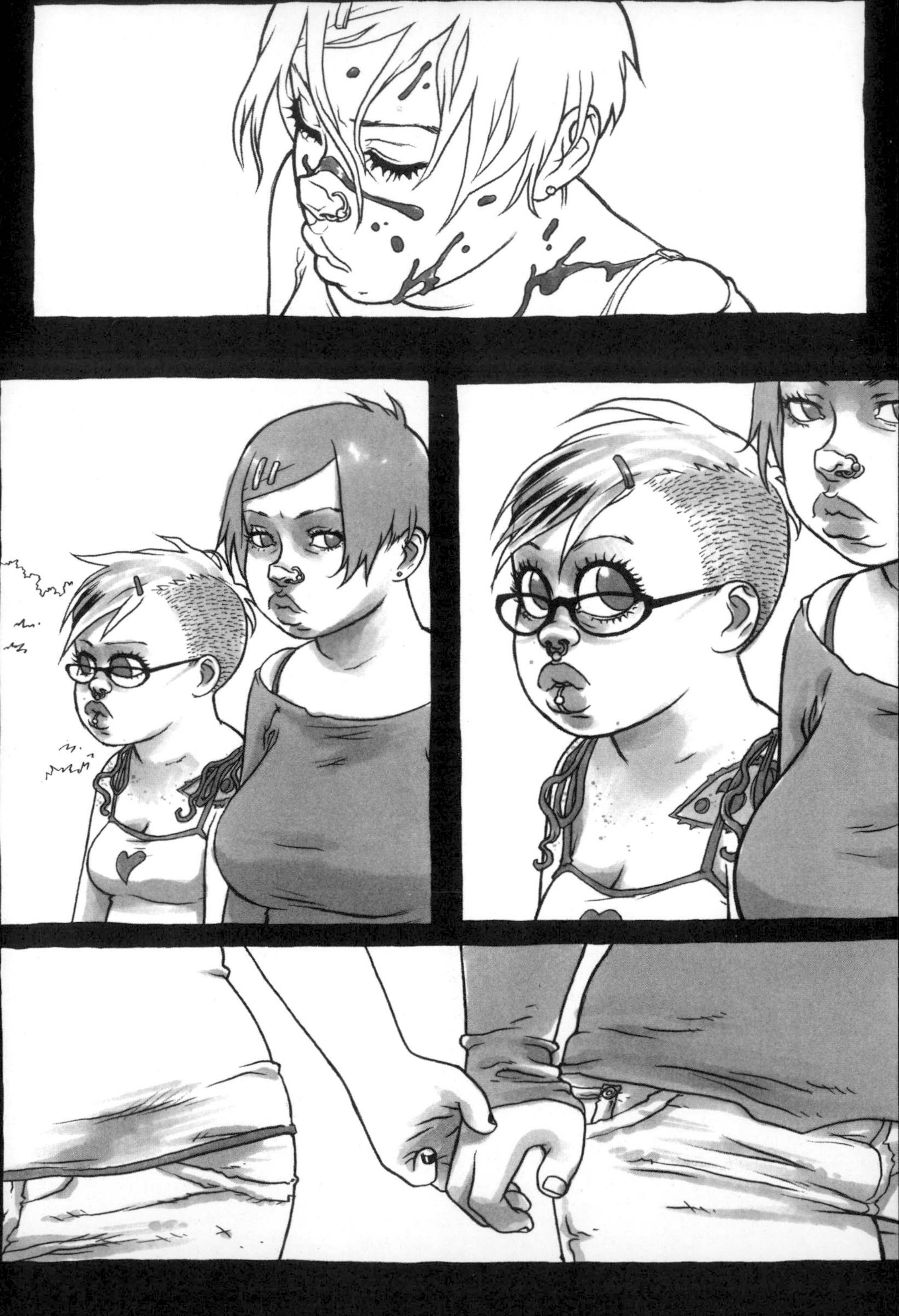

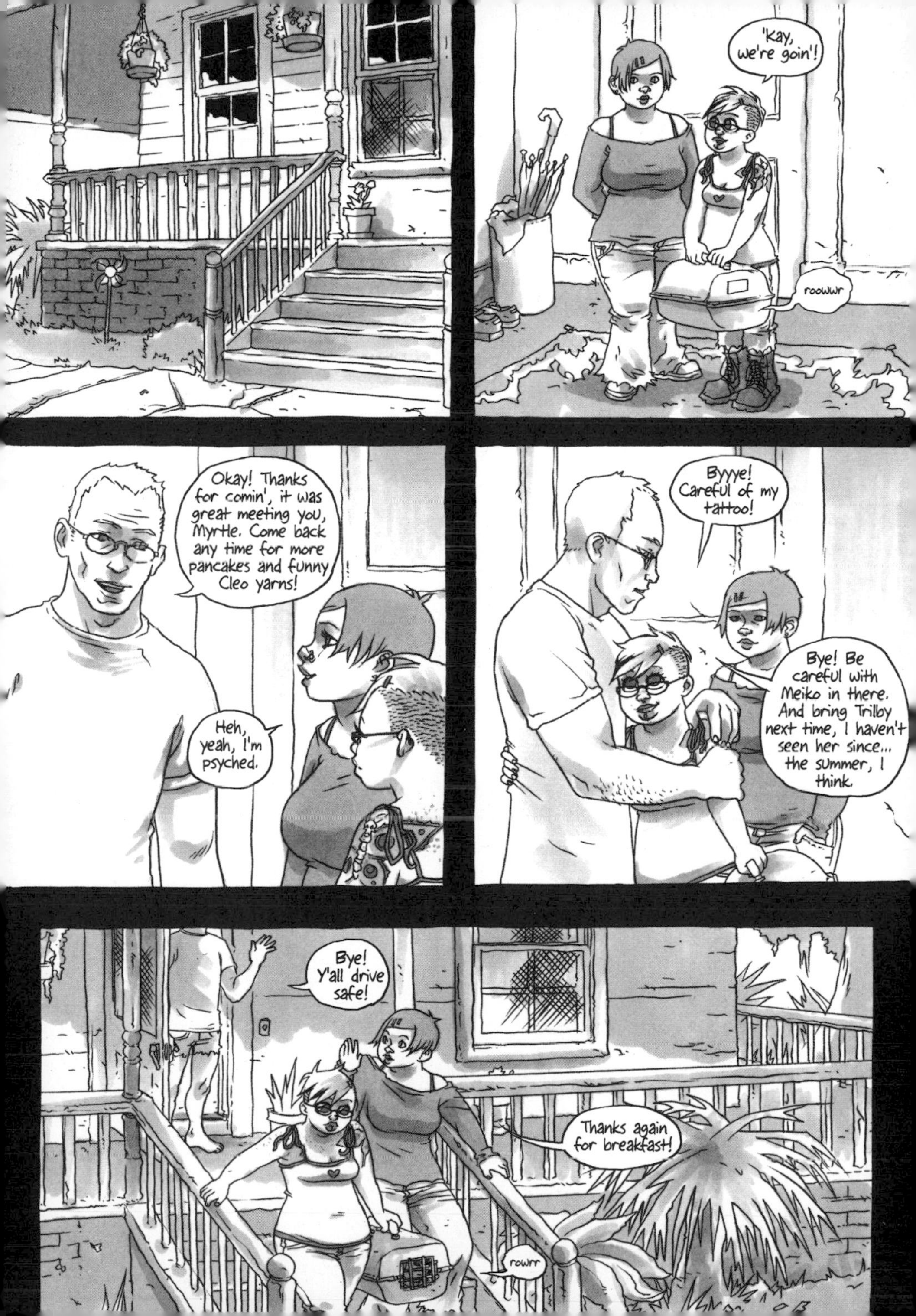
'Kay, we're goin'!
roowwr
Okay! Thanks for comin', it was great meeting you, Myrtle. Come back any time for more pancakes and funny Cleo yarns!
Heh, yeah, I'm psyched.
Byyye! Careful of my tattoo!
Bye! Be careful with Meiko in there. And bring Trilby next time, I haven't seen her since... the summer, I think.
Bye! Y'all drive safe!
Thanks again for breakfast!
rowrr

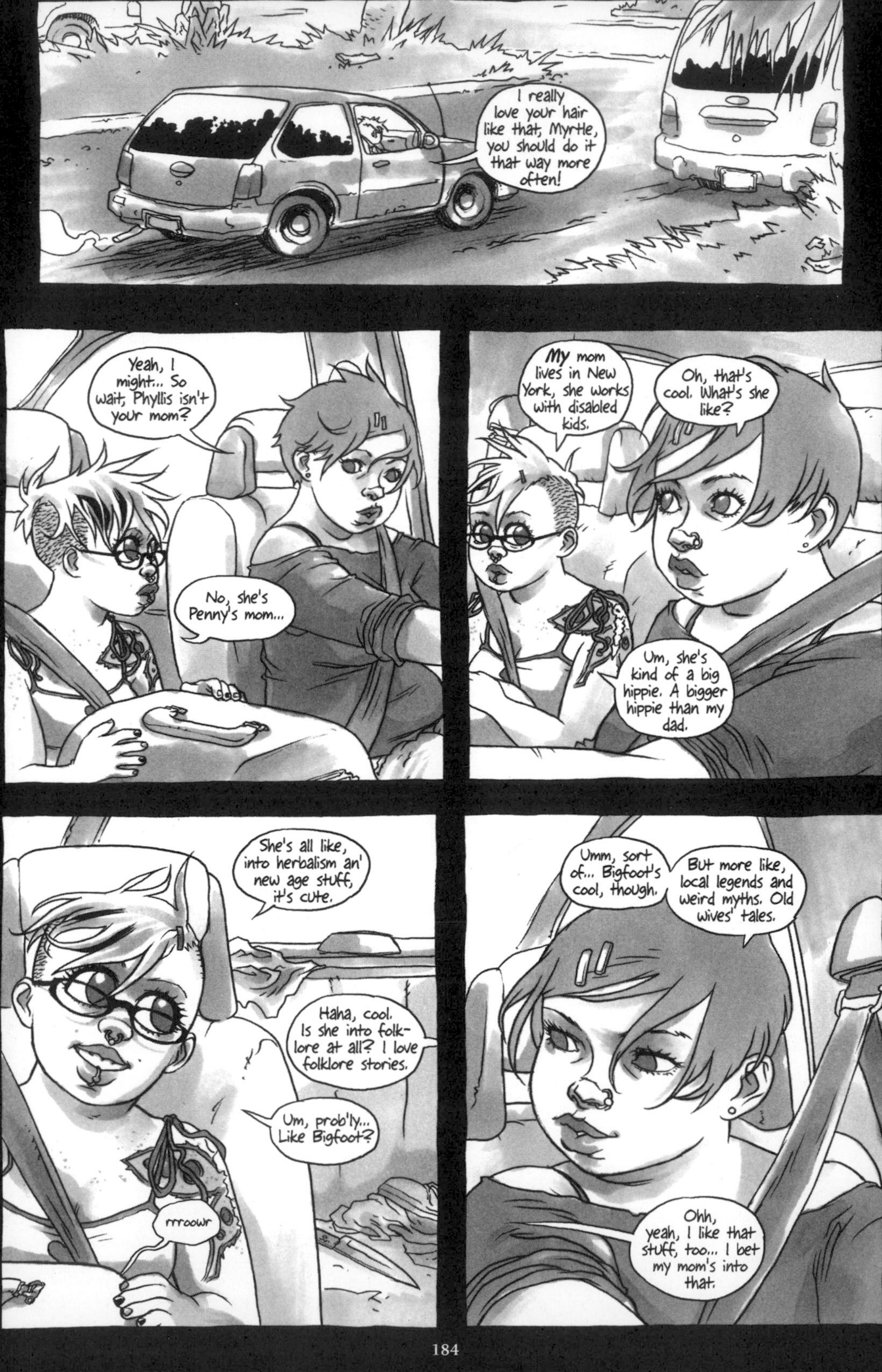
I really love your hair like that, Myrtle, you should do it that way more often!
Yeah, I might... So wait, Phyllis isn't your mom?
No, she's Penny's mom...
My mom lives in New York, she works with disabled kids.
Oh, that's cool. What's she like?
Um, she's kind of a big hippie. A bigger hippie than my dad.
She's all like, into herbalism an' new age stuff, it's cute.
Haha, cool. Is she into folk-lore at all? I love folklore stories.
Um, prob'ly... Like Bigfoot?
rrroowr
Umm, sort of... Bigfoot's cool, though.
But more like, local legends and weird myths. Old wives' tales.
Ohh, yeah, I like that stuff, too... I bet my mom's into that.

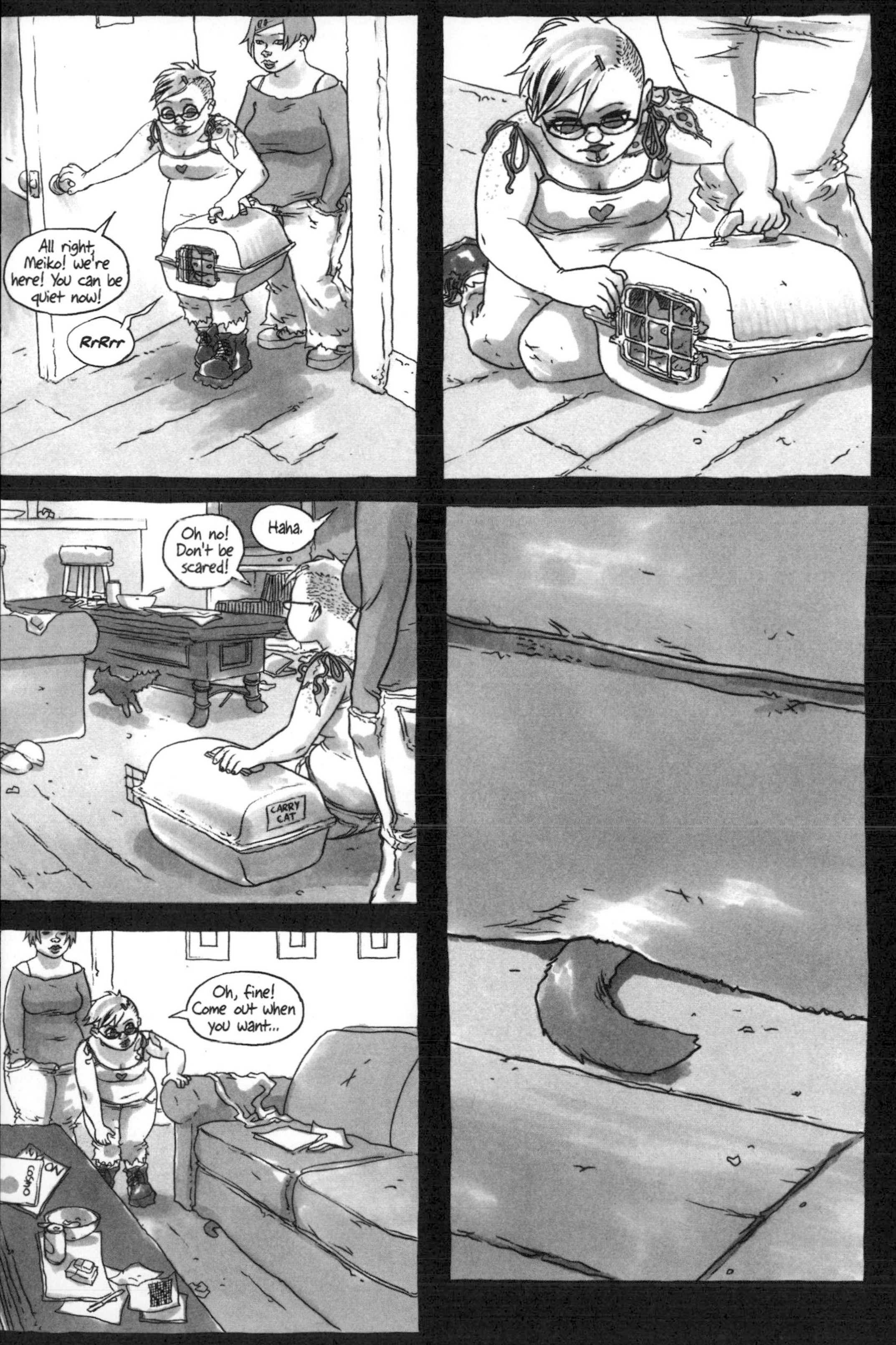
All right, Meiko! We're here! You can be quiet now!
RrRrr
Oh no! Don't be scared!
Haha.
CARRY CAT
Oh, fine! Come out when you want...
COSMO

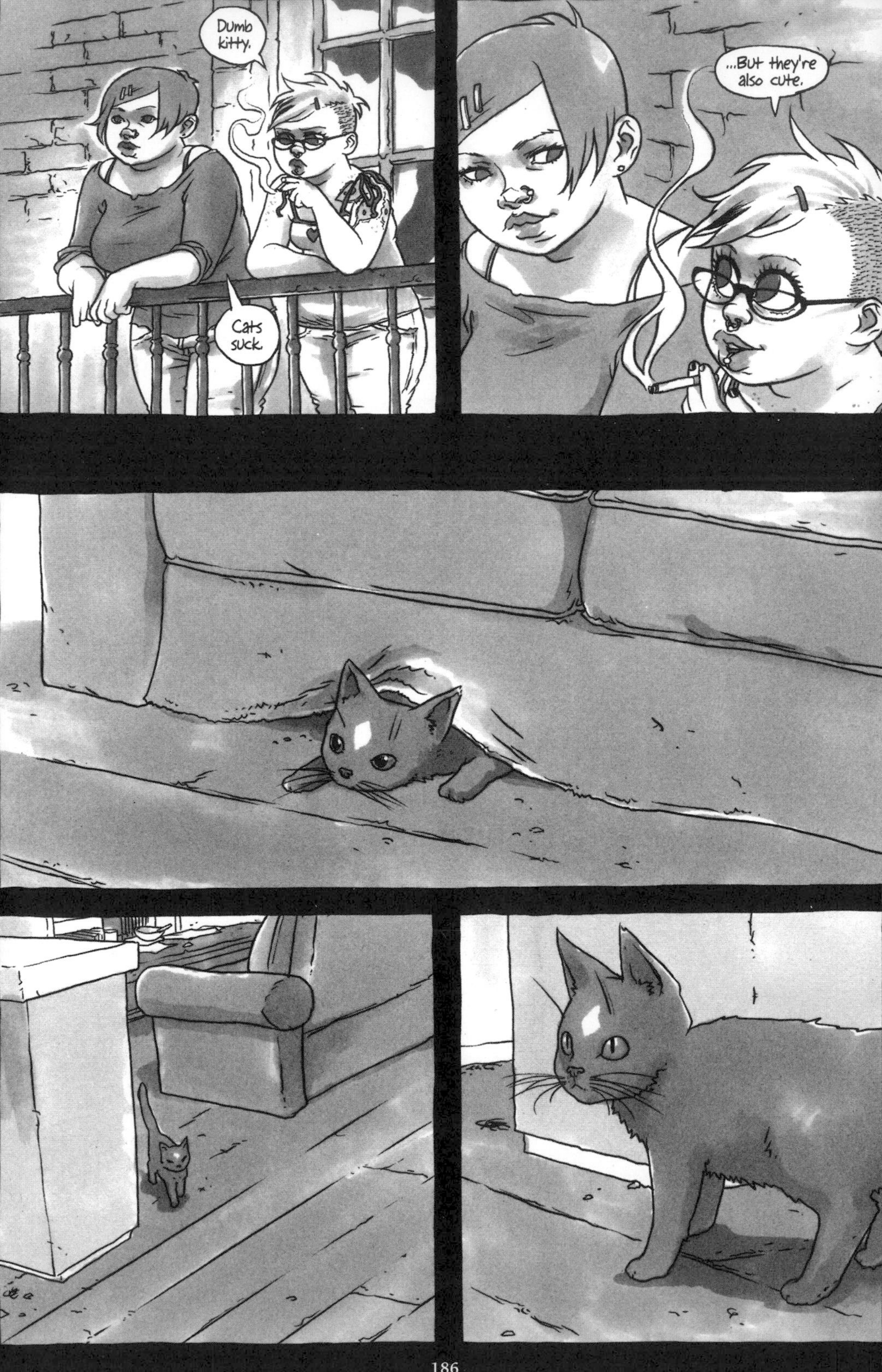
Dumb kitty.
Cats suck.
...But they're also cute.

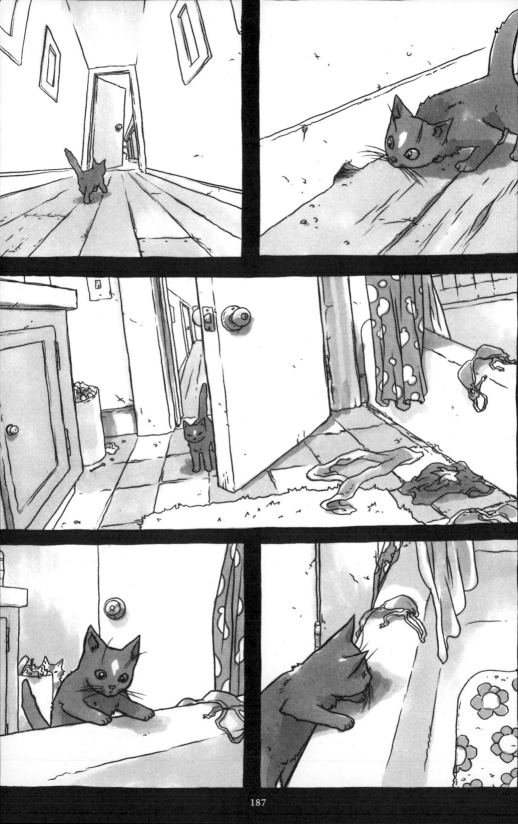

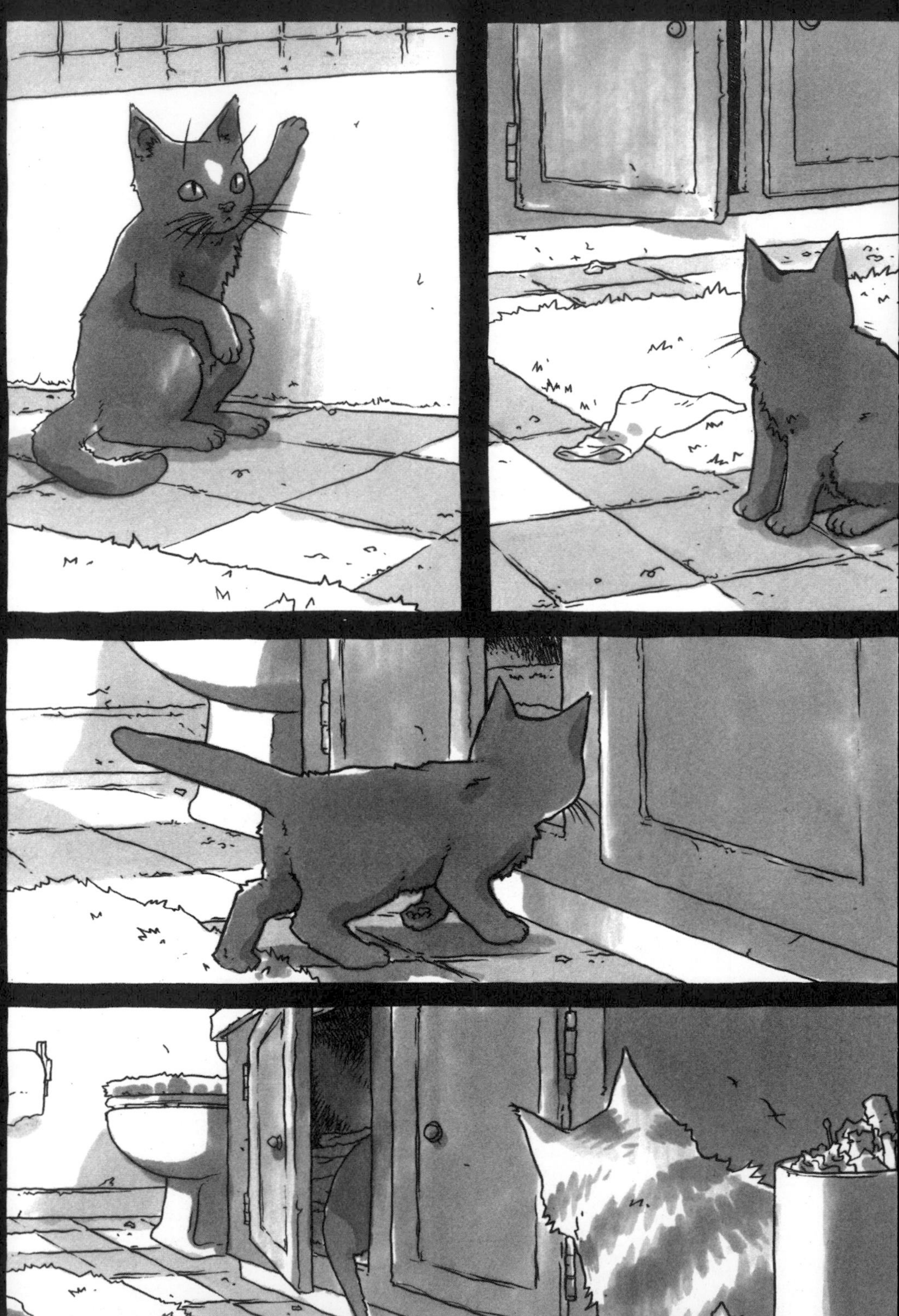

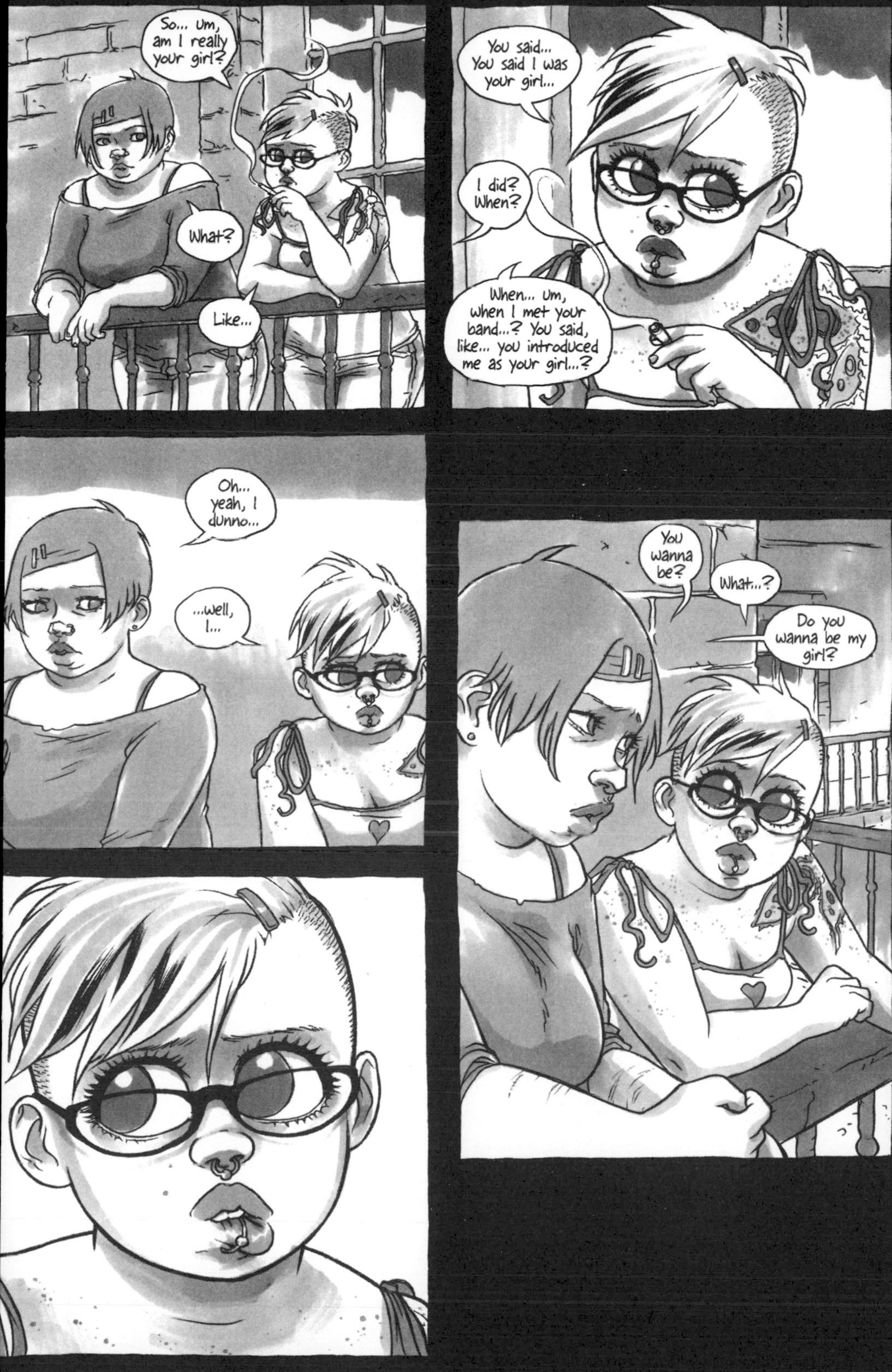
So... Um, am I really your girl?
What?
Like...
You said... You said I was your girl...
I did? When?
When... um, when I met your band...? You said, like... you introduced me as your girl...?
Oh... yeah, I dunno...
...well, I...
You wanna be?
What...?
Do you wanna be my girl?

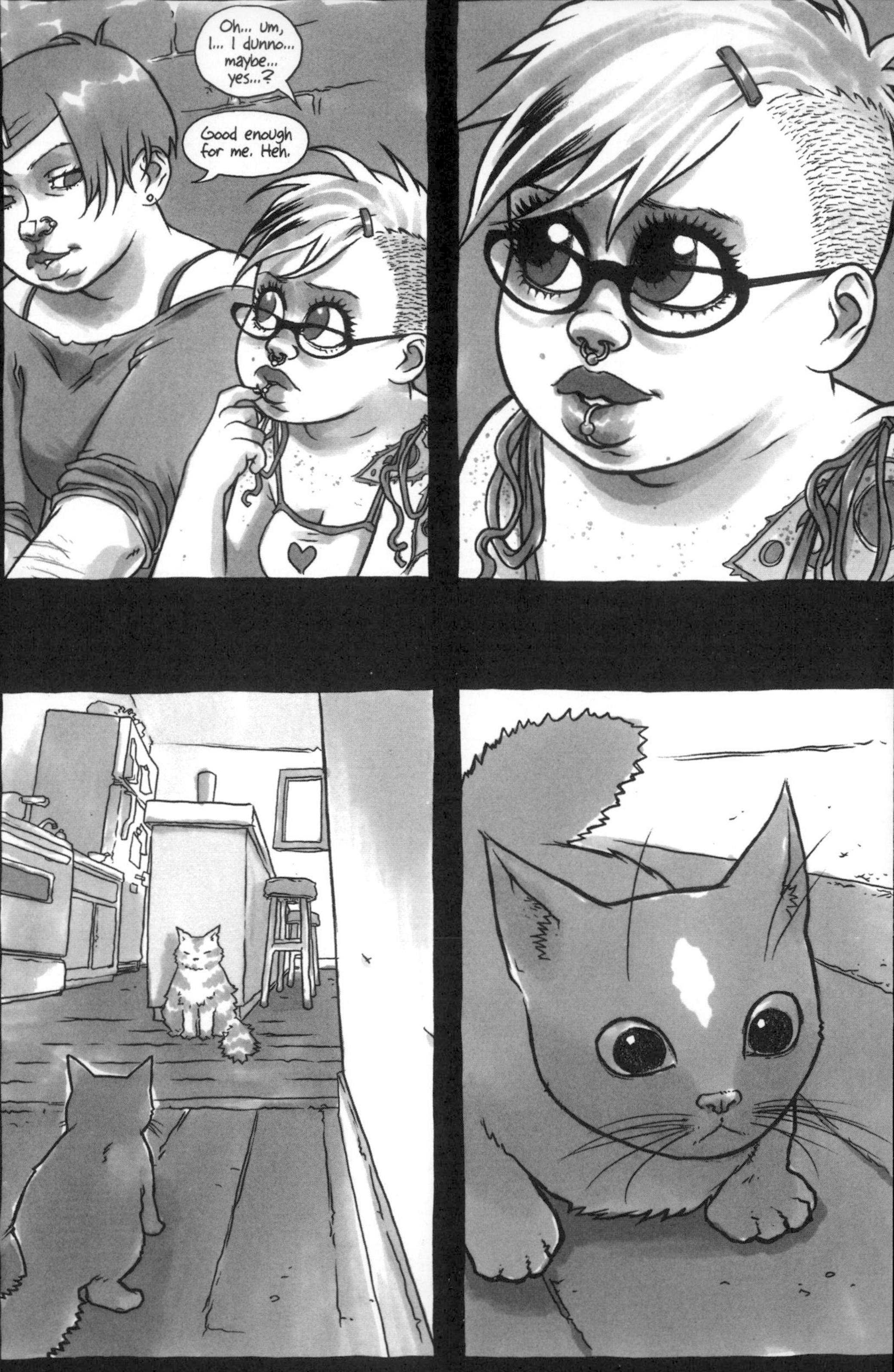
Oh... um, I... I dunno... maybe... yes...?
Good enough for me. Heh.

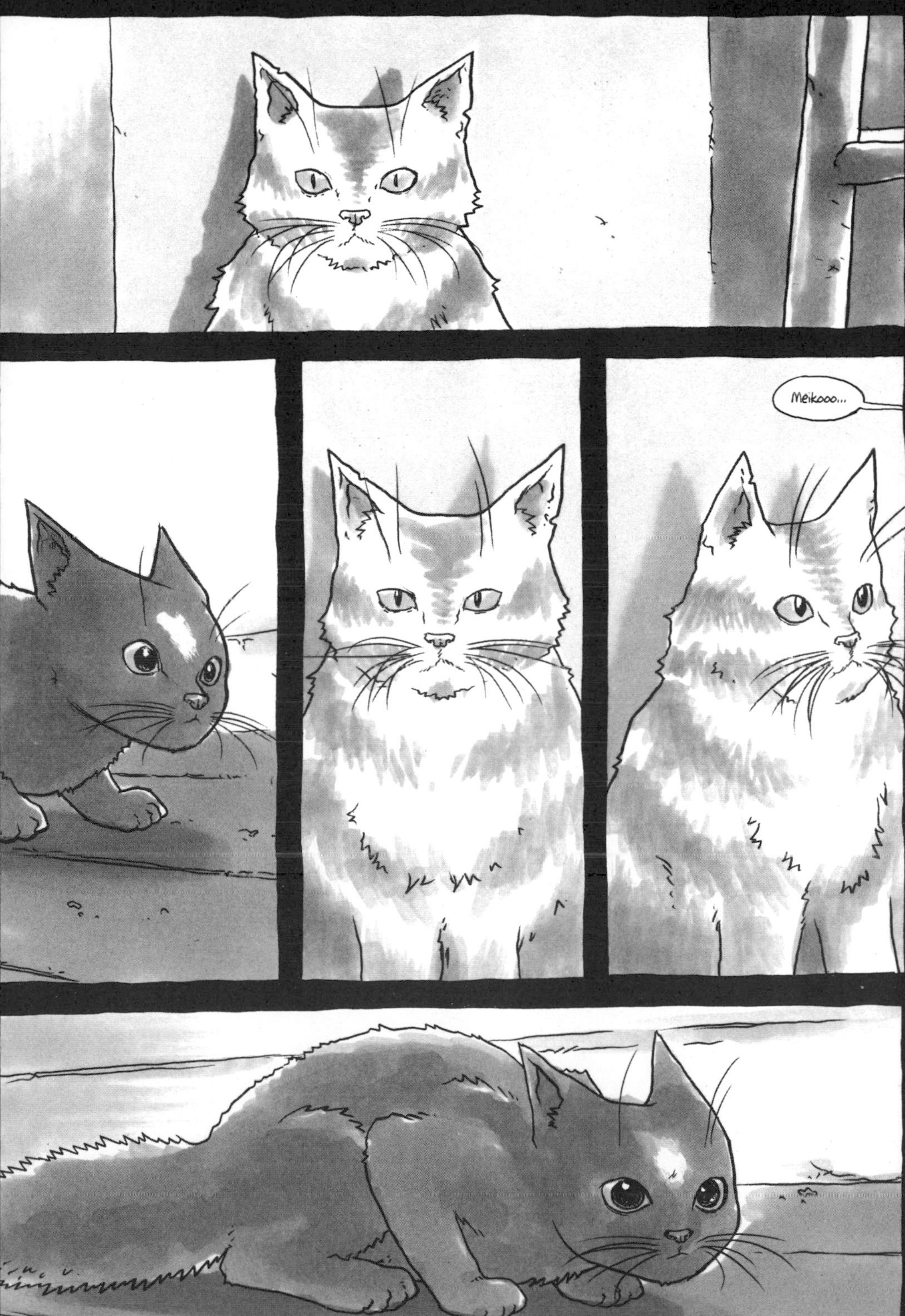
Meikooo...

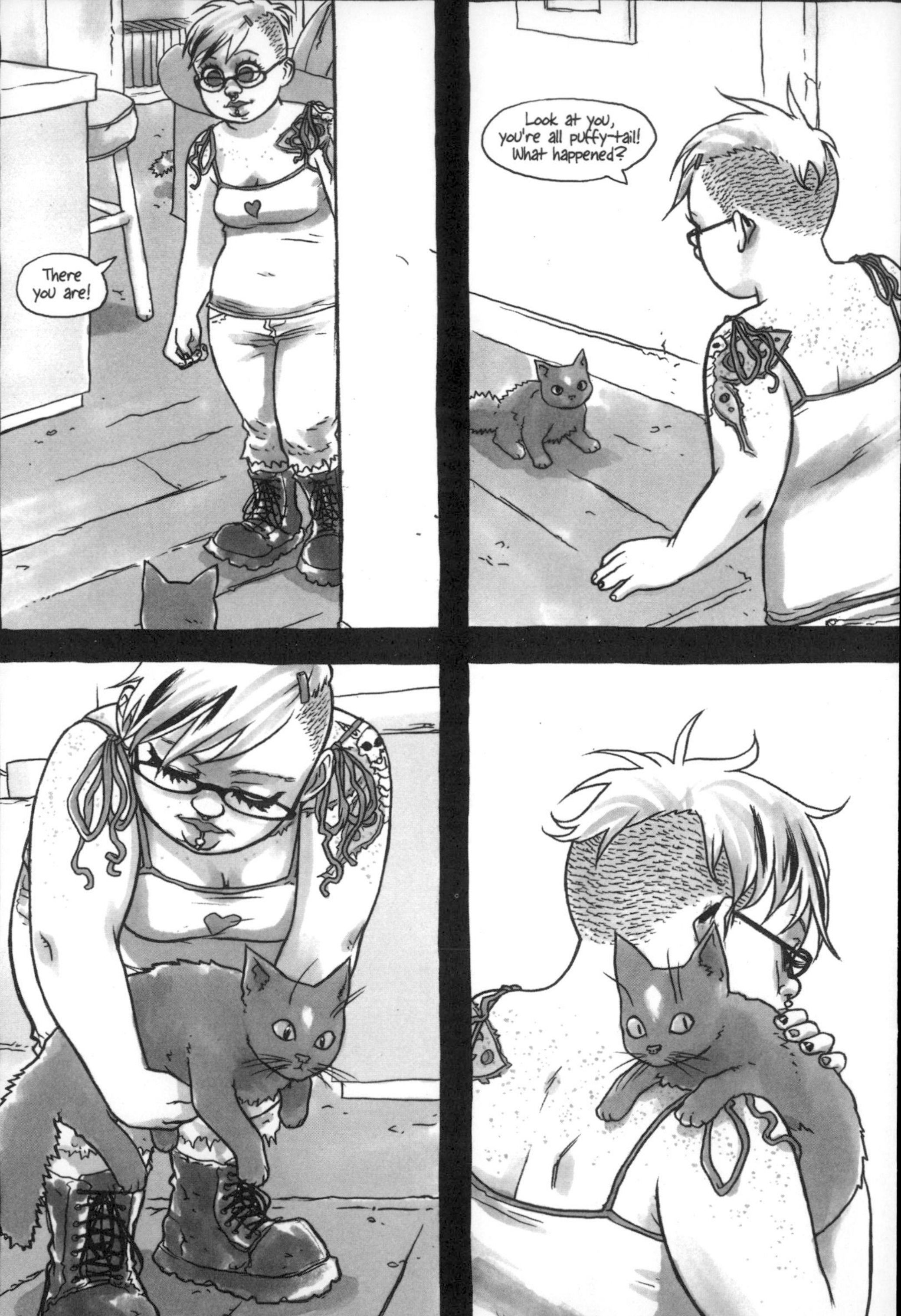
There you are!
Look at you, you're all puffy-tail! What happened?

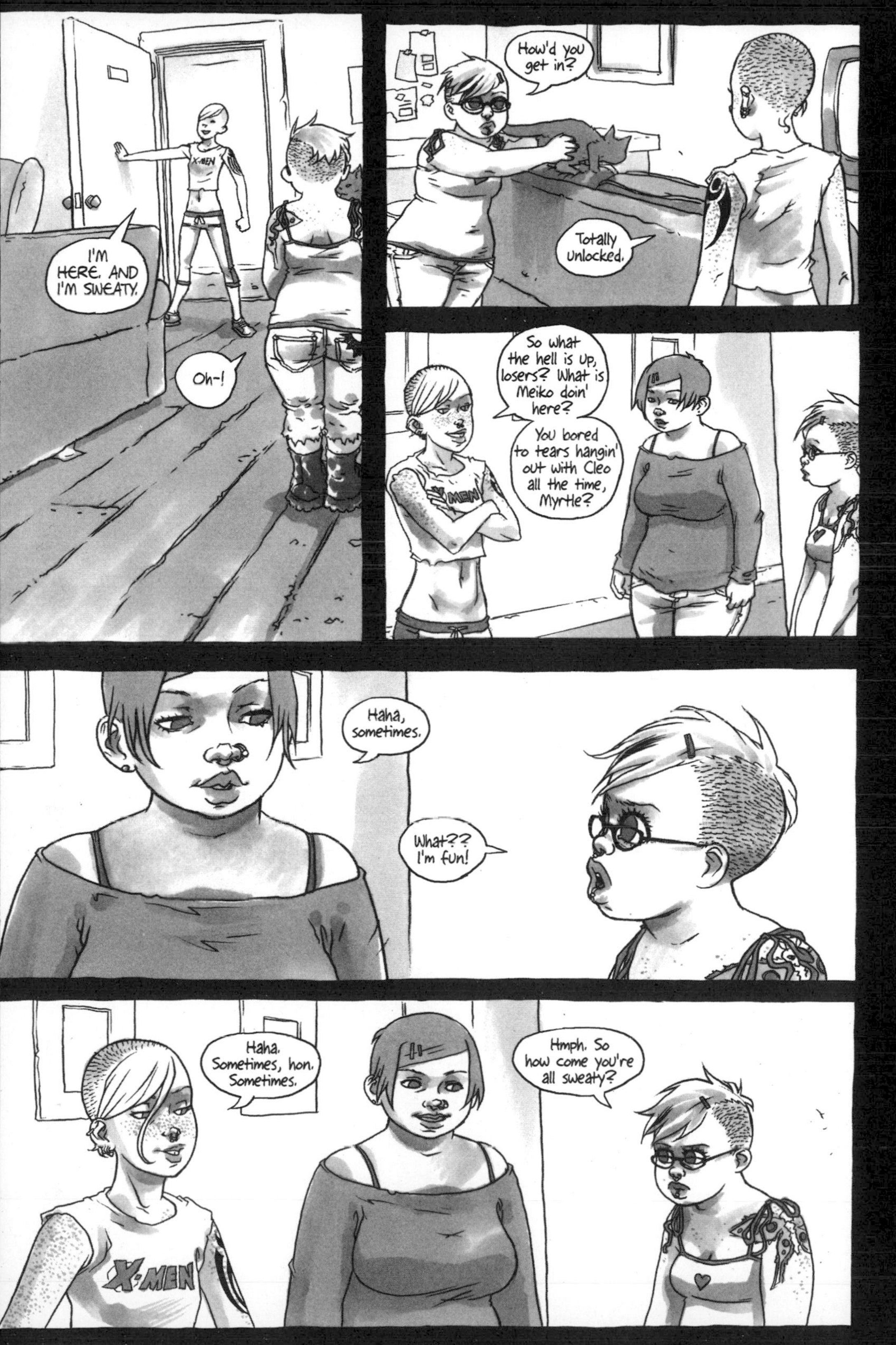
I'M HERE. AND I'M SWEATY.
Oh-!
How'd you get in?
Totally unlocked.
So what the hell is up, losers? What is Meiko doin' here?
You bored to tears hangin' out with Cleo all the time, Myrtle?
Haha, sometimes.
What?? I'm fun!
Haha. Sometimes, hon. Sometimes.
Hmph. So how come you're all sweaty?

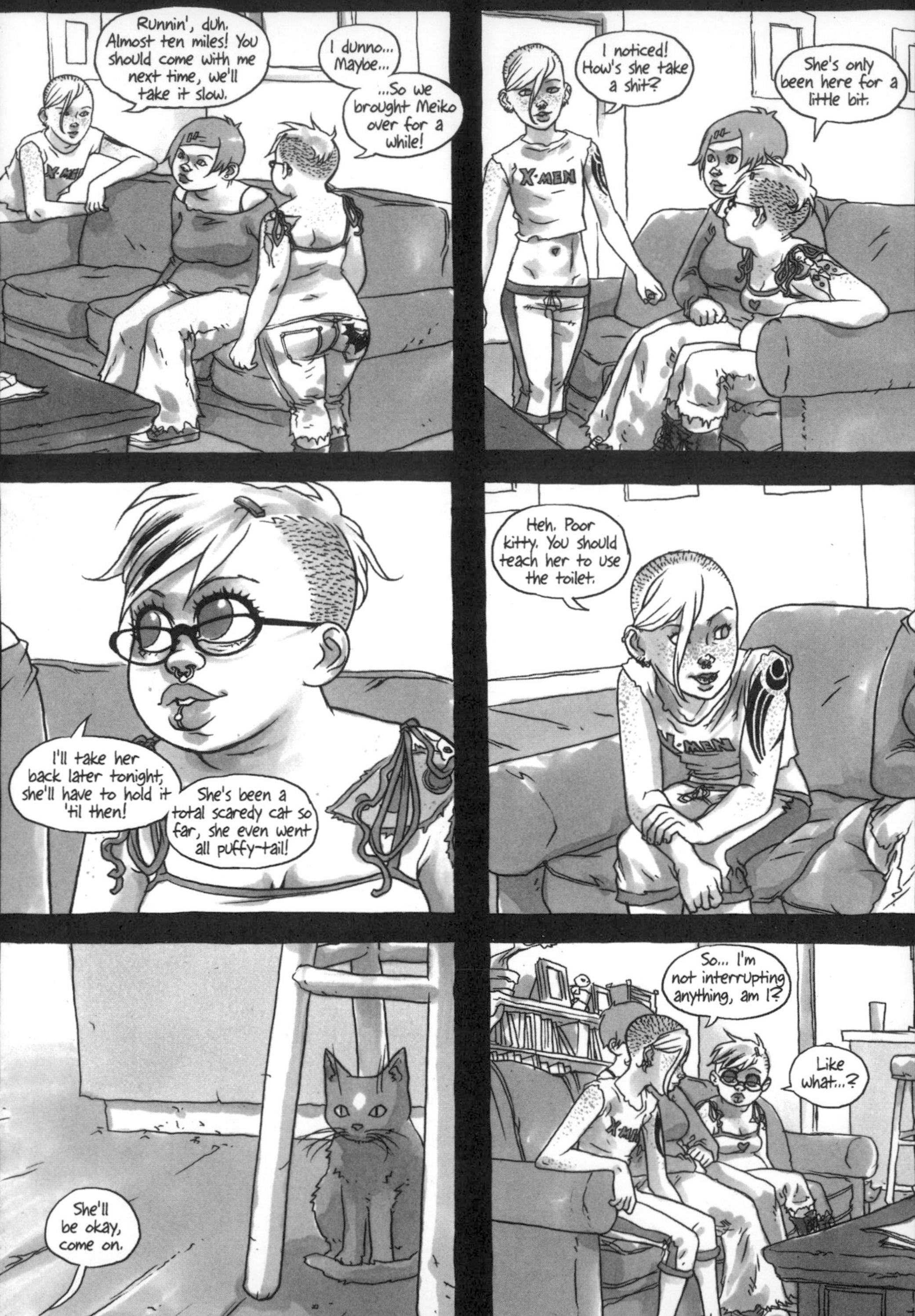
Runnin', duh. Almost ten miles! You should come with me next time, we'll take it slow.
I dunno... Maybe...
...So we brought Meiko over for a while!
X-MEN
I noticed! How's she take a shit?
She's only been here for a little bit.
X-MEN
I'll take her back later tonight, she'll have to hold it 'til then!
She's been a total scaredy cat so far, she even went all puffy-tail!
Heh. Poor kitty. You should teach her to use the toilet.
X-MEN
She'll be okay, come on.
So... I'm not interrupting anything, am I?
Like what...?
X-MEN

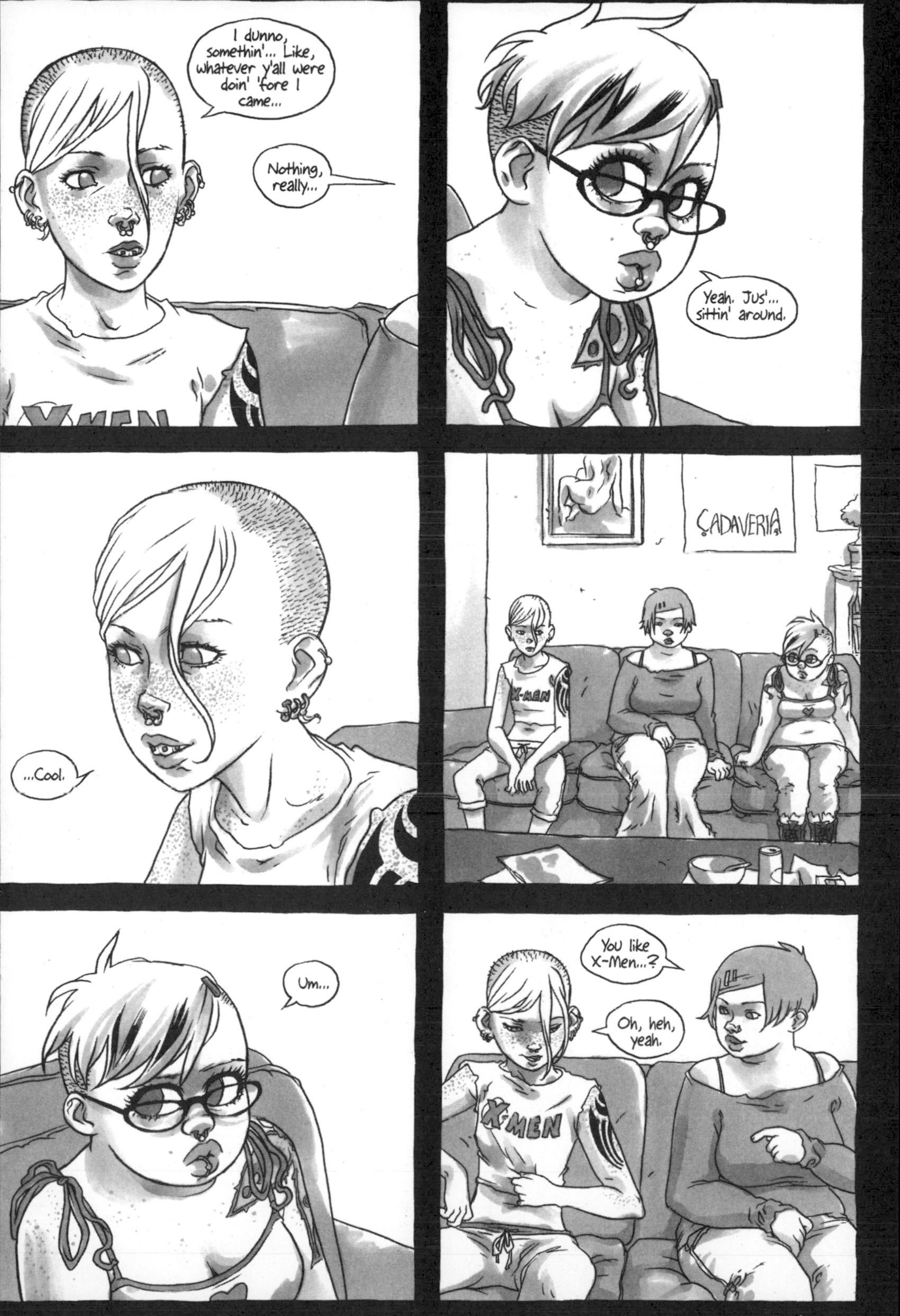

I dunno, somethin'... Like, whatever y'all were doin' 'fore I came...
Nothing, really...
Yeah. Jus'... sittin' around.
...Cool.
ÇADAVERIA
Um...
You like X-Men...?
Oh, heh, yeah.

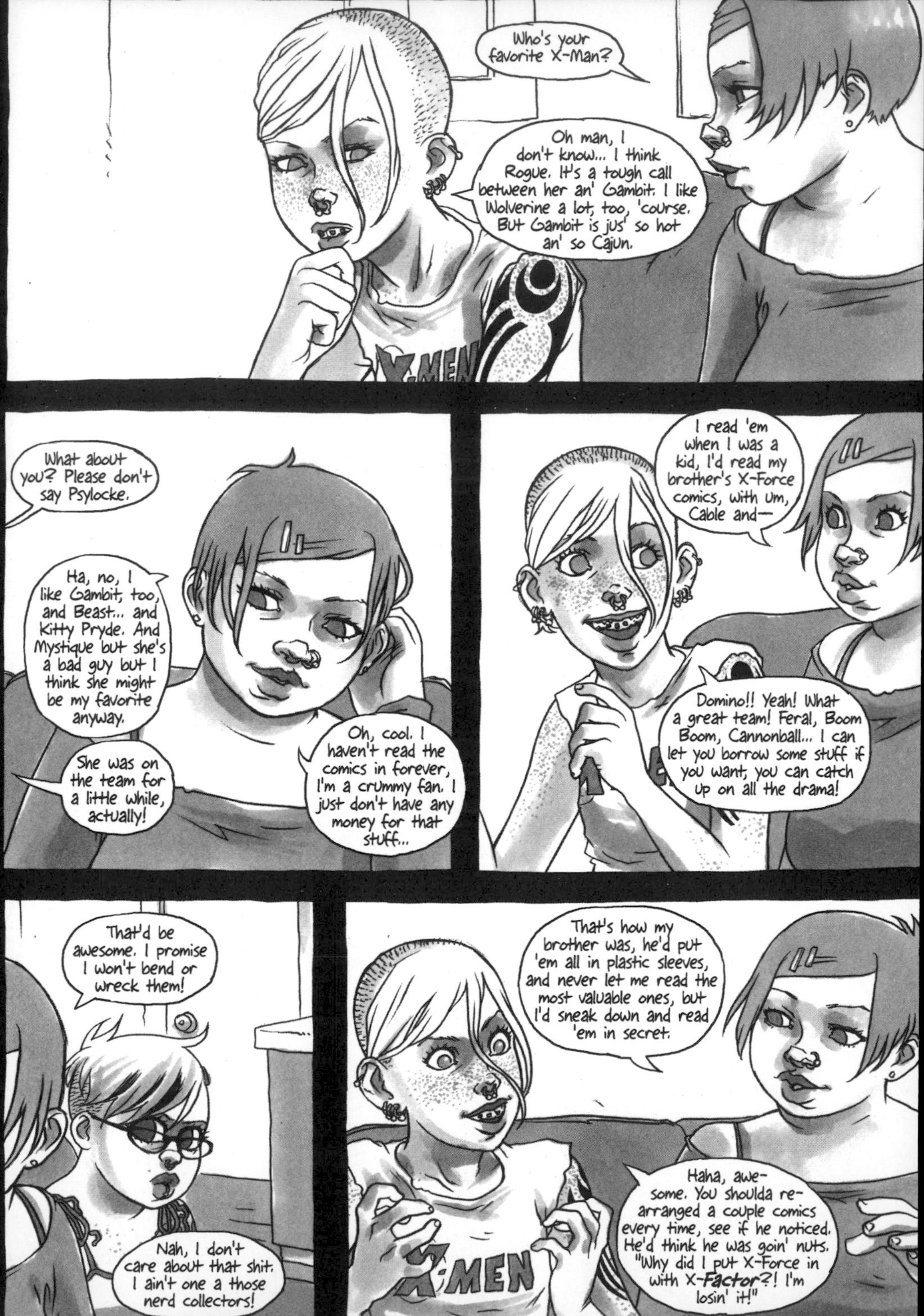
Who's your favorite X-Man?
Oh man, I don't know... I think Rogue. It's a tough call between her an' Gambit. I like Wolverine a lot, too, 'course. But Gambit is jus' so hot an' so Cajun.
X-MEN
What about you? Please don't say Psylocke.
Ha, no, I like Gambit, too, and Beast... and Kitty Pryde. And Mystique but she's a bad guy but I think she might be my favorite anyway.
She was on the team for a little while, actually!
Oh, cool. I haven't read the comics in forever, I'm a crummy fan. I just don't have any money for that stuff...
I read 'em when I was a kid, I'd read my brother's X-Force comics, with um, Cable and—
Domino!! Yeah! What a great team! Feral, Boom Boom, Cannonball... I can let you borrow some stuff if you want, you can catch up on all the drama!
That'd be awesome. I promise I won't bend or wreck them!
Nah, I don't care about that shit. I ain't one a those nerd collectors!
That's how my brother was, he'd put 'em all in plastic sleeves, and never let me read the most valuable ones, but I'd sneak down and read 'em in secret.
X-MEN
Haha, awe-some. You shoulda re-arranged a couple comics every time, see if he noticed. He'd think he was goin' nuts. "Why did I put X-Force in with X-*Factor*?! I'm losin' it!"

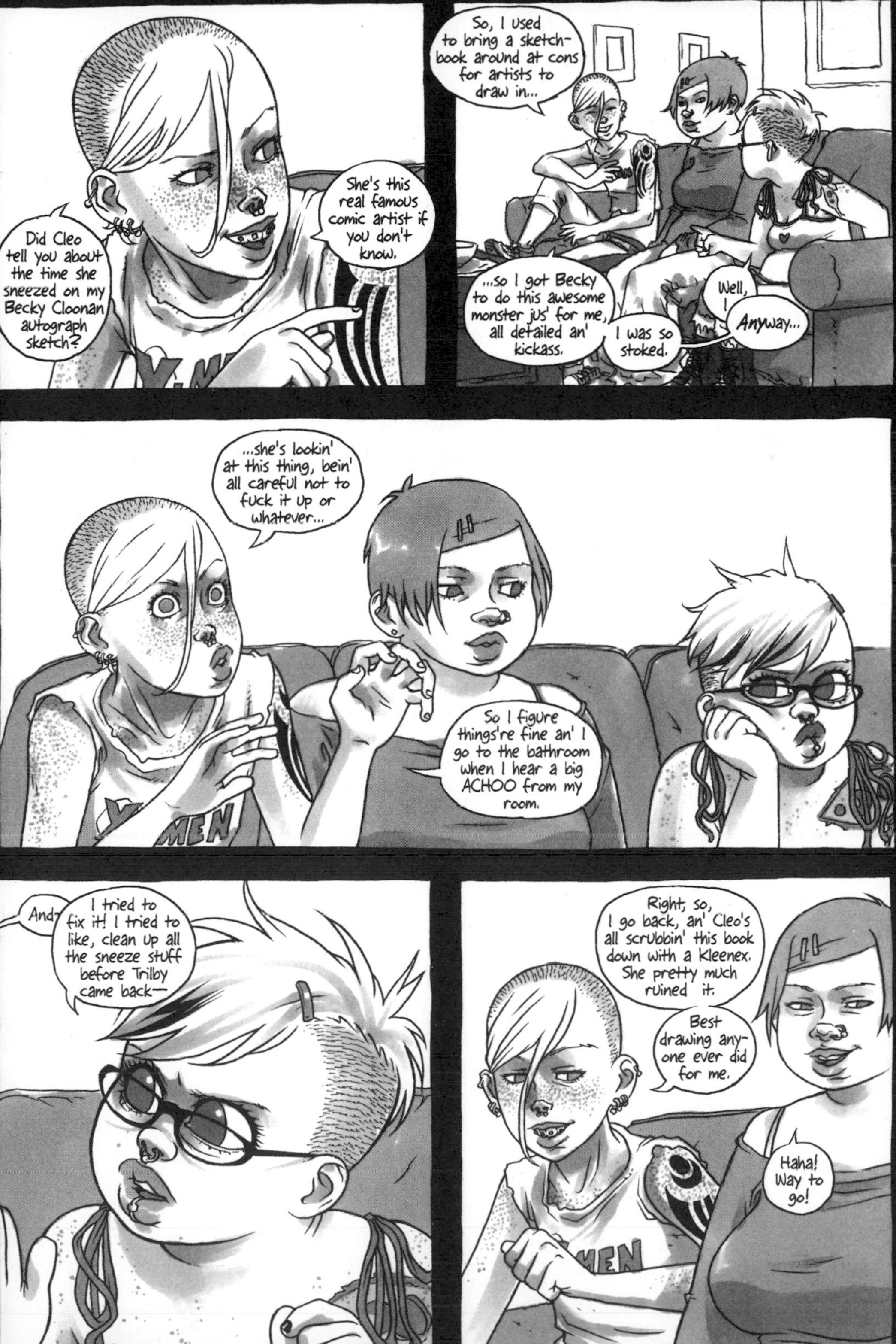
Did Cleo tell you about the time she sneezed on my Becky Cloonan autograph sketch?
She's this real famous comic artist if you don't know.
So, I used to bring a sketch-book around at cons for artists to draw in...
...so I got Becky to do this awesome monster jus' for me, all detailed an' kickass.
I was so stoked.
Well, I
Anyway...
...she's lookin' at this thing, bein' all careful not to fuck it up or whatever...
So I figure things're fine an' I go to the bathroom when I hear a big ACHOO from my room.
And
I tried to fix it! I tried to like, clean up all the sneeze stuff before Trilby came back—
Right, so, I go back, an' Cleo's all scrubbin' this book down with a Kleenex. She pretty much ruined it.
Best drawing any-one ever did for me.
Haha! Way to go!

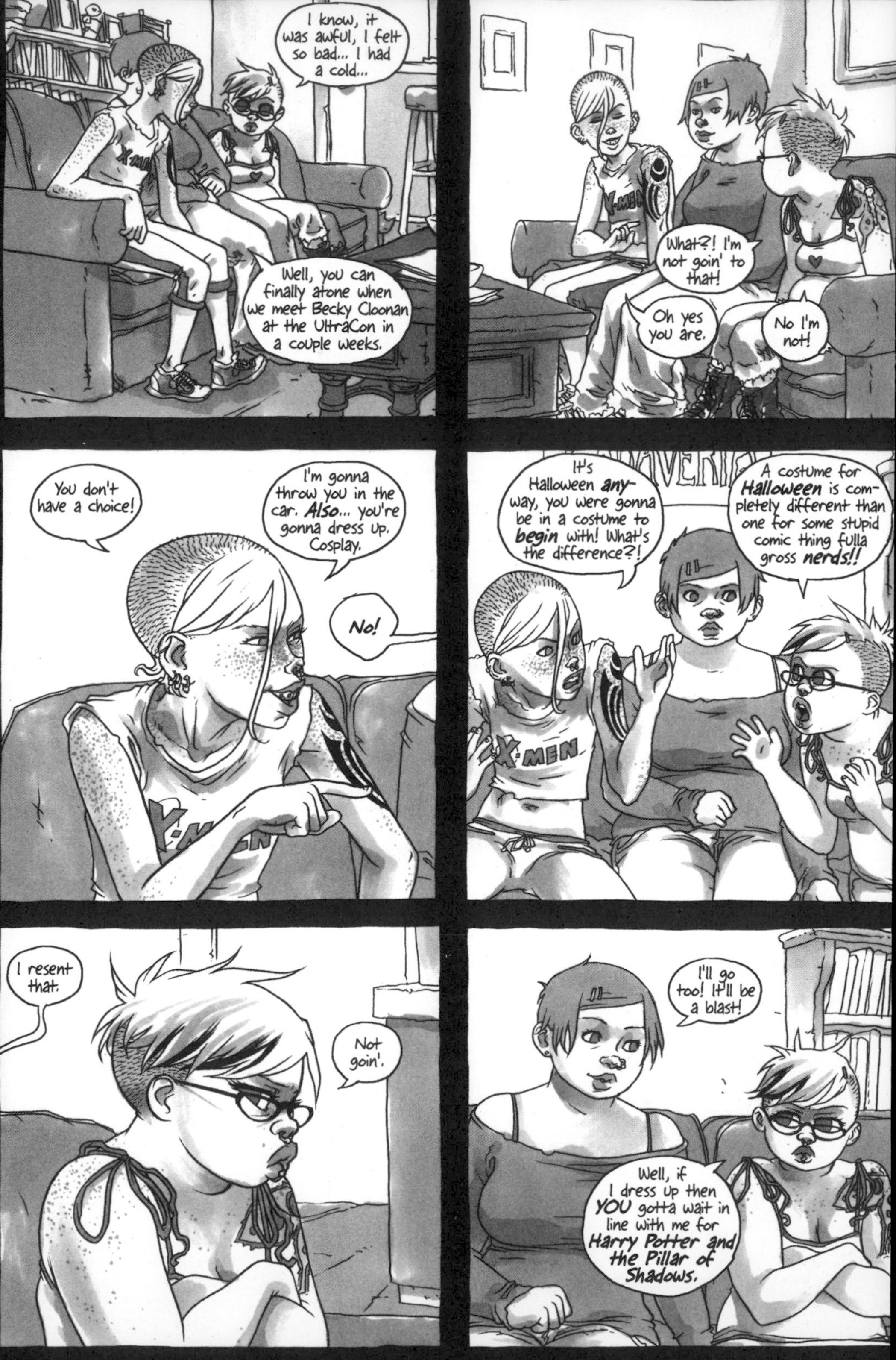

I know, it was awful, I felt so bad... I had a cold...
Well, you can finally atone when we meet Becky Cloonan at the UltraCon in a couple weeks.
What?! I'm not goin' to that!
Oh yes you are.
No I'm not!
You don't have a choice!
I'm gonna throw you in the car. **Also**... you're gonna dress up. Cosplay.
No!
It's Halloween **any**-way, you were gonna be in a costume to **begin** with! What's the difference?!
A costume for **Halloween** is completely different than one for some stupid comic thing fulla gross **nerds!!**
I resent that.
Not goin'.
I'll go too! It'll be a blast!
Well, if I dress up then **YOU** gotta wait in line with me for **Harry Potter and the Pillar of Shadows.**

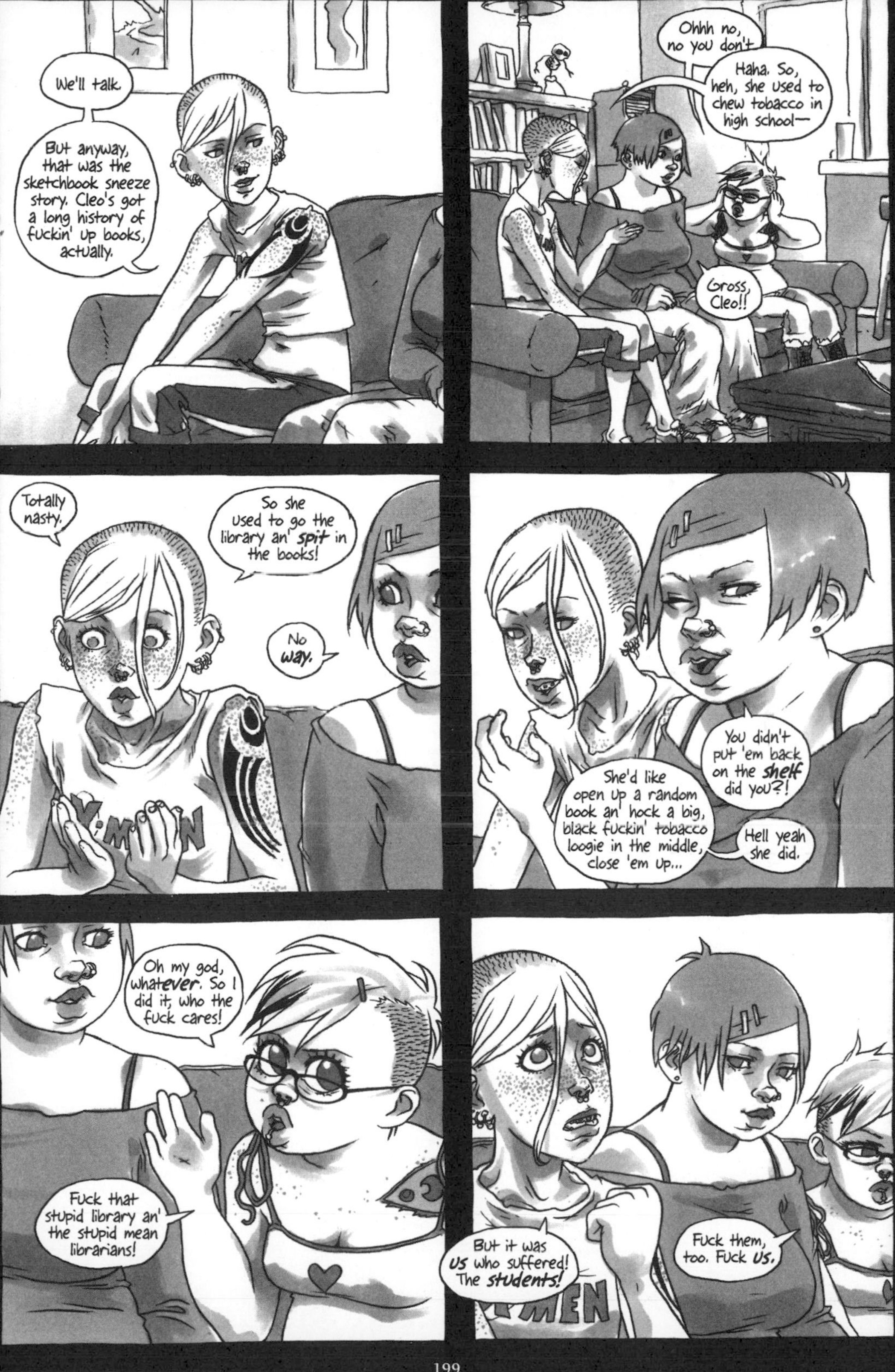
We'll talk.
But anyway, that was the sketchbook sneeze story. Cleo's got a long history of fuckin' up books, actually.
Ohhh no, no you don't
Haha. So, heh, she used to chew tobacco in high school—
Gross, Cleo!!
Totally nasty.
So she used to go the library an' *spit* in the books!
No *way.*
She'd like open up a random book an' hock a big, black fuckin' tobacco loogie in the middle, close 'em up...
You didn't put 'em back on the *shelf* did you?!
Hell yeah she did.
Oh my god, what*ever*. So I did it, who the fuck cares!
Fuck that stupid library an' the stupid mean librarians!
But it was *us* who suffered! The *students!*
Fuck them, too. Fuck *us.*

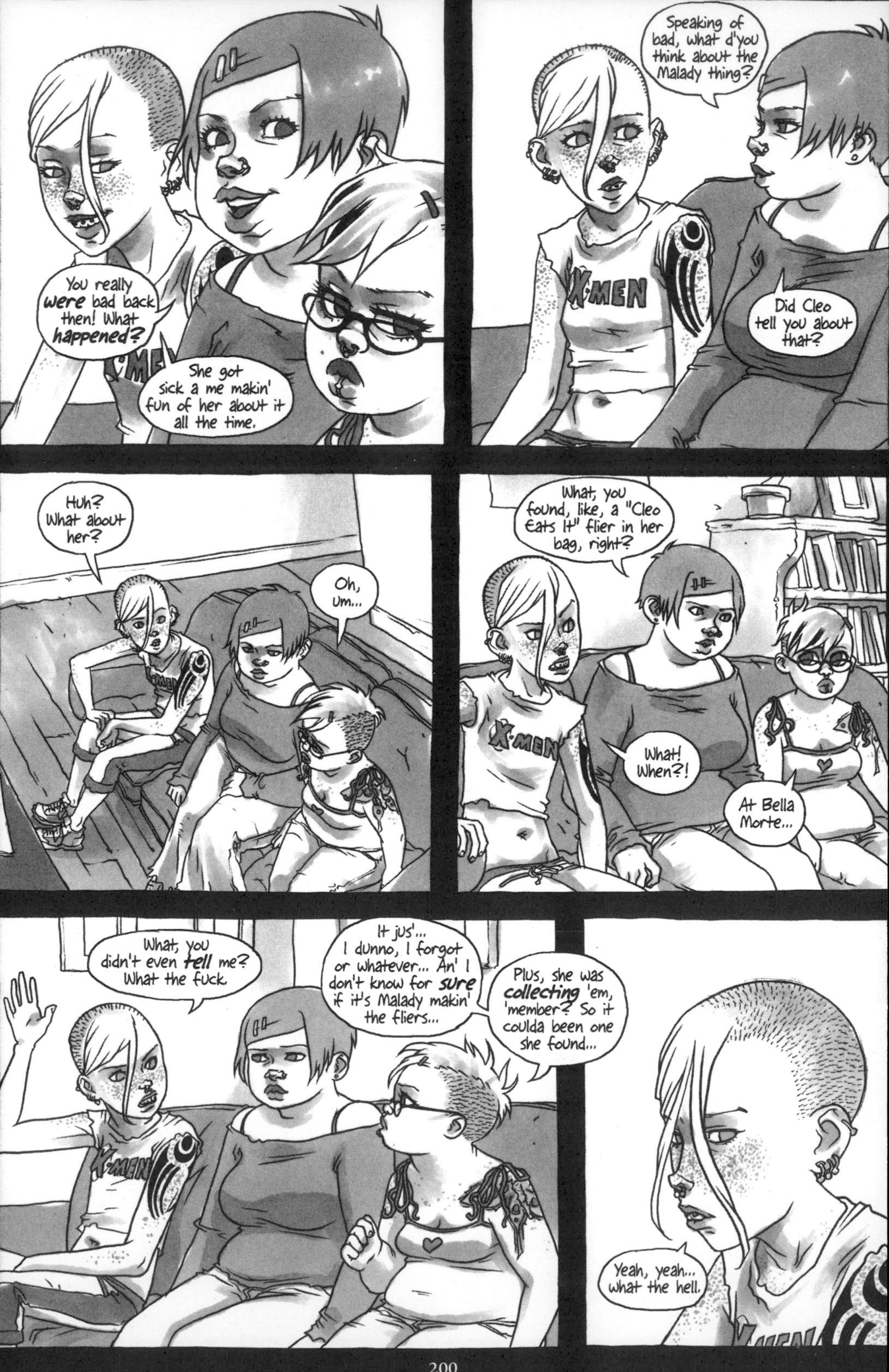
You really **were** bad back then! What **happened?**
She got sick a me makin' fun of her about it all the time.
Speaking of bad, what d'you think about the Malady thing?
Did Cleo tell you about that?
Huh? What about her?
Oh, um...
What, you found, like, a "Cleo Eats It" flier in her bag, right?
What! When?!
At Bella Morte...
What, you didn't even **tell** me? What the fuck.
It jus'... I dunno, I forgot or whatever... An' I don't know for **sure** if it's Malady makin' the fliers...
Plus, she was **collecting** 'em, 'member? So it coulda been one she found...
Yeah, yeah... what the hell.

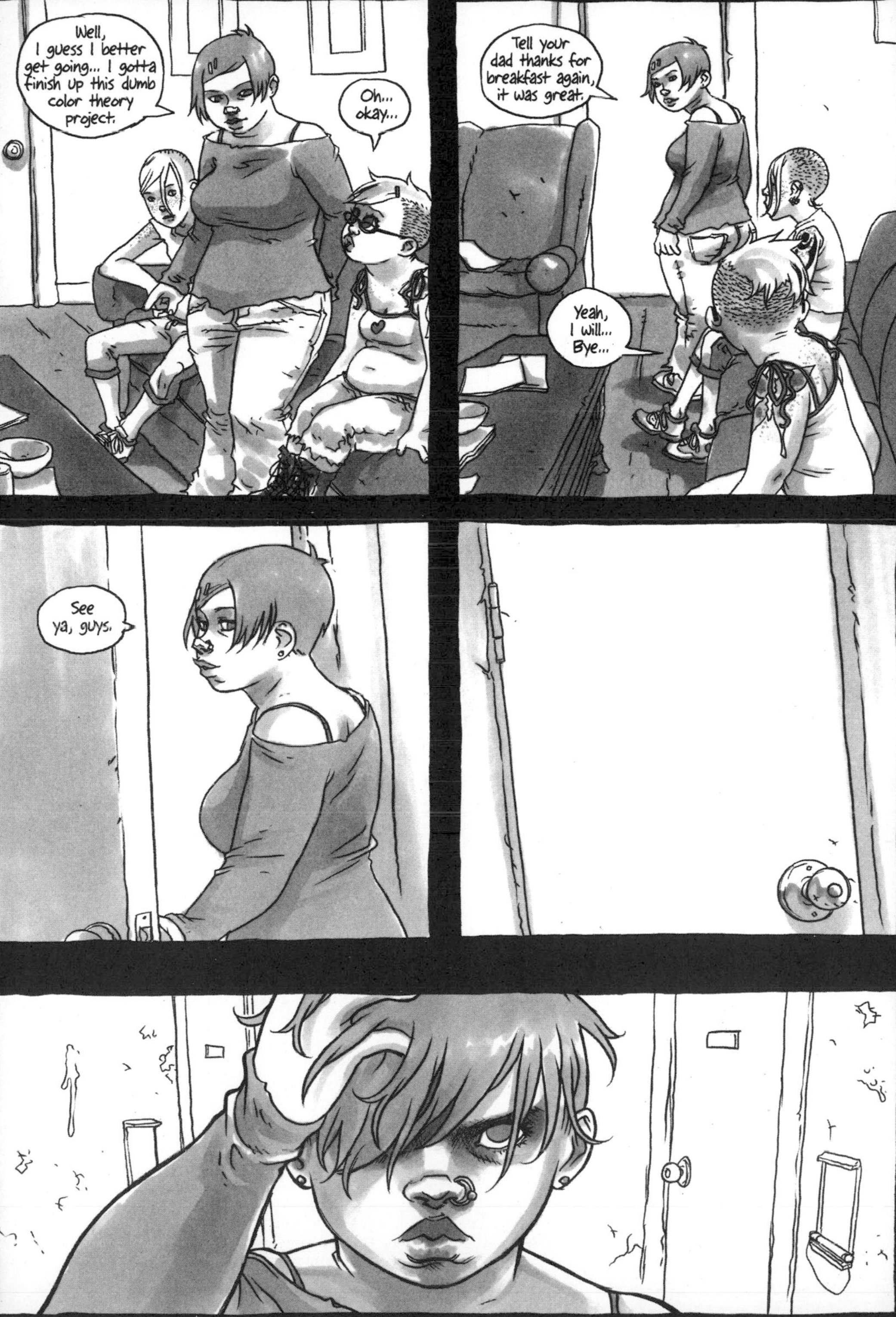
Well, I guess I better get going... I gotta finish up this dumb color theory project.
Oh... okay...
Tell your dad thanks for breakfast again, it was great.
Yeah, I will... Bye...
See ya, guys.

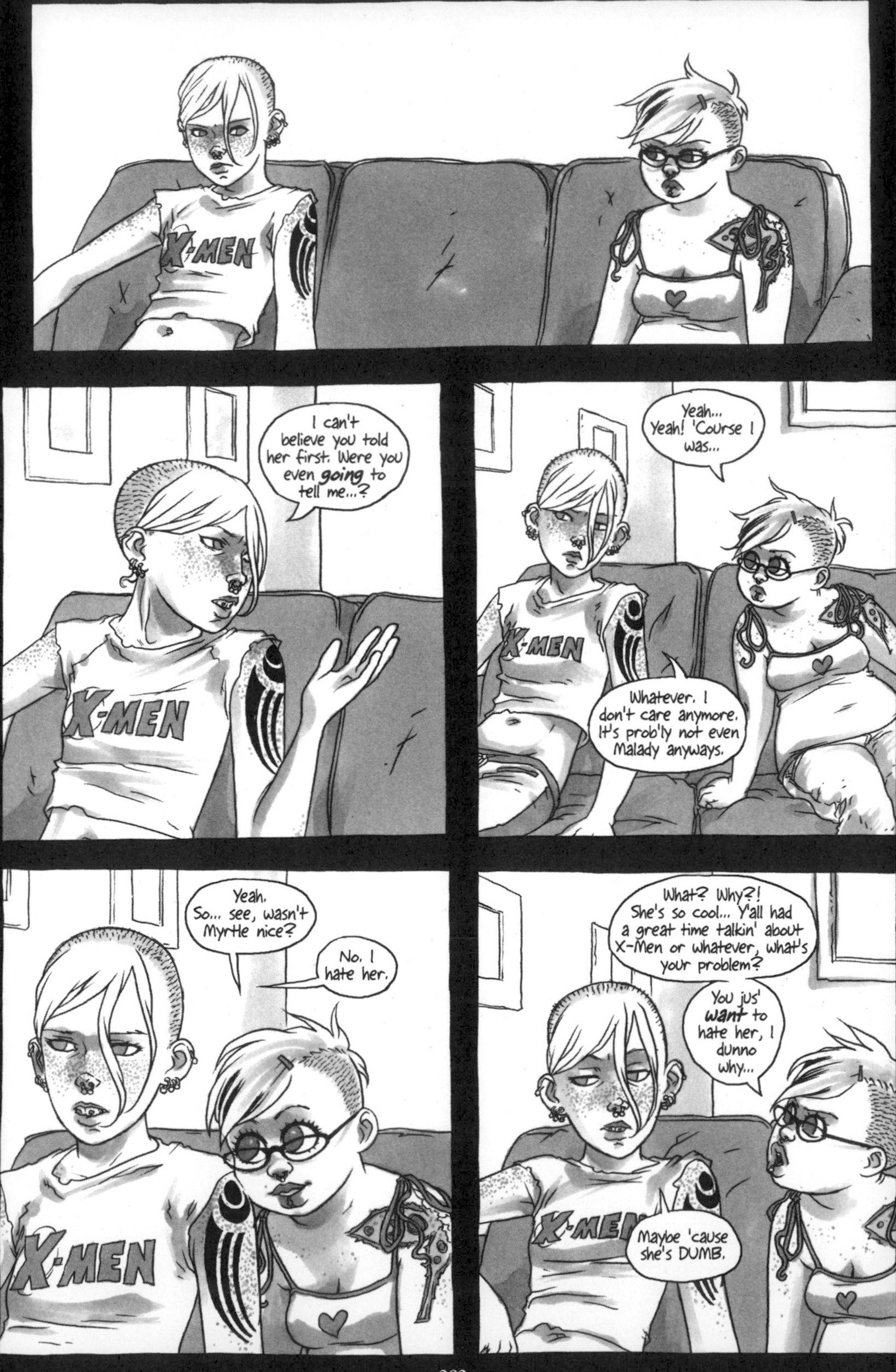
X-MEN
I can't believe you told her first. Were you even going to tell me...?
X-MEN
Yeah... Yeah! 'Course I was...
X-MEN
Whatever. I don't care anymore. It's prob'ly not even Malady anyways.
Yeah. So... see, wasn't Myrtle nice?
No. I hate her.
X-MEN
What? Why?! She's so cool... Y'all had a great time talkin' about X-Men or whatever, what's your problem?
You jus' want to hate her, I dunno why...
Maybe 'cause she's DUMB.

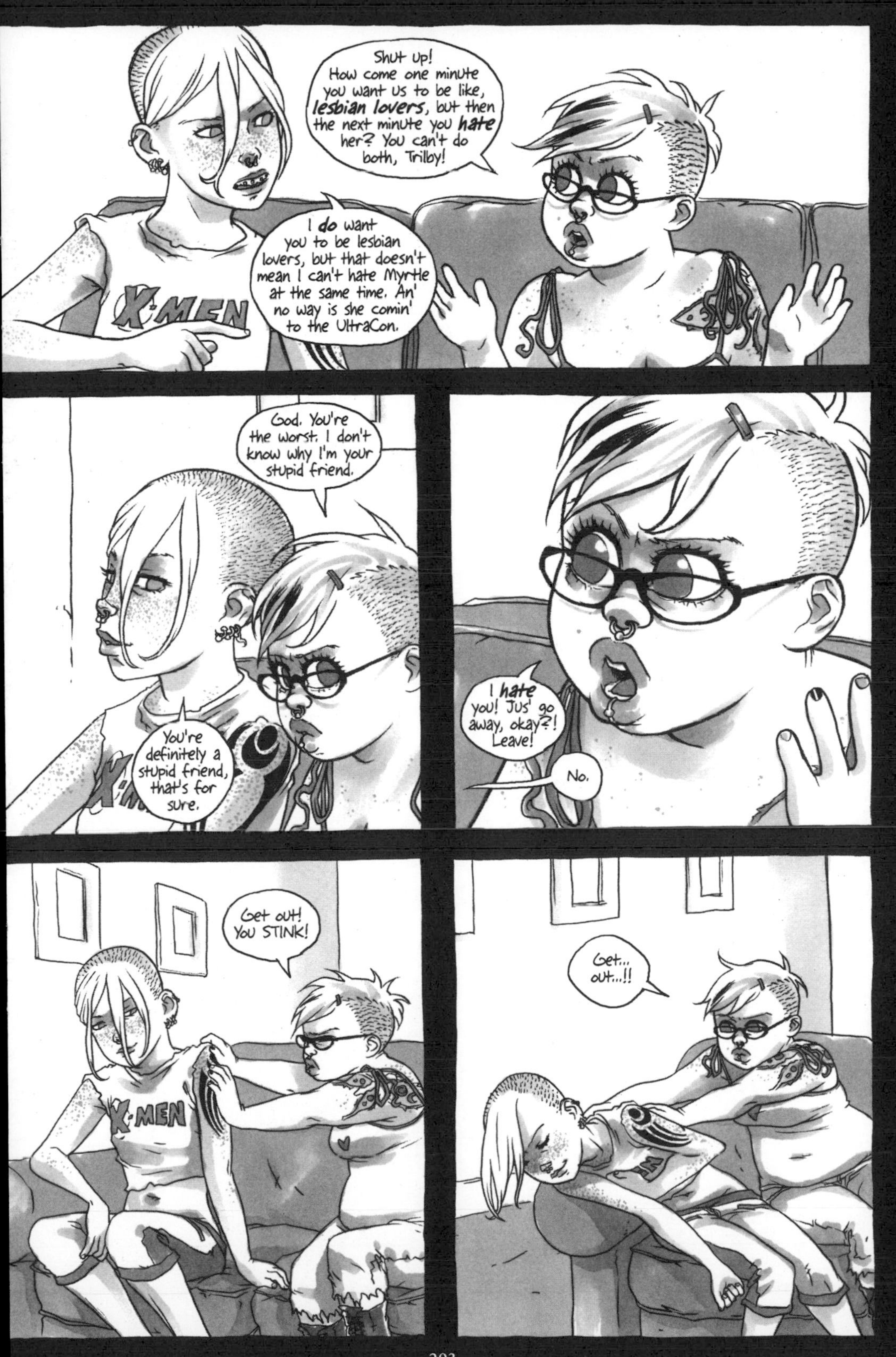
Shut up! How come one minute you want us to be like, **lesbian lovers**, but then the next minute you **hate** her? You can't do both, Trilby!
I **do** want you to be lesbian lovers, but that doesn't mean I can't hate Myrtle at the same time. An' no way is she comin' to the UltraCon.
God. You're the worst. I don't know why I'm your stupid friend.
You're definitely a stupid friend, that's for sure.
I **hate** you! Jus' go away, okay?! Leave!
No.
Get out! You STINK!
Get... out...!!

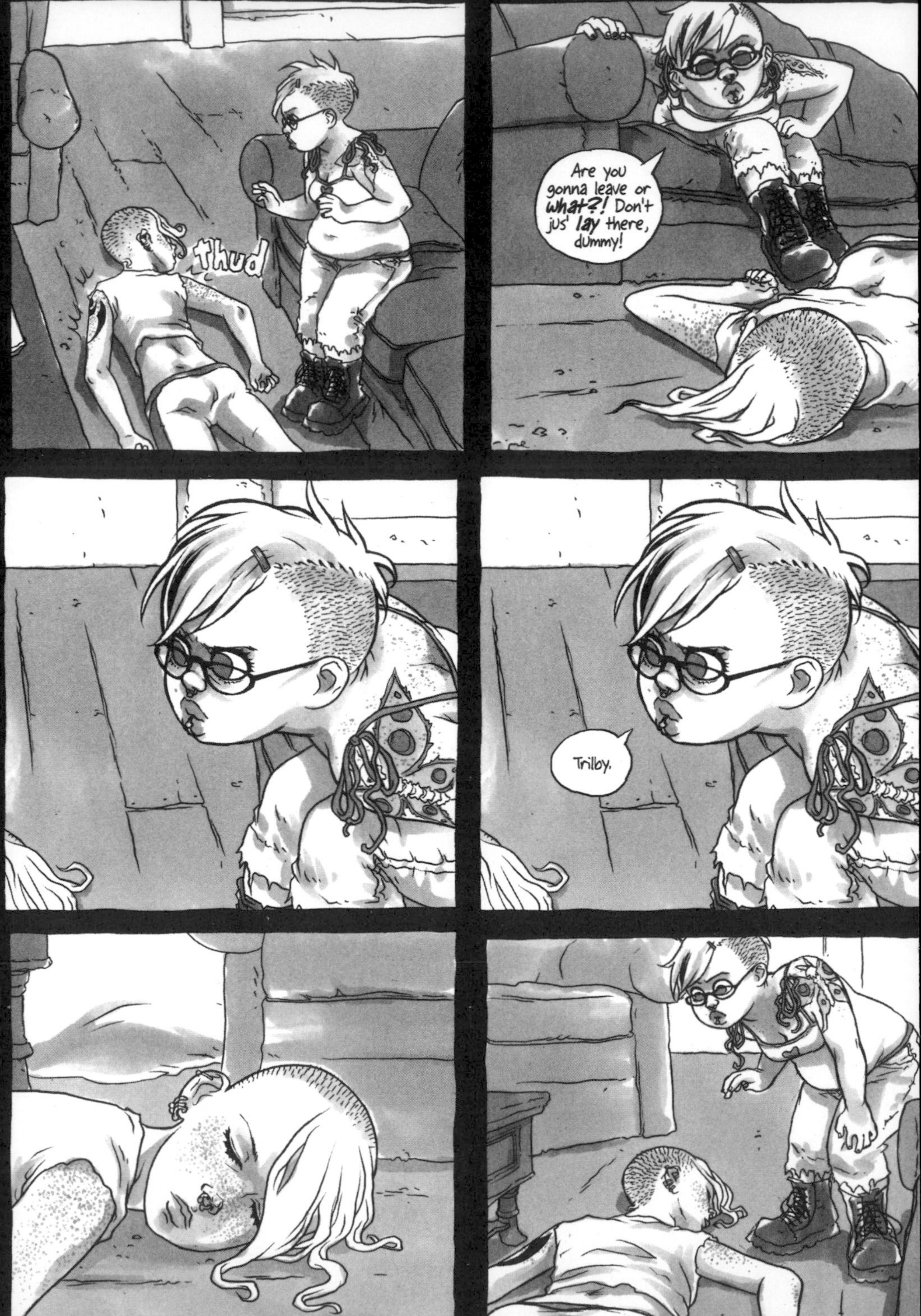
thud
Are you gonna leave or what?! Don't jus' lay there, dummy!
Trilby.

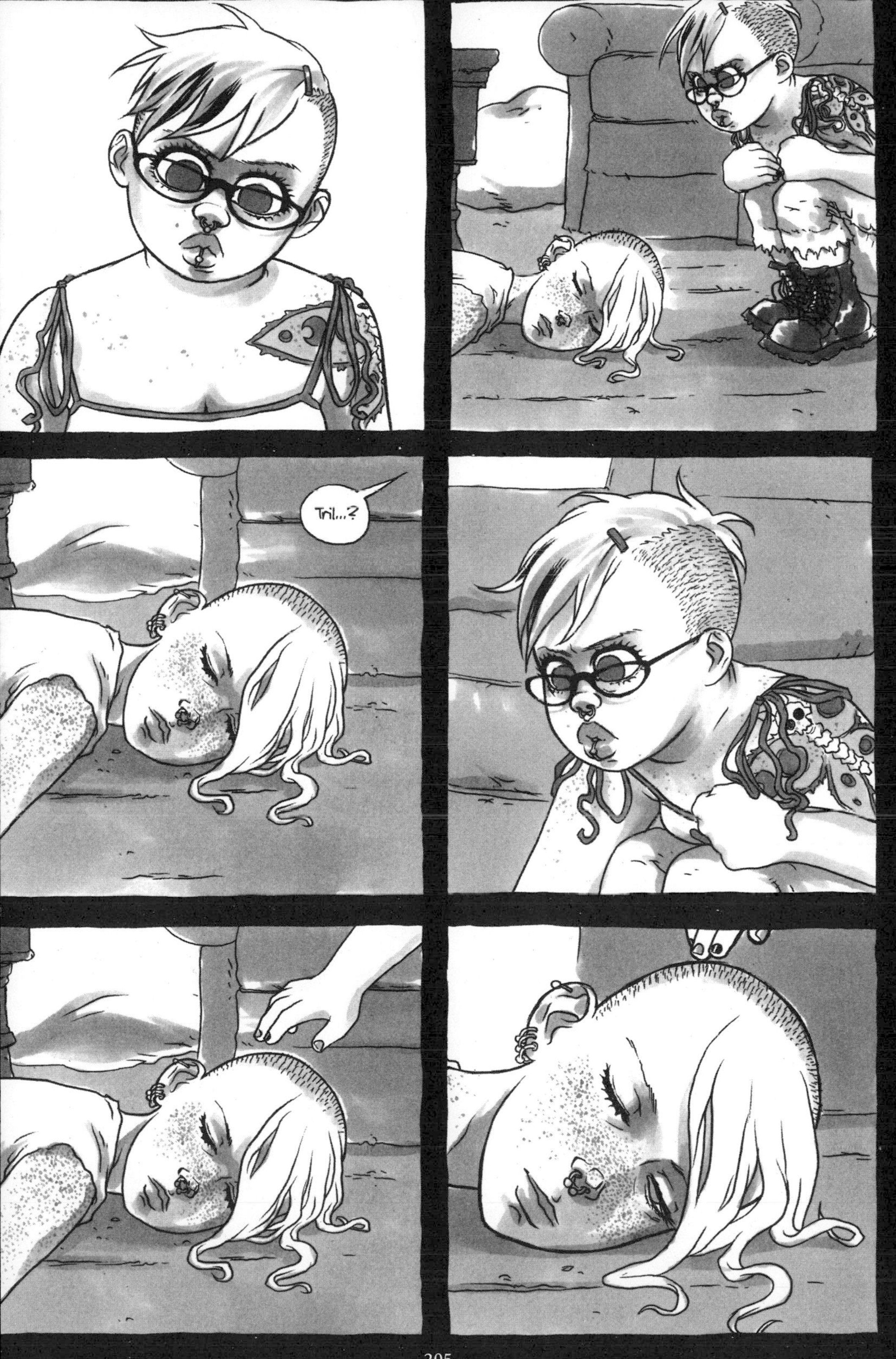
Tril...?

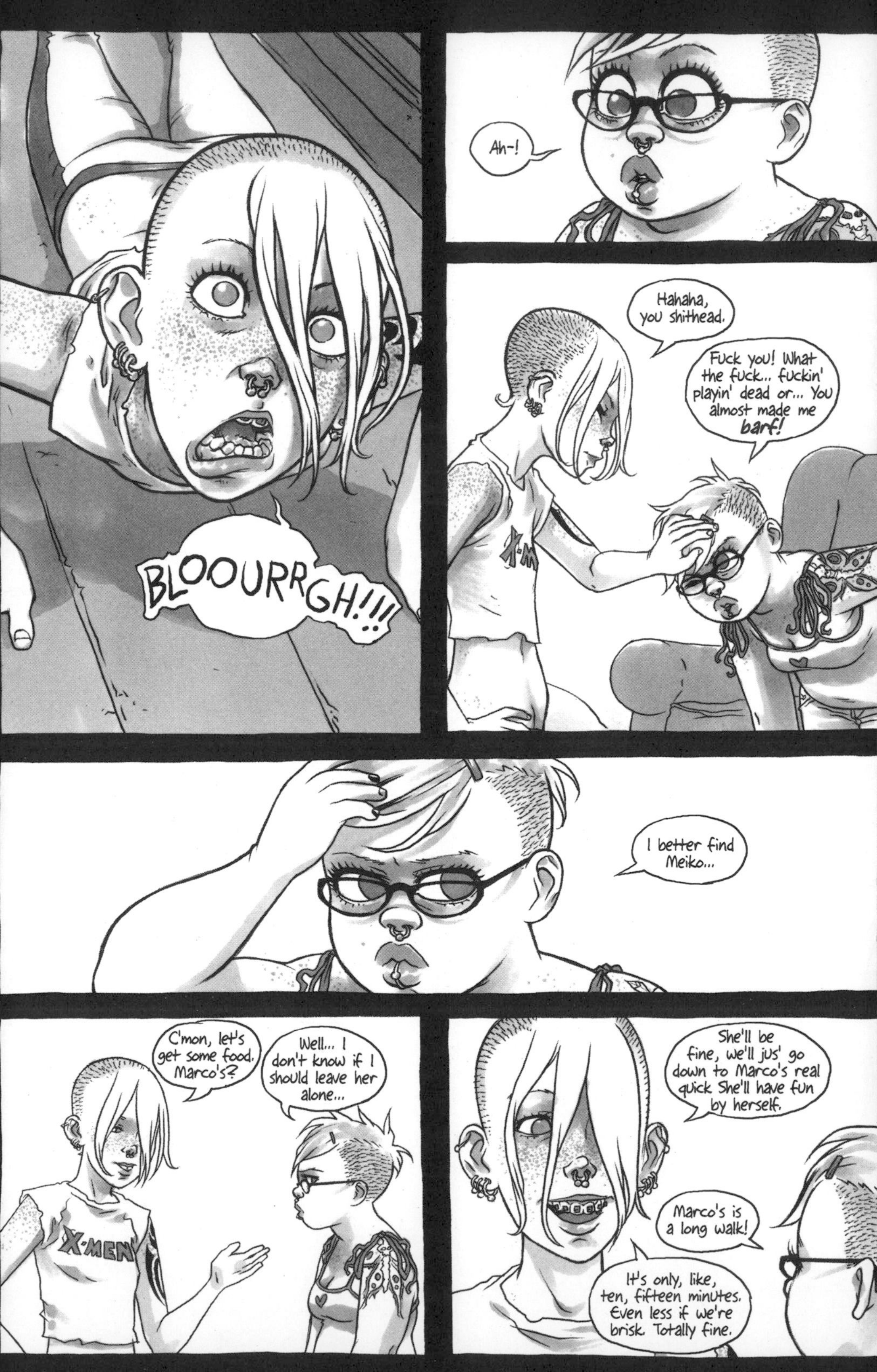
BLOOURRGH!!!
Ah-!
Hahaha, you shithead.
Fuck you! What the fuck... fuckin' playin' dead or... You almost made me **barf!**
I better find Meiko...
C'mon, let's get some food. Marco's?
Well... I don't know if I should leave her alone...
She'll be fine, we'll jus' go down to Marco's real quick She'll have fun by herself.
Marco's is a long walk!
It's only, like, ten, fifteen minutes. Even less if we're brisk. Totally fine.

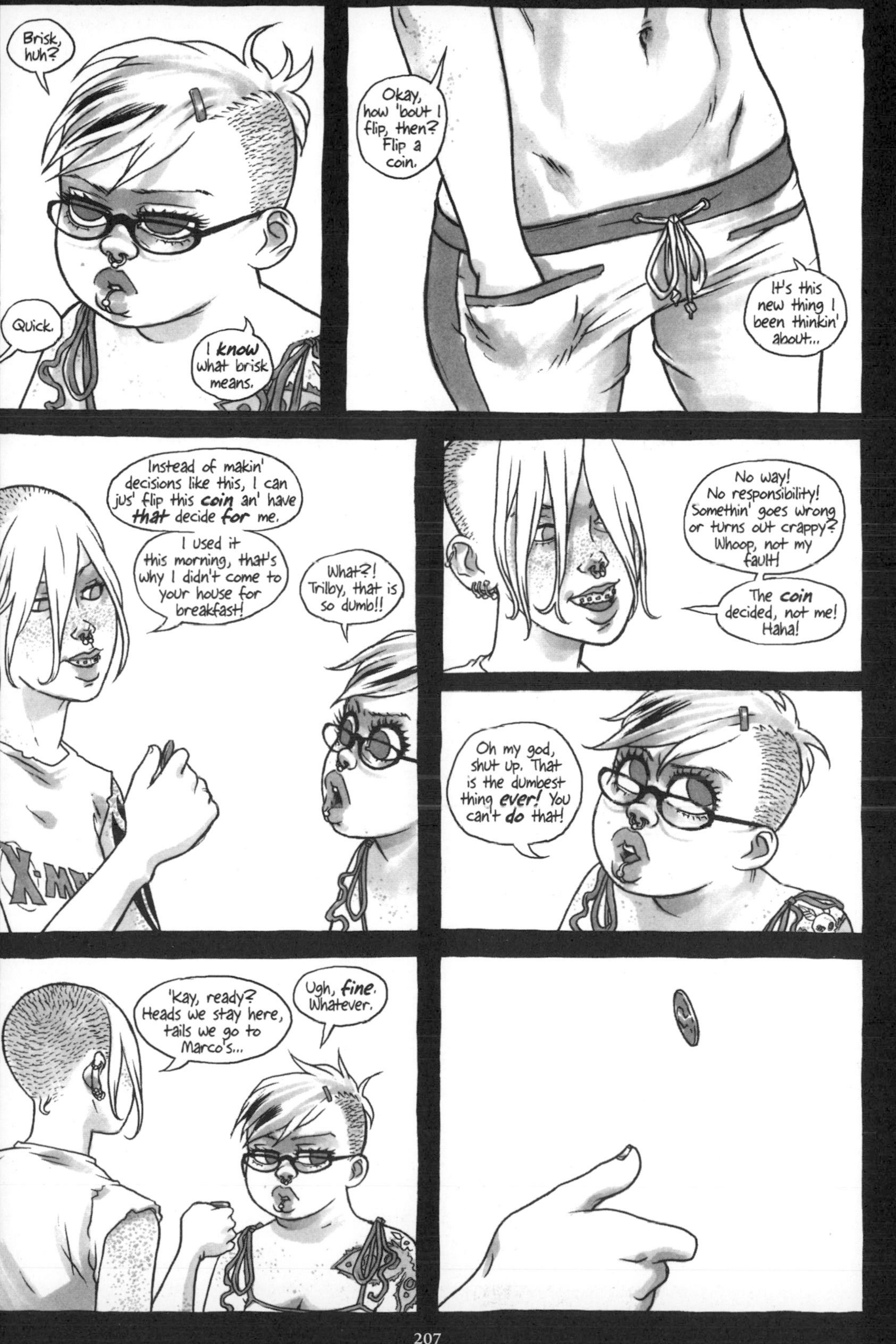
Brisk, huh?
Quick.
I know what brisk means.
Okay, how 'bout I flip, then? Flip a coin.
It's this new thing I been thinkin' about...
Instead of makin' decisions like this, I can jus' flip this coin an' have that decide for me.
I used it this morning, that's why I didn't come to your house for breakfast!
What?! Trilby, that is so dumb!!
No way! No responsibility! Somethin' goes wrong or turns out crappy? Whoop, not my fault!
The coin decided, not me! Haha!
Oh my god, shut up. That is the dumbest thing ever! You can't do that!
'Kay, ready? Heads we stay here, tails we go to Marco's...
Ugh, fine. Whatever.

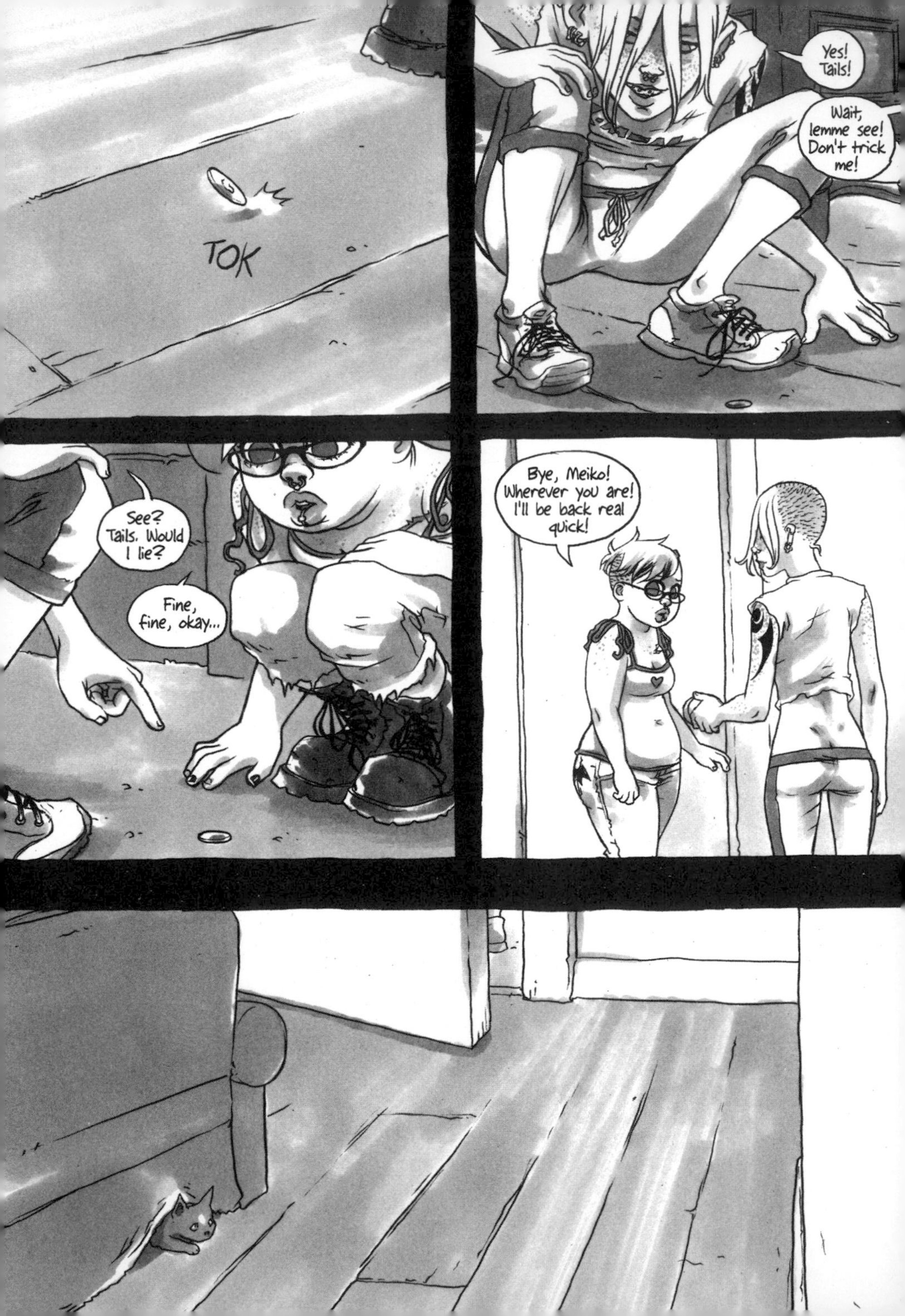
TOK
Yes! Tails!
Wait, lemme see! Don't trick me!
See? Tails. Would I lie?
Fine, fine, okay...
Bye, Meiko! Wherever you are! I'll be back real quick!

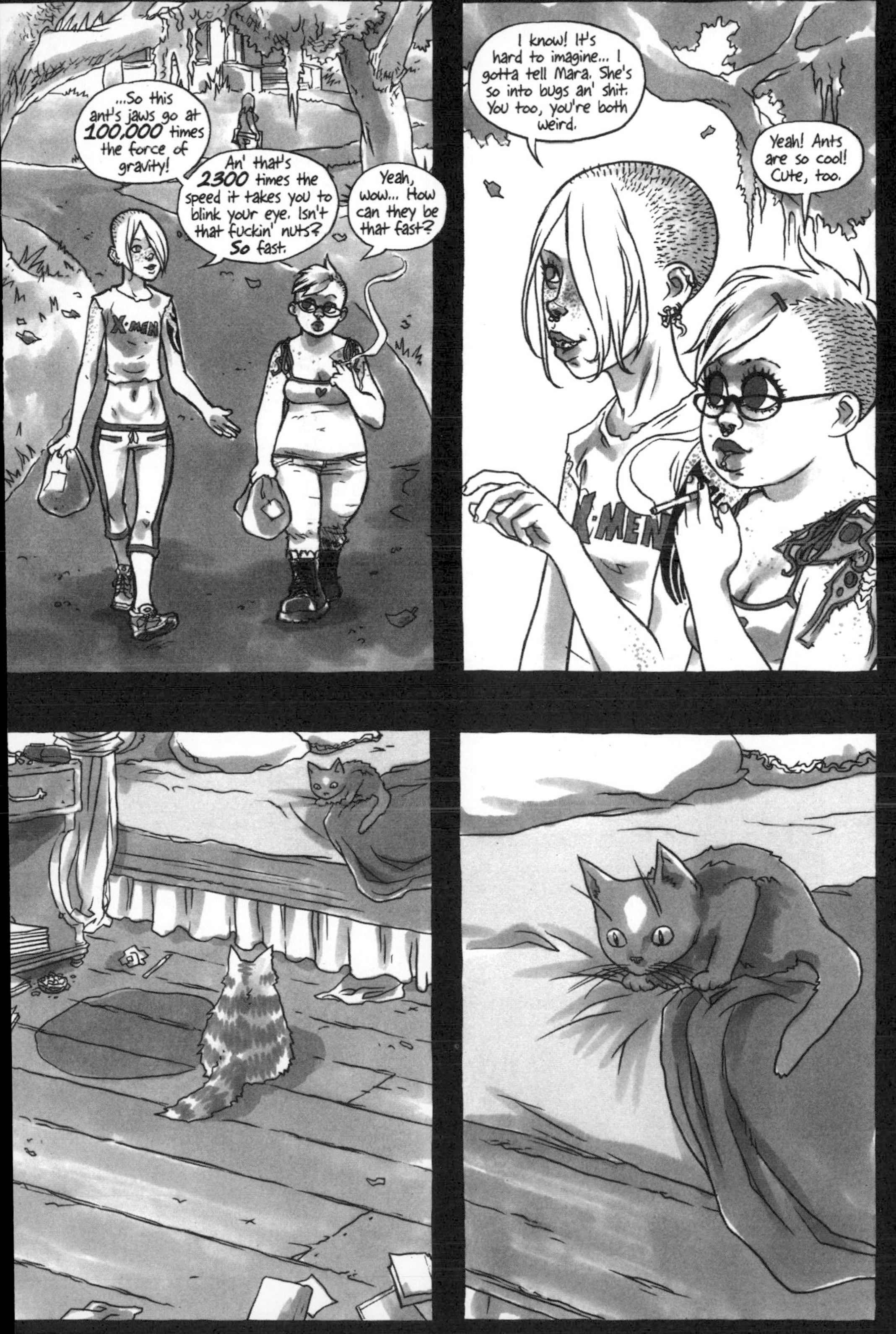
...So this ant's jaws go at 100,000 times the force of gravity!
An' that's 2300 times the speed it takes you to blink your eye. Isn't that fuckin' nuts? So fast.
Yeah, wow... How can they be that fast?
I know! It's hard to imagine... I gotta tell Mara. She's so into bugs an' shit. You too, you're both weird.
Yeah! Ants are so cool! Cute, too.
X-MEN
X-MEN

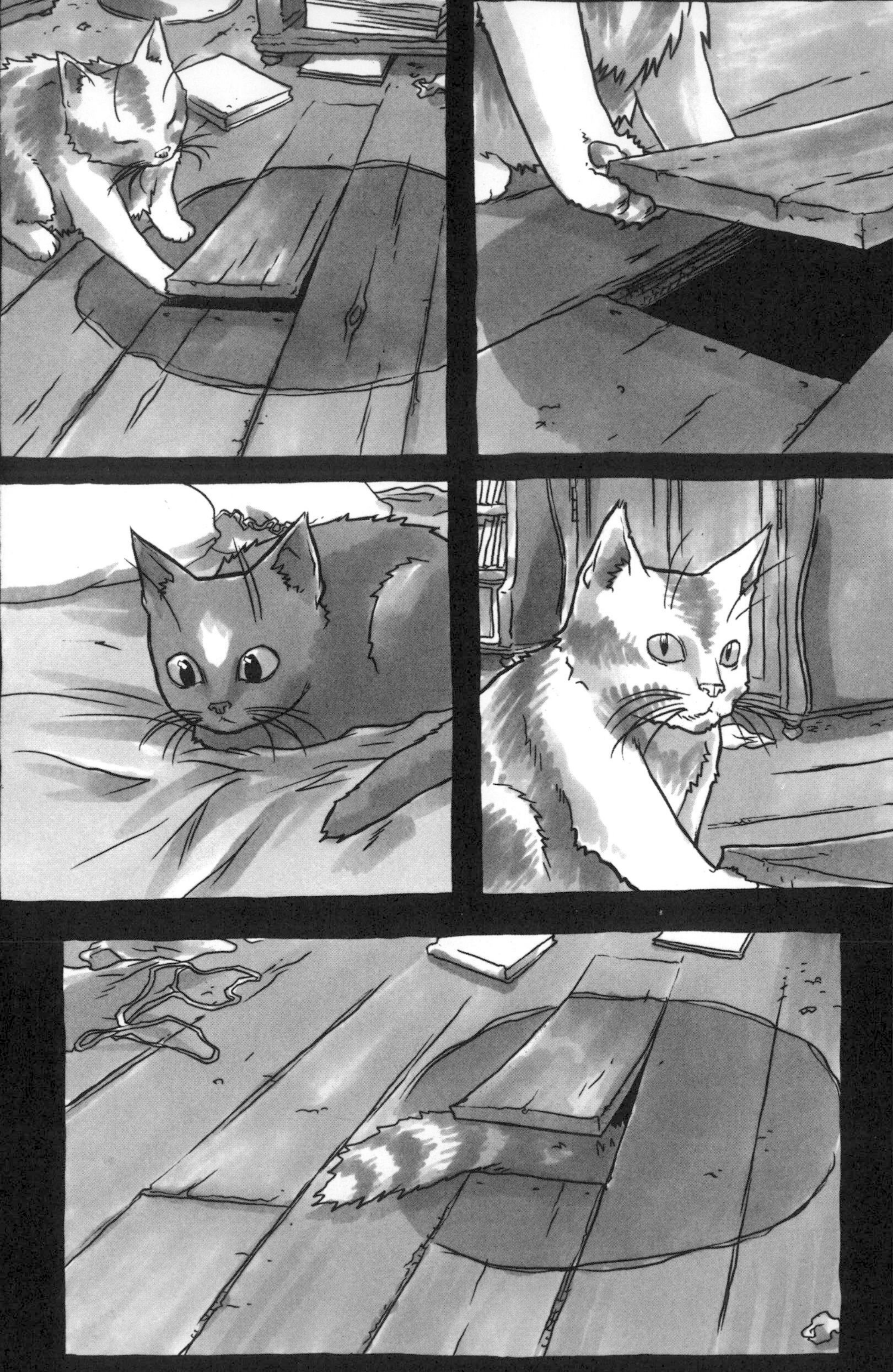

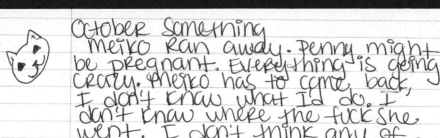

October something
Meiko ran away. Penny might be pregnant. Everything is going crazy. Meiko has to come back, I don't know what I'd do. I don't know where the fuck she went. I don't think any of the doors or windows were open, but I've checked the whole place and she's absolutely not here. Oh god, I don't know. Where is she?!!

Meiko came back! And then Penny! Oh my god! She's probably pregnant, but I just know she is! I really hope she keeps the baby, I want to be an aunt, and it would be cool to have a baby around. Everything sucks. I don't feel like writing ~~anymore~~ anymore.

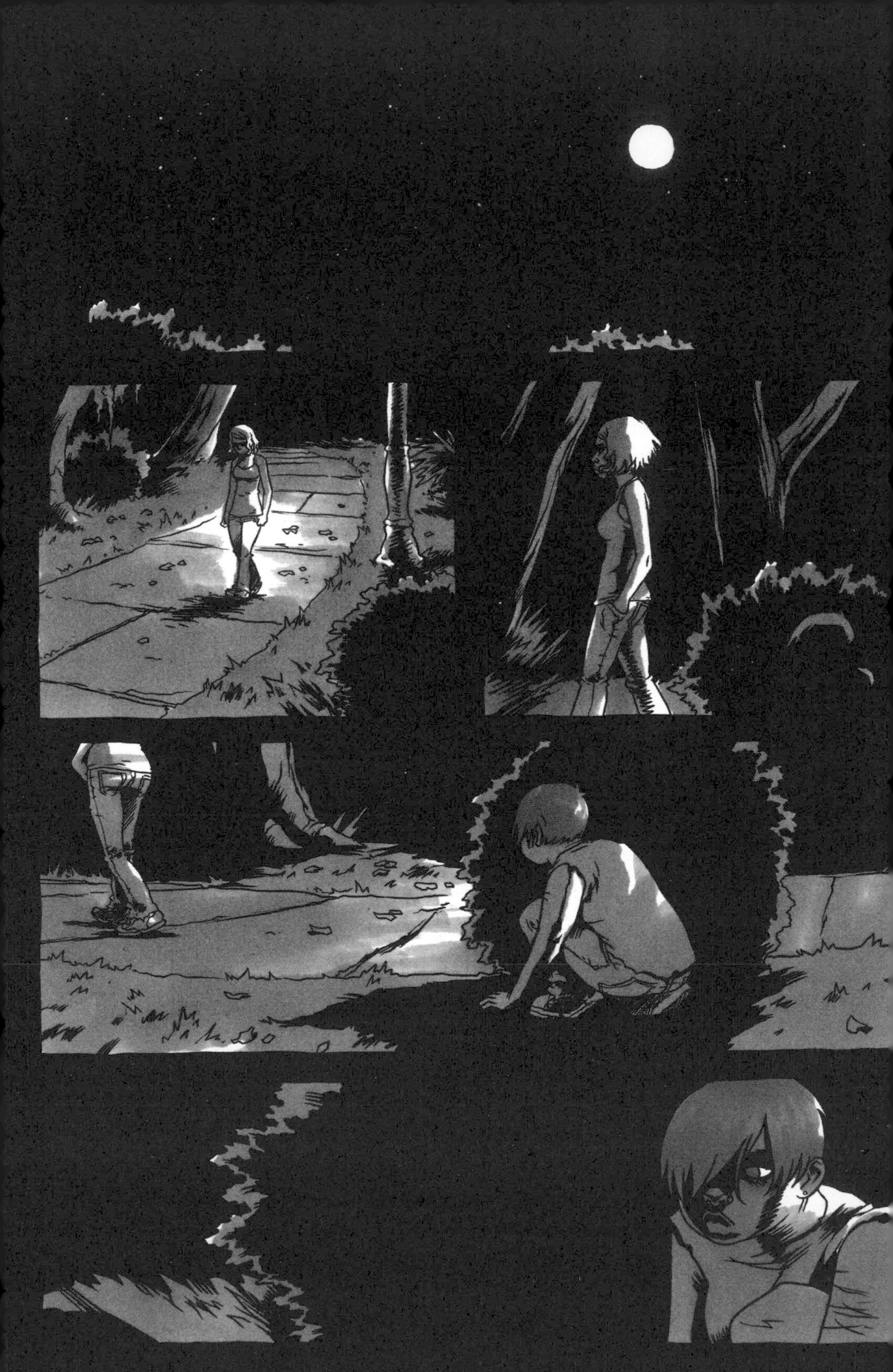

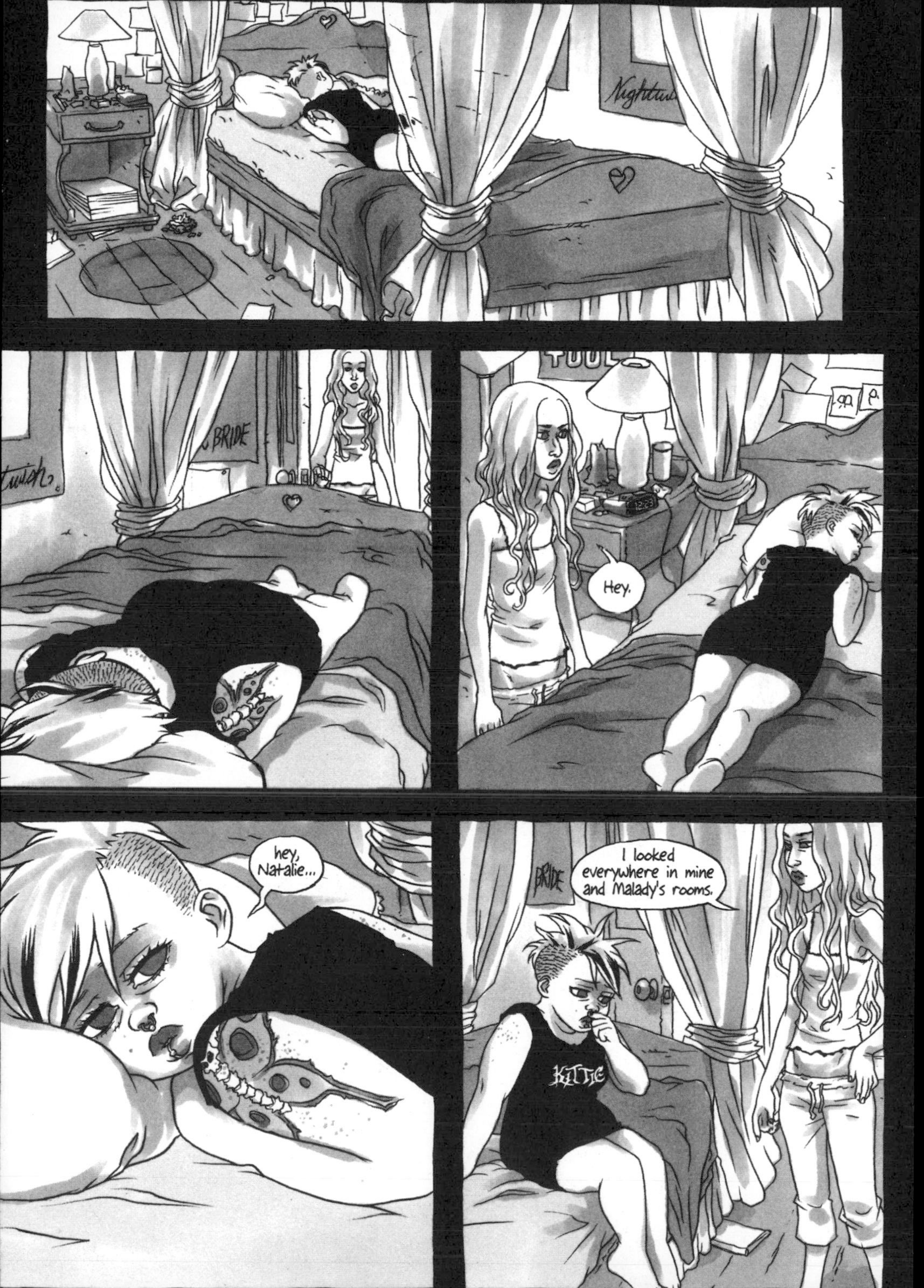
Hey.
hey, Natalie...
I looked everywhere in mine and Malady's rooms.

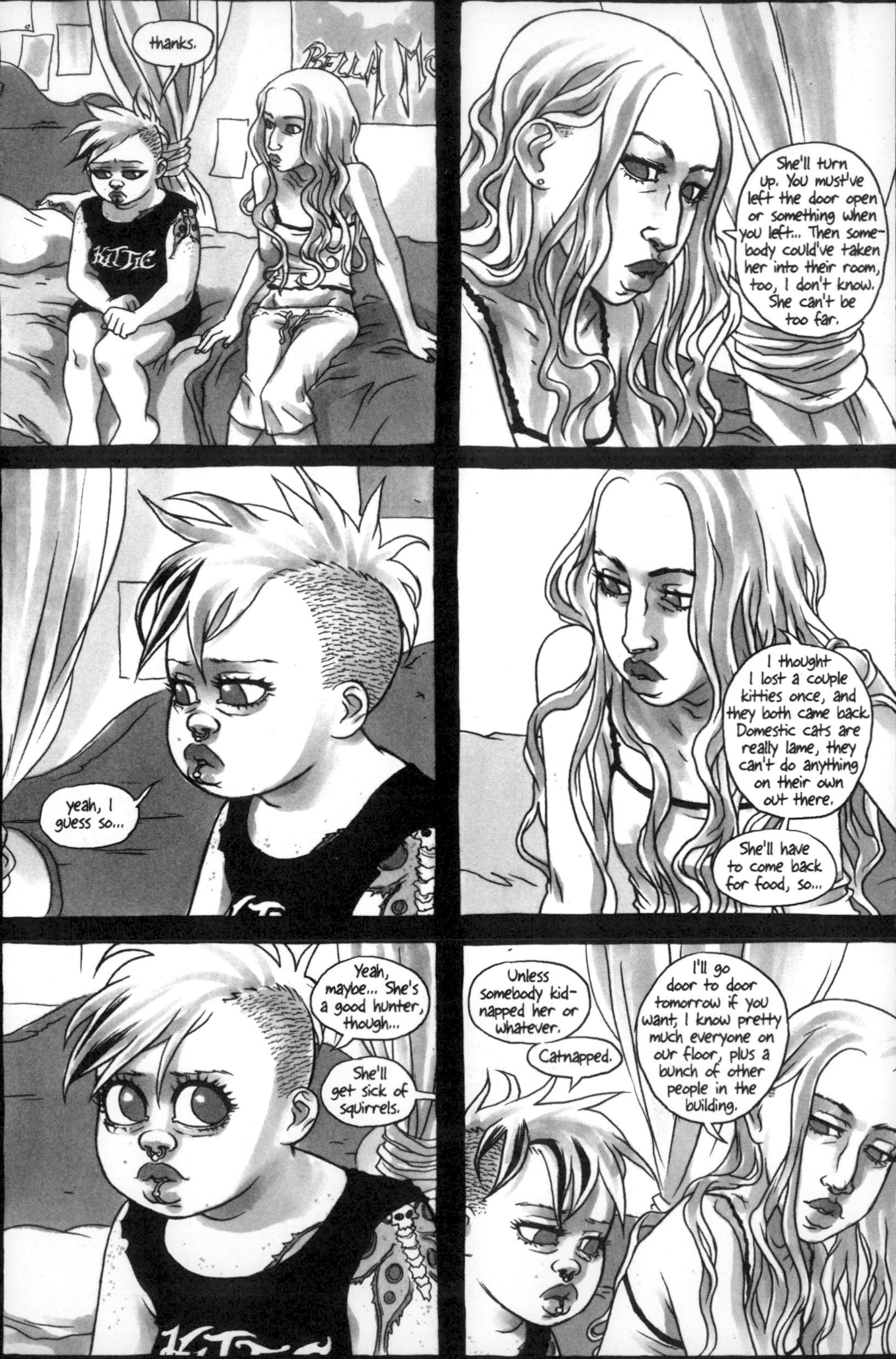
thanks.
BELLA MO
KITTIE
She'll turn up. You must've left the door open or something when you left... Then somebody could've taken her into their room, too, I don't know. She can't be too far.
yeah, I guess so...
I thought I lost a couple kitties once, and they both came back. Domestic cats are really lame, they can't do anything on their own out there.
She'll have to come back for food, so...
Yeah, maybe... She's a good hunter, though...
She'll get sick of squirrels.
Unless somebody kid-napped her or whatever.
Catnapped.
I'll go door to door tomorrow if you want, I know pretty much everyone on our floor, plus a bunch of other people in the building.

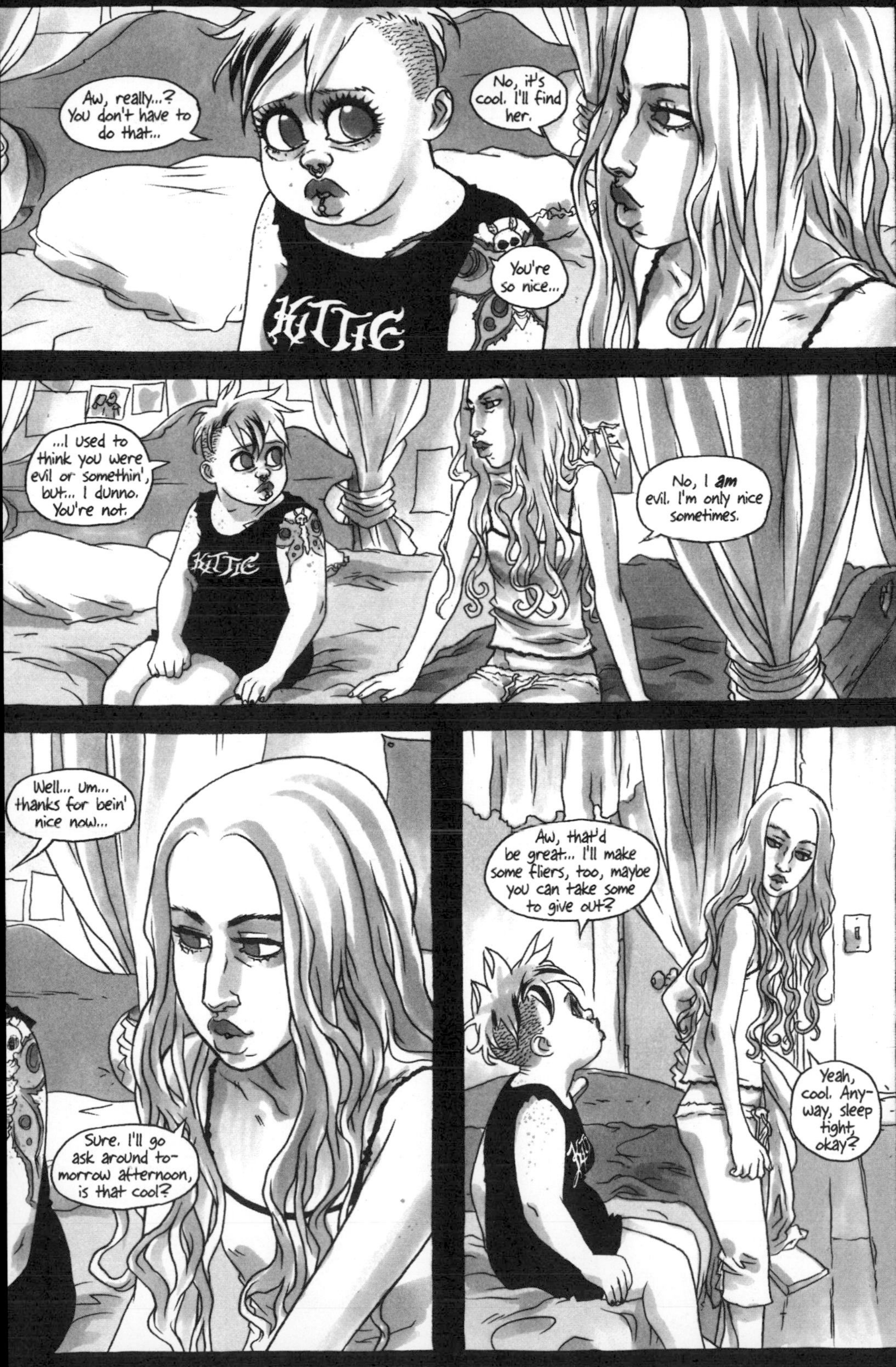

Aw, really...? You don't have to do that...
No, it's cool. I'll find her.
You're so nice...
KITTIE
...I used to think you were evil or somethin', but... I dunno. You're not.
No, I **am** evil. I'm only nice sometimes.
KITTIE
Well... um... thanks for bein' nice now...
Sure. I'll go ask around to-morrow afternoon, is that cool?
Aw, that'd be great... I'll make some fliers, too, maybe you can take some to give out?
Yeah, cool. Any-way, sleep tight, okay?

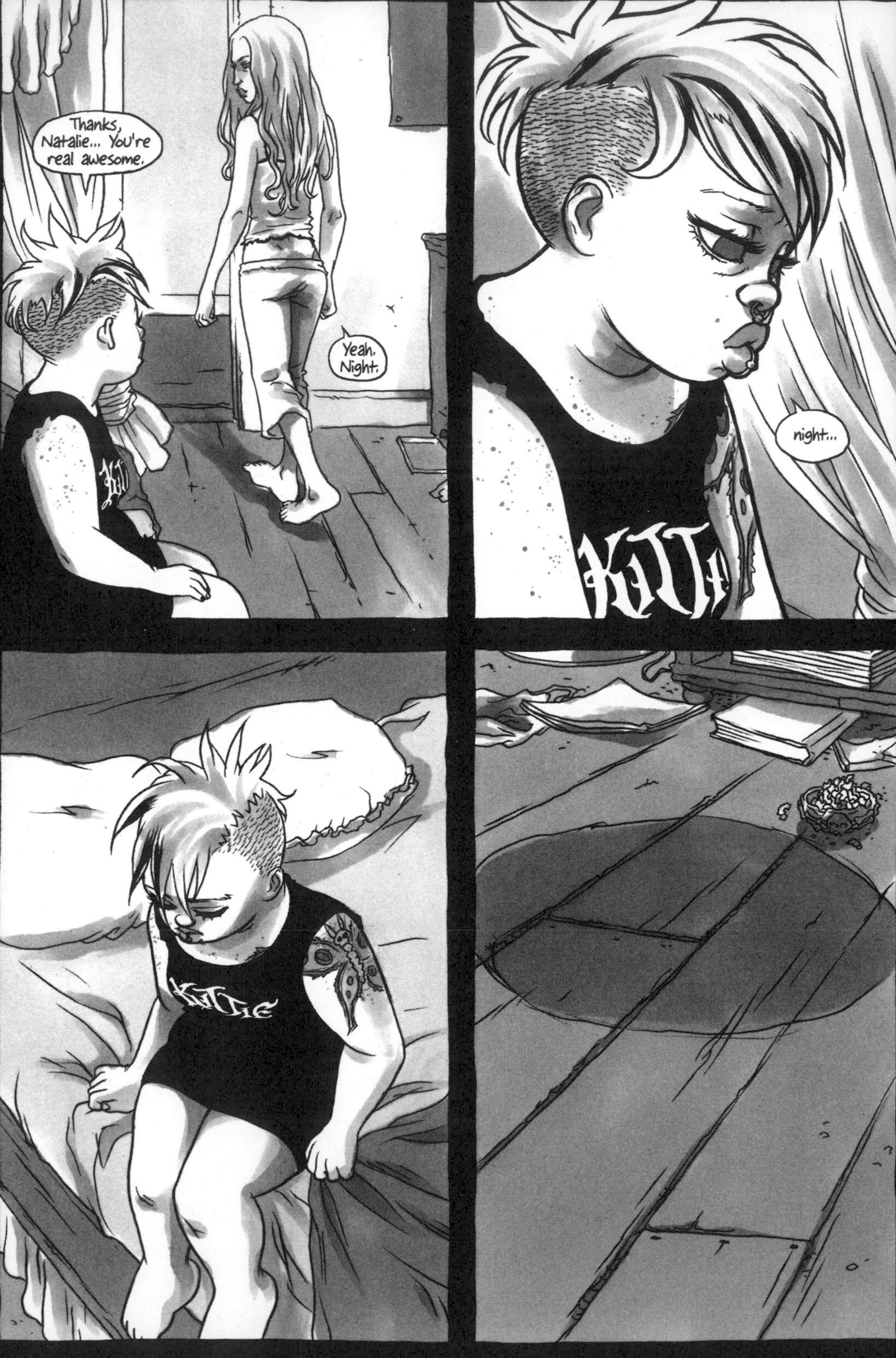
Thanks, Natalie... You're real awesome.
Yeah. Night.
night...

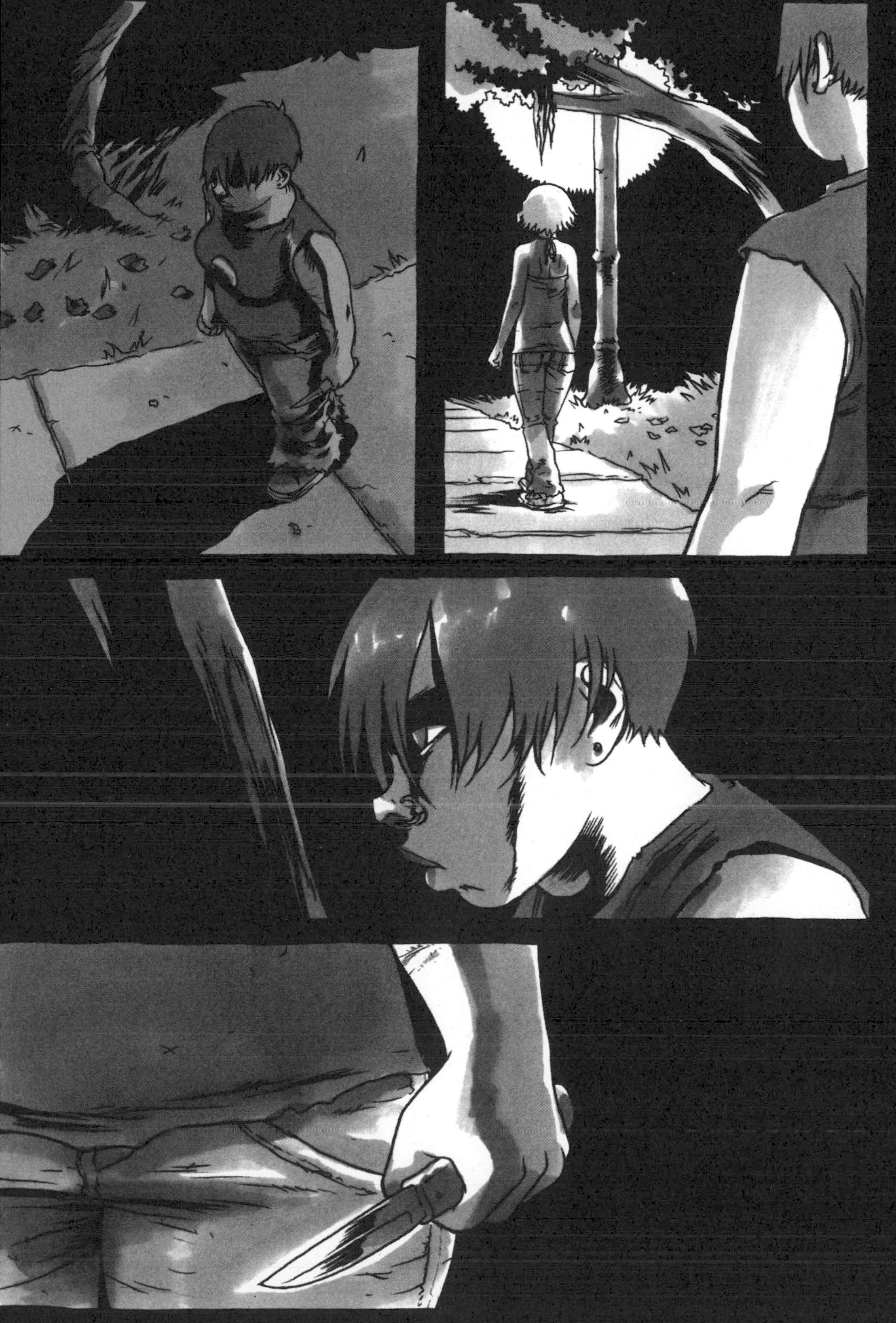

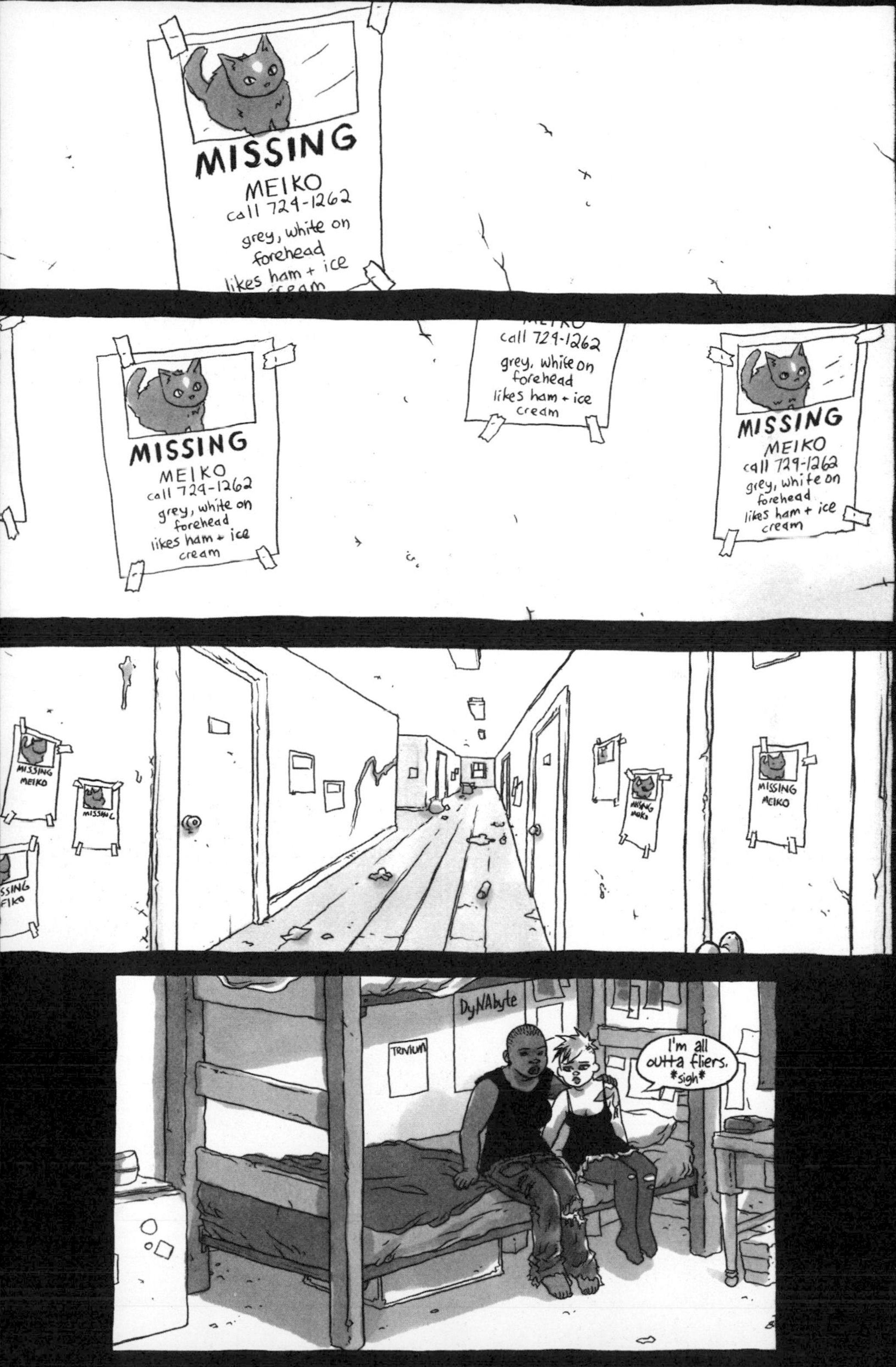
MISSING
MEIKO
call 729-1262
grey, white on forehead
likes ham + ice cream
call 729-1262
grey, white on forehead
likes ham + ice cream
MISSING
MEIKO
call 729-1262
grey, white on forehead
likes ham + ice cream
MISSING
MEIKO
call 729-1262
grey, white on forehead
likes ham + ice cream
MISSING
MEIKO
MISSING
MEIKO
DyNAbyte
TRIVIUM
I'm all outta fliers.
sigh

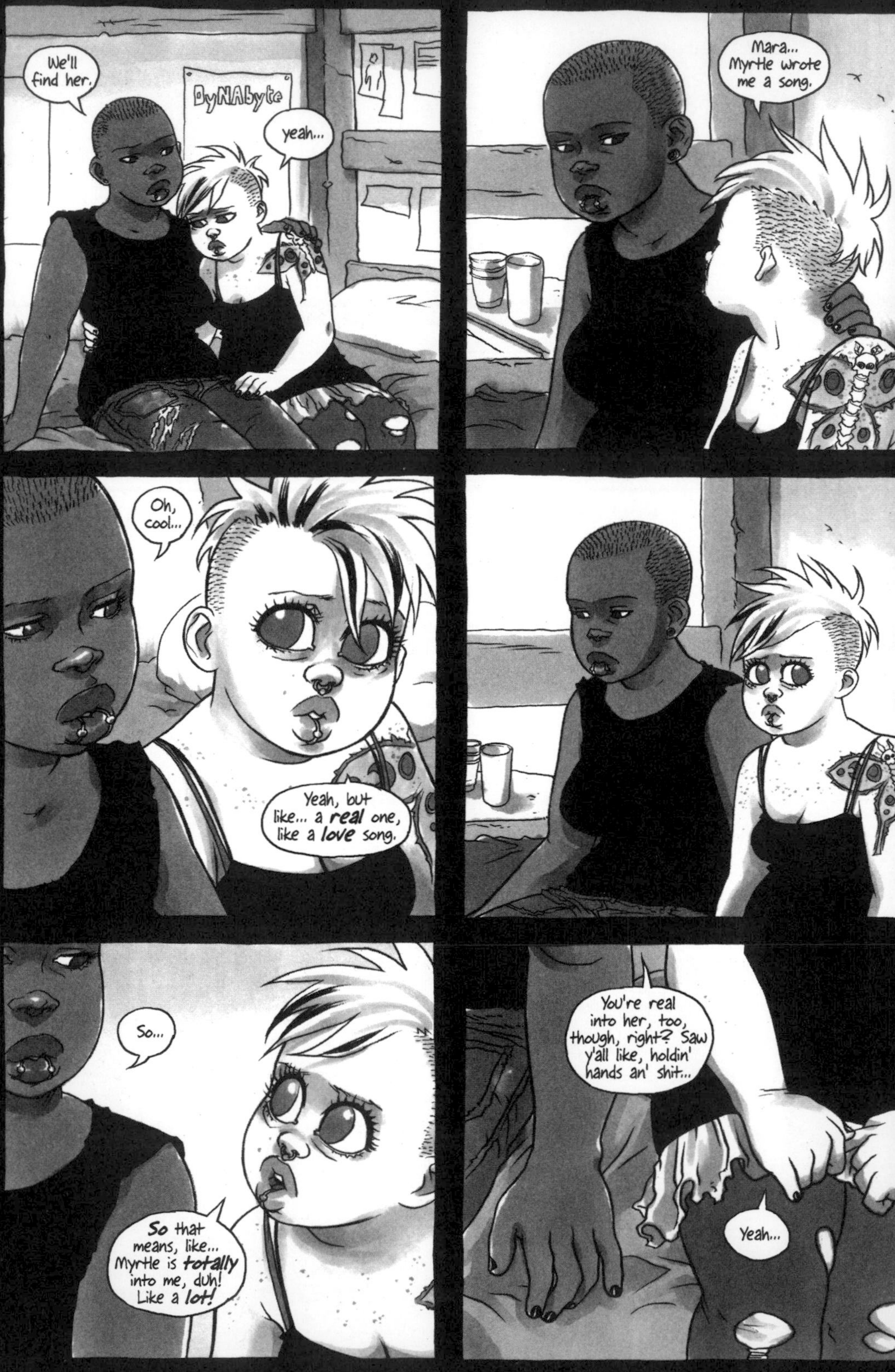

We'll find her.
yeah...
DyNAbyte
Mara... Myrtle wrote me a song.
Oh, cool...
Yeah, but like... a **real** one, like a **love** song.
So...
So that means, like... Myrtle is **totally** into me, duh! Like a **lot**!
You're real into her, too, though, right? Saw y'all like, holdin' hands an' shit...
Yeah...

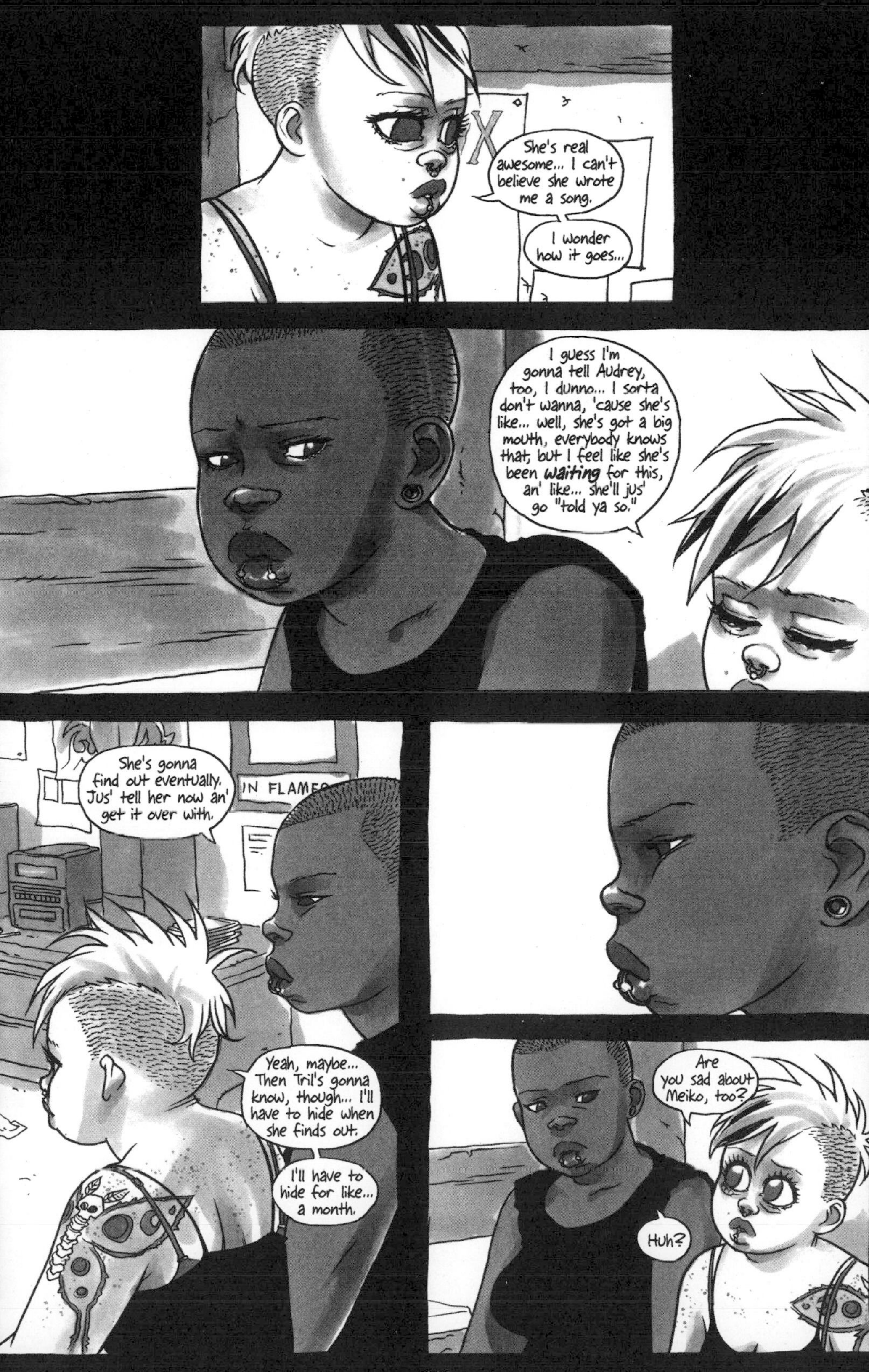
She's real awesome... I can't believe she wrote me a song.
I wonder how it goes...
I guess I'm gonna tell Audrey, too, I dunno... I sorta don't wanna, 'cause she's like... well, she's got a big mouth, everybody knows that, but I feel like she's been *waiting* for this, an' like... she'll jus' go "told ya so."
She's gonna find out eventually. Jus' tell her now an' get it over with.
IN FLAME
Yeah, maybe... Then Tril's gonna know, though... I'll have to hide when she finds out.
I'll have to hide for like... a month.
Are you sad about Meiko, too?
Huh?

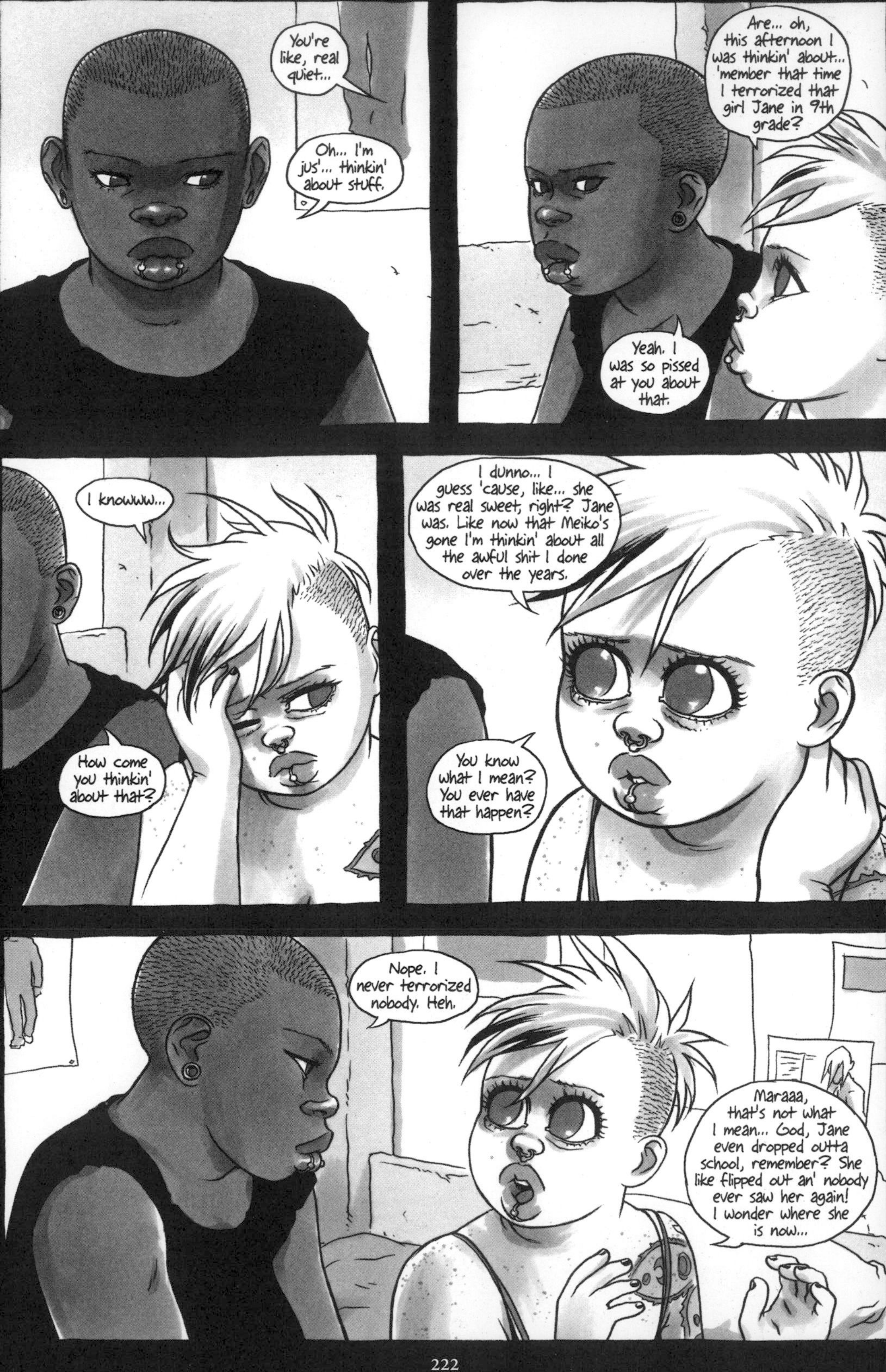
You're like, real quiet...
Oh... I'm jus'... thinkin' about stuff.
Are... oh, this afternoon I was thinkin' about... 'member that time I terrorized that girl Jane in 9th grade?
Yeah. I was so pissed at you about that.
I knowww...
How come you thinkin' about that?
I dunno... I guess 'cause, like... she was real sweet, right? Jane was. Like now that Meiko's gone I'm thinkin' about all the awful shit I done over the years.
You know what I mean? You ever have that happen?
Nope. I never terrorized nobody. Heh.
Maraaa, that's not what I mean... God, Jane even dropped outta school, remember? She like flipped out an' nobody ever saw her again! I wonder where she is now...

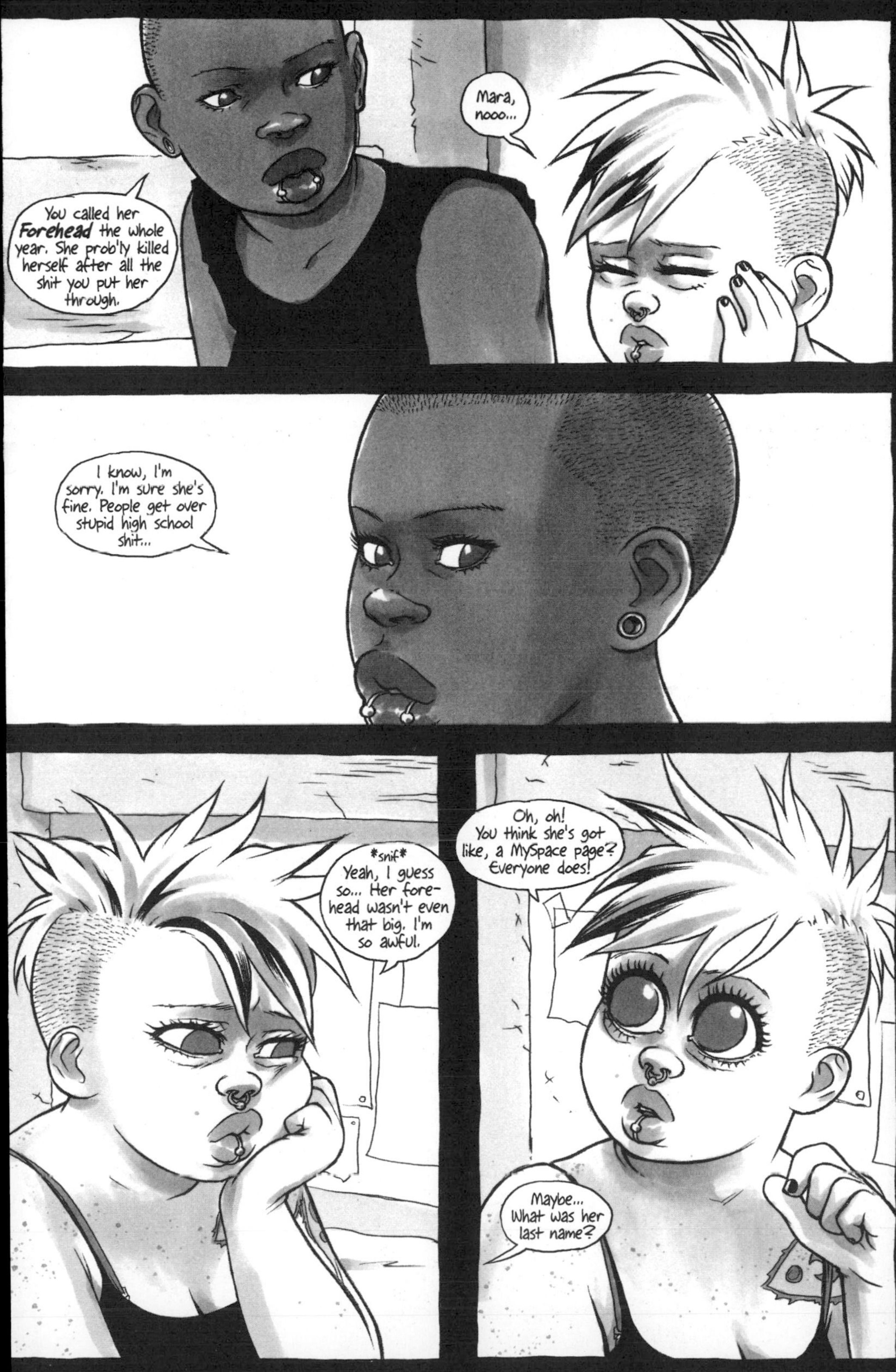
You called her Forehead the whole year. She prob'ly killed herself after all the shit you put her through.
Mara, nooo...
I know, I'm sorry. I'm sure she's fine. People get over stupid high school shit...
snif Yeah, I guess so... Her fore-head wasn't even that big. I'm so awful.
Oh, oh! You think she's got like, a MySpace page? Everyone does!
Maybe... What was her last name?

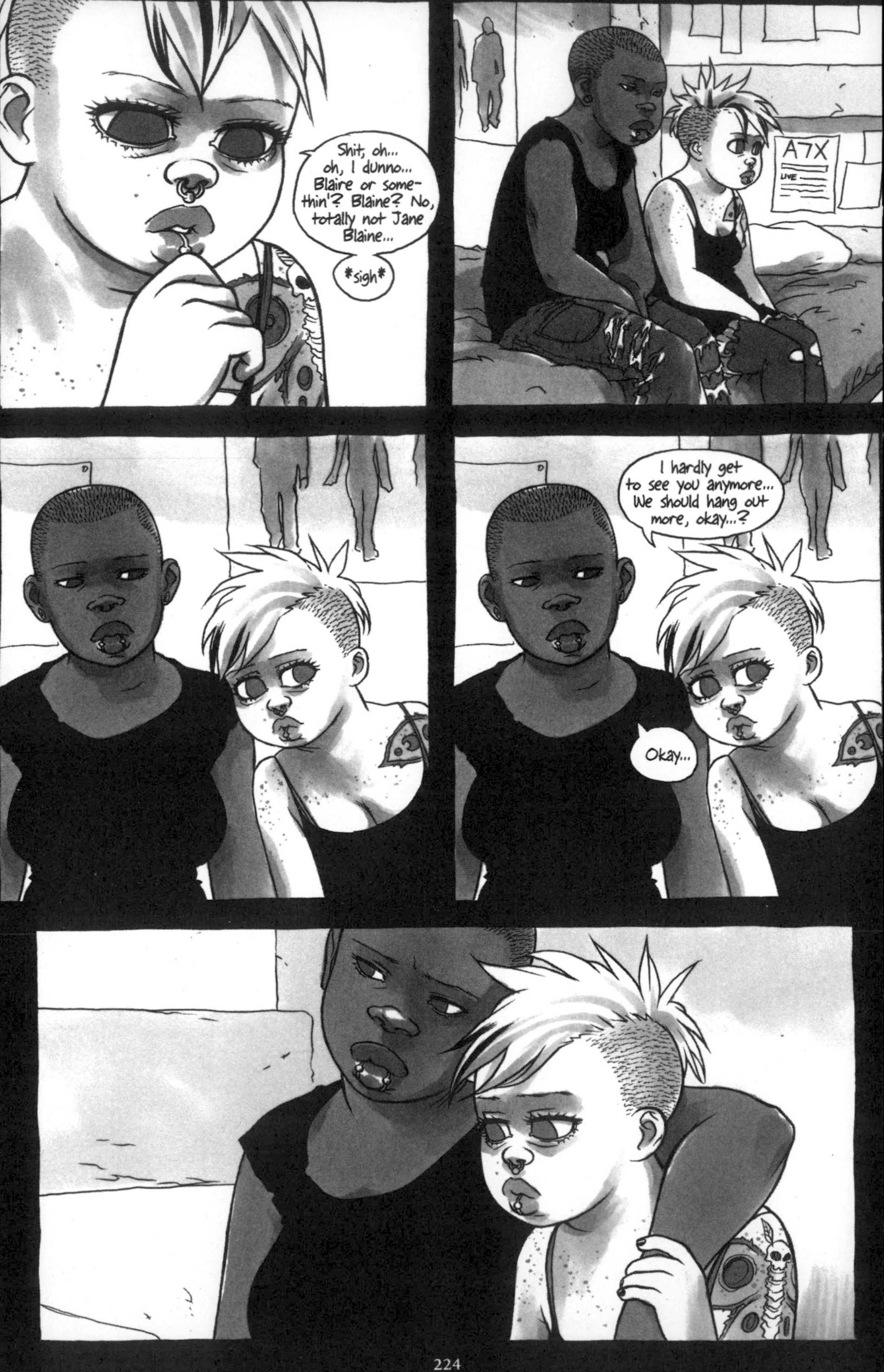

Shit, oh... oh, I dunno... Blaire or some-thin'? Blaine? No, totally not Jane Blaine...
sigh
I hardly get to see you anymore... We should hang out more, okay...?
Okay...

something breaks inside of me
something wicked
rise
screams lift into the air louder still
purge the demons from my mind

[Bella Morte]

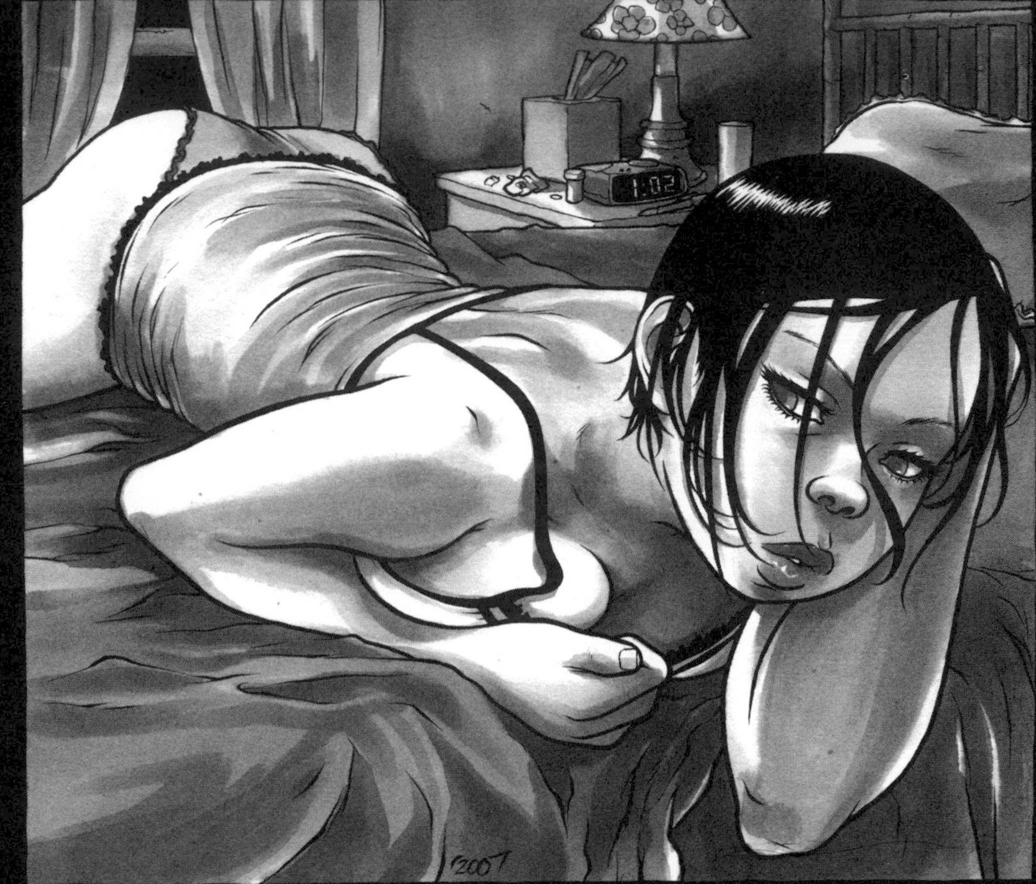
1:02
©2007

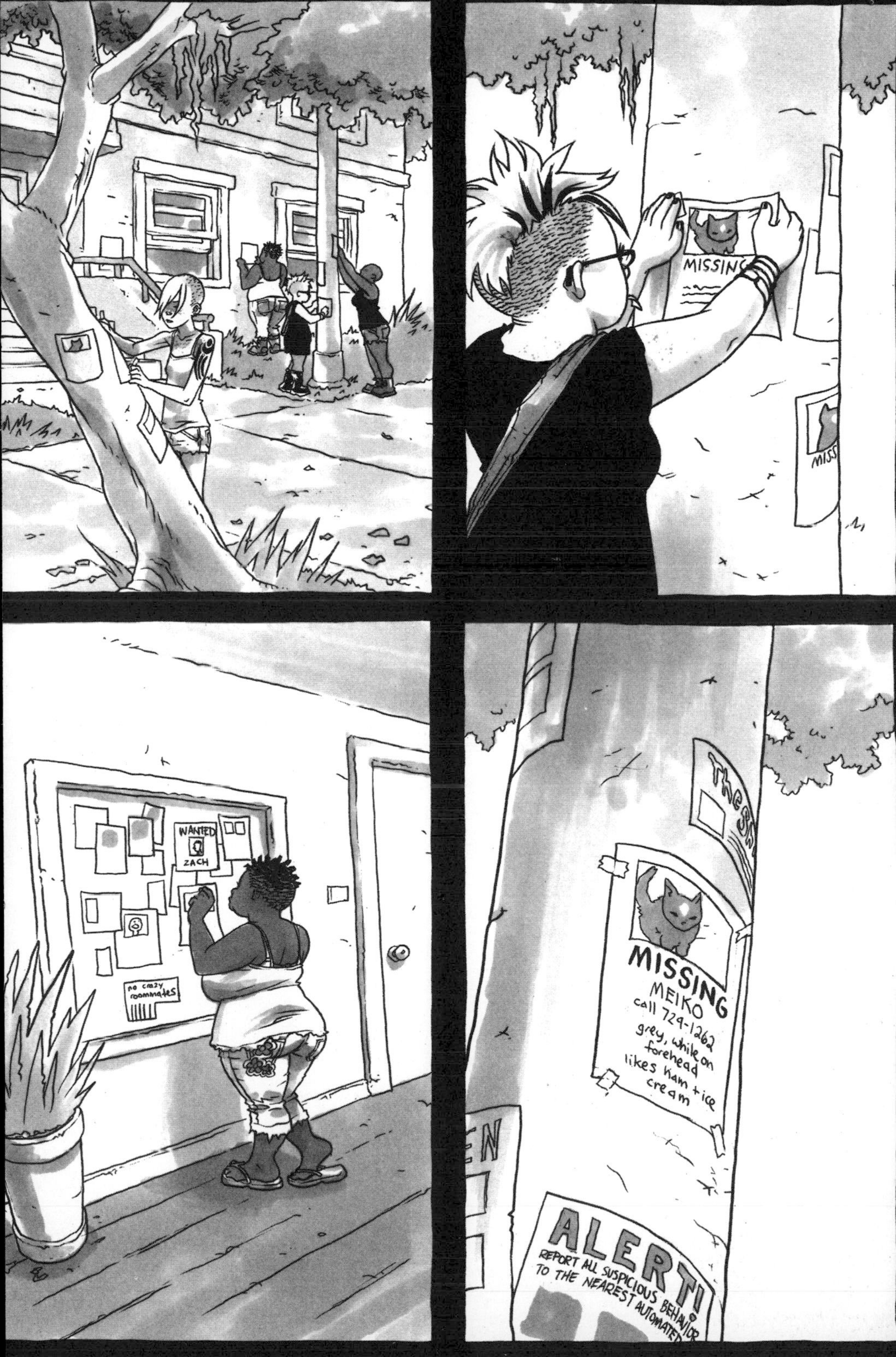
WANTED
ZACH
no crazy roommates
MISSING
MEIKO
call 724-1262
grey, white on forehead
likes ham + ice cream
ALERT!
REPORT ALL SUSPICIOUS BEHAVIOR
TO THE NEAREST AUTOMATED

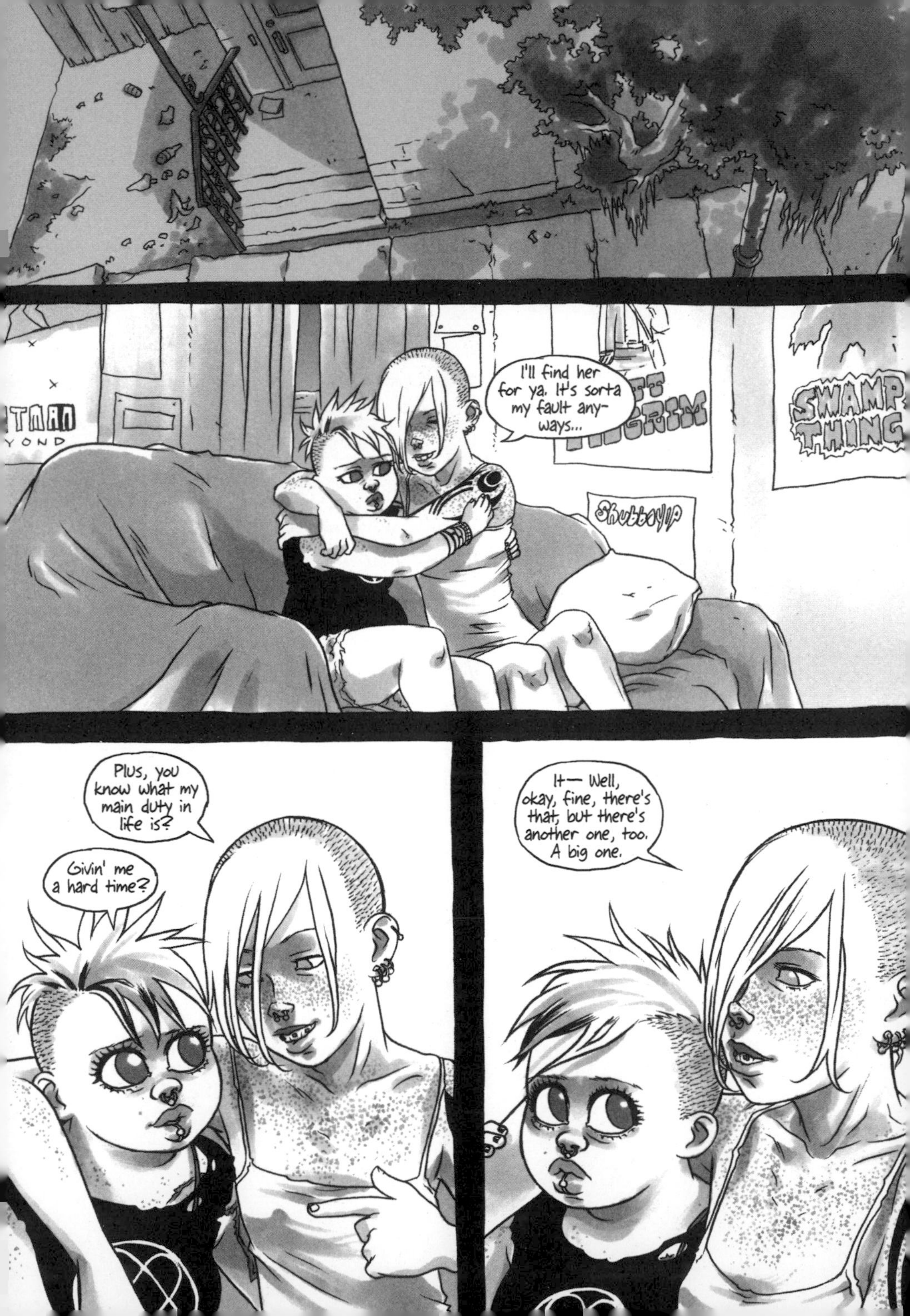

TMAN
YOND
I'll find her for ya. It's sorta my fault any-ways...
SWAMP THING
Shutterup
Plus, you know what my main duty in life is?
Givin' me a hard time?
It— Well, okay, fine, there's that, but there's another one, too. A big one.

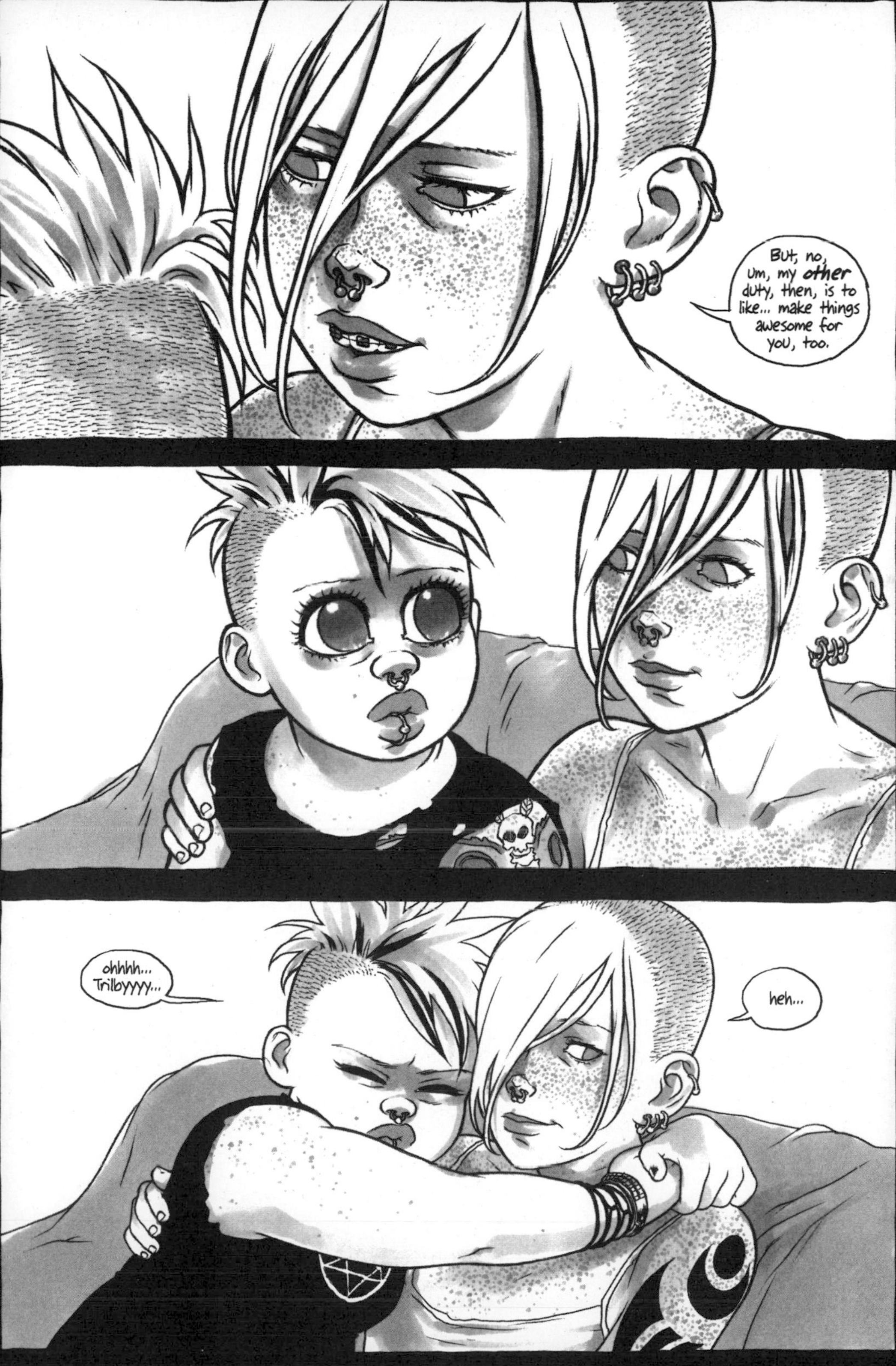
But, no, um, my **other** duty, then, is to like... make things awesome for you, too.
ohhhh... Trilbyyyy...
heh...

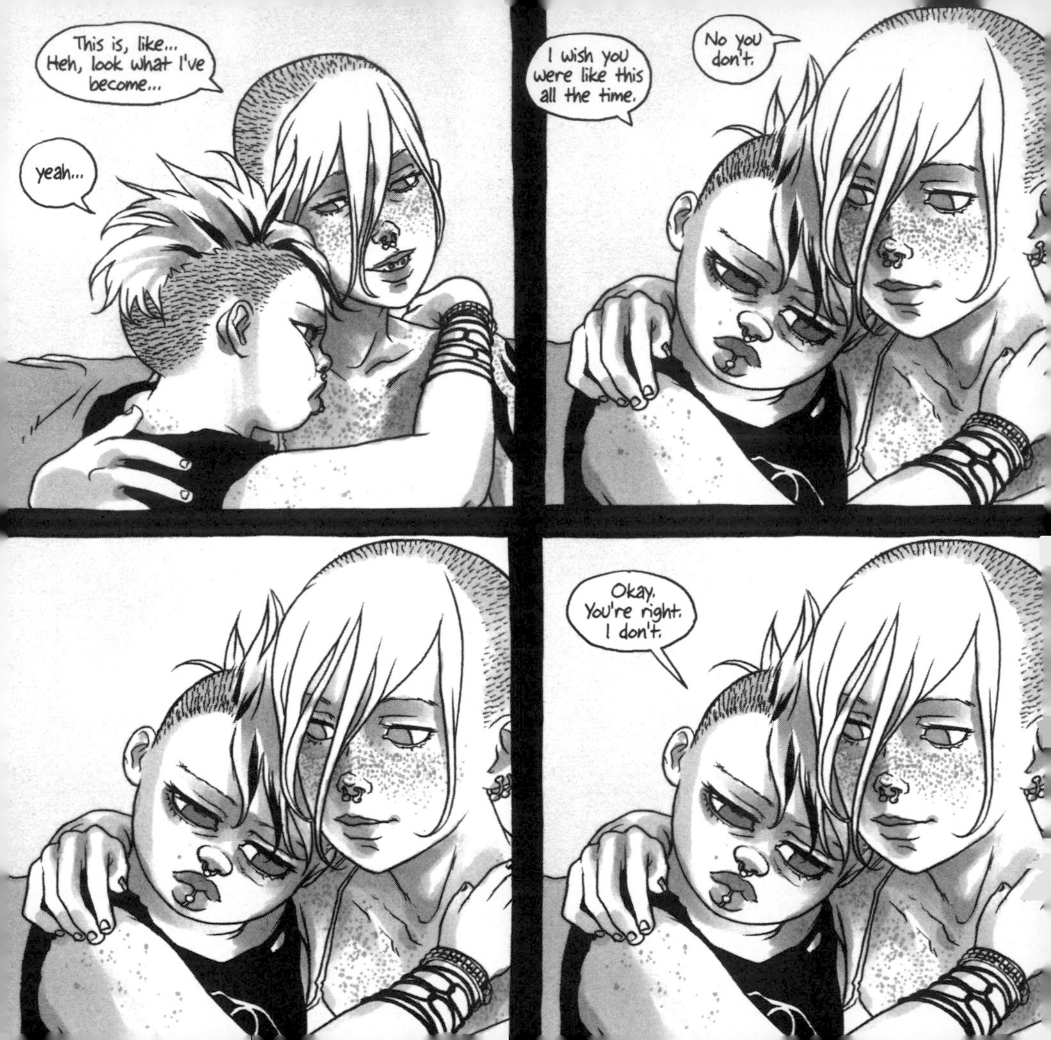
This is, like... Heh, look what I've become...
yeah...
I wish you were like this all the time.
No you don't.
Okay. You're right. I don't.

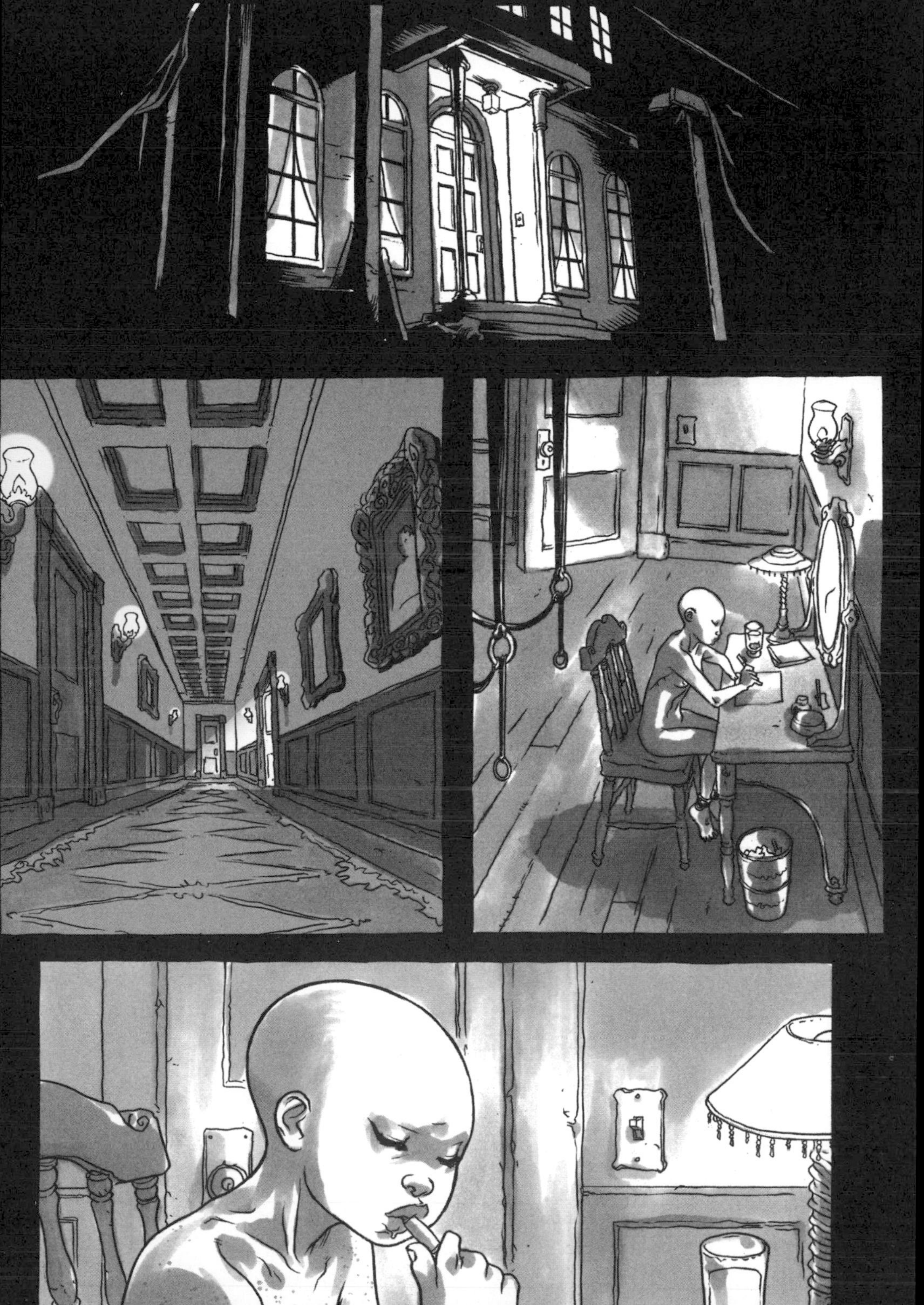

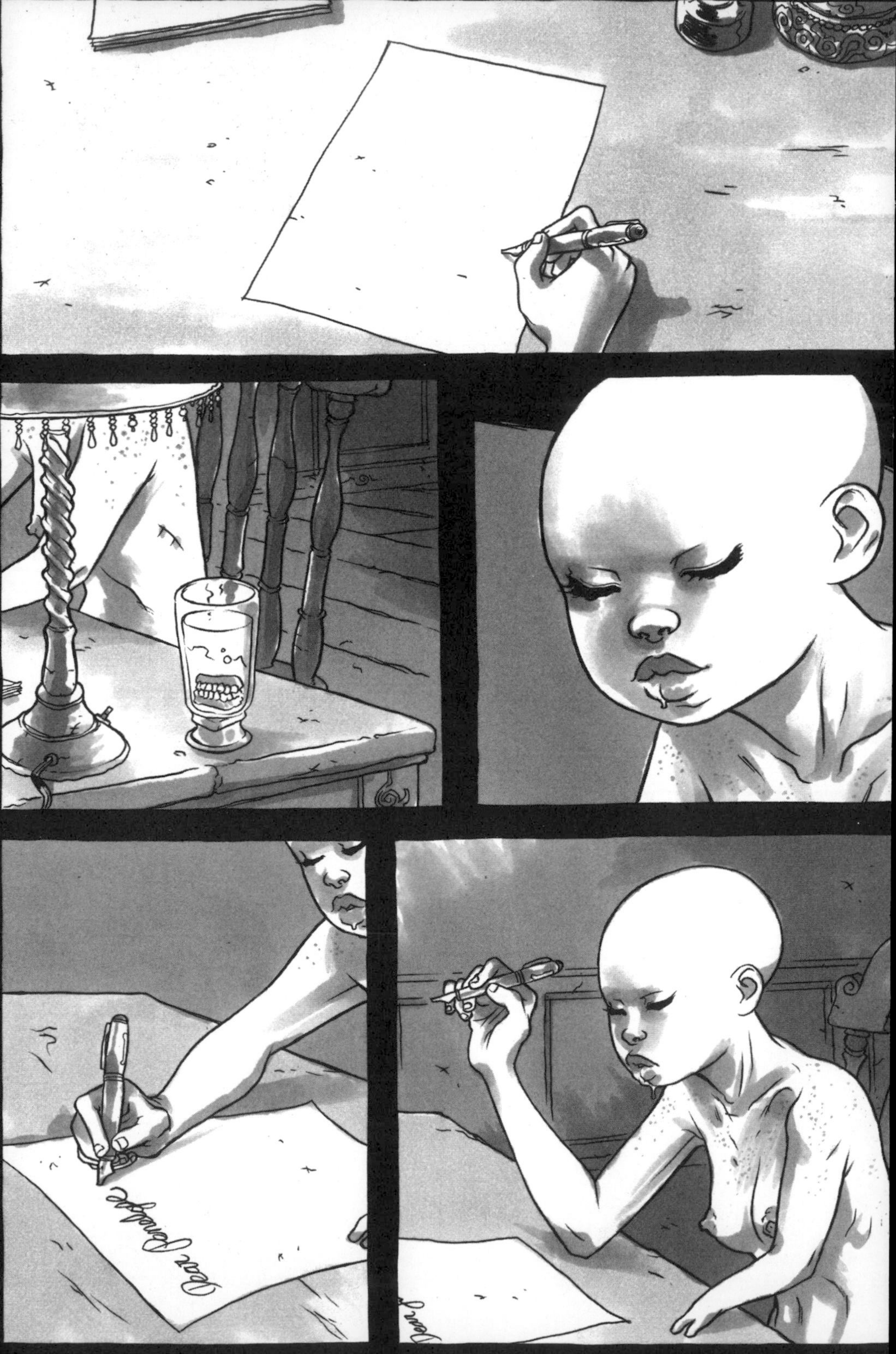
Dear Penelope

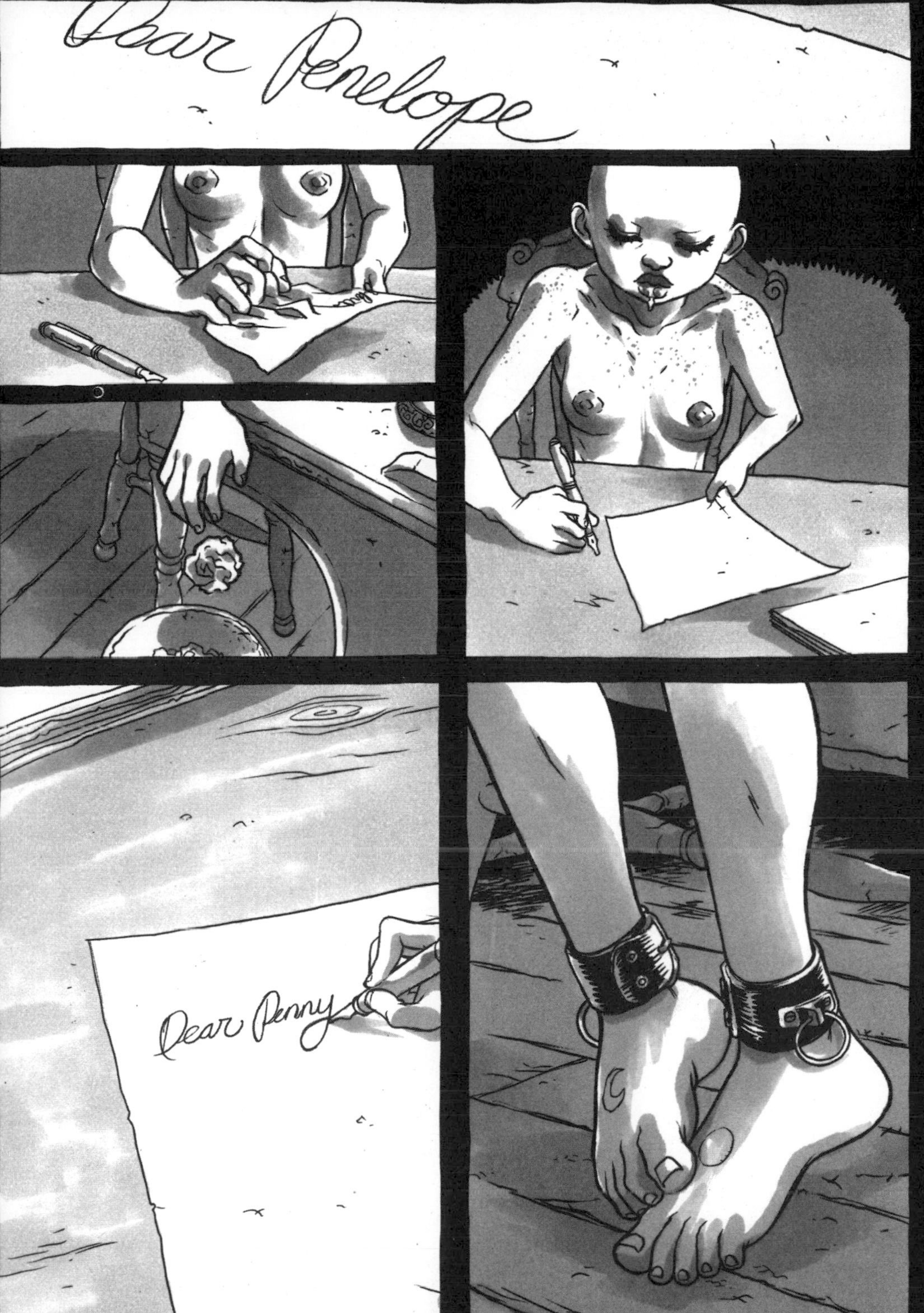
Dear Penelope
Dear Penny

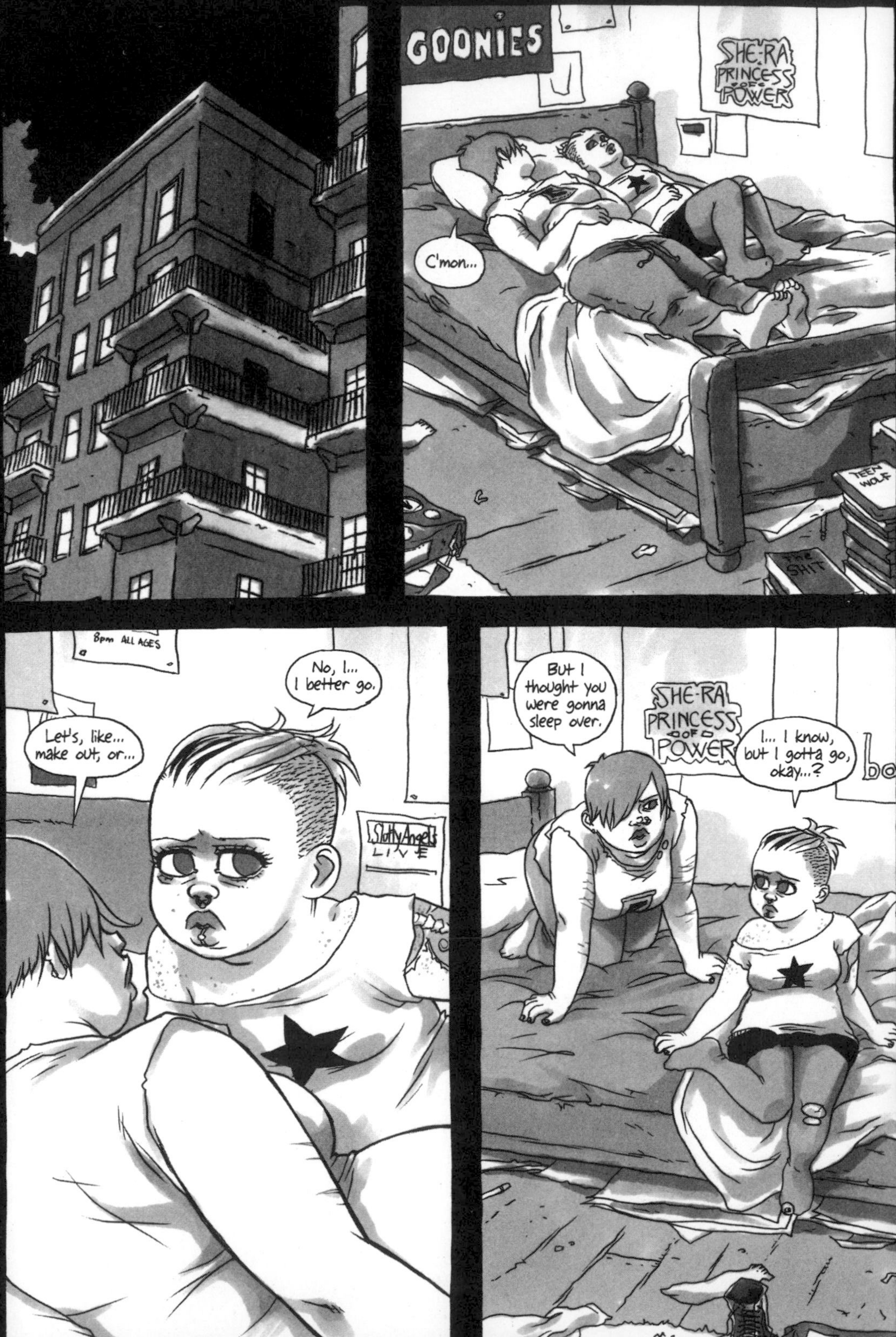
GOONIES
SHE-RA PRINCESS OF POWER
C'mon...
TEEN WOLF
THE SHIT
8pm ALL AGES
Let's, like... make out, or...
No, I... I better go.
Slutty Angels LIVE
But I thought you were gonna sleep over.
SHE-RA PRINCESS OF POWER
I... I know, but I gotta go, okay...?

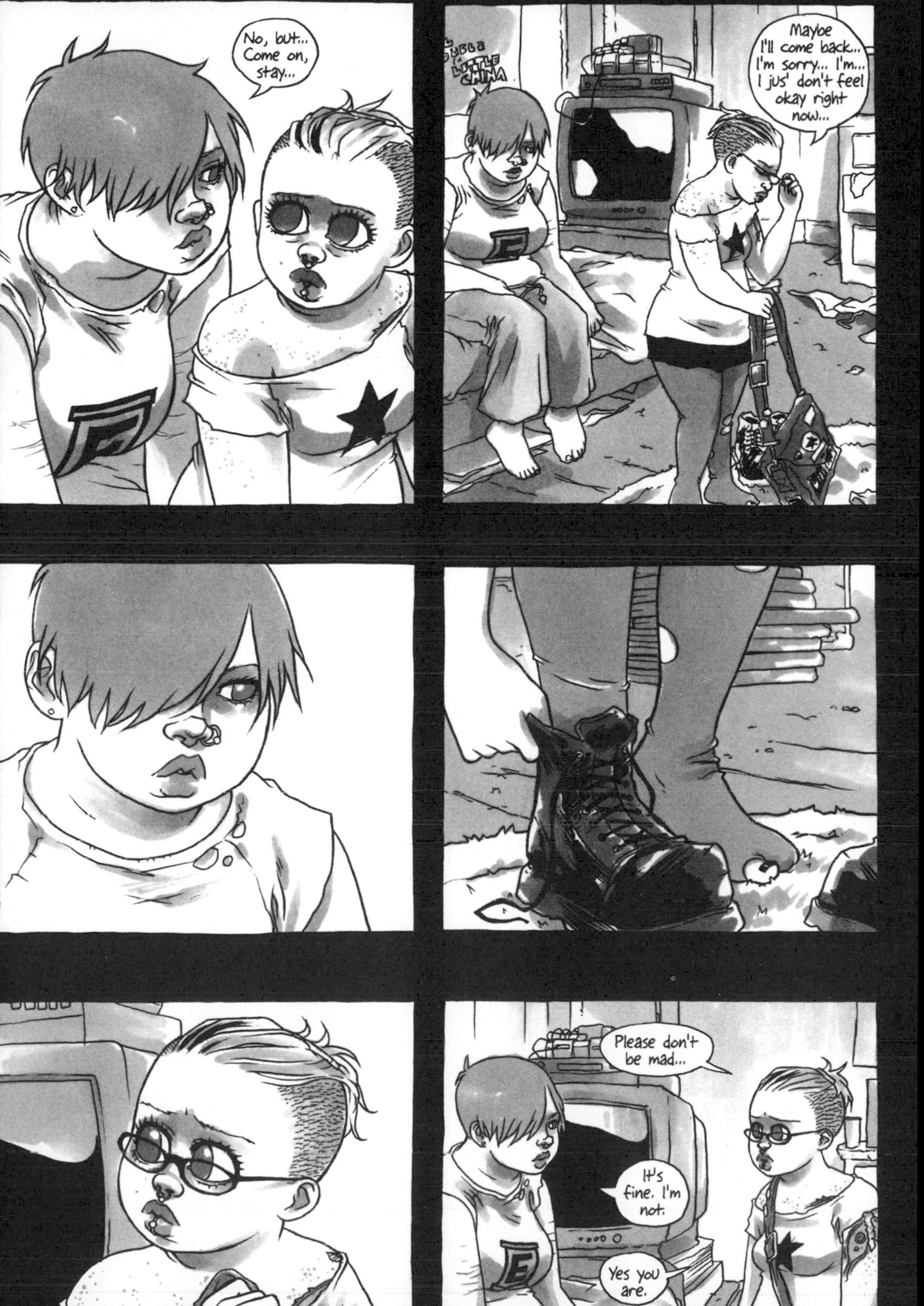
No, but... Come on, stay...
LITTLE CHINA
Maybe I'll come back... I'm sorry... I'm... I jus' don't feel okay right now...
Please don't be mad...
It's fine. I'm not.
Yes you are.

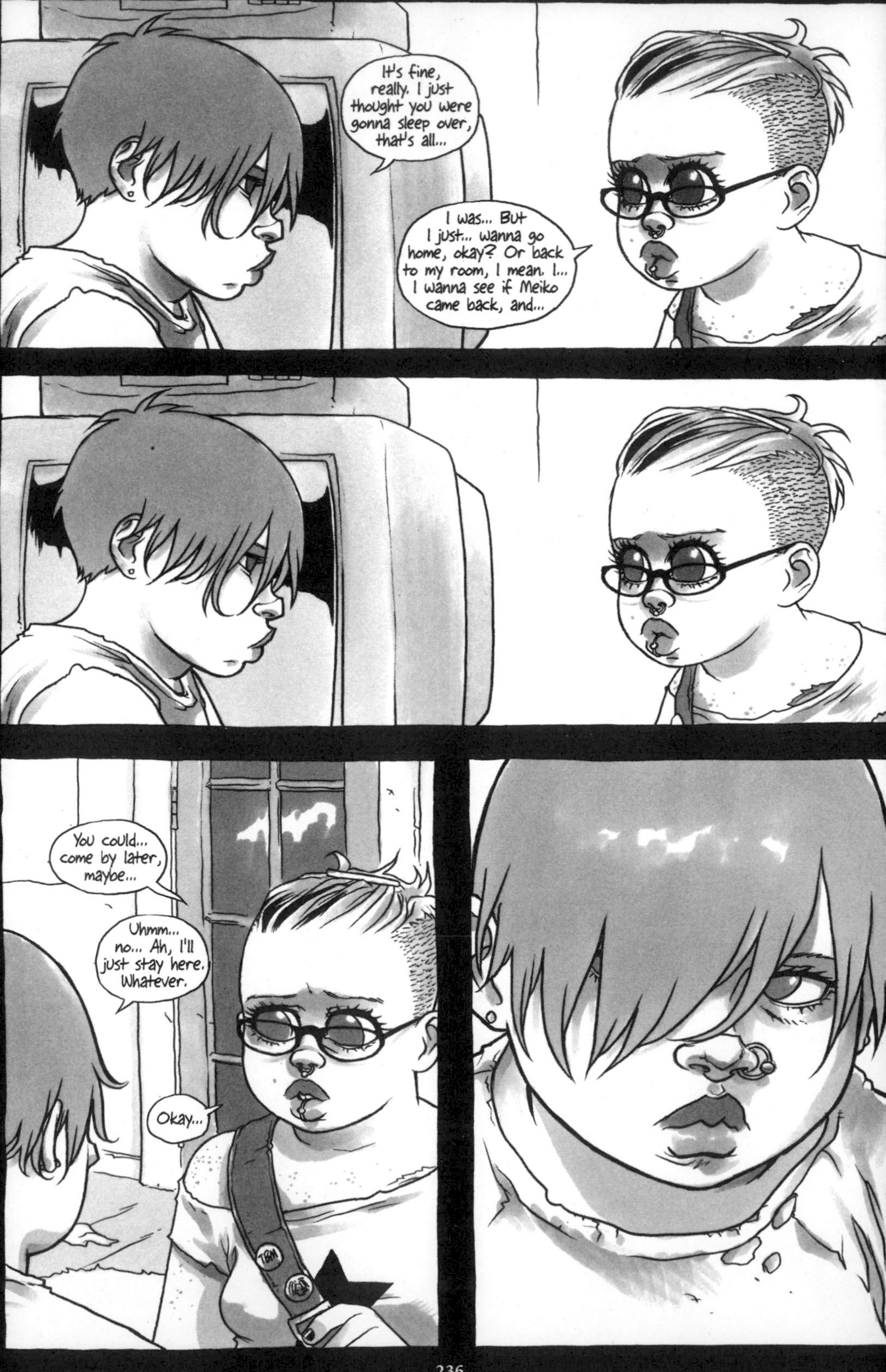
It's fine, really. I just thought you were gonna sleep over, that's all...
I was... But I just... wanna go home, okay? Or back to my room, I mean. I... I wanna see if Meiko came back, and...
You could... come by later, maybe...
Uhmm... no... Ah, I'll just stay here. Whatever.
Okay...

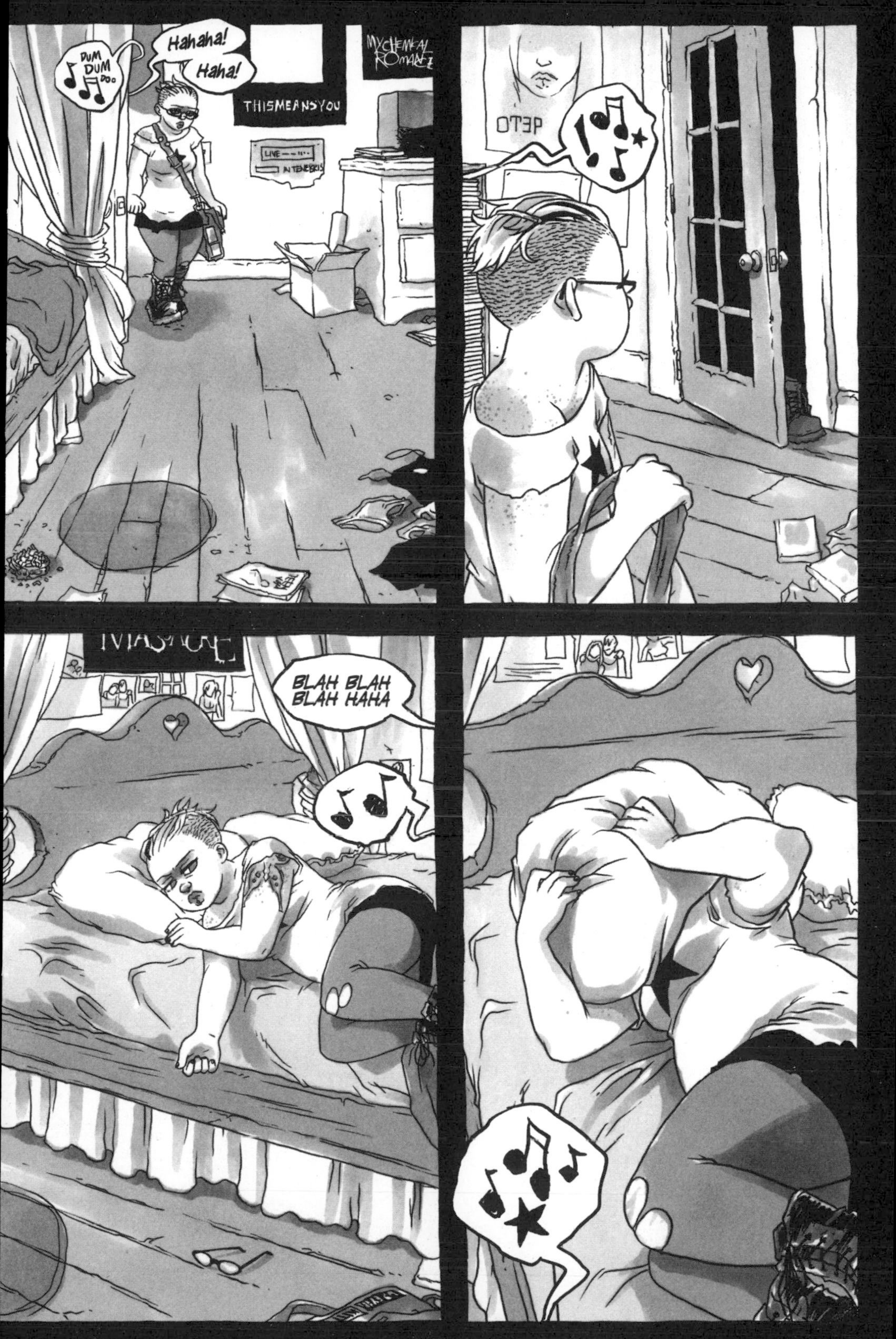
DUM DUM DOO
Hahaha! Haha!
MYCHEMICAL ROMANCE
THISMEANSYOU
LIVE
IN TENEBRIS
OTEP
BLAH BLAH BLAH HAHA

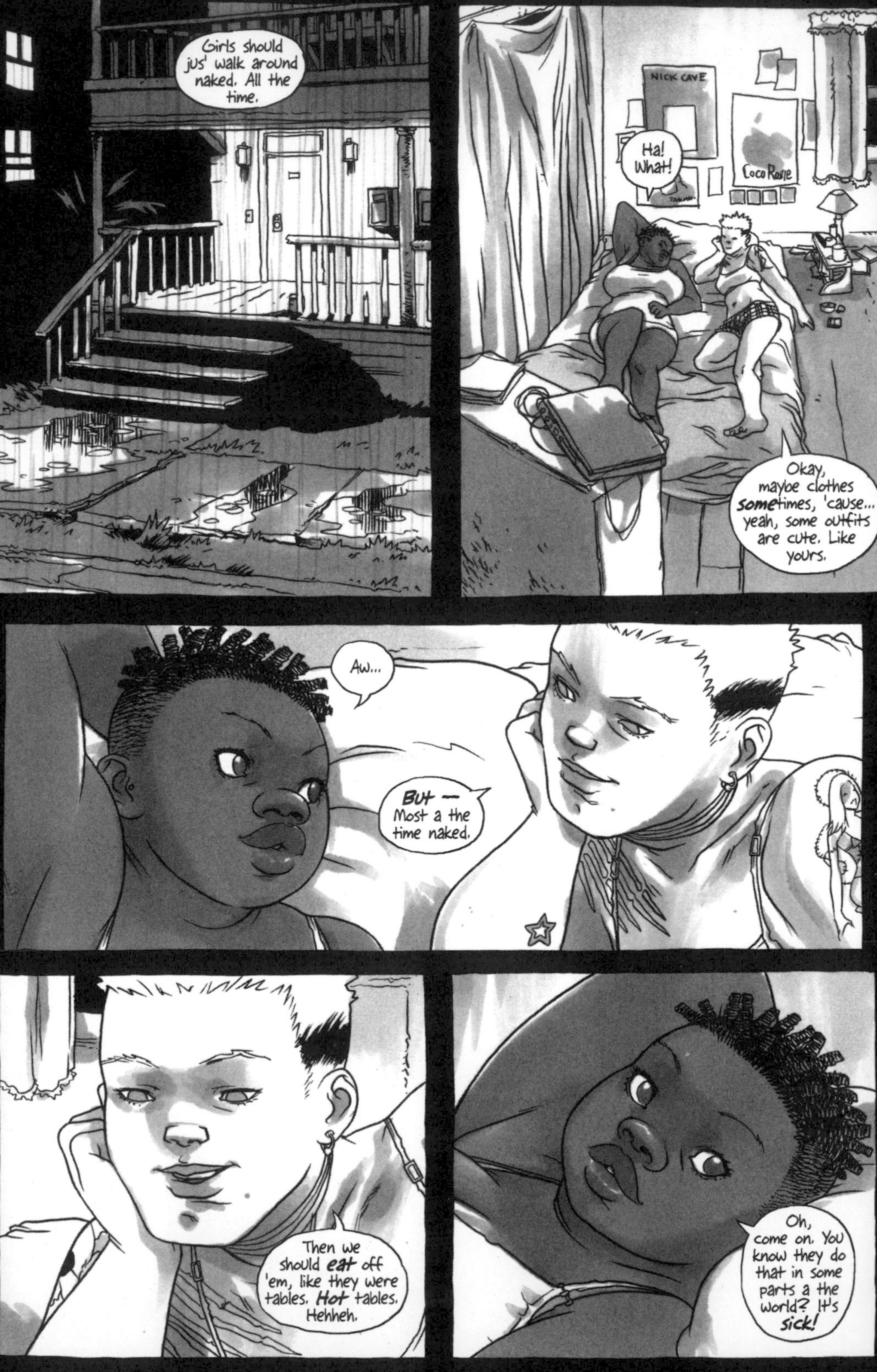
Girls should jus' walk around naked. All the time.
Ha! What!
NICK CAVE
Coco Rosie
Okay, maybe clothes **some**times, 'cause... yeah, some outfits are cute. Like yours.
Aw...
But — Most a the time naked.
Then we should **eat** off 'em, like they were tables. **Hot** tables. Hehheh.
Oh, come on. You know they do that in some parts a the world? It's **sick!**

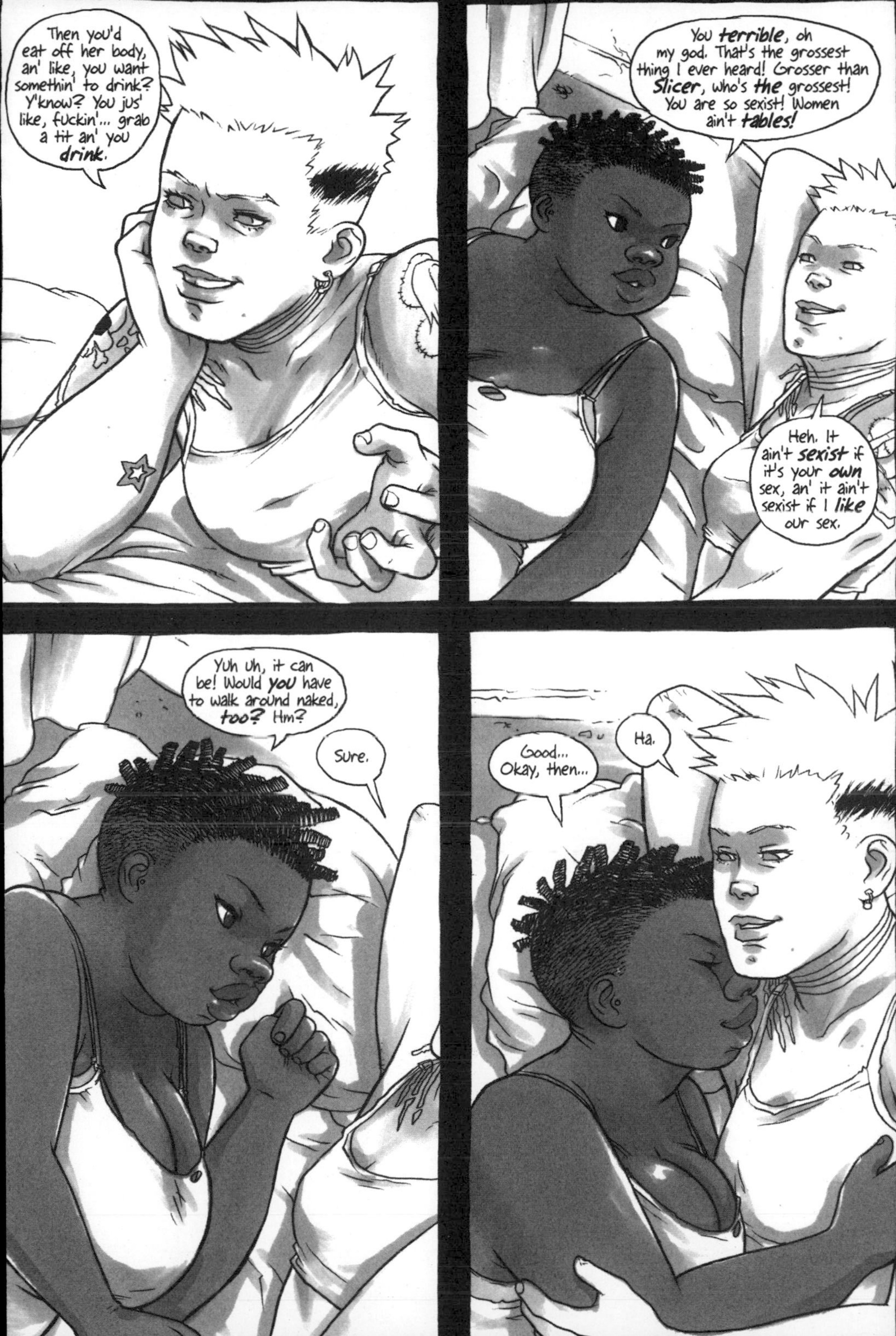
Then you'd eat off her body, an' like, you want somethin' to drink? Y'know? You jus' like, fuckin'... grab a tit an' you **drink**.
You **terrible**, oh my god. That's the grossest thing I ever heard! Grosser than **Slicer**, who's **the** grossest! You are so sexist! Women ain't **tables!**
Heh. It ain't **sexist** if it's your **own** sex, an' it ain't sexist if I **like** our sex.
Yuh uh, it can be! Would **you** have to walk around naked, **too?** Hm?
Sure.
Good... Okay, then...
Ha.

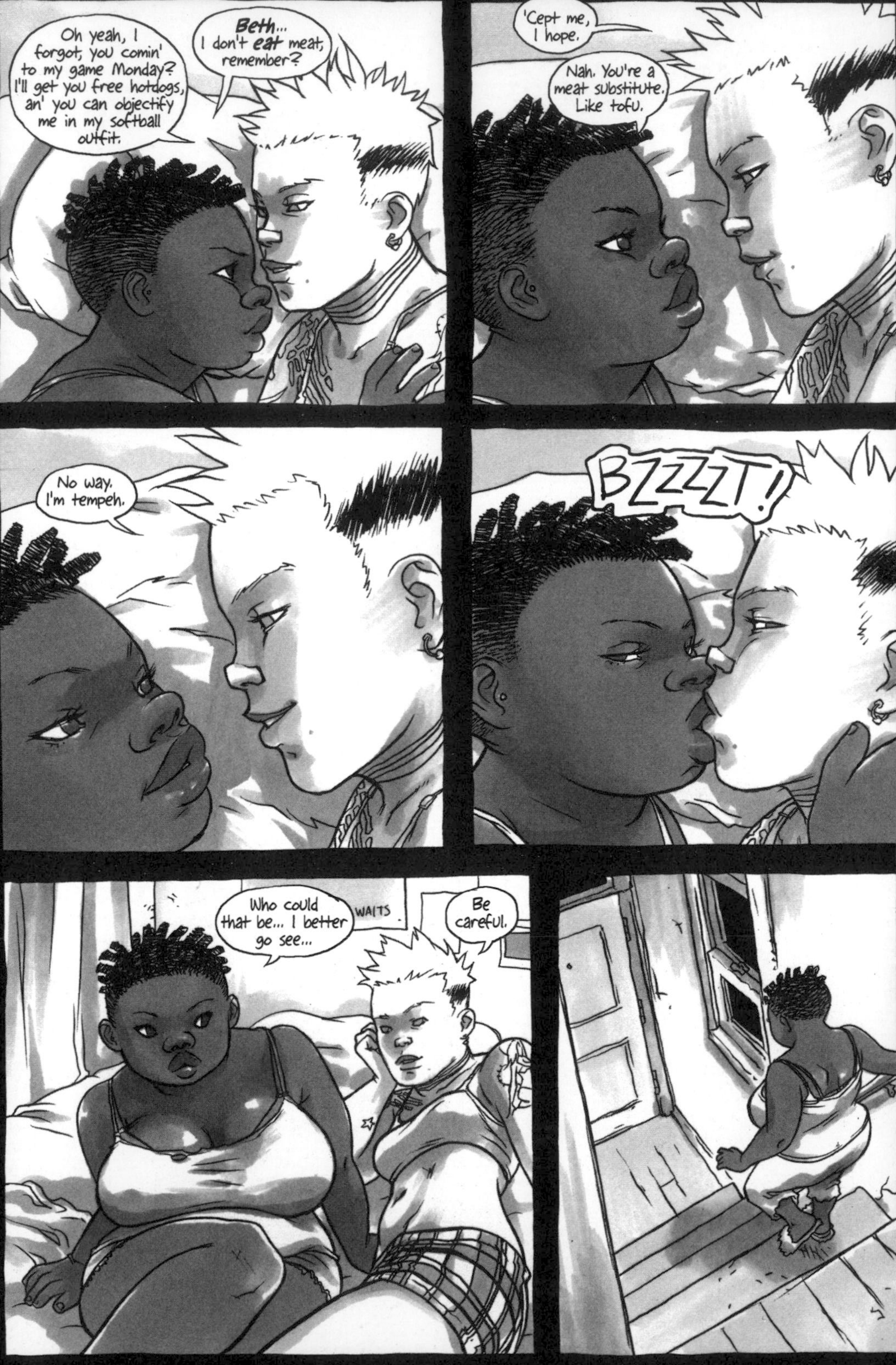

Oh yeah, I forgot, you comin' to my game Monday? I'll get you free hotdogs, an' you can objectify me in my softball outfit.
Beth... I don't eat meat, remember?
'Cept me, I hope.
Nah. You're a meat substitute. Like tofu.
No way. I'm tempeh.
BZZZZT!
Who could that be... I better go see...
WAITS
Be careful.

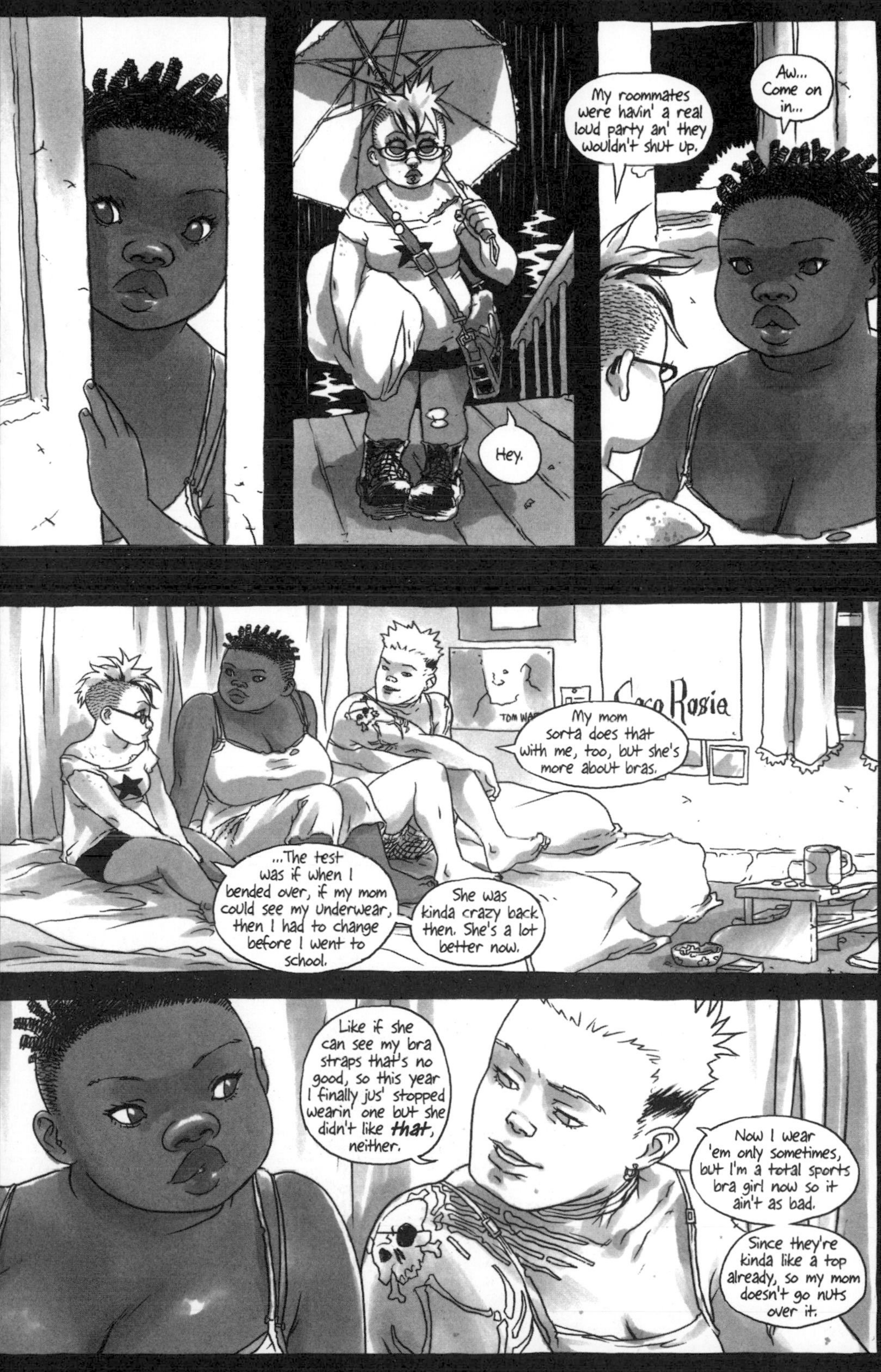
Hey.
My roommates were havin' a real loud party an' they wouldn't shut up.
Aw... Come on in...
Coco Rosie
TOM WA
My mom sorta does that with me, too, but she's more about bras.
...The test was if when I bended over, if my mom could see my underwear, then I had to change before I went to school.
She was kinda crazy back then. She's a lot better now.
Like if she can see my bra straps that's no good, so this year I finally jus' stopped wearin' one but she didn't like *that*, neither.
Now I wear 'em only sometimes, but I'm a total sports bra girl now so it ain't as bad.
Since they're kinda like a top already, so my mom doesn't go nuts over it.

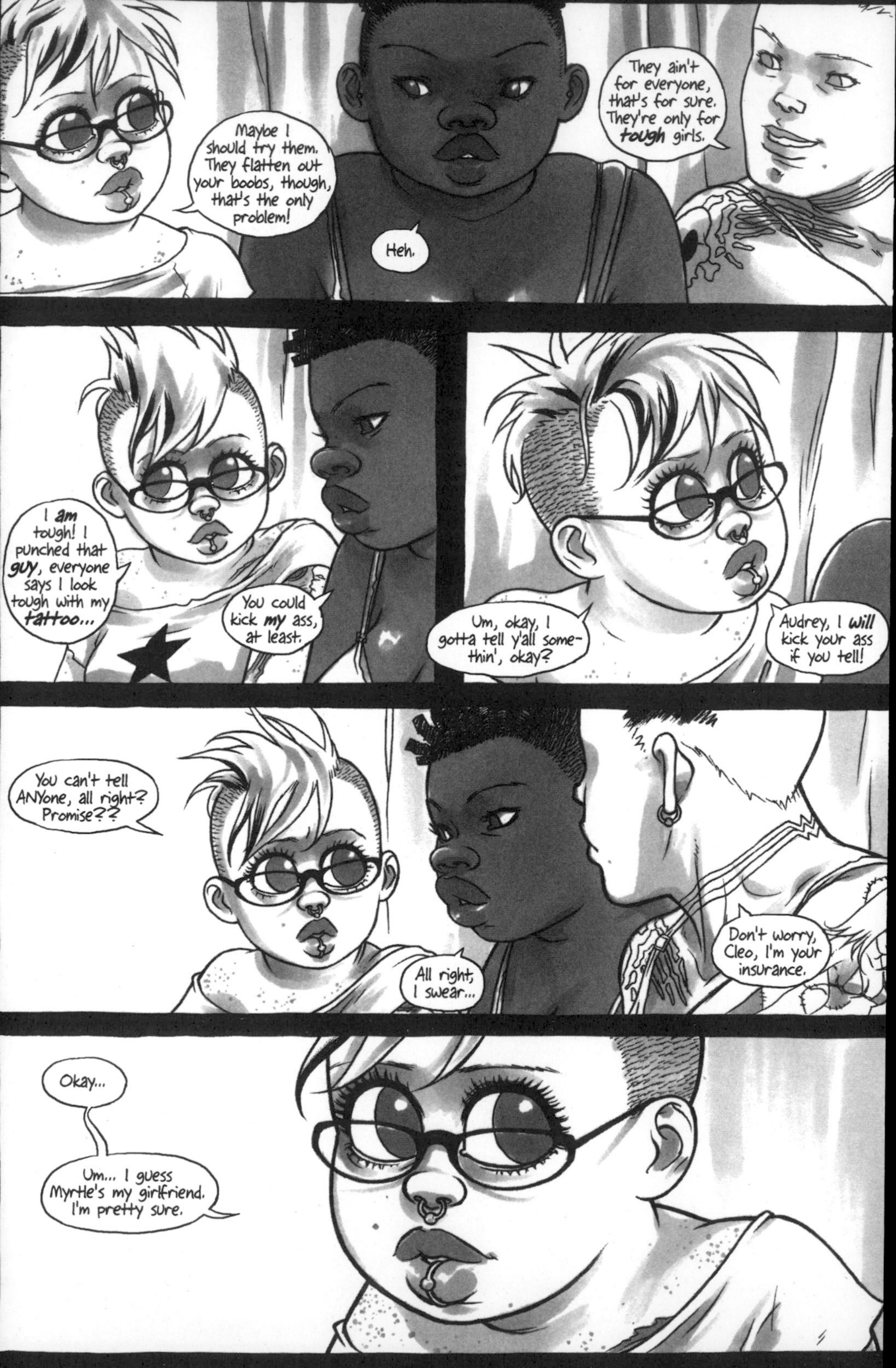
Maybe I should try them. They flatten out your boobs, though, that's the only problem!
Heh.
They ain't for everyone, that's for sure. They're only for tough girls.
I am tough! I punched that guy, everyone says I look tough with my tattoo...
You could kick my ass, at least.
Um, okay, I gotta tell y'all somethin', okay?
Audrey, I will kick your ass if you tell!
You can't tell ANYone, all right? Promise??
All right, I swear...
Don't worry, Cleo, I'm your insurance.
Okay...
Um... I guess Myrtle's my girlfriend. I'm pretty sure.

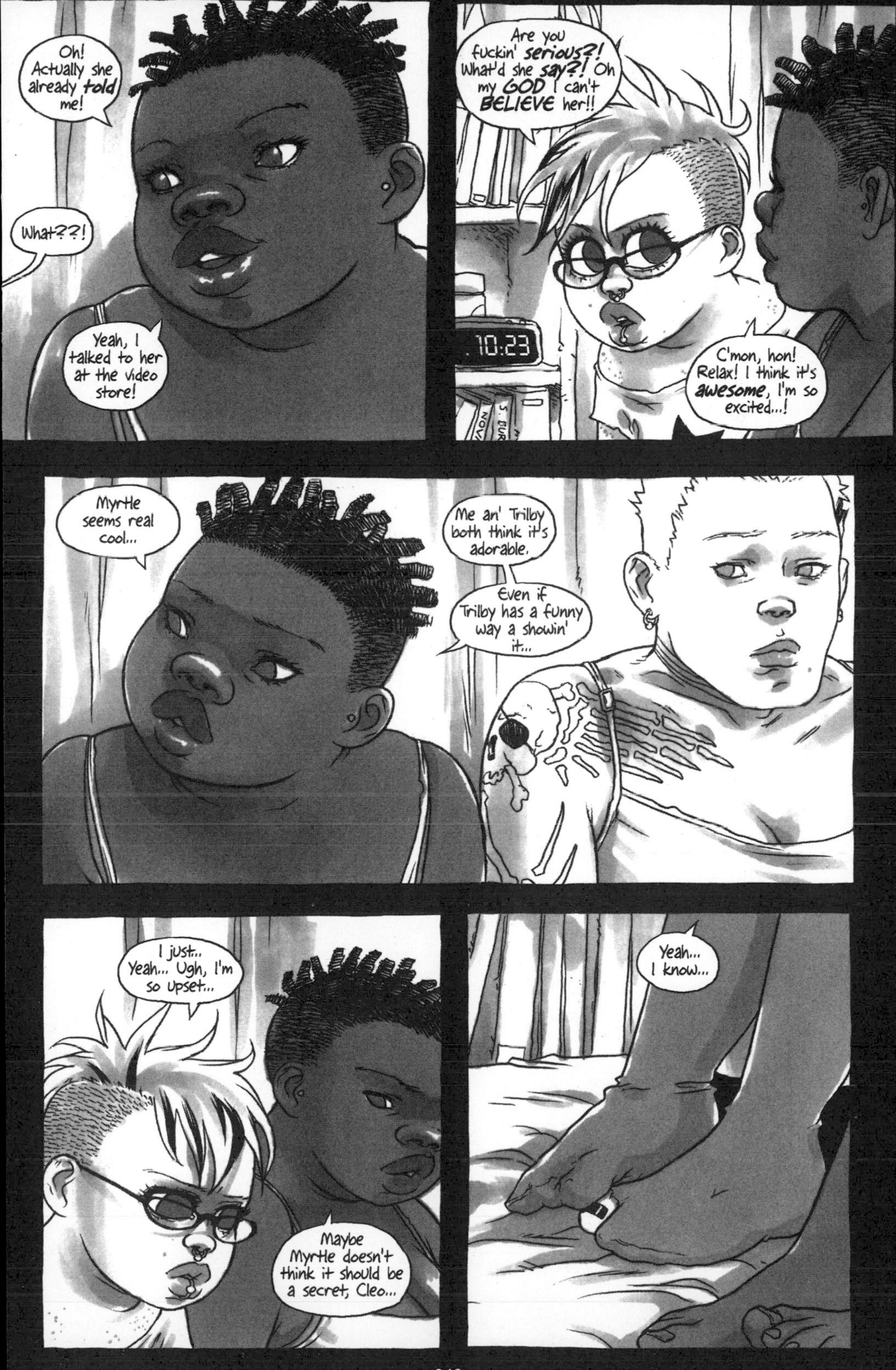
Oh! Actually she already told me!
What??!
Yeah, I talked to her at the video store!
Are you fuckin' serious?! What'd she say?! Oh my GOD I can't BELIEVE her!!
10:23
C'mon, hon! Relax! I think it's awesome, I'm so excited...!
Myrtle seems real cool...
Me an' Trilby both think it's adorable.
Even if Trilby has a funny way a showin' it...
I just... Yeah... Ugh, I'm so upset...
Maybe Myrtle doesn't think it should be a secret, Cleo...
Yeah... I know...

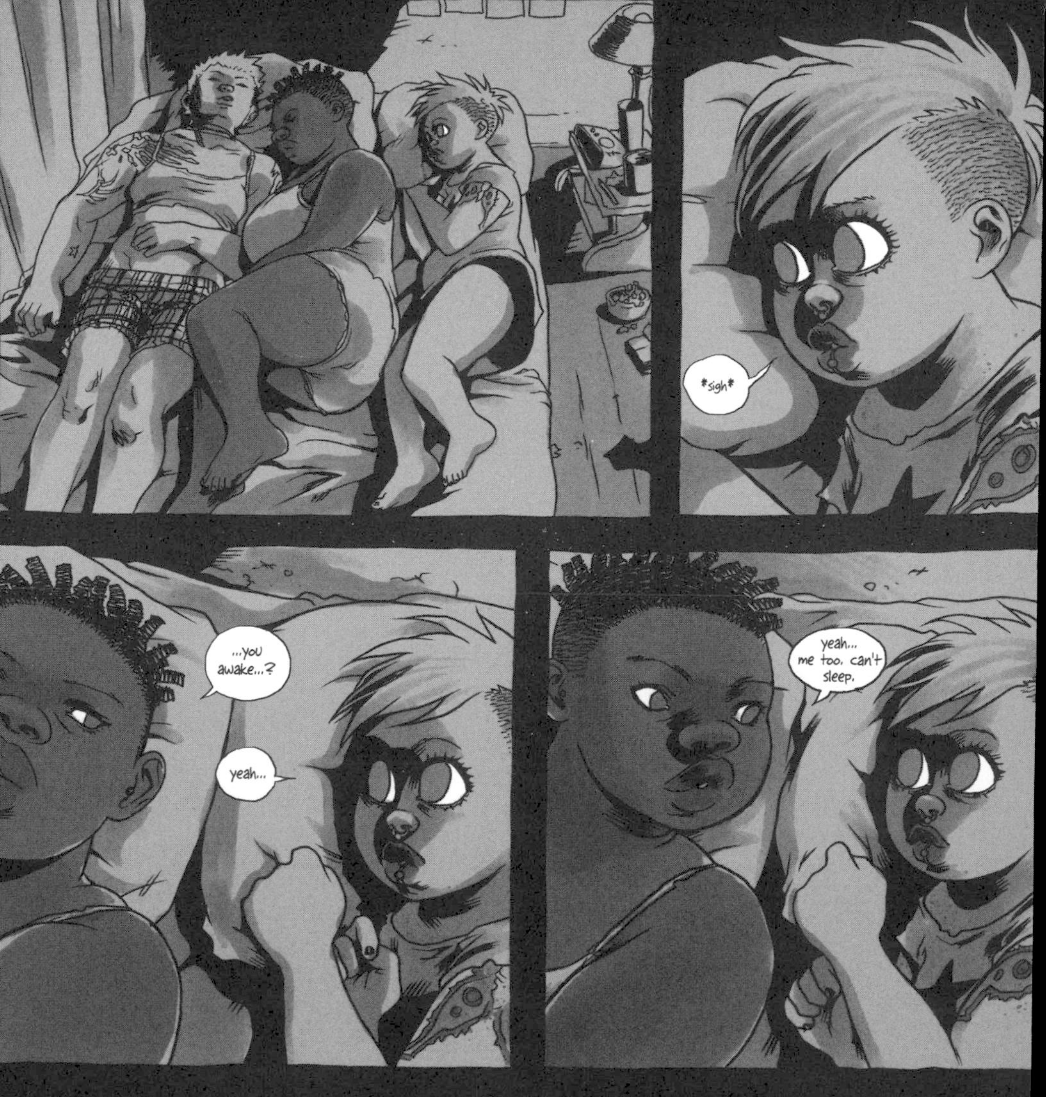
sigh
...you awake...?
yeah...
yeah... me too. can't sleep.

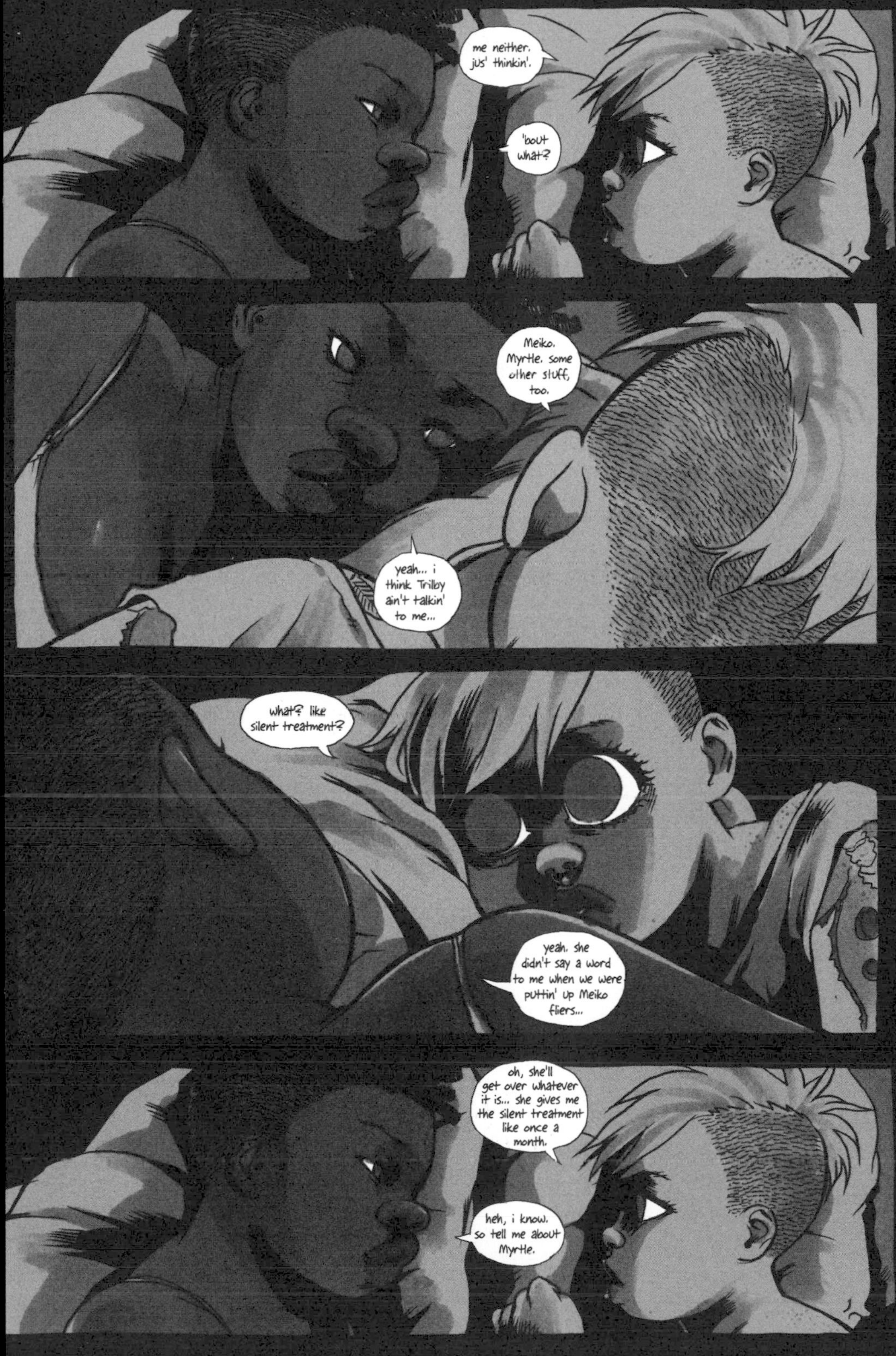
me neither. jus' thinkin'.
'bout what?
Meiko. Myrtle. some other stuff, too.
yeah... i think Trilby ain't talkin' to me...
what? like silent treatment?
yeah. she didn't say a word to me when we were puttin' up Meiko fliers...
oh, she'll get over whatever it is... she gives me the silent treatment like once a month.
heh, i know. so tell me about Myrtle.

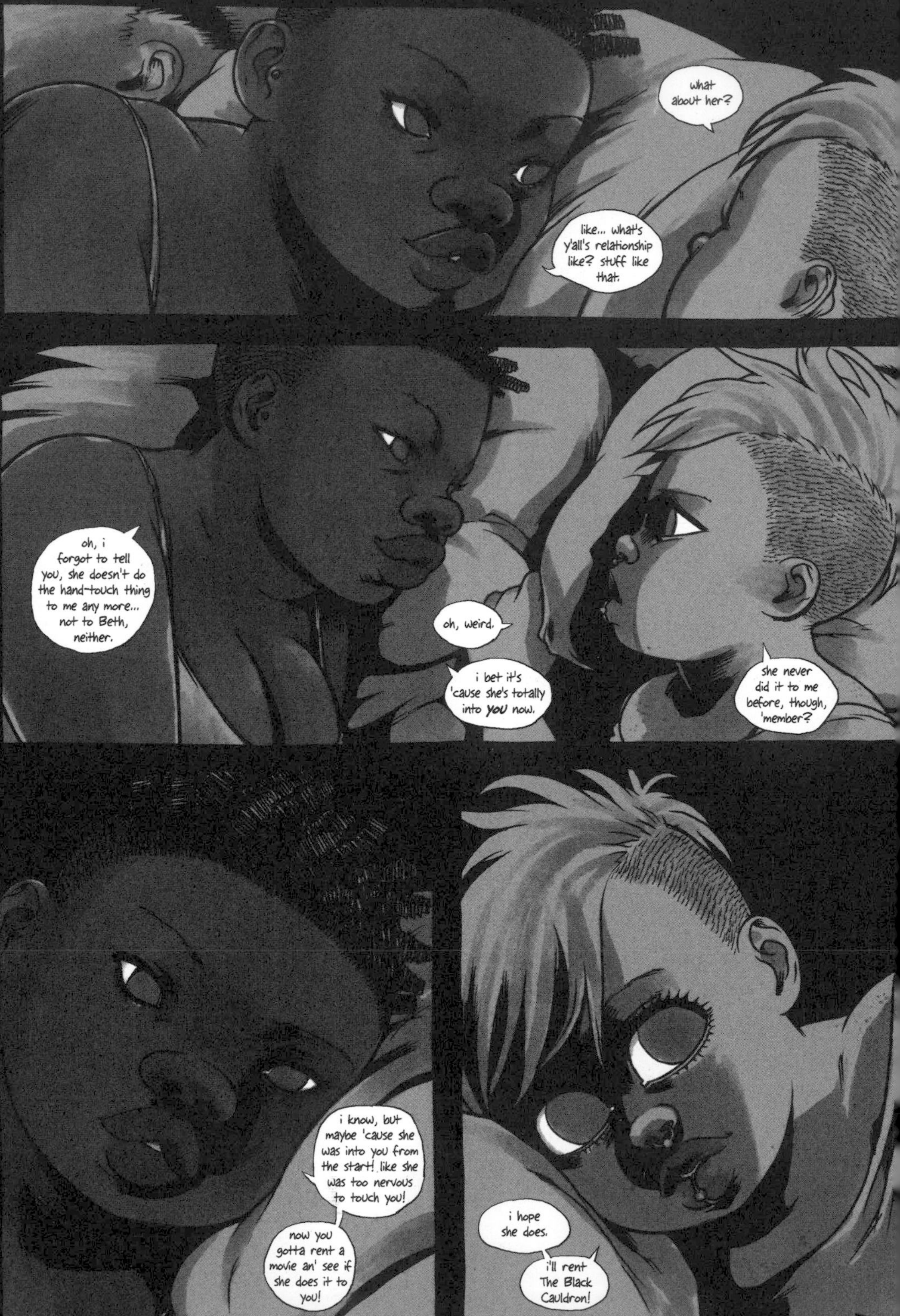
what about her?
like... what's y'all's relationship like? stuff like that.
oh, i forgot to tell you, she doesn't do the hand-touch thing to me any more... not to Beth, neither.
oh, weird.
i bet it's 'cause she's totally into *you* now.
she never did it to me before, though, 'member?
i know, but maybe 'cause she was into you from the start! like she was too nervous to touch you!
now you gotta rent a movie an' see if she does it to you!
i hope she does.
i'll rent The Black Cauldron!

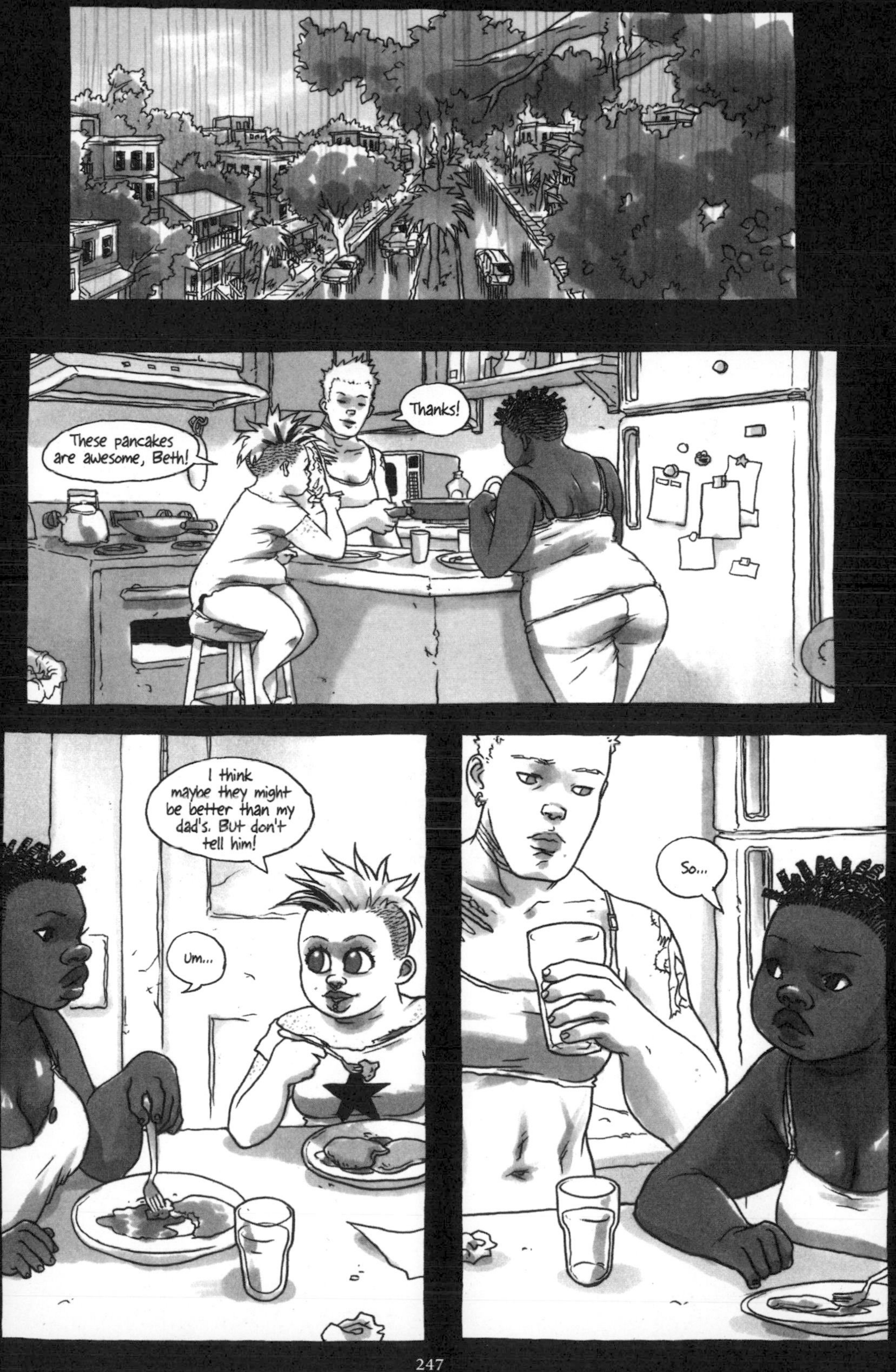
These pancakes are awesome, Beth!
Thanks!
I think maybe they might be better than my dad's. But don't tell him!
Um...
So...

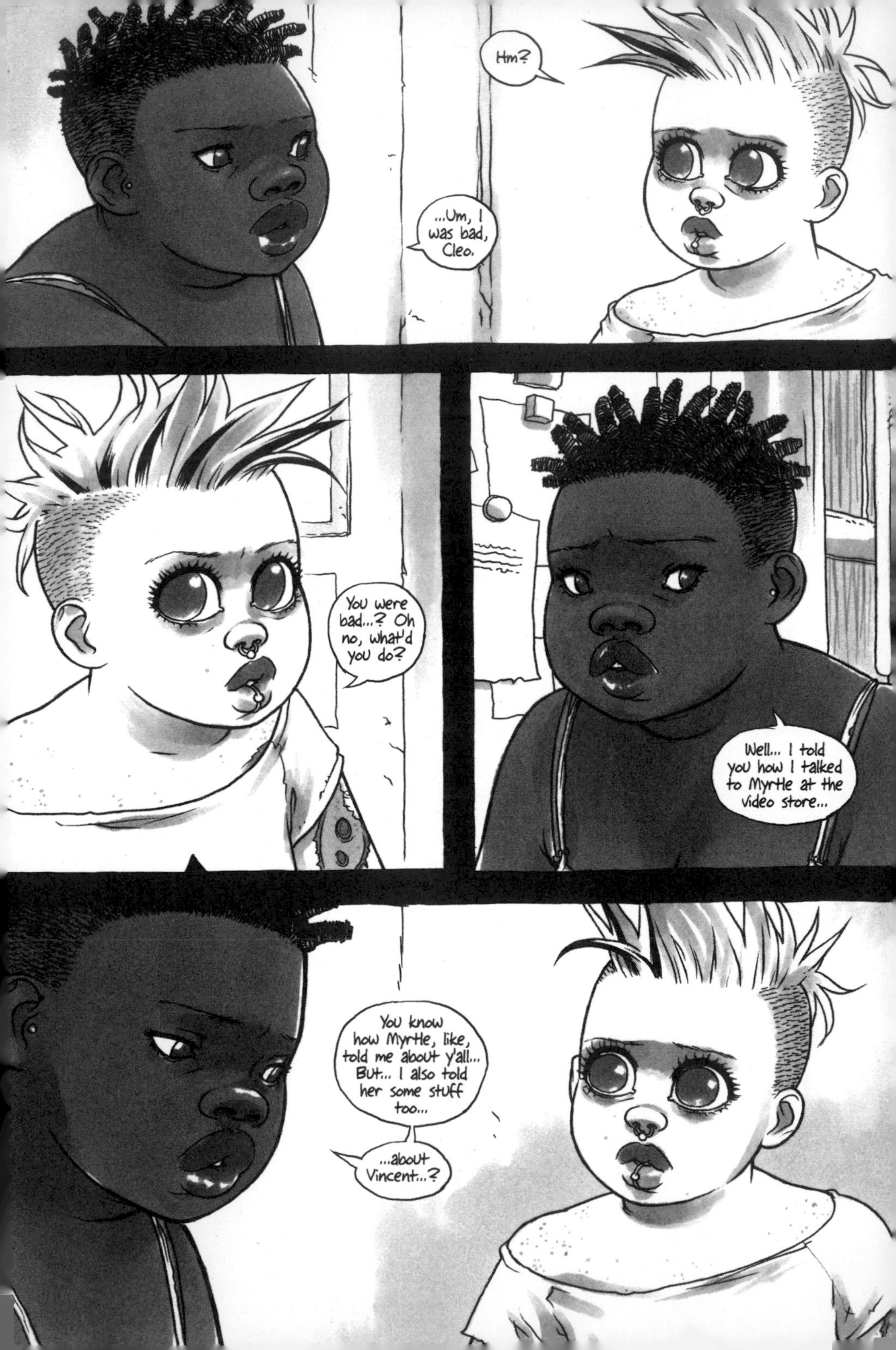
Hm?
...Um, I was bad, Cleo.
You were bad...? Oh no, what'd you do?
Well... I told you how I talked to Myrtle at the video store...
You know how Myrtle, like, told me about y'all... But... I also told her some stuff too...
...about Vincent...?

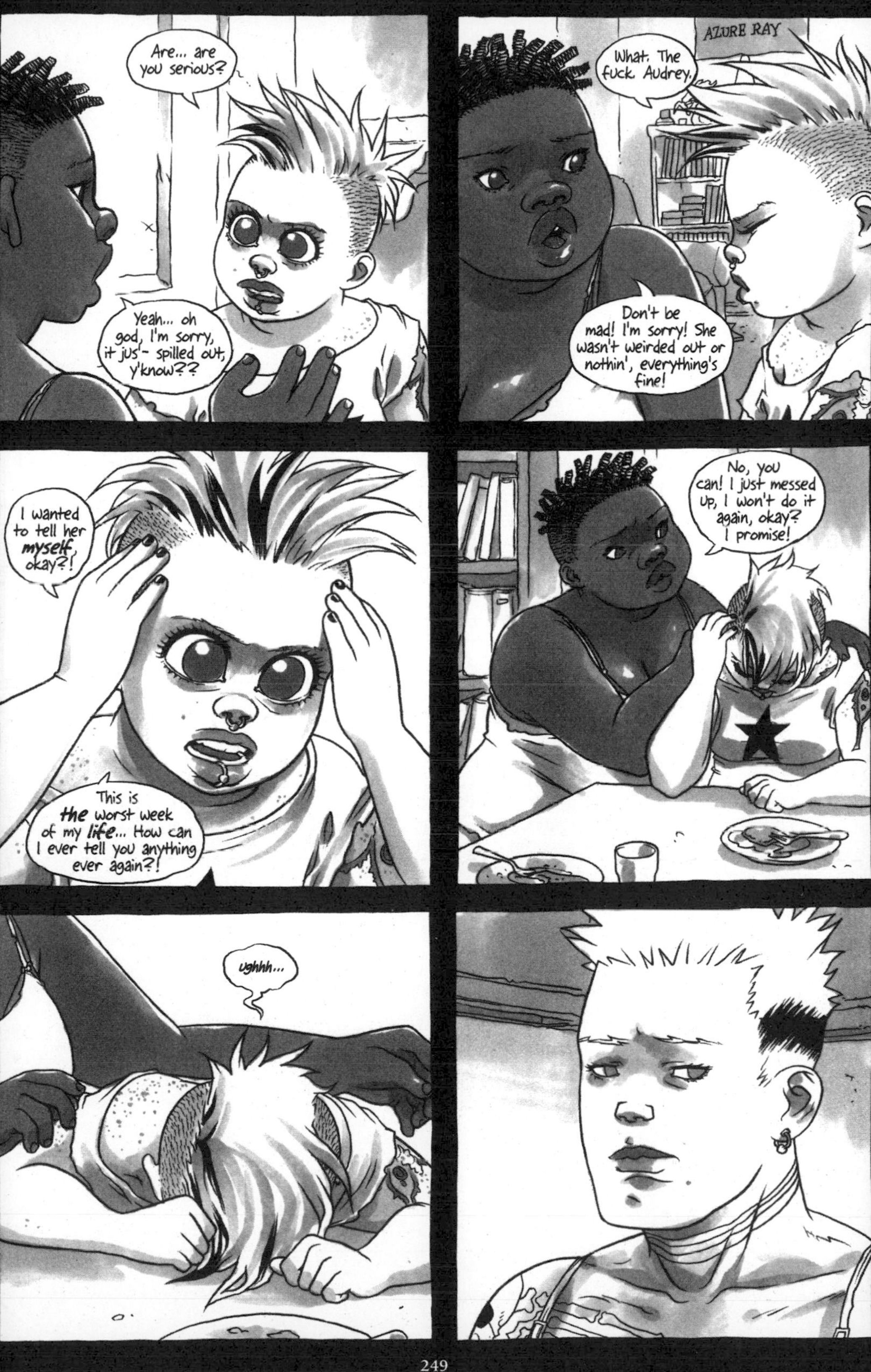
Are... are you serious?
Yeah... oh god, I'm sorry, it jus'- spilled out, y'know??
AZURE RAY
What. The fuck. Audrey.
Don't be mad! I'm sorry! She wasn't weirded out or nothin', everything's fine!
I wanted to tell her myself, okay?!
This is the worst week of my life... How can I ever tell you anything ever again?!
No, you can! I just messed up, I won't do it again, okay? I promise!
ughhh...

The Wonders At Your Feet

[friendtoroaches@gmail.com]

Recent Entries   Archive   Friends   User Info

mara's journal

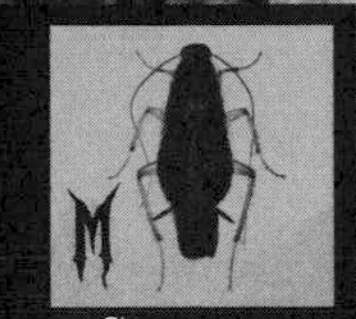

M

profile

October 19th, 1:22am

TREAD THE WORLD WITH STEEL AND BURNING BLADES

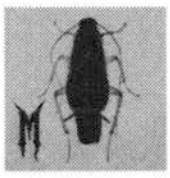

i got up even earlier today. and i went running. i haven't gone for a run in such a long time it felt like, at least since 10th grade i think. it was great except that i really felt the shit in my lungs, it's weird how i hardly ever noticed until now. i really have to quit, i'll never hack it in softball if i don't. i'd hit a homerun and collapse before i'd made it to third base. Cleo's been smoking longer than me, i don't know how she can take it. i think she usually smokes like over a pack a day but i smoke only about half a pack on good days. it's really gross. anyway the run was great, i'm doing it again tomorrow and i hope i can keep it up and start a routine to get in shape again. and then i'll figure out how to stop smoking. then i will rock. i'm sick of my friends and i know i was all talking about how i like being alone so much in my last post but i think i might look for some new friends. at least ones for casual hanging out, i don't know. it's hard to set up new close friendships with people you haven't already known for years from when you were a kid. i think i'm going to take another jog and then stop over at Bowden House and see if Natalie's there. i can't leave things with her hanging on my last two weird, awkward, shitty run-ins. it's going to be good this time.

mood: excited
current music: dynabyte - i'll rise

[0 comments | leave a comment]

October 16th, 3:47pm

THIS RIVER BANK HOLDS SECRETS

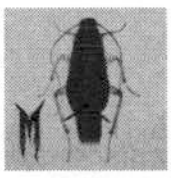

today i got up around 2pm, that's a good start. Cleo is seeing this girl Myrtle, i've mentioned her before. i didn't really think about it at first but i'm pretty much positive now that it's a romantic thing between them. Myrtle actually came up to the window in our European Romanticism class to bug Cleo. who does that? then after that i saw them holding hands. i guess it's cool. i think i'm going to start playing softball again. i walked past the field today and i got all nostalgic and remembering when i used to play. me and Trilby both played and i know Trilby still does so that might be weird with her on the team too. but i know i should really do this, i'm going to tryouts next week. i used to hit some killer home runs. it'll be great to be playing for the Wet Moon Worm Lizards again. maybe this means i'll have to stop smoking.

Trilby being with Martin, Cleo with Myrtle and Audrey with Beth sort of half makes me want to be with someone too, like this subconscious, passive peer pressure. nobody's actively trying to get me to do anything, but it's this presence that's still there. i like being the one single girl though, there's something appealing about it. when all my friends are off with their significant others i'm pretty much left alone, and while i sort of know my roomate Claire i don't really have anyone else to hang out with but i kind of like that, being forced to be by myself and entertain myself. it gives me a lot of time to do things i'd never normally do or read things i wouldn't normally think of to read. there's something also really cool about going out to eat by yourself. either in a restaurant or the dining hall. or even getting takeout alone is cool. i can't imagine myself dating anyone right now anyway, i can't imagine how anyone could really pull me out of this. everyone always rubs me the wrong way or i piss them off and everything goes down the shitter so i might as well keep to myself for now.

mood: nostalgic
current music: thismeansyou - river

[2 comments | leave a comment]

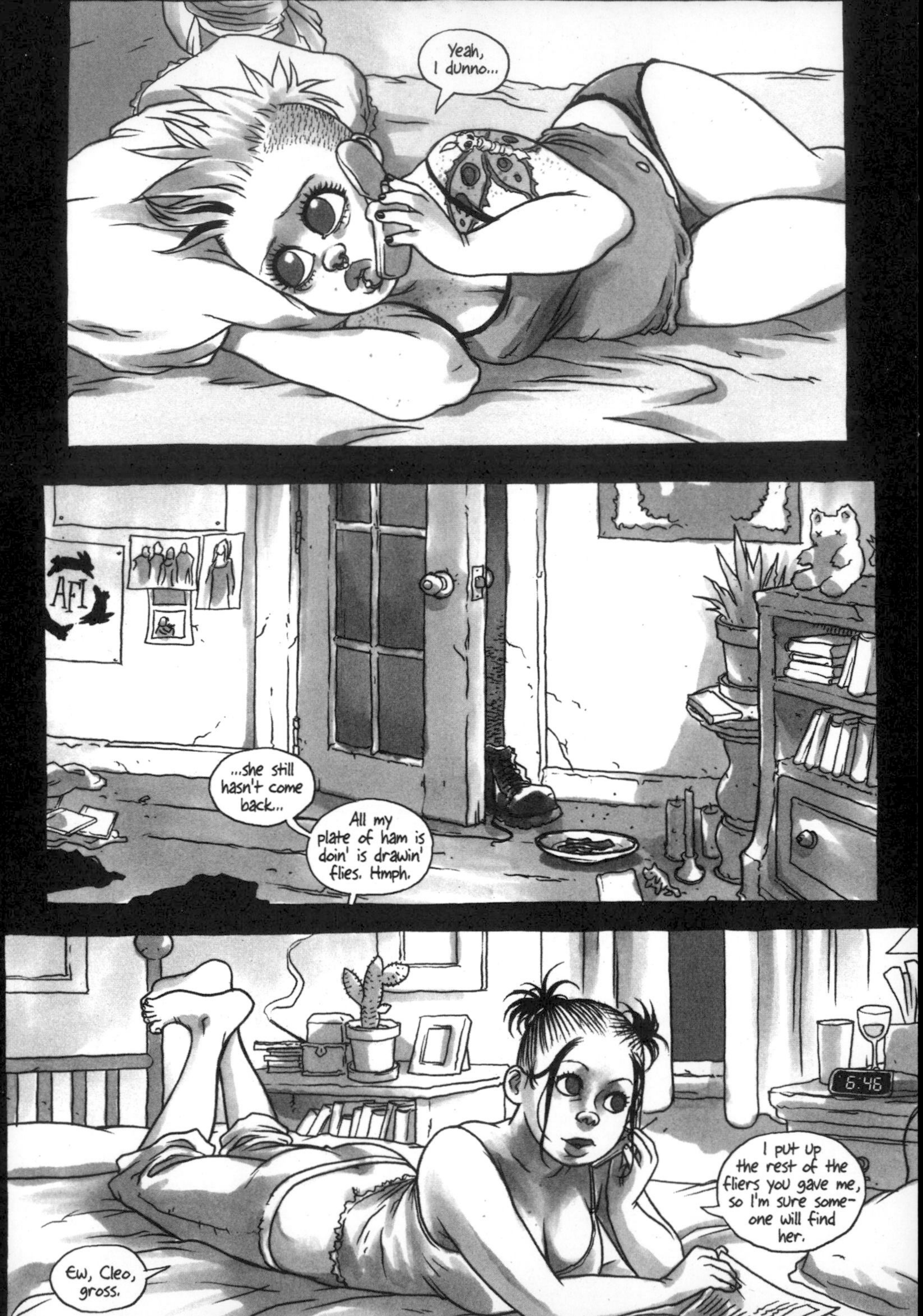
Yeah, I dunno...
...she still hasn't come back...
All my plate of ham is doin' is drawin' flies. Hmph.
AFI
6:46
I put up the rest of the fliers you gave me, so I'm sure someone will find her.
Ew, Cleo, gross.

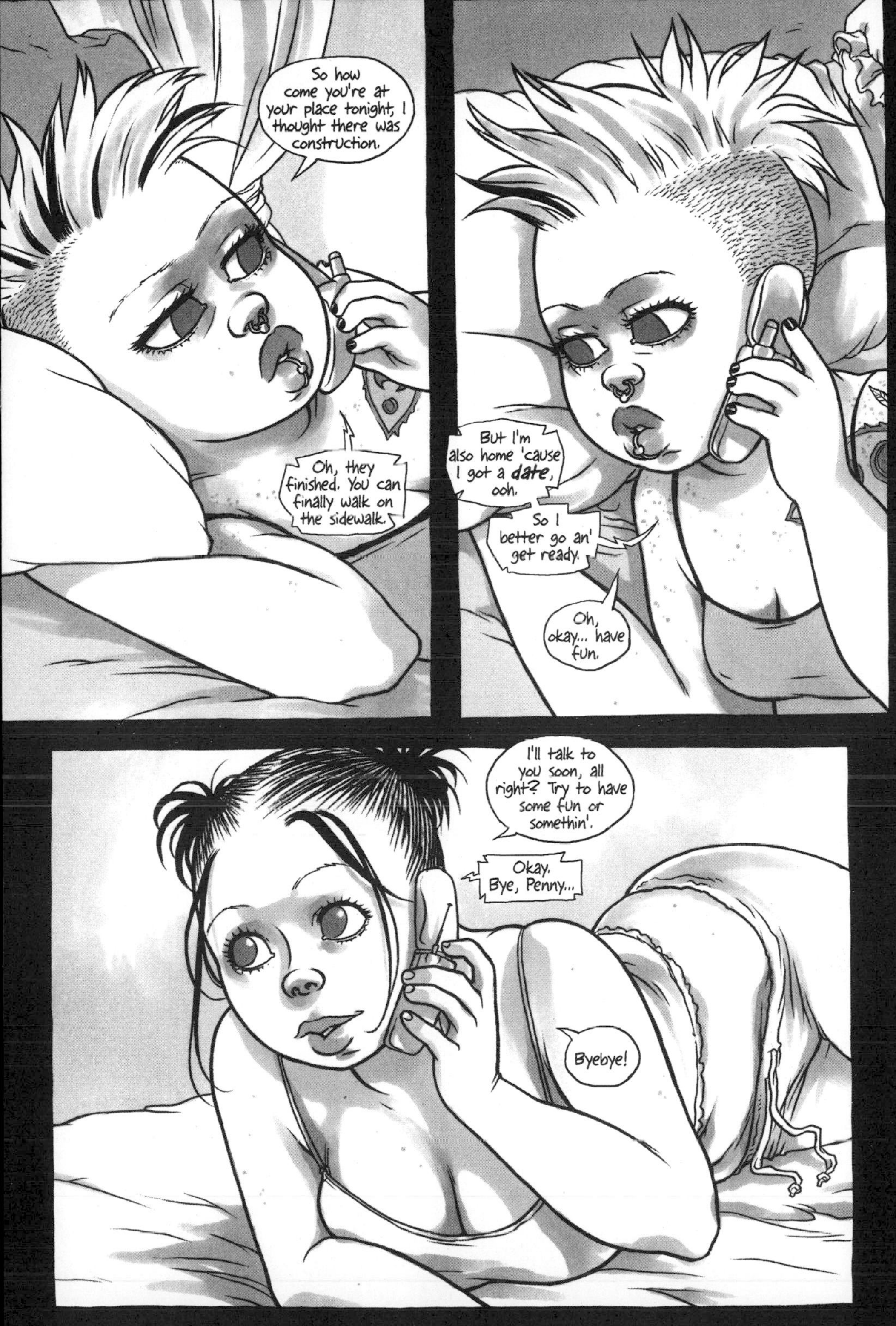

So how come you're at your place tonight, I thought there was construction.
Oh, they finished. You can finally walk on the sidewalk.
But I'm also home 'cause I got a **date**, ooh.
So I better go an' get ready.
Oh, okay... have fun.
I'll talk to you soon, all right? Try to have some fun or somethin'.
Okay. Bye, Penny...
Byebye!

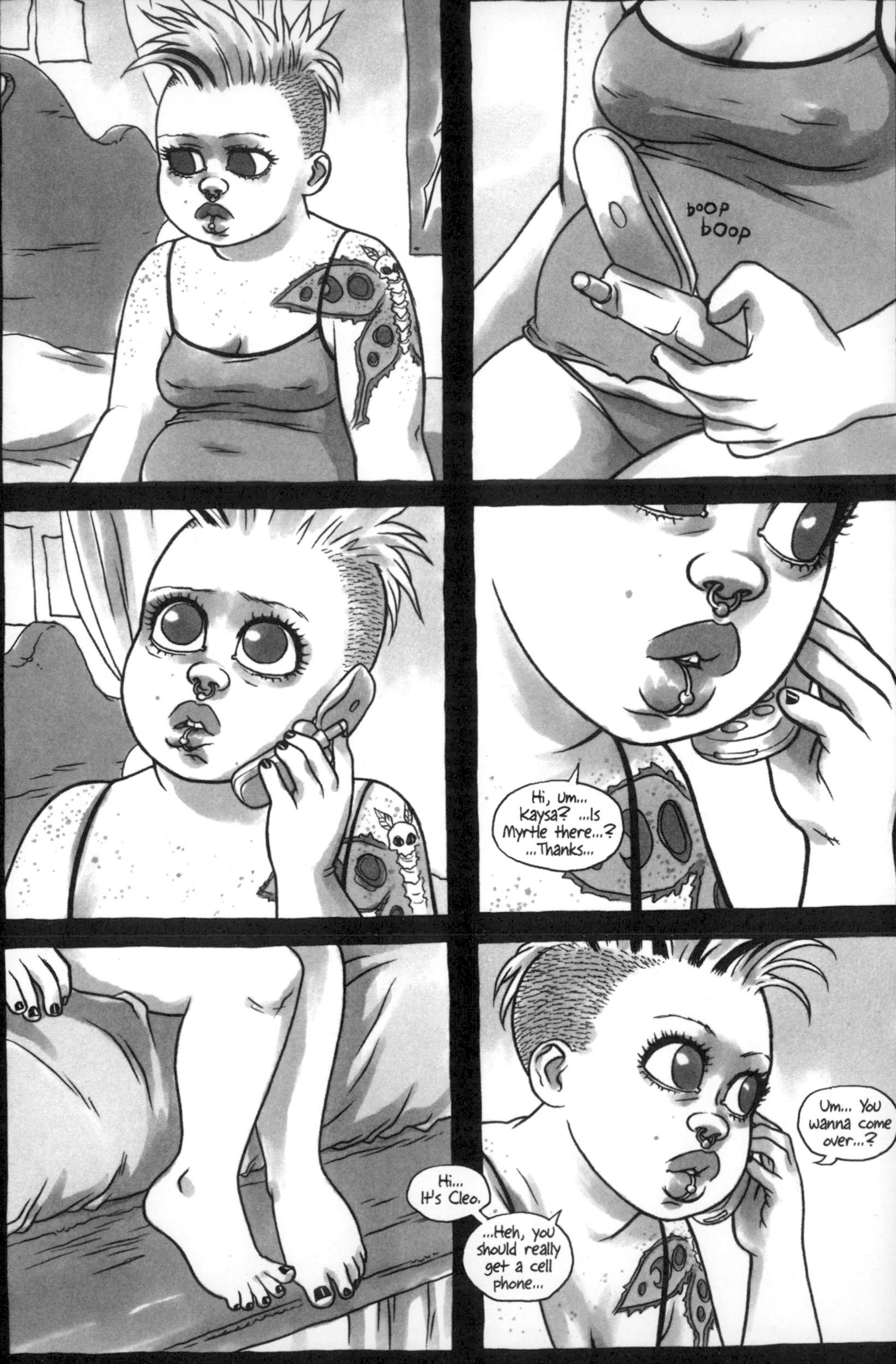

boop
boop
Hi, Um... Kaysa? ...Is Myrtle there...? ...Thanks...
Hi... It's Cleo.
...Heh, you should really get a cell phone...
Um... You wanna come over...?

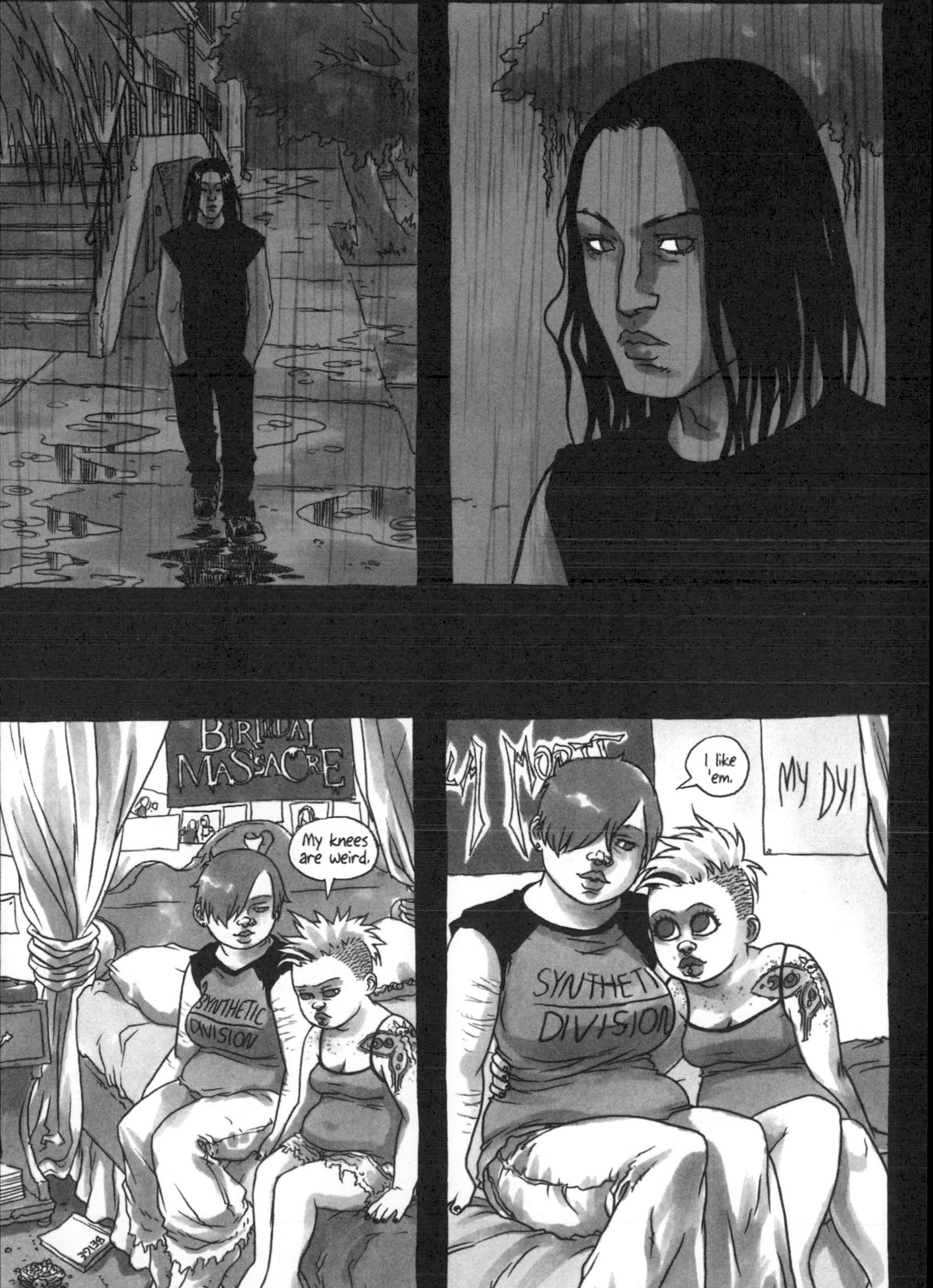
MASSACRE
My knees are weird.
SYNTHETIC DIVISION
I like 'em.
SYNTHETI DIVISION

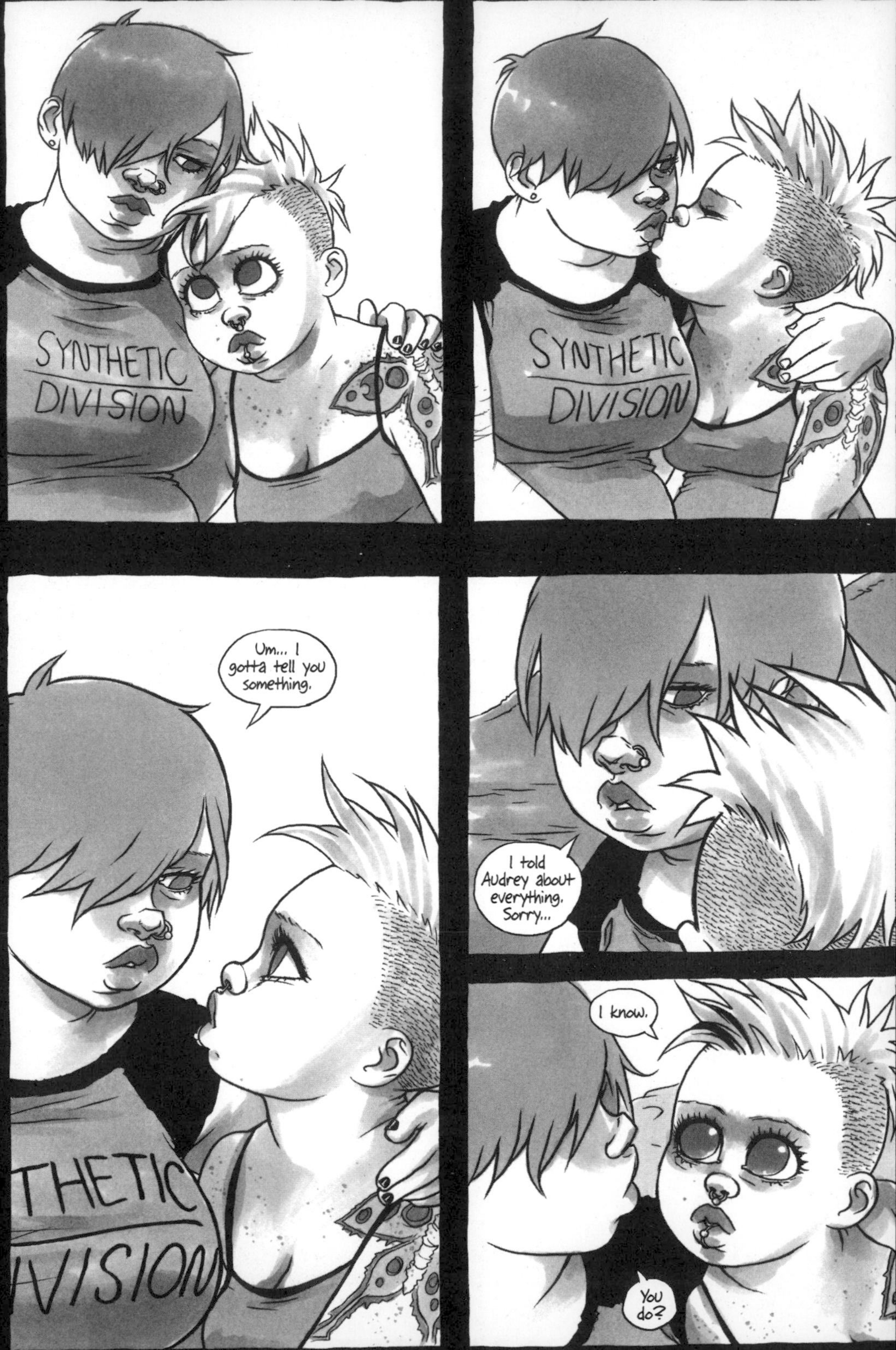
SYNTHETIC DIVISION
SYNTHETIC DIVISION
Um... I gotta tell you something.
THETIC IVISION
I told Audrey about everything. Sorry...
I know.
You do?

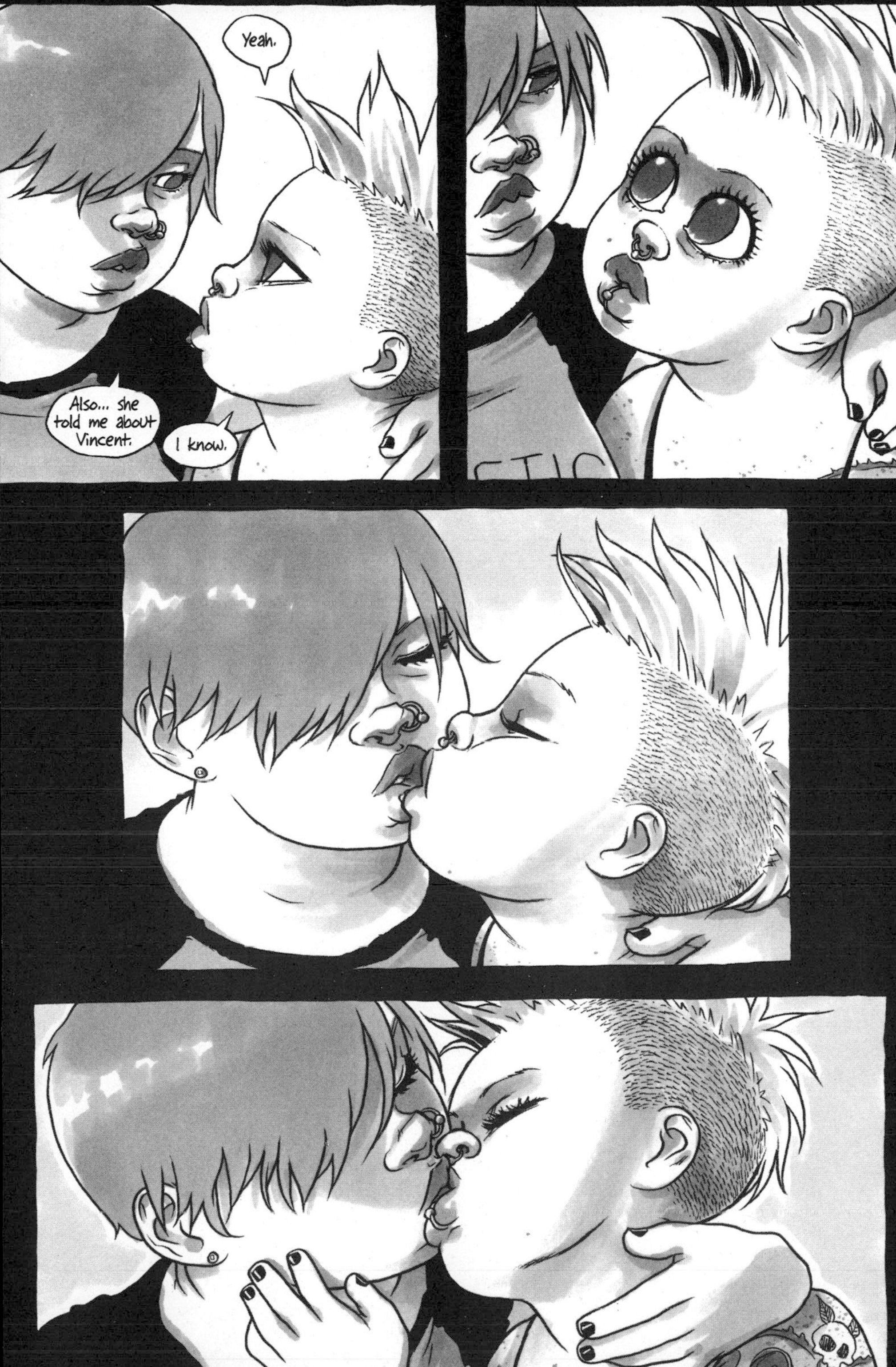
Yeah.
Also... she told me about Vincent.
I know.

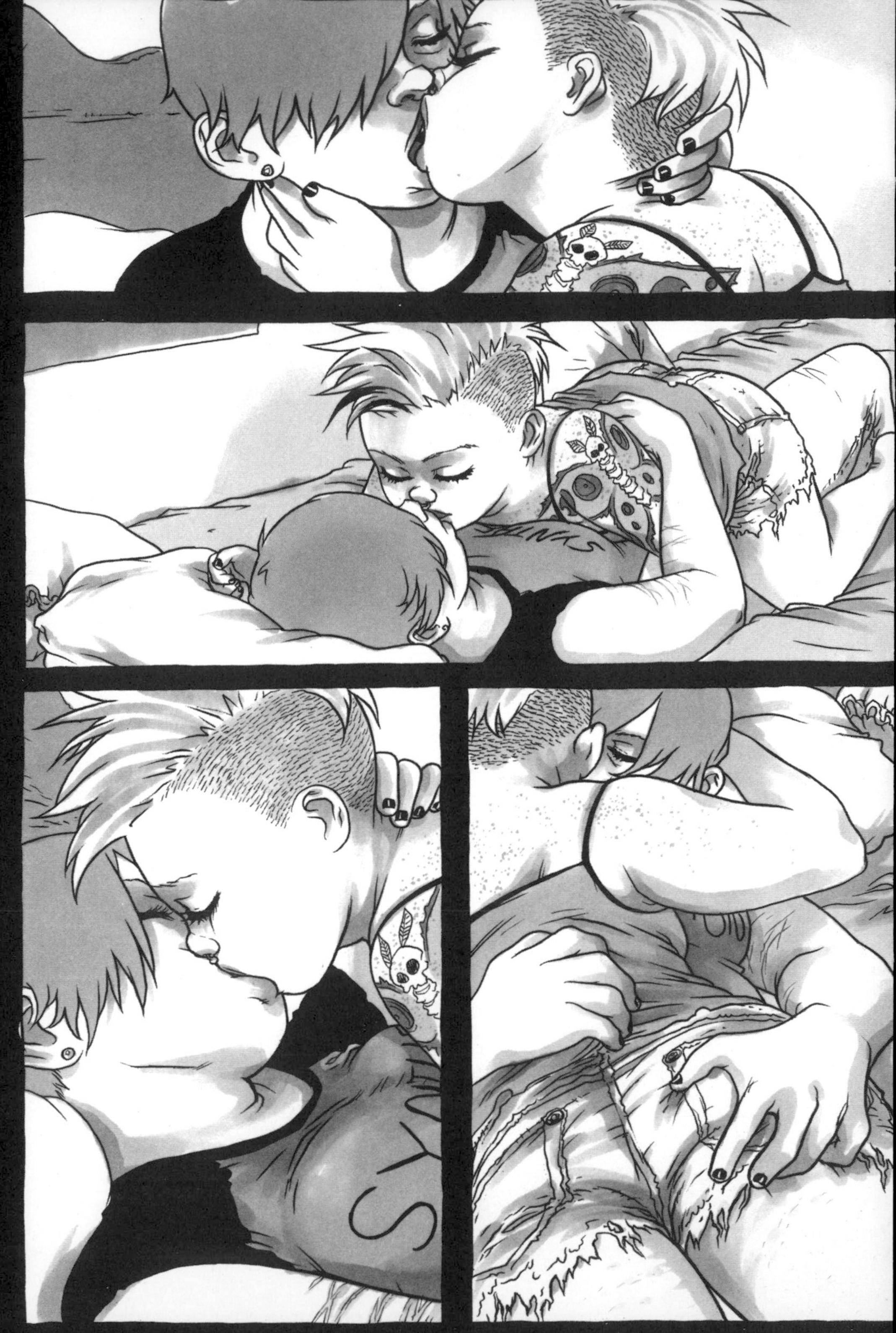

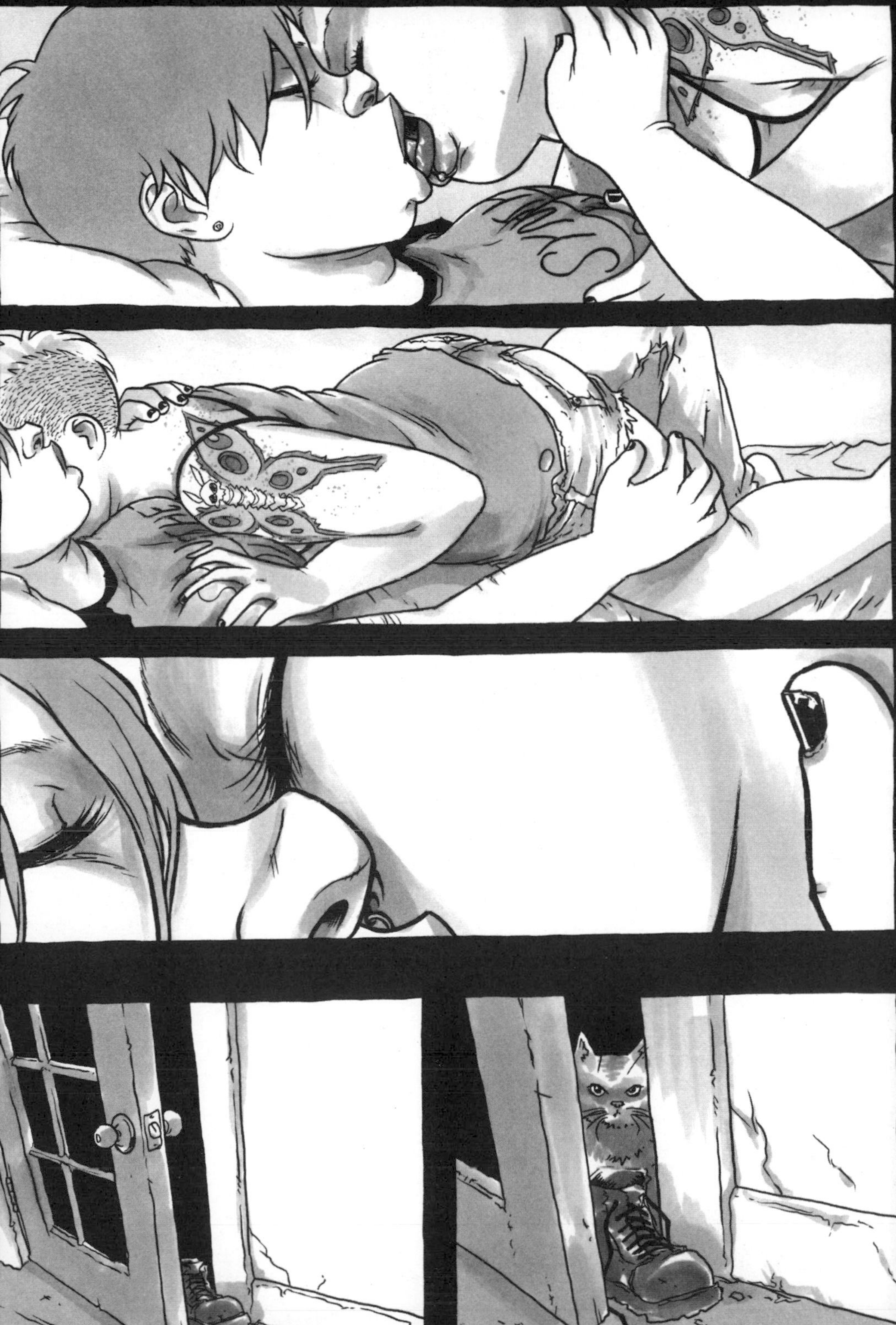

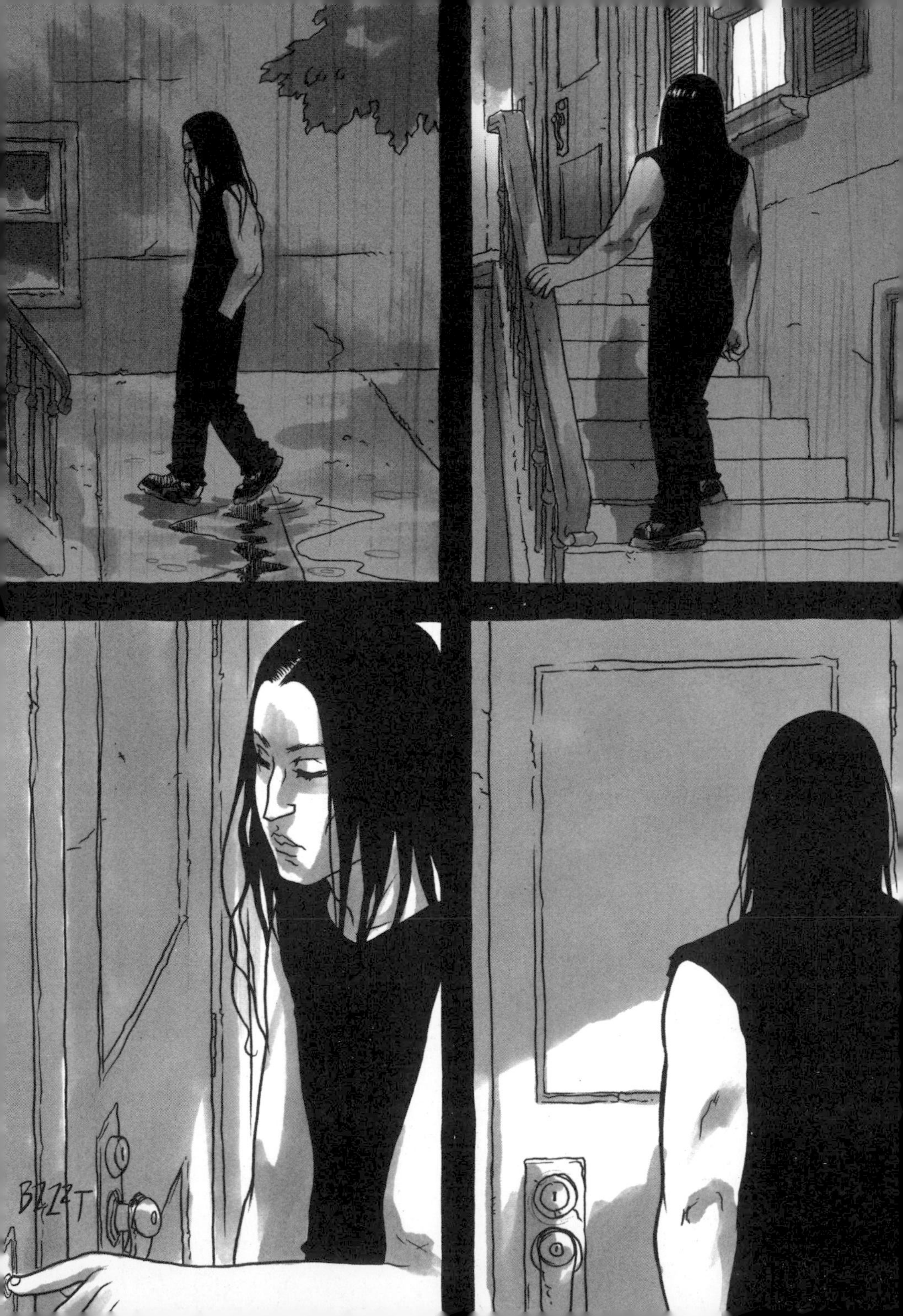
BZZZT

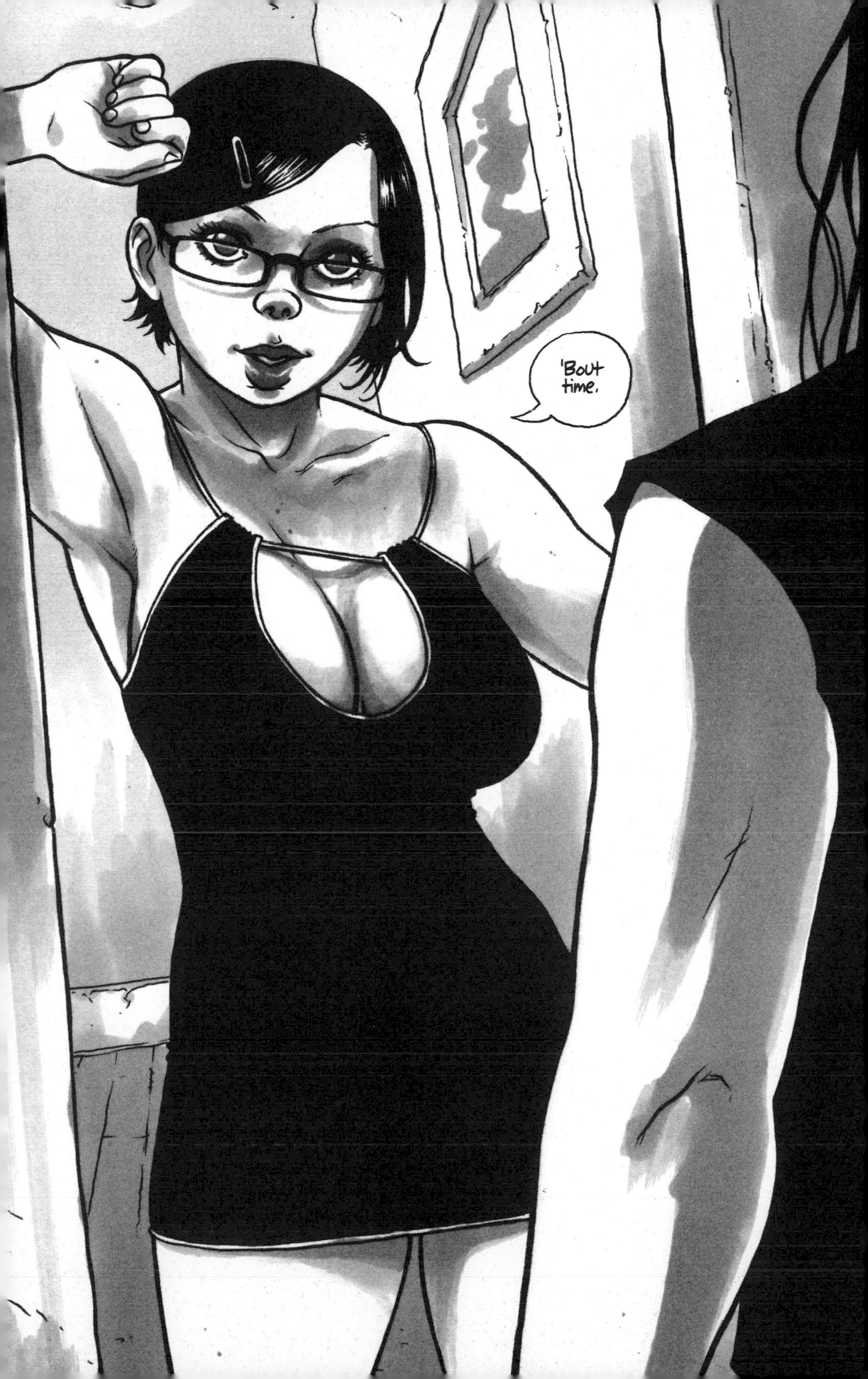
'Bout time.

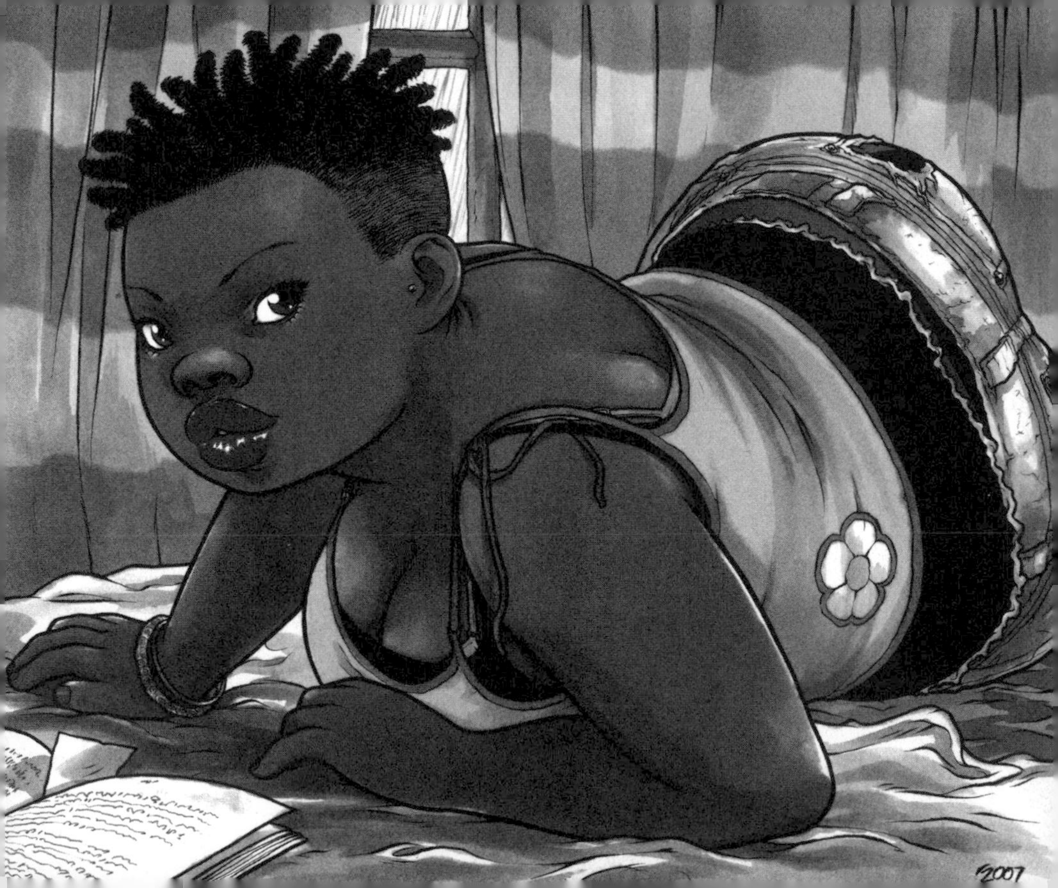
2007

WHO'S WHO IN WET MOON

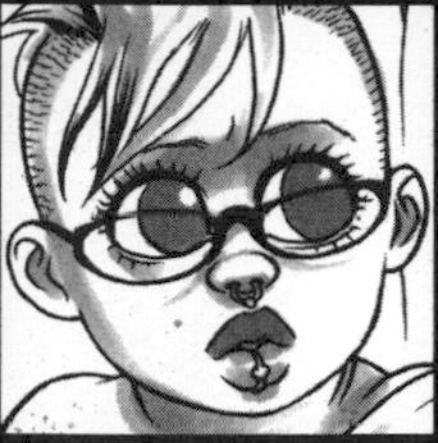
cleo lovedrop
(18)

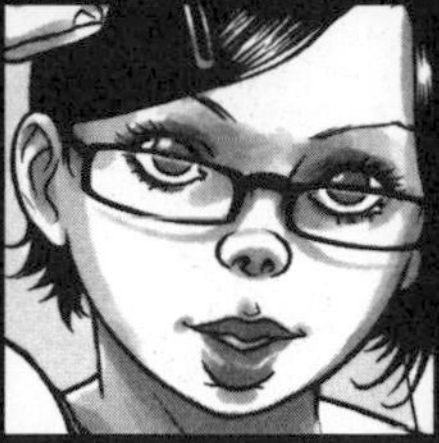
penny lovedrop
(23)

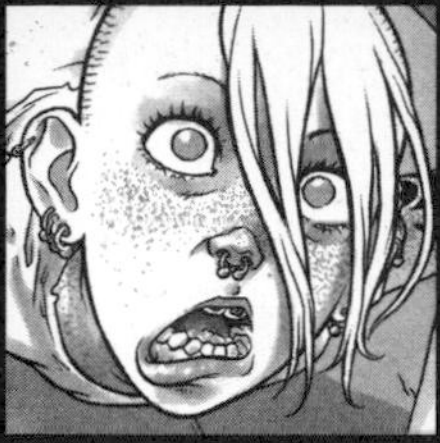
trilby bernarde
(18)

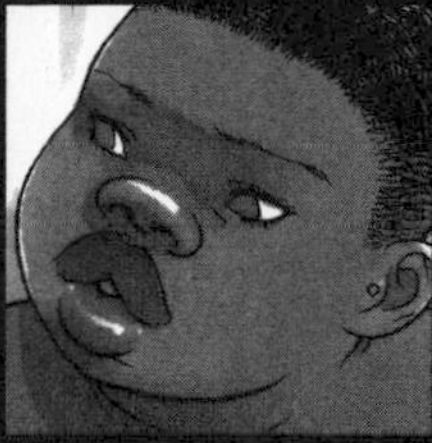
audrey richter
(19)

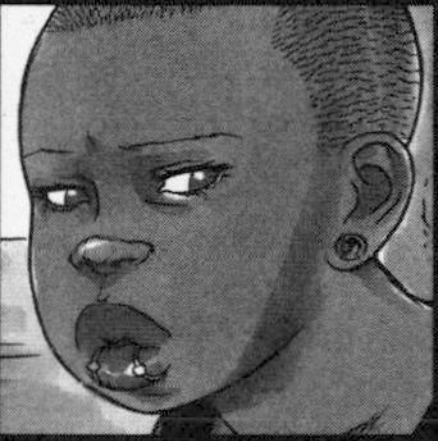
mara zuzanny
(18)

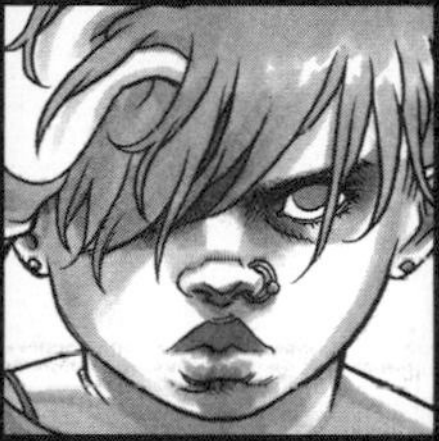
myrtle turenne
(19)

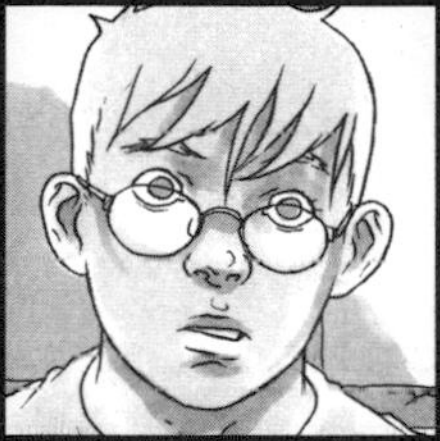
martin samson
(21)

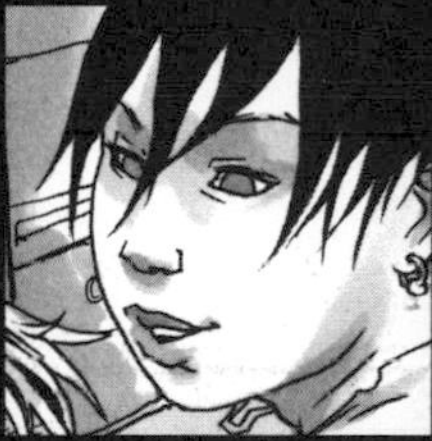
glen neuhoff
(20)

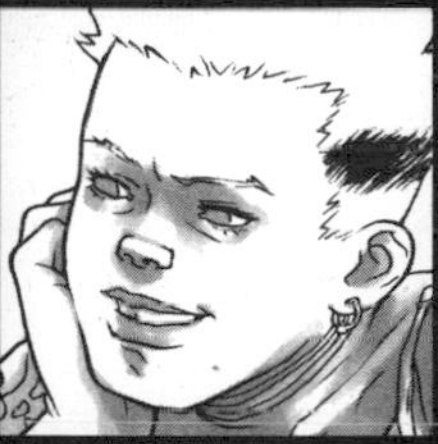
beth mckenzie
(17)

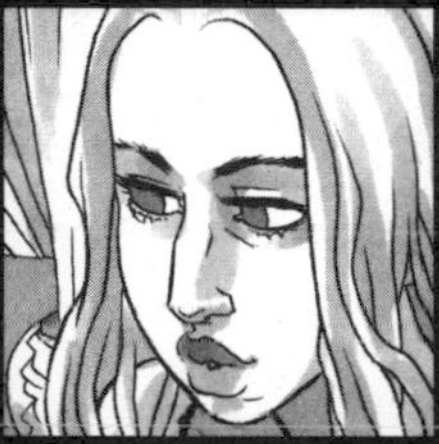
natalie ringtree
(21)

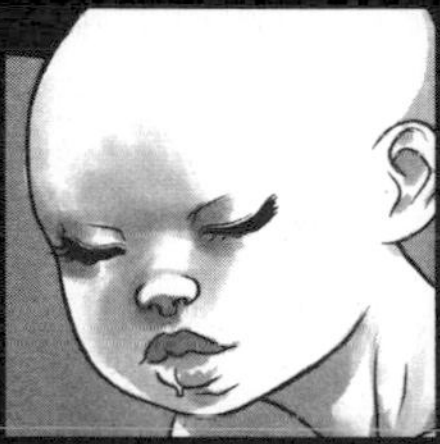
fern
(age unknown)

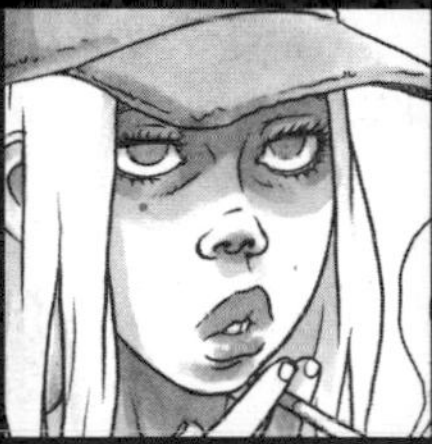
fall swanhilde
(15)

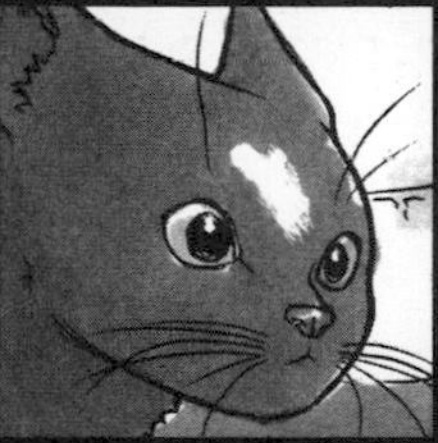
meiko
(5)

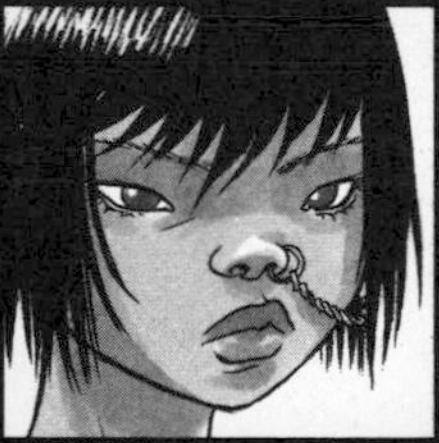
kinzoku
(19)

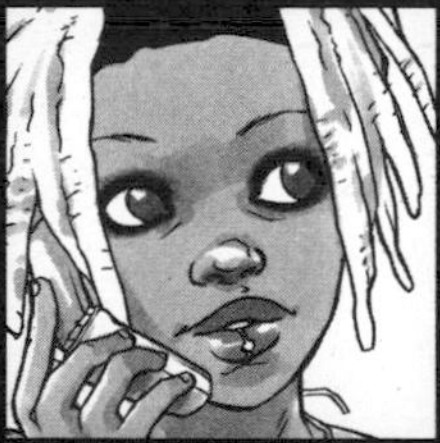
malady mayapple
(20)

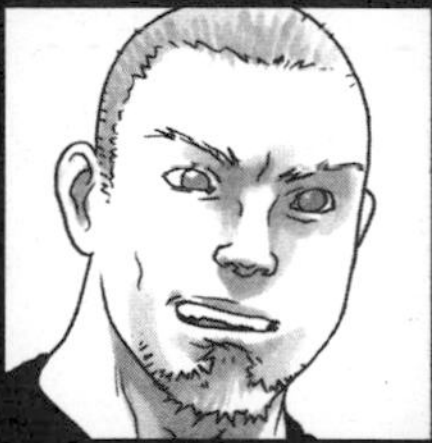
connor eakle
(23)

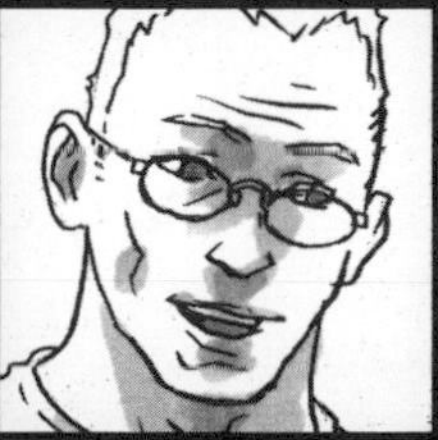
larry lovedrop

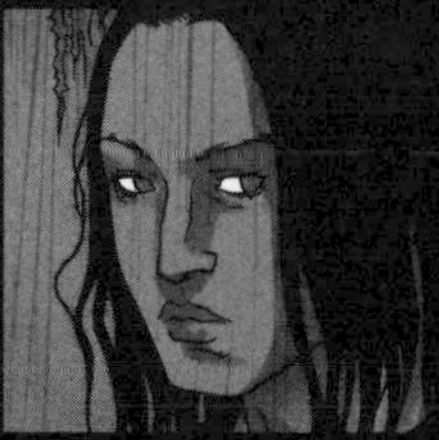
vincent verrier

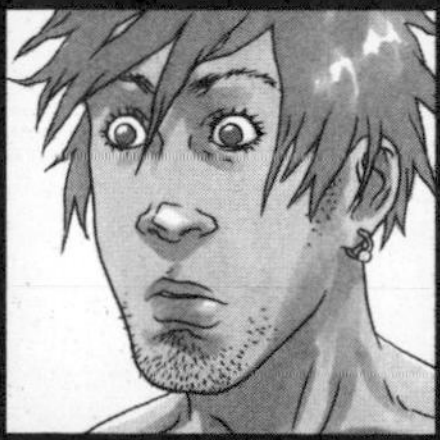
dale mcgovern

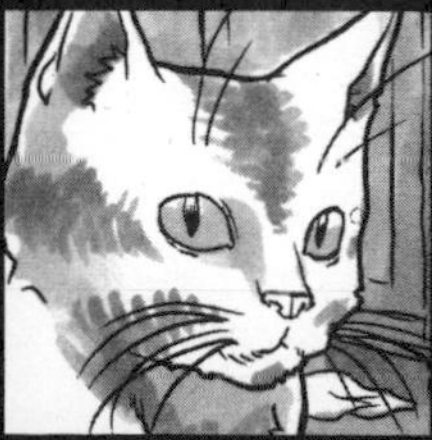
??

PENNY ANNE LOVEDROP

AGE: 20
SIGN: Gemini (June 11th)
HEIGHT: 5 ft. 9 in.
HAIR DYE: Ebony Shimmer
MAJOR: Interior Design
HOMETOWN: Wet Moon, Florida
MUSIC: Sarah McLachlan, Tori Amos, Death Cab For Cutie, Coldplay, John Mayer, Josh Groban, Bryn Christopher, Tegan and Sara, Feist
READING: Lisa Unger, Jodi Picoult, Donna Tartt
MOVIES/TV: Fargo, Sex And The City, Grey's Anatomy, Scrubs, Pride & Prejudice, The Fugitive, Oh Brother Where Art Thou, Titanic
LIKES: Wooden porches, milkshakes, quiet nights at home, long baths, horror novels, sushi, organizing parties and get-togethers, ambitious modern art, and sleeping all day
DISLIKES: Goats, people borrowing her stuff, anything medieval, steak, mutants, people humming/singing to themselves, tall audio speakers, people cracking their knuckles, activists, library books with writing in them, celery, rugs with tassels, movie theater crowds, people looking through her music collection, whistles, and pandas

FALL ANTONIA SWANHILDE

AGE: 15
SIGN: Libra (September 24th)
HEIGHT: 5 ft. 3 in.
HAIR DYE: none
MAJOR: none
HOMETOWN: Wet Moon, Florida
MUSIC: Metallica, Linkin Park, Sevendust, Manhole, Disturbed, Mudvayne, DMX, Coal Chamber, Breaking Benjamin, Hole
READING: nothing
MOVIES/TV: Saw, Final Destination 1-3, The Matrix, Half Baked, The Cave, anything with Johnny Depp, The Mighty Ducks
LIKES: Older guys, breaking the law, reality shows, chain smoking, swimming, ignoring people, Hello Kitty, and rollercoasters
DISLIKES: Societal conventions, showering, mayonnaise, blonde jokes, dragonflies, and mangoes (to which she's allergic)

BETH MCKENZIE

AGE: 17

SIGN: Sagittarius (December 10th)

HEIGHT: 5 ft. 5 in.

HAIR DYE: Bleach

MAJOR: none

HOMETOWN: Wet Moon, Florida

MUSIC: L7, Bikini Kill, Metallica, Fire Party, Joan Jett, Lita Ford, Otep, Human Waste Project, Danzig, Order of the Fly

READING: Twilight (but don't tell anybody)

MOVIES/TV: Terminator 2, Evil Dead 1 & 2, Aliens, Real World, Indiana Jones, Malcolm in the Middle, anything with Will Ferrell, Kill Bill, Pulp Fiction, Hostel, Dirty Dancing, Point Break, The Dark Half, Breakfast Club, Frankenhooker, anything with Piper Perabo, Return of the Living Dead 1 & 3, Basket Case, The Gore Gore Girls

LIKES: Pizza, big dogs, bikers, Whoopi Goldberg, softball (she plays for the Wet Moon Worm Lizards), Pabst Blue Ribbon, pirates, open graves, and stomping through the mud

DISLIKES: School, teachers, customers at the coffee shop where she works, centipedes, flossing her teeth, and see-through shower curtains

FERN

AGE: 20
SIGN: Scorpio (November 17th)
HEIGHT: 5 ft. 1 in.
HAIR DYE: none
MAJOR: unknown
HOMETOWN: Wet Moon, Florida (presumably)
MUSIC: Dead Can Dance, Miranda Sex Garden, Peter Murphy, Weird Al, Autumn's Grey Solace
READING: Dracula, true crime, Wuthering Heights, books about turn of the century serial killers, nonfiction books about biology and geography
MOVIES/TV: Bride of Frankenstein, Fiend Without A Face, the Shaggy Dog, any horror movie from the 1960s
LIKES: Kittens, pineapple, chains and hooks, old furniture, unopenable doors and what may be behind them, dead legends, applesauce, old dusty libraries, ancient tomes, curving staircases, listening, the moon, Halloween, expensive soap, and white bathroom tiles
DISLIKES: Profanity, carrot cake, wall-to-wall carpeting, and the sound of car horns

FURTHER REALMS OF FRIGHT

── PLAYLIST ──

BELLA MORTE — **BLEED AGAIN**

LOVE SPIRALS DOWNWARDS — **CITY MOON**

MIRA — **GOING NOWHERE**

DEPECHE MODE — **RUSH**

THISMEANSYOU — **RIVER**

THE BIRTHDAY MASSACRE — **GOODNIGHT**

IN THIS MOMENT — **ASHES**

DARK TRANQUILLITY — **THE WONDERS AT YOUR FEET**

SARAH MCLACHLAN — **FEAR**

THE CURE — **LOVESONG**

KITTIE — **LOVELESS**

CLAN OF XYMOX — **CONSOLATION**

DYNABYTE — **I'LL RISE**

FIELDS OF THE NEPHILIM — **MOONCHILD**

HOCICO — **SPIRITS OF CRIME**

L'AME IMMORTELLE — **FALLEN ANGEL**

BELLA MORTE — **THE COFFIN DON'T WANT ME,
AND SHE DON'T EITHER**

Way back in 2007, I was having problems with my wrist and thumb so I needed to find a new way to draw. I decided I'd do volume 3 in pencil, except that ended up causing tendonitis in my forearm because I'd grip the pencil too hard, so I basically drew the whole book with my hand in a withered claw like an old crone. I think it's obvious, the linework was sometimes jagged and stiff, but it was the best I could do. It was physically exhausting at times but I kept pushing myself to just get it done, not to mention it's the longest book I've ever done. Looking back on it I can't believe I did it all.

Second, since I was using pencil, that meant I couldn't use markers for greytones like I'd been doing since the markers would smudge the graphite, so I had to figure something else out and I didn't want to do digital greys. So, I came up with a kind of ridiculous method of photocopying the pencil pages and using the markers on the photocopies, which would preserve the pencilwork (for the most part, I eventually found out that the marker ink could also dissolve the photocopy ink), with the drawback of creating a ton of extra legwork and twice the amount of space needed to store all the pages. I also couldn't use ink wash on the photocopy paper since it was just flimsy printer paper, and a 250+ page book done all in Prismacolor markers is EXPENSIVE.

Third, and most importantly, was the huge shift in the visual style. Part of it was out of me trying to draw differently because my hand and arm hurt, but mostly I desperately wanted to differentiate the characters much more. I wanted them to all have distinct, immediately recognizable faces, so for better or worse I tried something totally new. I wanted to do something different and fresh and cut loose a bit. I still remember the backlash on my Deviantart page when I first posted artwork from *Wet Moon* Book 3, people HATED it! Like virulently so, I was getting people telling me I'd ruined their lives and people giving me ultimatums that if I didn't change the art back that they'd never look at my work again, and so forth. Back then Deviantart was a much different place than it is now, at least on my page, people were much more involved and vocal, so it reached a fever pitch at the time, it was almost shocking for me. Even now, ten years later, I still get messages once in a blue moon from someone angry at me for changing the look. It's pretty awesome, though, that people get that invested in my work. It's amazing even when the reactions are negative, and I definitely understood where people were coming from, but I had to follow my heart.

Anyway! Despite all the growing pains and frustrations and that looking back on the book I can only really see the mistakes, I'm still proud of *Wet Moon* Book 3, it was a huge accomplishment for me. I think it's the book where *Wet Moon* started to feel like I always wanted it to feel, and where I began to really figure things out. Every book I do is a learning experience, but *Wet Moon* Book 3 taught me the most.

SOPHIE CAMPBELL
December 2016

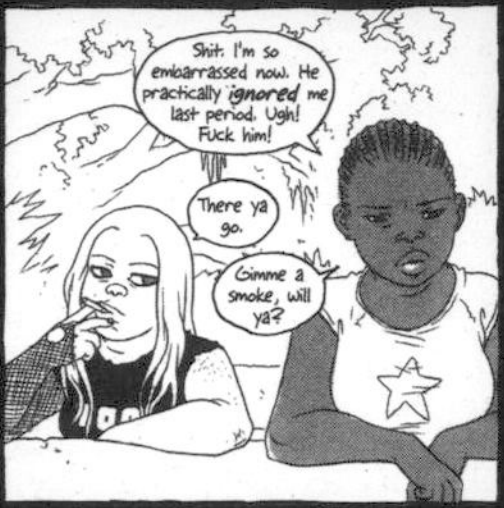
Shit. I'm so embarrassed now. He practically *ignored* me last period. Ugh! Fuck him!
There ya go.
Gimme a smoke, will ya?

PAGES 10-19: I love doing the high school flashback scenes so much, partly for nostalgic reasons since all of the interiors of the school are based directly on my high school, it's really fun putting my characters into environments that I know so well. And high school-age Cleo is hilarious, I should do an entire story about her someday, she's such a miserable bitch. I always have a blast writing and drawing her. My heart just breaks when I do flashback-era Mara, she's so sweet and trod upon.

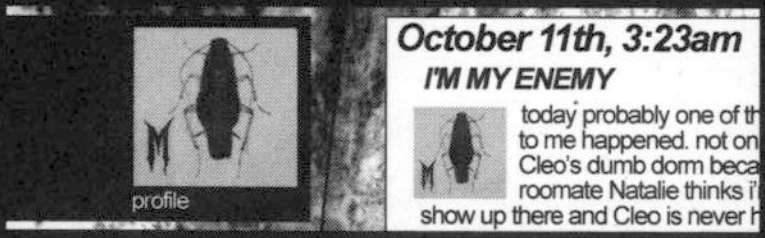
profile
October 11th, 3:23am
I'M MY ENEMY
today probably one of th
to me happened. not on
Cleo's dumb dorm beca
roomate Natalie thinks i'
show up there and Cleo is never h

PAGE 49: When I did this book, Livejournal was still a thing and I was posting there a lot so it felt natural to have the characters have their own blogs. I guess it's maybe the first thing in the series that obviously dates it and places the story in a particular time when up to that point it had been vague, but I don't think that's a bad thing. It gave me a really cool way to develop Mara, her inner life and what she's into, I loved coming up with her blog layout and title and what her user icon would be. I think it says a lot about her.

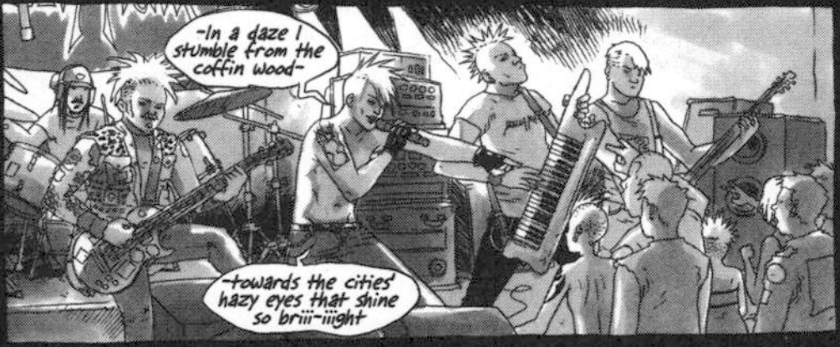
~In a daze I stumble from the coffin wood~
~towards the cities' hazy eyes that shine so briii~iiight

PAGES 60-67: Bella Morte! My favorite band! It was a difficult scene to draw but I loved doing it, and I'm acquainted with the band members so it was so awesome seeing their reactions to being in a comic. The *Wet Moon* goth scene had been represented by House of Usher in the first book but the Bella Morte concert is more in line with my own experiences, it was more personal and less cartoonish, a bit more real. Again, it's like the high school flashbacks, it was fun putting the characters into a place and situation that I was familiar with.

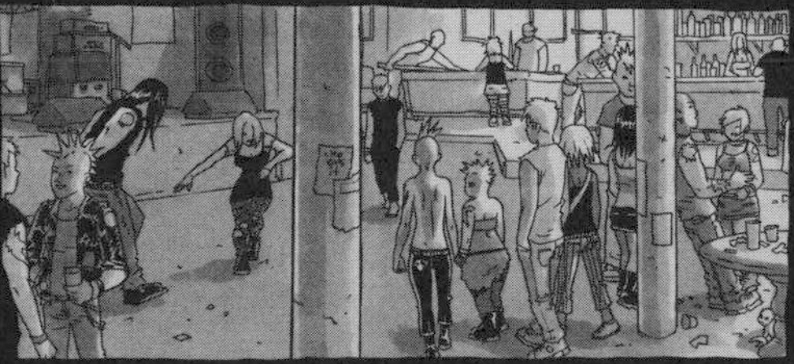

In the first panel on page 60, I tried to draw the "goth dance" that it seemed like everyone did, you guys know which dance I'm talking about?? I don't know if people still do it anymore but back then everyone did the same thing, regardless of what the song was.

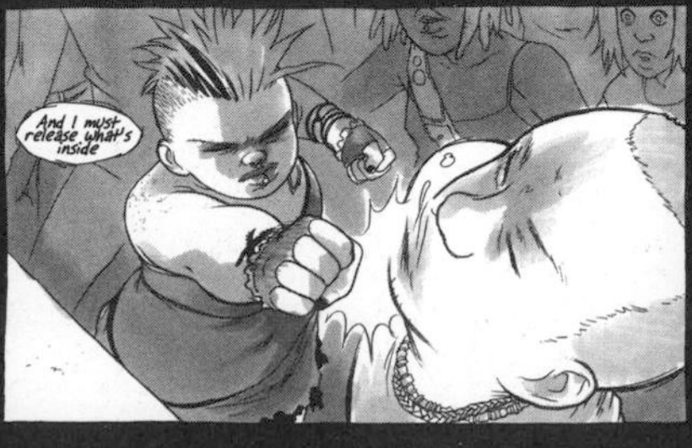
And I must release what's inside

Besides Bella Morte, the other cameo in this sequence is Kirk Gauthier, the guy who Cleo punches and knocks out. He's not around much anymore but he was a particularly excited fan of both Bella Morte and my work, he was a fixture of the Livejournal/ Deviantart era, so I thought it would be funny to put him in. He shows up again in volume 4.

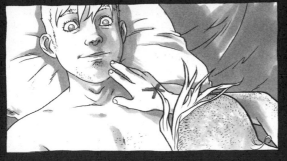

PAGES 80-88: The notorious blowjob scene! Originally, I was going to draw EVERYTHING and not have anything off-panel, I wanted to present sex in a way that wasn't pornographic or meant to be titillating, just a couple of regular dorky people messing around, treated no differently than any of the other things the characters did. Oni was actually cool with it, so I was all set to do it, but for whatever reason I started doubting it. I did a poll online and the overwhelming majority of people said yes to me drawing it uncensored, and whenever people want me to do one thing, I feel compelled to do the opposite, so I ended up keeping it all off-panel. I'm not sure if I regret it or not, part of me thinks I should've just drawn Martin's erect dick and Trilby going down on him, but maybe that just would've been too much. I don't know why but at the time I thought it was so funny to have dialogue from *Chronicles of Riddick* overlaid onto the scene.

...Yeah, brown like chocolate, haha. No! Hell yes I'm serious!

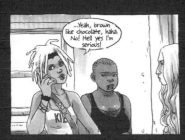

PAGES 116-117: I love Mara and Natalie's budding, awkward friendship. When I was going back through the book to do this commentary, I started laughing at Malady's dialogue in this scene. The thing about the Snickers in the VCR turning the TV screen brown is a real thing a guy I knew when I was a teenager claimed happened to him, I had to put it in the comic. I still find it funny, it's just so stupid.

See ya.

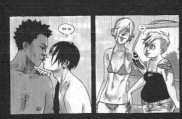

PAGE 136: I do not condone Cleo's reaction in panel 5 to Glen and Harrison kissing. A gay couple is not a novelty for you to fawn over, Cleo!

PAGES 204-206: This is one of my favorite scenes in the book, I really like how the pacing turned out and I always laugh to myself when I think about it.

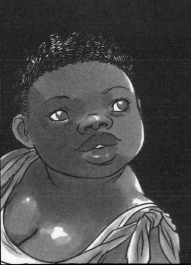

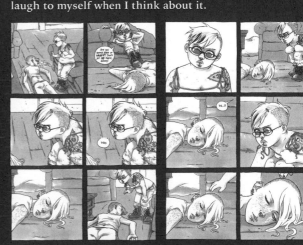

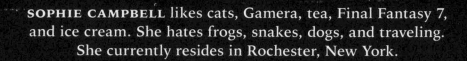

SOPHIE CAMPBELL likes cats, Gamera, tea, Final Fantasy 7, and ice cream. She hates frogs, snakes, dogs, and traveling. She currently resides in Rochester, New York.

FOLLOW SOPHIE AT:
—*twitter.com/mooncalfe1—mooncalfe.tumblr.com—*
—*mooncalfe-art.tumblr.com—shadoweyescomic.tumblr.com—*
—*cantlookbackcomic.tumblr.com—*